W9-CRK-817

Purnell's History of the 20th Century

Volume 3

Purnell's History of the 20th Century

Editor-in-Chief

A J P Taylor MA FBA

Fellow of Magdalen College Oxford

General Editor

J M Roberts MA DPhil

Fellow and Tutor at Merton College Oxford

Purnell: New York / London

Library of Congress
Catalog Card No 78-141357

Manufactured in Great Britain
by Purnell & Sons Limited
Paulton Bristol

Editor-in-Chief:
A.J.P.Taylor MA FBA

General Editor:
J.M.Roberts MA DPhil

International Panel of Consultants

Allan Angoff
BS in Jour, MS in LS
Director of Public Relations, Teaneck Public Library, New Jersey

K.D.Bracher
Professor of Contemporary History and Political Science at Bonn University

C.P.FitzGerald
Professor of Far Eastern and Chinese History at Canberra University

Henri Michel
Director of Research at the National Centre for Scientific Research (France) and Secretary-General of the International Committee of the Second World War

Robert Ochs
Professor of Modern History at South Carolina University

William J.Roehrenbeck
AB, BS in LS Director, Jersey City Public Library

Colonel A.M.Samsonov
Corresponding Member of the Soviet Academy of Sciences

Antonín Šnejdárek
Director of the Institute of International Politics, Prague

Rear-Admiral Baron Sadatoshi Tomioka
Chief of Shiryo-Chosakai (Historical Research Institute), Japan

Leo Valiani
Professor of History at the L.Einaudi Foundation, Turin

Claudio Veliz
Director of International Studies at Chile University

Scientific Consultant:
C.J.H.Watson
Fellow of Merton College, Oxford

Designed by:
Germano Facetti FSIA

Editors:
William Armstrong MA
Christopher Falkus BA

Deputy Editors:
John Grisewood BA
John Man BA

Assistant Editors:
Louise Black BA
Robert Stewart DPhil
Stephen Webbe BA
Simon Rigge BA
Roger Boulanger BA
Ruth Midgley BA

Editors' Assistants:
Gill Coleridge
Gila Curtis MA
Carolyn Rutherford

Editorial Assistants:
Sarah Salt
Sue Byrom
Penelope Maunsell

Art Director:
Brian Mayers DA MSIA

Art Editor:
Nicoletta Baroni

Designers:
Nicolas Sutton
Ken Carroll
Ewing Paddock
Roger Daniels
Tony Garrett

Design Assistant:
Monica Greenfield

Visual Aids:
Devised by Bruce Robertson
Drawn by Robert Chapman

Picture Research Co-ordinators:
Georgina Barker
Jasmine Gale

Picture Editor:
Bruce Bernard

Picture Research:
Evan Davies
Gunn Brinson
Shirley Green (USA)

Indexers:
H.A.Piehler
Barbara Heller
Isabelle Paton

Contents

Chapter 20

Introduction by J.M.Roberts

The whole of this Chapter is devoted to the war at sea. Although the future of naval warfare between Germany and Great Britain had been discussed endlessly before 1914, what happened was almost entirely unexpected. Although, too, so much time, money, and thought had been lavished on them, the fleets of dreadnoughts only once met to perform the role for which they were designed, the pitched battle. That meeting was at Jutland. It remains the only great sea-battle fought with guns between post-dreadnought capital ships. Although strategically decisive, in that the British retained the ascendancy in the North Sea which was the foundation of their strategy, its tactical and technical lessons were hard to evaluate. The score of ships sunk on both sides alarmed a British public opinion unprepared to believe that a new Trafalgar would not be won outright by the Royal Navy. We are presenting two articles on **The Battle of Jutland**, one by Vice-Admiral Friedrich Ruge, from the German point of view, one by Captain Donald Macintyre, from the British.

The other articles deal with what was to be the main theme of the naval war, the attack on commerce. Although there was to be an early burst of unrestricted warfare in 1915, British merchant ships were seriously threatened only by German surface raiders when the war began. R.K. Middlemas's article on **The Raiders** shows what damage they could do and what an important distraction they could be until hunted down. Necessarily, they tied down in search operations far larger numbers of ships than would have been necessary to master them had they been brought to battle. Herein lay their strategical value. Individual ships, of course, were not so dangerous as the one German squadron of any size at sea in 1914, that of Spee. This inflicted one damaging defeat on a British squadron at Coronel before it was itself destroyed near the Falkland islands, as Barrie Pitt narrates in **Revenge at Sea**.

With the raiders out of the way, the Royal Navy had no serious worries about protecting British merchant ships until the German U-boat campaign began in earnest. The use of the submarine as a commerce-destroyer was unexpected. Neither the German nor the British naval staff had seen this as the submarine's main role. The submarine's new employment grew out of the slow strangulation imposed on Germany by the increasingly complete British blockade. These developments are described by Captain S.W.Roskill in **Blockade**, an article which places in their true perspective the spectacular deeds of the raiders and the comings and goings of the battlefleets whose drama more easily won the attention of the public, then as now.

Karlsruhe—*a daring and dangerous raider*

Imperial War Museum

Dresden, *tracked down, shows the white flag*

Südd-Verlag, Munich

Survivors from the scuttled Dresden, *with the Chilean sailors who picked them up*

Imperial War Museum

Victim at Jutland—the German battle-cruiser Seydlitz, *torn by a British shell*

The War at Sea

1909 Naval powers agree at the London Naval Conference to exempt all property of a belligerent state except contraband from capture, but the convention is never ratified.

1911 Churchill became first lord of the Admiralty after the Agadir crisis; the Admiralty decides to blockade German home naval bases in the event of war.

1914 On outbreak of war, the British government declares its intention to abide by the terms of agreement at the London Conference and puts into operation the 'distant blockade' plan, designed to control exits from the North Sea.
Early August: *Königsberg* sinks the *City of Winchester*; *Karlsruhe* sinks merchant ship in the Caribbean.
11th August: *Goeben* escapes to Constantinople.
28th August: British raid of Heligoland Bight sinks three German light cruisers.
7th September: *Emden* travels through Sumatra channel and sinks nine ships within a week.
20th September: *Königsberg* attacks Zanzibar and sinks *Pegasus*.
21st September: *Emden* bombards Madras.
Throughout August and September *Karlsruhe* and *Dresden* terrorize waters off Brazil.
Late September: *Karlsruhe* and *Kronprinz Wilhelm* sink twenty ships.
14th October: Stoddart given command of north and mid-Atlantic and organizes pursuit of *Karlsruhe*.
Mid-October: Australian convoy ready to sail; *Emden* strikes again and, after sinking several other ships, sails into Penang and sinks the Russian cruiser *Zhemchug*.
1st November: at the battle of Coronel Spee destroys *Monmouth* and *Good Hope*.
4th November: news of the defeat reaches Great Britain and within the week *Invincible* and *Inflexible* are sent under Sturdee to chase Spee's squadron.
9th November: *Emden* destroyed after long running battle with *Sydney* of the Anzac convoy. Her captain ran her on to the reefs of the Cocos Islands.
7th December: Sturdee's squadron reaches the Falkland Islands.
8th-9th December: at battle of Falkland Islands British sink the *Scharnhorst*, *Gneisenau*, *Leipzig*, and *Nürnberg*; only *Dresden* remains of the German East Asia Squadron.

1915 24th January: battle of Dogger Bank costs the Germans the cruiser *Blücher* and drives the High Seas Fleet back to port where, except for a few cautious sorties, it remains for the rest of the year.
4th February: German government declares the waters around Great Britain a 'war zone' and begins first unrestricted submarine campaign, which lasts until August.
March: German admiralty sends the collier *Rubens* to refuel the *Königsberg*.
11th March: Great Britain issues the Reprisals Order, declaring that goods destined for Germany will be seized, even if they are being carried to a neutral country; neutral countries protest.
14th March: *Dresden* is scuttled at Juan Fernández.
7th May: *Lusitania* sunk by German submarine.
July: *Königsberg* destroyed on the Rufiji river in first air-sea operation ever mounted.

1916 January: Scheer becomes commander-in-chief of the High Seas Fleet.
February: Great Britain creates a ministry of blockade to prevent neutral ships from trading with the enemy and to ration imports into neutral countries, to prevent their being passed on to the enemy.
29th February: the ministry of blockade issues a statutory black list of firms with whom transactions are forbidden.
March: Germany renews 'extended' submarine warfare.
25th April: German navy bombards Lowestoft.
31st May: *Elbing*'s hit on *Galatea* starts the battle of Jutland.
1st June: battle of Jutland ends; the High Seas Fleet makes for harbour and repairs.
7th July: an order in council of the British government ends British commitment to the Declaration of London of August 1914.
August: Scheer leads High Seas Fleet out again and narrowly escapes being caught in another Jutland trap; Germany decides against a high seas battle.

1917 February: intensified unrestricted submarine warfare on merchant shipping brings the United States into the war in April.

The Naval War, 1914-15/R.K.Middlemas

The Raiders

The Royal Navy might be the most powerful in the world, but it could not – to the dismay of the British empire – guarantee the safety of Great Britain's world-wide shipping against a small number of daringly led German cruisers. To German soldiers in western Europe and in the snowbound trenches of the Russian front the names of* Emden, Karlsruhe, Dresden, *and* Königsberg *brought pride – and hope for the future

The exploits of the raiders, 1914-15. ***Below:*** Karlsruhe *and* Dresden *terrorized the coast of Brazil. When Spee summoned* Dresden *to meet him in the Pacific,* Karlsruhe *turned north. She was making for the rich British colony of Barbados, when, unaccountably, she blew up.* ***Bottom:*** Emden *wrought havoc in the Indian Ocean, once regarded as a British preserve. She sailed from Tsingtao through the Sumatra channel, sank nine ships, bombarded Madras, sank another ten ships near Ceylon, sailed into Penang harbour to sink more ships. Eventually, chased by* Sydney, *her captain ran her aground off the Cocos Islands*

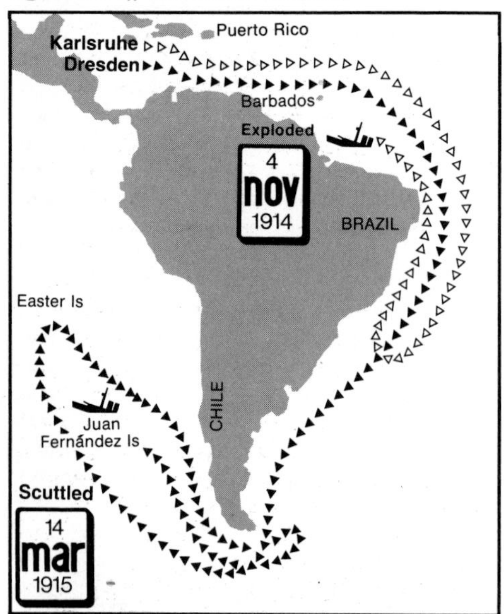

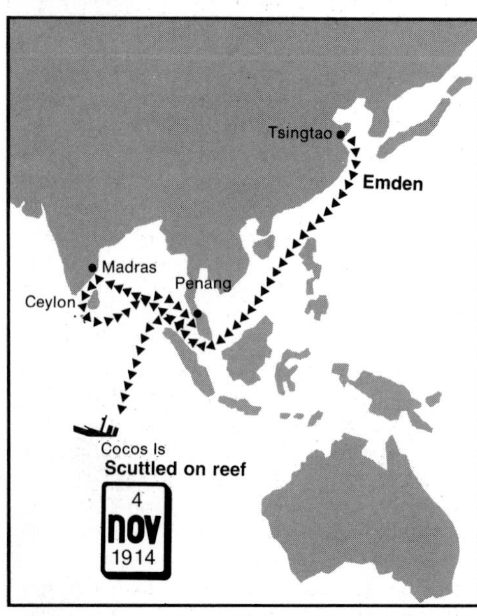

Until at least the 1890's, as an Englishman once said to Grand Admiral von Tirpitz, Germany 'was not a sea-going nation'. Plans for a navy, inspired as much by nationalism as by strategic needs, stagnated in disputes between the competing authorities, the admiralty, executive command, and the naval cabinet, between the Kaiser and the general staff. Even after Tirpitz gained the Kaiser's favour in 1892 and began to create the nucleus of the German navy, there remained the dilemma of what sort of force it should be. Was there to be a High Seas Fleet to wear down Great Britain (because there was never any doubt of the ultimate naval enemy) from a strong centralized position as Great Britain herself had done in the Napoleonic Wars? Or should they build fast cruisers, like 18th-century privateers, to destroy the enemy's trade and distract their main fleet as well?

German naval authorities argued about this crucial decision for ten years after 1895 – the year in which Tirpitz resigned because his battle fleet was being subordinated to the political arguments for cruiser warfare. Colonial ambition was proving a strong argument in favour of a far seas strategy. Not only were the new fast cruisers to fly the German flag in every port of the world, reinforcing pro-German sympathies in South America, Africa, and Asia, but they provided the defence of the scattered islands and territories proudly called the German 'empire'. Frequently they were the reason for acquiring them: Tirpitz himself negotiated the acquisition of the last of the treaty ports in China, Tsingtao, as a base for the East Asia Squadron.

The primacy given to cruiser warfare faded after Tirpitz returned. The second Navy Bill of 1900 outlined the need for a strong home fleet. But as a *quid pro quo* to the cruiser strategists, it also attempted to define an important role for the warships in the far seas: 'to represent the German navy abroad . . . and to gather fruits which have ripened as a result of the naval strength of the Reich embodied in the Home Battle Fleet'.

Until 1910 this policy backed a programme of building fast, well-armed cruisers and light cruisers, capable of from 24 to 27 knots and fitted with 4·1-inch and 6-inch guns which were, at that date, the most accurate for their size in the world. When, under the pressure of the race to build larger and larger capital ships, the emphasis changed, and all new cruisers were kept for the battle fleet, it was the cruisers of the period 1905-10 which were assigned to foreign stations. They were superior both in speed and gunnery to the equivalent British ships, although this was not obvious to either side before hostilities began. They were intended, however, not for direct action against warships, but to draw away vital units from the British Grand Fleet and leave the North Sea open to a blow from the German North Sea Fleet.

British strategy did not rely on a counterpart to the German cruisers. It was hard enough to get money to build battleships – even the dreadnoughts – and only enough new cruisers were laid down for home waters. This left a fair number of County Class cruisers, built in a period of bad naval design between 1895 and 1905, too costly to scrap, whose failings in speed and armaments were not shown until they were actually under fire. To make up these deficiencies, and to guard her immensely long trade routes and communications, Great Britain relied on the alliance with Japan – whose fleet could blockade Tsingtao, Germany's only effective Asiatic port – and on the combined forces of Australia and New Zealand, which were to neutralize Germany's Pacific colonies. No specific defences were provided for the Indian Ocean, which was felt to be a British preserve.

When war was declared, the main German strength lay in the East Asia Squadron, commanded by Vice-Admiral von Spee, which consisted of the heavy cruisers *Scharnhorst* and *Gneisenau* and three light cruisers *Emden, Leipzig,* and *Nürnberg*. In the Caribbean were two of the fastest light cruisers, *Karlsruhe* and *Dresden,* and in the Indian Ocean, based on German East Africa, *Königsberg*. In the Mediterranean there was *Goeben,* one of the finest battle-cruisers in the German navy, and *Breslau*. Finally, mainly in American or German ports, there were the great liners of the passenger fleet, ships of over 20,000 tons, capable of 25 knots, fitted with gun mountings, waiting for the signal to rendezvous with warships and collect their armaments.

The Allied defences appeared far greater on paper than they were in practice because of the immense distances to be covered. Eastern command was based in Hong Kong and Singapore and combined with the small, but modern, Australian fleet. The North Pacific was left to the Japanese; three cruiser squadrons and one French squadron defended the Atlantic; two obsolete squadrons in the Indian Ocean completed the preparations in the far seas. Churchill, the first lord of the Admiralty, and his staff were aware that the line was thin – they did not realize how severely it was to be tested.

Bibliothek für Zeitgeschichte, Stuttgart

The Königsberg, *which was to prove her superior speed and guns in the Indian Ocean*

Impressive initial successes

Immediately after the declaration of war, Germany chalked up an impressive list of successes. *Goeben* bombarded the French bases of Bône and Philippeville in North Africa and, with bewildering speed, evaded the French and British fleets in the Mediterranean (p. 478). She escaped to Constantinople where she was sold to the ostensibly neutral Turkish government. The persuasive force of her presence in Constantinople and, even more, the intrigues of her powerful commander Admiral Souchon, helped materially to bring Turkey into the war on the side of Germany in the autumn of 1914. Meanwhile, in early August, *Königsberg* sank the *City of Winchester* with most of the Ceylon tea crop on board, off the coast of Aden, and threatened the safety of the Suez route to India. Two armed liners escaped through the North Sea and another, *Kronprinz Wilhelm,* ran the blockade of the American ports, while *Karlsruhe* sank her first merchant ship in the Caribbean.

Before the British Admiralty had time to react to these threats, the necessities of the war on the Western Front made the job more difficult. After the retreat from Mons the demand for more power rose dramatically. As the front extended itself from the Channel to Verdun, Kitchener, the secretary of state for war, summoned the reserves, subordinating the Admiralty's other plans in order to escort home the vital battalions of the British army in India. Added to this were the divisions from Australia and New Zealand which, with *Königsberg* at large, would need to be escorted at least through the Red Sea. For weeks half the far seas squadrons were diverted from chasing the German cruisers.

But what might have been a great opportunity for the raiders was lost. One of the decisive battles of the war, the minor engagement in the North Sea off Heligoland on 28th August, in which the Germans lost three light cruisers, so disturbed the Kaiser that he shrank from endangering his cherished fleet again. A defensive strategy took the place of that worked out before 1914; a defective one as far as cruiser warfare was concerned. Instead of ordering immediate strikes at vulnerable points, German planning took account of the imminent loss of her Pacific bases, Samoa, Nauru, New Guinea, and Tsingtao, and the difficulties of supplying and coaling

Imperial War Museum

the raiders, rather than of their immense potential. Tirpitz wanted to order Spee home, but such was the atmosphere in Berlin that no orders were sent at all: Pohl, the chief of naval staff, said: 'it is impossible to tell from here whether the squadron will be able to choose against whom it will deal its dying blows'. Within a month of hostilities, the German admiralty had entirely abandoned the preparation of years, the network of colliers and supply ships, communications, and neutral sympathizers. The successes of the raiders in the autumn were obtained without even moral support from home.

The raiders harried two main areas, both vital to the British war effort: the mid-Atlantic and the Indian Ocean. The most vital British interests in August were the troop convoys from India through the Suez Canal. None of these were safe until the whereabouts of *Königsberg* were known. But Captain Looff and his ship had disappeared; he had gone back to German East Africa and did not emerge until 20th September when at dawn he attacked the quiet harbour of Zanzibar, shelled the port, and sank the British light cruiser *Pegasus*. In these anxious months, the calm of the waters between Australia and India, so long a British preserve, was shattered by the foremost raider of all, *Emden*.

'There are great prizes to be won'

Admiral von Spee had left Tsingtao on manoeuvres before war broke out and he was soon deprived of his base by the Japanese blockade. He foresaw the dilemma of his squadron: that if he stayed in the Pacific he must ultimately run out of coal or be destroyed by the Singapore and Japanese squadrons. Instead, he chose to sail round Cape Horn, break through the Atlantic defences, and run for home through the North Sea. But Karl von Müller, captain of *Emden,* asked permission to raid in the Indian Ocean. Spee wrote: 'A single light cruiser can coal from captured vessels and maintain herself for longer . . . as there are great prizes to be won there, I despatched the fastest light cruiser.'

Heavily disguised, with a false funnel, *Emden* crept through the Sumatra channel and began her raiding career on 7th September by sinking nine ships in a week. When the news reached London it produced consternation and a steep rise in insurance rates; and Australia and New Zealand demanded a strong escort for the Anzac troop convoy. Nothing could be given because of the war office priority for the Indian convoys endangered by *Königsberg*. On 21st September Müller carried the war on to enemy territory and bombarded the city of Madras by night, setting fire to the great oil tanks and, by the light of the blaze, destroying the harbour installations. He then turned south and in the seas around Ceylon, impudently within range of the defences of Colombo, captured or sunk another ten merchant ships. Loss of confidence and prestige caused bitter questions – what was the Admiralty doing? Australia and New Zealand bluntly postponed the convoy for three weeks.

Emden did not strike again until mid-October – just when the convoy, with an escort, was ready, and at a time when the war in South Africa against the German-backed rebels under Christian de Wet was at its most dangerous. Several more sinkings preceded one of the boldest strokes of the war: Müller sailed into the harbour of Penang on the Malay peninsula and sank the Russian light cruiser *Zhemchug* and a French destroyer. Combined with the steady toll taken in the Atlantic by *Karlsruhe* and the armed liners, and Spee's attack on the French colony of Tahiti, the raiders were achieving their object of distracting the enemy. By the end of October they had captured or sunk more than forty Allied ships.

Karlsruhe alone had accounted for nearly 100,000 tons of shipping. She had nearly been caught by Admiral Cradock's squadron in the Caribbean in early August, but she refuelled from the armed liner *Kronprinz Wilhelm* and escaped to Puerto Rico with almost empty bunkers. But thereafter Captain Kohler could easily evade pursuit in his 27½-knot ship, as Cradock wearily traversed the mid-Atlantic. In concert with *Dresden* during August and September, the two raiders terrorized the waters off the coast of Brazil where all the trade routes to South America converged. They held up cargoes of frozen meat in Argentine ports and gave a strong stimulus to pro-German feeling among neutral Latin American countries.

Then Spee summoned *Dresden* to meet him in the Pacific, luring Cradock south and leaving the West Indies open to *Karlsruhe* – a chance which Kohler did not miss. He drew his information about the sailings of merchant vessels from German intelligence in Brazil, the Argentine, and Chile, and waited for them to arrive. Working with *Kronprinz Wilhelm* he sank twenty ships in late September, taking what he needed from their cargoes and coaling at sea.

The extent of this damage was only realized when he landed 400 prisoners, and the pursuit was not fully organized until 14th October, when Admiral Stoddart was given overall command of the mid- and North Atlantic and the modern cruiser *Defence*. But Kohler was warned in advance; he sank two more rich cargoes and turned north, planning a spectacular blow to Allied morale in the heart of the West Indies, by destroying Barbados and Forte de France in Martinique.

So far, the only British successes had been the sinking of two armed liners, *Kaiser Wilhelm der Grosse* on the African coast, and *Cap Trafalgar* (by another armed liner, the Cunard *Carmania*) which disrupted supplies of coal to *Karlsruhe*. In the Pacific, all the German bases had been captured by combined operations with the dominions and Japanese. But the main danger was the unknown, powerful squadron of Spee, of which Admiral Cradock, now commanding the South Atlantic, was more aware than the British Admiralty. No one could know that Spee had decided to bring his ships home, if possible, intact. If he passed Cape Horn, Cradock reasoned, he could attack Capetown or even cross to head off the Anzac convoy. It was this which led him, at loggerheads with the Admiralty, to seek out Spee on the Pacific coast – and to the disastrous battle of Coronel. The first British naval engagement for a century ended on 1st November in almost total disaster.

At once the strategic picture changed. Spee must be destroyed. Two battle-cruisers were withdrawn from Jellicoe's Grand Fleet and despatched with such urgency that the fitters were left on board. A great concentration took place off the Brazilian coast and a net of steel was stretched on either side of Cape Horn. The Japanese and Australian fleets cut off the retreat to the Pacific. The urgency of the war in Europe was at last transferred to the far seas and finally ended the careers of the raiders: only as a result of a major humiliation was Pohl's gloomy prophecy fulfilled.

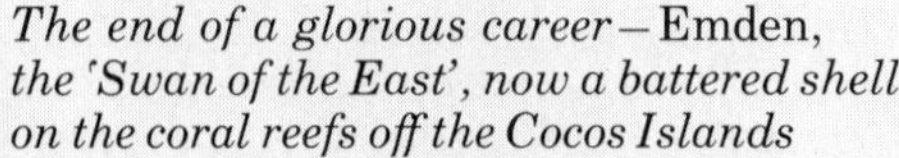

The end of a glorious career – Emden, *the 'Swan of the East', now a battered shell, on the coral reefs off the Cocos Islands*

End of the 'Swan of the East'

After two months of unparalleled havoc in the Indian Ocean, pursued by the game but ineffective Captain Grant in *Yarmouth, Emden*'s luck changed. Müller decided to attack the wireless station in the Cocos Islands to cut the trunk cables to Australia and South Africa, and ran straight into the path of the Anzac convoy which, heavily escorted, had at last left Perth. HMAS *Sydney,* under Captain Glossop, was detached in pursuit, and after a long running battle, Müller ran the ruined shell of *Emden,* the 'Swan of the East', on the coral reefs of the Cocos Islands. He was taken prisoner and, in unusual recognition, allowed to keep his sword.

Captain Kohler was meanwhile steaming towards Barbados. With all the Atlantic warships to the south, nothing could have saved the unsuspecting colony, but on a clear day, for no known reason, *Karlsruhe* suddenly exploded and was torn in two, sinking at once with the loss of her captain and most of the crew. It was ironic that, on the same day, the German admiralty cabled: 'Return home, your work is done.'

The danger of armed liners was also largely over. They had been, at best, an extravagant form of raider, fast but requiring immense quantities of coal. An organization for supplying them existed, run by Captain Boy-Ed of the German embassy in Washington, but the British warships waiting outside US territorial waters were too great a deterrent and the majority were interned. Only *Kronprinz Wilhelm* had a successful raiding career, sinking in six months some 60,000 tons of shipping. But although her speed was 25 knots she had to spend valuable weeks coaling at sea from captured colliers and, after November, was largely disregarded by the British forces concentrating on the threat at Cape Horn.

On 9th December came the news of the battle of the Falkland Islands in which Admiral Sturdee destroyed the whole of Spee's squadron except the raider *Dresden.* This was, practically speaking, the end of the war in the far seas. *Dresden* escaped along the myriad inlets of the Chilean coast but remained a hunted vagrant, finally tracked down and scuttled at Juan Fernández. The German colliers still slipped out from Brazilian ports to supply *Kronprinz Wilhelm* and another armed liner, *Prinz Eitel Friedrich,* which had escaped before the battle of the Falklands. Between them they took eighteen merchant ships during the winter but in March, for lack of coal, unable to undertake the long voyage home, they both ran in to Newport harbour in the United States and were interned. Six months later the recall of Captain Boy-Ed was demanded by the American government. His activities probably did more to swing American opinion against Germany than to create any lasting advantage for German seapower.

Königsberg alone remained. After the successful raid on Zanzibar Captain Looff had returned to his secret base, charted before the war, in the intricate muddy channels of the Rufiji river in German East Africa where he was tracked down and bottled in by a strong British squadron commanded by Captain Drury-Lowe. But *Königsberg* was out of range and hidden behind the forests and mangrove swamps, while her men were entrenched in efficient land defences. Supplies reached them from the interior. One of the channels was blocked by sinking an old collier, but others were open: *Königsberg* posed a unique problem and tied down three modern cruisers.

Primitive aircraft brought by ship from Capetown were able to locate her, but tropical rain and heat made them unusable. Both sides settled down to stalemate and nothing happened until March, when the German admiralty sent the collier *Rubens* to refuel the raider and give Looff the chance to break for the open sea and return home. After circling the north of Scotland and running down past the Cape, *Rubens* was sunk within a day's sail of the Rufiji. Looff sent half his men inland to help General von Lettow-Vorbeck in the war on Lake Tanganyika and abandoned hope of escaping. But *Königsberg* was still indestructible. More aircraft were sent out, and finally two monitors – flat gun emplacements, drawing only five feet of water. In the first air-sea operation ever mounted they steamed up river, firing indirectly at *Königsberg,* the fall of shot spotted from the air. At the first attack they were withdrawn, severely damaged. But the Germans were short of ammunition and the next assault, a week later, succeeded. The last of the German raiders was left, a riddled hulk on a mosquito-plagued shore, nearly a year after the start of the war.

The daring of the privateers

The raiders inherited the tradition of 18th-century privateers. Their orders debarred them from attacking warships except in emergency. German planning of bases, supplies of coal, and repairs was as efficient as the scattered nature of her colonies and the benevolence of neutrals would allow. But because of reverses in Europe, there was no subsequent strategy except, at the end, the order for recall. Yet, in the North Sea, few of the raiders would have had a use comparable to their value abroad. Events called in question the whole conception of far seas strategy. The German cruisers were superior in speed and gunnery to their British counterparts. *Karlsruhe* could have taken on Cradock's whole squadron and escaped – and if Spee, instead of turning away to preserve his ships had sailed straight into Port Stanley itself, he would have caught a fleet half at anchor, and sunk or severely damaged some of the best units in the British fleet, 6,000 miles from a British port. The German admiralty seems to have been dominated by calculations of sheer number. If the staff really believed the cruisers were doomed, they could have sent them down in crippling attacks on troop convoys or even harbours like Hong Kong. The courage and dash came from the raiders themselves, from Müller and Kohler, not from Berlin.

The war of movement took both sides by surprise. The effectiveness of the raiders, the daring of *Emden* and *Karlsruhe,* had not been foreseen. The needs of the army in Flanders overrode naval advice and it took Coronel to galvanize the British defences. Then the truth became clear: surface raiders had only a limited life. Submarines, two years later, were needed to bring Great Britain to the edge of starvation.

But the raiders meant something more. They pointed the contrast between war in the far seas and the struggles on the Western Front and the stagnation of embittered fleets facing each other across the North Sea. The raiders hit the headlines and the imagination. The gamekeeper's pursuit of the poacher did not. To German soldiers in Europe and in the snowbound trenches of the Russian Front the names of *Emden, Karlsruhe, Dresden,* and *Königsberg* brought pride and, above all, hope for the future, as operations contracted, grimly, to the war of attrition.

The Naval War, 1914 / Barrie Pitt

Revenge at Sea

The unthinkable had happened. The Royal Navy had been beaten in a naval battle. Reaction in Great Britain was immediate and drastic, and within a few days the powerful battle-cruisers **Inflexible** *and* **Invincible** *were heading into the south Atlantic – to seek revenge*

At the outbreak of war, the German East Asia Squadron under Vice-Admiral Graf Maximilian von Spee had been widely dispersed; but by 12th October all the most powerful ships, the *Scharnhorst, Gneisenau, Nürnberg* and *Leipzig* were gathered at Easter Island where they were joined by the light cruiser *Dresden*, which brought news of the British reaction to Spee's exploits to date, and thus gave him some idea of the forces being ranged against him.

These did not amount to much. If what *Dresden*'s captain told Spee was correct, the only British ships west of Cape Horn were the old armoured cruiser *Monmouth*, the modern light cruiser *Glasgow*, and the armed merchantman *Otranto*, while just east of the Horn at the British coaling base at Port Stanley on the Falkland Islands, the admiral commanding this tatterdemalion collection of ships, Vice-Admiral Sir Christopher Cradock, waited – presumably for more effective reinforcement – in the armoured cruiser *Good Hope*.

If this were all the naval opposition ranged for the moment against him, there was obviously no point in further delay; Spee coaled his squadron from colliers carefully collected beforehand at Easter Island, and on 18th October left – first for Más Afuera and then for the Chilean coast. He and his ships were forty miles off Valparaiso late on the afternoon of 30th October, and the following evening he learned that the British light cruiser *Glasgow* was at Coronel, 250 miles to the south.

National Maritime Museum, Greenwich

Bravely Gneisenau *and* Scharnhorst *fought their more powerful enemies in the battle of the Falkland Islands. But they were doomed. This picture painted by W.L.Wyllie, shows* Scharnhorst *and* Gneisenau *in action.* Scharnhorst *is sinking and* Gneisenau *will soon follow her. The British had taken their revenge for Coronel*

Detaching *Nürnberg* to pick up mail in Valparaiso, Spee took his squadron south in order to cut off the British cruiser, and perhaps to meet other British ships in company. By 1600 on Sunday, 1st November 1914, his ships were off Coronel, and at 1625 his lookouts sighted two ships away to the south-west; they were *Glasgow* and *Monmouth* and shortly afterwards these two were joined by *Good Hope* flying the flag of Admiral Cradock, and the armed merchantman *Otranto*. The two forces had found each other at last, and the first battle began in which ships of the German navy were ranged in line of battle against ships of the Royal Navy.

Everything favoured the German ships.

By 1800 the two battle lines were formed, and briefly there did appear some small advantage for the British: the setting sun was behind them, blinding the German gunners but lighting up the German ships into perfect targets. But the range was not close enough for the out-dated British guns, so at 1804 Cradock turned his ships four points towards his enemy – who with superior speed and room to manoeuvre turned away and kept out of range. Grimly, the British re-formed their battle line and assessed the odds against them – now shown up with ominous clarity; *Scharnhorst* and *Gneisenau* riding powerfully over the seas, the details of their high-placed heavy armament picked out by the westering sun, the seas racing along the towering sides and occasionally sweeping the foredecks.

Behind them came the light cruisers *Leipzig* and *Dresden*, and radio signals warned that *Nürnberg* was coming down fast from the north – but most fatal of all for the British, evening slowly crept over the sea from the east and touched the German battleline, greying it into the sea and the sky beyond. As twilight thickened, the moon came up behind heavy clouds, to show fleetingly through them, briefly outlining the German ships – and at last it seemed that *Scharnhorst* and *Gneisenau* were closing in. To the west, the afterglow of the sun made a fiery, yellow-shot tapestry of the windswept sky, against which the British ships now stood out in black, hard-edged clarity; nothing would help them tonight but their courage and the long tradition of the Royal Navy.

The massacre begins

At 1904 on Sunday, 1st November 1914, the 8·2-inch guns of the German East Asia Squadron at last opened fire on the British ships, at a range of 12,000 yards.

From the bridge of *Glasgow* were seen two lines of orange flashes from *Scharnhorst* and *Gneisenau*, and as the thunder of *Good Hope*'s 9·2s answered, grey-white mushrooms blossomed from the sea 500 yards short of the British ships, beautifully aimed, beautifully grouped.

Glasgow's pair of modern 6-inch guns fired experimentally into the darkness, but even while the gun controller was

Ullstein

Imperial War Museum

1 Admiral Spee's ships steam out of Valparaiso. In the far background are, from left to right, Scharnhorst, Gneisenau, *and* Leipzig. *In the foreground are Chilean warships. 2 German medal struck in commemoration of Spee's courage at Coronel and Falkland. With him are shown his two sons. One served on the* Gneisenau, *the other on the* Nürnberg. *Both were killed. 3 Cradock's flagship at Coronel, the armoured cruiser* Good Hope

4 Sunset, 1st November 1914. The opening of the battle of Coronel. The guns of the German East Asia Squadron open fire on the British ships. 5 Two hours later. Nürnberg *finds* Monmouth *and sinks her.* Otranto *has left the battle, and now* Glasgow *is fleeing.* Good Hope *has sunk. 6 The battle of the Falkland Islands, showing when the German ships sank.* Baden *and* Santa Isobel *were supply ships mopped up during the battle*

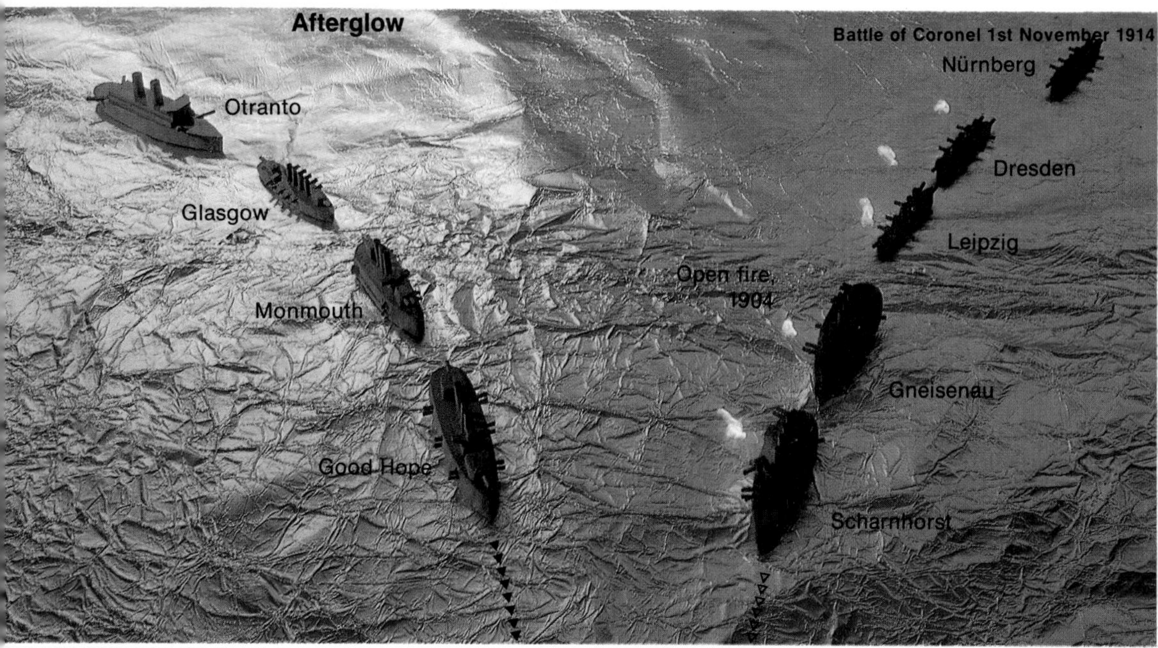

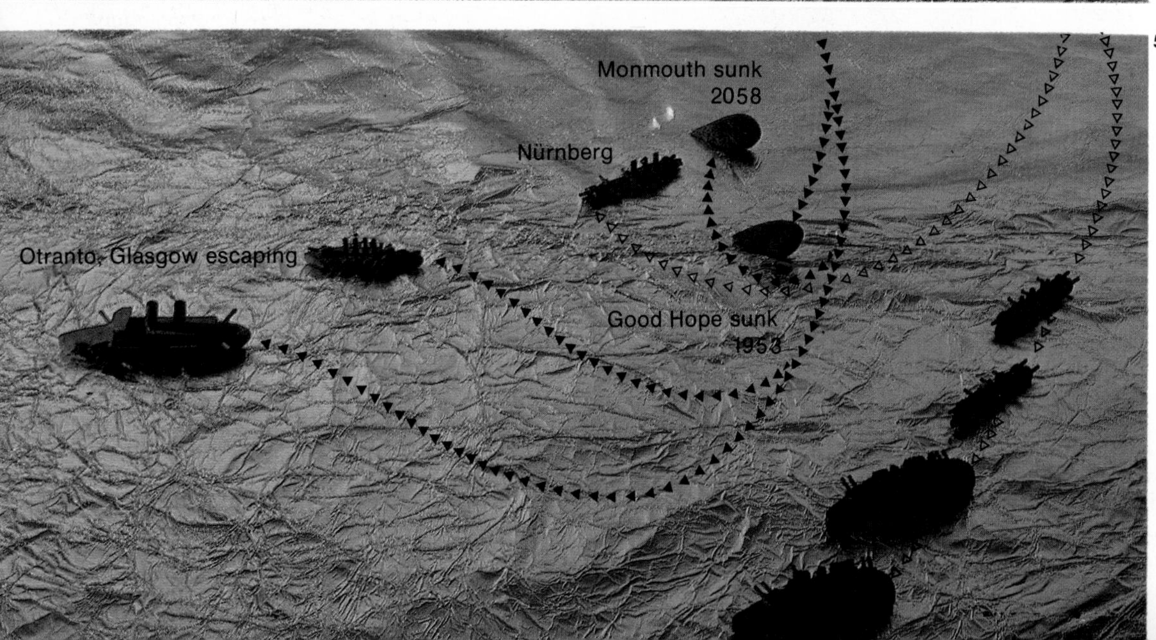

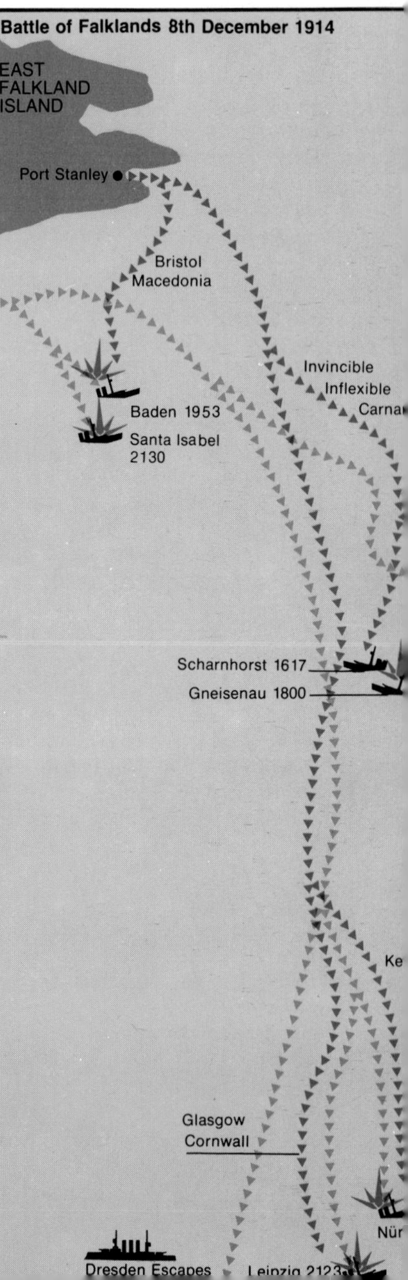

vainly searching the east for fall of shot, the orange lines sparkled again and then again – lengthened now as *Leipzig* and *Dresden* opened fire. Shell splinters whined shrilly overhead, the seas erupted around the British ships, *Monmouth* steamed ahead through a forest of water and *Good Hope*'s foredeck exploded in a sheet of flame which twisted the forward 9·2-inch gun into a hopeless knot of steel protruding from a turret like a blazing cauldron, and abruptly halved the British chance of harming the enemy at anything but short range. Before the mind could react, the next salvo arrived.

Monmouth's foredeck flared in hard-edged flame and black smoke billowed from sudden, sharp fires along her starboard side; *Good Hope*'s deck amidships threw up a fan of sparks, her upper bridge, mast-head, and foretop glowed redly as *Scharnhorst*'s high-explosive burst between them, and as the glow faded cordite flared on the deck, and stacked ammunition exploded whitely along the gun-flats.

Intent on closing the range and thus bringing his secondary armament into action, Cradock now led the British ships directly towards the German line – but Spee expertly held the range to his own advantage so that his ships remained unscathed while Cradock's took a dreadful punishment. *Monmouth,* especially, received the full attention of the guns of the *Gneisenau* – which had won the Kaiser's Gold Cup only months before – and began slowly to sag out of line as though beaten away by sheer weight of metal. Flames belched from her quarterdeck, water flooded through gaping holes in her bows, she listed badly to port and as darkness increased she disappeared to the south and her guns lapsed into silence.

Except for the endless flashes from their batteries, the German ships were now quite invisible from the British decks. Not so *Good Hope*; she flared like a beacon.

Since action had commenced the British flagship had received the undivided attention of the gunners aboard *Scharnhorst,* who were to prove as efficient as their colleagues aboard *Gneisenau.* At 1940, *Good Hope* was seen to slow and stagger under the rain of blows; her foredeck was ablaze, clouds of steam and smoke billowed around her, glowing sullenly, and her ports glowed redly from the fires in her crowded flats.

Then at 1942, as if in contempt for her own condition, *Good Hope* seemed to gather up her remaining strength, turn directly towards her antagonists and charge them. Abruptly, *Scharnhorst* and *Gneisenau* changed course slightly and shortened range to bring their full broadsides to bear – and, blanketed under a dreadful fire, *Good Hope* was at last brought to a halt and her last desperate throw defeated.

As though stunned, she drifted down silently between the lines.

Then the fires reached a main magazine and at 1953 – fifty minutes after the first salvo had been fired at her – *Good Hope* was shattered by an explosion which still lives in the memories of those who witnessed it. A broad column of flame rose upwards from between her main and after funnels until it towered two hundred feet above her decks, and in its awful light jagged and incongruous shapes soared up and away into the darkness, twisting and weaving in the blast, tumbling in the sudden vacuums.

Then the waves took the blazing hulk farther off into the darkness, the flames dwindled and all that remained of Cradock and his men drifted out of the battle.

A net of steel

This was virtually the end of the battle of Coronel. *Otranto* had already left the battle-line – ordered away by Cradock – and now *Glasgow,* after a vain attempt to succour *Monmouth,* fled to the south. At 2035, *Nürnberg* found *Monmouth* painfully making her way towards the Chilean coast and as the British ship made no attempt to strike her colours, had little choice but to reopen the action and finally sink her. At 2058 the waves finally closed over the stern of the British cruiser. There were no survivors – and none from the *Good Hope,* which was never seen again after she drifted from the battle. In two hours the Royal Navy had lost two ships and over 1,000 men and boys.

When the news reached Great Britain, the reaction was immediate and drastic. The first lord of the Admiralty, Winston Churchill, learned of the disaster at 1900 on 4th November, and immediately convened a meeting with the sea lords. As it happened, the position of first sea lord had just been taken over (for the second time) by Lord Fisher, and this doughty old man had no time for half measures – a characteristic which endeared him to Churchill.

Within a week the two battle-cruisers *Invincible* and *Inflexible* (as superior in speed and armament to *Scharnhorst* and *Gneisenau* as the German ships had been to *Good Hope* and *Monmouth)* had sailed from Devonport for the Falkland Islands, and they were joined on their voyage south by the County Class cruisers *Carnarvon, Cornwall,* and *Kent,* and the light cruisers *Bristol* and *Glasgow* (hurriedly patched up after her escape from Coronel in the dry dock at Rio). The squadron was under command of Vice-Admiral Sir Frederick Doveton Sturdee, and as it moved farther and farther south – searching all the time for Spee's ships in case they had already come around the Horn – his search line was lengthened every day by the addition of a host of colliers together with the armed merchantman *Orama,* and eventually by another cruiser, *Macedonia.*

Sturdee's augmented squadron reached the Falkland Islands on 7th December, and he ordered concentration in Port Stanley and the outer bay at Port William for coaling. After their long voyage, some of the ships needed to draw their fires for boiler examination, but *Glasgow* and *Carnarvon* coaled through the night, *Macedonia* patrolled outside the harbour, and at dawn on 8th December the colliers went alongside the battle-cruisers to begin filling their enormous demands for fuel.

To Sturdee, it thus seemed that within ten or twelve hours – twenty-four at the most – his entire squadron would be ready for sea again, to take up the search for the elusive German ships. This, of course, was his great problem, for with the enormous power at his disposal, there could be no doubt as to the outcome of a battle with the East Asia Squadron, once they were sighted. It was a problem rapidly solved.

Shortly after 0830 on the morning after his arrival at Port Stanley – while his capital ships were still coaling and two of his cruisers carrying out boiler examination – Sir Frederick was interrupted while shaving with the news that *Gneisenau* and *Nürnberg* were approaching the island and about twenty miles off, and the smoke from the other ships of Spee's command was visible on the horizon astern of them. It says much for the Vice-Admiral's *sang-froid* that his only comment was the classic 'Then send the men to breakfast'.

Spee's critical error

There is no way of being certain why Spee chose to attack the Falkland Islands, but there is little doubt about the fact that had he ordered an immediate attack on the British squadron as they lay at anchor in the two bays, he could have inflicted on them a defeat of staggering proportions – though probably at the cost of his own ships and certainly at the cost of using up all his remaining ammunition.

Fortunately for Sturdee, however, as soon as the captain of the *Gneisenau* reported the presence of a large number of British warships, Spee issued the order: 'Do not accept action. Concentrate on course east by south. Proceed at full speed.'

In doing so, the German admiral signed his own death-warrant and condemned his squadron to annihilation – though this fact did not become apparent to him or his men until 1000 when, to the dismay and astonishment of the observers aboard *Leipzig,* two pairs of tripod masts – the recognition mark of battle-cruisers were seen above the low-lying spit, proceeding towards Port William harbour.

From the British point of view, every

advantage favoured them. A long summer day stretched ahead, visibility was at its maximum, the sea calm, the sky clear and pale. By 1048 the whole squadron was at sea in a long line stretching eastwards from Port William–*Glasgow* in the lead, *Inflexible* and *Invincible* three miles astern, *Kent* two miles astern of them and *Cornwall* and *Carnarvon* as much again. The squadron's speed was 19 knots, the enemy were some twelve miles ahead and their calculated speed was only 15 knots.

The distance between the two adversaries inexorably lessened and at 1257 *Inflexible* fired the first shot of the battle of the Falkland Islands–at *Leipzig*, the lame duck of the German squadron. The shell fell well short, and only occasional sighting shots were fired during the next thirty minutes; then at 1320, Spee hoisted the signal: 'Light cruisers part company and endeavour to escape.' And the two armoured cruisers bravely turned to accept action from their formidable opponents.

As at Coronel by six o'clock in the evening, the main forces were now ranging broadside against broadside–but this was half past one in the afternoon, there were still eight hours of daylight left, and no mounting seas or storm clouds to complicate the hazards of war. *Invincible* opened fire against *Gneisenau*; *Inflexible* against *Scharnhorst*.

By this time, the British light and County Class cruisers had swung away from the main battle to chase the escaping German light cruisers, and Captain Allen aboard *Kent*, later wrote this description of the scene:

'With the sun still shining on them, the German ships looked as if they had been painted for the occasion. They fired as if they had but eight minutes in which to make a record battle-practice score and never have I seen heavy guns fired with such rapidity and yet with such control. Flash after flash travelled down their sides from head to stern, all their six and eight-inch guns firing every salvo.

Of the British battle-cruisers less could be seen as their smoke drifted from them across the range and not only obscured their own view but also the spectator's view of them. Nevertheless, they seemed to be firing incessantly, their shells hitting the German ships at intervals whereas all that could be seen of the German fire was that it straddled the British ships. Four or five times in the first twenty minutes the white puff of bursting shell could be seen among the clouds of brown cordite smoke in Gneisenau, *and she was seen to be on fire near her mainmast, but this soon disappeared.* (By permission of *Naval Review.*)

In addition to the greater weight of broadside and greater range of guns, the battle-cruisers had a further advantage–they were firing, for the first time in a naval battle, lyddite shell, and this new explosive wreaked dreadful havoc aboard the German ships. However Spee might seek to twist and turn, hoping for some sudden squall or mist patch in which to escape, the British battle-cruisers hung grimly on, unhurried but implacable, inexorably smashing his ships to pieces. All through the afternoon the battle continued, and aboard the British ships great admiration was felt for the perfect timing and grouping of the German gunnery, despite the chaos visible on the German decks.

By 1545 clouds of steam gushed upwards from *Scharnhorst*'s decks, the first and second funnels were leaning against each other, an enormous livid rent had been torn in the side plating below her quarterdeck and she was blazing fore and aft–but still her starboard batteries fired.

Her masts were gone, her bridge was wrecked, her magazines must have been almost empty, but still her ensign fluttered from a jury mast above the after control station. Then suddenly, just before 1600 her batteries ceased fire as though they had been switched off, and she was seen to turn eight points to starboard and come staggering across the seas towards her powerful antagonists. Behind her, *Gneisenau* swung across still firing rapidly, and as *Inflexible* re-engaged the farther ship, *Invincible* turned and headed for Spee's flagship. Less than 10,000 yards separated the two admirals, but it was soon evident that they would never meet, for *Scharnhorst*'s decks were a sea of fire, her speed fell away and she listed badly.

Just before 1610 her list took her deckrails under, water flooded inboard to quench the flames and she rolled on to her beams end. Through rents in her plating a few figures climbed laboriously and stood on her side-plates watching the battle-cruisers and the cold, impartial sea. Seven minutes later, *Scharnhorst*'s bows suddenly dipped, her stern came up, steam and smoke wreathed about her and with her flag still flying, she slid quickly under water and was gone, leaving only a huge yellow patch on the surface of the sea.

Fifteen minutes later, *Carnarvon* reached the spot and steamed directly through the stained waters. Neither survivors nor wreckage were visible.

By this time, *Invincible* had rejoined *Inflexible* and the two battle-cruisers turned their attention on *Gneisenau*.

The end was now a foregone conclusion, and as Sturdee had no intention of sustaining avoidable damage to either of his ships, he ordered them to stand off and take their time. Thus *Gneisenau*'s agony was protracted for another hour, by which time the destruction aboard beggared description.

Between the masts, her decks were beaten down to the armoured deck, and soon even this was torn open by plummeting shells. Her after-turret was jammed at ninety degrees, all the starboard casemate guns blown into the sea or pounded into shapeless masses of metal. Half her crew were dead or wounded, and shells had ended much suffering by exploding in the sick-bay and in the stokers' bathrooms where an emergency bay had been set up.

Then a shell from *Carnarvon* caused jamming of *Gneisenau*'s helm so that she slowly came round and, almost for the first time, the port batteries could come into action–though there was little enough ammunition left to fire. But there was some –enough to sting the battle-cruisers into re-opening fire and finishing *Gneisenau* as a fighting ship. Just before 1730 she lay almost motionless in the water, listing so badly that the seas flooded inboard through the lower gun ports.

Yet she was not sinking–and in order to ensure that nothing of value would fall into British hands, her captain gave the order for explosive charges between the inner and outer hull skins to be blown, and the stern torpedoes to be fired with the sluice gates left open. At a few minutes to six in the evening, *Gneisenau* seemed to shake herself and come fractionally out of the water; then she lay over at about ten degrees and began to settle. Her crew–what was left of them–gave three cheers for the Kaiser and then clambered across the decks to drop down into the icy waters alongside; and at two minutes after six, *Gneisenau*'s bows came up, keel uppermost, then slid down out of sight, leaving the seas littered with debris and struggling men. Only 187 of these, including seventeen officers but not *Gneisenau*'s captain, were picked up by British boats.

Of the remaining ships of Spee's command, *Nürnberg* was chased, caught, and sunk by *Kent* at 1927, *Leipzig* fought gallantly until 2123, against both *Cornwall* and *Glasgow*; and *Dresden* escaped for the moment. She reached Punta Arenas three days after the battle, passed through the Magellan Straits and played hide and seek with British pursuers until the morning of 14th March 1915, when she was found by *Glasgow* and *Kent* sheltering in Cumberland Bay on Juan Fernández Island.

But there was no battle. Tamely, her captain ran up a white flag, evacuated the crew ashore and then blew up the main magazine–and *Dresden*'s wreck still lies in the bay. After the fire and fury of the two battles, this was something of an anti-climax, but it should be remembered that *Dresden* was not an original member of the East Asia Squadron. Spee's captains all fought to the end, and went down with their ships.

The Naval War, 31st May–1st June 1916

Jutland

Here at last was the 20th-century Trafalgar: the long-awaited clash of the mighty dreadnoughts. As the two fleets collided in the North Sea and turned the full fury of their huge guns upon each other, the unexpected happened, suddenly, in many quarters. The story of this most controversial battle is told both by a British and a German naval historian.

British view/Captain Donald Macintyre

With the arrival of spring 1916, the First World War was eighteen months old. On land a decision had eluded the opposing armies; they had settled into a war of attrition bleeding both sides white. At sea the two most powerful fleets the world had ever seen faced each other across the North Sea, each eager to engage the other, but neither able to bring about an encounter on terms favourable to itself.

The British Grand Fleet, under Admiral Sir John Jellicoe, was concentrated at Scapa Flow, in the Orkneys, whence, it was calculated, the northern exit from the North Sea could be closed to the enemy, while the German fleet could still be intercepted and brought to battle should it threaten the British coasts. The British ability to read German coded radio mes-

Signals before the battle. 31st May 1916: the greatest battle fleet the world had ever seen steams into the North Sea to meet its German rival

Südd-Verlag, Munich

In one afternoon and evening the fate of the war hangs in the balance . . .

sages enabled them to obtain warning of any impending moves.

The German High Seas Fleet, numerically much inferior to its opponent, could contemplate battle with only a portion of the British Grand Fleet. From almost the beginning of the war its strategy had been aimed at forcing the British to divide their strength so that this might be brought about. Raids by the German battle-cruiser force, commanded by Rear-Admiral Hipper, on English east coast towns had been mounted. The failure of the Grand Fleet to intercept these had resulted in the Grand Fleet's battle-cruiser force, under Vice-Admiral Sir David Beatty, being based at Rosyth; and when Hipper again sortied in January 1915 he had been intercepted. In the battle of Dogger Bank which had followed, the German armoured cruiser *Blücher* had been sunk and the battle-cruiser *Seydlitz* had narrowly escaped destruction when a shell penetrated her after turret, starting a conflagration among the ammunition. Only flooding the magazine had saved her.

Further adventures by the High Seas Fleet had been forbidden by the Kaiser and the Germans had launched their first unrestricted U-boat campaign against Allied merchant shipping. For the rest of 1915 the High Seas Fleet had languished in port, chafing against its inaction.

But in January 1916, its command had been taken over by Admiral Reinhard Scheer who had at once set about reanimating it. Raids on the English coast were resumed. As before, the Grand Fleet, in spite of the warnings received through radio interception, had been unable to reach the scene from Scapa Flow in time to interfere. Jellicoe was forced to agree to his 5th Battle Squadron – the fast and powerful Queen Elizabeth-class ships – joining Beatty's Battle-cruiser Fleet at Rosyth.

When in May 1916, the U-boat campaign was called off at the threat of American intervention on the Allied side and the submarines recalled, Scheer had the conditions necessary for his ambition to bring about a fleet action on favourable terms by bringing the three arms of the fleet simultaneously into play. His surface forces were to sortie for a bombardment of Sunderland and lure the enemy to sea where his U-boats could ambush them, while his Zeppelin airships would scout far afield and so enable him to avoid any confrontation with a superior enemy concentration.

Plans were drawn up for the latter part of May; the actual date, to be decided at the last moment, would depend upon when the fleet was brought up to full strength by the return of the battle-cruiser *Seydlitz* from repairs caused by mine damage during a previous sortie, and upon suitable weather for the airships to reconnoitre efficiently. Meanwhile the U-boats, sixteen in number, sailed on 17th May for their stations off Scapa, Cromarty, and the Firth of Forth. Their endurance made the 30th the latest possible date. The *Seydlitz* did not rejoin until the 28th, however, and then a period of hazy weather set in, unsuitable for air reconnaissance.

Against such a development, an alternative plan had been prepared. Hipper's battle-cruiser force was to go north from the Heligoland Bight and 'trail its shirt' off the Norwegian coast where it would be duly reported to the British. Beatty's battle-cruiser fleet from Rosyth would come racing eastwards to fall into the trap of the High Seas Fleet battle squadrons, waiting some forty miles to the southward of Hipper, before the Grand Fleet from Scapa could intervene.

The trap is set

Such a plan – assuming an unlikely credulity on the part of the British – was naïve, to say the least, even allowing for the fact that the British ability to read German wireless signals was not realized. Nevertheless, when the thick weather persisted throughout the 28th and 29th, it was decided to employ it. On the afternoon of 30th May, the brief signal went out to the High Seas Fleet assembled in the Schillig Roads – 31GG2490, which signified 'Carry out Secret Instruction 2490 on 31st May'.

This was duly picked up by the Admiralty's monitoring stations and though its meaning was not known, it was clear from various indications that some major operation by the German fleet was impending. At once the organization for getting the Grand Fleet to sea swung into action; the main body under the commander-in-chief, with his flag in the *Iron Duke*, including the three battle-cruisers of the 3rd Battle-Cruiser Squadron, who had been detached there from Rosyth for gunnery practice, sailed from Scapa Flow; from the Cromarty Firth sailed the 2nd Battle Squadron, the 1st Cruiser Squadron, and a flotilla of destroyers. These two forces were to rendezvous the following morning (31st) in a position some ninety miles west of Norway's southerly point. When joined, they would comprise a force of no less than 24 dreadnought battleships, 3 battle-cruisers, 8 armoured cruisers, 12 light cruisers, and 51 destroyers. Beatty's Battle-Cruiser Fleet – 6 battle-cruisers, the four 15-inch-gun, fast Queen Elizabeth-class battleships, 12 light cruisers, 28 destroyers, and a seaplane carrier – was to steer from the Firth of Forth directly to reach a position some 120 miles west of the Jutland Bank at 1400 on the 31st, which would place him sixty-nine miles ahead of the Grand Fleet as it steered towards the Heligoland Bight. If Beatty had ▷548

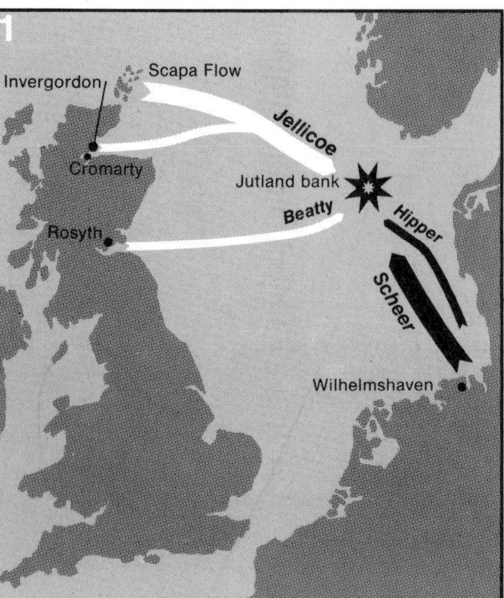

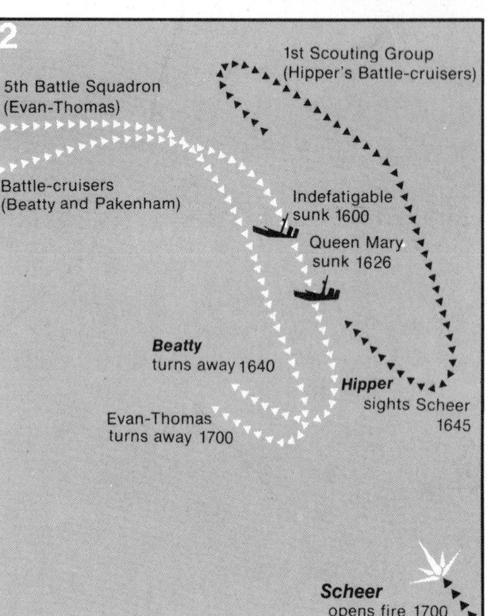

1 The titans weigh anchor and steam to battle stations on the Jutland Bank, 31st May 1916. 2 Battle-cruiser action, 1415-1800, 31st May. Lacking flash-tight magazines and betrayed by inadequate armour protection, Indefatigable *and* Queen Mary *exploded under a hail of fire from Hipper's ships. 3 First fleet action, 1815-1835. Scheer had manoeuvred into the worst possible situation for a fleet action. Only by ordering a simultaneous 'about turn' could he extricate himself from the trap so brilliantly sprung by Jellicoe. 4 Second fleet action, 1912-1926. The British battle fleet opened fire at 1912 but the engagement was broken off when Scheer executed a second 'about turn', at the same time launching a massed torpedo attack. Jellicoe promptly countered by turning his own battle line. 5 Loss of contact during the night of 31st May-1st June, 2100-0300. Scheer eluded Jellicoe and ran for home.*

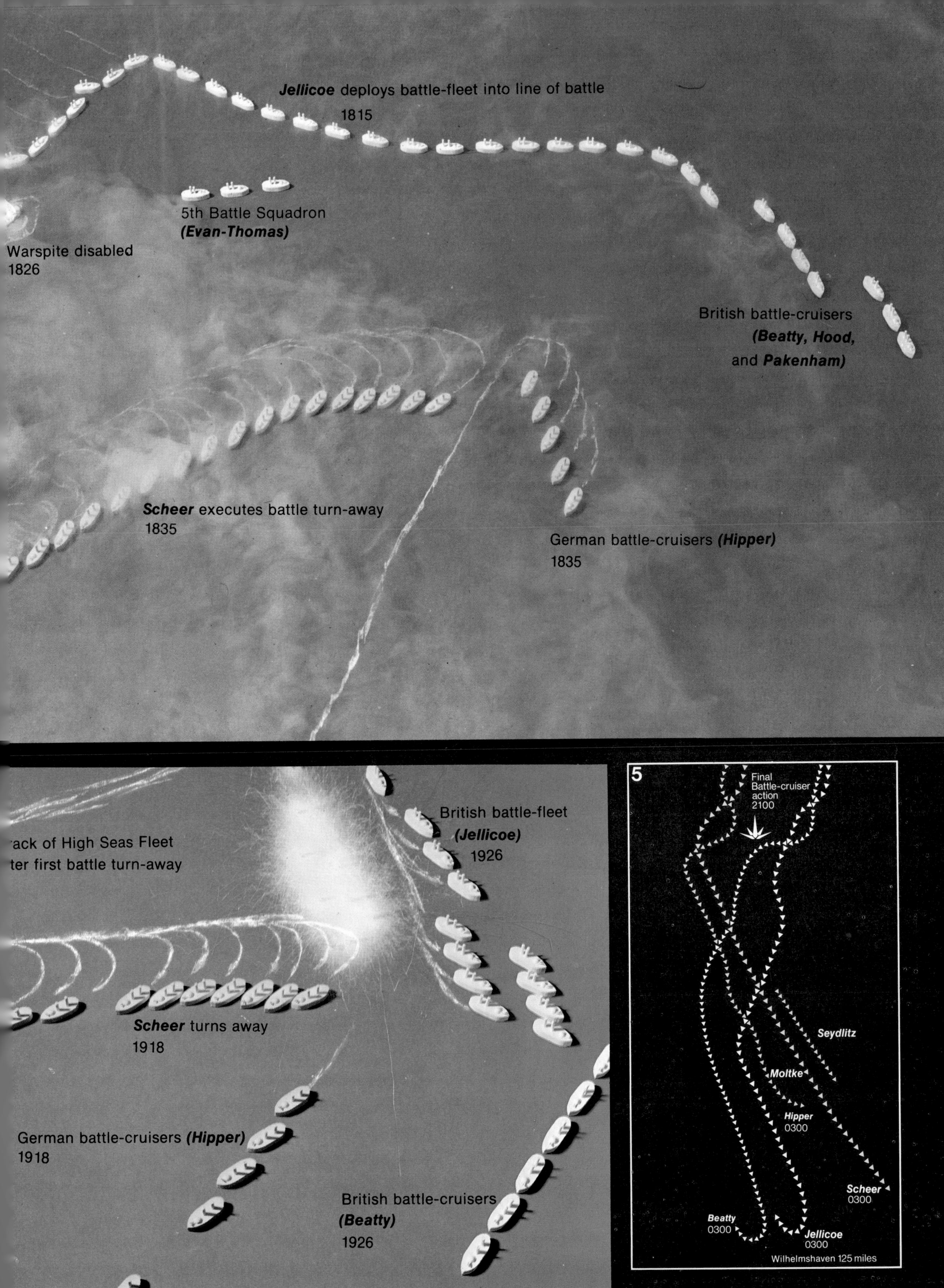
Jellicoe deploys battle-fleet into line of battle
1815
5th Battle Squadron
(Evan-Thomas)
Warspite disabled
1826
British battle-cruisers
(Beatty, Hood,
and Pakenham)
Scheer executes battle turn-away
1835
German battle-cruisers (Hipper)
1835
British battle-fleet
(Jellicoe)
1926
rack of High Seas Fleet
ter first battle turn-away
Scheer turns away
1918
German battle-cruisers (Hipper)
1918
British battle-cruisers
(Beatty)
1926
5
Final
Battle-cruiser
action
2100
Seydlitz
Moltke
Hipper
0300
Scheer
0300
Beatty
0300
Jellicoe
0300
Wilhelmshaven 125 miles

HMS Lion *leads cruisers* **Warrior** *and* **Defence** *into action (left) and battle-cruisers* **Princess Royal, Tiger,** *and* **New Zealand** *(right). Painted by W.Wyllie RA (Reproduced by permission of Earl Beatty)*

National Portrait Gallery

'Some Sea Officers, 1914-1918' painted by Sir Arthur S.Cope RA. Among them, left to right, are Beatty who led the battle-cruiser fleet at Jutland (left foreground), Sturdee (seated centre right), and Jellicoe, who was the commander-in-chief at Jutland (far right)

sighted no enemy by that time, he was to turn north to meet Jellicoe.

Thus, long before the first moves of Scheer's plan to lure Beatty out had been made, the whole vast strength of the British fleet was at sea. The schemer was liable to have the tables turned on him. The first aim of Scheer's project had already been missed. His U-boats had failed to deliver any successful attacks on the British squadrons as they sortied; furthermore their reports of what they had seen added up only to various isolated squadrons at sea and gave no warning that the Grand Fleet was at sea in strength.

At 0100 on 31st May, therefore, the first ships of Hipper's force – five battle-cruisers of the 1st Scouting Group *(Lützow* (flagship), *Derfflinger, Seydlitz, Moltke, Von der Tann),* four light cruisers of the 2nd Scouting Group, and 33 destroyers led by another light cruiser – weighed anchor and steered north past Heligoland and through the swept channels, leaving the Horn Reef light vessel to the eastward of them. They were followed, fifty miles astern, by Scheer, his flag in the *Friedrich der Grosse,* leading 16 dreadnought battleships, 6 pre-dreadnoughts, and accompanied by 5 light cruisers of the 4th Scouting Group and 39 destroyers led by a light cruiser.

By 1400 Hipper was abreast the Jutland Bank off the Danish coast – his scouting light cruisers spread on an arc extending from ahead to either beam, some seven to ten miles from the battle-cruisers. It was a clear, calm, summer day with visibility extreme but likely to become hazy as the afternoon wore on. Unknown to Hipper and equally ignorant of his presence, Beatty was fifty miles to the north-westward, zig-zagging at 19 knots on a mean course of east and approaching the eastward limit set for his advance, with his light cruisers scouting ahead in pairs. The signal to turn north was made at 1415 and was obeyed by all except the light cruiser *Galatea* which held on to investigate smoke on the eastern horizon. This came from a Danish merchantman and was simultaneously being investigated by the western-most of Hipper's light cruisers, the *Elbing.* The two warships thus came in sight of one another, reported, and fired the opening shots of the battle of Jutland.

The two battle-cruiser admirals turned at once towards the sound of the guns which soon brought them in sight of one another on opposite courses, when Hipper altered course to the southward to lead his opponents towards the advancing German battle squadrons. That these were at sea was still unknown to either Beatty or Jellicoe. The British radio monitoring stations had been led to believe that the High Seas Fleet was still in harbour, misled by an arrangement on the part of Scheer's staff which transferred the flagship's call-sign to a shore station so that the commander-in-chief would not be distracted by administrative matters.

The battle-cruisers open fire

The *Lion,* leading *Princess Royal, Queen Mary, Tiger, New Zealand* and *Indefatigable* (in that order), turned on a parallel course and at 1548 each side opened fire. Hipper was outnumbered, six ships to five. He would have been even more, perhaps disastrously, inferior, but for Beatty's impetuosity in racing at full speed into action without waiting for the 5th Battle Squadron, which was not only initially six miles farther from the enemy but, owing to signal confusion, failed to conform at once to Beatty's movements. By the time it did so, it was ten miles astern, and it was not until twenty-seven minutes after action had been joined that the 15-inch guns of the British battleships could open fire.

In the interval much had happened. Hipper's ships had quickly displayed a gunnery superiority over their opponents who were very slow to find the range. The *Lion, Princess Royal,* and *Tiger* had all been heavily hit before a single German ship had suffered; though the *Seydlitz, Derfflinger,* and *Lützow* were then each hit hard, the advantage had continued to lie with Hipper's ships and at 1600 Beatty's rear ship, *Indefatigable,* had blown up and sunk as shells plunged through into her magazines. Almost simultaneously the *Lion* had been only saved from a similar fate by flooding the magazine of her mid-ship turret when it was penetrated by a shell from the *Lützow.*

But now, at last, the 5th Battle Squadron *(Barham, Valiant, Warspite, Malaya,* lying in that order) was able to get into action. Their gunnery was magnificent. The two rear ships of Hipper's line were quickly hit. Disaster must have overwhelmed him but for a defect of the British shells, some of which broke up on impact instead of penetrating the armour. Nevertheless, it seemed impossible Hipper could survive long enough for Scheer's battle-squadrons, still over the horizon, to come to his rescue. In spite of this the German battle-cruisers continued to shoot with deadly accuracy and at 1626 the *Queen Mary,* betrayed, like the *Indefatigable,* by her inadequate armour, blew up.

Meanwhile, a destroyer battle had been raging between the lines, the flotillas on each side moving out to attack with torpedoes and meeting to fight it out with guns. Of all the torpedoes fired, one only, from the British *Petard,* found a billet in the *Seydlitz,* but did not damage her enough to put her out of action. Two British destroyers were sunk.

The fast-moving battle had left the majority of Beatty's scouting cruisers behind, except for Commodore Goodenough's 2nd Light Cruiser Squadron which by 1633 had succeeded in getting two miles ahead of the *Lion.* At that moment to Goodenough's astonished gaze the top masts of a long line of battleships hove in sight.

Battle-cruiser Seydlitz *on fire during the battle. Although heavily damaged by torpedo and shellfire she was not put out of action*

In the radio rooms of the ships of the British fleet, the message, which all had almost despaired of ever hearing, was taken in: 'Have sighted enemy battle fleet, bearing SE. Enemy's course North.'

Hipper had been saved in the nick of time, and his task of luring Beatty brilliantly achieved. Goodenough's timely warning, however, enabled the latter to escape the trap. Before the enemy battle fleet came within range, Beatty reversed course to the northward. The 5th Battle Squadron held on for a while to cover the damaged battle-cruisers' retreat. By the time they turned back themselves they came under heavy fire from the German battle squadrons and *Malaya,* in particular, received damaging hits. In reply they did heavy damage to the *Lützow, Derfflinger,* and *Seydlitz,* as well as hitting the leading German battleships.

The situation had now been reversed, with Beatty drawing the enemy after him towards a superior force the latter knew nothing of—the Grand Fleet, pressing southwards at its best speed of 20 knots. Jellicoe's twenty-four battleships were in the compact cruising formation of six columns abeam of each other, with the fleet flagship leading the more easterly of the two centre columns. Before encountering the enemy they would have to be deployed into a single battle line to allow all ships to bring their guns to bear. If deployment was delayed too long, the consequences could be disastrous. To make a deployment by the right method, it was essential that the admiral should know the bearing on which the approaching enemy would appear.

For various reasons—discrepancy between the calculated positions of the two portions of the fleet and communication failures—this was just what Jellicoe did not know. And, meanwhile, the two fleets were racing towards each other at a combined speed of nearly 40 knots. Even though Beatty's light cruisers had made visual contact with Jellicoe's advanced screen of armoured cruisers at 1630, though the thunder of distant gun-fire had been audible for some time before the *Marlborough,* leading the starboard column of the Grand Fleet battleships, sighted gunflashes through the gathering haze and funnel smoke ahead at 1750, and six minutes later Beatty's battle-cruisers were sighted from the *Iron Duke* racing across the line of Jellicoe's advance—and incidentally spreading a further pall of black smoke—it was not until nearly 1815 that at last, in the nick of time, the vital piece of information reached the commander-in-chief from the *Lion:* 'Enemy battle fleet bearing south-west.'

Jellicoe's vital decision

During the next minute or so, through the mind of Jellicoe as he stood gazing at the compass in its binnacle on the bridge of the *Iron Duke,* sped the many considerations on the accurate interpretation of which, at this moment of supreme crisis, the correct deployment and all chances of victory depended. The decision Jellicoe made—to deploy on his port wing column on a course south-east by east—has been damned and lauded by opposing critics in the controversy that was later to develop.

To the appalled Scheer, as out of the smoke and haze ahead of him, between him and retreat to his base, loomed an interminable line of dim grey shapes from which rippled the flash of heavy gunfire, and a storm of shell splashes began to fall round the leading ships of his line, there was no doubt. His 'T' had been crossed—the worst situation possible in a fleet action. Fortunately for him a counter to such a calamity, a simultaneous 'about turn' by every ship of the battle columns—a manoeuvre not lightly undertaken by a mass of the unwieldy battleships of the day—had been practised and perfected by the High Seas Fleet. He ordered it now, and so, behind a smoke screen laid by his destroyers extricated himself from the trap so brilliantly sprung by Jellicoe.

His escape was only temporary, nevertheless. Between him and his base was a force whose full strength he had been unable as yet to determine, which he must either fight or somehow evade.

While the trap was thus being sprung on Scheer, some final spectacular successes had been achieved by the Germans. Of the 5th Battle Squadron, the *Warspite,* with her helm jammed, had charged towards Scheer's battle line and before she could be got under control again, had been severely damaged and forced out of action. Jellicoe's advanced screen of armoured cruisers had been caught at short range by Hipper's battle-cruisers and the leading German battleships as they emerged from the smoke haze. The *Defence* had been overwhelmed and blown up, the *Warrior* so heavily damaged that she staggered out of action to sink on her way back to harbour. Then the German battle-cruisers had encountered the three battle-cruisers attached to the Grand Fleet. In a brief gun duel at short range, the Germans had suffered many hits and further damage; but in reply had sunk the *Invincible* whose magazine was penetrated in the same way as in the *Indefatigable* and *Queen Mary.*

This was the last major success for the Germans, however. They had fought magnificently and, with the aid of superior ship design and ammunition, had had much the better of the exchanges, though the *Lützow* was by now fatally crippled, limping painfully off the scene, and only the stout construction and well-designed compartmentation of the other battle-cruisers was saving them from a similar state. But Scheer was now desperately on the defensive, though he had not yet realized that it was the whole Grand Fleet he had encountered. As soon as his initial retreat brought relief from the concentration of fire on his van, he reversed course once again in the hope of being able to cut through astern of the enemy to gain a clear escape route to the Horn Reef lightship and safety behind his own minefields. Once again he ran up against the immense line of dreadnoughts of which all he could see in the poor visibility to the eastward was the flickering orange light of their broadsides. Once again he had hastily to retire or be annihilated.

While he was extricating himself he launched his much-tried battle-cruisers on a rearguard thrust and his destroyer flotillas to deliver a massed torpedo attack. The former miraculously survived a further hammering before being recalled. The latter launched a total of twenty-eight torpedoes at the British line. More than any other single factor they were to save the High Seas Fleet from disaster, robbing Jellicoe of the fruits of the strategic masterpiece he had brought about.

The counter to the massed torpedo attack by destroyers, which could be backed by long-range torpedo fire from retreating battleships, had been carefully studied. There were several alternatives; the only one sufficiently effective in Jellicoe's opinion, was a simultaneous turn away by his own battle line. This was promptly carried out – a turn of 45 degrees.

Contact lost

The two battle fleets were now on widely diverging courses and rapidly ran out of range and sight of one another. By the time the twenty-eight torpedoes had been avoided – not one scored a hit – and the British battle line turned back to regain contact, more than fifteen miles separated Jellicoe and Scheer. Sunset was barely half an hour away. Yet there was time in the long summer twilight ahead for the battle to be renewed on greatly advantageous terms for Jellicoe if he turned at once to an interception course. That he did not do so until too late for various reasons, not the least of which was the failure of his scouting forces to keep him informed of the enemy's position and movements, was to be the central feature of much criticism.

The van of the German battle fleet came, in fact, briefly into view from the nearest British battleship division at the moment that Jellicoe, who was not willing to accept the uncertain fortunes of a night action, ordered a turn away and the adoption of a compact night cruising disposition. The opportunity was let slip, never to return.

Nevertheless, at this stage, as night settled down over a calm sea, the outlook for Scheer was bleak, indeed. Between him and his base was an overwhelming enemy force. Unless he could get past it during the night, the battle must be resumed at daybreak and, with a long summer day ahead, it could only spell annihilation for him. He decided his only hope was to try to bludgeon his way through, regardless of consequences. To his fleet he signalled the course for the Horn Reef Light at a speed of 16 knots, adding the instruction that this course was to be maintained at all costs.

Jellicoe, having formed his night disposition and ordered his flotillas (many of whom had not yet been in action) to the rear, was steering a course slightly converging with that of Scheer but at a knot faster. From Jellicoe's point of view, Scheer had the choice of two routes – to the entrance of the channels which began at the Horn Reef Light or southward into the German Bight before turning eastward round the mined areas. The extra knot would keep the Grand Fleet between Scheer and the latter. If he chose the former he must pass astern of Jellicoe's battle squadrons, where he would encounter the massed British flotillas which could be counted on to inflict severe losses and to keep Jellicoe informed.

In the event the British flotillas failed to do either of these things. The pre-dreadnought battleship *Pommern* and a light cruiser were their sole victims in a series of night encounters, and they passed no information of the position and course of the enemy. On the other hand Scheer's message to his fleet was intercepted by the Admiralty and was passed to Jellicoe, though a further message in which Scheer asked for airship reconnaissance of the Horn Reef area at dawn which would have clinched the matter, was withheld.

In the absence of certain knowledge of the enemy's movements, Jellicoe held on through the night. Scheer crossed astern of him and by daylight was safe, a development which seemed little short of miraculous to the German admiral.

The battle of Jutland was over. Controversy as to its outcome was to rage for decades. The bald facts, of which German publicity made the most in claiming a great victory, while the British Admiralty's communiqué did nothing to explain or qualify them, showed that a superior British force had lost three capital ships, three cruisers, and a number of destroyers against one battle-cruiser, a pre-dreadnought battleship, four cruisers, and some destroyers sunk on the German side.

Even to-day more than fifty years since the battle, it is not easy to strike a balance sheet of victory and defeat. British losses were largely the result of inferior armour protection in their battle-cruisers, which had been accepted in favour of mounting bigger guns, the advantage of which had been lost through faulty design of armour-piercing shells. Even so, one of the surviving German battle-cruisers only reached harbour in a sinking condition, another was a hideous shambles with 200 casualties, bearing witness to the pounding they had

London Express

Imperial War Museum

Above: *German cruiser* Blücher *sinking in battle of Dogger Bank, January 1915.* ***Below:*** Iron Duke, *Jellicoe's flagship*

Imperial War Museum

Imperial War Museum

Above: *Beatty's flagship* Lion *firing first shots in the battle.* ***Below:*** Derfflinger, *the battle-cruiser that sank* Invincible

Above: *Battle-cruiser* Indefatigable *going into action at Jutland.* ***Below:*** *Battleship* Warspite *laid up in dry dock*

Above: *Battleship* Malaya *of the 5th Battle Squadron.* ***Below:*** *Battle-cruiser* Invincible. *Blew up like* Indefatigable

received even from defective shells.

The High Seas Fleet was no longer fit for battle on the morning of the 1st June 1916 and could only make for harbour and repairs, fortunately close at hand. The Grand Fleet was largely intact and ready to renew the fight. Jellicoe may be said, perhaps, to have lost the battle of Jutland. Scheer can hardly be judged to have won anything but an escape from annihilation.

So much for the immediate results of the encounter. They do not add up to a victory for either side. In the larger context of the war at sea as a whole, it is no easier to weigh the results. When Scheer led the High Seas Fleet out once again in August 1916 (except for *Seydlitz* and *Derfflinger,* still under repair), he narrowly escaped being caught in a second Jutland trap, with no safe base under his lee this time, in spite of Zeppelin reconnaissance aloft. Both Scheer and the Kaiser's general headquarters were finally convinced that the risks to be faced in attempting to bring about a sea fight were unacceptable. The High Seas Fleet, built at such cost to challenge Great Britain's seapower, was ordered back on to the defensive. The fatal decision was taken to revert to the unrestricted submarine warfare which was to bring America into the war.

It is true, of course, that the High Seas Fleet kept 'in being', forced the continued maintenance of the huge Grand Fleet, absorbing many thousands of trained seamen and a hundred destroyers which could have been more profitably employed combating the U-boats. On the other hand, that same High Seas Fleet, its ships lying idle in harbour, the morale of its crews sinking, degenerated into a centre of discontent and revolution. In August 1917 Scheer had to quell an open mutiny. A year later, when ordered to sea by its new commander, Hipper, it flared into revolt and led the disintegration of the Kaiser's Germany. This, too, can be accounted one of the consequences of Jutland – perhaps the most important when reviewing the whole war.

German view / Vice-Admiral Friedrich Ruge

Jutland was the last of many naval battles fought by long lines of closely spaced big ships with heavy guns. Its tactical details are well-known, for each ship kept a log. Its results were inconclusive. It was the climax of the Anglo-German naval rivalry, with the scuttling of the German fleet at Scapa Flow three years later as the anti-climax.

This rivalry, which cost both nations dearly, was at least partly caused by the fact that the Germans did not fully realize the implications of seapower. In their difficult position in central Europe they needed a navy of some strength to balance the fleets of the Franco-Russian alliance. But from their inferior strategic position in the south-eastern corner of the North Sea they could neither protect their overseas trade nor attack the sea routes vital to Great Britain. When war broke out in 1914 the Royal Navy was not compelled to attack the German bases but could content itself on the whole with a distant blockade from Scapa Flow.

In the first two years of the war there were a number of operations and clashes in the North Sea which did not change the situation, since neither side wanted to give battle too far from their own bases. In 1916 this changed to some extent. Admiral Reinhard Scheer, the new commander-in-chief of the German High Seas Fleet, was more aggressive than his predecessors. On the Allied side, the Russians felt the blockade heavily and clamoured for the British to force the Baltic so that they might receive ammunition and raw materials which they needed desperately. An operation of that kind had no prospects of success, however, as long as the High Seas Fleet was intact. Therefore it was decided that stronger efforts should be made to bring it to battle. The Grand Fleet under Admiral Sir John Jellicoe had been considerably reinforced by new ships. In spring 1916 it was almost twice as strong as the German fleet.

Early in March, the German fleet made a sortie into the southern North Sea and came within sixty miles of Lowestoft. On 25th March British light forces operated south of Horn Reef, and aircraft from a seaplane-carrier tried to bombard airship sheds. Bad weather prevented contact of the heavy ships. On 25th April German battle-cruisers bombarded Lowestoft. Early in May the British repeated the attempt to attack airship sheds. Both fleets were at sea, but no contact was established.

For the second half of May, Admiral Scheer planned an operation with all his forces. The battle-cruisers were to bombard Sunderland, and twelve submarines were stationed off the British bases to attack the squadrons of the Grand Fleet when they put to sea. Scouting by airships was necessary for the German fleet to avoid being cut off by superior forces. When the time ran out for his submarines after two weeks at sea and the weather remained unfavourable, Scheer compromised on a sweep of his light forces through the Skagerrak backed up by the battle fleet. Shortly after midnight of 30th to 31st May 1916 the German scouting forces (5 battle-cruisers, 5 light cruisers, and 30 destroyers under Rear-Admiral Hipper) left Schillig Roads near Wilhelmshaven, soon followed by the battle fleet (16 new and 6 old battleships, 6 light cruisers, and 33 destroyers). ▷ 552

The Grand Fleet at sea

At that time the Grand Fleet was already at sea, course set for the Skagerrak, too. The bombardment of Lowestoft had roused public opinion, the situation of the Russians had deteriorated, and Jellicoe now planned to set a trap for the German fleet. Light cruisers were to sweep through the Skagerrak deep into the Kattegat; in the meantime the main forces would take up position near Horn Reef to meet the Germans who were sure to come out in order to intercept the British cruisers operating in the Kattegat.

In the early afternoon of 31st May occurred the first of the incidents which greatly changed the course of the events. The British battle-cruiser fleet, under Vice-Admiral Sir David Beatty in *Lion*, changed course from east to north to rendezvous with the battle fleet under Admiral Jellicoe in *Iron Duke.* At 1430 *Lützow,* flying Admiral Hipper's flag, was only forty-five miles east of *Lion* steering a slightly converging course. Contact would have been made considerably later but for a small Danish steamer plodding along between the two forces. Two German destroyers and a British light cruiser were dispatched to examine her. Soon the first salvoes were fired; the first hit (a dud) was made by *Elbing* on *Galatea.*

Within minutes wireless messages informed the admirals of the situation. Signals went up, Hipper swung his force round, and Beatty soon followed suit. The crews were alerted by bugles sounding action stations, guns and powder rooms were manned, steam was raised in reserve boilers, and damage parties assembled deep down in the ships. The gunnery officers climbed to their elevated positions, received ready reports from turrets, range-finders, and fire-control-stations, and then reported their batteries ready for action to their captains. Now a hush of expectancy fell over the great ships while the distance decreased by nearly a mile a minute.

At first, sight was obscured by the smoke of the cruisers. Then these fell back on their battle-cruisers, and the huge shapes of the adversaries came into each other's sight, but only for the few men whose duty was to watch the enemy. Almost all the technical personnel and most of the sailors fought without seeing an enemy ship.

Hipper faced heavy odds, ten ships with heavier guns against his five. His plan was simple: to draw the enemy to Scheer's battle fleet, which was following at a distance of fifty miles. His smaller calibres (11- and 12-inch as against 12-, 13-, and 15-inch in the British ships) made it imperative for him to get comparatively close before opening fire. He offered battle on a north-westerly course, reversed course when Beatty tried to cut his force off, and with a few terse signals coolly manoeuvred his fine ships through the danger zone. At 1548 they were at the right distance (16,500 yards) and in perfect order. The *Lützow* opened fire.

Beatty's ships started answering quickly but they were not yet in formation to use all their guns. Because of delays in signalling, the four powerful and fast battleships of the Queen Elizabeth-class had fallen astern and were out of range. Conditions for a gunnery duel were perfect: visibility was good, especially to the west, and there was hardly any seaway.

First blood to the Germans

The first salvoes all appear to have fallen wide, perhaps because the range-takers were more interested in the details of their foes than in measuring the distance exactly. After three minutes the Germans obtained hits on *Lion, Princess Royal,* and *Tiger.* Because the first target in sight had been light cruisers, the gunnery officer of *Lützow* had given orders to load shells detonating on impact. For reasons of ballistics he did not change over to armour-piercing shells. *Lion* was hit twelve times and suffered heavy casualties, but minor injuries only, except for one shell which penetrated the roof of a turret, killed the gun crews, and ignited powder-bags. The turret-commander, Major Harvey of the Royal Marines, was fatally wounded but before he died he ordered the magazines to be flooded and thus saved the ship.

Now disaster struck the rear of the British line. Here *Indefatigable* and *Von der Tann* fought an even match. At 1604, *Indefatigable,* hit by two salvoes in quick succession, erupted in a violent explosion, turned over to port and disappeared in the waves. *Von der Tann* had fired fifty-two 11-inch shells in all. Twenty minutes later a similar fate overtook *Queen Mary* who had come under the concentrated fire of *Derfflinger* and *Seydlitz.* After vehement detonations she capsized and went down with her propellers still turning. *Tiger,* the next astern, barely avoided crashing into the wreck.

In spite of these losses the situation now eased for the British. The magnificent 5th Battle Squadron, ably handled by Rear-Admiral Evan-Thomas, came up and took the rear ships of the German line under fire. When one of the projectiles, weighing almost a ton, struck *Von der Tann* far aft, the whole ship vibrated like a gigantic tuning-fork. Hipper increased speed and distance and sent his destroyers to the attack. They were met by British destroyers, and in the ensuing mêlée *Nomad* and two Germans were sunk. At the same time 1630 the 2nd Light Cruiser Squadron under Commodore Goodenough sighted smoke to the south-east and, soon after, a seemingly endless column of heavy ships surrounded by light cruisers and destroyers.

Now the tables were turned. Under heavy fire Beatty reversed course and steered to the north to draw the High Seas Fleet to the British Battle Fleet. *Barham* and *Malaya* received several hits which did not, however, impair their speed, but, *Nestor,* attacking the German van with some other destroyers, was sunk. When her boatswain was rescued with other survivors he was mainly disgusted at the smallness and squalor of the coal-burning torpedo-boat which had picked him up.

All through these events the British Battle Fleet had been steadily drawing nearer, in cruising formation with its twenty-four battleships in six divisions, these in line abreast, screened by armoured and light cruisers and destroyers. The 3rd Battle-Cruiser Squadron, under Rear-Admiral Hood in *Invincible,* was twenty-five miles ahead and far to the east of its calculated position. Jellicoe, 'the only man who could lose the war in an afternoon', was now faced with the decision on which course to form his divisions into single line ahead. In all war games and exercises the rule had been 'towards Heligoland'. Yet the reports he received were incomplete and contradictory, it was impossible to get a clear picture of the situation. At the last moment, when Beatty's battle-cruisers came in sight, Jellicoe ordered his division to turn together to port to the north-east. In this way he gained a favourable position for crossing the enemy's T. He was unintentionally assisted by the 3rd Battle-Cruiser Squadron, which almost missed the Germans, but now closed in from the east and brought the German van between two fires. The light cruiser *Wiesbaden* soon lay dead in the water. For hours the battle raged around her, she was fired upon by many British ships, but did not sink until 0200 on 1st June. Only one survivor was picked up, two days later.

The delay in forming the line of battle put part of the screen and the 5th Battle Squadron in a difficult situation at what was later called 'Windy Corner'. Making room for Beatty's battle-cruisers to go to the van of the line, some armoured cruisers came into range of the German battleships. *Defence* blew up in view of both fleets; *Warrior* was saved a similar fate by the chance intervention of *Warspite.* The 5th Battle Squadron was forced to counter-march and came under the fire of several battleships. After a hit *Warspite*'s rudder jammed; she turned towards the German line, thus masking *Warrior,* who was able to creep away, but sank on the next morning. *Warspite* almost collided with *Valiant*

2

Imperial War Museum

4

Imperial War Museum

The equivocal result of the battle of Jutland was paid for by both sides with damaged ships and wounded men. 1 Seydlitz *in dry dock after the battle, her iron sides blasted by British shells. 2 The British light cruiser* Southampton. *She had suffered heavily in the furious clash between the rival light cruisers on the night of the 31st May-1st June. 3* Friedrich der Grosse, *flagship of the German line. 4 Rear-Admiral Hipper, whose battle-cruisers were the first to open fire in this clash of giants*

5 Admiral Scheer—caught in a trap—managed, with luck and skill, to extricate his fleet. 6 Hipper's flagship, the battle-cruiser Lützow. *7 Heroic death on the high seas—a German postcard. While his ship sinks under him, the sailor holds the flag of the German navy high, and a Valkyrie holds out a laurel wreath and waits to carry him to Valhalla, the reward of faithful warriors. 8 The wounded after the battle of Jutland in* HMS Castor, *painted by Jan Gordon. 8,500 men lost their lives during the battle*

5

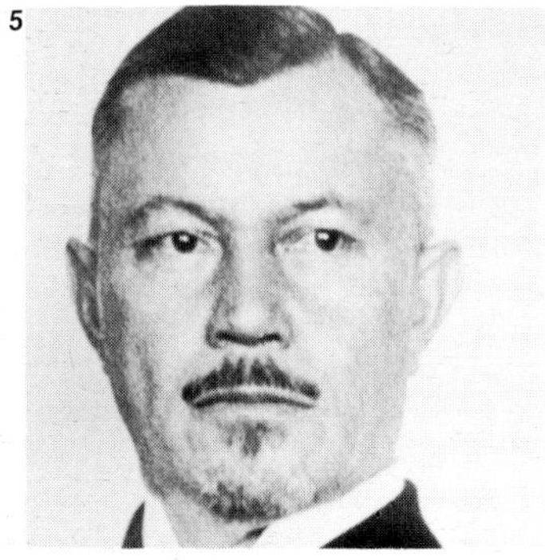

6

8

Imperial War Museum

and made two full circles at high speed before her rudder was in working order again. Heavily damaged she was ordered home and reached Rosyth after evading the attack of a German submarine.

Visibility was now generally decreasing and greatly varying as a result of masses of funnel and artificial smoke. For the commanders-in-chief it was most difficult to gain a reliable picture of the actual situation from their own limited observations (radar was not yet invented) and the reports of their subordinates. For a few moments Scheer toyed with the idea of splitting his line to take Windy Corner under two fires. However, there was no battle signal for this promising but unusual procedure, his van was evidently hard pressed, and so he continued with his battleships in line ahead. With the loss of the destroyer *Shark* the 3rd Battle-Cruiser Squadron had inflicted heavy damage on the Germans and now took up station at the head of the British line followed by Beatty's battle-cruisers.

For more than half an hour the German ships could see no more than the flashes of the enemy guns. Then at 1830 visibility suddenly improved, *Lützow* and *Derfflinger* sighted *Invincible,* the leading ship, at a distance of 9,500 yards and sank her in a few minutes. There were only six survivors, among them the gunnery officer who, as he said, 'merely stepped from the foretop into the water'.

At that time Scheer ordered a battle turn reversing course to get his ships out of the overwhelming enemy fire. Beginning from the rear the heavy ships had to turn to starboard in quick succession until single line ahead was formed on the opposite course. Light cruiser squadrons and destroyer flotillas had to conform. This manoeuvre was all the more difficult because the fleet was now disposed almost in a semi-circle, but it was successful, supported by a destroyer attack on the centre of the British line. The fleets drew apart, and the fire slackened and then ceased altogether. A German destroyer was crippled and sank later, and the battleship *Marlborough* received a torpedo-hit which reduced her speed.

The German fleet now steamed to the west south-west, and the British fleet slowly hauled round to the south. With its higher speed it had a good chance of cutting off the Germans from their bases. Scheer sensed this even though contact had been lost completely. Therefore he ordered another battle turn to the old course with the express intention to deal the enemy a heavy blow, to surprise and confuse him, to bring the destroyers to the attack, to facilitate disengaging for the night, and, if possible, to rescue the crew of the *Wiesbaden.* The execution of this plan has been criticized but there is no doubt that Scheer succeeded in getting his fleet out of a difficult situation although his van suffered heavily.

The German thrust was directed against the British centre. The attacking ships soon came under heavy fire without being able to reply effectively because visibility was better to the west and favoured the British gunnery. Scheer saw his fleet rush into a wide arc of gun flashes and decided to support the destroyer attack by the battle-cruisers while the battle fleet executed its third battle turn. To the battle-cruisers he made the well-known signal, 'Ran' ('At them'), which meant charging regardless of consequences. *Lützow* could not take part because after twenty-three hits she was far down by the bow and could steam no more than 15 knots. So *Derfflinger* led that death ride. Her captain transmitted Scheer's signal to all battle stations and was answered by a thundering roar, gun crews shouting, stokers banging their shovels against bulkheads. The destroyers went in, fired torpedoes, and retreated, the battle-cruisers then turned after receiving numerous hits. Not a single torpedo reached a target, for Jellicoe turned away. Contact ceased again and a lull in the battle followed. Both fleets hauled round to the south until their courses converged. The Germans proceeded in inversed order and in several columns, the British in single line ahead, sixteen miles long.

At sunset (2020) the terribly mauled battle-cruisers again came under the fire of the leading British battleships, the old ships of the II Battle Squadron under that of the British battle-cruisers. The Germans were silhouetted against the western horizon, their opponents were hardly visible to them. As a British officer later wrote: 'I sighted an obsolete German battleship firing in a desultory way at apparently nothing.' All the German columns turned to the west; the British did not follow but took up night-cruising order, the battleships in divisions abreast, destroyer flotillas following in their wake, course south-east, speed 17 knots. Jellicoe intended to put himself between the Germans and their bases and to renew the battle at daylight. Scheer collected his units practically on the same course which took some time, and at 2300 headed south-east for Horn Reef, speed 16 knots. Because of the heavy odds against him, he wanted to fight a renewed battle nearer to his bases. It was another whim of fate that, as a consequence, the German main body crashed through the British flotillas which were not looking for the enemy but were waiting for the day battle. In contrast the German destroyers searched in vain for the heavy ships of the enemy.

The night actions

During the short northern summer night there were numerous clashes. They started with a furious fight between light cruisers at short distance. *Dublin* and *Southampton* suffered heavy damage and casualties; the obsolete *Frauenlob* was hit by a torpedo and sank with most of her crew. Next the 4th Destroyer Flotilla, led by *Tipperary,* converged upon the German van, came under the fire of half a dozen battleships, and turned away in disorder firing torpedoes and leaving *Tipperary,* burning fiercely, behind. When the battleships turned to starboard to avoid the torpedoes, the light cruiser *Elbing* was rammed and remained stopped with flooded engine-rooms. The battleship *Nassau* tried to ram the destroyer *Spitfire*: they collided on nearly opposite courses, and the destroyer bounced off the side armour of her robust opponent leaving part of her bridge behind. With her forecastle a shambles, *Spitfire* succeeded in limping home.

Both sides resumed course and soon met again. In the intense fire *Broke,* and immediately afterwards *Contest,* rammed *Sparrowhawk,* which kept afloat to the morning. This time a torpedo crippled the light cruiser *Rostock.* Half an hour later, shortly after midnight, the unlucky 4th Flotilla encountered the same ships for the third time and lost *Fortune* and *Ardent.* Most of the other destroyers were damaged, it was no more a fighting unit.

A short time later a large ship approached the centre of the German line from port. It was the armoured cruiser *Black Prince.* She had probably been damaged when *Defence* blew up, and had tried to follow the battle fleet. Too late she turned away, and in minutes was a blazing pyre. Without firing a single shot she disintegrated.

These clashes saved the 6th Battle Squadron from an encounter with German battleships. It lagged behind because torpedo damage prevented *Marlborough,* the flagship, from keeping up 17 knots. As it were the German van passed no more than three miles astern at around 0100. A little later it hit the rear of a line of thirteen destroyers belonging to four flotillas. *Turbulent* was sunk, others damaged, the Germans carried on. At early dawn, after a calm of an hour, they were sighted and attacked by the 12th Flotilla. The German ships succeeded in evading a great number of torpedoes but the old battleship *Pommern* was hit and broke in two after several detonations.

The great battle was over. At 0300 the Germans were approaching Horn Reef, the British battle fleet, thirty miles to the south-west, reversed course, neither commander-in-chief was inclined to renew the fight. Jellicoe went north to look for

Left: *Fatally wounded, with the gun's crew dead and dying around him, Boy 1st Class John Travers Cornwell (aged 16) remains at his post on* HMS Chester *during the battle of Jutland and earns a posthumous VC. From the painting by Sir Frank Salisbury*

German stragglers. However, *Lützow, Elbing,* and *Rostock* had already been scuttled after German destroyers had taken their crews off. Both fleets steered for their bases. The *Ostfriesland* struck a mine in a field laid a few hours earlier by *Abdiel* but reached port without assistance.

The battle changed neither the ratio of strength between the two fleets nor the strategic situation. The British blockade continued, and Russia remained cut off from the supplies she needed urgently. The tactical advantage was with the Germans: they had inflicted about double their own losses on a greatly superior opponent. The fleet was proud of this achievement, and Scheer was willing to go on baiting the British. On 19th August 1916 both fleets were again in the North Sea but missed each other by thirty miles. However, it was evident–and Scheer said so in his reports–that the war could not be decided by this strategy. The situation on the fronts deteriorated after Allied offensives, and lack of food was painfully felt at home. Therefore the German government declared unrestricted submarine warfare two weeks before the Russian revolution broke out. The submarines did great havoc to Allied shipping, but brought the United States into the war.

As to the High Seas Fleet it did not

The losses in battle

	British	German
Battle-cruisers	3	1
Armoured cruisers	3	-
Old battleships	-	1
Light cruisers	-	4
Destroyers	8	5
	tons 112,000	tons 61,000
Killed	6,000	2,500

remain inactive in port as has been alleged. In April 1918 it made its last sweep to the latitude of Bergen/Shetlands. But its main duty was now to support the submarine war by protecting the minesweepers and by giving its best young officers and ratings to the submarine arm. Other reasons for the sudden break-up of this efficient fighting force in November 1918 were psychological mistakes, malnutrition, and subversion, aggravated by the hopeless political and military situation of Germany.

The Naval War, 1914-16 / Captain S.W.Roskill

Blockade

The outcome of the war was at stake in this struggle – for each nation could have been strangled by a successful blockade. On her side Great Britain had the vigilance and numerical superiority of the Royal Navy. Germany had the devastating effectiveness of her U-boats

Left: *A painting of British dazzle-ships by Edward Wadsworth. The camouflage was intended to confuse German attackers.* ***Below:*** *Dutch cartoonist Raemaekers shows the Kaiser under pressure of the Royal Navy's blockade.* ***Bottom:*** *Germany nursing her latest offspring, a submarine, while the Kaiser and Admiral Tirpitz smile down benignly from their portraits*

Ulk/Tasiemka

Warring states have from the earliest times endeavoured to deprive their enemies of seaborne supplies. But blockade in its modern form dates only from the beginning of the 17th century when Hugo Grotius, the famous Dutch jurist, put forward the claim for *'Mare Liberum'* – the Freedom of the Seas. This meant that ships flying the flag of a neutral nation, and the goods they carried, should be exempt from seizure by belligerents. The British reply was that he who commanded the sea automatically acquired the right to control all traffic passing over it, regardless of nationality. Thus was born the claim to 'Belligerent Rights', which remained a cardinal feature of British maritime policy for more than two centuries, but was always very unpopular with neutral nations.

In 1856 the Declaration of Paris, an appendage to the treaty ending the Crimean War, was signed. It abolished privateering, from which Great Britain had suffered serious losses in earlier wars; but as it exempted the property of a belligerent state from capture, except in the case of contraband, it went a long way towards accepting Grotius's doctrine. The situation remained unchanged until the winter of 1908-09 when, shortly after the conclusion of the second Hague conference, the principal naval powers met in London and formulated the Declaration of London. This document attempted to define contraband of war by dividing commodities into three classes – absolute contraband, conditional contraband, and free goods. Though it accepted that foodstuffs carried in neutral ships might be declared contraband, such commodities as oil, raw cotton, and rubber were classed as free goods.

Though the Bill giving the Declaration of London the force of law was passed by the Liberal majority in the House of Commons it was thrown out by the House of Lords. Nonetheless, shortly after the outbreak of war in 1914, the Asquith government announced its intention of adhering to its terms. This seemingly short-sighted and gratuitous acceptance of a self-imposed handicap probably arose from the desire to placate opinion in neutral countries, and especially the USA. But it is also true to say that no nation realized at the time that in total war between industrialized countries economic pressure would prove an extremely powerful, perhaps decisive weapon.

There are two types of blockade – usually described as naval blockade and commercial (or economic) blockade. The two types, however, nearly always overlap – that is to say a naval blockade also has commercial implications, and *vice versa*. A naval blockade is enforced by stationing warships off an enemy port with the object of preventing his warships coming out, or of engaging them if they do try to escape. This form of blockade was brought to a fine art by the Royal Navy in the Napoleonic War, and contributed greatly to the defeat of imperial France.

A commercial blockade, on the other hand, aims to cripple the enemy's economy and starve his people into submission by seizing all goods destined to him, even if they are consigned to a neutral nation in the first place, and regardless of the ownership of the ship carrying the goods. The procedure followed begins with the recognized right of a belligerent to 'visit and search' a ship on the high seas, continues with the detention of the cargo if it is believed to be contraband, and ends with the condemnation of the cargo, and possibly of the ship as well, before a nationally constituted Prize Court.

Prior to the Agadir crisis of 1911 (p. 394) the Asquith government, preoccupied as it was by a far-reaching programme for social and electoral reform, paid comparatively little attention to defence policy or to the strategy to be employed should the threat of war with Germany and her allies (Austria-Hungary and Italy) materialize. But shortly after the crisis, Winston Churchill became first lord of the Admiralty, and under his vigorous direction naval policy and plans became a live issue. The Committee of Imperial Defence (CID), an advisory body of which the prime minister was chairman, began to meet more frequently, and one of its subcommittees reviewed the susceptibility of the Central European powers to the economic pressure of a blockade, and the means required to apply such pressure.

At about the same time, the Admiralty considered the strategy to be employed against the powerful German High Seas Fleet, based in the southern North Sea, and the detached squadrons of cruisers which the German navy had stationed overseas – especially in the Mediterranean and the Pacific. Although the 1908 War Orders had reaffirmed the ancient principle that the Royal Navy's primary function was 'to bring the main German fleet to decisive action', and so secure command of all the seas and oceans, the Admiralty recognized that the High Seas Fleet might well not fall in with such a purpose. Therefore that fleet must be neutralized by a naval blockade of its home bases. The same principle applied to the much less well developed bases used by the detached cruisers, such as Tsingtao on the north east coast of China and the Austrian bases in the Adriatic.

By the early years of the 20th century technical progress, and especially the development of the mine, the submarine, the torpedo, and aircraft had obviously made the old concept of close blockade on the Napoleonic War model totally obsolete. Nonetheless, there was in British naval circles a good deal of hesitation about abandoning what was regarded as a well-tried and provenly effective strategy. Not until the middle of 1912 was close blockade replaced by what was called an 'observational blockade' of the Heligoland Bight. This was to be enforced by a line of cruisers and destroyers patrolling the North Sea from the south-west coast of Norway to the Dutch coast, with heavy squadrons from the main fleet in support to the north and west. But this idea proved short-lived, since it was plainly impossible to patrol a 300-mile-long line effectively, by night and day, in winter and summer.

The blockade plan laid down

A month before the outbreak of war the observational blockade was therefore abandoned in favour of a 'distant blockade' designed to control the exits from the North Sea. This was made possible by the geographical chance which has placed the British Isles like a breakwater across the passages leading from the outer oceans to the German seaports and naval bases on their North Sea and Baltic coasts. The British plan was that the Channel Fleet, based chiefly on the Thames estuary ports, Dover, and Portsmouth, would close the Straits of Dover, while the much more powerful Grand Fleet would be based on Scapa Flow in the Orkneys and would throw out a line of cruisers or armed merchant cruisers (called the Northern Patrol) to watch the remote and stormy waters between the Shetland Islands, Norway, and Iceland. Such was, in brief outline, the final naval blockade plan which was brought into force in August 1914.

But recent technical developments had a much wider influence than merely to render the concept of close blockade obsolete. They all, but especially the mine, proved potent instruments of blockade in their own right, and both sides laid large numbers of mines, and disposed submarines in the approaches to the other side's ports and bases for this purpose. Unfortunately, the early British mines, like their torpedoes, were extremely inefficient, and it was not until 1917, when an exact copy of the German mine was produced in quantity, that the Royal Navy was provided with an efficient mine.

The Admiralty always expected that the enemy's reply to the British blockade would, as in all earlier wars, take the form of an attack on commerce by cruisers and armed merchantmen. This was a perfectly legal form of warfare, subject to the regulations incorporated in the Hague Conventions regarding the safety of the crews of captured merchant ships; and the German surface raiders in fact showed humanity in their observance of those regulations. Before the war the CID reviewed the measures necessary to keep shipping moving despite the possibility of capture, and recommended that the State should receive eighty per cent of the insurance premiums required to cover war risks on merchant ships and stand eighty per cent of the losses. The Treasury, however, was not at first willing to accept such an intrusion into the field of private enterprise, and the War Risks Insurance scheme did not actually come into force until the outbreak of war.

By July 1915 all the German raiders which had been at sea at the beginning of the war had been destroyed (p. 538). Allied (mainly British) seapower so dominated the outer seas and oceans that German trade had been brought to an almost complete halt immediately war broke out – except in the Baltic. Many German merchant ships sought refuge in neutral ports, and the transfer of cargoes destined for Germany to neutral ships began at once. Freight rates rose very sharply, and the neutral nations began to reap enormous profits. These developments stimulated British concern over the emasculation of Belligerent Rights by the Declarations of Paris and London. The first step taken to restore the earlier state of affairs was to issue Orders in Council transferring various commodities from the 'free goods' to the contraband list, and in 1915 the distinction between conditional and absolute contraband was all but wiped out.

On 20th November 1914 a small British merchant ship was sunk by a German submarine in the North Sea and the crew left in the boats – contrary to the Hague Conventions. Other sinkings by submarines soon followed, and thus was ushered in an entirely new element in the German attack on trade – and one for which the Royal Navy was almost totally unprepared. Plainly the implications were very serious. On 11th March 1915 the British government issued an Order in Council, generally referred to as the 'Reprisals Order', since it was made in reprisal for the illegal use of submarines. It declared that goods which could be shown to be destined for Germany were liable to seizure, even though the vessel carrying them was bound for a neutral port.

This led to strong protests from the neutrals, and especially from the USA, regarding interference with what they regarded as legitimate – and of course highly profitable – trade. The USA never moved from the position that the Reprisals Order was illegal – until they themselves were at war. But the real reason for the issue of the order was that the British government was aware that the Scandinavian countries and Holland were importing vastly greater quantities of goods which were on the British contraband list than they had taken before the war. Obviously the surplus was being passed direct to Germany, and the shipping services of the neutral nations were thus replacing the immobilized German merchant fleet. The leak through the blockade via Italy was never serious, and when she entered the war on the Allied side in May 1915 it stopped altogether. But with the Scandinavian countries and Holland the leak was very large indeed, and it did not prove easy to stop it.

In home waters the British blockade was operated through contraband control stations in the Orkneys and the Downs (the anchorage in the Channel between the Goodwin Sands and the coast), and ships intercepted were sent into one or other unless their cargoes were above suspicion. In 1915 the Northern Patrol cruisers intercepted 3,098 ships, and in the following year 3,388. Those sent in for examination totalled 743 and 889 respectively. Many neutral ships called voluntarily at the examination stations, and they were given priority for clearance; but there were always some to whom the prospect of high profits outweighed the risks involved in not conforming with the British regulations. When flagrant cases came to light a series of seizures in prize would probably be organized. For example the very high shipments of lard from USA to Scandinavia were stopped by the seizure of four cargoes in rapid succession in October and November 1914.

Ruffled neutral feathers

On the outbreak of war the CID set up a 'Trading with the Enemy Committee' to control imports through neutral countries; but its procedure proved too slow and cumbrous, and its functions were therefore taken over in March 1915 by the War Trade Intelligence Department, which collected evidence regarding consignees, studied the scale of neutral imports of all commodities and generally 'acted as a clearing house for the collection, analysis, and dissemination of economic data relating to enemy and neutral trade'. The Exports Control Committee under the Intelligence Department was responsible for issuing import and export licences to shippers, and ruffled neutral feathers were

1

Bibliothek für Zeitgeschichte, Stuttgart

2

Imperial War Museum

3

Ullstein

often smoothed by purchasing detained cargoes instead of seizing them in prize.

Nonetheless, difficulties with neutral nations sometimes became acute. Intercepted ships were often subject to long delays, and sometimes they were sunk while being taken into port under British armed guard. After the war the British government paid full value plus five percent accrued interest on all ships sunk in such circumstances. Because of neutral susceptibilities the British government had to move with caution and moderation, especially in dealings with the USA, where the anti-British lobby was powerful and vociferous. The process of keeping American public opinion sweet was, however, aided by German ruthlessness – notably over the sinking of the great Cunard liner *Lusitania* (p. 521) on 7th May 1915 with a heavy loss of civilian lives including 128 Americans.

The German reply to the tightening British blockade was to declare on 4th February 1915 the whole of the waters around the British Isles a 'War Zone' in which any ship might be sunk without warning. Thus began the first unrestricted submarine campaign. It lasted until August, when the rising tide of neutral protests caused the German government to order a return to less flagrantly illegal methods. However, the substantial tonnage sunk by submarines in that phase (748,914 tons in the whole of 1915) caused great anxiety in Allied circles, and should have provided an opportunity to find the proper antidote – namely convoy. Such, however, was not the case, since the Admiralty remained stubbornly opposed to convoy.

The winter of 1915-16 saw a revival of German surface ship raiders; but this time disguised merchantmen instead of warships were employed. Altogether five such ships were sent out, and one of them (the *Möwe*) made two cruises and sank 122,000 tons of shipping. Two were caught right at the beginning of their careers, but the others proved skilful and elusive enemies. Like their predecessors of the cruiser period they caused considerable delay and dislocation to shipping, and the last of them was not eliminated until early in 1918.

Despite the success achieved by the first unrestricted submarine campaign, the situation as regards the blockade and counterblockade at the end of 1915 was not unfavourable to the Allies. This was the more fortunate because in all theatres of military operations that year was one of unmitigated defeat and disaster for their

1 German raider Möwe. *A disguised merchantman, it made two cruises and sank 122,000 tons of shipping. 2 A German submarine detains a merchant vessel at sea. 3 Armed tanker burning after attack by German U-boat*

Imperial War Museum

British Q ship B2. Posing as unarmed merchantmen, Q ships sailed in submarine-infested waters shelling unwary German submarines with their concealed guns

cause (p. 512). True, there was a shortage of shipping, caused partly by excessive requisitioning by the service departments; but the flow of supplies of all kinds had been kept up, and losses of merchant ships, which had totalled 855,721 tons during the year, had been replaced by newly built and captured vessels.

With complete deadlock prevailing on the Western Front, the commercial blockade of Germany had obviously gained in importance. Accordingly in February 1916 the British government set up a new Ministry of Blockade under Lord Robert Cecil to co-ordinate the political and administrative measures necessary to cripple the Central powers' resources. The new ministry, working closely with the War Trade Intelligence Department, gradually built up world-wide control over the movement of all merchant ships and the shipment of cargoes. Consular shipping control officers were installed in all important ports, and they transmitted to London a stream of information regarding the true shippers and consignees of cargoes. With this knowledge in hand the ministry was able to compile a list of firms known to be trading with the enemy, and great ingenuity was shown in exerting pressure to curb their activities. Because bunkering facilities in many overseas ports were British-controlled it was possible to deprive ships of coal and other essential supplies when they called. The location of the greater part of the world's banking and insurance business in London enabled credit and insurance cover to be refused to firms whose activities were not above suspicion. And British control over most of the world's wireless and cable communications made it improbable that such activities would long remain uncovered. Finally, if a ship did sail with an illicit cargo, the Admiralty would be asked to take special steps to intercept it; and if that succeeded condemnation in prize was virtually certain.

But the Ministry of Blockade did not only work to prevent shipment of contraband cargoes. Neutral nations' imports were rationed with increasing stringency at a figure no greater than they had taken before the war; and goods which were particularly vital to the enemy war effort, such as the special minerals (wolfram and tungsten, for example) used in weapon and armour plate manufacture, were controlled by the pre-emptive purchase of the whole available supply.

One of the first actions of the Ministry of Blockade was to issue (29th February 1916) a 'Statutory Black List' of firms in neutral countries with whom all transactions were forbidden. This aroused strong American protests – since a number of the firms were American. In the following month a system known as 'Letters of Assurance' for approved shippers was introduced. These were always referred to as 'Navicerts' (from the code word used in cables referring to them), and possession of such a letter ensured a ship unhindered passage through the blockade. Encouragement was given to shippers to arrange with London for advance booking of cargoes, which would then be approved or disapproved by the Contraband Committee.

Neutral shipowners were also given every encouragement to order their ships to call in voluntarily for examination at Scapa Flow and the Downs or at Halifax, Alexandria, and Gibraltar where additional stations were set up. In 1916 no less than 1,878 neutral vessels called in voluntarily, 950 were intercepted and sent in, and only 155 (some five per cent of the total) successfully ran the blockade. New Orders in Council were issued to increase the stringency of the blockade – notably that of 7th July 1916 which repealed the Declaration of London Order in Council of August 1914. Throughout 1916 the effectiveness of the Allied machinery of commercial blockade steadily increased.

The Germans did not, of course, take this escalation of Allied blockade measures lying down. In March 1916 they renewed the unrestricted submarine campaign, and again quickly achieved a fairly high rate of sinkings – 126,000 tons in April. However, they once again caused the loss of American lives, and the resultant protests produced a temporary lull. In September they tried again, and despite the wide variety of measures introduced by the Admiralty to combat the submarine menace – minefields, nets, surface patrols, and the much advertised 'mystery' or 'Q-ships' – German submarines sank nearly 147,000 tons of shipping in October. The implications were plainly very serious, since if the upward trend continued the loss to be anticipated in 1917 would exceed 2,000,000 tons. Furthermore the total Allied shipping losses in 1916 amounted to 1,237,634 tons, which was nearly fifty per cent higher than in the previous year; and, finally, the rate of sinking of U-boats had not been satisfactory in relation to the speed at which new ones were built. From the beginning of the war to the end of 1916 only forty-six had been sunk.

But if the closing months of 1916 brought little comfort to those responsible for maintaining the flow of Allied supplies, to the German people the implication of that year's developments were far more threatening. Though their armed forces had not yet suffered appreciably, since they were given priority for all available supplies, the condition of the civilian population was beginning to deteriorate seriously. The 1915 and 1916 harvests had been bad, due chiefly to lack of imported fertilizers, the conquered territories in eastern Europe had failed to replace supplies from overseas, home producers of foodstuffs were withholding their produce or selling it on the extensive black market, the calorific value of the civilian ration was falling steadily, and the shortage of clothing was becoming increasingly acute. With the winter of 1916-17 approaching – it was to be remembered in Germany as the 'Turnip Winter' – the outlook was grim indeed.

Such was the state of affairs that led the German government to adopt the desperate expedient of renewed submarine warfare on merchant shipping in February 1917; and that led to the entry of the USA into the war, and so to the utter defeat of the Central powers.

The Allies on the Offensive

Chapter 21

Introduction by J.M.Roberts

In 1916, each of the main combatant nations made great efforts to achieve a decisive victory. Each failed, with huge losses, although the Russians had the greatest partial success. But the effort exhausted the Tsarist army. The Russian soldier was already bowing under the strain of two and a half years' warfare with inadequate supplies, bad planning, a depleted officer corps, a shattered transport system, and a chronic shortage of weapons and ammunition. After their last great success under Brusilov, the exhausted Russian armies were suddenly called to cover a new front extending to the Black Sea. It was to be too much. The battles on the Eastern Front in 1916 are analysed by J.N.Westwood in **The Brusilov Offensive**.

The Russian effort, though followed by disappointment, had probably saved the French army. Alistair Horne, in **Verdun and the Somme**, describes the terrible fighting of the summer in the west. The German strategy of deliberately destroying the French will to fight in a great battle of attrition at Verdun came near to success. The diversion of troops to face Brusilov was one factor thwarting it. Another was the persistence of the British army in sustaining its offensive on the Somme in the teeth of enormous losses. Both these battles were to leave scars for decades to come. The memory of the forts of Verdun inspired the faith in the passive strategy of the Maginot line, and Great Britain's generals in the Second World War were determined that the British army should never again squander its blood as it had done in 1916.

By the autumn the war was beginning to wear out men and institutions under which it had opened. The implications for Great Britain are described by C.L.Mowat in **Britain Organizes for Total War**; the old, unchallenged assumptions about government and the economy were one by one found inadequate to maintain the struggle. New leaders were needed, too. In this Chapter there are the profiles of the three under whom Great Britain, France, and Germany were to fight out the rest of the war. **Ludendorff** was the first to take power, though his virtual dictatorship came to an end just before the end of the war, because he preferred to resign before he was associated with defeat. His opponents, **Lloyd George** and **Clemenceau**, were both veteran politicians, not soldiers. Both had radical backgrounds and both inspired much distrust. Yet both also succeeded in inspiring their countrymen as others had failed to do, and in convincing them that after terrible suffering they could still win the war. With warfare no longer a matter of professional armies, but demanding the physical and psychological mobilization of whole populations, theirs was a decisive contribution.

Ullstein

Ambulance at German field hospital is wrecked during a British bombardment,

Ulk/Tasiemka

German cartoon derides Brusilov's offensive. He examines tree of victory with neutrals

Syndication International

Girl munition workers parading for Lloyd George when he visited Wales, August 1918

Great Britain

1914 8th August: Defence of the Realm Act gives government wide measure of control over persons and property; government takes control of the railways.
November: employers and unions sign the Crayford Agreement on 'dilution' of labour.

1915 March: Treasury Agreement clears up union opposition to 'dilution' by providing safeguards.
25th May: Asquith government reorganized as a coalition; the War Committee takes over the conduct of the war; Lloyd George becomes minister in the new ministry of munitions.
July: coal miners in South Wales go on strike.
June: legislation controls licensing hours of public houses.
During the year seventy-three 'national factories' are built, and the government takes control of the meat exports of Australia and New Zealand.

1916 January: conscription of unmarried men introduced.
March: industrial troubles on the Clyde lead to the arrest and deportation of the leaders of the Clyde Workers' Committee.
May: Conscription extended to married men.
1st December: South Wales coalfield put under government control.
7th December: Lloyd George becomes prime minister; he forms the War Cabinet and creates the ministries of labour, food, and shipping.

1917 1st January: food production ministry created to encourage agriculture.
March: all coal mines put under control of the Coal Controller.
March: prime ministers of the Dominions assemble as the Imperial War Cabinet.

1918 April: government takes over flour mills.

Western Front

1915 2nd December: Joffre appointed supreme commander of the French forces.
6th December: Joffre holds conference of Allied commanders; plans are formed to co-ordinate a summer offensive.

1916 21st February: Germans begin bombardment of Verdun and first assault troops move forward.
22nd February: main German infantry attacks Verdun.
24th February: second line of the French defences falls.
25th February: Radtke takes fort of Douaumont just outside Verdun.
May: the Germans finish clearing the left bank of the Meuse.
2nd June: Germans take Fort Vaux.
5th June: Kitchener lost in *HMS Hampshire*.
26th June: Haig's preliminary bombardment of the Somme begins.
1st July: British attack on the Somme begins.
11th July: Germans make last assault on Verdun.
14th July: Rawlinson attacks by night.
30th August: after Falkenhayn's resignation, Hindenburg appointed German chief of staff.
15th September: Haig decides to use tanks in third major Somme offensive; they are all scattered or destroyed.
2nd November: French recapture Douaumont and Vaux.
13th November: British take Beaumont-Hamel.
18th November: battle of the Somme ends.
12th December: Nivelle replaces Joffre.
18th December: battle of Verdun ends.

Eastern Front

1916 19th March-30th April: after battle of Lake Naroch Russians withdraw with heavy losses.
14th April: Tsar replaces Ivanov with Brusilov; Brusilov proposes an attack on all fronts.
15th May-3rd June: Austrians make successful offensive against the Italians in the Trentino.
4th June: Brusilov's Offensive is launched.
8th June: Brusilov takes Lutsk.
9th June: Evert informs Brusilov that he will postpone his attack until 18th June.
18th June: instead of attacking towards Wilno, Evert moves south towards Baranowicze; he is then sent to join Brusilov.
10th August: Brusilov Offensive comes to an end.
17th August: Rumania signs alliance with Russia.
27th August: Rumanian troops strike north towards Transylvania, and in early September take Hermannstadt and Kronstadt.
7th-9th October: Austro-German forces retake Kronstadt.
23rd October: Mackensen takes Constanta.
6th December: Germans take Bucharest; Rumanians hemmed in area around Jassy.

Western Front, February-November 1916/Alistair Horne

Verdun and the Somme

Few before the First World War could have visualized the atrocious slaughter that was to take place at Verdun and the Somme. The total of British, French, and German dead, wounded, and missing in these battles was well over 1,500,000. Other casualties were the French and German commanders, the British and French prime ministers —and most of the idealism left in the war

The year 1916 was the watershed of the First World War. Beyond it all rivers ran in changed directions. It was the year that saw German hopes of outright victory vanish, and the Allied prospects of winning the war with their existing tactics and resources—without the United States—disappear. It was the last year in which Russia would be a powerful military force, and by the end of it Great Britain would have assumed the principal burden on the Western Front. It was also the last year in which the 'Old World' of pre-1914 still had a chance of surviving by means of a negotiated, 'stalemate' peace; it would have been as good a year as any to have ended the war. Finally, 1916 was the year of heavy guns, and—with the exception of the cataclysm of 1918—the year that brought the highest casualty lists.

On land in 1916 there were two battles which more than any others came to symbolize the First World War for the post-war generation: Verdun and the Somme. Verdun was the occasion of Germany's only deviation—between 1915 and 1918—from her profitable strategy of standing on the defensive in the west and letting the Allies waste themselves against an almost impregnable line at unimaginable cost.

By the end of 1915 deadlock had been reached along a static front stretching from Switzerland to the Channel. The Germans had failed, at the Marne (p. 456), to win the war by one sledge-hammer blow against their numerically superior enemies, while suffering three-quarters of a million casualties. In attempting to repulse them from her soil, France had lost 300,000 killed and another 600,000 wounded, captured, and missing. Great Britain's naval might had proved impotent to wrest the Dardanelles from Turkey. Isolated Russia staggered on from defeat to defeat, yet still the Central powers could not bring the war to a decision in the limitless spaces of the east.

But on neither side had these early losses and disillusions impaired the will to fight on. Civilian resolution matched military morale. The opposing troops of France and Germany were no longer the green enthusiasts of 1914, nor yet the battle-weary veterans of 1917-18; they represented the best the war was to produce. In the munitions industries of both sides, artillery programmes had also reached a peak. In Great Britain Kitchener's army of conscripts was about to replace the lost 'First Hundred Thousand'.

On 2nd December, 1915, Joffre, the 'victor of the Marne', was appointed supreme commander of French military forces throughout the world. A sixty-three year-old engineer with little experience of handling infantry, he was now incomparably the most powerful figure on the Allied side and his new ascendancy enabled him to concentrate everything on the Western Front. Four days later Joffre held an historic conference of the Allied commanders at his HQ in Chantilly. From it sprang plans for a co-ordinated offensive by all the allies the following summer. By then, for the first time, there would be an abundance of men, heavy guns, and ammunition. The principal component of this offensive would be a Franco-British 'push' astride the river Somme. Forty French and twenty-five British divisions would be involved. There were no strategic objectives behind this sector of the front; Joffre's principal reason for selecting it was his instinct that he could be most assured of full British participation if they went over the top arm in arm with the French—*'bras dessus bras dessous'*.

Sir Douglas Haig, who had also just taken over command of the British forces in France from General French, would have preferred to attack in Flanders (a preference which was to reassert itself with disastrous consequences a year later). However, after a meeting with Joffre on 29th December, he allowed himself to be won over to the Somme strategy. But on the other side of the lines, the chief of the German general staff, General Erich von Falkenhayn—a strange compound of ruthlessness and indecision—had his own plans. The Germans were to beat the Allies to the draw.

To bleed France white

Prospects would never again seem so bright for German arms as at the close of 1915. In mid-December Falkenhayn prepared a lengthy memorandum for the Kaiser in which he argued that the only way to achieve victory was to cripple the Allies' main instrument, the French army, by luring it into the defence of an indefensible position. Verdun, perched precariously at the tip of a long salient, about 130 air miles south-east of where Joffre intended to attack on the Somme and just 150 miles due east of Paris, fulfilled all of Falkenhayn's requirements.

Verdun's history as a fortified camp stretched back to Roman times, when Attila had found it worth burning. In the 17th century Louis XIV's great ▷ 565

Opposite page: *Verdun burning, 26th March 1916. A painting by Francois Flameng.* ***Below:*** *French soldier wearing gas mask mounts guard at an entrance to Fort Souville, Verdun. The fort, part of the main French defence line on the east bank of the Meuse, consistently defied capture*

Südd-Verlag, Munich

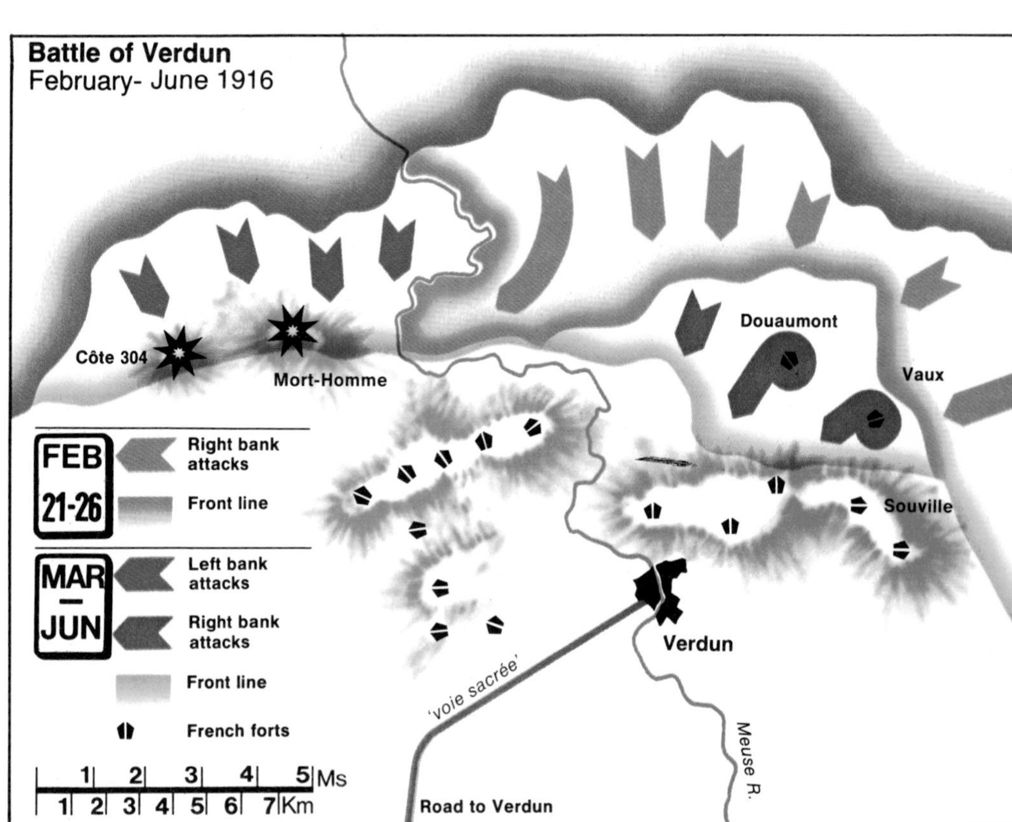

1 Raemaekers cartoon. Crown Prince Wilhelm tells his father: 'We must have a higher pile to see Verdun.' 2 The battle-ground. 3 German soldier using a flame-thrower at Verdun. By Max Rabes

engineer, Vauban, had made Verdun the most powerful fortress in his cordon protecting France; in the Franco-Prussian War of 1870 it had been the last of the great French strongholds to fall, surviving Sedan, Metz, and Strasbourg. After 1870 it had become the key bastion in the chain of fortresses guarding France's frontier with Germany. In 1914, Verdun had provided an unshakable pivot for the French line, and without it Joffre might not have been able to stand on the Marne and save Paris.

From his knowledge both of her history and character, Falkenhayn calculated that France would be forced to defend this semi-sacred citadel to the last man. By menacing Verdun with a modest outlay of only nine divisions, he expected to draw the main weight of the French army into the salient, where German heavy artillery would grind it to pieces from three sides.

In Falkenhayn's own words, France was thus to be 'bled white'. It was a conception totally novel to the history of war and one that, in its very imagery, was symptomatic of that Great War where, in their callousness, leaders could regard human lives as mere corpuscles.

The V Army, commanded by the Kaiser's heir, the Crown Prince, was appointed to conduct the victorious operation. Day and night the great cannon and their copious munition trains now began to flow toward the V Army from all other German fronts. Aided by the railways behind their front and the national genius for organization, preparations moved with astonishing speed and secrecy. By the beginning of February 1916 more than 1,200 guns were in position – for an assault frontage of barely eight miles. More than 500 were 'heavies', including 13 of the 420mm 'Big Bertha mortars', the 'secret weapon' of 1914 which had shattered the supposedly impregnable Belgian forts. Never before had such a concentration of artillery been seen.

Verdun lay less than ten miles up the tortuous Meuse from the German lines. Most of its 15,000 inhabitants had departed when the war reached its gates in 1914, and its streets were now filled with troops, but this was nothing new for a city which had long been a garrison town.

In notable contrast to the featureless open country of Flanders and the Somme, Verdun was surrounded by interlocking patterns of steep hills and ridges which provided immensely strong natural lines of defence. The key heights were studded with three concentric rings of mighty underground forts, totalling no less than twenty major and forty intermediary works.

Each was superbly sited so that its guns could dislodge any enemy infantry appearing on the superstructure of its neighbour. With concrete carapaces eight feet thick, staunch enough to resist even the German 'Big Berthas', some of the major forts – such as Douaumont – were equipped with heavy artillery and machine-guns firing from retractable steel turrets. Outlying blockhouses linked by subterranean passages made them able to repel an attack from whatever direction it might come, and in their shell-proof cellars each could house as much as a battalion of infantry.

These forts lay between five and ten miles from Verdun itself. Between them and no man's land stretched a protective network of trenches, redoubts, and barbed wire such as was to be found throughout the whole length of the Western Front. Verdun deserved its reputation as the world's most powerful fortress. In theory.

In fact – despite, or perhaps because of, its reputation – by February 1916, Verdun's defences were in a lamentable state. The fate of the Belgian forts had persuaded Joffre to evacuate the infantry garrisons from the Verdun forts, and remove many of their guns. The troops themselves had become slack, lulled by many months spent in so quiet and 'safe' a sector, whose deceptive calm was deepened by the influence of one of the nastiest, rainiest, foggiest, and most enervating climates in France. The French soldier has never been renowned for his ardour for digging in, and the forward lines of trenches at Verdun compared poorly with the immensely deep earthworks the Germans had constructed at their key points on the Western Front. And, in contrast to the seventy-two battalions of elite storm troops, the Crown Prince held ready for the attack, the French trenches were manned by only thirty-four battalions, some of which were second-class units.

One outstanding French officer, Lieutenant Colonel Emile Driant, who commanded two battalions of *chasseurs* in the very tip of the salient, actually warned the French high command of the impending attack and the bad state of the Verdun defences. For this impertinence, his knuckles were severely rapped; the imperturbable Joffre paid little attention.

'Sauve qui peut!'

After a nine-day delay caused by bad weather (the first serious setback to German plans), the bombardment began at dawn on 21st February. For nine appalling hours it continued. Even on the shell-saturated Western Front nothing like it had ever been experienced. The poorly prepared French trenches were obliterated, many of their defenders buried alive. Among the units to bear the brunt of the shelling were Driant's *chasseurs*.

At 4 that afternoon the bombardment lifted and the first German assault troops moved forward out of their concealed positions. This was, in fact, but a strong patrol action, testing like a dentist's probe for the weakest areas of the French front. In most places it held. The next morning, the brutal bombardment began again. It seemed impossible that any human being could have survived in that methodically worked-over soil. Yet some had, and, with a heroic tenacity that was to immortalize the French defence during the long months ahead, they continued to face the unseen enemy from what remained of their trenches.

On the afternoon of 22nd February the Germans' first main infantry wave went in. The defenders' front line buckled.

L'Illustration

General Philippe Pétain in 1916. From warrior-hero he later turned defeatist

Driant was shot through the head while withdrawing the remnants of his *chasseurs*. Of these two battalions, 1,200 strong, a handful of officers and about 500 men, many of them wounded, were all that eventually straggled back to the rear. But the French resistance once again caused the German storm troops to be pulled back, to await a third softening-up bombardment the following morning.

On 23rd February, there were signs of mounting confusion and alarm at the various HQs before Verdun. Telephone lines were cut by the shelling; runners were not getting through; whole units were disappearing from the sight of their commanders. Order and counter-order were followed by the inevitable consequence. One by one the French batteries were falling silent, while others shelled their own positions, in the belief that these had already been abandoned to the enemy.

24th February was the day the dam burst. A fresh division, flung in piecemeal, broke under the bombardment, and the whole of the second line of the French defences fell within a matter of hours. ▷ **566**

During that disastrous day, German gains equalled those of the first three days put together. By the evening it looked as if the war had again become one of movement – for the first time since the Marne.

Between the attackers and Verdun, however, there still lay the lines of the forts – above all, Douaumont, the strongest of them all, a solid bulwark of comfort behind the backs of the retreating *poilus*. Then, on 25th February, the Germans pulled off – almost in a fit of absent-mindedness – one of their greatest coups of the entire war. Acting on their own initiative, several small packets of the 24th Brandenburg Regiment, headed by a twenty-four-year-old lieutenant, Eugen Radtke (who, though seriously wounded later on, still lives in Berlin today), worked their way into Douaumont without losing a man. To their astonishment, they discovered the world's most powerful fort to be virtually undefended.

In Germany church bells rang throughout the country to acclaim the capture of Douaumont. In France its surrender was rightly regarded as a national disaster of the first magnitude (later reckoned to have cost France the equivalent of 100,000 men). Through the streets of Verdun itself survivors of broken units ran shouting, *'Sauve qui peut!'*

At his headquarters in Chantilly even Joffre had at last become impressed by the urgency of events. To take over the imminently threatened sector, he dispatched Henri Philippe Pétain, France's outstanding expert in the art of the defensive. No general possessed the confidence of the *poilu* more than Pétain. Now – in tragic irony – this uniquely humanitarian leader was called upon to subject his men to what was becoming the most inhuman conflict of the whole war. Pétain's orders were to hold Verdun, 'whatever the cost'.

But the German attack was beginning to bog down. Losses had already been far heavier than Falkenhayn had anticipated, many of them inflicted by flanking fire from French guns across the Meuse. The German lines looped across the river to the north of Verdun, and, from the very first, the Crown Prince had urged that his V Army be allowed to attack along both banks simultaneously. But Falkenhayn – determined to keep his own outlay of infantry in the 'bleeding white' strategy down to the barest minimum – had refused, restricting operations to the right bank. Now, to clear the menace of the French artillery, Falkenhayn reluctantly agreed to extend the offensive across to the left bank, releasing for this purpose another army corps from his tightly hoarded reserves. The deadly escalation of Verdun was under way.

Mission of sacrifice

The lull before the next phase of the German offensive enabled Pétain to stabilize the front to an almost miraculous extent. He established a road artery to Verdun, later known as the Voie Sacrée, along which the whole lifeblood of France was to pour, to reinforce the threatened city; during the critical first week of March alone 190,000 men marched up it.

The Crown Prince now launched a new all-out attack along the left bank toward a small ridge called the Mort-Homme, which, with its sinister name, acquired from some long-forgotten tragedy of another age, was to be the centre of the most bitter, see-saw fighting for the better part of the next three months. On this one tiny sector a monotonous, deadly pattern was establishing that continued almost without let-up. It typified the whole battle of Verdun. After hours of saturating bombardment, the German assault troops would surge forward to carry what remained of the French front line. There were no longer any trenches; what the Germans occupied were for the most part clusters of shell holes, where isolated groups of men lived and slept and died defending their 'position' with grenade and pick helve.

'You have a mission of sacrifice,' ran the typical orders that one French colonel gave to his men. 'Here is a post of honour

Below: *German troops at Verdun scramble up the soft earth of a devastated trench to launch a grenade attack*

where they want to attack. Every day you will have casualties . . . On the day they want to, they will massacre you to the last man, and it is your duty to fall.'

At Verdun most fell without ever having seen the enemy, under the murderous non-stop artillery bombardment, which came to characterize this battle perhaps more than any other. 'Verdun is terrible,' wrote French Sergeant-Major César Méléra, who was killed a fortnight before the armistice, 'because man is fighting against material, with the sensation of striking out at empty air . . .' Describing the effects of a bombardment, Paul Dubrulle, a thirty-four-year-old Jesuit serving as an infantry sergeant (also later killed), said: 'The most solid nerves cannot resist for long; the moment arrives where the blood mounts to the head; where fever burns the body and where the nerves, exhausted, become incapable of reacting . . . finally one abandons oneself to it, one has no longer even the strength to cover oneself with one's pack as protection against splinters, and one scarcely still has left the strength to pray to God.'

Despite the heroic sacrifices of Pétain's men, each day brought the sea of *Feldgrau* a few yards closer to Verdun. By the end of March, French losses totalled 89,000; but the attackers had also lost nearly 82,000 men. Even once they had taken the Mort-Homme, the Germans found themselves hamstrung by French guns on the Côte 304, another ridge still farther out on the flank. Like a surgeon treating galloping cancer, Falkenhayn's knife was enticed ever farther from the original point of application. More fresh German divisions were hurled into the battle – this time to seize Côte 304.

Not until May was the German 'clearing' operation on the left bank of the Meuse at last completed. The final push towards Verdun could begin. But the Crown Prince was now for calling off the offensive, and even Falkenhayn's enthusiasm was waning. The strategic significance of Verdun had long since passed out of sight; yet the battle had somehow achieved a demonic existence of its own, far beyond the control of generals of either nation. Honour had become involved to an extent which made disengagement impossible. On the French side, Pétain – affected (too deeply, according to Joffre) by the horrors he had witnessed – was promoted and replaced by two more ferocious figures: General Robert Nivelle and General Charles Mangin, nicknamed 'The Butcher'.

By now men had become almost conditioned to death at Verdun. 'One eats, one drinks beside the dead, one sleeps in the midst of the dying, one laughs and sings in the company of corpses,' wrote Georges Duhamel, the poet and dramatist, who was serving as a French army doctor. The highly compressed area of the battlefield itself had become a reeking open cemetery where 'you found the dead embedded in the walls of the trenches; heads, legs and half-bodies, just as they had been shovelled out of the way by the picks and shovels of the working party'. Conditions were no longer much better for the attacking Germans; as one soldier wrote home in April under the French counter-bombardment: 'Many would rather endure starvation than make dangerous expeditions for food.'

On 26th May a 'very excited' Joffre visited Haig at his HQ and appealed to him to advance the date of the Somme offensive. When Haig spoke of 15th August, Joffre shouted that 'The French Army would cease to exist if we did nothing by then.' Haig finally agreed to help by attacking on 1st July instead. Although Haig entertained vague hopes of a breakthrough to be exploited by cavalry, neither he nor Rawlinson – whose 4th Army were to fight the battle – had yet arrived at any higher strategic purpose than that of relieving Verdun and 'to kill as many Germans as possible' (Rawlinson).

Meanwhile, at Verdun the beginning of a torrid June brought the deadliest phase in the three-and-a-half-month battle, with the Germans throwing in a weight of attack comparable to that of February – but this time concentrated along a front only three, instead of eight, miles wide. The fighting reached Vaux, the second of the great forts, where 600 men under Major Sylvain Eugène Raynal in an epic defence held up the main thrust of the German V Army for a whole week until thirst forced them to surrender.

The Suicide Club

Then, just as Vaux was falling, the first of the Allied summer offensives was unleashed. In the east, General Brusilov struck at the Austro-Hungarians with forty divisions, achieving a spectacular initial success. Falkenhayn was forced to transfer troops badly needed at Verdun to bolster up his sagging ally. Verdun was reprieved; although in fact it was not until 23rd June that the actual crisis was reached. On that day, using a deadly new gas called phosgene, the Crown Prince (reluctantly) attacked towards Fort Souville, astride the last ridge before Verdun. At one moment, machine-gun bullets were striking the city streets. Still the French held but there were ominous signs that morale was cracking. Just how much could a nation stand?

Two days later, however, the rumble of heavy British guns was heard in Verdun. Haig's five-day preliminary bombardment on the Somme had begun.

Because of her crippling losses at Verdun, the French contribution on the Somme had shrunk from forty to sixteen divisions, of which only five actually attacked on 1st July, compared with fourteen British divisions. Thus, for the first time, Great Britain was shouldering the main weight in a Western Front offensive. Of the British first-wave divisions, eleven were either Territorials or from Kitchener's 'New Armies'. Typical of the latter force was one battalion which had only three 'trained officers', including one who was stone deaf, another who suffered from a badly broken leg, and a sixty-three-year-old commanding officer who had retired before the Boer War. These new amateur units of 'civvies' had been trained to advance in rigid parade-ground formations that would have served well at Dettingen – straight lines two to three paces between each man, one hundred yards between each rank in the assault waves. In their rawness, their leaders did not trust them to attempt any of the more sophisticated tactics of infiltration such as the Germans and French had evolved at Verdun – despite a recommendation by Haig himself. French farmers were reluctant to allow their fields to be used for badly needed extra infantry training. But what 'K's' men

French troops attempt to take up position under fire in the Helby defile at Verdun

lacked in expertise, they more than made up for in zeal and courage.

The Somme meanders through a flat, wide, and marshy valley. In the areas where the battle was to be fought, there are few geographical features of any note, except the high ground running south-east from Thiepval to Guillemont. This lay in German hands, and was the principal tactical objective for Rawlinson's 4th Army. The British, therefore, would everywhere be fighting uphill; whereas opposite General Fayolle's 6th Army, the French faced more or less level ground. The Germans had superb observation points gazing down on the British lines, their excellence matched only by the depth of their fortifications.

In the nearly two years that they had sat on the Somme, they had excavated dugouts and vast dormitories out of the chalk

Ullstein

Verdun landscape: bombardments left shattered woods and pockmarked hillsides

as deep as forty feet below ground, comfortably safe from all but the heaviest British shell. Ironically, the British, by their policy of continual 'strafing' (in contrast to the prevalent German and French philosophy of 'live and let live'), had provoked the defenders to dig even deeper. When captured, the German dugouts astonished everybody by their depth and complexity. The German line on the Somme was, claims Churchill, 'undoubtedly the strongest and most perfectly defended position in the world'.

British security surrounding the Somme offensive was by no means perfect. Among other indiscretions, the press reported a speech made by a member of the government, Arthur Henderson, requesting workers in a munitions factory not to question why the Whitsun Bank Holiday was being suspended. In his diary for 10th June, Crown Prince Rupprecht, the German army group commander, wrote: '. . . This fact should speak volumes. It certainly does so speak, it contains the surest proof that there will be a great British offensive before long. . . .' Abundantly aware of just where the 'Big Push' was coming, for several weeks previously the German defenders had industriously practised rushing their machine-guns up from the dugouts. This had been perfected to a three-minute drill, which would give the Germans an ample margin on 'Z-day' between the lifting of the British barrage and the arrival of the attacking infantry.

For five days Rawlinson's artillery preparation blasted away without let-up (Haig would have preferred a short preliminary bombardment)—thereby dissipating what little element of surprise there still remained. By British standards of the day, it was a bombardment of unprecedented weight. Yet on their much wider front they could mount not nearly half as many heavy guns as the French; and they had nothing to compare with the French 240mm mortars and 400 'super-heavies' with which Foch (French northern army group commander) had equipped Fayolle. A depressing quantity of the British shells turned out to be dud; while defective American ammunition caused so many premature explosions that some of the 4.5 howitzer gun crews nicknamed themselves 'the Suicide Club'. The fire-plan also suffered from the same inflexibility which characterized the training of the new infantry. Through sheer weight of metal, large sections of the German front-line trenches were indeed obliterated, their skeleton outposts killed. But down below in the secure depths of the dugouts, the main body of the German defenders sat playing *Skat* while the shelling raged above.

The worst shortcoming of the five-day bombardment, however, was that it failed in its essential task of breaking up the barbed wire through which the British assault waves were to advance. Divisional commanders appear to have known this, but to have kept the knowledge to themselves. On the eve of the 'Big Push', Haig wrote in his diary with the misguided optimism that was to be found at almost every level prior to 1st July: 'The wire has never been so well cut, nor the Artillery preparation so thorough. I have seen personally all the Corps commanders and one and all are full of confidence. . . .'

At 0245 hours on 1st July a German listening post picked up a message from Rawlinson wishing his 4th Army 'Good Luck'. A little less than five hours later there was suddenly a strange silence as the British bombardment ended. Somewhere near a hundred thousand men left their trenches at this moment and moved forward at a steady walk. On their backs they carried their personal kit—including a spare pair of socks—water bottles, a day's rations, two gas masks, mess tins and field dressings, as well as rifle, bayonet, 220 rounds of ammunition, and an entrenching tool. Some also carried hand grenades or bombs for a trench mortar. The minimum load was 66lb; some men were laden with as much as 85 to 90lb. It was about to become a broiling hot day.

'. . . They got going without delay,' wrote the commanding officer of a battalion of the Royal Inniskilling Fusiliers;

'No fuss, no shouting, no running, everything solid and thorough—just like the men themselves. Here and there a boy would wave his hand to me as I shouted good luck to them through my megaphone. And all had a cheery face . . . Fancy advancing against heavy fire with a big roll of barbed wire on your shoulders! . . .'

Seen from the defenders' point of view, a German recorded that the moment the bombardment lifted:

'. . . Our men at once clambered up the steep shafts leading from the dug-outs to daylight and ran for the nearest shell craters. The machine-guns were pulled out of the dug-outs and hurriedly placed into position, their crews dragging the heavy ammunition boxes up the steps and out to the guns. A rough firing line was thus rapidly established. As soon as in position, a series of extended lines of British infantry were seen moving forward from the British trenches. The first line appeared to continue without end to right and left. It was quickly followed by a second line, then a third and fourth. They came on at a steady easy pace as if expecting to find nothing alive in our front trenches. . . .'

Reading from left to right along the line, the British forces involved in the principal offensive were the 8th, 10th, 3rd, 15th, and 13th Corps, while below them on the river Somme itself came the French 20th and 35th Corps. General Hunter-Weston's 8th Corps had the most difficult task of all—the terrain was particularly difficult—and, because of its inexperience, it was the corps about which Haig had entertained the most doubts. With the 31st Division holding its left flank, the Yorks and Lancs were encouraged to see ahead of them numerous gaps in the wire opened up by the shelling. But at the moment of reaching them, they were scythed down by devastating machine-gun fire from the weapons which the Germans had rushed up from their dug-outs. It was an experience that was to be repeated innumerable times that day. By early afternoon the 31st Division had lost 3,600 officers and men, of whom only eight were prisoners. ▷ 571

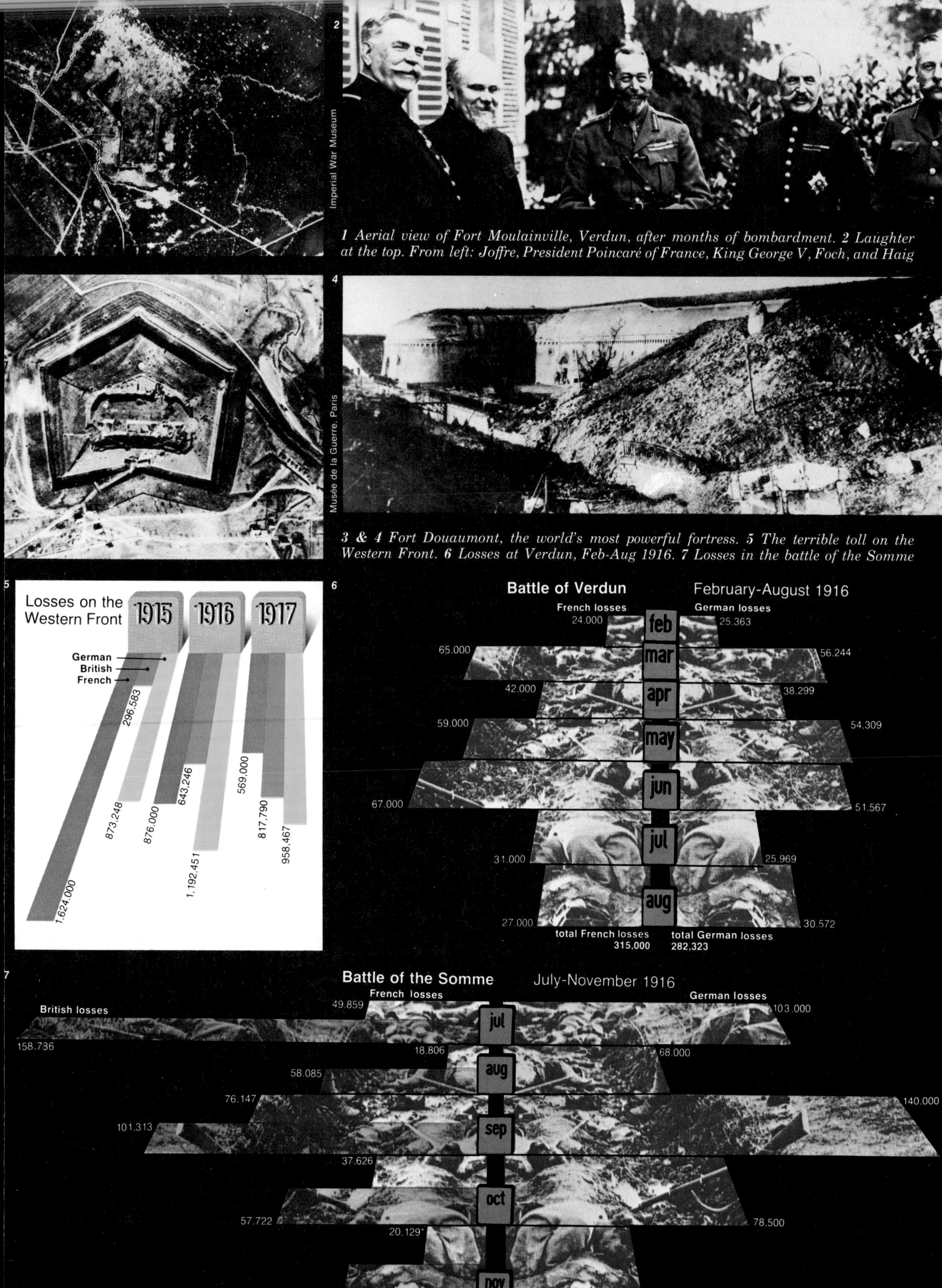

1 Aerial view of Fort Moulainville, Verdun, after months of bombardment. 2 Laughter at the top. From left: Joffre, President Poincaré of France, King George V, Foch, and Haig

3 & 4 Fort Douaumont, the world's most powerful fortress. 5 The terrible toll on the Western Front. 6 Losses at Verdun, Feb-Aug 1916. 7 Losses in the battle of the Somme

Bayer. Armeemuseum, Munich

1 Painting of the Somme battlefield, Colincamps to Fouquevillers, from a German balloon. 2 A British military policeman escorts a German prisoner captured in November, 1916

Imperial War Museum

3 A British heavy howitzer battery in action on the Somme. 4 The farthest extent of the Allied advances in the battle of the Somme. The offensive lost impetus amid rain and mud, capturing nothing of strategic importance. 5 Abandoned British trench in the Fricourt salient, September 1916. Flints and chalk are spilling out of the rotting sandbags

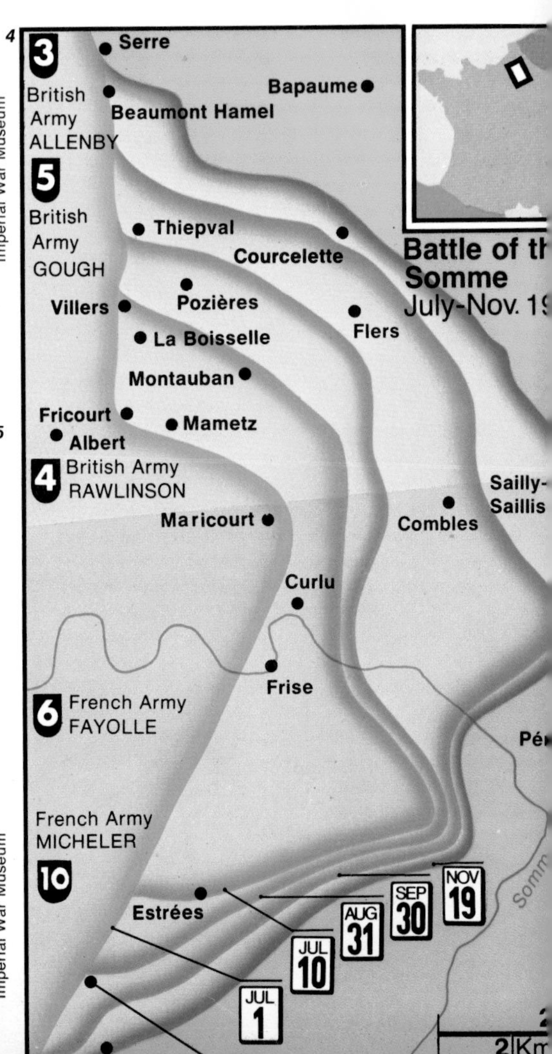

Imperial War Museum

Imperial War Museum

Next to it, the 29th Division, recently returned from Gallipoli, had the task of rushing the 'Hawthorn Redoubt' after an immense mine had been detonated under it. But the mine had been timed to go off ten minutes before zero hour; giving the German machine-gunners plenty of time to reoccupy the crater. Moving across no man's land the Royal Fusiliers could see ahead of them the bodies of their first waves festooning the uncut wire; all that came back from this one battalion was 120 men. The divisional commander, in a supreme understatement, noted that his men had been 'temporarily held up by some machine-guns', and pushed up another brigade; one battalion found itself so obstructed by the dead and the endless lines of wounded that it physically could not get forward. Attacking unsuccessfully but with fantastic courage at Beaumont-Hamel, the Newfoundlanders won their greatest battle honour: in a matter of minutes 710 men fell.

Also at Beaumont-Hamel, troops that had captured the Heidenkopf position were tragically shot down by the second wave, unaware that the German strong-point was already in British hands.

By nightfall, the 8th Corps alone had lost 14,000 officers and men without even broaching the main objective. It had taken only twenty-two prisoners. For the 10th, the 3rd, and part of 15th Corps the story of bloody failure was much the same:

'I get up from the ground and whistle,' recalled an officer commanding an Irish battalion in the second wave. 'The others rise. We move off with steady pace. I see rows upon rows of British soldiers lying dead, dying or wounded in no man's land. Here and there I see the hands thrown up and then a body flops on the ground. The bursting shells and smoke make visibility poor. We proceed. Again I look southward from a different angle and perceive heaped up masses of British corpses suspended on the German wire, while live men rush forward in orderly procession to swell the weight of numbers in the spider's web. . . .'

The Highland Light Infantry went into battle behind their pipers. Swiftly their leading companies invested the German trenches, but while they were still exulting at their success, hidden German machine-guns opened fire. Within little more than an hour of the beginning of the attack, half the HLI were killed or wounded, bringing the assault to a sudden halt.

Opposite Thiepval, the 36th (Ulster) Division came tantalizingly, tragically close to achieving success. Better trained than most of Rawlinson's units, the Inniskillings managed to advance a mile in the first hour of the attack, attaining the top of the ridge and capturing the Schwaben Redoubt, an important strongpoint in the German first-line. But, following the experiences of 1915 when so many field officers had been killed off, it was Haig's orders that no battalion commanding officers or second-in-commands should go in with their men in the first wave. Thus there was no one senior enough to consolidate the Ulstermen's fine success. Communications with the rear were appalling. Runners sent back for fresh orders never returned. Precious time was thrown away, while the Germans recovered their balance. When finally a reserve brigade was sent up to reinforce the Inniskillings, it too had no senior officers with it; with the result it advanced too fast, running into its own artillery barrage, where it lost something like two-thirds of its soldiers. That evening, of the 10th Corps' 9,000 losses, over half came from the Ulster Division – a fact which was long to cause bitterness against the neighbouring English units. The division was left clinging precariously to the German front line.

On the 3rd Corps' front, the 8th Division was another unit to suffer appalling casualties in return for very little progress. It lost a shocking total of 1,927 officers and men killed; one of its battalions, the 2nd Middlesex, lost 22 officers and 601 men, another – the 8th Yorks and Lancs – 21 and 576 respectively, out of an average of 27-30 officers and roughly 700 men to a battalion.

Over the whole British front, only Congreve's 13th Corps, next door to the French, registered any notable success that day. Attacking through Montauban, it captured the entire HQ of the German 62nd Regiment; making a total bag of 1,882 prisoners (compared with the 8th Corps' 22). At Montauban, the cellars were found to be filled with German dead; apparently killed by the French heavy mortars.

Fighting in hell

Indeed, for all the incredible fortitude of Kitchener's men, it was the French who won the laurels on 1st July. The terrain opposite them was admittedly much more favourable, the defences weaker; they had more and heavier guns, which had smashed up even some of the deepest enemy dug-outs; their infantry moved with greater skill and flexibility; and they had the advantage of a certain degree of surprise. After the losses inflicted at Verdun, German intelligence could not believe that the French were capable of making a serious contribution on the Somme. To reinforce this belief, Foch cleverly delayed the French attack until several hours after the British.

By early afternoon, Fayolle's troops had taken 6,000 prisoners, destroyed the whole of the German 121st Division's artillery, and come close to making a breakthrough. Péronne itself was threatened. General Balfourier, commanding the 'Iron' (20th) Corps which had saved Verdun in February, urged Congreve on his left to join him in continuing the advance. But Congreve would budge no farther. Above him, Rawlinson was bent more on consolidation than exploitation. Thus Balfourier, with his left flank hanging in the air, was unable to advance either. It was not until 10 o'clock that night that Rawlinson made any attempt to push reserves up to the areas of least resistance. What prospect there had been of capitalizing on any success gained during the 1st July was swiftly lost; the Germans were soon replacing the machine-guns destroyed that day.

When the casualties were counted, the British figures came to 60,000, of which the dead numbered 20,000. Most of the slaughter had been accomplished by perhaps a hundred German machine-gun teams. 1st July was one of the blackest days in British history. Even at Verdun, the total French casualty list for the worst month barely exceeded what Great Britain had lost on that one day. Fayolle lost fewer men than the defending Germans.

Haig had no idea of the full extent of the British losses until 3rd July and neither he nor Rawlinson quite knew why some efforts had succeeded and others failed. On the 3rd Haig ordered Rawlinson to attack again; this time rightly trying to follow up the good results achieved on his southern sector. But the guns were now short of ammunition, and the losses on 1st July greatly reduced the strength of the new blows. That night it rained, and the next day 'walking, let alone fighting, became hellish'.

On 14th July, Rawlinson – chastened by the terrible casualties his army had suffered – decided to try something new. He would attack by night. Describing it caustically as 'an attack organized for amateurs by amateurs', the French predicted disaster. Haig, equally dubious, caused the attack to be postponed twenty-four hours – a delay that diminished the chances of success. Nevertheless, throwing in six brigades which totalled some 22,000 men, Rawlinson after a short hurricane bombardment punched out a salient four miles wide and a thousand yards deep, breaching the Germans' second line – and thereby briefly restoring the element of surprise to the Western Front. A French liaison officer telephoned the sceptical Balfourier: *'Ils ont osé. Ils ont réussi!'*

Once again, however, the fruits of victory were thrown away by poor communications and the painful slowness to react of the British command. As at Gallipoli, there was a horrifying absence of any sense of urgency. The cavalry were waiting in the wings, but too far back to be available to exploit any gains, and not until mid-after-

Snark International

British go over the top in the Somme battle. Their dead bodies were to festoon the wire

noon that day was it decided to push up the already battle-weary 7th Infantry Division. Thus nine valuable hours were wasted, and darkness was falling when at last the British cavalry and infantry reserves attacked. By then the shaken Germans had rallied.

Deeply disappointed, Haig now settled for a long-protracted 'battle of attrition'. Writing to the government, he declared his intention 'to maintain a steady pressure on Somme battle . . . proceeding thus, I expect to be able to maintain the offensive well into the Autumn. . . .' All through August and into September the bloody slogging match continued. As seen by the Australian official history, Haig's new technique 'merely appeared to be that of applying a battering-ram ten or fifteen times against the same part of the enemy's battle-front with the intention of penetrating for a mile, or possibly two . . . the claim that it was economic is entirely unjustified'. By the end of the summer, one level-headed Australian officer was writing '. . . we have just come out of a place so terrible that . . . a raving lunatic could never imagine the horror the last thirteen days. . . .'

Meanwhile, however, Verdun had been finally and definitively relieved by the dreadful British sacrifices on the Somme. On 11th July, one last desperate effort was mounted against Verdun, and a handful of Germans momentarily reached a height whence they could actually gaze down on Verdun's citadel. It was the high-water mark of the battle, and – though not apparent at the time – was perhaps the turning point, the Gettysburg of the First World War. Rapidly the tide now receded at Verdun, with Falkenhayn ordering the German army to assume the defensive all along the Western Front.

At the end of August Falkenhayn was replaced by the formidable combination of Hindenburg and Ludendorff.

Visiting the Somme, Ludendorff criticized the inflexibility of the defence there; '. . . Without doubt they fought too doggedly, clinging too resolutely to the mere holding of ground, with the result that the losses were heavy. . . . The Field Marshal and I could for the moment only ask that the front line should be held more lightly. . . .' It was a prelude to the strategic withdrawal to the 'Hindenburg Line' in the following spring.

'A pretty mechanical toy'

On the Somme, 15th September was to become a red-letter day in the history of warfare. Haig decided to throw into a third major attack the first fifty newly invented tanks. Rejected by Kitchener as 'a pretty mechanical toy but of very limited military value', the tank had been developed under the greatest secrecy and crews trained with similar security behind a vast secret enclosure near Thetford in Norfolk. Even the name 'tank' was intended to deceive the enemy. Its inventors begged the army not to employ the first machines, however, until they were technically more reliable; while even Asquith visiting the front on 6th September thought it: '. . . a mistake to put them into the battle of the Somme. They were built for the purpose of breaking an ordinary trench system with a normal artillery fire only, whereas on the Somme they will have to penetrate a terrific artillery barrage, and will have to operate in a broken country full of shell-craters . . .'

But Haig was determined. Historians will long continue to argue whether he was right or not; on Haig's side, the Cambrai raid the following year tends to prove that the surprise value of the tank had not entirely been thrown away, and undoubtedly, sooner or later, it would have had to be tried out under battle conditions.

On the day of the attack, only thirty-two of the original fifty tanks reached the assembly area in working order; twenty-four actually went into battle, and most of these broke down, became bogged, or were knocked out. At Flers the tank showed what it could do, and the infantry advanced cheering down the main street of the village behind four solitary machines. But once again poor communications between front and rear gave the Germans a chance to reorganize before success could be exploited. By the evening of the 15th all the tanks were either scattered or destroyed. With them vanished the last of Haig's three opportunities on the Somme; Montauban on 1st July, Rawlinson's night attack on the 14th, and Flers on 15th September.

Now the equinoctial rains turned the battlefield into a slippery bog. But, pressed by Joffre, Haig stuck out his Celtic jaw and soldiered on, in the mystic belief that – somehow, somewhere – an exhausted foe might suddenly break. The British army was equally exhausted. Conditions became even more appalling. In November, a soldier wrote: '. . . Whoever it is we are relieving, they have already gone. The trench is empty . . . Corpses lie along the parados, rotting in the wet; every now and then a booted foot appears jutting over the trench. The mud makes it all but impassable, and now, sunk in it up to the knees, I have the momentary terror of never being able to pull myself out . . . This is the very limit of endurance. . . .'

In a last attack on 13th November, shattered Beaumont-Hamel was finally captured. Having won the bloodily disputed high ground, the British were now fighting their way down into the valley beyond – condemning themselves to spend a winter in flooded trenches. Nothing of any strategic value had been attained. The 'Big Push' was over.

At Verdun in the autumn, Nivelle and Mangin recaptured forts Douaumont and Vaux in a series of brilliant counter-strokes – plus much of the territory gained so painfully by the Crown Prince's men. By Christmas 1916 both battles were finished. After ten terrible months Verdun had been saved. But at what a cost! Half the houses in the city itself had been destroyed by the long-range German guns, and nine of its neighbouring villages had vanished off the face of the earth. When the human casualties came to be added up, the French admitted to having lost 377,231 men, of whom 162,308 were listed as dead or missing. German losses amounted to no less than 337,000. But, in fact, combined casualties may easily have totalled much more than 800,000.

What caused this imprecision about the slaughter at Verdun, as well as giving the battle its particularly atrocious character, was the fact that it all took place in so concentrated an area – little larger than the London parks. Many of the dead were never found, or are still being discovered to this day. One combatant recalled how 'the shells disinterred the bodies, then reinterred them, chopped them to pieces, played with them as a cat plays ▷ 576

2

Imperial War Museum

1 Australian Royal Field Artillery pass by 4.7 gun during the Somme battle.
2 Germans captured in the battle of Morval.
3 Somme: Dead German with live grenades

4

Imperial War Museum

4 British troops supporting the first assault wave near Morval on the Somme.
5 French troops marching to positions in the battle. ***6*** *A guide awaiting a patrol*

6

Imperial War Museum

***Previous page:** Under lowering night skies French military traffic winds along the Voie Sacrée at Verdun. The whole life-blood of France poured along this artery to reinforce the threatened city. Painting by Georges Scott (Musée de la Guerre, Paris)*

Imperial War Museum

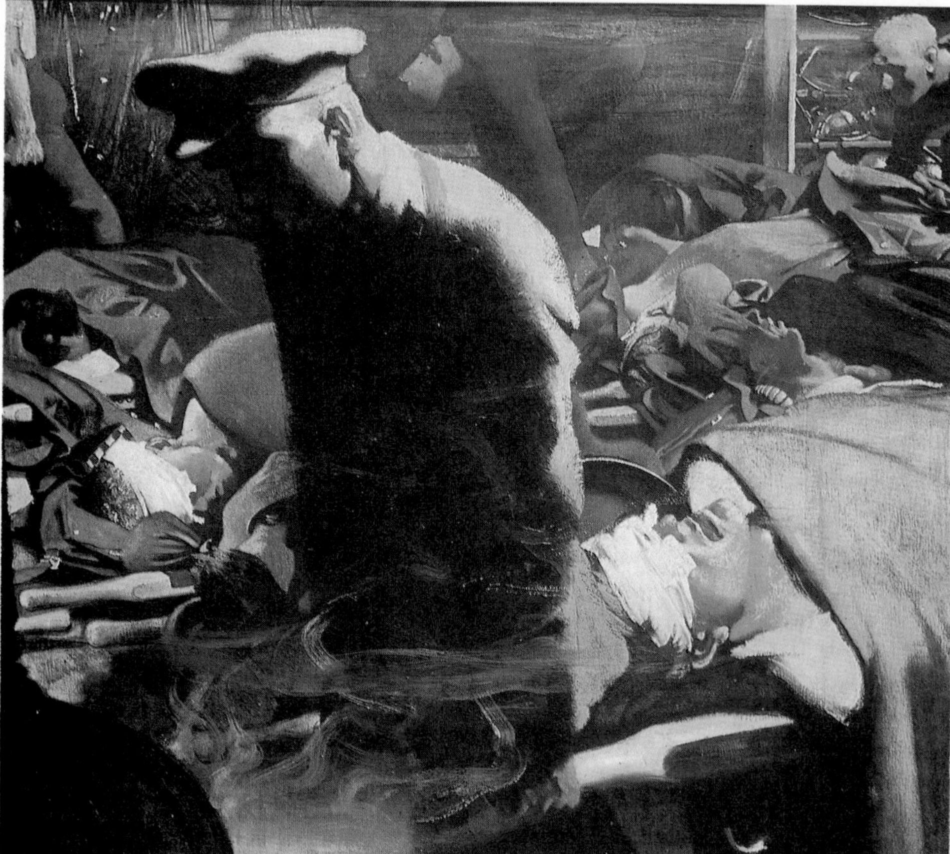

Imperial War Museum

*Painters capture the meaning of these sacrificial battles. **Left:** 'Paths of Glory' by C.Nevinson. **Bottom left:** 'Gassed and Wounded' painted by Eric Kennington*

with a mouse'. Inside the great sombre *Ossuaire* at Verdun lie the bones of more than 100,000 unknown warriors.

On the Somme, the British had lost some 420,000 men; the French about 200,000 and the Germans probably about 450,000 – although a miasma of mendacity and error still surrounds the exact figures. On the battlefields of Verdun and the Somme, there also expired the last flickers of idealism; yet the war would go on.

The casualties of the two battles included among them the highest warlords on both sides. Falkenhayn had fallen; then Joffre, to be replaced (disastrously) by Nivelle, and Asquith by Lloyd George; a few months later Premier Briand's head would also topple. Because of the appalling extent to which Verdun had 'bled white' his own army, Falkenhayn's grim experiment had failed. Yet, in its longer-range effects, it contained an element of success. As Raymond Jubert, a young French ensign, wrote in prophetic despair before he was killed at Verdun: 'They will not be able to make us do it again another day; that would be to misconstrue the price of our effort. . . .' The excessive sacrifices of the French army at Verdun germinated the seeds of the mutinies that were to sprout in the summer of 1917, thereby making it finally plain that the war could no longer be won without American troops.

In many ways Verdun and Somme were the First World War in microcosm, with all its heroism and futility, its glorious and unspeakable horrors. They were indecisive battles in an indecisive war. Of the two, Verdun undoubtedly had the greater historical significance. Years after the 1918 Armistice this Pyrrhic victory of the 20th century continued to haunt the French nation. From the role the forts at Verdun had played, France's military leaders (headed by Pétain) drew the wrong conclusions, and the Maginot Line – with all its disastrous strategic consequences in 1940 – was born.

Spiritually, perhaps, the damage was even greater. More than three-quarters of the whole French army passed through the hell of Verdun – almost an entire generation of Frenchmen. Nobody knew this better than Pétain who, years after the war, remarked that at Verdun 'the constant vision of death had penetrated him (the French soldier) with a resignation which bordered on fatalism'.

For a symbol of what Verdun did to France, one need hardly search beyond the tragic figure of Pétain, the warrior-hero of 1916, the resigned defeatist of 1940.

Eastern Front, June-December 1916 / J.N.Westwood

The Brusilov Offensive

One of the most successful of the Allied campaigns took place on the Eastern Front in 1916 when Brusilov's armies smashed through the Austrians. It was the only victory of the war to be named after a commander. But, unfortunately for the Russians, the victory was probably too successful . . .

After its great retreat of autumn 1915 the Russian army, which had withdrawn in good order though with great losses, settled down on a new line. This ran from north to south for over 500 miles, from Riga on the Baltic through the Pinsk marshes to the Rumanian frontier. In the north it faced the Germans under Ludendorff, in the south the Austrians under Archduke Frederick. The line was divided into three fronts (army groups). The northernmost of these was the North-West Front, commanded by the same Kuropatkin who in the Russo-Japanese War had specialized in the tactic of the mis-timed retreat (p. 68). The next sector was the West Front commanded by General Evert, who was also to manifest a dislike for offensive actions. Finally there was the South-West Front commanded by another master of timidity, General Ivanov.

Major-General Alekseyev who, as chief of staff to the commander-in-chief (Tsar Nicholas), was responsible for the Russian operations, was one of the better generals of the First World War – but his front commanders certainly were not. That men of their outlook held such responsible positions was, on the one hand, an indictment of the Russian political situation: with the Tsar, weak-willed in any case, out of touch at the front, the conduct of affairs at Petrograd (as St Petersburg was now called) was dependent more and more on the intrigues of the Tsarina and her favourites, and this circle tended to oppose the appointment of men of strong character and intellectual energy. On the other hand, there was another reason why so many Russian officers were unaggressive: the victory of 1812 over Napoleon had by now, aided by Tolstoy's dramatic and erroneous interpretation in *War and Peace,* entered the Russian tradition as a victory won by a great general called Kutuzov who had deliberately retreated in order to win the war. Thus there existed a concept – conscious and subconscious – of victory through retreat, which is why so many Russian generals seemed reluctant and over-anxious in attack.

During the winter of 1915-16 the Russian army was slowly restored to fighting condition. The deficiencies in 1915, the lack of rifles, of ammunition, of boots, and of properly-trained soldiers, would not be repeated in 1916. In early 1916 rifles were being produced at the rate of 10,000 per month; most front-line units had their full complement of field and machine-guns; ammunition, except perhaps for the heaviest guns, was being delivered fast enough to build up stocks for a full summer campaign; the quiet winter months had given time for proper training of recruits – although the shortage of good experienced officers could not be remedied so easily. The Red Cross detachments organized by local civilians were doing much to maintain front-line morale, not least because they made it their business to provide for many of the physical and recreational needs which the war ministry had so obviously neglected.

The last battle of 1915 had been a minor Russian offensive in the south, aimed at helping the Serbian army, which had been driven into retreat when Bulgaria declared war. In the winter an inter-Allied military conference held at Chantilly in France laid plans for the 1916 summer campaign. Russia was to play a relatively small part in these plans, because of the heavy losses she had sustained in 1915: the main Allied offensive was to be on the Somme, and was to be preceded by a small diversionary attack made by the Russian army. However, the Germans disturbed this scheme by their massive attack on Verdun in February: not for the first time – nor the last – Russia was called upon to save her western allies by mounting a hastily-planned offensive to draw German divisions from the west to the east. In March and April a Russian army of the West Front, with artillery support whose intensity surprised the Germans, attacked through the mud of the spring thaw and overcame the German advanced lines. Ludendorff brought up reinforcements, for some reason the Russian GHQ withdrew its heavy artillery and aircraft from the sector, and the Russian soldiers were left almost defenceless in shallow marsh trenches, without gas masks. Unable to withstand the prolonged barrage of gas and high-explosive shells, and sustaining great losses, the Russians, still singing their hymns, were driven back to their start line in one day.

This disaster – the battle of Lake Naroch – was a relatively minor action, and the Russians were already planning bigger things, both to honour their pledge to the Allies (for the Somme operation was still scheduled) and to take pressure off the French, who were bearing heavy losses and in a desperate situation at Verdun. On 14th April the Tsar had presided at a meeting of the front commanders at GHQ. By this time the pessimistic Ivanov had been replaced by General Alexey Brusilov, who as an army commander had distinguished himself in the 1915 retreat even

General Alexey Brusilov. He later claimed that if his fantastically successful offensive had been properly exploited, Russia could have won the war for the Allies. Even if he had not won the war he probably prevented the Allies losing it

Novosti

though he was a champion of an offensive strategy.

Brusilov risks his reputation

At the 14th April meeting the idea of attacking on the West (Evert's) Front was discussed. Both Evert and Kuropatkin declared that they preferred to stay on the defensive, alleging that there was not enough heavy artillery and shells to start an offensive. Brusilov disagreed, and recommended attacks on all fronts. This latter proposal was made in view of the superior rail communications on the German side of the line. By quickly shifting troops from a quiet sector the German command could easily reinforce that part of its line under threat: if the Russian attack came not at one point but at several this would be more difficult, especially as it would be hard to divine which of the attacks was intended to develop into the main thrust.

It was finally agreed that an offensive would be launched at the end of May, and that Brusilov's South-West Front would make the first move but that the main thrust would in fact start soon afterwards on Evert's West Front and be directed towards Wilno.

As he left this meeting Brusilov was told by a colleague that he had been unwise to risk his reputation by offering to launch an offensive. Unperturbed by this pessimism, he returned to his South-West Front to make the most of his six-week preparation time. He decided not to concentrate his forces but to ask each of the generals commanding his four armies to prepare an attack; with preparations being made at four places on his 200-mile sector of the line the enemy would be unable to anticipate where the main blow would fall. In previous actions, as Brusilov was well aware, both the place and the time of an attack had seemed to produce no surprise, so, in addition to avoiding troop concentrations, he took the precaution of dismissing newspaper correspondents. Also, since he suspected that the Tsarina was a careless talker, he avoided telling her the details of his plan.

The Austro-Hungarian line which Brusilov was preparing to break through was strongly fortified, consisting in most parts of three defensive belts one behind the other at intervals of one or two miles. Each belt had at least three lines of full-depth trenches, with fifty to sixty yards between each trench. There were well-built dugouts, machine-gun nests, sniper hideouts, and as many communication trenches as were needed. Before each belt there was a barbed wire barrier, consisting of about twenty rows of posts to which were attached swathes of barbed wire, some of which was very thick and some electrified or mined. Brusilov's aircraft had made good photographs of these defences and the information was transferred to large-scale maps so that, as was shown later, the Russian officers had as good maps of the opposing line as had the Austrians. Moreover, although during the preparation period most of the soldiers were kept well behind the line, the officers spent much time in advanced positions studying the terrain over which they would fight. Meanwhile, with odd sighting shots the gunners were able to get the range of their prescribed targets, and shell stocks were building up. Trenches to serve as assembly and jumping-off points were dug near to the front-line Austrian trenches, in some places getting as close as one hundred or even seventy-five yards. Because this was to be a widely dispersed effort and not a conventional hammer-blow attack, no reserves were assembled.

While his four army commanders were each planning the details of their respective attacks, Brusilov was in touch – frequently acrimonious touch – with GHQ on the question of timing. On the one hand, Evert was declaring that his West Front attack, for which Brusilov's was only a preliminary diversion, needed more preparation time. On the other hand, to the urgent situation at Verdun was now added the rout of the Italian army by the Austrians at Trentino: unless Russia could do something to relieve the pressure Italy would be driven out of the war and the Central powers would be able to bring even greater strength against Verdun. In the end, 'Brusilov's Offensive', as it was later called (it was the only victory during the First World War named after a commander) was launched on 4th June.

The Archduke's birthday party

Three of Brusilov's four armies broke through at once, aided by thorough artillery preparation, surprise, and the alacrity with which the Czech elements of the Austro-Hungarian army offered themselves as grateful prisoners of war. Brusilov's main thrust was towards Lutsk and Kovel. The former was taken on the 8th: the Archduke Josef Ferdinand was forced by Russian shells to abandon his birthday party which he was celebrating there. With three deep and wide gaps in their line the Austrians were soon in full and fast retreat. However, the ever-reluctant Evert was still unwilling to start his own attack and on 9th June Brusilov learned that this attack would be postponed until the 18th. By this time Ludendorff was desperately trying to organize a counter-attack, and scraping together German units which he sent south to stiffen the demoralized Austrians. Fortunately for Austria, Brusilov's main thrust, confused by unclear instructions from GHQ, advanced in two directions at once, and thus lost the chance of capturing Kovel.

On 18th June Evert's promised attack towards Wilno did not materialize. Instead, that general made a minor, ill-prepared, and unsuccessful advance farther south at Baranowicze. By now it was clear that GHQ would do what Brusilov had always opposed: instead of attacking on the West Front it would send Evert's troops to Brusilov, believing that the latter with these reinforcements would be able to exploit his success fully. As Brusilov expected, as soon as the Germans noticed these Russian troop movements they felt able to transfer their own troops southwards and, because they had better railways, got there first. In this way the German command was able to make the best possible use of its scanty resources. Despite a renewed push at the end of July, Brusilov made less and less headway as he found more and more German units opposing him. In general, the Brusilov Offensive came to an end about 10th August, by which time the Austrians had lost not only vast areas of territory but also 375,000 prisoners of war, not to speak of killed and wounded. But Russian casualties already exceeded half a million.

Brusilov later claimed that if his wildly successful offensive had been properly exploited, Russia could have won the war for the Allies. It does seem very possible that if Evert had carried out the main attack as planned (thus occupying those German troops which in fact were sent to help the Austrians) Brusilov would have been able to drive Austria out of the war – which almost certainly would have entailed the surrender of Germany before the end of 1916. In any case, Brusilov's Offensive achieved all the aims which it had been set, and more: Austrian troops in Italy had to abandon their victories and rush north to fight the Russians, and the Germans were forced to end the Verdun operation and transfer no less than thirty-five divisions from France to the Eastern Front. Even if Brusilov had not won the war, he probably stopped the Allies losing it.

Persuading Rumania

In mid-August, just as Brusilov's Offensive was slowing down, it was brought to a definite end by the decision of Rumania to abandon her neutrality and join the Allies, her first step in this direction being to sign a military alliance.

Right from the beginning of the war Allied diplomacy had been busy in Rumania. The Russian effort in this respect was two-pronged and, in view of the Tsar's habit of acting independently of his ministers, it is possible that neither prong knew what the other was doing. ▷ **580**

1 The Brusilov Offensive. The main thrust towards Lutsk and Kovel sent the Austrians reeling, but Evert failed to attack on the West Front.
2 Painting of Austrian soldiers on the South-west Front, by Karl Sterrer

Novosti

3 Russian troops on the Galician Front, 1916. 4 Austrian field gun in the Rumanian mountains.
5 Russian troops in helmets of French design sight a machine-gun during the Brusilov Offensive

Radio Times Hulton

Novosti

The conventional weapon in this diplomatic campaign was the Russian ambassador in Bucharest, who enjoyed a certain influence in Rumanian political circles. But his talents were well matched by the Rumanian statesman Brătianu, who was long able to postpone a decision. Rumania at this time had well-balanced ties with both Russia and the Central powers, and public opinion was more or less equally split between those who favoured the Allies and those who supported Germany and Austria. It seems likely that most Rumanians were behind Brătianu in his efforts to delay a decision until the bandwagon of ultimate victory had moved unmistakably in one direction or another.

Below: Fund raising for Rumania. British poster depicts a serene King Ferdinand of Rumania warding off the sinister outline of the Kaiser in pickelhaube. *Rumania declared war on Austria on 27th August 1916*

Russia's second agent in Bucharest was less correct than the ambassador, but may have been more effective in the long run. This was Rear-Admiral Veselkin, who from his miniature flagship *Rus* commanded the Danube Flotilla of the Russian Imperial Navy. This flotilla, directly controlled by GHQ, had been formed in 1914 by arming Danubian steamers and adding a few gunboats from the Black Sea Fleet. Its purpose had been to keep Serbia supplied, but after that nation was overrun it had little to do, apart from engaging in intrigues to push Rumania into war on Russia's side.

Veselkin was a witty, open-hearted, and eloquent officer, popular with his colleagues and, more important, a favourite of the Tsar. Whether he dabbled in genuine cloak-and-dagger activities is doubtful: the mysterious packages which he entrusted to transient Russians for strictly personal delivery to the Tsar contained not secret documents but merely Nicholas's favourite kind of Rumanian smoked sausage. But certainly he devoted all his spare time to the persuasion of the Rumanians. He had been entrusted with two million roubles' worth of jewellery which he distributed as 'gifts' to influential Rumanians and their wives. However, this was little compared to the wealth at the disposal of the German agents (who admittedly needed large sums to bribe railwaymen to turn a blind eye on the thinly-disguised war materials passing through on their way from Germany to Turkey). In mid-1916 it seemed that the pro-German party in Rumania was still strong enough to thwart Russian efforts.

In any case, some influential Russians believed that a neutral Rumania was more advantageous than an allied Rumania. Both the Russian naval and military attachés were sending mournful accounts of Rumania's unpreparedness for any serious war, and other Russian officials had the foresight to realize that an Allied Rumania would ask for help which Russia could not spare. However, a change of Russian foreign ministers was followed by what was virtually an ultimatum setting Rumania a time limit in which to make up her mind: the success of Brusilov's Offensive—then in progress—had encouraged this Russian move while at the same time providing an extra inducement for Rumania to choose the side of the Allies.

Rumania at war

Thus it came about that on 17th August Rumania signed the military alliance which had been pressed upon her, and then immediately began to disprove the belief—still current among the great powers fifty years later—that an ally is inevitably better than a neutral. The Allies had hoped that the more than half-a-million-strong Rumanian army would be sent south against Bulgaria, and then perhaps join up with their own forces at Salonika. However, Rumanian appetites in the direction of Bulgaria had already been satisfied by the Treaty of Bucharest of 1913 which had ended the Balkan War (p. 404). On the other hand, Rumania still had desires (termed 'national aspirations') for Austrian Transylvania. So, on 27th August, to the consternation of friends and enemies alike, Rumania struck north.

Germany, which had been hoping that the Rumanian government would procrastinate just a little longer, was ill-placed to meet this new threat: help had already been sent to Austria to stop Brusilov, the western Allies were starting their Somme offensive at the same time as their forces at Salonika were becoming more active. So at first the Rumanian army carried all before it, capturing the capital of Transylvania in early September. However, by tight organization and by taking great risks in scraping together reinforcements from quiet sectors of other fronts, the German high command did just manage to master the situation. Falkenhayn attacked the Rumanians in Transylvania, while Mackensen went through Bulgaria and attacked the new enemy from the south, forcing the Rumanians to relinquish their Dobrudja territory. It now became evident that the Rumanian army was even worse trained and worse equipped than the pessimists had claimed, and in any case the easy-going Rumanian officers were ill-adapted to modern warfare. The Rumanians called for Russian help, and it was Russian troops which inflicted a temporary check on Mackensen in mid-September. Before the end of the month, despite Russian diversionary pressure farther north, the two German armies were threatening the heart of Rumania. In the south Mackensen drove his enemy over the Danube, while the Rumanian forces which had so cheerfully invaded Transylvania a month previously, were now in full retreat. On 23rd October Mackensen captured the key Black Sea port of Constanta, and in early December Bucharest fell. The Rumanian army was now finished for the time being: it occupied a small part of Rumanian territory around Jassy and was being reorganized by a French general in the hope of better days to come.

By this time two Russian armies were involved in Rumania, and it was not long before a quarter of the Russian army was devoted to this area. The Russian front had now, in effect, been extended to the Black Sea: no longer was there a safely neutral Russo-Rumanian frontier, so that for Petrograd at least the Rumanian alliance had proved to be of negative value. For Germany, once the immediate crisis was over, the entry of Rumania was a blessing: she now occupied the wheatlands and oilfields of that country and had better communications with her ally Turkey. Moreover, rightly or wrongly, the German high command had been anticipating the entry into the war of Holland and Denmark on the Allied side, and the rout of Rumania convinced it that these two countries were now unlikely to risk the same fate.

The Rumanian opportunists did the best they could to retrieve their country's fortunes: they declared peace in May 1918 but rejoined the Allies on the eve of their final victory.

Great Britain, May 1915-November 1918 / C.L.Mowat

Britain Organizes for Total War

New men at the top, new powers for the government, new organizations – all were needed to gear the nation for an all-out effort

'We are going to lose this war', Lloyd George told Colonel Maurice Hankey, the all-important but unobtrusive secretary of the cabinet's War Committee, some time in November 1916. And indeed 'this war' was going very badly, and no end, let alone victory, seemed in sight after more than two years of fighting.

Herbert Asquith, the Liberal prime minister, seemed to many to be unsuited for his task. His virtues, equanimity, patience, a certain lack of imagination, a readiness to wait for the right moment to decide and to act, had served well in the 'constitutional crisis' of 1909-11, less well during the Ulster rebellion of 1912-14 (p. 412). Now they seemed irrelevant: '. . . with the war going badly, the Prime Minister appeared positively wooden . . . the passive spectator of events, fundamentally unwilling . . . to alter the course of the juggernaut he had helped set in motion,' a later commentator wrote. Asquith had retained the cabinet of twenty-one members and had resorted to improvised bodies, a war council, then the Dardanelles Committee, then a War Committee, to deal with wartime administration and policy; but he had not given these committees the necessary authority. The final decisions, after another round of argument, still rested with the cabinet. There was no one to direct and co-ordinate the general management of the war. Kitchener, 'an ageing ignorant man armed only with a giant's reputation', was put in as secretary of war and left both to direct strategy and to organize his voluntary armies without informed criticism from outside; and Asquith's failure to demand information and to co-ordinate the plans of the War Office and Admiralty had contributed to the Dardanelles disaster (p. 506). The system of 'business as usual', applied to munitions and supplies, helped to bring about the 'shell scandal' of May 1915. The coalition government which Asquith had formed at that time had brought in Conservatives and Labour MPs to share responsibility; and in fact problems of war production and administration were tackled much more effectively when this had been done. There remained, or seemed to remain (and in war, psychology is a vital factor), a lack of drive and grasp of purpose.

With the main parties already within the government, change could come only from within. Lloyd George alone 'had a passion to win the war', and as minister

A queue forming outside Southwark Town Hall after Lord Derby's recruiting campaign 1915

Radio Times Hulton

The King's Royal Rifle Corps on a recruiting march in 1915

Paul Popper

Young Britons entering a No-Conscription Fellowship meeting

of munitions (May 1915-June 1916), and then, after Kitchener's death, as war secretary, he had grappled with the production of arms and the transport services, and was ready, indeed desperately anxious, to have a wider scope for initiative. But as Asquith wrote to Bonar Law, the Conservative leader, 'he lacks the one thing needful—he does not inspire trust'. No change of direction could be made without the support of the Conservatives and they, in particular, distrusted Lloyd George. But there were notable exceptions: Bonar Law, the cautious, melancholy leader, aware of his precarious authority within his own party, and adventurers like Carson, the Ulster leader, Milner, the rabid imperialist, and Northcliffe, the overweening press lord, who saw in Lloyd George a kindred spirit. What was needed was a go-between, to bring together those who, acting together, could produce a change of direction. And one was at hand: Max Aitken (later Lord Beaverbrook). It was at Aitken's country house, Cherkley (near Leatherhead), that Bonar Law and Lloyd George met after Kitchener's death; Bonar Law's support persuaded Asquith to appoint Lloyd George to the War Office—a portent for the future.

Lloyd George takes over

The political crisis which brought Lloyd George to the premiership on 7th December 1916 occurred inside a week—or rather a week-end—but it had really begun early in November when Carson quarrelled with Bonar Law over some trivial matter and was followed by almost half the Conservatives. Aitken went into action to save his friend Bonar Law: a series of meetings, calls, dinners followed. Lloyd George had his own reasons for wanting a change (and had been in touch with Carson and Milner): his authority at the War Office was limited by the independent position of the chief of the general staff, Sir William Robertson, who worked against Lloyd George and leaked information to the press. Lloyd George wanted a small and effective war cabinet for the direction of the war, with himself as the working chairman, though Asquith as prime minister would be the formal head. On 25th November Bonar Law, Lloyd George, Carson, and Aitken met at Bonar Law's London house, Pembroke Lodge, and agreed to put forward to Asquith the plan for a war cabinet. Asquith's reply on the 27th was a polite rejection.

Lloyd George, confident of Bonar Law's support, though of little else, now acted. On 1st December he wrote to Asquith, again proposing a war cabinet. Asquith declined. Bonar Law, dining with Aitken at the Hyde Park Hotel, decided that he must see Lloyd George that evening. 'I had the means of finding Lloyd George at that time at any hour of the day or night, and I knew he was dining at the Berkeley Hotel,' wrote Aitken in his long and fascinating story of the crisis. They hauled Lloyd George out of his dinner party. Bonar Law decided that night to hold firm in supporting Lloyd George. Next day the *Daily Express* and the *Daily Chronicle* came out in criticism of the government and called for a 'war council': for this Aitken was responsible, though not for other newspaper comment favourable to Lloyd George. Similar comment in the Sunday papers increased the annoyance of Bonar Law's Conservative colleagues, and they came to a meeting at Pembroke Lodge, on Sunday 3rd December, in an angry mood. They believed that Asquith was indispensable as prime minister and preserver of national unity, and wanted to turn Lloyd George out. They passed a resolution calling on Asquith to resign because 'in our opinion the publicity given to Mr Lloyd George's intentions makes reconstruction from within no longer possible', and declared that they would themselves resign if Asquith refused. The intention was to enable him to form a new government with or without Lloyd George. However, when Bonar Law told him of the resolution that afternoon, Asquith took fright at the word 'resignation'. He decided to compromise with Lloyd George over his plans and that night published a notice that the government was being reconstructed.

On Monday 4th December, Asquith changed his mind. Several Liberal ministers advised him to stand firm, and Lord Curzon and other Conservative ministers promised him support, Curzon pledging himself not to take office under either Lloyd George or Bonar Law. Asquith was also annoyed by an editorial in that morning's *Times*, which he wrongly attributed to Lloyd George. He sent Lloyd George a note that evening again rejecting his plan. Lloyd George resigned. After discouraging advice from both Liberal and Conservative ministers, Asquith also resigned. Bonar Law saw Lloyd George a little later; again, they agreed to act together, each to support the other in forming a government.

At the Palace that night (5th December) the King asked Bonar Law to form a government. For this Asquith's support was essential. Asquith refused, and Bonar Law resigned the commission. Lloyd George was given the task next day, and succeeded. He had the support of Bonar Law, of course, and the other Conservatives (Curzon forgot his pledge). Balfour, the ex-prime minister, who had been ill during the crisis, agreed at once to join. So did many Liberals, whose support was canvassed by Dr Christopher Addison. And Lloyd George won round the Labour leaders, promising the party a larger share in the government.

These events had important consequences, and not only in the direction of the war. The Liberals were split, a large number following Asquith into opposition. The decline of the Liberal Party has been attributed to this division and blamed on Lloyd George's conspiracy and seizure of power. Four points must be made. There is such a thing as legitimate ambition. Lloyd George was convinced that he could save his country and win the war; stalemate, the reckless, hopeless outpouring of life, seemed the alternative. If he split with Asquith, Asquith equally split with him; by refusing to join a new government Asquith perpetuated the split—whether because, as he said, he could serve the country more effectively in opposition, or because he believed that Lloyd George would fail and he would be recalled to office untrammelled, makes no difference. There are many reasons, besides those of personalities, which underlie the Liberal decline. And, lastly, Lloyd George would never have gained office without the support of the Conservatives, and particularly of Bonar Law—but equally, he could not have succeeded without the support of the press and the public—which believed, without necessarily liking or admiring him, that he had the vision and power which the country needed.

Radio Times Hulton

Once-exempt married men are called to the colours, June 1916

Imperial War Museum

Shells pile up. Shortages resulted in a munitions ministry

The War Cabinet

Lloyd George at once formed his proposed War Cabinet. Carson (who became first lord of the Admiralty) was not a member; instead, Lloyd George chose Curzon and Milner, men of great ability who represented important sides of the Conservative party, Bonar Law and Arthur Henderson (Labour). None of these except Bonar Law, who was chancellor of the exchequer, had departmental responsibilities. The War Cabinet met almost daily (200 days in the first 235), devoting itself to over-all problems of strategy and administration. For three periods in 1917 and 1918 it was reinforced by the prime ministers of the Dominions, becoming the Imperial War Cabinet. This was a large and imaginative development, though it did not survive the war.

Lloyd George's reorganization of the government for total war was a combination of drive, information, and co-ordination. At the top was the War Cabinet, with its own secretary (Hankey) and secretariat, its agenda and minutes; hitherto, the cabinet had had no secretariat, no official records (the system survived the war and peacetime cabinets continued to keep minutes). Much of the work of the War Cabinet was done by committees of which one or other of its members was in charge. At the other end came the regular government departments, reinforced by new ministries (Labour, Food, Shipping, Pensions) and innumerable departments and committees. The essential link between the two ends was provided partly by committees, partly by the prime minister's enlarged number of secretaries. These bright young men, often called the 'garden suburb' (because of the huts they were housed in) and disliked as interfering and superior persons, were Lloyd George's 'leg men', co-ordinating the work of the War Cabinet with the other layers of government. Many of them came from Milner's old 'Kindergarten' which had helped to reorganize South Africa after the Boer War: Lionel Curtis, Philip Kerr (later Lord Lothian), Leopold Amery, Waldorf Astor. Among their many functions was the gathering of precise information and statistics, information either lacking altogether or buried in departments isolated from each other. Thus one secretary was Joseph Davies, a statistician from the South Wales coal trade, whose work on the statistics of ship sinkings and farm production was of the highest value. Only in the co-ordination of political and military strategy did the system fail to achieve full success, largely because of the mutual distrust of Lloyd George and the generals – a difficulty Churchill overcame in the Second World War.

War and welfare

Before looking at the effects of these new arrangements we should notice that much had already been done, piecemeal, to gear the nation for total war. By the Defence of the Realm Act ('Dora'), passed on 8th August 1914, the government had taken powers to make regulations of the widest scope over persons and property. Almost everything was subject to government regulations from the internment of aliens and the taking over of factories to street lighting or the whistling for cabs. An early problem was trade union opposition to the replacement ('dilution') of skilled labour in engineering works and shipyards by the employment of less skilled men and of women. An agreement was made between the employers and the unions in November 1914 (the Crayford Agreement), but difficulties continued until the 'Treasury Agreement' was made at a conference in March 1915 presided over by Lloyd George (then chancellor of the exchequer). Dilution was accepted but with certain safeguards, and on condition that after the war working conditions would return to normal; disputes were to be arbitrated, strikes outlawed. Plenty of room remained for friction, and the unions, by supporting government measures, were accused of deserting the workers and were challenged by a shop stewards' movement. The worst troubles were in the engineering works and shipyards on the Clyde, and culminated in the arrest and deportation (to Edinburgh) of David Kirkwood and other leaders of the Clyde Workers' Committee in March 1916. Industrial conscription, though talked of, was never introduced; but there were regulations controlling the employment and discharge of workmen – in particular a system of leaving certificates by which, if withheld, his employer could prevent a worker from moving to another job. Wage increases and bonuses averted many disputes, but there were some strikes – for example, a coal strike in South Wales in July 1915. The railways were taken under government control at the start of the war and put under an executive committee of the leading managers. Shipping and the ports were progressively controlled under a system of requisitions and licensing. The South Wales coalfield was put under government control on 1st December 1916. Government purchases built up stocks of sugar, wheat, meat, and hides; for example, the government took over the entire meat exports of Australia and New Zealand in 1915. Drunkenness and absenteeism led the government into controlling licensing hours through the Central Control Board (Liquor Traffic) created in June 1915; early in 1916 the board took over all licensed premises in three districts, Enfield Lock, Carlisle and Gretna, and Invergordon. Government control of the public's drinking habits, through licensing laws, is one of the so far permanent legacies of the First World War.

The most spectacular advance was in munitions manufacture. The War Office and Admiralty were slow to expand the channels through which they traditionally procured equipment. Lloyd George early took up the question, and Asquith appointed a special committee in October 1914, but its work was thwarted by Kitchener. The 'shell scandal' of May 1915 followed newspaper reports from the front of the shortage of ammunition. When, soon afterwards, Asquith formed his Coalition government, Lloyd George took over a new Ministry of Munitions. Within a year he had built up a department whose headquarters staff alone numbered 25,000. Businessmen, engineers, and economists were drawn in, a network of local committees created; huge orders were placed at home and abroad, often in anticipation of far greater demands than the service chiefs recognized; firms were persuaded to change over to munitions production. New 'national factories' were built, 73 in 1915, 218 by the end of the war.

Three inter-related consequences followed. In munitions work, as in industry and transport generally, women were employed in place of men; the status of women was raised, and their emancipation

Below: *Women war workers servicing a lorry chassis, 1917. In munitions work, industry, and transport, women were employed in place of men. Their status was raised and emancipation advanced by the war*

advanced by the war. Equally, the new field of industrial welfare developed. Building factories in new areas and transferring workers, particularly women, to them brought the need for amenities hitherto thought unnecessary: canteens, nurseries, rest rooms, hostels, billeting arrangements. Lloyd George created a welfare section of the ministry of munitions and put in charge of it Seebohm Rowntree, a pioneer in new methods of management. And to protect war workers in the future, unemployment insurance which had been started in a small way in the National Insurance Act of 1911 was extended in 1916 to all workers in munitions and a wide range of related industries. War and the welfare state were as closely linked between 1914 and 1918 as they were between 1939 and 1945.

Conscription for military service was the other side of the coin. The pre-war army and the Territorials were recruited from volunteers. Kitchener continued to raise volunteer armies, and enlisting became a patriotic duty. War production suffered when skilled men joined the colours, though a system of badges encouraged many to stay at work without stigma to their patriotism. The toll of life in the campaigns of 1915 soon made it clear that volunteering, besides being wasteful and undiscriminating, would fail to keep up the strength of the army. Kitchener resisted conscription, however, and so did many Liberals, so that the demand for it, pushed by the Conservatives, nearly split Asquith's government. Asquith first bought time by getting Lord Derby to head a recruiting scheme (October 1915) under which men would 'attest' their willingness to serve, and if rejected on personal grounds, or because they were needed on the Home Front, would be issued with khaki armbands. No married men were to be called up until the unmarried had been taken. When it was clear that many unmarried men had not attested, a conscription bill was introduced in January 1916, imposing service on unmarried men not subject to exemption. This, too, proved inadequate, and a second act in May 1916 applied conscription to all men between the ages of eighteen and forty-one. As an afterthought some provisions were added for conscientious objectors; many were allowed to do civilian work of national importance, many others served prison sentences, including a hard core of 985 'absolutists'.

Leviathan

All this organization for war, widely ramified by the end of 1915, was extended and knit together under Lloyd George's government in 1917. Industrialists like Lord Inverforth, Lord Leverhulme, Lord Rhondda, Albert Stanley (Lord Ashfield), and Sir Joseph Maclay were brought in to head new ministries or offices. Rationing of meat, sugar, butter, eggs was introduced in 1918, more because of queues and hoarding than because of actual shortages of supply. Flour mills were taken over in April 1918. Agricultural production was encouraged by the new Food Production Department (created 1st January 1917) under the Board of Agriculture. The government empowered itself to seize and cultivate unoccupied or badly farmed land. Guaranteed prices were offered, and agricultural wages raised under local wages boards. Some two million acres of grassland were ploughed up for grain crops. All coal mines were put under the Coal Controller in March 1917 (sequel to control in South Wales). By the end of the war the nation was at full stretch, and no sphere of life was outside the rule of war.

The wartime controls and organization were swept away within three years. Other effects remained. Lack of price control, rising prices, matched more or less by increased wages, produced inflation: in December 1918 the index of retail food prices stood at 229 (1913=100). Many new fortunes had been made, but there were also the 'new poor' who lived on fixed incomes or slowly rising salaries; working men, and particularly unskilled and semi-skilled workers, were better off unless unemployment overtook them. At the same time taxation took a much larger share of the national income, eighteen per cent after the war compared to seven and a half per cent before. The budget, which in 1913 was under £200 millions, allowed for expenditure of £2,579 millions in 1918. Income tax had been raised from 1s. 8d. in the £ to 6s.; surtax had been raised, and the exemption limit lowered from £5,000 to £2,000; and excess profits were taxed at eighty per cent. Here, as in the extent of the government's powers, the scale of its operations and the number of its civil servants and workers, Leviathan, big government, had taken over, never to retreat.

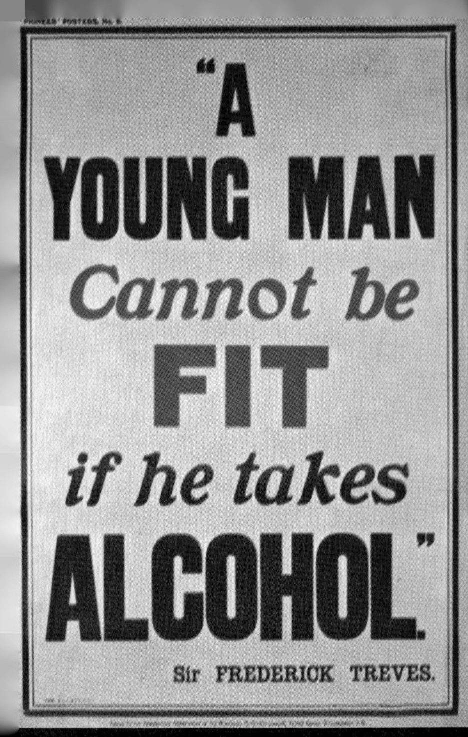

Radio Times Hulton

Above: *Temperance poster. Drunkenness and absenteeism led to government control of drinking habits.* ***Right:*** *Helpers on the agricultural front.* ***Below:*** *Munitions poster*

THE WAR OF MUNITIONS

HOW GREAT BRITAIN HAS MOBILISED HER INDUSTRIES

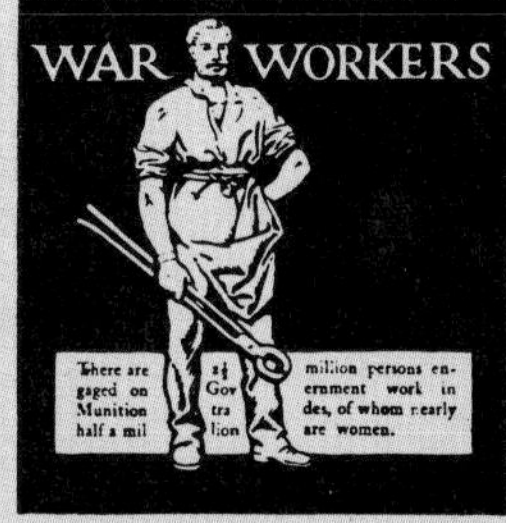

SINCE the outbreak of war in August, 1914, Great Britain has grappled with the task of munitionment with astonishing success, and to-day she is one great Arsenal. Not only has she maintained her armies at the Front with ever-increasing supplies, but she has also materially assisted in the munitioning of her Allies. Despite the fact that more than five million men have been drafted to the Colours, she has raised a vast industrial army which is ceaselessly engaged upon the production of munitions. Her industries have been mobilised and placed upon a war footing, countless new factories have been erected, many old factories have been adapted for war purposes, and the output of munitions in the British Isles has been enormously increased. The workshops of Britain are at war, and they will know no truce till victory is secure.

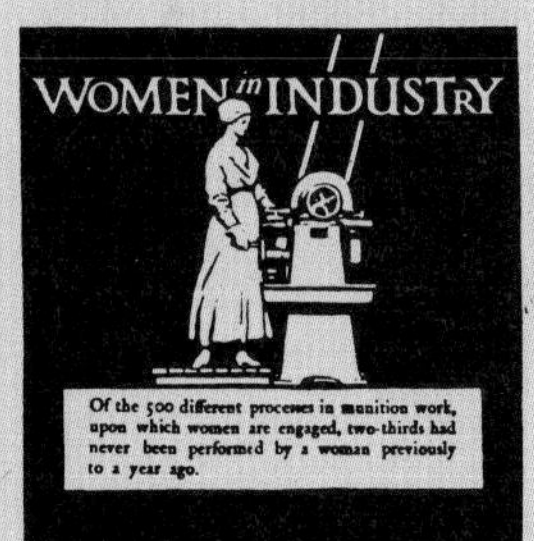

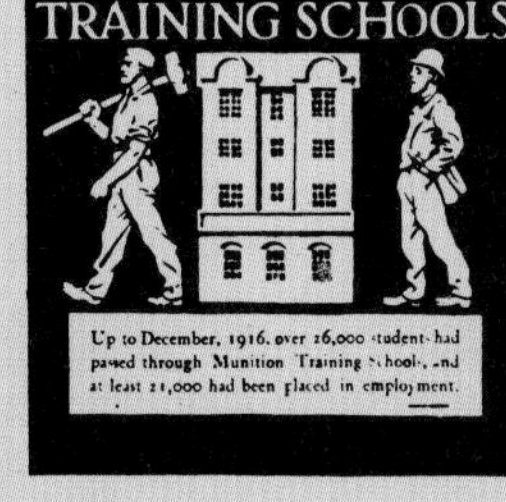

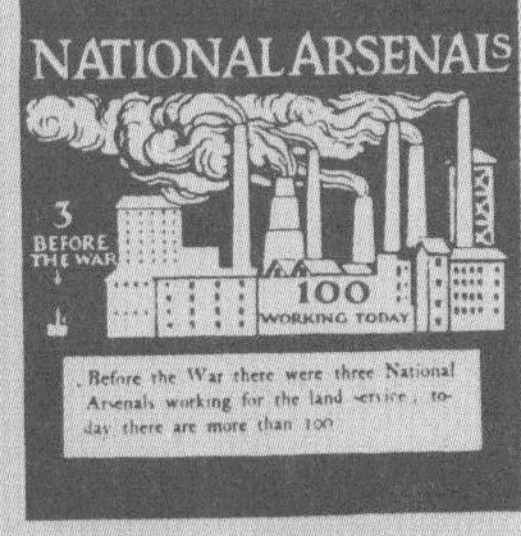

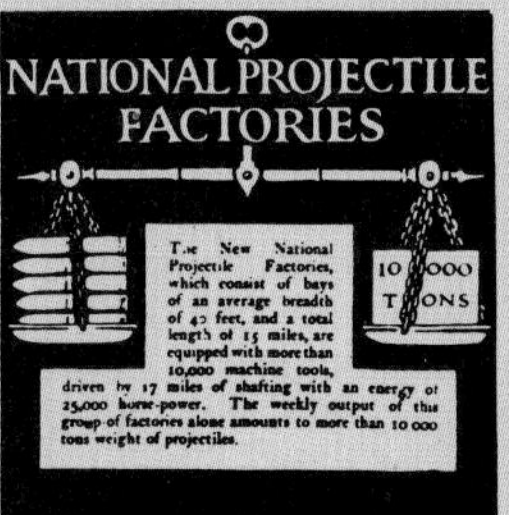

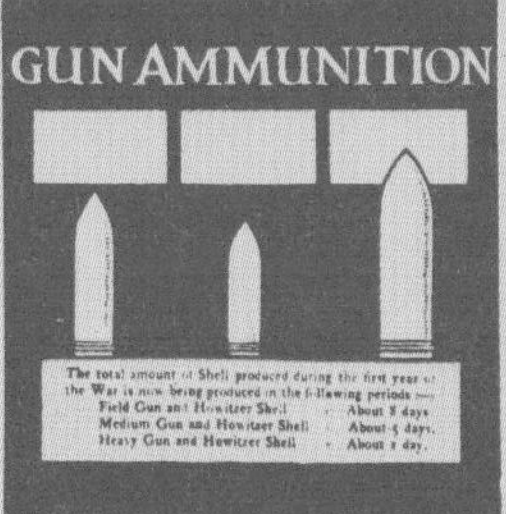

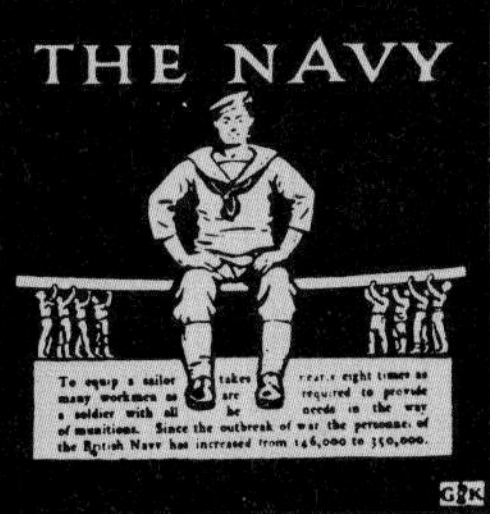

Great Britain, France, and Germany, 1916

The New Leaders

1916 brought a change of leadership in Great Britain and Germany. The men who were conducting their country's war efforts at the end of the year were: Lloyd George, a Welshman, and Ludendorff, a middle-class German general. In 1917, a former radical prime minister, Clemenceau, took office in France. They were very different from the traditional leaders of the past. But they were to lead their countries in the ruthless pursuit of total victory for the rest of the war

Radio Times Hulton

David Lloyd George / Kenneth Morgan

At Buckingham Palace on the evening of 6th December 1916, at an hour of supreme national crisis, David Lloyd George accepted the King's commission to form a government to win the war. So, at the age of fifty-three, Lloyd George reached the climax of an astonishing and dramatic career that had made him for over a decade the most colourful and controversial figure in British public life.

From the start, he had been an outsider in politics: a Welsh Baptist in a system run by and for the English ruling classes, a relatively poor man from a humble home thrusting his way through an aristocratic world. He had first emerged in the 1890's as a fiery young Nonconformist radical, dedicated to overthrowing the supremacy of the parson and the squire over the farming community. During the Boer War (1899-1902, p. 13), he was a passionate opponent of British imperialism. When the Liberal Party came to power in 1905, he was the voice of radical dissent in the cabinet, first as president of the Board of Trade, later (from 1908) as chancellor of the exchequer. In this last office, he was the champion of social reform, of old age pensions, of the 'People's Budget', of national insurance, and other measures which helped to lay the foundations of the welfare state. Deep passions were stirred by his onslaughts on the landlords and on the House of Lords. And yet this extreme radical could also be the master of compromise: no one had a more notable record as conciliator in industrial disputes. It was said that he 'could charm a bird off a bough'. In 1910 he had even proposed a coalition government to promote social reform and rearmament.

When the First World War broke out in August 1914, Lloyd George was from the start a major figure in the great controversies that surrounded its course. Although he had been most reluctant to endorse a declaration of war, even as late as 2nd August 1914, he now threw himself unsparingly into a ruthless pursuit of total war, whatever the cost. He knew nothing of military affairs at first hand: in the past, he had been absorbed almost entirely in domestic rather than in foreign affairs. But his genius saw at once that this was a different kind of conflict, a total war, fought not just between armies but between peoples and civilizations. Here the intuition of a Welsh outsider might find a way through when the conventional wisdom of the generals would break down.

With Churchill, Lloyd George was throughout 1915 a vehement 'Easterner', urging a peripheral strategy in the Balkans and the eastern Mediterranean, instead of the useless stalemate on the Western Front. He developed an instinctive distrust of Robertson, the chief of the imperial general staff, and Haig, the commander-in-chief, which later events were to confirm. When Asquith's government was turned into a coalition in May 1915, Lloyd George took over the vitally important post of minister of munitions. Here he could employ all his dynamism and eloquence to provide mortars and machine-guns, and the 'mountains of shells' for which he had called. His 'men of push and go' helped transform the industrial sectors of the economy from a peacetime to a wartime basis. At the same time, he improved conditions for working men (and women) in the munitions factories, seeing that welfare and warfare went hand in hand. It was now total war at last.

As 1916 wore on, Lloyd George's impatience with Asquith's leadership became more acute. He was deeply disturbed by Asquith's delays in introducing general conscription in the early months of the year, and by his irrational faith in Kitchener, who in Mrs Asquith's view was only 'a magnificent poster'. When Kitchener was drowned at sea in June, Lloyd George succeeded him at the War Office. But his dissatisfaction continued. The war still went badly, notably, he thought, in the failure to launch a new expedition to Salonika or to aid Rumania, a 'little five-foot-five nation' like Wales itself. The climax came in the complicated political crisis of 1st-6th December 1916. On the 7th Lloyd George was able to find enough support to form an all-party government, and Asquith was pushed into opposition.

From the outset it was clear that Lloyd George's premiership marked a new era in British government. He set up a new war cabinet of only five members to run the war, a small and efficient body with its own secretariat, all under the direct control of the prime minister himself. But more important than the change in the machinery of government in December 1916 was the change in the style of leadership. The new premier seemed, in contrast to the fallen Asquith, alien and remote. His household at No 10 Downing Street was strange to English eyes—frugal,

Welsh in speech, with occasional evenings of hymn-singing around the hearth. He had little patience with high society and little faith in the 'experts'. His friends were drawn from outside the usual political circles – newspaper magnates and self-made industrialists prominent among them. Now there seemed in Great Britain a new will to victory, which the new leader's eloquence could harness. At the Aberystwyth National *eisteddfod* earlier in the year, he had urged his countrymen to sing during the gravest crisis of the war, as the nightingale sang in the darkest hour of the night. Buoyant, self-confident, the world crisis was now his opportunity.

Georges Clemenceau / J.M.Roberts

Snark International

On 20th November 1917, Georges Clemenceau presented himself to the Chamber of Deputies as the new prime minister of France. Called to office at last by an old enemy, Poincaré, President of the republic, he took up his new duties at a dark moment, but it was only because things looked so black that he was prime minister at all. Frenchmen with long memories remembered a man whose career had opened with great promise. Yet, somehow, time after time, it had run to seed in disappointment.

Clemenceau had been born in 1841, in a passionately republican family which still honoured the memory of the great heroes of the Revolution. He could remember his father being taken off in a Black Maria by the police of Napoleon III; as a young medical student in Paris he ran secret printing-presses and was soon prosecuted for it by the police. He was already committed to the republic as an ideal, and after 1871 he was faithful to the republic as an institution. Although deeply sceptical, Clemenceau, like a later great Frenchman, always cherished a certain idea of the grandeur of France. Unlike de Gaulle, however, Clemenceau saw France as the standard-bearer of reason and rationalism and the citadel of the republican democracy.

Besides passionate beliefs he had other qualities which were likely to make a mark. He was fearless and willingly met his political and personal enemies on the duelling-ground. He soon earned his nickname 'The Tiger'; both a fine speaker and a fluent stylist, he was at his best in bitter invective. He had wide intellectual and artistic interests which appealed to the bourgeois elite of the Third Republic. His gifts should have brought him great success. Yet, indisputably, they did not.

During the siege of Paris in 1870 he was mayor of Montmartre. Nearly lynched himself, he failed to save the lives of officers seized by the enraged populace at the beginning of the Communard insurrection; it was years before gossip about this incident ceased to dog him. In the early years of the Republic he at first followed Gambetta, but soon moved over to become the leader of the radical left in the Chamber. He made many enemies as ministry after ministry fell apart under the hammering of his oratory. When he made a mistake, backing a war minister who turned out to be a would-be military dictator, his enemies were delighted. He was already acquiring the reputation of a man who was without judgement and unsound.

His enemies' chance came with the explosion of a great scandal. A company set up to build a canal in Panama collapsed in 1892. Friends of Clemenceau were deeply implicated in shady financial and political transactions connected with it. He could not explain away his relationship with them. At a time when anglophobia was rife in France, he was a known friend of Great Britain and was subjected to slanderous reports that he was a British agent. In his constituency he was greeted by peasants howling 'Aoh, yes', in heavily accented English and was soundly defeated. It seemed that his career was over.

He earned his living as a journalist. Then another scandal offered him the chance of getting back into politics. This was the Dreyfus Affair (p. 93). His violent advocacy of Dreyfus's innocence took him back to the Chamber and the struggle with his old enemy, clericalism. Detested by the right, in 1906 he became minister of the interior, a post in which he then won the hatred of socialists by his skill and brutality in handling labour troubles. The left had now gone far beyond the once extreme Clemenceau; he harried the socialists. When he became prime minister in October 1906 another disappointment followed. Although in office for three years, he achieved almost nothing except the further embitterment of the social problem and the strengthening of his dubious repute as a strike breaker. Clemenceau retired to the Senate to grumble about his successors.

But once again a crisis saved Clemenceau. In 1914 he had refused office so that he should not be muzzled in criticizing the conduct of the war. Fiercely patriotic, he used his newspaper and his position as president of the Senate Commission on the army to castigate and criticize incompetence and slackness. There was ambition in this. He longed to be prime minister and worked off personal vendettas in his investigations. But his contribution to morale was enormous. To all excuses and evasions he replied, implacably, 'the Germans are at Noyon'.

Finally, there was no one else to turn to. In the great ministry which began in November 1917, Clemenceau the politician was at last overshadowed by Clemenceau the statesman. He paid little attention to parliamentary politics and acted more or less as a dictator. At seventy-six, he was the oldest of the war leaders. He left the details to dim and shadowy ministers whose names have been forgotten, and to a great French patriot, Georges Mandel, his omniscient *chef du cabinet.* There were scandals and protests, as socialists, defeatists, German agents, and former ministers were scooped up pell-mell in his purges. Clemenceau was untroubled by the outcry: if the firing-squads of Vincennes helped to save the Republic in danger, they were justified. And they did. Meanwhile, the prime minister spent his happiest and some of his most valuable days in fortnightly visits to the trenches. One day a soldier gave him a bunch of flowers gathered on the battlefield. They remained, in a shell-case, in Clemenceau's room until the day of his death and his will directed that they should be buried with him. They are a reminder of the feeling that Clemenceau always strove to conceal under a biting cynicism. They may also stand for the key to the success of Clemenceau as a war leader: finally, at last, he found in the war a role which reconciled him to his countrymen.

Ludendorff / K.H.Janssen

Radio Times Hulton

'The war is lost,' cried Kaiser Wilhelm II when he heard of Rumania's astounding declaration of war on the Central powers.

So great was the shock that he lost confidence in the faithful chief of his general staff, Erich von Falkenhayn, and sacrificed him as scapegoat for the defeats of the summer of 1916. The court consoled the Kaiser with the promise that Germany could still be saved by her national heroes Hindenburg and Ludendorff.

The old Field Marshal von Hindenburg, who had defeated the Russians at Tannenberg, was an even more popular father-figure than the Kaiser. Only the initiated knew that he really owed his fame to his chief of staff, General Erich Ludendorff. Without the latter Hindenburg would have been insignificant and helpless; at the same time he himself, with his imperturbable serenity and his sagacious humour, was the ideal complement to the younger, highly emotional and impetuous Ludendorff. For this reason the post of chief of the general staff now had two occupants: Hindenburg carried the outward responsibility while the true leader of the German army in the field – indeed the secret dictator of Germany – was henceforth Ludendorff, in the guise of 'First Quartermaster General'.

However, there were a few people at general headquarters who expected no good to come of Ludendorff's appointment. Colonel von Marschall, in those August days, put in writing his view that 'Ludendorff in his limitless ambition and pride will wage war until the German people are totally exhausted; and then the monarchy will have to take the blame'. Ludendorff's colleague and later successor, General Groener, summed Ludendorff up perfectly: *'Er ist ganz Soldat – aber gar kein Diplomat'* ('He is everything of a soldier – but nothing of a diplomat'). The court was horrified by the general's coarse tone when dealing with the Kaiser. And older, tradition-conscious soldiers stood aghast when Hindenburg – at the instigation of Ludendorff and his following of young colonels – publicly issued orders and reproofs to the chancellor. In contrast to the Allies, whose peoples granted extraordinary powers to civilians like Lloyd George and Clemenceau, in Germany Kaiser and government bowed before the brute will of a soldier. After only three months the chancellor, Bethmann Hollweg, was complaining of Ludendorff's continual attacks: 'At the core of it lies a dictatorial thirst for power and a consequent intention to militarize the whole political scene.'

By an irony of fate it had been Bethmann Hollweg himself who had helped Ludendorff to power. Long before the misguided majority, the chancellor had realized that Germany could not dictate peace to her enemies, but could at best arrive at one on the basis of the *status quo ante.* But he did not believe he could answer to the people for these 'meagre, rotten peaces' once the most popular soldier had been placed at the head. 'Even if we lost a battle, which God forbid, our people would accept it as long as Hindenburg was in command; similarly they would accept any peace graced by his name.' This was a fatal error, for in fact statesmanship stepped down when the power-obsessed but totally unpolitical Ludendorff took control.

Ludendorff overestimated wildly not only himself but also the strength of the German people. Even when he was responsible just for a section of the Eastern Front he had showed not the slightest appreciation of the problems of a high command that was only managing to live from hand to mouth through a three-front war for which Germany was far too weak. Falkenhayn was calculating on a long war of attrition; for this reason he was trying to be sparing with his reserves of men and materials. Ludendorff, on the other hand, who wanted 'just to win again', could only attribute to envy and jealousy Falkenhayn's refusal of the six divisions he needed to conquer Riga and Petrograd. The general seriously believed that Falkenhayn's conduct of the war was leading Germany to disaster. Not only because he aspired to the levers of power, not only because he considered himself a better commander, but also out of patriotic conviction, Ludendorff intrigued with the chancellor until they achieved Falkenhayn's downfall. 'I can only love or hate,' he said at the time, 'and General von Falkenhayn I hate. To work with him is impossible for me.'

Ludendorff's 'crusade'

But Ludendorff could not work with anyone who did not share his unlimited will to win. And, indeed, even he had to admit after a few weeks that the German army had so exhausted itself in the bloody battles at Verdun and the Somme that it would be incapable of any further offensive in the coming year – even the Central powers' successful campaign against Rumania could not hide that. For him too the only possible chance of victory now lay in the ruthless submarine war against Great Britain's overseas trade. Although the politicians feared rightly that such warfare, which was contrary to international law, would drive the United States of America into the enemy's camp, Ludendorff on 9th January 1917 launched the submarine war, promising himself results within a few months. Until then he hoped to hold out by mobilizing all the available resources of the German people – the sick, the war-wounded, children, women – for total war ('He who does not work shall not eat either').

Following the pattern of the Munitions of War Act Germany, too, was now going to double and treble her production of guns and munitions. But Ludendorff overlooked the fact that Great Britain commanded quite different sources of raw materials from Germany, who was cut off from her overseas connexions. Production targets were not reached, and many construction projects had to be abandoned half way through. It was all very well for the general to make the Reichstag pass a 'Law concerning service to the Fatherland', rendering all male Germans between the ages of sixteen and sixty liable for service; but he was soon forced to realize that one cannot command an economy like an army. Also it proved impossible, in the face of resistance from the trade unions, to introduce a blanket compulsion to work. Moreover, Germany no longer had the resources at the same time to replace her war casualties (a million and a half in 1916 alone), to man new divisions, and to fill new jobs with trained workers.

In the end Ludendorff fell back on the idea of utilizing the Polish and Belgian 'human material'. In the autumn of 1916, to the plaudits of German heavy industry and heedless of world opinion, he had Belgian workers rounded up in thousands like cattle and deported to Germany in goods trains. Only worldwide protests gave the civil government the courage to put a stop to this slave traffic. Over the Polish question, however, it surrendered abjectly to the pressure of the military. On 5th November 1916, at Ludendorff's insistence, the Central powers declared Poland independent, even though the slight chance then existing of making a separate peace with Russia was thereby wrecked. But instead of the expected 750,000, only 5,000 Poles turned up at the German recruiting offices.

Ludendorff's 'crusade' for total victory over all Germany's enemies only led to available resources being overstrained and exhausted – a situation which had to rebound sooner or later. The political leadership had naturally opposed this course; but it was powerless against an alliance of military and public opinion, a majority in the Reichstag, heavy industry and Junkerdom, all of which were well pleased by Ludendorff's dictatorship. Already by the end of 1916 the military leadership was working towards the chancellor's downfall; however, they let him carry on in the hope that, if he remained even after the submarine war had been declared, his international prestige would impress the neutral countries favourably. But from the end of 1916 until his fall in the summer of 1917 Bethmann Hollweg was only chancellor by Ludendorff's leave. 'Never before was a harder task suddenly imposed on a man by Fate,' wrote Ludendorff, looking back at his life in 1916. Too true. For he aspired to the impossible – a German victory. *(Translation)*

Revolutionary Implications of the War

Chapter 22

Introduction by J.M.Roberts

Nationalism had never previously achieved successes such as were given to it within a few years by the Great War. In the end it swept away the old multi-national dynastic European empires and led to the reorganization of central and eastern Europe on the national lines which are still the basis of the states which exist today.

Many of these changes came because a few devoted and indefatigable leaders seized the chance the war offered them. While it was still going on, they exploited the leverage available to them because of the quarrels of the great powers. Four of these leaders are the subject of profiles in this chapter. **Venizelos**, the Greek, dreamed of reconstituting an Aegean empire at the expense of Turkey. **Masaryk**, the Czech, convinced President Wilson of the justice of his people's claim to independence of the Habsburgs. **Piłsudski**, the Pole, used first the Central powers and then the Entente to advance his countrymen's interests. **De Valera**, the Irishman, exploited the legendary contribution of the 1916 rebels to lead an intransigent Irish national movement.

That the only important armed national rising against any of the great powers in Europe should be in Ireland, where British rule was mild by the standards of Habsburg or Romanov, was ironical, though understandable. Constantine FitzGibbon describes **The Easter Rising** in this chapter. Its significance was not that it achieved any immediate success. It failed in all its military objectives. But the long-term effects were considerable. Before the Rising the nation, though supporting Home Rule, did not support the extremists who went out to fight in 1916. After the Rising came a remarkable change of sentiment in Ireland: the old Irish Parliamentary Party, which up to then had had the support of the majority of Irishmen, was finished; the extreme Sinn Feiners now held the centre of the stage. The Easter Rising was the first and the greatest blow in the Irish Revolution. It was a revolution which inspired and foreshadowed revolutionary movements in Asia and in Africa. The leaders of Indian nationalism were greatly encouraged by the Rising, and as Christopher Falkus shows in **India at War**, the tide of nationalism was rising in India.

A very different sort of revolution is described in the article on **Lawrence and the Arabs**, by Major-General J.D.Lunt. The desert Arabs who revolted did so less under the influence of ideas drawn from the European doctrine of nationalism than as followers of their traditional tribal leaders. The man who moulded their enthusiasm into a movement of major strategic significance was T.E.Lawrence, about whom a personal legend was to grow.

Imperial War Museum

The surrender of Jerusalem, 9th December 1917. British soldiers mingle with Turks

Imperial War Museum

Countess Markievicz surrenders after the Rising. She was then put in Holloway Gaol

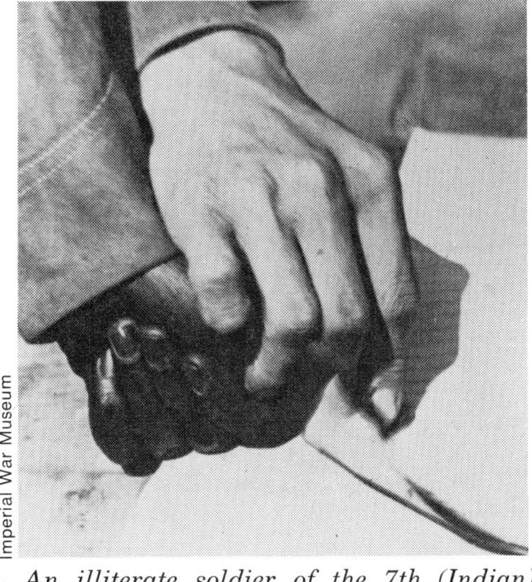
Imperial War Museum

An illiterate soldier of the 7th (Indian) Division makes his mark on a pay sheet

Arabia

1916 5th June: princes of Hejaz rise against their Turkish overlords.
October: Storrs and Lawrence approach Abdulla and Feisal; Turks strengthen Medina.
1917 6th July: Lawrence, with Auda abu Tayi, takes Aqaba; Feisal places himself under Allenby's command.
9th December: Allenby enters Jerusalem.
1918 January: Lawrence advances through mountains of Moab and fights a fierce battle at Tafila.
In the spring Allenby crosses the Jordan, but the British fail to take Salt and the Arab attack on Ma'an fails.
17th September: Arabs attack Deraa railway junction.
19th September: British offensive against Turkish forces begins.
1st October: Feisal takes Damascus.
31st October: Allies sign Armistice with Turkey.
1919 Lawrence goes to the Versailles peace conference to plead for Arab independence.

Ireland

1905 Sinn Fein holds first annual convention.
1910 Irish Republican Brotherhood founds *Irish Freedom*.
1913 Irish Volunteers founded as a counter-poise to the Ulster Volunteers.
Connolly organizes his Citizen Army after an ITGWU strike is broken by strong-arm methods.
1914 On the outbreak of war Redmond accepts postponement of Home Rule; IRB decides that there must be an Irish insurrection before the end of the war.
1916 21st April: Casement lands from German submarine near Tralee in County Kerry and is arrested.
British navy intercepts German arms ship *Aud* carrying arms for the rebels.
23rd April: Wimborne orders the arrest of nationalist leaders; MacNeill calls for cancellation of the rising, but Pearse determines to continue.
24th April: Easter Rising begins; Pearse proclaims provisional government of Irish Republic from the captured General Post Office; the attempt to seize Dublin castle fails; the British call for reinforcements.
28th April: Pearse and Connolly surrender.
3rd May: Pearse executed in Kilmainham Gaol.
12th May: Connolly executed in Kilmainham.

Nationalism

Eamonn de Valera
1915 March: de Valera appointed commandant in Irish Volunteers.
1917 July: de Valera elected for East Clare.
October: de Valera replaces Griffith as president of Sinn Fein.
1918 December: de Valera effectively achieves leadership of the nation in the general election.
1919 3rd February: Michael Collins organises de Valera's escape from Lincoln Gaol.
1st April: at second session of Dail Eireann de Valera elected Priomh-Aire.

Eleutherios Venizelos
1910 October: Venizelos becomes Greek prime minister.
1912 March: Venizelist Liberals win 150 out of 181 seats.
1915 1st March: Venizelos proposes Greek troops aid Allies at Gallipoli.
25th September: Venizelos flees to Crete and proclaims a revolution.
1918 September: 250,000 troops engaged in Macedonia.
1920 November: Venizelos defeated at the polls.

Thomas Masaryk
1891 elected as member of the Young Czech Party to the Reichrat.
1906 accused but acquitted of anti-religious offences.
1917 May: Masaryk goes to Russia to plead Czech and Slovak cause.
1918 he goes to the United States on a similar mission.

Józef Pilsudski
1914 6th August: Pilsudski attempts to foment national uprising in Russian Poland.
1917 July: *Pilsudski* is interned in Magdeburg for refusal to swear oath of allegiance to the Reich.

India

1917 June: Indian government interns Mrs. Besant.
July: Edwin Montagu replaced Austen Chamberlain at the India Office.
20th August: Montagu announces that the British government aims to establish responsible government in India.
1918 influenza epidemic scourges India.
1919 13th April: Amritsar massacre.

Arabia, 1916-18/Major-General James Lunt

The Arabs and Lawrence

In the harsh world of the Arabian desert, T.E.Lawrence – Al Auruns as the bedouin called the small, fair-haired, blue-eyed man who led them – created two myths. To Englishmen he himself became an ambiguous hero, a figure of adventurous glamour who invited detractors and controversy. To Arabs he offered a vision of Arab unity that carried them to Damascus and helped Allenby defeat the Turks – a vision which has haunted the Middle East ever since

Opposite page: *Painting of T.E.Lawrence in Arab dress by Augustus John. He fixed the bird-like mind of the bedouin on a stable course and shared their hardships* ***Below:*** *Mecca to Aqaba, June 1916-July 1917. Mecca fell to Sherif Hussein's forces on June 10th 1916 and on 6th July 1917, Lawrence, with Auda abu Tayi, took Aqaba.* ***Bottom:*** *Aqaba to Damascus, July 1917-October 1918. Damascus fell to Lawrence and Feisal on 1st October 1918*

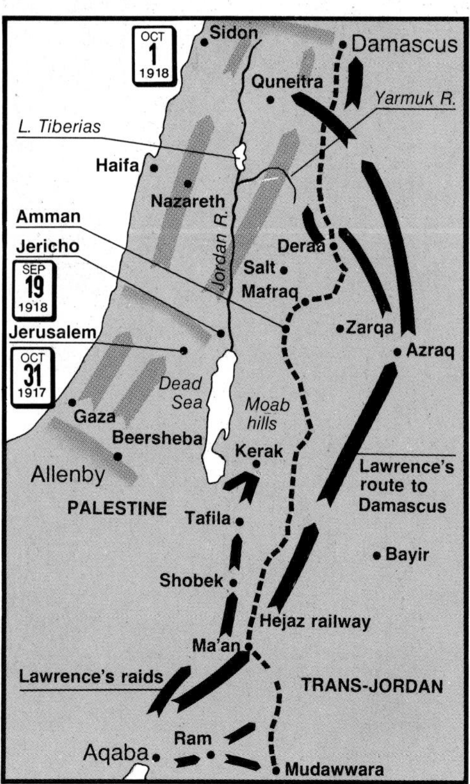

Arabia, the land with which T.E.Lawrence will always be associated, is reputed to be a harsh and barren mistress, rewarding those who serve her with sickness of the body and distress of the mind. Lawrence's connection with the Arabs brought him at least as much pain as profit, and was in large measure responsible for his decision to retire at an early age from public life, once he judged that his work for the Arabs had been completed.

He is one of the most interesting personalities of his times, as well as one of the most controversial. He possessed the ability to achieve distinction in many fields, and yet, after flashing across the skies like a comet, he chose to become a recluse. Here again he was original, choosing neither the monastery nor the hermit's cave, but the anonymity of life in the ranks as a private soldier, first in the Royal Air Force, then the army, and then once more in the RAF. He believed himself immune from most human weaknesses, renouncing women, drink, and tobacco, but he worshipped speed. A few months after his final retirement from the RAF in 1935, he was riding his motorbike along a Dorset lane when he came upon two cyclists and in a vain attempt to avoid them, crashed and met his death.

A man so varied in accomplishment, so complex in character, so untrammelled by convention, inevitably invited hostile criticism. Richard Aldington, the poet and novelist, sought to destroy the Lawrence legend finally and for ever in his *Lawrence of Arabia* (1955), but he wrecked his case by confusing his facts. Others, too, have belittled his contribution to Allenby's victory in Palestine, arguing that Lawrence was at most a gifted leader of guerrillas. Some believed that his desire for anonymity was inspired as much by a clever understanding of the media of publicity as by any genuine desire to withdraw from the hurly-burly of public life. But Lawrence was not an ordinary man. He did not fit, nor did he wish to fit, into the 'establishment'. If fame is a natural ambition, he achieved it, both in the world of action and in letters. If success is to be judged by the acquisition of wealth, he despised it; if it is to be determined by rank or status, he ignored it. The fact that throughout his life he enjoyed the friendship of such men as Churchill, Shaw, Liddell Hart, Wavell, E.M.Forster, and Trenchard is sufficient to demolish the charges brought against him by Aldington. These were not men who admitted to their friendship the charlatan and the braggart.

The untidy subaltern

Thomas Edward Lawrence was born at Tremadoc in North Wales in 1888. He was the second son of Thomas Chapman, a rather eccentric Anglo-Irishman who later changed his name to Lawrence, and who subsequently inherited a baronetcy. T.E. Lawrence was born out of wedlock, a fact which undoubtedly affected him psychologically, but there is no evidence to suggest that he took the matter as seriously as Aldington has alleged. He discussed his illegitimacy quite openly with his more intimate friends. His father had sufficient private means to live comfortably, but not ostentatiously, and T.E.Lawrence gave early evidence of ability above the average. He learned to read at the age of four, and was learning Latin at six. He contributed towards the cost of his education by winning scholarships, first to Oxford High School, and then to the University. He was an omnivorous reader, with a particular interest in medieval and military history, and archaeology.

While reading history at Jesus College, Lawrence travelled in the Levant visiting Crusaders' castles, and subsequently took a first-class degree. Having been awarded a travelling scholarship, he joined D.G. Hogarth's expedition excavating Carchemish, and also worked with the archaeologist (Sir) Leonard Woolley. This brought him into contact with the Arabs, for whom he discovered he had a natural affinity, and he learned their language and as much as he could about their history and customs. On the outbreak of war in 1914, he tried to join the army, but was rejected at first, because he was below the minimum height of five feet five inches. It was several months before he was given a commission and employed in the intelligence branch of the general staff, where his knowledge of Arabic led to his posting to the 'Arab Bureau' at GHQ in Egypt. He was then a very junior and young-looking subaltern, whose untidiness in uniform and unconcern with the niceties of military protocol were not calculated to endear him to the more orthodox among his superiors.

The war against the Turks was going badly at the time. Their attack on the Suez Canal had been easily repulsed, but the ponderous British advance across Sinai had ground to a halt opposite Gaza. The failure at Gallipoli was fresh in men's

Above: *Painting of Australian troops at Rumani, Sinai, August 1916 The second Turkish attack on the Suez Canal was foiled here*

Below: *Feisal's tribesmen enter Damascus, October 1918. The Turks were now in flight*

Imperial War Museum

Below: *One of Lawrence's desert warriors*

Below: *Typical follower of Lawrence. 'Al Auruns' won the love and respect of such men*

memories, and was soon to be followed by Townshend's surrender at Kut in Mesopotamia (p. 529). In south-west Arabia the Turks had advanced to the gates of Aden, where they were to remain for the rest of the war. They may have been corrupt and incompetent, but they were not faring too badly against the might of the British empire. It was at this moment, 5th June 1916, that the Hashimite princes of the Hejaz chose to rise against their Turkish overlords. The Arab Revolt, or, as some would prefer it, the Arab Awakening, had begun.

As a military operation, it was no more likely to succeed than some of the more recent military undertakings of the Arabs, in which performance has fallen far short of promise. Mecca, Jidda, and Taif were quickly captured, but the Arabs failed to take Medina, the principal Turkish garrison. The revolt lost impetus, and in the meantime the Turks sent reinforcements down the Hejaz railway, which the Arabs failed to interdict. In October 1916 the British sent Mr (later Sir Ronald) Storrs, accompanied by Lawrence, to investigate the situation at first-hand, and to consult with the Amir Abdullah, second son of Sherif Hussein, ruler of the Hejaz, whose tribal levies had captured Taif the previous month.

After preliminary discussions with Abdullah, Lawrence was dispatched to visit his younger brother, the Amir Feisal, whose tribesmen had been repulsed at Medina, but who was lying up in the hills nearby. The two men established an almost immediate *rapport,* but it was clear to Lawrence that Feisal's ill-disciplined and badly-armed tribesmen were no match for the Turks in conventional positional warfare. Meanwhile, the Turks continued to reinforce Medina, and the unruly bedouin, disappointed in their hopes for loot, began to drift back to their tents in the desert.

Lawrence was completely untrained in military staff work, but he at once appreciated that the key to the strategic situation was the Hejaz railway. So long as this continued operating, the Turks would be able to build up sufficient strength to reconquer the Hejaz. Moreover, the Arabs, although natural guerrillas, lacked the discipline, and even the will, to fight a pitched battle against the Turks, however incompetent the Turkish leadership. Some other use must be made of their natural military qualities and their ability to operate for long periods in the desert, and this could best be done by abandoning the siege of Medina and carrying the campaign into the north, raiding the railway, the Turks' lifeline, and reducing the flow of reinforcements to a trickle. Lawrence was not the first military leader in history to understand the potentialities of guerrilla warfare when operating against a conventionally-minded enemy, nor has he been the last, for Mao Tse-tung has been equally successful in China, and Giap in Vietnam. But he must at least be given the credit for appreciating how best the Arab Revolt could be harnessed to assist the Allied cause, and at the same time achieve the Arabs' aim, which was to win their independence from foreign rule.

In pursuit of his aim to tie down as many Turks as possible in the Hejaz, Lawrence launched a series of raids against the single-line, wood-burning railway linking Medina with Damascus. He sought not to destroy the railway, but to impede its working, and to compel the Turks to deploy an ever-increasing number of troops to guard it. Fakhri Pasha, the Turkish commander in Medina, lacked initiative, remaining static behind his defences, and clamouring for more and more reinforcements. As they trickled down to him, Lawrence moved steadily farther north, joining forces with the Trans-Jordan tribes, and carrying his raids against the railway nearer to the main British front in Palestine. On 6th July 1917, in company with the famous desert raider, Auda abu Tayi, and his Howeitat tribesmen, he captured Aqaba from the rear, having first overwhelmed a Turkish battalion moving down from Ma'an to reinforce Aqaba.

Feisal then moved his headquarters to Aqaba, which was nearer to the main front than Wejh on the Red Sea, and with Sherif Hussein's permission placed himself under the command of General Allenby, who had taken over command in Palestine. The mainly tribal contingents of Feisal were provided with a stiffening in the shape of armoured cars and light artillery; small detachments of British, French, and Indian troops were sent to Aqaba to support the Arabs; and above all, arms, ammunition, and gold were provided to keep the Arab tribesmen in the field. Allenby intended to employ the Arabs to protect his open flank east of the river Jordan, and to hinder Turkish attempts to reinforce their armies in Palestine. He also realized the political appeal of the Arab Revolt, and planned to harness it to his aim of destroying the Turkish armies, containing as they did large numbers of Arab officers and many thousands of Arab conscripts.

To Damascus

The British attack on the Gaza-Beersheba line was planned for early November 1917. The Arabs were asked to cut beforehand the Damascus-Haifa railway in the Yarmuk gorge, west of the junction of Deraa in Syria, in order to impede the flow of reinforcements to Palestine. The raid involved an approach march from Aqaba of over 350 miles through the desert, but the final stretch was through cultivated country where the peasants gave the Turks warning. The operation was unsuccessful, and nearly a disaster, but the raiders managed to get away and destroyed sections of the railway north of Amman before retreating to Aqaba. Meanwhile, Allenby had successfully broken through the Turkish defences and was advancing on Jerusalem.

Lawrence was present when Allenby entered Jerusalem on 9th December 1917. He greatly admired Allenby, just as Allenby, at their first meeting, had immediately appreciated Lawrence's qualities. He was also unmoved by Lawrence's preference for wearing Arab dress, a practice that reduced many British regular officers to apoplectic fury. Allenby now required the Arabs to move north from Aqaba, through the hills east of the Jordan valley, and establish contact with the British near Jericho. Lawrence thereupon advanced through the mountains of Moab, fighting a fierce battle at Tafila in January 1918, a masterpiece in minor tactics which resulted in the annihilation of a Turkish battalion. However, a farther advance to Kerak and beyond was prevented by the bitterly cold weather which affected the Arabs' morale.

Allenby crossed the Jordan in the spring of 1918 and attempted to capture Salt on the Trans-Jordan plateau. This failed, as did the Arab attack on Ma'an, intended to coincide with the British attack, but large sections of the railway were permanently destroyed and the Turkish army in the Hejaz was effectively isolated. Lawrence had set off for the north to link up with the British, but this too had failed, and he established himself far out in the desert at the oasis of Azraq. There he waited for the main British offensive to begin.

The British attack was due to start on 19th September 1918. Allenby had asked that it should be preceded by a diversionary attack by the Arabs on the important railway junction of Deraa. This was carried out under Lawrence on 17th September with complete success. When, two days later, Allenby fell with massive strength on the Turkish army, its way of retreat through Deraa to Damascus was blocked. Moreover, Lawrence and Feisal, moving north, had raised the tribes south of Damascus. The Turks gave no quarter, nor did they receive any from the Arabs, as they struggled in hopeless confusion across the Jordan into Syria. Feisal entered Damascus in triumph, and for some weeks Lawrence was responsible for civil and military order in the city. On 31st October 1918 an armistice was concluded with Turkey. ▷594

It has sometimes been said of Lawrence's campaign in the desert that it was 'a sideshow within a sideshow'. This may be true if war consists of a counting of heads, or 'cipherin' ', as Robert E.Lee described it, but Wavell, in his semi-official history of the Palestine Campaign, certainly does not underrate the valuable contribution made by the Arabs under Lawrence's leadership to Allenby's victory. He makes it clear that a force of barely 3,000 Arabs tied down 50,000 Turks at a crucial moment, and compelled the Turkish high command to deploy some 150,000 troops 'spread over the rest of the region in a futile effort to stem the tide of the Arab Revolt'. As General Glubb has since written: 'To the student of war, the whole Arab campaign provides a remarkable illustration of the extraordinary results which can be achieved by mobile guerrilla tactics. For the Arabs detained tens of thousands of regular Turkish troops with a force barely capable of engaging a brigade of infantry in a pitched battle.'

Al Auruns

When Lawrence arrived in the Hejaz he was junior in rank and untrained in formal military matters. It is the measure of his strategic insight that he was able to perceive how best the Arab Revolt could be utilized to assist the British strategy in the Middle East, and his understanding of the characteristics of Arab tribesmen enabled him to employ them to the best advantage in the war against the Turks. Whatever may be said to the contrary, and there has recently been published a book by an Arab author which seeks to belittle the part played by Lawrence in the Arab Revolt, anyone with experience of the Arabs as soldiers will know that they would never have chosen such tactics of their own volition. They would have met the Turks head-on, and they would have been defeated.

The way in which Lawrence established his leadership over the Arabs is a fascinating study in itself. He proved to them time and again that he could out-match them in their own hardiness. No people live in a harsher environment than the bedouin tribesmen of Arabia. Lawrence lived in the same fashion as they did, enduring the same hardships, and demanding no favours. He rode his camels harder, and farther, and for longer periods, than his Arab companions were accustomed to do. He trained himself to be patient during the interminable, and often fruitless, discussions around the coffee hearth. He ate their food, and drank their water, and suffered in consequence from a succession of debilitating stomach ailments. He was never a fluent Arabic speaker, like Glubb for example, nor could he hope to pass himself off as an Arab, as Leachman did in Nejd; his piercing blue eyes, fair hair, and skin would soon have given him away. He could appreciate the Arabs' virtues without overlooking their weaknesses, as some Englishmen have done when subjected to the persuasive charm of the bedouin. No one who has lived with the bedouin can forget the attractive side of their characters, but very few men have possessed the ability to fix their bird-like minds on a stable course. Lawrence succeeded in doing this, and no amount of critical hindsight can detract from the part he played in maintaining the impetus of the Arab Revolt.

His work with the Arabs did not end with the conclusion of the armistice in 1918. He believed passionately that his own honour was committed to obtain for them the independence for which they had fought. He understood the force of Arab nationalism as did few others at that time. The Turks had hopelessly under-estimated the strength of the movement for Arab unity, just as the British and the French were to do in later years. The ramshackle Ottoman empire had no other solution for Arab nationalism than repression, but the Arabs' desire for unity is a burning faith, however distant its fulfilment may seem. Statesmen and politicians in London and Paris might scoff, but Lawrence was a visionary, and he understood the Arabs' longing. He gave himself body and soul to help them in their quest. This brought him into conflict with his own government after the war, since the aim of Great Britain and France was to substitute their influence for Turkey's in the Middle East.

Lawrence accompanied the Arab delegation to the Peace Conference at Versailles as an adviser, and found himself ensnarled in the tortuous negotiations conducted by Great Britain and France earlier in the war to carve up the former Turkish empire in Arabia into respective spheres of influence for themselves. It has been a dirty game, as power politics so often is, and Lawrence was soon to learn that pledges made in the stress of war are as likely to be overlooked as honoured after the peace. His practice of wearing Arab dress aroused hostile comment. It was far too unconventional for British tastes, but it was as good a way as any for Lawrence to demonstrate to the Arabs which side he was backing. Nonetheless, despite all his efforts, the outcome of the negotiations could have been predicted. The French received mandates in Syria and the Lebanon, and they at once ejected Feisal from his throne in Damascus. The British were given mandates in Iraq, and in Palestine and Trans-Jordan. Feisal was in due course to be given a throne in Iraq, and Abdullah in Trans-Jordan, but there had been left a legacy of bitterness which has soured our relations with the Arabs ever since.

Lawrence was far from fit at the time, either physically or mentally. His physical resistance had been lowered by his years in the desert. He had been scarred mentally by the vicious sexual assault he had suffered at the hands of the Turkish commandant in Deraa, where he had been captured while reconnoitring the town. He had managed to escape, his identity still not suspected, but not until after he had been subjected to appalling indignities and a merciless beating. Exhausted though he was, he fought his hardest for the Arabs at Versailles. After the peace treaty had been concluded, and there was nothing more he could do in an official capacity, he resigned from the army, and in letters and articles in the press sought to persuade the British government to honour its obligations and give the Arabs real, instead of sham, independence.

Adviser to Churchill

His vision of the Commonwealth was years ahead of his time, though he expressed himself in contemporary terms. 'This new Imperialism,' he wrote in *The Round Table* in 1920, 'involves an active side of imposing responsibility on the local peoples. . . . We can only teach them by forcing them to try, while we stand by to give advice. . . . We have to be prepared to see them doing things by methods quite unlike our own, and less well; but on principle it is better that they half do it than that we do it perfectly for them.' Much blood, treasure, and heart-ache would have been saved had the colonial powers understood the truth of this. The Middle East was in a turmoil, while Curzon's policy at the Foreign Office was out of tune with the times, old-fashioned imperialism that had had its day. The situation only improved when the Colonial Office assumed responsibility for the Middle East. Churchill was the minister, and he took Lawrence with him as adviser on Arab affairs to a conference convened in Cairo in 1921.

The outcome of the conference was regarded at the time as being entirely satisfactory, almost universally so among the British, and only to a lesser extent among the Arabs. In Churchill's words in *The Aftermath,* 'The Arabs and Colonel Lawrence were appeased by the enthronement of King Feisal at Baghdad; the British Army, which had been costing thirty millions a year, had been brought home; and complete tranquillity was preserved under the thrifty Trenchard'. Lawrence, writing in 1932 a second inscription in the copy of *The Seven Pillars of Wisdom* he had presented to Churchill, had this to say: 'And eleven years after we set our

Press Association

T.E.Lawrence in RAF uniform. He was killed in 1935 riding his motorbike along a Dorset lane when, coming upon two cyclists, he crashed in a vain attempt to avoid them

hands to making an honest settlement, all our work still stands: the countries having gone forward, our interests having been saved, and nobody killed, either on our side or the other. To have planned for eleven years is statesmanship.' Unhappily, Anglo-Arab relations, which seemed 'set fair' in 1932, were soon to be wrecked on the rocks of Palestine, and Lawrence was fortunate in being spared witnessing the collapse of all he had striven for.

He had been elected a Fellow of All Souls in 1919, and most of his spare time immediately after the war was devoted to the writing of his book, *The Seven Pillars of Wisdom*. His style is modelled on Doughty's in *Arabia Deserta,* and it is curiously stilted in places, but he manages to catch, and convey, the spirit of Arabia as no other book, apart from the Bible, has succeeded in doing. Whether or not posterity remembers Lawrence as a gifted strategist and brilliant guerrilla leader, his name will live in his epic literary account of the Arab Revolt. But although he wrote unashamedly for literary fame, he did not seek fame in other fields. In 1922 he enlisted in the ranks of the RAF, taking the name J.H.Ross, and sought his personal seclusion in the barrack-room. He described his experience in the ranks in *The Mint,* written in 1928, which was rather too strong meat for some people's tastes.

The newspapers tracked him down, and unwelcome publicity forced him to leave the RAF. He promptly re-enlisted in the Royal Tank Corps under the name of T.E.Shaw, which he later adopted by deed poll, but found himself more suited to the RAF than the army. He wangled himself back into the RAF in 1925, pulling every string he could in order to overcome bureaucratic resistance, and he served in India from 1927 to 1929. After India Lawrence was at first posted to the flying-boat station at Cattewater near Plymouth, before being sent to Calshot on the south coast, where he indulged his love of speed by working with high-speed air-sea rescue launches. He invented his own engine and spent hours tinkering with his motor-cycle to get more power out of it. All this time he was corresponding, as a leading aircraftsman, with the great in the land, and on every imaginable kind of topic from cabbages to kings. He was a brilliant letter-writer, as the publication of *The Letters of T.E.Lawrence to his Friends* has shown. These friends came from all walks of life, and he devoted as much care to a letter to an old comrade from the ranks as he did to one addressed to Field-Marshal Allenby, or George Bernard Shaw.

It was an extraordinary situation, and it is certainly arguable whether a man so gifted is justified in shutting himself away from the world, and avoiding his responsibilities. 'No man is an island,' wrote Donne, but that is what Lawrence was determined to be. Perhaps he had nearly come to terms with himself by the time his service in the RAF ended early in 1935. He had had time to work the bitterness and disillusionment out of his system, and he could hardly have expected to insulate himself from the rapidly-growing menace of Nazism. Had he lived, it is almost certain that Churchill would have sought—even commanded—his services. The two men had high regard for each other. But it was not to be, for he was killed the same year in May. He was only forty-seven.

Nearly twenty years after his death, while I was serving with the Arab Legion in Jordan, I retraced many of his journeys and operations, and sought out those who had ridden with him across the desert with Damascus as their lodestar. They were growing few and far between, and most of those I met had reached the stage where memory fails. But in a bedouin tent I found one elderly sheikh who had ridden with Lawrence to Deraa, and I asked what he had thought of him. For a while he was silent, staring out from the tent into the distance, and then he turned to me and said quietly—'Of all the men I have ever met, *Al Auruns* was the greatest Prince.'

Ireland, 1916-18 / Constantine FitzGibbon

The Easter Rising

***Below:** Raging fires silhouette the Dublin rooftops at the height of the Rising. Indiscriminate British artillery bombardments had started the conflagrations which laid waste large tracts of Dublin and wreaked millions of pounds' worth of damage. **Centre:** A row of British infantrymen fire on the Four Courts from behind an improvised barricade. It was no longer a police action but full-scale war in which no attempt was made to spare the civilians. **Bottom:** After the Rising, rebels in a British gaol. The Irish suffered some thousand casualties in the Rising and hundreds were imprisoned*

Topix

George Morrison

George Morrison

The rebels knew they could not win. They were denounced by most of their countrymen. Yet this heroic, sacrificial gesture changed the history of Ireland – and perhaps the world?

The circumstances that led to the Irish rebellion of 1916 are of an intense complexity, historical, social, political, and perhaps above all psychological. Sean O'Faolain, that fine Irish writer, has written of his country: 'Most of our physical embodiments of the past are ruins, as most of our songs are songs of lament and defiance.' The Easter Rising was a complete failure, which left large parts of Dublin in ruins; yet without it Ireland might never have been free of English rule. The leaders, alive, had very few supporters even among the Irish patriots; dead, they became and have remained their country's heroes. It was a great historical paradox, and one that to this day the British have perhaps never really understood. Had they understood it, it is conceivable that the British might still have an empire, since the overthrow of British rule in Ireland became the model, the prototype, for the overthrow of imperial British might in Asia, in Africa, and elsewhere.

The historical complexity, from the British point of view, can be traced to a general misunderstanding of the Irish character and of Irish desires. The English were bewildered by the fact that most Irishmen, and all educated Irishmen, spoke English, and wrote it, as well as, and often better than, most Englishmen. They were further bewildered by the fact that a very large proportion of the Irish governing class was of English or Norman ancestry. In 1916, the English had not grasped the fact that for two centuries – since the brutal smashing of the old Irish governing class and the theft of their lands – it was precisely these people, Grattan, Tone, Parnell and so on, who had led the Irish in their longing to be free of alien rule. And the reason for this gross misunderstanding was that the English in England did not realize that the Irish way of life was in many ways – at least in terms of human relationships – culturally superior to the English way, less brutal, less materialistic, more spiritual, more dignified, with infinitely less snobbery and class distinction, directed more towards human happiness than to the acquisition of wealth or objects. Always technologically backward, the Irish were overwhelmed in the course of a thousand and more years by waves of conquerors. If those conquerors remained in Ireland, they became, as the English would and did say, seduced by the ease and pleasure of an Irish attitude that looks for charm, gaiety, and wit rather than for profit: they became 'more Irish than the Irish'.

And this the English, in England, dismissed as fecklessness. The fact that the Irish had different values from their own was regarded as funny – and the 'stage Irishman' was created in London. The fact that English might had always, eventually, crushed Irish rebellion was remembered; the fact that Irishmen had fought with immense distinction in all the major armies of Europe, and not least in that of Great Britain, was often forgotten. From the point of view of Whitehall at the turn of the century Paddy-and-his-pig was an essentially comical, child-like figure. He should know, in English terms, his proper station in life. Perhaps, at a pinch, the Anglo-Irish (an odious and meaningless term) might administer this province of Great Britain, but Paddy, never.

On the other hand, these people were politically troublesome and, furthermore, the English of the late Victorian age were a decent lot on the whole. During the Great Famine of 1846 the English liberals had let Ireland starve in the interests of their *laissez-faire* ideology – to have fed them would have interfered with the workings of the free market so far as corn chandlers were concerned – but later second thoughts prevailed. The Irish were to be given partial sovereignty over their own affairs, and a Home Rule Bill was passed. But then the First World War began. Home Rule was postponed until victory over the Germans should have been achieved. Paddy wouldn't mind, why should he? Paddy would join the British army, as he had always done and as scores of thousands of Irishmen did. Paddy wouldn't understand – and many, perhaps most, did not.

Mounting a revolution

But some Irishmen did understand. The most important of these were the members of the Irish Republican Brotherhood or IRB (which must not be confused with the Irish Republican Army, or IRA, a later creation). The IRB had been formed in 1858. It was a secret society which probably never numbered more than 2,000 including those Irishmen who belonged to it and who lived in England, America, or elsewhere. The majority of its members were what might be loosely called 'intellectuals' and in this, in their determination, and in their secrecy they bore a certain resemblance to their Russian contemporaries, Lenin's small Bolshevik Party. However, their aims were political rather than economic. They were patriots, dedicated to the ideal of national independence, and were prepared to use all means – including force – to achieve this ▷599

Above: *One of the banners run up on the General Post Office, Dublin, after it had been seized by the rebels for their headquarters*

Below: *Irish Volunteers drilling in Dublin, 1915. One thousand men from this primitive army challenged the might of Great Britain*

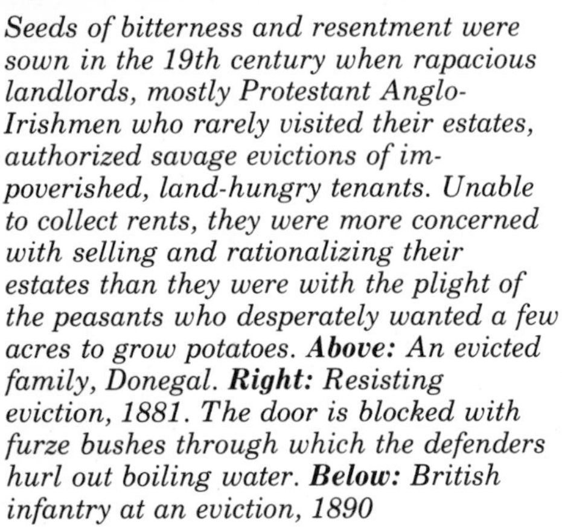

George Morrison

Seeds of bitterness and resentment were sown in the 19th century when rapacious landlords, mostly Protestant Anglo-Irishmen who rarely visited their estates, authorized savage evictions of impoverished, land-hungry tenants. Unable to collect rents, they were more concerned with selling and rationalizing their estates than they were with the plight of the peasants who desperately wanted a few acres to grow potatoes. ***Above:*** *An evicted family, Donegal.* ***Right:*** *Resisting eviction, 1881. The door is blocked with furze bushes through which the defenders hurl out boiling water.* ***Below:*** *British infantry at an eviction, 1890*

end. They provided, as it were, the general staff of the mass movement for Irish freedom from British rule, and their fortnightly publication, *Irish Freedom* (founded in 1910), advocated complete republican government for the whole of Ireland. It is significant that all the men who signed the proclamation of an Irish Republic on Easter Monday were members of the IRB.

When the First World War began, John Redmond, the leader of the Irish Nationalist Party and Parnell's heir, immediately proclaimed his acceptance of the postponement of Home Rule, both for himself and for his followers. These included the Irish Volunteers, perhaps then some 200,000 strong (of whom maybe a couple of thousand were trained and armed). This force had been created in November 1913 as a counter to the Ulster Volunteers (p. 412), which were originally formed to fight against Home Rule. The Ulster Volunteers were also prepared to postpone a struggle that had recently seemed both inevitable and imminent, and from the North of Ireland as from the South scores of thousands of young men went off to fight, and only too often to die, in Flanders. As volunteers. Indeed, Redmond suggested to the government in London that they could remove all British troops from Ireland: his Volunteer force and the Ulster Volunteers were quite capable of seeing that there were no disturbances in Ireland throughout the period of the war.

The IRB had other ideas. At a meeting of their supreme council, as early as August 1914, the decision was taken – in secret of course – that there must be an Irish insurrection before the end of Britain's war with Germany. Until Easter Week 1916 the active members of the IRB were fully occupied in mounting this revolution.

They had at their disposal brains, a fairly considerable amount of money – mostly from Irish Americans – and little else. They had to act through the Irish patriotic organizations, over many of which they had obtained partial control, and if the rising were to be a military success they had to acquire arms, either from British arsenals, or from abroad, which meant in effect from Germany. The balance sheet was roughly as follows: apart from Ulstermen and certain landlords and industrialists, the people of Ireland wanted their freedom from British rule. However, the people were temporarily agreeable to the Home Rule solution, even though the postponed bill gave Ireland less than Dominion status in fiscal and other matters. Furthermore, the farming community, even more important in Ireland then than it is now, was doing very well out of the war. Thus the IRB could rely on very considerable emotional sympathy but little, if any, practical help from the mass of the people. And since the Irish are in some measure a volatile race, there was no telling how they would react to a rising. Certainly the Roman Catholic Church would be against such a deed: and the parish priests were and are very powerful spokesmen in Ireland.

So far as fighting men went, any insurrection would seem doomed to certain defeat. Redmond's huge numbers of Volunteers were mostly unarmed, or were fighting for the British in France. However, some of those who remained in Ireland and were armed and trained could be relied upon. Their chief-of-staff was the historian Eoin MacNeill, and their commandant a schoolmaster in his early thirties named Patrick Pearse. Both of these men were members of the IRB, but as events will show they did not see eye to eye on tactics. The Volunteers were scattered throughout Ireland.

Resources of David and Goliath

The other para-military force was James Connolly's Irish Citizen Army. Connolly was a socialist who in 1896 had founded the Socialist Republican Party. He was a trained soldier. In 1908 James Larkin had created the Irish Transport and General Workers' Union. When that union organized a strike in 1913, and the strike was broken by strong-arm methods, Connolly decided that a workers' defensive force was needed and created his Citizen Army. It was led by himself and by an ex-British Army officer named Jack White. It has been said that this was the most efficient military force at the disposal of the Republicans. It was, however, very small. When it came to the actual fighting, it was only some 250 men who went out, as opposed to about 1,000 from the Volunteers.

Supporting these was the women's organization. Countess Markievicz – an Irishwoman, born a Gore-Booth, and of aristocratic ancestry – was one of the most prominent. She fought as an officer of the Citizen Army throughout the Easter Rising for she was not only a patriot but a socialist. There were also the so-called 'Fianna Boys', lads who enjoyed the manoeuvring before the Rising, as most boys would, and who also showed guts and resourcefulness when the real thing happened. They were messengers, runners, and so on.

Against them they had what was, on paper at least, a most formidable force.

To maintain their control over Ireland, the British relied primarily on the Royal Irish Constabulary, an armed police force, living largely in barracks, and some 10,000 strong. They were almost all Irishmen, knew their districts thoroughly, and were in 1916, with a very few exceptions, entirely loyal to the Crown. They were well trained, well equipped, only moderately unpopular (the Irish do not love police forces), and well informed. English HQ was Dublin Castle, and 'the Castle' relied on the RIC for its field intelligence.

In Dublin itself the police were not armed, though of course there were arms available. They numbered about 1,000 and were organized on the model of the London police. The Special Branch was concerned with politics. Through its investigations, and general infiltration of Irish republican politics, the Castle was supposed to know what the IRB was planning. The Special Branch did not seem, however, to have been particularly good at this job, nor to have infiltrated the IRB to any great extent. On the other hand the blame may rest with those in the Castle to whom they sent their reports. The evaluation of intelligence is infinitely more important than its accumulation.

And behind those 'occupation' forces there was a large British army in Ireland and what, in wartime and in Irish terms, were almost infinite reserves in Great Britain. If it were a mere question of manpower, the Irish had not a hope.

As for fire-arms, the David and Goliath ratio was even more vivid. Before the outbreak of the First World War the Ulster Volunteers had bought some 35,000 German rifles, the Irish Volunteers about 1,000. And of course the British army had everything, including artillery of all sorts. The Irish made an attempt to rectify this by getting rifles from Germany. Sir Roger Casement, an Irishman with a distinguished past, went to Germany from neutral America. He was to bring the weapons for the Easter Rising that the IRB had agreed on. His mission was a failure. British naval intelligence had broken some German cyphers. The British navy was thus able to intercept the German ship carrying the guns. Casement himself was immediately arrested when he came ashore from a U-boat near Tralee, in County Kerry, on Good Friday. Later the English tried him and hanged him as a traitor. The guns on which the Irish had been relying, even for this forlorn hope, had not arrived. Were they still to go on?

It is here that the different personalities and attitudes become important. We must pause to look at the men, English and Irish, involved; and also at the whole meaning of *Sinn Fein*.

Sinn Fein is usually translated as 'ourselves alone', and this is perhaps the best rendering in English of a complicated Irish concept. It means, first of all and above all, independence from British rule. But since Irish history was in those days so much bound up with contemporary Irish politics, it had a secondary meaning. For many centuries the Irish had hoped for the help of England's enemies to get rid of the ▷600

George Morrison

Patrick Pearse, in barrister's robe and wig

George Morrison

***Above:** MacNeill – attempted to stop Rising*
***Below:** Lord Wimborne – lord-lieutenant*

George Morrison

***Below:** Countess Markievicz – a socialist*

George Morrison

English. The Spaniards and the French had let them down as the Germans were to do in 1916. This was not so much because Britain's enemies lacked the anxiety to defeat Britain in Ireland but because of geographical-military complications (tides, prevailing winds, and so on). Thus *Sinn Fein* also meant that the Irish must rely upon themselves alone in order to rid themselves of their British rulers. For the British, in the years to come, the 'Shinners' were to be the epitome of violent republicanism in Ireland. In fact the party, which only had its first annual convention as late as 1905, was essentially democratic. It had run a parliamentary candidate (who was defeated) in the Leitrim election of 1908. But as time went on it gained an increasing number of the extremists from Redmond's Nationalist Party. Arthur Griffith, its leader and also the editor of the *United Irishmen,* was never a fanatic. He believed in constitutional tactics – and was thus far less of an extremist than many of the IRB leaders – but, unlike Redmond's and Parnell's old party, he no longer trusted the alliance with the Liberal Party in Great Britain. Ourselves alone. To many young men it was a most attractive idea.

The British rulers were, on the whole, a shadowy lot. The Liberal government in London was inevitably devoting almost all its attention to the gigantic struggle on the Continent. Since Ireland appeared so placid in 1916, neither the best politicians nor by any means the best British soldiers were in the country. Augustine Birrell was Chief Secretary. Possessed, it was said, of extreme personal charm, he was a *belle lettrist* whose books, now forgotten, enjoyed in their time considerable esteem. He appears to have regarded his job in Dublin – which might be described as active head of the administration – as something of a sideline to his career as a *littérateur,* and spent a very large proportion of his time being charming in London. His principal Assistant Secretary, responsible for political affairs, was a civil servant experienced in colonial administration, Sir Matthew Nathan. He seems to have had little comprehension of the Irish temperament and to have been happiest behind his desk, dealing with routine paperwork. The general officer commanding the British army in Ireland was a Major-General Field. He, even more, seems to have had no idea of what was going on in Ireland at all. And finally there was Lord Wimborne, the lord-lieutenant and the King's representative, who presided over the British administration as a sort of constitutional monarch with all the powers, and most of the limitations, that that implies. However, he knew Ireland well. He had sponsored the land act of 1903, which had pacified the Irish countrymen by further advantageous changes of the tenant-landlord relationship. He was popular with the Irish governing class, as was Birrell; but, unlike his Chief Secretary, he did not at all care for the situation that was developing.

The British intelligence services had, as we have seen, infiltrated the various Irish 'resistance' movements. The Volunteers, it must be assumed, had few secrets not known to Dublin Castle. And the Castle knew that a rising was planned to take place as soon as possible after the landing of Casement and his German guns. On 21st April 1916, Casement landed and was immediately arrested. Wimborne, who was to have gone to Belfast, cancelled his visit and on Sunday the 23rd, that is to say only a matter of hours before the Rising took place, demanded of Nathan that he immediately arrest 'between sixty and a hundred' of the Irish leaders. Had this been done successfully, it seems unlikely that any Rising would have taken place *at that time.* However, it was probably too late for a mere police action by that date. The men of the Citizen Army and the more militant Volunteers were under arms and ready to fight. As it was, Nathan persuaded his 'constitutional monarch' that there was no need for action. And Birrell was in London.

It would seem probable that Nathan's intelligence service had briefed him as to what was happening within the high command of the Volunteers after the news of Casement's arrest, that he knew Eoin MacNeill had decided that without the guns the Rising must be cancelled or at least postponed. What Nathan presumably did not know was that this decision finally split the Volunteers, and that the IRB was almost solidly behind Patrick Pearse and those other Irish patriots who were prepared to go ahead with the Rising even in these disadvantageous, indeed well-nigh suicidal, circumstances. All this sounds very neat and staff-officerish when put down on paper, but of course the reality was far more chaotic, involving a clash of multiple personalities, orders and counter-orders, and very considerable bitterness. Indeed MacNeill's decision to call off the Rising, and Pearse's to go ahead, was really the death-knell of the Volunteers and of the Nationalist Party whose armed force they were supposed to be. After the Rising, the political leadership of those hostile to British rule in Ireland passed to *Sinn Fein,* while those who fought in Easter week became the nucleus of the Irish Republican Army.

Certainly MacNeill's last-minute proclamation that the Rising be cancelled – he had boys bicycling all over the country, and even announced this supposed non-

Some Irishmen chose to fight for 'country' rather than 'king'

George Morrison

Above: *A Dublin tram bedecked with British recruiting slogans, 1915. Home Rule now had to await German surrender. Paddy wouldn't mind, why should he? Paddy would join the British Army as he had always done – and as scores of thousands of Irishmen did.* ***Left:*** *Citizen Army parading outside Liberty Hall. When James Connolly assumed command of the Army he hung this provocative banner outside the building. The small Citizen Army contributed some 250 men to the rebel force.* ***Below:*** *Recruiting poster inviting young Irishmen to share the carnage of the trenches and die for Great Britain. By 1916 there was fierce opposition to conscription. Men felt they owed nothing to Great Britain. It was her war, not Ireland's*

Imperial War Museum

For a week a handful of rebels convulsed Dublin

Radio Times Hulton

Above: *Embattled rebels in the General Post Office, Sackville Street, Easter Monday, 1916*

National Museum of Ireland, Dublin

Above: *British troops searching the gutted GPO, 3rd May 1916. The rebels evacuated it when red-hot and just about to collapse.* ***Below:*** *Dublin slum-dwellers jeered at the rebels and carried off charred timbers from devastated buildings in Sackville Street as firewood*

Press Association

happening in the Sunday papers—cannot possibly have been unknown to Nathan. He must have taken into account the fact that a few hot-heads were likely to ignore this order: he must also have known that the vast bulk of the Volunteers would breathe a sigh of relief and that the clergy—to whom the English have often attached an exaggerated political importance in Ireland owing to their ubiquity and their marked difference from the Anglican clergy in England—would support MacNeill and the mass of his supporters, content with the promise of eventual, diluted Home Rule. The handful of extremists could be dealt with—though not at all as easily as the English thought—by the overwhelming forces arraigned against them. No special precautions were taken, despite Lord Wimborne's fully justified fears. Indeed, on Easter Monday, the first day of the Rising, a great many British officers were at Fairyhouse Races.

The Easter Rising was suicidal. Patrick Pearse was well aware of this. Before ever it happened he said to his mother: 'The day is coming when I shall be shot, swept away, and my colleagues like me.' When his mother enquired about her other son, William, who was also an extreme nationalist, Pearse is reported to have replied: 'Willie? Shot like the others. We'll all be shot.' And James Connolly is said to have remarked: 'The chances against us are a thousand to one.' On the morning of the Rising, when asked by one of his men if there was any hope, he replied, cheerfully: 'None whatever!'

It was hard for the staff officers and colonial administrators of Dublin Castle, accustomed to weighing possibilities so far as their own actions were concerned, to realize that a group of men, perhaps 1,250 strong (the Citizen Army took no notice of MacNeill), was prepared to fight and die in such circumstances. But they should have been wiser in their age: Langemarck was recent, Verdun was going on, the Somme was about to happen. Seldom in history have men been so willing, indeed so eager, to throw away their lives for an ideal, almost any ideal, and the Irish ideal had long roots. The men went out and fought.

Easter week

The essence of the Irish plan was to seize certain key points in the city, and hold these for as long as possible, thus disrupting British control of the capital. It was then hoped that one of three things might happen: the country might rise in sympathy; the British might realize the ultimate impossibility of controlling Ireland and pull out; and last and faintest of hopes, the Germans might somehow come to the rescue of the rebels. Since the rebels had no artillery of any sort, their ▷**606**

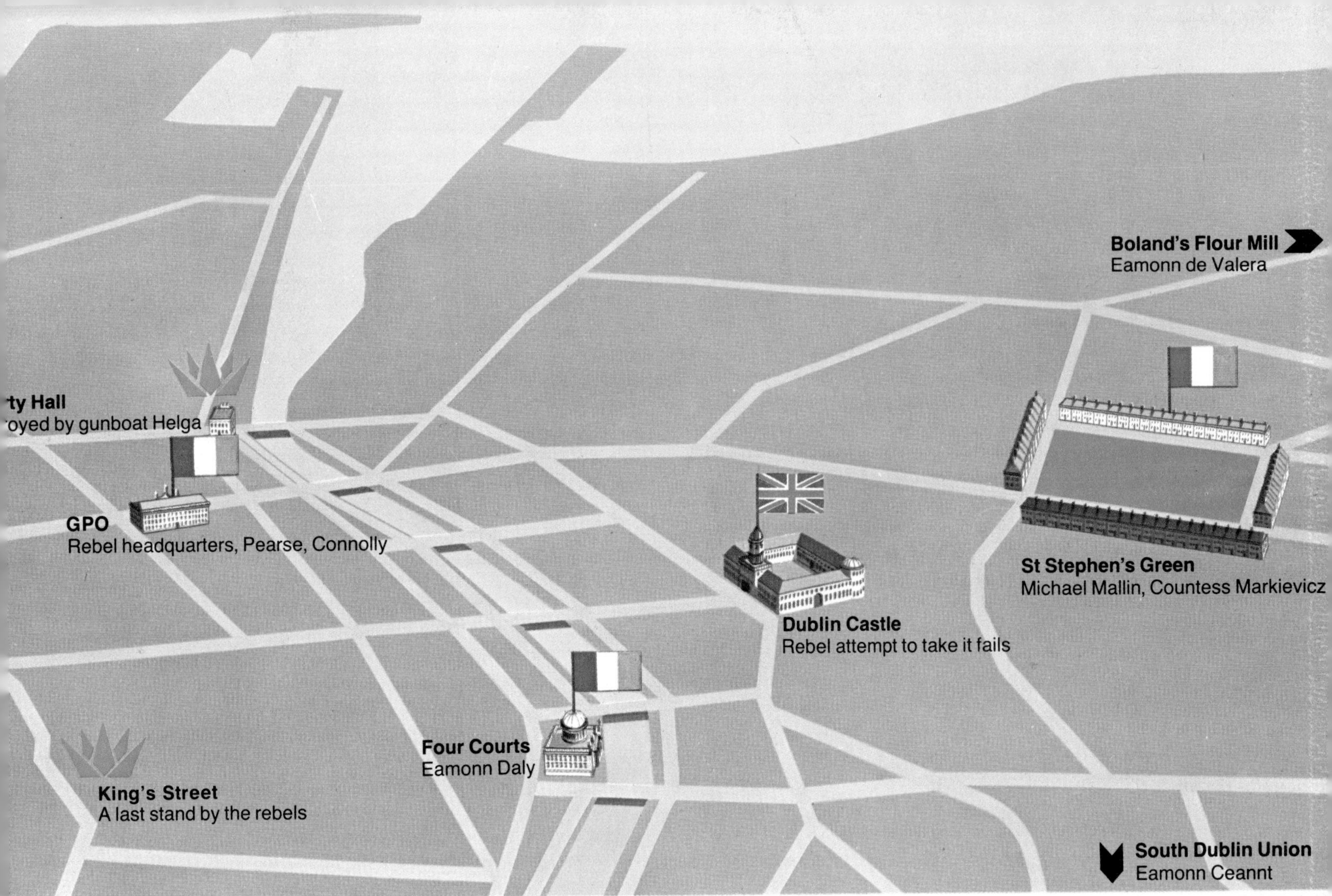

Boland's Flour Mill
Eamonn de Valera

ty Hall
royed by gunboat Helga

GPO
Rebel headquarters, Pearse, Connolly

St Stephen's Green
Michael Mallin, Countess Markievicz

Dublin Castle
Rebel attempt to take it fails

Four Courts
Eamonn Daly

King's Street
A last stand by the rebels

South Dublin Union
Eamonn Ceannt

Above: *A bird's eye view of Dublin at the time of the Rising, Easter 1916, showing the principal strong points occupied by the rebels*

Below: *'O'Connell Street after the Bombardment' by Joseph McGill. Connolly imagined the British would not shell their own property*

1

Dublin Civic Museum / Photo: Alan Spain

1 Mementoes of resistance and revolt. Top row, left to right: Parnell on matchbox; badge and cap badge of Irish Volunteers; Pearse medallion; postcard depicting Pearse reading the proclamation of the provisional government. Bottom row, left to right: British military pass, 1916; Parnell memorial badge; Irish Volunteers button; 'Daughter of Erin' badge and Home Rule demonstration shamrock, 1912. 2 Pictured after the Rising: the women who fought so bravely during the siege of the GPO. 3 'The Surrender of Countess Markievicz' painted by Kathleen Fox. 4 Plaque in Kilmainham Gaol commemorating the rebel leaders who were executed. 5 Portrait of Eamonn de Valera on an Irish Volunteers banner. Opposite: de Valera under arrest. His life was spared because he was of American birth

3

Dr Karl Mullen

George Morrison

strong-points could only hold out provided that the British did not use their artillery. Connolly and the socialists hoped that the British would, for capitalist reasons, not bombard Dublin and thus destroy their own – or largely their own – property. This, too, was an illusion.

H-hour was 12 noon and since this was a Bank Holiday there were crowds in the streets who witnessed the small bodies of Volunteers and of the Citizen Army marching, armed, through the city to seize their various strongpoints. It went, on the whole, remarkably smoothly. Five major buildings or groups of buildings were seized north of the River Liffey, nine south of it, and some of the railway stations were occupied. Headquarters were established in the massive General Post Office in Sackville Street (now O'Connell Street) from which Irish flags were flown and where Patrick Pearse announced the creation of a provisional government of the new Irish Republic. With him in the Post Office were Connolly as military commander, Joseph Plunkett (a very sick man), The O'Rahilly, Tom Clark, Sean MacDermott, and other leaders. There, too, was a young man named Michael Collins. The rebels immediately set about preparing the Post Office against the attack which they expected almost at once. The four other principal strong-points seized were the South Dublin Union, a congeries of poor-houses and the like (commanded by Eamonn Ceannt); the Four Courts, the headquarters of the legal profession, where heavy law books were used as sandbags (Eamonn Daly); St Stephen's Green, where trenches were dug and barricades of motor-cars erected (Michael Mallin and Countess Markievicz); and Boland's Flour Mill, which covered the approach roads from Kingstown, now Dun Laoghaire, where any reinforcements from England would almost certainly disembark (Eamonn de Valera).

An attempt to seize Dublin Castle failed. An attempt to capture a large quantity of arms and ammunition from the arsenal in Phoenix Park known as the Magazine Fort was only partially successful and merely a few rifles seized. On the other hand, the rebels successfully cut telephone lines, and the Castle was for a time almost isolated. A further success was that a troop of Lancers which attempted to charge down Sackville Street was repulsed with casualties.

The British had been taken by surprise and were now almost completely in the dark. The Castle immediately ordered troops up from the Curragh and other camps outside Dublin and appealed to London for reinforcements. There, Lord French was commander-in-chief. He was an Irishman and an ardent Unionist. He immediately ordered that no less than four divisions be alerted for transfer to Ireland. British policy was in fact thrown into reverse. Appeasement of the Irish was out; the rebels were to be crushed, rapidly, and massively. But if the British in Dublin were in the dark, so were the rebels. They had no wireless links either between the strong-points they had seized or with the outside world. Communication by runner became difficult and eventually impossible when the fighting reached its peak.

From a military point of view, Tuesday was comparatively calm. The British were closing in cautiously. Their strategy was to throw a cordon around that area of Dublin where the rebels' strong-points were, then cut that area in two, and finally mop up. They moved artillery and troops into Trinity College, a natural fortress which the rebels had failed to seize, though they had planned to do so. The reason was the small number of fighting men available. Looting began by the crowds. Martial law was declared. British reinforcements arrived at Kingstown. A mad British officer, a Captain Bowen-Colthurst, had three harmless journalists shot 'while trying to escape' – a phrase to become hideously familiar, and not only in Ireland. The atrocities had begun.

Dublin burns, Dubliners starve

By Wednesday morning the rebels were outnumbered twenty to one. The British now began to attack in earnest. Their first major action was to destroy Liberty Hall, the headquarters of the Labour Party and of the trade unions, by shellfire from the gunboat *Helga*. As it happened, the rebels had anticipated this, and the building was entirely empty. The British gunfire was inaccurate and many other buildings were hit and many civilians killed. The army also was using artillery: a 9-pounder gun was fired against a single sniper. Dublin began to burn, and the Dubliners to starve, for there was no food coming into the city. This was no longer a police action but full-scale war in which no attempt was made to spare the civilians. Meanwhile, British reinforcements marching in from Kingstown were ambushed by de Valera's men and suffered heavy casualties, but by dint of numbers forced their way through. St Stephen's Green had been cleared of rebels, who retreated into the Royal College of Surgeons, and established a strong-point there.

On Thursday the new British commander-in-chief arrived. Since Ireland was under martial law, he held full powers there. This was General Sir John Maxwell, a soldier of some distinction who had returned the month before from Egypt, where he had been commander-in-chief of the Anglo-Egyptian armies. Although he numbered the Countess Markievicz among his relations, he had no knowledge of the

Patrick Pearse surrendering to the British

REBEL LEADERS
SURRENDER.

THREE PRINCIPALS
TRIED AND SHOT.

OTHERS ARRESTED & HELD FO
TRIAL UNCONDITIONALLY.

SERIOUS FIGHTING ALL ROUND THE CIT

HEAVY CASUALTIES IN DEAD AN
WOUNDED.

CENTRE OF DUBLIN DEVASTATED BY FIRE
PALATIAL BUILDINGS IN ASHES.

The Sinn Fein insurrection, which broke out in Dublin City on Easter Monday a noon, has been effectively quelled.

The positions of vantage which the rebels took up in various parts of the city wer reduced, and the leaders unconditionally surrendered.

Thomas J. Clarke, P. H. Pearse, and Thomas Macdonagh, three of the signatorie to the poster proclaiming an Irish Republic, have been tried by court-martial an

Above: *Headline in the* Irish Independent
Below: *Liberty Hall, Citizen Army HQ, in 1917. It was shelled by the gunboat,* Helga

***Left:** Kilmainham Gaol, Dublin. The forbidding '1916 Corridor' where rebel leaders were imprisoned after the abortive Easter Rising. A number of rebels, including Pearse and Connolly, faced firing-squads in the gaol's execution yard. Connolly, shot in the ankle by a British sniper during the Rising and unable to stand, was executed in a chair*

Photo: Alan Spain

current political mood in Ireland, and, indeed, as events were to prove, did more to undermine British rule in Ireland than all the rebels put together. He had been ordered by the British prime minister, Asquith, to put down the rebellion with all possible speed. And this he did regardless of political consequences.

The reinforcements from England were now in action. These were largely untrained men, and when they discovered that many of the men of the Irish Republican Army—as the rebels now and henceforth styled themselves—were not in uniform (how could they be?) they began shooting male civilians on sight.

On that day (Thursday) attacks were made on Boland's Mill, the men in the South Dublin Union were forced to give ground, and there was shelling of the General Post Office, which began to burn from the top down. Connolly was wounded twice. The first wound he hid from his men: the second was more serious, for one foot was shattered and he was in great pain. With the aid of morphia he carried on, directing the battle as best he could. The Dublin fires were now great conflagrations. With the streets full of small-arms fire and the water supplies often cut, these could not be dealt with. Still, no major rebel strong-point surrendered.

On Friday Connolly ordered the women who had fought so bravely to leave the General Post Office building, which was now cut off and burning. Later that day he and Pearse and the remaining rebels escaped from a building that was by now almost red-hot and about to collapse. They found temporary refuge nearby, while the British continued to shell the empty building. All knew that the end was near. A last battle was fought for King's Street, near the Four Courts. It took some 5,000 British soldiers, equipped with armoured cars and artillery, twenty-eight hours to advance about 150 yards against some 200 rebels. It was then that the troops of the South Staffordshire Regiment bayoneted and shot civilians hiding in cellars. And now all was over. On Saturday morning Pearse and Connolly surrendered unconditionally.

Like so much else about the Easter Rising, casualties are hard to estimate. It would seem that those of the British were about 500; those of the Irish, including civilians, about twice that figure. Material damage was estimated at about £2½ million. Large parts of Dublin lay in ruins.

When, on Sunday, the arrested rebels were marched across Dublin from one prison compound to another, they were at times jeered at and booed by the crowds, and particularly in the slum areas. The mass of public opinion had been against the rebels before the Rising and remained so until the reprisals began. ▷608

George Morrison

Left: The rebellious capital was not allowed to forget that British military might had crushed the Easter Rising. Tanks clatter past the saluting base during General French's peace parade, Dublin 1919

On the direct orders of the cabinet in London, reprisals were swift, secret, and brutal. The leaders were tried by court martial and shot: only when they were dead were their deaths announced. Among those thus killed were Willie Pearse, who was no leader and who, it was generally believed in Ireland, was killed because he had followed his famous brother; the invalid Plunkett; and, most disgusting of all to Irish minds, Connolly, who was dying and who had to be propped up in bed for the court martial in his hospital room. He was shot in a chair, since he could not stand. A wave of disgust crossed all Ireland. That wave did not subside when Asquith defended these measures in the Commons; nor when he realized that a mistake had been made, and sacked Maxwell.

When London at last understood that its methods were uniting all Ireland against Britain, there was yet another change of British policy. Many of the three thousand-odd men arrested after the Rising were released from British gaols. They returned to Ireland and began immediately to reorganize a new and more powerful IRA, now with the backing of the people. This was a gesture of appeasement by Lloyd George, the new prime minister, who called an Irish Convention intended to solve 'the Irish problem'. Since *Sinn Fein* boycotted the Convention, it was a complete failure. Again British policy was thrown into reverse, and the leaders of the new independence movement were arrested in the spring of 1918. Michael Collins, however, escaped arrest, though there was a price on his head, dead or alive, which eventually reached the sum of £10,000. He was to be the great guerrilla leader in the next round of the struggle. The Irish leaders, with much backing from the United States, both emotional and financial, set about creating a viable alternative government which could and did take over when the British should have at last seen that they could not win. *Sinn Fein* triumphed, and won most of the Irish seats in the 1918 election. The elected members, however, formed their own 'parliament', *Dail Eireann,* rather than sit in Westminster. Collins drew up a strategy of resistance, first passive, then obstructive, and finally active, which has since been pursued elsewhere against British imperialism, and indeed against the imperialisms of other nations. And in January of 1919 the first shots of the new rebellion were fired in County Tipperary.

The Easter Rising was a total failure. And yet it was a total success. After Easter week 1916 permanent English rule in Ireland became an impossibility. One tragedy was a triumph. Other tragedies were to follow. But the Irish achieved it, and alone.

Four Nationalist Leaders

The First World War was a midwife of revolution. And this can be clearly seen in the careers of four European nationalist leaders—de Valera, Venizelos, Masaryk, and Pilsudski. The war was vital to them and their countrymen. The opportunities which were offered and taken were to shape the history of post-war Europe

1 Eamonn de Valera—as a commandant during the Easter Rising, there was little hint of the power and adulation that were to come. 2 Eleutherios Venizelos—in self-imposed exile he watched his dream of a Greater Greece crumble. 3 Thomas Masaryk—a propagandist and conspirator in the cause of racial justice and human rights. 4 Józef Pilsudski—discovered that national unity created by the euphoria of independence had little substance

1 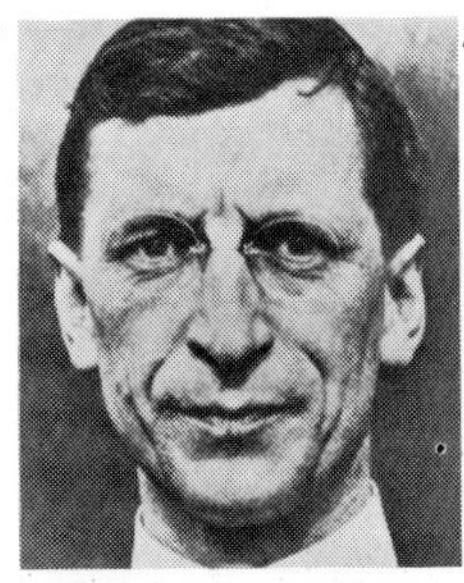

2 

3 

4 

EAMONN DE VALERA —'politician by accident'

David Thornley

If most revolutionaries are to some extent 'politicians by accident', the description is especially applicable to the men who carried on the 1916 struggle into its second phase of guerrilla war and international diplomacy. Mostly young men, often in their twenties, and without administrative experience, they came into their inheritance as the result of the prompt liquidation by General Maxwell's firing squads of almost the entire middle-age group of revolutionary leaders. And they were propelled into politics by a movement whose sole aim was independence and which had correspondingly avoided all but the most generalized ideas of social obligation.

Of no one was this more true than Eamonn de Valera. Born in New York on 14th October 1882 of a Spanish father and an Irish mother, he was sent back to Ireland at the age of two to be reared by a maternal uncle. A solemn, industrious child, he succeeded, through family self-sacrifice, part-time jobs, and scholarships, in educating himself to the attainment of the BA, BSc degrees of the old Royal University. He was drawn into nationalism through his devotion to the Irish language, joined the Irish Volunteers on its foundation in November 1913, and by the time of the rising had risen to the rank of commandant, with specific responsibility for the important Boland's Flour Mill outpost.

But there was still little hint of the power and adulation that were to come. At this period he was a teacher of mathematics, a tall, ascetic figure, withdrawn, and a poor speaker—which in a sense he always remained, his later magnetism being physical rather than rhetorical. In neither of the main organs into which revolutionary feeling was channelled was he in the top hierarchy. In the Volunteers, although appointed commandant in March 1915, he had remained outside the inner circle of the leadership; in October 1915 he refused Tomas MacDonagh's pressing invitation to join the executive council of the Volunteers. And of the Irish Republican Brotherhood, which master-minded the Rising, he was a passive member.

But a succession of factors, some of them deriving from the development of his personality and experience, some of them wholly coincidental, swept him to the leadership of the revolutionary movement in the period between May 1916 and April 1919. The first was the sheer fact of his survival. The first of the executed leaders was shot on 3rd May, the last on 12th May, the day after de Valera's own condemnation. By then a revulsion of public feeling, plus his American birth and arguable citizenship, saved his life. At once the aura descended upon him of 'the last surviving commandant' of the Easter Rising. The title was not quite technically accurate, but his seniority among the survivors was unquestionable and gave him, as Convict 95 in Dartmoor, and later in Lewes gaol, the *de jure* leadership of the Volunteer prisoners. Indeed, by comparison with many of them, he possessed, at thirty-four, the additional seniority of age. For over a year he occupied his time with mathematics and the maintenance of discipline and morale among his fellow-convicts.

Meanwhile, Irish opinion slowly changed. The heroism of the Volunteers and the savagery of the executions in the face of protests from sources as disparate as George Bernard Shaw and the *Manchester Guardian* pointed up the sacrificial role of Pearse and his little band. The continued failure of the Irish Parliamentary Party to make the smallest progress towards the peaceful attainment of independence except under the threat of partition discredited it. The Irish Republican Brotherhood was revived and reorganized by men like Michael Collins, back in Ireland in December 1916 with the first batch of 600 freed internees. Sheer war-weariness and the shadow of the introduction to Ireland of military conscription to sustain Great Britain's wasting armies fomented anti-British feeling. In February 1917 in Roscommon *Sinn Fein,* on an abstentionist platform and with Volunteer support, captured its first seat from the Irish Parliamentary Party; in May in Longford it took its second. In June the last of the prisoners were released. Cheering crowds greeted them as they stepped off the boat at Dun Laoghaire. For none was the reception so ecstatic as for de Valera. He was at once pressed into the *Sinn Fein* candidature in a third by-election in East Clare, and in July he was elected.

His informal public status as the surviving leader of the revolutionary tradition was now generally taken for granted. To give it formal expression he needed to assume the leadership of its institutional organizations, the Volunteers, *Sinn Fein,* the Irish Republican Brotherhood, and ultimately the revolutionary government. He never achieved leadership of the third, which remained effectively under Collins's control, and this dichotomy was to contribute not a little to subsequent divisions. But within two years the leading positions in the other three were his. In October 1917 *Sinn Fein* held its tenth convention. This meeting abandoned Griffith's constitutional ideas in favour of an outright republican programme; Griffith stood down as president and de Valera was unanimously chosen to replace him. The Irish Volunteers nevertheless remained an independent and at times sceptical military movement, but the crucial personal status of de Valera, who had already been chosen as the spokesman of the released officers on the night of their return to Dublin, was further emphasized when the Volunteer Convention of November 1917 also elected him its president.

There remained only the leadership of the nation itself. This was effectively achieved in the general election of December 1918. De Valera himself was again in an English prison, but this, as with so many Irish leaders before him, served only to enhance his popularity. Mass excitement, the barrenness of the Parliamentary Party, Irish-American money, and enthusiastic organization, rising occasionally to intimidation, by the young men of the Volunteers, overcame the handicaps of censorship and the imprisonment of the principal leaders. *Sinn Fein* destroyed the old Party and won 73 seats out of 105. In January 1919 the nucleus of these members who were at liberty constituted themselves the first *Dail Eireann* (Assembly of Ireland) and declared the independence of Ireland. They appointed only an acting head of state; they were waiting for de Valera. They did not have long to wait; on 3rd February Collins successfully organized de Valera's rescue from Lincoln gaol and he was smuggled back to Ireland more than ever the symbol of Ireland's will to freedom. The second session of *Dail Eireann* was convened on 1st April and de Valera was formally elected *Priomh-Aire*. The precise meaning of that Irish term was to cause more than semantic confusion three years later. Some were to argue that it meant no more than the first minister of the Dail, others that it symbolized the Presidency not merely of the nation but of a formally-constituted sovereign republic. But that problem was in the future, as were civil war, imprisonment, the loss of power, and its recapture. In May 1919 de Valera set out on a publicity campaign to the United States; here he would sharpen his already developing tactical skill in the toughest school there was – Irish-American politics. Whatever *Priomh-Aire* meant, the bespectacled mathematician to whom Pearse entrusted the command of the 3rd Battalion of the Dublin Brigade in March 1915 was now the Chief, and the Chief he was to remain.

ELEUTHERIOS VENIZELOS
– and the dream of a Greater Greece

Michael Llewellyn Smith

A tall, thin man with a white beard, a black skull-cap, rimless glasses, infinite charm, and 'an inexhaustible eloquence', in Lord Curzon's words, 'which leaves no chink for a reply'. Such was Venizelos in the heyday of his power and influence, at the Paris Peace Conference in 1919. The mandate for a Greek occupation of Smyrna and its hinterland which he obtained at Paris was the reward for four years of unwavering support for the Allied cause in the First World War – support which Venizelos analysed with candour in a speech in September 1915: 'It must be understood that the great powers, every one of them, are out for their own interests. But over the Eastern Question, where our own interests lie, the two Western powers are, to my mind, those whose interests concur with our own.' This self-interested backing of the side which, providentially, won, together with his three-year battle against a King of Greece who thought differently, won Venizelos a reputation as the greatest Greek statesman since Pericles, which even his shattering defeat at the polls in 1920 did not affect. The Greek people were dismissed as ungrateful, ready as always to turn to their greatest men and rend them.

Imperial War Museum

Venizelos arrives at Salonika. Within weeks Venizelist troops were fighting with the Allied forces along the Macedonian Front

Venizelos preached a Greek renaissance which British philhellenes – men like Harold Nicolson at the Foreign Office, steeped in the classical tradition – wanted to believe in. Certainly Venizelos's first four years in office gave grounds for confidence in his powers. He left his native Crete in September 1910, to become prime minister of Greece within a month of his arrival on the mainland. In the next four years he succeeded in changing the face of the country, and almost doubling its surface area and population. First proving his 'respectability' by dropping the anti-dynastic tendencies which were expected of him by the Military League of revolutionary officers which brought him to power, and working in harmony with the King, he proceeded to build up support among the Greeks of all classes who were tired of the factional politics of his predecessors and the national humiliations of the last few years. The Venizelist Liberals won 150 out of 181 seats in March 1912.

Venizelos's appeal was a nationalist appeal, to all Greeks, for a national regeneration. Uninterested in theories of government, lacking any rigid political philosophy, he devoted his energies to the reorganization and strengthening of Greek institutions in preparation for the fulfilment of Greece's national dream – the expansion of the Greek kingdom so as to include all those parts of the Ottoman empire which the Greeks regarded as theirs by historical and ethnological right – Epirus, Macedonia, Thrace, the islands, Smyrna, and finally even Constantinople itself. This dream was the 'Great Idea' which, as the Greeks saw it, Venizelos had come from Crete to fulfil. The triumphantly successful Balkan Wars of 1912-13 (p. 404), in which Greece extended her boundaries northwards to include Ioannina and southern Epirus, Salonika and western Macedonia, were a great leap forward towards its fulfilment. Venizelos, as architect of the alliance of Balkan states which launched the successful crusade against the Turks, shared the popularity for victory with Prince Constantine, commander of the victorious Greek army, who became King on the assassination of his father in newly liberated Salonika in 1913.

Thus at the outbreak of the First World War Venizelos presided over a country which needed a period of peace and quiet, as he himself admitted, in order to digest its territorial gains. The war, however, which Venizelos rightly saw would lead to the final disintegration of the Ottoman empire, gave Greece an unrepeatable opportunity to extend her frontiers still farther and embrace the still unredeemed Greeks of Thrace and Asia Minor. Venizelos's policy was, therefore, to support the Entente powers in the hope that the Allies would uphold Greek claims on Ottoman territory after the war. The view of the King, who believed that the Central powers would win, was that Greek neutrality should be preserved at all costs.

On 1st March 1915, in an attempt to engage Greece on the side of the Entente powers, Venizelos proposed to commit

Greek troops in support of the forthcoming Allied landing at Gallipoli. The King rejected the proposal, and Venizelos resigned. In the elections which followed Venizelos was returned with 184 out of 310 seats. In October, however, having attempted once more to commit Greece to war by inviting an Allied expeditionary force to land at Salonika, he was again dismissed by the King, who was by now opposed to Greek involvement even in the event of a Bulgarian attack on Serbia, with whom Greece had a defensive alliance.

The division of the country into Royalists and Venizelists was now acute and bitter. The King was obliged to impose his views through successive puppet Royalist governments. Allied pressure on the Greeks, and violations of Greek sovereignty by the Allied army at Salonika, became more and more flagrant – and for this Venizelos was later to be blamed. But it was not until summer 1916, when the Bulgarians invaded Macedonia and occupied Kavalla, and the Greek garrison of 8,000 men, laying down their arms, was sent to internment in Germany – all to maintain the dogma of neutrality – that Venizelos acted. On 25th September he fled to Crete, proclaimed a revolution, and ten days later, on arrival in Salonika, formed a pro-Allied 'Provisional Government'. Within weeks Venizelist troops were fighting with the Allies on the Macedonian Front. For eight months Greece was physically divided into a Venizelist and a Royalist camp; then the Allies, losing patience with the King, forced him to vacate the throne and retire to Switzerland, and reinstated Venizelos as prime minister over a united Greece. At last the country, freed from the blockade instituted by the Allies against Royalist Greece, was able to devote all its energies to war. By September 1918, 250,000 Greek troops were engaged in Macedonia, and played a brave part in the offensive which broke through the Bulgarian Front. Through this useful contribution to the Allied war effort Venizelos hoped to justify Greece's claims at the peace conference. In his success he overreached himself, claiming and gaining Smyrna and western Asia Minor, and thus committing Greece to a far more arduous war, against a rejuvenated Turkey, and to defeat.

In his unbounded faith in the vigour and 'civilizing mission' of the Greeks, Venizelos was a nationalist; but his nationalism was undisturbed by the extent of foreign influence and interference in Greek affairs. From his experience in Crete he knew how far Greek policy was affected by the pressures of the great powers. He knew that Greek finances, ever since the Graeco-Turkish war of 1897 had been controlled by an international financial commission. His reaction to this was not to complain of exploitation, or speak of 'Greece for the Greeks', as his opposite number Kemal fought for 'Turkey for the Turks'. On the contrary, Venizelos tried, by co-operating to the full with the Western powers, to *use* them to further his policy of Greek expansion. Thus during his first premiership he summoned a French military mission and an English naval mission to reorganize the Greek army and navy. Thus he supported the Allied powers. Thus after the armistice, in order to strengthen his claim on Allied gratitude, he sent two divisions of Greek troops to support the disastrous French expedition to south Russia, although no Greek interest was involved. Thus, because the island was British, he did not press the Greek claim to Cyprus at the conference. All this he did to win the support of France and Great Britain.

Spellbound by Venizelos's vision of a Greater Greece spanning two continents, his admirers often forgot that Greece remained in fact a war-weary, economically fragile, bitterly divided country, longing for peace. Venizelos's colleagues, in his absence in Paris, did nothing to heal the divisions, and the opposition spoke convincingly of oppression and persecution of Royalists. Venizelos reassured his friends in Paris that as soon as the peace was settled he would devote himself, with startling results, to internal affairs. For the Greeks that was too long to wait. At the general elections of November 1920 Venizelos fell, his Royalist enemies triumphed, and King Constantine returned to Greece. In self-imposed exile in western Europe, Venizelos watched his dream of a Greater Greece crumble in September 1922 when the Greek army was broken by Turkish troops, and Smyrna went up in flames. This for Greece was the end of the great war, and the end of five centuries of dreams. Venizelos died in France in 1936.

Ulk/Tasiemka

Sarcastic German cartoon depicts Venizelos as a puppet of the Allies. It asserts 'he will be 'first played with and then broken'

THOMAS MASARYK
– father of Czechoslovakia

Elizabeth Wiskemann

Thomas Masaryk's parents were German-speaking working people of Slav descent; they lived in Austrian Moravia near Hungarian Slovakia from which they came. After some elementary schooling they managed to send their son to the German grammar school in Brno, and later he embarked upon a classical course at the University of Vienna. He was prodigiously intelligent and industrious, and uncompromisingly upright. He picked up Czech and Slovak at an early age, and soon read French, Russian, and English. His marriage in 1878 to Charlotte Garrigue, an American girl studying music in Leipzig, brought him closer to the English-speaking world. In 1879 he began to teach philosophy in the University of Vienna. Finally, after publishing a book on the sociology of suicide, in 1882 Masaryk was appointed to lecture in Prague, a city which he then scarcely knew, at the new Czech University. His first lecture there was on the philosopher Hume and his scepticism, a new subject for a Central European university. He introduced another novelty by inviting his students to his home and taking a helpful interest in their lives. At the same time he was soon directing two periodicals in addition to writing on philosophy, history, and politics.

His name first became known to a wide public in 1886 when he helped to expose as forgeries some Czech manuscripts claimed to derive from the early Middle Ages. As a Czech patriot he repudiated faked origins, but many Czechs denounced him as a traitor to his people. This controversy drew him into the racial quarrels of Austria-Hungary in those days. Masaryk advocated what he called a realist's approach and was followed as a realist by two leading young men, Kramář and Kaizl. The three of them were elected as members of the Young Czech Party to the Austrian Parliament or Reichsrat, in 1891. As a deputy Masaryk mostly spoke on educational matters, but he also expressed advanced views on universal suffrage for men and women, and on social reform. He was in fact too liberal for the Young Czechs, who were chauvinist, and in 1893 he resigned from the Reichsrat and also from the Bohemian Diet to which he had belonged.

In the following years, back at the University in Prague, Masaryk became a centre of attraction not only for the more liberally-minded Czech students, but also for Croats and Serbs who looked to him for advice over their own national problem, that of the Southern (or Yugo) Slavs. Serb and Croat students from Bosnia (occupied by Austria-Hungary since 1878) and Herzegovina were forbidden by the authorities there to visit the University of Prague, but some of them came to Masaryk's lectures. Masaryk, who felt himself to be a Slovak rather than a Czech, also in the 'nineties helped the Slovak nationalists to survive the oppressive rule of the Hungarians. Thus he became the leading intellectual of the Slavonic nationalities in Austria-Hungary. This was an important part of his preparation for the future. In the world of those days it was almost unprecedented that a man should rise from the lowest ranks of society to Masaryk's eminence.

Masaryk waged two typical battles for enlightenment in 1899 and 1906 respectively. In 1899 he, who had grown up in the anti-semitic atmosphere of provincial Austria in the 1860's, protested against the sentence to death of a Jew called Hilsner who was accused of a ritual murder: the sentence was commuted to penal servitude for life and was ended only by the amnesty of 1916. In 1906 Masaryk himself was charged with anti-religious offences, for he had 'accused Catholicism of being a degenerate religion which needs politics for its defence'. The case against him broke down and he was acquitted. Throughout both episodes he was ferociously attacked and showed unshaken courage.

In 1907 Masaryk was again elected to the Reichsrat, this time as a 'progressive realist'. A year later Austria-Hungary annexed Bosnia and Herzegovina (p. 214). This was a blow to South Slav aspirations, for it brought the direct subjection of many more Serbs and Croats to the Habsburg monarchy and seemed a step backwards in the evolution of the nationalities. Masaryk condemned this move out of hand; it had been greeted with enthusiasm by the Austrian Pan-Germans as a triumph for them. The annexation was followed by the arrest of fifty-three Croats as Pan-Serb agents; they were brought to trial at Zagreb in May 1909. Some of them were former students of Masaryk and he spoke in their favour in the Reichsrat. In the end no death sentences were pronounced and a case was brought later in the year in Vienna against Dr Friedjung. The latter was the author of an article in the *Neue Freie Presse* on 24th March 1909: this had accused the Zagreb defendants of conspiracy, quoting 'official' documents which Masaryk was able to prove had been forged.

Thus on the eve of the First World War Masaryk had challenged the chief vested interests in Austrian life, the chauvinist Germans and the Catholic Church. It is not surprising that even he, since the retrograde measure of the annexation of Bosnia, had developed bitter feelings against the Habsburg monarchy. Although he would have regarded any attempt to establish an independent Czechoslovakia as unrealistic before the war, he decided that the possibility of destroying Austria-Hungary must be used once war had broken out. The dynasty had failed to reconcile its nationalities, and it was clear to Masaryk that if the Central powers won the war the dominion of the Germans and Magyars over the Slavs and Rumanians was likely to be accentuated.

At the age of sixty-four Masaryk set out to plead the cause first and foremost of the Czechs and Slovaks, but also of the others, before the outside world. He went first to Switzerland, then to Paris and London, then, in May 1917, to Russia, and finally, in 1918, to the United States. In the cause of racial justice and human rights Thomas Masaryk became a propagandist and even a conspirator. His idea of propaganda was, however, unusual: 'not to abuse the Germans, not to underestimate the enemy, to distort nothing, and not to exaggerate; not to make empty promises and not to beg for favours; to let facts speak for themselves. . . .' His former pupil Edvard Beneš, was his representative

Thomas Masaryk with volunteers for the Czech force in the French army at the recruiting camp, Stamford, Connecticut, 1918

Fotoarchiv Vhu, Prague

in Paris. Unlike some of their countrymen, Masaryk and Beneš had always looked to the Western powers for leadership, rather than to Slavonic Russia; thus the Russian revolution did not disturb their plans, although it meant disentangling a Czech volunteer army from Russia. Both the Czech leaders were social reformers but not Marxists.

In December 1918 he returned to Prague where his supporters had taken over from the Austrian authorities. A democratic republic was founded with German, Magyar, and Ruthene citizens to whom the new Minorities Treaty and the Czechoslovak constitution guaranteed education and justice in their own languages. It should be noted that many of the new Czechoslovak officials were former Austrian ones and often administered the regulations in much the same way but in reverse.

JÓZEF PIŁSUDSKI *–the indomitable Pole*

Antony Polonsky

The First World War radically changed the nature of the 'Polish Question'. For the first time since 1815 all three powers which had effected the partition of Poland were at war, and it soon became clear that the struggle would be a long one. As the conflict dragged on, both sides looked to the Poles for support. The promises each made, in an attempt to outbid the other, raised again the issue of Polish national status.

The political orientations of the different Polish groupings had become crystallized in the decade preceding the outbreak of the war (see p. 46). Piłsudski and his followers had seen in the revolutionary crisis in Russia between 1904 and 1907 the opportunity they had longed for to launch a new insurrection to regain Poland's lost independence. Piłsudski even went to Japan in 1904, during the Russo-Japanese War, to seek support from the Japanese high command. During the revolution he assumed control of the almost completely autonomous 'Military Organization' of the Polish Socialist Party (PPS), and led a series of attacks on Russian government outposts which culminated in the seizure of the railway station at Bezdany, north of Wilno, in September 1908.

Piłsudski's devotion to terrorism and his belief in the precedence of national liberation over social revolution provoked considerable dissatisfaction within the PPS. By 1906 it had become obvious that his activities would not spark off a national revolt; in addition, the strength of the Russian revolutionary and socialist movements was contradicting his view that Russia was one uniformly reactionary mass. The discontent within the PPS came to a head at the party's 9th Congress in November 1906, when a large group seceded, creating the Polish Socialist Party –Left Wing. This group advocated close co-operation between the Polish and Russian revolutionary movements and held that the establishment of a constituent assembly in Warsaw would satisfy Polish national demands. Yet, even so modest a proposal was to prove a bar to co-operation with Rosa Luxemburg's Social Democracy, absolutely opposed to any notion of Polish national separateness.

Piłsudski himself was dissatisfied with the results of terrorism and became more and more convinced that only war between the partitioning powers, which by now seemed increasingly likely, could change Poland's position. But he saw that if Polish desires were to be given any consideration, a Polish military force, capable of playing an independent part in such a conflict, would have to be created. Already in June 1908 he had formed the League of Active Struggle to organize and train military units. Soon afterwards he moved to Galicia (Austrian Poland) where political conditions were least restrictive and where the Austrian government was not unsympathetic to his anti-Russian aims. His pre-war military activity reached its peak in November 1912, with the formation of the Provisional Committee of Confederated Parties Demanding Independence which united in support of a Polish independent military force almost all the Galician parties except the Conservatives (a grouping of large landowners) and the National Democrats. By the outbreak of the war, in spite of Piłsudski's disputes with the Committee and the internal divisions which plagued it, it could put nearly 7,000 Polish Legionaries in the field.

The National Democrats, under Dmowski, had bitterly opposed Piłsudski's attempts to initiate a national revolt in 1905, regarding them as a futile and dangerous echo of the activities of the 19th-century gentry revolutionaries. Dmowski even followed Piłsudski to Japan to dissuade the Japanese from giving him any assistance. In the elections for the First Duma in March and April 1906 the National Democrats won every seat in Russian Poland (the Congress Kingdom). But although they had some success in convincing both Russian public opinion and some officials that Polish aspirations were not necessarily hostile to the interests of the Russian state, their activity had little practical result. Nevertheless, by 1914 they had become the strongest political force both in the Congress Kingdom and in Prussian Poland, where a policy of germanization was being energetically pursued during this period. In Galicia they were less successful. Their pro-Russian orientation was unpopular, and politics here were still to a great extent dominated by the Galician Conservatives. This group, mainly upper class and landowning in its support, which had been instrumental in obtaining self-government for Galicia in the 1860's, advocated strong links with the Habsburgs. The most it demanded in national terms was the incorporation of the Congress Kingdom into Austria-Hungary. National Democratic strength grew in Galicia, particularly after the introduction of universal suffrage in 1907.

On the outbreak of war, Piłsudski attempted to foment a national uprising in Russian Poland. On 6th August 1914 he crossed the Austro-Russian border near Cracow with his troops, hoping in this way to gain a certain freedom in relation to the Central powers, whom he had not consulted before acting. His plans failed utterly. The Poles in the Congress Kingdom, for the most part sympathetic to the National Democrats and even to the Russian war effort, greeted his troops with a mixture of hostility and indifference. He was thus faced with the alternative of either disbanding his legions or co-operating with the General National Committee, a rival organization set up in Galicia by the pro-Austrian Conservatives at the beginning of the war. He decided on co-operation, and became still firmer in his resolve when the Central powers' successful offensive in the summer of 1915 led to the Russian evacuation of the Congress Kingdom. It is true that Piłsudski still had serious reservations about the Austrians (indeed, by August the Germans were tentatively suggesting to Austria that she eventually annex the Congress Kingdom) and that he tried to prevent the Central powers from recruiting Polish soldiers in Russian Poland, but he was probably sincere when he wrote to Władysław Jaworski, a leading Galician Conservative, in August 1915: '. . . the political aim of the War . . . was and is the incorporation of Galicia and the Congress Kingdom into the framework of the Austro-Hungarian Monarchy.'

Piłsudski remained true to the policy of turning to Austria until mid-1916, when the increasing weakness of Austria and the hostility of the Hungarians, the Germans, and the Austrian army to the Austro-Polish solution had become evident. Already in August 1916 Bethmann Hollweg, the German chancellor, had forced the Austrians to agree to the setting up of an 'independent' Polish state. Piłsudski now became convinced that a satisfactory resolution of the 'Polish Question' depended on an agreement with Germany. When the Germans established a rump Polish state on 5th November 1916, Piłsudski supported their action; however, he demanded the setting up of a civilian government before he would help in the creation of an army. When this condition was met in January 1917 by the formation of a Provisional Council of State, he went ahead. He realized very quickly, however, that the Germans were interested only in a puppet state, and he refused to take the oath of allegiance to the Reich which was demanded of the army, and counselled his supporters to follow his example. In July 1917 he was arrested and interned in Magdeburg for the duration of the war. After his arrest the Council of State, soon renamed the Regency Council, was controlled by groups in the Congress Kingdom similar in character to the Galician Conservatives.

Since the beginning of the war the point of view of the National Democrats had also undergone important changes. Already in 1912 a secret party conference with delegates from all three parts of Poland meeting in Cracow had decided that in the event of war the party would support the Entente powers. Thus in August 1914 the party accepted enthusiastically the Manifesto to the Poles issued by Grand Duke Nicholas, which promised the Poles national unification under the sceptre of the Romanovs. In November it formed a pro-Entente Polish National Committee to counteract the influence of the pro-Austrian General National Committee. The Polish National Committee strongly attacked the Piłsudski legions and formed Polish units, the so-called Gorczynski legions, to fight beside the Russian forces. Yet once again little was achieved, and the self-government promised to the Congress Kingdom had still not been granted when the Russians were forced to withdraw.

The situation changed somewhat after the February Revolution of 1917. The Provisional Government of Prince Lvov issued a manifesto on 30th March 1917 promising to set up a Polish state composed of the Congress Kingdom, Galicia, and Prussian Poland linked to Russia in a military union. However, it was clear that Russia was by now a less significant part of the Allied coalition, and in August 1917 the Polish National Committee moved to western Europe. It was first reconstituted in Lausanne, then adopted Paris as its headquarters, where it was headed by Dmowski himself. During 1918 the Allies committed themselves to the re-establishment of a Polish state and in November recognized the Polish National Committee as the future government.

Yet although the National Democrats had gained recognition abroad as the predominant Polish group, in Poland itself Piłsudski was in a strong position. His internment in Magdeburg allowed him to return to Poland in November 1918, following the collapse of the Central powers, with the aura of a martyr and the reputation of an indomitable fighter for independence, unsullied by compromises. When the Austrian occupying authority in the southern part of the Congress Kingdom collapsed, the PPS, the Galician Polish Socialist Party, and a number of radical peasant groups set up a People's Government in Lublin led by the veteran Galician Socialist, Ignacy Daszyński, which was intended to supplant the still existing Regency Council established by the Germans in Warsaw. However, when Pilsudski returned from Magdeburg, he was rather surprisingly recognized by the Regency Council as its legal successor. He also enjoyed the overwhelming support of the armed forces maintaining the Lublin government. As a result, Daszyński resigned, acquiescing in the formation of a new People's Government controlled by Piłsudski.

Piłsudski decided to try to come to terms with the National Democrats. He accepted the formation of a compromise government headed by Ignacy Paderewski and agreed that the delegation of the Polish National Committee, with some Piłsudski-ite additions, should represent Poland at Versailles. Nevertheless, the next few years were to show that the bitter antagonisms of the pre-war and wartime period could not be overcome so easily, and that the illusion of national unity created by the euphoria of independence had little substance.

Below: *Piłsudski leading the Polish Legion across the frontier between Austrian Poland and Russian Poland on 6th August 1914*

Snark/Photothèque Laffont

India, 1914-18/Christopher Falkus

India at War

Indians, spontaneously, and almost unanimously, embraced Great Britain's cause in the war. Nearly one million men fought on the Western Front, in East Africa, and in the Middle East and it was scarcely any wonder that they considered such efforts entitled them to higher status in the empire

The outbreak of the First World War found India in a state of political unrest. Growing dissatisfaction with her status as a dependency was expressed by increasing demands for self-government, an aspiration shared by both 'moderate' and 'extremist' members of the National Congress. This body, formerly little more than a glorified debating society for educated Indians, was rapidly becoming a focus of agitation as the British government persisted on an exasperating course. For no clear policy regarding India's future had been laid down, though some statesmen made matters worse with remarks like that of Lord Milner in 1908: 'The idea of extending what is described as colonial self-government to India which seems to have a fascination for some untutored minds, is a hopeless absurdity.' The Germans hoped for great things from Indian discontent, and in the years before the war tried to spread ideas of rebellion among the Indian people. There were many in Great Britain who shared the opinion of author William Archer that 'the moment Britain gets into trouble elsewhere, India, in her present temper, would burst into a blaze of rebellion'.

But in the event these fears proved groundless. Many Indians still prized the imperial connexion and some members of Great Britain's Liberal government showed themselves more tolerant of Indian hopes than imperialists like Milner, or the autocratic Curzon, who described them as 'fantastic and futile dreams'. Edwin Montagu, for example, later to become secretary of state for India, did not condemn the winds of change out of hand: 'A new generation, a new school of thought, fostered by our education and new European learning has grown up, and it asks "what are you going to do with us?" '

Encouraged by what they hoped was a growing sympathy for their aims, the Indians, spontaneously, and almost unanimously, embraced Great Britain's cause in the war. Offers of military and financial help poured in from all over the subcontinent both within and outside the territory of British India. The great Indian princes pledged their services and made massive financial donations. Nepal offered its resources; even the Dalai Lama in Tibet offered a thousand troops; while the Congress expressed enthusiastic support. Instead of having to reinforce India to combat sedition, Great Britain was able to denude India of almost all of her troops and equipment, while Indian forces were able to take their places on the battlefield before contingents from the dominions were trained and ready. In unfamiliar, bitterly cold conditions Indians reached the Western Front during the critical winter of 1914, symbolizing not only the wider imperial contributions which were to follow but also, in their own eyes, their right to be considered as free and equal members of a community fighting in a common cause. Altogether over 800,000 Indian soldiers fought on the Western Front, in East Africa, and in the Middle East. Their fatal casualties numbered 65,000, and their economy was brought to the verge of bankruptcy. It was scarcely any wonder that they considered such efforts entitled them to a higher status within the empire they were sacrificing so much to maintain.

Initial response in Great Britain was slightly incredulous. The public was both surprised and dazzled by the nature of India's effort and *The Times* wrote in 1914 that 'the Indian Empire has overwhelmed the British nation by the completeness and unanimity of its enthusiastic aid'. Nationalists in India were quick to emphasize what they expected in return. The famous theosophist Mrs Annie Besant, social worker, radical, and sometime Christian, atheist, and Hindu, said at the Congress in 1914 that India was 'not content to be any longer a child in the nursery of the Empire . . . She is showing the responsibility of the man in the Empire. Give her the freedom of the man in India'.

Perhaps British statesmen were at fault in allowing Indian expectations to rise too rapidly. Whatever the reason, a mood of uneasiness replaced the excitement of the early months. Educated Indians noted with concern that the imperial government could not be persuaded to define their long-term plans for India. Agitation increased when Mrs Besant and Mr Bal Gangadhar Tilak, the extremist leader, launched 'home rule' movements. Muslims in India were disconcerted by Turkey's entry on the side of the Central powers. Projected schemes for some kind of imperial parliament or council alarmed Indians who feared that their affairs would be controlled not only by Great Britain but by the white dominions. In view of the humiliating racialist policies pursued by South Africa and Australia this was not a pleasant prospect.

By 1917, though most Indians continued loyal to the empire, tension was rising as Great Britain remained silent on plans for Indian self-government. Moderates were struggling to restrain the militant policies of extremists. Sir Satyendra Sinha, the

Below: Blunt Indian recruiting technique. The accompanying exhortation read: 'This soldier is guarding India. He is guarding his home and his household. Thus we are guarding your home. You have to join the army.' Nearly a million men joined up, suffering 65,000 casualties, while India was brought to the verge of bankruptcy

Imperial War Museum

A woman offers flowers to British Indian troops marching through Paris, 14th July 1915

great moderate leader, had already appealed for 'a frank and full statement of the policy of the government as regards the future of India so that hope may come where despair holds sway and faith where doubt spreads its darkening shadow'. All the diverse elements in Indian society were slowly uniting at least in their insistence on a definition of British aims. The Hindu-dominated Congress signed a concordat with the Muslim League; the Maharajah of Bikaner approved of 'the legitimate aspirations of our brother Indians'; Mrs Besant continued her agitation to such an extent that the Indian government foolishly had her interned in June 1917. Demonstrations against this action threatened an ugly situation when, in July 1917, Edwin Montagu replaced Austen Chamberlain at the India Office. On 20th August he made a pronouncement which was of epoch-making importance for the whole empire. In the Commons, he defined his government's aim as 'the progressive realization of responsible government in India as an integral part of the British empire'.

Exactly what the British government was committed to, and by when, was unclear. But obviously some form of parliamentary government was foreshadowed.

It cannot be denied that by the time of this announcement a great deal of India's earlier enthusiasm for war had been allowed to evaporate. Nevertheless, despite her enormous sacrifices and frustrations, the war ended with Indian opinion on a rising tide of expectancy. War fever had been rekindled after the Russian collapse threatened to open a land route for German armies to march on India; Montagu's declaration, and his subsequent arrival to make an on-the-spot report, aroused new hopes; the principles of self-determination preached in Europe seemed applicable to India; even the future nationalist leader, Mahatma Gandhi, was opposed to the activities of Tilak and Mrs Besant. In July 1918 he wrote, in support of the war effort, 'seek ye first the recruiting office, and everything will be added unto you'.

But of course there were difficulties. The British government was, perhaps inevitably, expected to make her intangible promises a reality too quickly. Failure to grant self-government was rapidly to alienate Gandhi and begin a new era in non-violent agitation. The very impetus given to nationalist aspirations alarmed the Muslims who feared a Hindu-dominated administration. A more sombre mood rapidly took the place of earlier hopes, darkened by the Amritsar massacre and by the terrible epidemic of influenza which killed more Indians than had perished in more than four years of war. This mood was rarely to be absent from Indian politics in the inter-war period.

Chapter 23

Introduction by J.M.Roberts

'Business as usual', a slogan said to have been launched by Winston Churchill, was one the British used with pride in the early months of the war. They drew from it reassurance; things were going to go on much as before, with, perhaps, a little added excitement. But as the war unrolled, one settled institution after another was shaken to its foundations. Every side of the national life was gradually permeated by the business of war-making. In every country the story was the same. This slow but tremendous revolution is the subject of this Chapter.

Christopher Falkus's article on **The Dominions at War** shows how widespread in a purely geographical sense were these repercussions. It was at first sight extraordinary that the domestic politics of Australia and Canada should be disturbed by a quarrel over the way Habsburgs treated their Slav subjects. Yet this happened, because of the nature of the British empire at that time and the relations of the dominions to the mother country. It was full of significance for the future; the dominions were not to forget the cost to them of involvement in Great Britain's war.

The home fronts of the European combatants showed, even more quickly, startling changes in both economic and social life. Colin Cross's article on **The Meaning of Total War** outlines the most important changes in Great Britain, France, and Germany down to the end of 1916. After that time, with the intensifying of the war (of which the adoption of conscription by Great Britain may be taken as the supreme symbol) these changes were accelerated. In 1918 men would find themselves living in a world undreamed of in 1914. And this was even more true for women. In **Women at Work and War** Louise Black describes the war's lasting impact on one half of the human race.

When so many rapid and violent changes occurred in the external world of material culture and institutions, it was inevitable that culture and artistic life should also respond to them. The cultural history of the war is a vast theme. Here we can discuss only two of its many aspects. T.G.Rosenthal's article on **War and the Artist** describes the response of the visual and plastic arts to the war. **The War Poets** are the subject of an article by Michael Llewellyn-Smith.Perhaps because of the concentration of emotion which it can impose, poetry has claim to be, of all the arts, the one in which the Great War left behind most of enduring value. To English readers that legacy is easily available in the poems of Owen, Sassoon, Blunden, and Graves. To remind our readers of what is available in other languages, we have printed also a poem by Apollinaire.

Ulk/Tasiemka

German cartoon ridiculing British reliance upon Australia, as 'England's last hope'

Roger Viollet

A French family amuses itself in a cellar during a night air raid alert in Paris

Imperial War Museum

British girls humping coke. Behind every fighting soldier—three civilian workers

British War Poets

'The subject of it is War, and the pity of War,' wrote Wilfred Owen in his preface to the book of poems he was writing in the trenches. The British poets appointed themselves spokesmen for the generation who died in northern France, gassed, demoralized by shell shock, their lives thrown heedlessly away by ignorant patriotism. The following poems show the preoccupations of these poets of the trenches.

Anthem for Doomed Youth

What passing-bells for those who die as cattle?
  Only the monstrous anger of the guns.
  Only the stuttering rifles' rapid rattle
Can patter out their hasty orisons.
No mockeries for them; no prayers nor bells,
Nor any voice of mourning save the choirs—
The shrill, demented choirs of wailing shells;
And bugles calling for them from sad shires.

What candles may be held to speed them all?
  Not in the hands of boys, but in their eyes
Shall shine the holy glimmers of goodbyes.
  The pallor of girls' brows shall be their pall;
Their flowers the tenderness of patient minds
And each slow dusk a drawing-down of blinds.

Wilfred Owen
(By permission of Mr Harold Owen and Chatto & Windus Ltd)

The General

'Good morning, good morning' the general said,
When we met him last week on our way to the line.
Now the soldiers he smiled at are most of them dead,
And we're cursing his staff for incompetent swine.
'He's a cheery old card,' grunted Harry to Jack
As they slogged up to Arras with rifle and pack.

But he did for them both by his plan of attack.

Siegfried Sassoon
(By permission of the author)

Break of Day in the Trenches

The darkness crumbles away—
It is the same old druid Time as ever.
Only a live thing leaps my hand—
A queer sardonic rat—
As I pull the parapet's poppy
To stick behind my ear.
Droll rat, they would shoot you if they knew
Your cosmopolitan sympathies
(And God knows what antipathies).
Now you have touched this English hand
You will do the same to a German—
Soon, no doubt, if it be your pleasure
To cross the sleeping green between.
It seems you inwardly grin as you pass
Strong eyes, fine limbs, haughty athletes
Less chanced than you for life,
Bonds to the whims of murder,
Sprawled in the bowels of the earth,
The torn fields of France.
What do you see in our eyes
At the shrieking iron and flame
Hurled through still heavens?
What quaver—what heart aghast?
Poppies whose roots are in man's veins
Drop, and are ever dropping;
But mine in my ear is safe,
Just a little white with the dust.

Isaac Rosenberg
(By permission of the author's literary estate and Chatto & Windus Ltd)

1

BERNOT

Snark/René Dazy

2

Bibliothek für Zeitgeschichte, Stuttgart

Great Britain, France, and Germany, 1914-18/Colin Cross

The Meaning of Total War

'Keep the home fires burning' sang the British Tommies at the front in the first years of the war. But even at home the war had its effects. Ersatz coffee, coupons and war loans, paper money and censored newspapers were superficial signs of strain. Other changes were more profound. And over everything hung the shadow of the casualty lists, appearing with terrible monotony week after week

On 5th September 1917 Miss Barbara Adam, a twenty-year-old student at Cambridge University, married Captain Jack Wootton, aged twenty-six. According to the conventions of their era and class, neither was yet ready for marriage. It was simply because of the war that their families gave consent.

They had a twenty-four-hour honeymoon in the country and then a night at the Rubens Hotel, London, before Captain Wootton set off from Victoria Station to join his regiment at the front. Five weeks later, without his wife ever having seen him again, he died of wounds. The army sent his blood-stained kit to Mrs Wootton and she resumed her studies at Cambridge. She went on to make a considerable public career, ending as one of the first women to become a member of the House of Lords. She married again. Yet, describing her brief first marriage in her autobiography half a century later, she wrote that she still avoided any occasion for entering the Rubens Hotel.

In ordinary times, such a story would stand out as being especially tragic. But during the First World War it was routine; something of the kind happened to tens of thousands of couples. The most direct and most devastating result of the war was the wholesale killing of young men. Great Britain lost 680,000, France lost 1,300,000 and Germany lost 1,700,000. The point is not that the total numbers were particularly large—the warfare of the 1939-45 period accounted for many more deaths—but that the casualties were almost all of the same kind. It was as if some Pied Piper had travelled across Europe carrying off the young men.

There were so many widows and bereaved parents that, in Great Britain, a movement was started to make white the colour for mourning, lest the streets appear too gloomy. This did not catch on and the old mourning rituals were curtailed to a simple armband or dropped altogether. They never really returned. The Germans were rather more traditional. 'For weeks past the town [Berlin] seems to have been enveloped in an impenetrable veil of sadness, grey in grey, which no golden ray of sunlight seems to pierce, and which forms a fit setting for the white-faced, black-robed women who glide so sadly through the streets,' wrote Countess Evelyn Blücher, in her diary for 27th December 1915.

1 Parisians queuing for coal in the Place de L'Opéra, March 1917. While their menfolk died women queued for the necessities of life. 2 A Hyde Park investiture. Widows and next of kin seen waiting to receive posthumous awards. There were very few families who did not know personal grief. 3 Horatio Bottomley, 1915. Popular jingoistic orator. He made patriotism pay, earning some £27,000 as a private enterprise recruiter

It would be false, however, to suppose that the mood in the combatant countries was one entirely of gloom. By 1916 the expectation cherished at the beginning by both sides, that the war would be a short one, had faded. But each side, convinced that it was fighting in self-defence against an evil enemy, was confident of ultimate victory. The roistering energies which over the previous period had revolutionized the European way of life were now turned inwards, to destruction. The war was not so much the end of 19th-century Europe as its consequence.

Land of Hope and Glory

The deepest impact was upon Great Britain where the war acted as an accelerator and distorter of social changes which had already begun in the unstable Edwardian period.

The key decision, from which every other change derived, was the novel one of creating a mass British army on a scale comparable to the gigantic conscript forces on the mainland of Europe. That army was intended to end the war by overwhelming Germany on the Western Front. (Unfortunately neither its training nor its higher leadership matched the enthusiasm of its recruits.)

During the first two years of the war the whole resources of public propaganda were used to recruit the army. The country was saturated with patriotic appeals. 'Land of Hope and Glory' became a second national anthem. 'God Save the King' was introduced as a customary item in theatre and cinema performances, a custom which still survives. Kitchener's poster 'Your King and Country Need YOU', with its pointed finger, can still be counted as the most memorable piece of outdoor advertising ever designed. Every locality had its own recruiting committee. There were private-enterprise recruiters, notably the outrageous Horatio Bottomley. Some clergymen preached sermons urging young men to join the army. Music-hall stars ended performances with patriotic tableaux and appeals for recruits. Military bands paraded the streets and young men fell in behind them to march to the recruiting sergeant. 'We don't want to lose you, but we think you ought to go' became an important popular song. The basic pay was a shilling a day, and many recruits did their first drills in public parks, with civilian spectators proudly looking on.

It became embarrassing to be a male civilian of military age. An admiral in Folkestone started a movement organizing girls to present white feathers to young men they saw in the streets in civilian dress. In one case, it was said, a winner of the VC got one while on leave. Some women went a stage farther. The romantic novelist, Baroness Orczy, founded the 'Women of England's Active Service League', every member of which pledged herself to have nothing to do with any man eligible to join up who had not done so. She aimed at 100,000 members; she actually achieved 10,000, and sent the names of all of them to the King.

The flaw, which by 1916 had become glaringly apparent, was that an army on such a scale required enormous industrial support to equip and clothe it. At least three civilian workers were required for every fighting soldier. By 1915 the shortage of artillery shells had become a national scandal and even so elementary a thing as soldiers' boots was presenting problems. Thousands of skilled workers had followed the band into the army and they were hard to replace.

The government takes over

So, on a makeshift and temporary basis, began the characteristically 20th-century phenomenon of wholesale government direction of industry, Lloyd George as minister of munitions directing the initial stages. Until the war the condition of the economy had been considered hardly more the responsibility of the government than the weather. Even socialists had thought more about distributing wealth and resources than about managing them. Although after the war most of the controls were to be removed, the idea remained that the government was ultimately responsible for the economy.

To an increasing extent party politics and elections were to centre around economic questions. Unemployment between the wars was to become a political issue on a scale which would previously have been impossible. Recruitment propaganda also had some influence in this direction. It was hinted, without any precise explanation of how it was to come about, that the military defeat of Germany would raise British living standards. The soldiers who came back tended to look to the politicians to raise them.

The aim in 1915 and 1916 was to create a tri-partnership of government, trade

Ullstein

Soup kitchen for the people of Berlin, 1917

Musée de l'Armée, Brussels

Above: *Fashions rising to the occasion – a French reflection on German privations.*
Below: *Boiling bones for fats, Berlin 1917*

Ullstein

unions, and employers in which output, wages, and profits would be settled by negotiation instead of by the free play of the market. This had the incidental effect of increasing the size, status, and power of the unions. Instead of being pressure groups in the class war, they tended to become a recognized organ of the community, with rights and responsibilities to the whole nation as well as to their own members. Their membership rose dramatically, from 4,100,000 in 1914 to 6,500,000 in 1918; and when the soldiers returned it shot up to over 8,000,000. The effect was permanent (although numbers were to fall later) and it was one factor in the post-war displacement of the Liberal Party by the Labour Party.

By 1916 the war had become a way of life. The streets were curiously silent; the German bands and itinerant salesmen who in 1914 had enlivened them were now gone. There were short skirts and widows and multitudes of young men in uniform. For an army officer in uniform to have appeared in a tram or bus would in 1914 have been unknown; by 1916 it was commonplace for subalterns with their toothbrush moustaches to be handing their fares to girl conductors. Every issue of every newspaper carried lists of names of men who had been killed. Soldiers on leave sought to enjoy themselves before they died and nightclubs, previously furtive, almost unmentionable places, had become prominent features of the London scene. There were said to be 150 in Soho alone; in them the customers danced to the new jazz music which had just crossed the Atlantic. The older institution, the public house, had begun to decline; under emergency legislation the government had regulated the hours at which they could serve liquor and the phrase 'Time, gentlemen, please' had entered the language. The daytime thoughts of the nation were of the permanent battle which was being waged from trenches in France; sometimes in southern England the actual sound of the guns could be heard as a distant thunder.

Deadlock and disappointment

France and Germany, unlike Great Britain, had long prepared for the war in the sense that they had for generations run a system of universal military service and could, without improvisation, immediately mobilize a mass army. Neither, however, had reckoned on a long war. The German aim was a quick knock-out of France and then a switch of forces to the east to defeat the armies of archaic Tsarist Russia. The French, equally, had looked forward to dashing victories and the reconquest of the provinces of Alsace and Lorraine which they had lost to Germany forty-four years earlier. The outcome, a deadlock in France,

Musée de l'Armée, Brussels

Above: *German poster exhorting women to save hair for making machine belting.* ***Left:*** *Berliners exchange firewood for potato peelings, Berlin 1917*

Above: *Substitute for rubber. Sprung metal 'tyres' on a German car.* ***Left:*** *Parisians in a bread queue, 1917. Despite hardships there was bread for all.* ***Below:*** *German poster appeals for aluminium, copper, brass, nickel, tin*

Bibliothek für Zeitgeschichte, Stuttgart

was a disappointment to both sides.

The fighting on the Western Front was on French (and Belgian) soil, so that the French, unlike the Germans and the British, were on their home ground. Much of the industrial north-east of France was under German occupation. The result was that the French became less idealistic about the war than the British and Germans; they saw it as a plague rather than as an adventure. It was not until late 1917 that they found in Clemenceau an apt warlike leader. The French were drearily conscious of having been defeated in the initial battles of 1914, and by 1916 they feared that they were bleeding to death. The following year large segments of the French army were to mutiny in favour of a negotiated peace. German propaganda to the effect that Great Britain was willing to fight to the last Frenchman had its effect; the Germans actually subsidized the leading French left-wing paper, the *Bonnet Rouge*.

There was in France a special wartime drabness, save among the minority of industrial workers and their employers who made more money than ever before. In Paris the politicians quarrelled and at the front the soldiers died in thousands. Unlike the British and Germans, the French felt a widespread distrust of both politicians and generals, a distrust justified by some of the facts. There was no proper attempt at financial or industrial management. Since the richest industrial area was under German occupation, France had to rely upon imports from Great Britain, the United States, and Japan for the sinews of war and these were paid for by contracting debts. The internal debt also grew—in 1915 French revenue from taxes was actually lower than the ordinary peacetime level—and more and more paper money was printed. A crudely inefficient method was adopted by the government to finance munitions production. It lent capital, interest-free, to entrepreneurs; this, naturally, gave them enormous profits at the public expense. Few proper accounts were kept and by 1916 there was virtually no reliable information on the state of the public finances.

The mass French army consisted largely of peasants conscripted from their smallholdings and sent to the front. The women left behind continued to work the holdings, but the total food output, in peacetime sufficient to meet French needs, fell sharply. By 1916 sugar had become a luxury, there were two meatless days a week, and restaurants were restricted to serving three courses. According to historic practice, the government concentrated on controlling the supply and price of bread, and success in this was the civil population's great palliative; no matter what other hardships existed, there was bread for all. Other matters of price control and rationing were left to the departmental prefects, with the result that what supplies were available oscillated around France to the *départements* which momentarily allowed the highest prices. The Paris municipality incurred huge losses through trading in food; they were written off as 'insurance against public disorder'.

Paris in the early 20th century was at its peak as the international capital for the arts, culture, and the amenities of luxurious living. Every cultivated European and American regarded Paris as in some way his spiritual home. The war, if anything, increased this prestige. Although the street lights were extinguished and the city was on the edge of the war zone, Paris acquired extra glamour as an international city. By an odd compromise, the *Opéra* was allowed to stage performances on condition that the audiences did not wear evening dress.

The war struck deeply into French family and social life. The depreciation in money – by 1916 the cost of living had risen by forty per cent – was beginning to wreck the *rentier* class which, by tradition, had its savings in fixed interest bonds. Secure employment as a public official had, until 1914, been the most respectable thing to which a Frenchman could aspire. By 1916 the officials were losing their social prestige and being overtaken by businessmen, a process which was to continue.

French war-weariness, which was already apparent in 1916, seemed to sap the spirit of the nation. In the occupied sector the people were cowed by strict German administration; there was no attempt at a resistance movement. Although eventually France emerged as a nominal victor, and got back her lost provinces, there remained a loss of national confidence and a deep-rooted distrust of war. The seeds of the disaster of 1940 were being sown.

Ersatz *coffee and 'means-test' clothes*

In Germany in 1916 something still remained of the elation caused by the great victories of 1914. With the United States not yet in the war and the Russian empire obviously crumbling, it was reasonable for Germans to expect victory. The strategy was to be defensive in the west until forces could be brought from the Russian front to overwhelm the French and the British.

The main effect of the war on the national life was, apart from the enormous casualties, the shortages caused by the British blockade. Bread rationing had started as early as January 1915, and there was an agonizing dilemma, whether to use scarce nitrates to fertilize agricultural land or to make explosives. Generally the claims of

German appeal for acorns, chestnuts, 1917

Bibliothek für Zeitgeschichte, Stuttgart

the explosives got priority and so agricultural production, which in any case was insufficient for the nation's needs, declined. Further difficulty came because of bad weather – the winter of 1916-17 was known as the 'turnip winter' because early frosts had spoiled the potato harvest.

German ingenuity concentrated on producing substitute – '*ersatz*' – foods and some, although they sound dreadful, were quite palatable. It was possible to make an eatable cake from clover meal and chestnut flour. '*Ersatz*' coffee, made from roasted barley, rye, chicory, and figs, became a national drink. Schoolchildren were lectured on the need for thorough mastication to prevent the substitutes from harming their digestions.

The virtual dictator of the German economy was the Jewish industrialist, Walther Rathenau, a brilliant administrator brought in by the war office to organize supplies for the army. Step by step Rathenau brought the principal industries under government control and set up an elaborate bureaucracy to run them. As in Great Britain, this was public control without public ownership, but Rathenau's methods were more thorough than those of the British; government 'kommissars' participated in the actual management of companies, and the plan allotted everyone his place. In 1916 the Rathenau machine had reached the peak of its efficiency and the whole of Germany was organized for fighting the war.

To accompany Rathenau's economic planning there were elaborate rationing schemes, with everyone ticketed and docketed for what he was entitled to receive. Clothes were distributed in part on a 'means-test' system – a customer had to prove to an official that he needed a new suit.

The political effect of the war was still, in 1916, to reinforce confidence in the German imperial system. Germany consisted of twenty-five states, each with its ruling dynasty, the whole under the dominance of the largest state, Prussia, of which the Kaiser was King. It was an authoritarian and hierarchical system with a strong infusion of democracy – the imperial parliament was elected on universal manhood suffrage. (In Great Britain only fifty-eight per cent of adult males had the right to vote.) Although a strong Social Democrat opposition existed in parliament, the imperial and hierarchical system worked because the average German worker trusted his social superiors and was willing to vote for them.

Even the Social Democrat deputies had voted in favour of war credits. The military victories had engendered further confidence in the system and war weariness had hardly begun. Shortages, hardships, and even casualty lists were tolerable as the price of a certain German victory.

Of course the vast self-confidence of 1916 turned out to be a mistake. Within two years the Kaiser and the authorities under him were simply to vanish from German politics. German success and German power proved to have been a delusion. The psychological shock was to be enormous and lasting and it helped to cause the strange and national mood in which so eccentric a figure as Hitler was able to rise to power.

Debts and death

All the combatant countries financed the war by loans rather than by taxation. In Great Britain, for example, the highest wartime rate of income tax reached only 6s. in the pound. The theory was to lay the cost of the war upon the future generations it was being fought to protect. What it really meant was that, instead of being taxed outright, people subscribed to war loans and so received the right to an annual payment of interest.

After the war, France was to lessen the burden of debt by allowing the franc to depreciate in value. Germany got rid of it altogether in the great inflation of 1923. In Great Britain, however, where the value of money remained stable or even increased, the war debt was a continuing burden which contributed towards a sense of national ill-being and inability to afford costly projects, either for military defence or for the promotion of living standards.

But the greatest single effect of the war, clearly apparent in 1916, was the killing of young men. Public imaginations exaggerated the effect of the casualties far beyond statistical realities. In Great Britain and Germany, particularly, appeared a cult of youth which has continued ever since. There was impatience and even contempt for the past. Jeremy Bentham's plea that we should look to our ancestors, not for their wisdom, but for their follies became the fashionable mode of thought, and even half a century later it is still continuing.

Home fronts and society, 1914-18/Louise Black

Women at Work and War

'The ordinary male disbelief in our capacity cannot be argued away,' wrote a tired Englishwoman trying to persuade Russian officers to let her start up field hospitals in Rumania. 'It can only be worked away.' During the First World War munition girls and policewomen, Métro workers and bank clerks worked it away

The new Amazon—French war-time postcard. As their husbands, brothers, and sweethearts went off to die, the women came forward to 'do their bit' for their countries

'"That men must fight and women must weep" is an old story now being told again,' mourned *The Lady* in August 1914. Alongside patterns for that autumn's becoming tea-gown appeared instructions for making bandages. 'Old underwear can be cut up into good-sized handkerchiefs which are often so useful to the man in action. For instance he can wrap his handkerchief round a superficial wound and go on.'

It was a gentle note. The militant feminists reacted more positively. Mrs Pankhurst and her formidable daughter, Christabel, diverted their crusading energy to the war effort, and 'the Cause' was

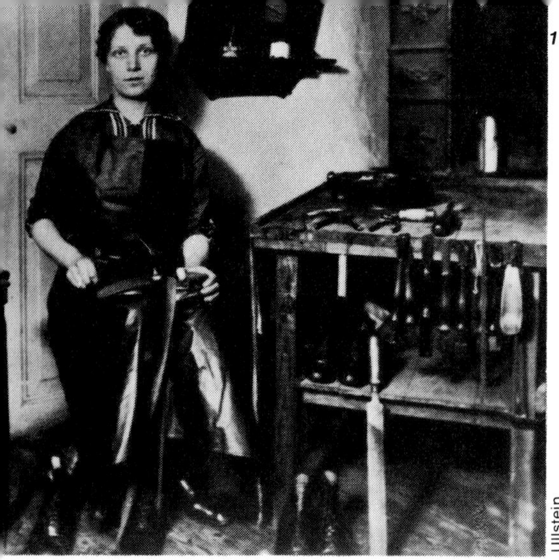

1

Ullstein

2

Imperial War Museum

3

Imperial War Museum

1 German lady shoemaker. Shortage of labour introduced many women to unaccustomed trades. 2 Workroom of a British war hospital supply depot, painted by J.B.Davis. 3 War working party, painted by J.B.Gibbs. Well-bred leisured ladies volunteered for hard work sewing comforts and uniforms, or serving in canteens. 4 Munition girls painted by E.F.Skinner

5

Roger Viollet

4

By gracious permission of H.M. The Queen

5 French tram driver. 6 'A Land Girl Ploughing' by Cecil Allen. On the Continent the peasants' wives took over in the fields. The British were startled by the land girls, who worked as hired farm hands. By the end of 1917 there were 260,000 women, part-time and full-time, in the Land Army. 7 Woman in the uniform of the City of London Red Cross ambulance column

6

Imperial War Museum

7

Imperial War Museum

In factories, hospitals, public services, women's work was winning the praise of society

almost overlooked in their impassioned appeals to British patriotism. Mrs Fawcett, the head of the National Union of Women's Suffrage Societies, approached the situation more sedately: 'Let us,' she said, prove ourselves worthy of citizenship whether our claim is recognized or not.' Many of the able and under-valued women who formed the backbone of the movement for women's rights saw the war as an opportunity to use their abilities to the full. Within a week the London branch of the NUWSS had converted itself into a women's employment agency in response to the thousands of women wanting to know where they could 'do their bit' for King and country. But as yet there was little for them to do, except gather 'comforts' for the wounded, and welcome Belgian refugees.

'The doctors is ladies'

The most obvious opening for women was in the hospitals. In August 1914 Mrs St Clair Stobart offered the services of the Women's Convoy Corps to the British Red Cross. They rejected her offer. In the same month Dr Elsie Inglis, founder of the Scottish Women's Suffrage Federation, suggested to the War Office that Scottish Women's Hospital Units should be formed for overseas service. Her offer was also refused. Nothing daunted, Mrs Stobart and Dr Inglis set to work and got together teams to go to Serbia. Dr Flora Murray and Dr Louisa Garret Anderson did not bother to go to the British authorities, but offered the services of an all-woman hospital to the French, who accepted with alacrity. By September a team of women doctors and nurses, most of them veteran suffragettes, was installed in the Hotel Claridge, Paris; the ladies' cloakroom had been converted into an operating theatre, and men suffering from sepsis, tetanus, and shock, were gazing up at the gilded halls and writing home that 'the doctors is ladies'.

In 1915 they were offered a hospital in London at Endell Street by the British authorities. A total of about 26,000 patients passed through the hospital before it was closed in 1919, and the high standards it maintained, and the excellence of its surgeons, in particular of Dr Anderson herself, excited the admiration not only of their grateful patients but also of the authorities themselves.

Dr Inglis and her all-woman team took part in the fight against the typhus epidemic in Serbia in 1915, and in the flight of the Serbian nation to the sea. As soon as she could she returned to help the Serbian units fighting with the Russians in Rumania. 'We do not see much of the glamour of war here,' she wrote. But her exploits showed a curious mixture of practicality and love of adventure, hard work and heroism. Few of the women who went to war had to cope with the problems Dr Inglis coped with (these varied from difficulties over transport, which not all her skilled lies could quite extort from the Russians, to the behaviour of Mrs X, a transport driver, who had taken to dressing like a man and flirting with the local Rumanian peasant girls). Few got as far from home as Russia. Few died of overwork. None received such a tribute – the Serbs dedicated a public fountain to the woman who had wanted every village to have clean drinking water, and whom some had come to venerate as a saint.

But for many of the women from the upper and middle classes who volunteered in their thousands for the Voluntary Aid Detachments and the other nursing services the war provided the same opportunity for useful action and patriotic adventure as it had for Dr Inglis.

For lower-class women the immediate effect of the war was unemployment. Large numbers of women had been employed in the cotton mills and cotton suffered a rapid slump. Many more were in luxury trades related to dress-making. In the hectic months of the autumn of 1914 the demand was for cartridge belts and khaki, not gloves and embroidery. In London women's employment dropped by ten and a half per cent in October.

In Germany the government had foreseen the problem, and enlisted the help of Dr Gertrude Baumer, the head of the *Bund Deutscher Frauenvereine,* one of the largest women's rights organizations in Germany. An order was issued organizing women district by district for 'the duration of the war', and making them responsible for providing cheap eating places, setting up nurseries, and helping the government to 'keep up an even supply of foodstuffs, and controlling the buying and selling of food'. Within the first month of the war the *Frauendienst* (as this wartime organization of women was called) had set up workrooms in all the larger cities to cope with the problem of unemployment. In the Berlin workrooms alone 23,000 women were employed within a week, sewing cartridge belts, bread sacks, and sheets for hospitals.

In Great Britain the only initiative to relieve the plight of unemployed women was taken by Queen Mary who hastily re-christened her Needlework Guild Queen Mary's Workshops. In the workshops women were employed at 3d an hour for a maximum of forty hours a week. Though this was condemned as 'sweated labour' (a weekly wage of 10s was intended to be less than that of regularly employed women, who supposedly earned 11s 6d a week) it was better than nothing.

By the summer of 1915 the situation had

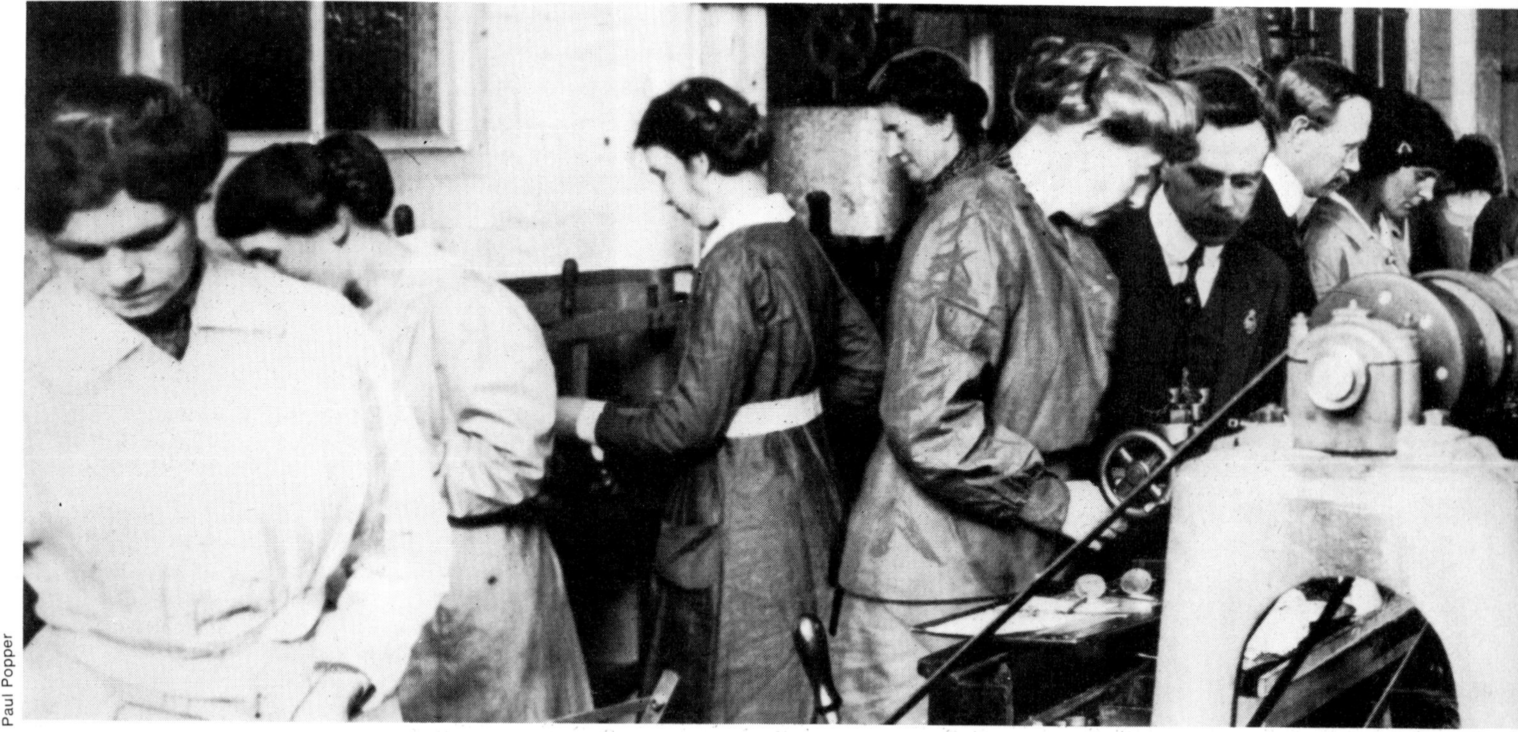
Paul Popper

changed completely. As the men went to the trenches to die in their thousands, the women had to take over. In France, Great Britain, and Germany the munitions factories demanded more and more workers. Women who had been unemployed moved in. Only in Great Britain does this appear to have caused hostility. The trade unions were sharply opposed to the threatened competition of unskilled and, in particular, female labour, which had always been cheaper than their own. At some factories the men refused to work with women, and in March 1915 the government had to promise that wage rates would be protected, and that women doing the same job as men would be paid the same piece rates. Furthermore, it was specifically stated that after the war the pre-war practices of industry would be restored. In July 1915 Lloyd George appealed for women to work in the munitions factories. The response seemed enormous. The increase of women in industry in Great Britain was in fact about 800,000, most of them employed in the munitions industry. Sixty per cent of those in the shell industry were women.

The skill and the patriotism of the women workers were praised rapturously in the British press. Women, it turned out, could work in the supposedly unfeminine world of the engineering industry as efficiently as men. Where manual dexterity was required they could work more efficiently. Where the work was too heavy or too complicated, it had been reorganized. In France the numbers of women employed in industry forced the introduction of mass-production techniques, in Great Britain they accelerated it.

The general attitude of the country was reflected in the instruction issued to the munitionettes in Woolwich Arsenal. 'A munition worker is as important as the soldier in the trenches and on her his life depends.' 'Output. Anyone who limits this is a traitor to sweethearts, husbands, and brothers fighting.' Under the pressure of patriotism and the war the munition girls were working twelve-hour shifts seven days a week. But since the making of shells was essential for the country, the government was at least careful of its workers. Women welfare supervisors were compulsory in the danger zones of the munitions factories, and recommended whenever large numbers of women were employed. They insisted on better cloakroom facilities, better rest rooms, ambulance rooms where accidents and illness could be treated immediately and better health regulations. There was constant supervision of those working with dangerous materials, and the food in the canteens was checked for its nutritional value. Many of the girls, despite their hard work, were healthier than they had been before.

The vast numbers of women workers, many of them working several miles from their homes, had to have somewhere to live. Sometimes whole new residential areas were built. Sometimes they lived in hostels. Nurseries also had to be found, and some of them were partly financed by the ministry of munitions. The nurseries became a recognized institution.

But it was not only in the munitions factories that women replaced men. They ran the Métro in Paris, the buses in London; they hammered plates on to ships in the Clyde, and worked in the shipbuilding plants of the German navy. They acted as electricians, plumbers, undertakers. Two of Lloyd George's secretaries were women and over 200,000 extra women were employed in government establishments. Over 1,300,000 more women were employed in Great Britain in July 1918 than in 1914, and it was estimated that 700,000 of these were directly replacing men.

In Great Britain women also became police and served in the forces. Volunteer policewomen discouraged 'provocative loitering', and indecent behaviour in cinemas, parks, pubs, and the darkened streets. By 1916 the Women's Police Service had been sought out by town authorities and the ministry of munitions, and was proving invaluable in controlling crowds during air raids and helping checking that munition girls obeyed the safety regulations.

The first of the women's forces, the Women's Army Auxiliary Corps, was organized in 1917 to replace fit men doing jobs in what was called the line of communications. Although some drove ambulances, most were employed in the kitchens, the offices, and as gardeners in the cemeteries. They wore smart khaki uniforms, with peaked caps and skirts a daring twelve inches off the ground, slept in dormitories, and were submitted to drill and discipline by their officers. By the end of the war about 57,000 had enrolled. About 3,000 women served in the Women's Royal Naval Service and about 32,000 in the Women's Royal Air Force.

Women's battalions were also formed in Russia in early 1917. They were on guard in the Winter Palace the night the Provisional Government surrendered to the Bolsheviks.

The 'restless feeling'

When the war was over most of the women went quietly or reluctantly back to their original jobs, or to their homes. The figures for women employed in 1921 were no larger than those in 1914. Women had not won the right to equal pay or equal opportunity.

Despite the agreement that men and women should be paid equally for piece work, women had still usually been paid less than men. In the National Shell Factories women earned up to £2 4s. 6d. a week, men up to £4 6s. 6d. Women had usually worked under the supervision of men. Although women had occasionally been promoted, where they were available, men were automatically preferred. Few women had managed to get any lengthy training. The NUWSS had established a training school for oxy-acetylene welders, and by December 1917 there were twice as many women as men in forty government-run training schools for engineering work. But these were exceptions. Women had remained a source of comparatively unskilled and temporary labour.

A new feminine occupation—women training for work in the engineering industry

Similarly 400,000 women had left domestic service during the war, but in the mass unemployment for women that followed the return of the troops, most probably returned to their old jobs. There were no fewer servants after the war than before it. But, as one of the bus conductresses, who were mainly recruited from the better class of domestic servants, put it: 'The Company has promised all the men who are fighting that their places shall be kept open and we would not have it otherwise . . . but it's going to be a big problem. You see . . . we have all got a contagious restless feeling.'

The contagious restless feeling, the desire for the new way of life they had experienced was not easily buried. Though prices in Great Britain had doubled, many working-class women had been earning up to four times as much as they had earned before the war. Their children were better clothed, better fed, and in better health.

Even more important than the money was their increase in self-respect. The *New Statesman* commented 'they appear more alert, more critical of the conditions under which they work, more ready to make a stand against injustice than their pre-war selves or their prototypes'.

This was reflected in the increasing figures of trade union membership. The National Federation of Women Workers increased its membership to 50,000, but the total number of women in trade unions increased from 350,000 before the war to nearly 600,000 by the end of 1917. On the whole women tended to join the mixed general unions rather than the NFWW, and their admission into most unions (though not all) gradually made separate trade unions for women seem redundant. In France there was the same general tendency. Trade union activity among women increased, more women became prominent trade unionists, and the need for separate trade unions for women lessened.

In some ways the upper classes had gained even more. The nurses, the VAD's, and the WAAC officers, had been liberated from their restricted and over-protected lives. Any idea that it was unladylike to work was dissipated in the wave of patriotic fervour, and 'those peaceful days in the Midlands when one had lived for one's amusement and to kill time seemed to date back to one's infancy. The war turned one topsy-turvy, altered one's whole outlook on life. I felt I could never be "pre-war" again. None of us ought ever to have been like that'. Some went nursing only for a good time or to get their names into society papers. 'Miss Flapperton' was a recognized figure. But many led a tougher life than they had ever known. They left the shelter of the parental wings, and self reliance had to take the place of protection. There was much greater freedom between the sexes. During the war men and women were 'so thrown into daily contact with each other that conventional notions of a certain reserve as between the sexes have been very largely modified'. Chaperones disappeared, and so did the delicate ignorance in which upper-class girls were kept.

The outward signs of their freedom were flaunted gaily. Many used language that would have shocked their mothers; many started to wear cosmetics, smoking became widespread, and women bought drinks in public houses. Before the war short skirts and brassières had come in. During the war they completely ousted long dresses and camisoles. Well-meaning committees tried to discourage Land Girls, who, like most women doing heavy work or working outside, wore trousers, from wearing them off duty, but without success.

In defiance of the ever-present casualty figures, England was gripped by a feverish gaiety. 'Give the boys on leave a good time' was the universal sentiment. As one woman remembered it: 'If these young women who, as they read the casualty lists, felt fear in their hearts, did not seize experience at once, they knew that for many of them it would elude them for ever. Sex became both precious and unimportant: precious as a desired personal experience; unimportant as something without implications.' Young girls were gripped by 'khaki fever' and hovered round army camps. By the end of the war the illegitimacy rate had increased by thirty per cent. The marriage rate also increased sharply. Many marriages swiftly contracted, swiftly broke up. There were three times as many divorces in 1920 as in 1910.

The vote

Women's participation in the war effort had definitely shaken society. 'It would have been utterly impossible for us to have waged a successful war,' said Lloyd George, 'had it not been for the skill and ardour, enthusiasm and industry which the women of this country have thrown into the war.' In both Germany and France women talked more hopefully of getting the vote. In Great Britain they got it. The voting laws had to be changed to enfranchise the soldiers who were either not entitled to vote at all under the old system, or who had disfranchised themselves by moving from their homes to distant factories or the front. Women were enfranchised at the same time, though an age limit of thirty was imposed so that they would not become a majority of the electorate as they were of the population.

'Topping about your bill,' said the younger nurses to the veteran suffragettes at the Endell Street Hospital. The old valour for 'the Cause' had gone. To the short-skirted, self-reliant, uninhibited war girls of 1918 the romantic hysteria of the Pankhursts' championship of pure victimized women was as irrelevant as *The Lady's* advice on handkerchiefs. 'The ordinary male disbelief in our capacity,' Elsie Inglis had written from Rumania, 'cannot be argued away. It can only be worked away.' It had been. Women had been acknowledged as equal citizens. But most of all, women's understanding of what they were, and what they would like to be, had radically changed.

The Arts, 1914-18/T.G.Rosenthal

War and the Artist

The horrors and futility of the war provided artists with new and terrible subject matter. Different lessons, increasingly bitter and disillusioned, could be drawn from it

National Gallery of Canada *(Detail)*

The First World War, as everyone knows, was the 'war to end wars', and because of this somewhat feeble built-in excuse allowed itself to become, in human terms, one of the biggest wars in history. Out of such a self-styled definitive war, one would expect, some kind of definitive artistic statement. But, alas, just as the war itself was not the last word, nor was the art it produced. The moral is, of course, all too obvious; to make great art you need not great wars but great artists. The Peninsular War in Spain was a mild skirmish compared to Flanders Field, but it had Goya to chronicle it and etch into our memories images of war, such as the firing squad scene in *The Third of May,* which make the 20th-century equivalent seem feeble by comparison.

Only once in this century have we had an artistic statement of comparable force and then again it came from a Catalan, Pablo Picasso. But, perhaps significantly, *Guernica,* the delineation of the destruction by German bombers of the ancient capital of the Basques, was a part of the Spanish Civil War. It was a direct and specific protest against one direct and specific event that could burn itself into the mind of a great creative artist in a way that no part of that huge sprawling shambles which was the First World War ever could. In many ways the First World War was so ungraspable and so amorphous that it took the writers to do it full justice because they could more readily distil its essence into words than the painters could into visual images.

Yet, if there is no portrait of a soldier from the First World War to match Leonardo's drawing of a *Condottiere* and if there is no evocation of the undoubted physical excitement of war to compare with Uccello's *The Battle of San Romano,* the First World War did, nevertheless, yield a very large number of works of art which deserve to be remembered as much for themselves as for their subject matter.

There are basically two kinds of war art; the purely 'artistic' done with no motives other than to create good art and, perhaps, simultaneously preach an appropriate message and the 'official' art which sets out to record for governments, for regiments, or for posterity, particular military engagements or groups of people and which also sets out, often too frequently, to propagandize at the same time.

A typical piece of official art is Sir William Orpen's massive group portrait *A Peace Conference at the Quai d'Orsay.* This is routine, somewhat dull academic work containing conventional portraits of the victorious world leaders, Clemenceau, Lloyd George, and Woodrow Wilson. Neither this picture, nor its companion piece by the same artist, *The Signing of Peace in the Hall of Mirrors, Versailles, June 28th 1919,* can be called, in any acceptable sense of the word, art. Yet both pictures record factually what those momentously bungled scenes must have looked like to the detached observer; what they fail to do is re-create the heady, pompous, and self-satisfied atmosphere, and the exquisitely subtle hypocrisy which dominated the aftermath of the war.

Similarly there is no artistic joy to be had in looking at the serried and immaculately dressed ranks of official portraits of admirals and generals that one finds in war museums and portrait galleries the world over. Almost invariably the portraitist takes the easy way out and paints, often with much bravura, the uniform and the decorations and surmounts them with the best looking head he can produce in the circumstances. This, and the Great War produced an inordinate quantity of this kind of portraiture, is patriotism, glorification of the military leader, and anything else one cares to call it; but it is not art. Only rarely did the official or semi-official portrait produce anything of genuine intrinsic artistic quality. Oddly enough it was some of the lesser known theatres of war whose artistic by-products were the most interesting.

The desert war, for instance, produced a number of fascinating portraits, either during its progress or in retrospect. One of the most painted characters was T.E. Lawrence, Lawrence of Arabia (p. 590), and there are numerous studies of him, notably Eric Kennington's romanticized head and shoulders bust and Augustus John's much more ambiguous and enigmatic oil painting of the quasi-mystical, quasi-charlatan, desert leader in full Arab dress. The same campaign gave rise to Sydney Carline's painting of Turkish troops being bombed at Wadi Fara and to the bust of Feisal by Meštrović. Ivan Meštrović, who was Serbia's leading sculptor and probably that country's only 20th-century artist of European stature, also did a moving bust of Elsie Inglis. This bust is a memorial to a heroic woman who organized ambulance and other medical services on the ▷632

Left: *'The First German Gas Attack at Ypres' by William Roberts.* ***Opposite page:*** *Perhaps the most important single English war painting—'Merry-go-round' by Mark Gertler, painted after the Somme, 1916. D.H.Lawrence described it as 'a terrifying coloured flame of decomposition'*

1 ▷
Collection Richard Zeisler, New York (Detail)

1 'The Armoured Train' by Severini, a Futurist who was fascinated by speed, the machine, and by violence. Here he is excited by the force of the train, the shapes of weapons. 2 'La Mitrailleuse'—French machine-gunners painted by an Englishman, C.R.W.Nevinson

5 ▽

▷2
Imperial War Museum

Tate Gallery, London

National Gallery of Canada △ 3

National Gallery of Canada *(Detail)* ▽ 4

3 'Sappers at work: a Canadian Tunnelling Company' by David Bomberg. 4 'Some Day the People Will Return' by F.H.Varley, a battlefield not of glory but a waste of uprooted tombstones. 5 'A Battery Shelled' by Wyndham Lewis. This most important war painting shows a strong influence of Cubism

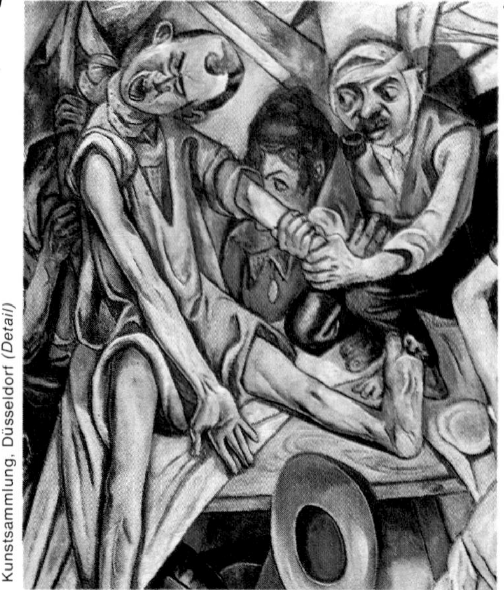

1 'We are making a New World' by Paul Nash—an ironic title for a picture of the devastation war had brought to the old world. 2 'The Night' by the German Expressionist, Max Beckmann. The war had imprinted on his mind images of killing and the wounded

Serbian, Rumanian, and Russian fronts, and died in 1917 after leading a unit across Russia. It is, in a sense, official art but it is executed by a powerful and mature sculptor, and is thus infinitely more effective than the academic sculpture spawned by the war and its millions of casualties.

Sculpture has always presented particular problems for the 'official' artist since, at least until the 1920's, sculpture was traditionally a more rigid and disciplined art form than painting and, consequently, fewer liberties could be taken. Good war sculpture is therefore extremely rare and, all too often, one is restricted to life-size, or larger-than-life-size, models of artillery or machine-guns as memorials to the fallen. One of the few sculptors who managed to do work which was not wholly traditional was the American-born Jacob Epstein. His portrait of Admiral of the Fleet Lord Fisher is a distinguished piece of portrait sculpture by any standards and succeeds in bringing out the formidable intelligence and personality of the architect of the modern British navy in the first quarter of this century. Another Epstein bronze, *The American Soldier,* displays the classic difficulty of the military form, since even Epstein can do nothing with the unyielding shape of the steel helmet, but when one gets below the helmet one sees the vigour of the sculptured face.

The official art of the Great War obviously had its limitations, and the most interesting art engendered by the war is that born of genuine conviction rather than a government commission. Thus, in France, for example, most of the best artists seemed to spend their war fighting rather than painting, and much of France's war art is therefore official and bad. A perfect example is *The Restoration of Alsace-Lorraine to France* a lithograph by Maurice Greiffenhagen. This is simply crude, bombastic propaganda showing two shawled girls, fetters sundered, clasping the noble, sword-carrying and buxom figure of the eternal Marianne. Other artists, however, contributed rather more although Picasso did surprisingly little. It is hard to think of any Picasso work directly connected with the First World War apart from his delightful 1916 drawing of the artist and poet Guillaume Apollinaire in uniform and with his head-wound bandaged.

But Braque, with Picasso the co-founder of Cubism, and one of the artists who fought in the war is quoted as saying, 'I was very happy when, in 1914, I realized that the army had used the principles of my Cubist paintings for camouflage.' One can see why Braque thought as he did, since the pre-war Cubist pictures painted by him and Picasso were, in their colouring and their fragmentation, not at all unlike camouflage netting and sheeting, being predominantly brown, green, and grey. That, apparently, was a case of art affecting war. For Fernand Léger it was the other way round. Léger fought in the French Engineers Corps and both his service in the army and his contact with the machinery of war had a profound influence on his post-war artistic development. Douglas Cooper, in his book on Léger, has quoted him as saying that: 'I was dazzled by the breach of a 75-millimetre gun which was standing uncovered in the sunlight: the magic of white light on metal. This was enough to make me forget the abstract art of 1912-1913.' It is difficult to say how much Léger's work after 1918 owes to the war and how much simply to the paraphernalia of the mechanistic age in which he lived. Clearly, however, he became obsessed with the harsh shapes of industrial products and the most often repeated images in his work are those of cylinders, pistons, and rods which belong to the battlefield almost as much as they belong to the factory. A typical example is his work of 1916 entitled *Soldier with Pipe.*

A French painter who recollected the war in retrospect was Georges Rouault. In his remarkable series of etchings entitled *Miserere* and *Guerre,* Rouault included one or two subjects which recalled the war with dreadful poignancy, most notably in *Mon Doux Pays, où êtes-vous?* (My sweet homeland, what has become of you?). This grim, brooding picture epitomizes the destruction of France, with its shattered buildings still burning and its gaunt soldiers lying listlessly in the foreground, wounded, bewildered, and apathetic. Another French artist who recalled the horrors of the Great War was Georges Leroux who, in *L'Enfer* (Hell), re-creates the inferno of battle with broken and uprooted trees, fire and explosions, mud-filled shell-holes and twisted corpses. In many ways this painting is typical of the art of the Great War in that it records the horrors without too much questioning. It was the English war artists, as we shall see later, who raised the largest doubts about this whole disastrous period.

One of the paradoxes of the time was the artistic role of the Germans. Strangely enough this ultra militaristic nation produced hardly any war art of any distinction, despite the fact that the period from about 1914 to 1933 was one of the most exciting in the whole history of German painting. Significant German artists like Lovis Corinth and Max Liebermann did some etchings for the German Red Cross and there is a good etching by Otto Dix called *Lens Bombed* which is a classic piece of Expressionist drawing, filled with terror and foreboding. But there are relatively few paintings of any distinction which deal with the war. One of the few exceptions is, in fact, only loosely connected: Max Beckmann's *The Night.* Beckmann fought in the war and was invalided out, after a spell in hospital, and the memory of the maimed and wounded was, for him, an indelible one. *The Night* is a nightmarish composition. The images of torture, wounding, and killing are clearly inspired partly by his dread of the Second World War, whose seeds he already saw in the late 1920's, and partly by his haunting remembrance of the First.

In Italy there were a number of artists who wanted Italy to come to the aid of France. These included in particular, men like Marinetti and Carrà, who were the pioneers and theorists of Futurism, a short-lived art movement which came to an end early in the war. A leading member of the Futurist group was Gino Severini, who has contributed two notable paintings to the art associated with the First World War. In *Guns in Action* he has managed to combine a visually exciting picture with a witty composition, using actual artillery

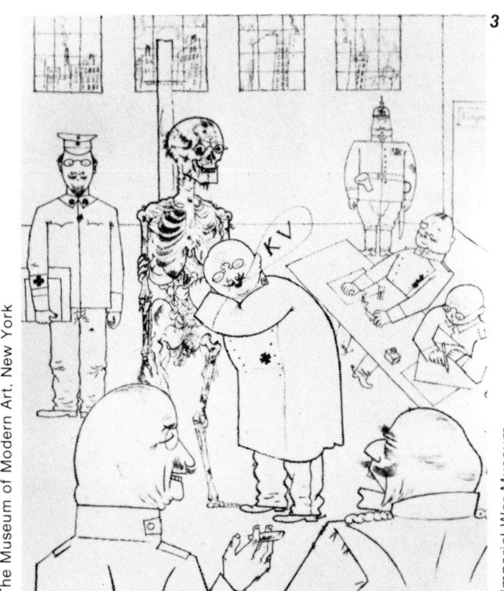

The Museum of Modern Art, New York

Imperial War Museum

Imperial War Museum

3 'Fit for Active Service' says the doctor of the skeleton. German cartoon by George Grosz. 4 Admiral Fisher—sculpture by Jacob Epstein. 5 Official art, factually correct, but not evocative: William Orpen's 'The Signing of Peace in the Hall of Mirrors, Versailles, June 28th 1919'

phrases and humorous corruptions of those terms. His other major war picture, *The Armoured Train,* is much more straightforward, and juxtaposes the force of the train, the shapes of the weapons and the typical, explosive fragmentation of Futurism to make an image of great excitement and power. The metaphysical painter Giorgio de Chirico also made his contribution, in the form of a splendid version of *Hector*. This work, done in 1916, could well be interpreted as an ironic call to arms. The martial figure of Hector is shown sightless, faceless and, presumably, brainless, consisting only of his metal armour and, instead of having a proud military bearing, standing slumped forward, needing the support of struts. Apart from being an archetypal de Chirico, *Hector* is also a telling image of war.

Understandably, because of her relatively late entry into the war, the United States' contribution to the visual arts of the First World War is not a very substantial one. The most important American artist of the period was the society painter John Singer Sargent who painted a huge canvas during his visit to the front in 1918 called *Gassed.* It shows the Dressing Station at Le Bac-de-Sud on the Doullens-Arras Road and measures 7 ft 6 ins by 20 ins. Painted in predominantly subdued, gas-like colours of mustard, brown, and green it is an ambitious picture in which files of wounded, blinded, and bandaged men, clinging to each other, walk through groups of similarly afflicted soldiers lying on the ground on either side of the road. It is a brave effort at a major work of art but it fails because the grandness of scale is not matched by any equivalent grandeur of either design or emotion. Yet it is, for all that, an honest attempt to record the disasters of war and, in a sense, a tribute to the pull of the war itself that this sophisticate, who became rich from painting the beautiful and the famous on both sides of the Atlantic, should endure the discomfort of the war to paint what he did.

The Canadians, who came into the war much earlier, made a quite remarkable contribution to the art of the period, chiefly because they had two outstandingly talented artists in F.H.Varley, a direct descendant of the English painter John Varley, and Wyndham Lewis. Lewis, the founder of Vorticism, the founder-editor of *Blast,* iconoclastic novelist and brilliant draftsman, painted some quite remarkable war scenes. His *A Battery Shelled* of 1918 is probably one of the most important pictures to come out of the First World War. It shows the influence of Cubism and does not yet show the distinctive characteristics of the Vorticism that was to come later. It is remarkable for the division between the calm of the observers on the left and the chaos of the running men on the right, and for the stylization of the figures, the guns and the buildings, apparently fragmented, but actually integrated. Varley's major painting is *Some Day the People will Return.* This monumental battlefield picture is a kind of visual counterpart to the second act of Sean O'Casey's anti-war play *The Silver Tassie.* It actually bears a strange relationship to O'Casey's stage directions: 'a scene of jagged and lacerated ruins . . . spiky stumps of trees which were once a small wood. Every feature of the scene seems a little distorted from its original appearance'. The irony of Varley's title is hammered home by the fact that a large part of his shattered landscape is a graveyard erupting with fragmented and grotesquely leaning tombstones.

Perhaps the most remarkable contribution to the art of the First World War is that of the British artists, not least because British art is, with a few obvious exceptions, less highly developed than in the European countries. Yet, for some reason, that old cliché about war bringing out the best in people applies more to British painters than to anyone else. C.R.W.Nevinson, for example, is a relatively unimportant English painter, but the war enabled him to paint a handful of pictures which entitle him to a respectful backward glance from his successors. His *La Mitrailleuse* (The Machine Gun) is a marvellous evocation of men in battle and *La Patrie* (The Fatherland) is probably his major work.

Paul Nash is another painter who did his best work during the First World War, as one can see from his deeply ironical *We are Making a New World* in which he almost brutally displays the destroyed old world which is the legacy of the war to end wars. Nash and Nevinson excelled in the depiction of the desolate, non-active aspects of war. David Bomberg, on the other hand, brilliantly caught the frenetic quality of hurried military activity in *Sappers at Work: a Canadian Tunnelling Company* and William Roberts has exactly caught the moment of horrified confusion in *The First German Gas Attack at Ypres.*

In some ways the most important single English war painting of this period is Mark Gertler's symbolic *Merry-go-round* in which a group of military and civilian figures are hopelessly caught on the vicious circle of the roundabout which goes on crazily turning for ever. Gertler painted this picture in 1916 after the tragedy of the Somme. When D.H.Lawrence saw it he wrote to Gertler that it was 'a terrible and dreadful picture . . . a terrifying coloured flame of decomposition'. *Merry-go-round,* with its robot-like figures, mindlessly revolving and going nowhere, is a coherent and protesting voice crying out against the wickedness of war. It is the voice of the non-participant shouting at those too stupid to see the needless waste.

The war pictures of Stanley Spencer are altogether different. His moving series of paintings in Burghclere Chapel is a series of semi-visionary and visionary recollections of his own military service as a hospital orderly, first in England and then in Macedonia, and then, for a brief period, as an infantryman, also in Macedonia. For him the military life is a strange mixture of floor scrubbing and of soldiers being resurrected after dying in battle.

All these painters, in their widely differing ways, have set down the few glories and the many horrors of the Great War which, whatever else it may have failed to achieve, did produce some very interesting art. But perhaps the last word should be left to that Swiftian caricaturist George Grosz who served in the German army during the First World War. In his cartoon *Fit for Active Service* a half-witted doctor is pronouncing a skeleton fit for military duty.

Political, 1914-18 / Christopher Falkus

The Dominions at War

Although the fate of the war would have to be decided in Europe, this was bound to be a world war. This survey shows how the war affected the dominions of the British empire: Australia, New Zealand, Canada, and South Africa

Australians wave an enthusiastic farewell to troops leaving Melbourne to help preserve the 'security of the Empire'. They were to win for Australia a sense of national identity and national pride

The Great War was a world war from the moment of Great Britain's entry on 4th August 1914. For she declared war not only on behalf of the 45,000,000 inhabitants of the British Isles, but also of the 400,000,000 members of a far-flung empire which was near the zenith of its extent and self-confidence. Within that empire the self-governing dominions could, if they chose, decline active support. But none did choose, and soon troops were on their way from remote corners of the world to battlefields many thousands of miles from home. Canadians, Australians, New Zealanders, and South Africans, representing the dominions, took their places in the trenches beside their European allies, as did the Sikhs, Gurkhas, Mussalmans and many more from the Indian sub-continent (p. 615).

The participation of the British empire involved all the non-European continents in the war, and in time the entry of Japan and the United States would transform it into a global conflict on a grand scale. Inevitably such a war brought a whole series of problems. In countries far from the

Western Front it was sometimes difficult to promote that sense of urgency needed for supreme effort. The vagaries of colonization had left some countries, like South Africa and Canada, with ethnic divisions which threatened grave crises under the stresses of war. In India growing nationalism foreshadowed a transformation in the character of the empire, while for all 'emerging' nations the question was raised of the part they were to play in the post-war world.

This article will deal with the effect of war on the political developments and ambitions of the dominions of the British empire which, geographically, were among the numerous countries on the perimeter of the conflict. A full list of participants—active and passive—would include not only the dominions and colonies of Great Britain but also the colonies of other European powers as well as numerous South and Central American countries who declared war in the wake of the United States. These were Cuba, Panama, Brazil, Guatemala, Nicaragua, Costa Rica, Haiti, and Honduras, while Siam, Liberia, and China also declared war on the Central powers. The contributions of the dominions considered here, while statistically smaller than those of the leading nations, were nevertheless of great significance, and emphasize the merging of European history into that of a widening world.

Australia

More than most other countries of the empire, Australia was able to boast that she entered the war a united people. The majority of her 5,000,000 inhabitants were bound by strong ties of race and sentiment to the mother country, and the major political parties vied with each other in expressions of support for Great Britain's policy. Joseph Cook, the Liberal leader, said: 'Whatever happens, Australia is part of the Empire right to the full. When the Empire is at war, so is Australia at war. All our resources are in the Empire and for the preservation and security of the Empire.' His Labour opponent, Andrew Fisher, declared that 'should the worst happen, after everything has been done that honour will permit, Australia will stand behind the mother country to help and defend her to our last man and our last shilling'. Such statements echoed the country's eager, even exuberant, mood. The governor-general cabled that there was 'indescribable enthusiasm and entire unanimity throughout Australia in support of all that tends to provide for the security of the Empire in war'.

The outbreak of war coincided with an election which resulted in a decisive Labour victory. Fisher was thus called upon to preside over the early stages of a war effort which involved measures quite out of keeping with Australian experiences and traditions. Sweeping powers over aliens, settlers of enemy origin or recent ancestry, censorship of the press, and control of publications were acquired by such measures as the War Precautions Act which gave the government authority to impose virtually a military regime. Inevitably the exercise of such authority in a country proud of its democratic way of life caused problems. Overzealous censorship, for example, caused friction between the government and press, while at times the rights of states seemed threatened by the powers of the federal government. When the Queensland premier, T.J.Ryan, spoke against conscription the federal government forbade publication of the speech and seized numerous copies. Ryan thereupon initiated action against the government for alleged violation of the rights of his sovereign state and found himself summoned before a Brisbane police court on charges of having prejudiced the public interest. The charges and counter-charges were allowed to drop, but Ryan's speech was nevertheless printed in the Parliamentary Debates with the 'censored' extracts appearing in heavy type.

Dealing with aliens was no great problem for Australia and only in the later stages of the war was there much prejudice shown against Germans in matters of employment and other forms of discrimination. South Australia, and other states to a lesser extent, assisted the war effort by appointing committees to replace traditional Germanic place-names with neutral or patriotic substitutes like Mount Kitchener in place of Kaiserstuhl.

These were trivial matters, however, compared with the great crisis of Australia's war effort, the struggle over conscription.

As the first enthusiasm faded, and as the Western Front added to the toll of Gallipoli, Australia was faced with a man-power shortage which had become acute by the end of 1916. Recruiting figures dropped so rapidly that, whereas in June 1915, for example, recruits had numbered over 12,000, a year later the figure was little more than half that. To one man, at least, it was clear that something would have to be done: that man was William Morris Hughes, the former attorney-general, who became prime minister in October 1915.

Hughes was one of the most colourful, as well as capable, statesmen in Australian history. Born into a poor Welsh family, at an early age he emigrated to Australia, where he studied law, entered politics, and with the aid of administrative gifts and fervent oratory rose to the highest position at a critical time. In more ways than one his career resembled that of his great contemporary, Lloyd George, though even the latter would probably have been incapable of Hughes's characteristic effrontery when, at the post-war peace conference, he was rebuked by no less a figure than President Wilson for his insistence on retaining New Guinea. Wilson said: 'Mr Prime Minister of Australia, do I understand your attitude aright? If I do, it is this, that the opinion of the whole civilized world is to be set at naught. This conference, fraught with such infinite consequences to mankind for good or evil, is to break up with results which may well be disastrous to the future happiness of 18 hundred millions of the human race, in order to satisfy the whim of 5 million people in this remote southern continent whom you claim to represent.' Hughes smartly replied: 'Very well put, Mr President, you have guessed it. That's just so.'

In March 1916 Hughes visited Great Britain for four months, a visit which, with the passage of time, has taken on the qualities of legend. His aggressive, uncompromising speeches made him a figure of international fame and the Australian press rejoiced in the triumphs of their leader. He spoke of 'the happy privilege of Australians now in France to fight alongside the men of my native country'. He declared that 'we must win! We are fighting for a deathless principle. And though we walk for a time through the valley of the shadow of death, yet our cause is right and it shall prevail'. Such words hit the right note when Great Britain herself was searching for resolute leadership, and the *Evening Standard* asked 'who are the two men amongst us today wielding the biggest sway over the minds and the hearts of the British people? Surely Mr Lloyd George and Mr W.M.Hughes, the Australian prime minister. Both are Welshmen of fervid imagination who appeal by their eloquence, their fire, their patriotism'.

But on his return Hughes was to embark on a policy which split, not only his party, but the nation, and threatened seriously to jeopardize the Australian war effort. This policy, to extend compulsory service to overseas duty, met with a humiliating rebuff in a national referendum held in October 1916. The Australian people rejected his proposals by a majority of over 72,000, though for reasons which are not easy to discover. Hughes enjoyed the support of the press and of most prominent figures which, together with his own Herculean labours, indicated a 'Yes' majority. But the combination of war-weariness, remoteness from the main areas of conflict, a developing and perhaps healthy national tradition of defeating the government on referenda, all combined to defeat the forecasts. In addition there was the remorseless figure of Dr Mannix, Roman Catholic coadjutor archbishop of Melbourne, cam-

Right: The empire recruits its heroes – a British poster of 1915. The bodies of Anzacs on the beaches of Gallipoli, and of Indians on the Western Front, bore abiding testimony to the union of the British empire with the mother country

paigning tirelessly against conscription. He did not scruple to play on Irish feelings in the aftermath of the Easter Rising (p. 596), or to suggest that Australia had already done more than her fair share in the war.

The referendum divided party and nation. Anti-conscriptionists resigned from the government; Hughes left the Labour party. He was able to carry on only with the support of the Liberals, and when his government shortly became a Nationalist coalition, headed by himself but maintained by his political opponents, his position was indeed strangely similar to that of the prime minister of Great Britain.

Hughes's Nationalists won an overwhelming victory in the 1917 election, which encouraged him to appeal once more for powers to enforce conscription. By this time recruiting figures had dropped to below half the figure of 7,000 a month considered necessary. The prime minister said bluntly: 'I tell you plainly that the government must have this power. It cannot govern the country without it, and will not attempt to do so.' Yet again he was disappointed, this time by an even larger adverse vote. He resigned as he had promised, but, with no alternative government possible, came back on the following day with the identical cabinet which had resigned with him. Compulsion was now impossible, and the government tried to make the best of things with a vigorous recruiting campaign. But they were hampered by growing opposition, particularly from trades unionists and a militant body called International Workers of the World, which demanded immediate peace through negotiation. It is probable that a serious division within Australian society on the war issue was averted only by the unexpected collapse of the German armies in the autumn of 1918.

Australia's political crisis was to remain significant long after the conclusion of the war. But despite these troubles her contribution to the final victory was remarkable. Her proportion of troops in the field and of casualties sustained compared favourably with those of other dominions and of Great Britain herself. Moreover in the 'Anzac spirit' she discovered, in conjunction with the New Zealanders, a sense of national identity as well as of national pride.

New Zealand

The First World War presented fewer problems in New Zealand than in the other dominions. Her political life was not disrupted by minority problems, social cleavages, or conscription debates. The country as a whole vigorously supported the war, and compulsory overseas service was adopted in 1916 not because of any lack of recruits but out of a sense of 'fair play'. The coalition government which had been created the previous year reflected no crisis, as in Great Britain and Australia, but rather the desire for national unity at a time of national effort.

By 1914, New Zealand politics were undergoing a process of transition. Until recently the Liberal party had reigned supreme under the impetus given by the extraordinary Richard Seddon – gross, uncultivated, far from high-principled, yet firmly entrenched prime minister from 1893 to 1906. His successor, Joseph Ward, continued to enjoy a success which had been built on strong support from the farmers, and it was a right-wing defection among the farmers which allowed the recently created Reform Party to form its first government in 1912.

The prime minister, William Ferguson Massey, was in many ways an uninspiring figure. He continued the 'Seddon tradition' of lack of refinement and intellectualism, but was without Seddon's overpowering personality. Narrow, bigoted, but resolute and energetic, Massey managed to remain prime minister continuously for thirteen years, though it is probable that Ward, his coalition partner and treasurer, exercised a greater control in wartime.

New Zealand entered the war with alacrity. Her traditions, recent though they were, were decidedly imperialistic. She had urged Great Britain to pursue a more active policy in the Pacific and her adoption of compulsory military service for home defence in 1909 involved calling up all males over the age of 12. She took pride in being the first dominion to offer troops, and throughout the war maintained a 'pro-British' sentiment which has become part of her national characteristic. She is regarded as considerably more 'British' than her Australian neighbour.

There was little social unrest to hamper her war effort. In the years preceding 1914 there had been, it is true, some violent incidents when Massey ruthlessly crushed a series of strikes. But the Labour movement, which would one day destroy the Liberals, was in its infancy; only half a dozen Labour members formed a party in opposition to the war. On the whole the war was a period of prosperity for New Zealand's agriculture. Her promise to feed Great Britain was profitable to both sides of the agreement, and her exportable wool, meat, and dairy produce was commandeered by the government to be sold at guaranteed high prices. The military effort was, for a country with such a small population, astonishing.

Altogether about 120,000 New Zealanders saw active service, of whom 17,000 were killed – a vast number of young men whose loss was severely felt in the difficult inter-war years. The Maoris, at first understandably reluctant to enlist, served with distinction, whether as volunteers or conscripts. Despite the smallness of her population and her distance from Europe, New Zealand's contribution to the Allied victory was far from negligible.

New Zealanders were proud of their effort in the war. The performance of their troops at Gallipoli (p. 506), their occupation of German Samoa, their voice in the counsels of the empire and in the League of Nations all assisted that growth of identity so important in the evolution of a colony into a nation.

Canada

As in Australia and New Zealand, in Canada both major political parties were outspoken in their support for the war. The Conservative prime minister, Sir Robert Borden, said that 'as to our duty, we are all agreed: we stand shoulder to shoulder with Britain and the other British Dominions in this quarrel, and that duty we shall not fail to fulfil as the honour of Canada demands'. Sir Wilfrid Laurier, leader of the Liberals and spokesman for the majority of French Canadians, claimed that 'this war is for as noble a cause as ever impelled a nation to risk her all upon the arbitrament of the sword'.

Such assertions hid a fundamental division in Canadian society which was to loom larger as the war progressed. The so-called Anglo-Canadians, together with British-born immigrants, had a vastly different outlook from that of the insular, tightly-knit community of French-speaking *Canadiens*. Naturally enough the French-speaking settlers felt less attachment to the British empire than their countrymen. Less obviously, but equally important, the French community retained fewer ties with their own 'mother country' and their support for the war was, on the whole, passive rather than overtly enthusiastic. This situation was not helped by the attitude of the administration. The minister of militia, Sam Hughes, made no pretence of his disgust at the low recruiting figures from the French-speaking provinces. Efforts to create specifically *Canadien* forces were usually obstructed; English was uniformly adopted as the language of command; and *Canadien* recruits seemed to suffer almost insuperable difficulties when it came to promotion.

These problems lay in the future, however, when Canada, in common with the rest of the empire, embarked on her struggle of unprecedented magnitude. Borden's greatest tasks, as he saw them, were two-fold. First he had to mobilize the nation for war, second, to ensure that his country participated in the direction of the effort to which he committed so many of ▷ **639**

THE EMPIRE NEEDS MEN!
AUSTRALIA
CANADA
INDIA
NEW ZEALAND
Arthur Wardle
All answer the call.
Helped by the YOUNG LIONS
The OLD LION defies his Foes.
ENLIST NOW.

Imperial War Museum

1 Maori butcher at his work in France.
2 Australian recruiting poster. In the earlier part of the war as many as 12,000 Australians volunteered each month.
3 Canadians at the time of the battle of the Somme tend German wounded

Imperial War Museum

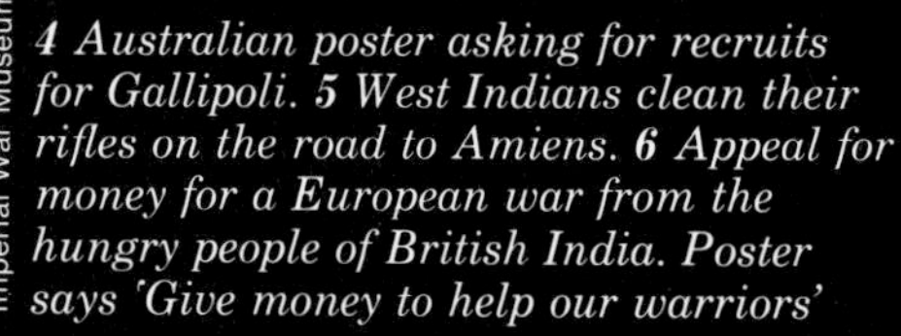

Imperial War Museum

4 Australian poster asking for recruits for Gallipoli. ***5*** *West Indians clean their rifles on the road to Amiens.* ***6*** *Appeal for money for a European war from the hungry people of British India. Poster says 'Give money to help our warriors'*

Imperial War Museum

Imperial War Museum

7

8

Imperial War Museum

Radio Times Hulton

7 *Canadian recruiting poster.* 8 *General Botha (sitting on the stool) personally directs operations in South West Africa.* 9 *An Australian and a New Zealander make friends with children on Lemnos, a base for soldiers fighting at Gallipoli*

9

Imperial War Museum

11

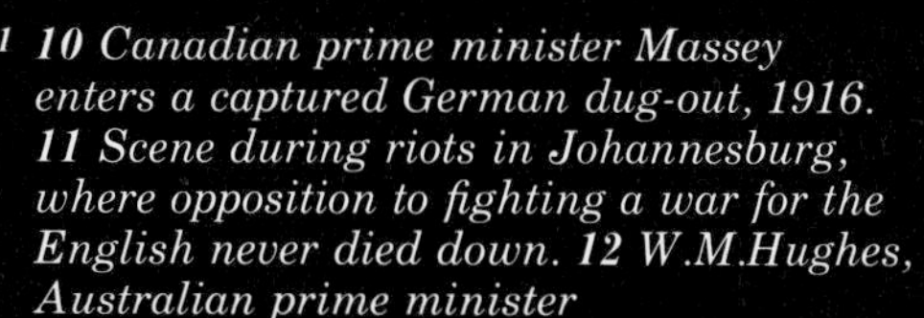

10 *Canadian prime minister Massey enters a captured German dug-out, 1916.* 11 *Scene during riots in Johannesburg, where opposition to fighting a war for the English never died down.* 12 *W.M.Hughes, Australian prime minister*

Radio Times Hulton

12

Library of Victoria, Melbourne

Great Britain's declaration of war brought 450,000,000 peopl from all continents into the conflict

his country's resources. Raising sufficien troops was far from easy. Canadiar traditions were non-military and her pre-war permanent army numbered a mere 3,000. No doubt a feeling of security due to the nearness of her powerful neighbour with its protective Monroe Doctrine played its part in this lack of preparedness but it meant that Canada felt the war-time dislocation even more severely thar other countries.

In view of her traditions Canada's achievements were formidable. Though the target of 500,000 troops had become evidently unattainable by 1917, Canada played her full share in the war effort Lloyd George's verdict on the quality of the Canadian troops after their exploits on the Somme in 1916 (p. 562) was that they 'played a part of such distinction tha thenceforward they were marked out as storm troops; for the remainder of the war they were brought along to head the assaul in one great battle after another. Whenever the Germans found the Canadiar Corps coming into the line, they preparec for the worst'.

With his country performing such feats Borden considered that he should play some part in formulating the policies for which his troops were committed. Wher told by Bonar Law, the colonial secretary that his schemes were impractical he retorted that 'it can hardly be expected tha we shall put 400,000 or 500,000 men in the field and willingly accept the position of having no more voice and receiving nc more consideration than if we were toy automata. Any person cherishing such ar expectation harbours an unfortunate anc even dangerous delusion. Is this war being waged by the United Kingdom alone, or is it a war waged by the whole Empire?' Such language had its effect, and after Lloyc George became prime minister in December 1916 the dominions found themselves consulted to a much greater extent. Ar Imperial War Cabinet was set up in March 1917, the same month for which an Imperial War Conference was summoned. I was Borden, appropriately enough, whc moved the famous resolution at the conference, claiming for the dominions a 'righ to an adequate voice in foreign policy anc in foreign relations'. After the war, Borden led the dominions' demands for representation at the peace conference and fo their individual membership of the League of Nations.

But while Sir Robert was demanding more influence for Canada, his country was being torn by a grave crisis over conscription ir 1917. The enormous losses sustained ir Europe during the previous year made man-power shortages general throughout all belligerent countries. Recruiting figures high in the early months of the war, fel alarmingly until they were less, month by month, than the casualties. By 1917 not only was conscription an urgent problem, but party politics had been renewed in a way which lent considerable bitterness to the struggle.

The growing opposition of the *Canadiens,* which was fostered by the treatment of their recruits, long-standing grievances over the exclusive use of English in schools in Ontario, and a series of frauds at governmental level all helped to create a dangerous political climate. Moreover, Laurier was determined to maintain the separate identity and different ideals of the French-Canadians, and these seemed threatened, not only by conscription, but by the coalition government advocated by the prime minister. So the Liberal leader fought the Military Service Act every inch of the way until it became law in August 1917; but the issue split his party and Borden was able to form his coalition in October with the help of Liberal defections. Moreover in the December elections, fought, like the parliamentary battle, over conscription, along racial lines, Laurier was heavily defeated by the government. Quebec, however, solidly supported him with 62 out of 65 seats. There is much truth in the accusation that the election was at least partly influenced by 'shameless manipulation'. For example, special legislation enfranchised those who were most committed to the war and therefore likely to be conscriptionist, but disenfranchised others who would be expected to vote the other way. In addition the soldiers' vote, which was solidly conscriptionist, was distributed in those provinces where it was most likely to show the best results for the government.

Perhaps the worst feature of the conscription crisis was that the political victory committed the country to a goal it was unable to achieve. Mass pleas for exemption, together with evasion and desertion cut the projected figure of 100,000 by nearly forty per cent, and most of those were too late to reach Europe anyway. Quebec was, of course, the most recalcitrant province, but farmers and trades unionists were to be found objecting in all parts of Canada.

So Canada's war effort was achieved at the cost of a deepening antagonism within her mixed population. But she had at least managed to sustain that effort without major disunity on the issue of the war itself. This no doubt had its effect on bringing the insular *Canadiens* to a fuller realization of the part they were compelled to play in world events. And that part had significantly grown when, in these years, Canada took the lead in asserting that the daughters of the mother country had come of age.

South Africa

South Africa's role in the war was dominated by two factors peculiar to her among the dominions. She alone had a military front line bordering her territory; and she alone had a large minority of settlers not only opposed to war but actively seeking a German victory as a means of throwing off the British connexion.

Causes of unrest in South Africa are not hard to discover. Memories of the Jameson raid and the Boer War (p. 13) remained strong, particularly among the Dutch farmers of Transvaal and the Orange Free State. All their lives these men had learned to regard the British as their chief enemies, and it was too much to expect that the grant of dominion status in the Union of 1910 would at once dispel the antagonism of generations. That despite these cleavages the Union remained intact under the stresses of war was due in large measure to the loyalty of two men. Louis Botha and Jan Smuts, South Africa's greatest soldier-statesmen, both pursued a policy of uniting their country within the framework of empire. The extent of their success must rank both men in the forefront of the world's leaders of the 20th century.

The existence of a strategically important German colony in South West Africa made any prospect of South African neutrality impossible. On the contrary, Great Britain immediately asked South Africa to undertake the conquest of the neighbouring territory, and Botha, the prime minister, was quick to agree. But his initial plans were scarcely completed when operations had to be suspended. For a serious rebellion among anti-British and pro-German elements threatened to undermine the war effort and perhaps to topple the government itself. The rebels included soldiers of the calibre of Colonel Maritz, commander of the frontier forces, General Beyers, and General de Wet. Suppressing this revolt was thus South Africa's first major achievement of the war, though the personal anguish of Botha, as he relentlessly pursued those who had formerly been comrades-in-arms against the British, can only be imagined. Smuts, the minister of defence, who directed from headquarters this destruction of former colleagues, said that 'few know what Botha went through in the rebellion. He lost friendships of a lifetime, friendships he valued perhaps more than anything in life. But Botha's line remained absolutely consistent. No one else in South Africa could have stuck it out. You wanted a man for that . . .'

Botha's statesmanship was never more clearly revealed than by his measures after the surrender of the rebels in February 1915. He was so lenient that only one man was executed – surely a record for a large-scale revolt in wartime. Meanwhile, he was able personally to conduct a campaign against German South West Africa, which has been called 'one of the neatest and most successful campaigns of the Great War'. Troops were also sent under Smuts to co-operate with British and Indian troops in German East Africa against the redoubtable Lettow Vorbeck, a campaign which was virtually over when Smuts left for London to represent his country at the Imperial War Conference.

Arriving in March 1917, Smuts originally intended to stay only a few weeks. He remained in Europe for two-and-a-half years, proving himself both militarily and politically among the ablest and most visionary of the British government's advisers. He was consulted by Lloyd George on tactics and strategy in Europe, spoke on imperial affairs so effectively that he was dubbed 'Orator for the Empire', recommended the creation of an independent command for the RAF, and was even used to end a strike of Welsh miners at Tonypandy. On that famous occasion he quietened the tumult by asking the miners to sing. They returned the compliment by returning to work. Lloyd George paid tribute to him as a man of 'rare and fine gifts of mind and heart', and that 'of his practical contributions to our councils during these trying years it is difficult to speak too highly'.

Besides serving on their own continent, South Africans also saw duty in the Middle East and on the Western Front where they enjoyed some notable triumphs. In all, some 136,000 white South Africans saw active service in a greater variety of conditions than the troops of any of the other dominions. But while the troops were winning distinction, and Smuts was earning unique prestige as an imperial statesman, Botha was severely troubled at home. Republicans, hostile to the empire, kept up constant pressure. Their party, the Nationalists, led by J.B.M.Hertzog, continually tried to obstruct the prosecution of the war, even to the extent of opposing, in 1918, Botha's motion hoping that God would grant victory to Great Britain.

South Africa's war effort had very mixed results. On the one hand the Union remained intact, South African prestige grew with the magnitude of her efforts, and her statesmen demonstrated the calibre which could be brought to British councils from distant parts of the empire. But numbers of her population remained unreconciled to the imperial connexion, and many who sought to protect the Afrikaner against the British extended this policy to seek greater protection for the white South African against the black. The war deepened rifts in South African loyalties and foreshadowed later internal developments which were to have important consequences for the nation's future.

The War Poets

When you see millions of the mouthless dead
Across your dreams in pale battalions go,
Say not soft things as other men have said . . .
Charles Sorley, killed in the battle of Loos, 1915

'The very phrase *War Poet,*' wrote Osbert Sitwell, a war poet himself, in *Noble Essences,* 'indicates a strange twentieth-century phenomenon, the attempt to combine two incompatibles. There had been no War Poets in the Peninsular, Crimean or Boer wars. But war had suddenly become transformed by the effort of scientist and mechanician into something so infernal, so inhuman, that it was recognised that only their natural enemy, the poet, could pierce through the armour of horror . . . to the pity at the human core.' There was a further, more prosaic reason for the phenomenon: this was the first war which sucked a whole generation into battle. The likelihood of a young poet fighting in the Crimea was slight. Almost the only young men of letters who escaped the First World War were those who were medically unfit, like Aldous Huxley.

The war generated two kinds of verse, belonging to a written and an oral tradition. The editor of an anthology of war poetry which appeared in 1916 referred to the 'scores of slim volumes and hundreds of separate poems' which had come from men in the army – most of them officers. Most of this verse is now totally forgotten. To the oral tradition belong the songs produced for and by the ordinary soldiers of each country involved in the war, and especially perhaps the British. Ironic, funny, obscene, and self-mocking, these songs are a wonderful reflection of the private soldier's views of the generals, the trenches, the food, the shells, his mates, and himself. They helped to make the almost intolerable tolerable. 'Send out the army and the navy, but for God's sake don't send me.' Exactly. Though some songs became universal, there were regimental preferences depending on temperament and origin. 'The men were singing,' wrote Robert Graves in *Goodbye to All That,* his account of his experiences in the war. 'Being mostly from the midlands, they sang comic songs rather than Welsh hymns: *Slippery Sam, When we've Wound up the Watch on the Rhine,* and *I do like a S'nice S'mince Pie* . . . The Second Welsh would never have sung a song like *When we've Wound up the Watch on the Rhine.* Their only songs about the war were defeatist:

I want to go home,
I want to go home.
The coal-box and shrapnel they whistle and roar,
I don't want to go to the trenches no more,
I want to go over the sea
Where the Kayser can't shoot bombs at me.
Oh, I
Don't want to die,
I want to go home.

This was the voice of the 'men'. It is the first category, the written verse, which most people mean when they speak of war poetry. Osbert Sitwell's quotation refers to a conception of war poetry which developed only towards the end of the war, when the full horror of it could not be camouflaged in rhetoric. In August 1914 the poetical voices which the public wished to hear were romantic, patriotic, and innocent. Convinced as each nation was of the rightness of its cause, it wished to have this confirmed by the poets. After a peace which had lasted in western Europe since 1871, no one, and poets no more than anyone else, knew what war would be like. Hence the idealization of war and death in much of the verse produced in the first months of the war. In England Rupert Brooke thanked God. In France the socialist, Charles Péguy, who had been warning his countrymen of the German menace since the Morocco crisis of 1905 (p. 135), had just time to respond to the war – 'Heureux ceux qui sont morts dans une juste guerre!' ('Happy are they who died in a just war') – before falling in the battle of the Marne.

Many European poets half-welcomed the war, not merely as an opportunity for self-sacrifice in a just cause, but in a deeper sense. In Russia Valery Bryusov in the decade 1900 to 1910 had called, in *The Coming Huns,* for some great catastrophe to purge a world grown rotten. In Germany Stefan George, anxious for the regeneration of German youth, whom he saw as corrupted by the false material values of the age, had foreseen, approvingly, a 'Holy War'. The war when it came fulfilled the prophecies of George and of many others.

Though some of these men would have claimed personally to abhor violence, they helped to create an atmosphere in which violence – and violence on a cosmic scale – was expected. The Futurists, led by the Italian poet, Filippo Marinetti, went farther. Marinetti's Futurist Manifesto of 1909 proclaimed the necessity of a new art drawing inspiration from the new and unforeseen, the rhythms of machines, the beauty of aggression. War for Marinetti was the bloody and necessary test of a people's force, 'the world's only hygiene'. It was as if men were tiring of peace.

The 'hygienic' view of war, echoed by Brooke in his reference to 'swimmers into cleanness leaping', was common. War was

Below: *Charles Péguy (sitting on right), a French poet who had warned his country of the impending German menace. 'Happy are they who died in a just war,' he wrote. He died in 1914, in the battle of the Marne*
Bottom: *Rupert Brooke, spokesman and symbol of the generation of young men who volunteered gladly at the outbreak of war. To him the war seemed to offer an opportunity to cleanse Europe from the stagnation and corruption of peace*

Bibliothèque Nationale, Paris

Radio Times Hulton

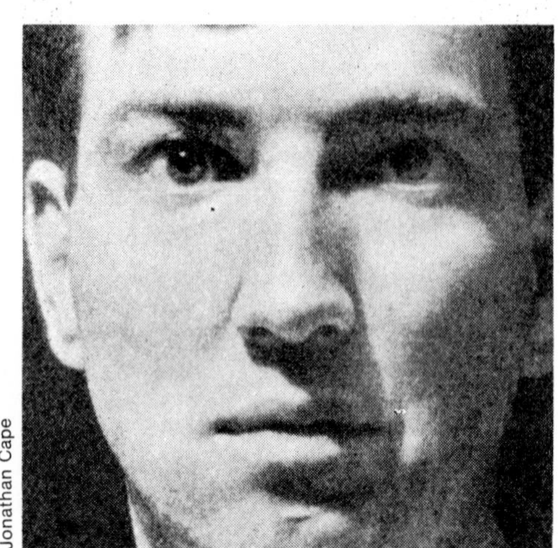
Jonathan Cape

Robert Graves. He, like other British poets in the trenches, wanted to tell of the real horrors of war, realistically

to be a kind of surgical operation on the rotten body of a society corrupted by materialism and complacency. A new, young, better society would emerge from under the knife. On these grounds, and as a release from uncertainty, the war could be welcomed. Even those who saw the magnitude of the catastrophe laboured to extract some good from it. The English poet, Wilfred Owen, wrote of 'the need /Of sowings for new Spring, and blood for seed'.

Disillusion, of course, followed. On the Western Front the slaughter on the Somme in the summer of 1916 destroyed for ever the romantic innocence with which the young had gone to war. The process of disenchantment is seen most clearly in the British poets, who set out in 1914 with perhaps more illusions than their continental cousins, and reacted more sharply in consequence. Every country had its soldier poets. Only among the British did war poetry develop an autonomous life of its own, so that one can fairly speak of a 'school' or 'movement'. Of the continental poets caught up in the war, some took it as their subject, others, preoccupied by aesthetic demands of their own conception of poetry, preserved the 'purity' of their art by retreating into silence or writing on other themes.

Thus the history of war poetry on the continent is the history of individuals. In Russia the moving descriptions of the Eastern Front by Viktor Khlebnikov, who served as a private, and the condemnation of the 'capitalist' war by Mayakovsky, were overtaken by the revolution, which undammed a torrent of verse from these two and their elders. Here, is seemed for a time, was the rebirth for which poets had been calling. In Italy, which came into the war late, the veteran romantic poet, Gabriele d'Annunzio, devoted his immense energy and rhetorical talents to involving his country on the side of the Allied powers, pointing to the example of France, who had 'donned her purple robe of war, / Ready to sing like a lark / On all the peaks of death'. He devoted the war years to playing the part of the poet-hero, the superman of action, losing an eye when crash-landing his aircraft, seeing his hour of glory when he captured Fiume in defiance of his own government in 1919. The war poems of Giuseppe Ungaretti expose with quiet honesty the morbid vanity of d'Annunzio's cult of blood and death.

France had her celebrator of war as Italy had d'Annunzio—Drieu la Rochelle, who found in the war a gratifying escape from bourgeois mediocrity to a life in which he hoped to find vitality, danger, and chivalry. War became his religion: 'Guerre . . . il faut que je m'abandonne à toi, corps et biens . . . Je ne saurais plus vivre hors de toi'. (War . . . let me abandon myself to you, body and all . . . I couldn't live without you now.) Such mystical enthusiasm was mercifully rare. It is lacking in France's greatest war poet, Guillaume Apollinaire, who wrote about the war, as he wrote about everything else, simply because it happened to him; too humane to glorify it; too honest to suppress its strange moments of beauty—

Ah Dieu! que la guerre est jolie
Avec ses chants ses longs loisirs.

(Ah God! how pretty war is
With its songs and its long hours of leisure)

He was too engrossed in the exploration of his own sensations and reactions to the war to preach about it. Apollinaire, a corpulent, generous figure, the champion of Picasso and the Cubists, was already an established poet at the outbreak of war.

Bibliothèque Nationale, Paris

A drawing by Apollinaire of himself as an artillery-man. He was a vivid reporter in poetry of the experience of war

After some unavoidable delay—being the son of a Polish mother and Italian father, he had to take out naturalization papers before he could join the French army—he enlisted in the ranks, was promoted sub-lieutenant in November 1915, and served at the front from then on. To the surprise of his literary friends, he adapted himself easily to army life. Neither the danger nor the tedium of war dulled his vitality. He bombarded his friends with letters and postcards in verse from the front:

The war-enthusiast D'Annunzio. Italian cartoon captioned: 'If we had guns as big as his mouth we'd have no trouble'

Je t'écris de dessous la tente
Tandis que meurt ce jour d'été
Où floraison éblouissante
Dans le ciel à peine bleuté
Une canonnade éclatante
Se fane avant d'avoir été

(I write to you from under the tent
While this summer day is dying
In which like a dazzling blossoming
In the hardly bluish sky
A cannonade bursts out
And fades before it has ever been)

Yet, though he was one of the most vivid reporters of the experience of war, he remained apart from it, not engaged in the way that Sassoon and Owen were morally engaged. After a head wound from a shell fragment ended his war service on 17th March 1916, Apollinaire lived out the war in Paris, and was adopted as the hero of the *avant-garde,* the 'little magazines', *Sic* and *Nord-Sud,* the young poets such as André Breton, Paul Eluard, and Louis Aragon, now serving in the army, who a few years later were to assist at the birth of Surrealism. It was for his techniques, his joyful experimentation, and his modern sensibility (he once wrote that artillery gave birth to the modern literary spirit) that these men took him as leader, not for his attitude to the war. Their poetic concerns, and his, were aesthetic. Thus Aragon, who won the *Croix de Guerre* in 1917, was later to reproach himself for passing through the war without writing a single word about it. Apollinaire died of Spanish 'flu on 9th November 1918.

The graceful, exuberant spirit of Apollinaire is very far from the spirit of the British war poets. When the war broke out in August 1914, men were agreed that it would not last long; it would be over in months. This made it easy for young men

Radio Times Hulton

Siegfried Sassoon: a recklessly brave soldier, an angry satirist of the 'callous complacency' of the patriots at home

like Rupert Brooke to see the war as a short, clean, painless break with the complacent materialism of the past. There is in the early war poems a paradoxical insistence on the irrelevance of death. We find it in *Into Battle* of Julian Grenfell, who died of wounds on 27th May 1915:

And life is colour and warmth and light,
And a striving evermore for these;
And he is dead who will not fight;
And who dies fighting has increase. . . .
The thundering line of battle stands,
And in the air death moans and sings,
But Day shall clasp him with strong hands,
And Night shall fold him in soft wings.

We find it also in the work of Brooke himself, who after his early death from septicaemia on a hospital ship in the Aegean was taken to be the ideal representative of the brave youth of Great Britain who sacrificed their lives:

War knows no power. Safe shall be my going,
Secretly armed against all death's endeavour;
Safe though all safety's lost; safe where men fall;
And if these poor limbs die, safest of all.

Brooke never experienced the trenches; he died in April 1915, just missing the Gallipoli campaign. It is therefore unfair to reproach him with failing to appreciate the awful reality of modern war. No one appreciated this before it was experienced. The point is that Brooke was typical. He expressed the thoughts of 'the plain recruit who had not the gift of a style', in the words of C.E.Montague, himself a far from plain recruit (he dyed his grey hair in order to be accepted into the army); of the 'officer-class' volunteers, at any rate. And when these views ceased to appeal to the fighting men as they discovered what war was really like, they continued dear to those at home who had lost their sons. Twenty thousand copies of Brooke's *1914, Five Sonnets* were printed in 1915.

After the Somme, a new, tougher group of poets began to make their voices heard. These men—Edmund Blunden, Robert Graves, Wilfred Owen, Herbert Read, Isaac Rosenberg, Siegfried Sassoon, and others—had a number of points in common. They were all, except Rosenberg, junior officers—among whom casualties were heaviest. They all hated the war, hated the profiteering and the jingoist propaganda of wartime Great Britain, and wished to confound the lies and the complacency with a true vision of the trenches. Blunden described the difficulty thus: 'Among the multitudes of us shipped to the Pas de Calais a few months before the Great Push (or Drive) of the British army in 1916, I was a verse-writer; my interests were not yet changed from what life had formed before all this chaos . . . In May and June 1916, in my notebooks, the grimness of war began to compete as a subject with the pastorals of peace. By the end of the year, when madness seemed totally to rule the hour, I was almost a part of the shell-holes, of ruin and of mortification. But the stanzas then written were left in the pocket-book: what good were they, who cared, who would agree?' To spread the bad news was hard. 'National interests were, understandably, in the way.'

Harold Owen—Chatto & Windus

Wilfred Owen, the greatest of the British war poets. 'I shall be better able to cry my outcry, playing my part'

Charles Sorley, killed in the battle of Loos. He was the first poet who tried to express the futility and horror of the war

The precursor of these poets, Charles Sorley, who was killed in the battle of Loos in 1915, and who was the first to present an image of the war which came near to comprehending its full horror and futility, left behind him a sonnet:

When you see millions of the mouthless dead
Across your dreams in pale battalions go,
Say not soft things as other men have said...

His successors had to find a language and a style for the hard things they had to say. When Graves first met Sassoon near Béthune, and showed him some of his poems, Sassoon 'frowned and said that war should not be written about in such a realistic way. In return, he showed me some of his own poems. One of them began:

Return to greet me, Colours that were my joy,
Not in the woeful crimson of men slain . . .

Siegfried had not yet been in the trenches. . . . I told him . . . he would soon change his style'.

Sassoon did. By 1917 he was totally opposed to the war. His verses were circulating rapidly among his fellow poets, but had not filtered through to the consciousness of the public. Sassoon, a recklessly brave soldier, decided to make a direct protest against the war. Having discussed his stand with the editor of *The Nation*, which was banned from foreign circulation on the grounds that its attitude to the war prejudiced recruiting, and with Bertrand Russell, whose opposition to the war lost him his Cambridge fellowship, Sassoon made public a statement repudiating the war.

Sassoon's statement was not pacifist, but a protest at the continuation of this particular war. The other trench poets, though they too had turned 'against the war', continued to fight; and even Sassoon, in the end, went back to war. Wilfred Owen moved close to pacifism, writing in a letter in 1917, that he now understood 'that one of Christ's essential commands was: passivity at any price! Suffer dishonour and disgrace, but never resort to arms. Be bullied, be outraged, be killed; but do not kill. . . . Am I not myself a conscientious objector with a very seared conscience?' But the desire to stand by his men in the trenches, the feeling that the true protest against the war could come only from those engaged in it, overcame the pacifism. 'I shall be better able to cry my outcry, playing my part.'

And though the trenches were desolate, in some ways home seemed even worse. England moved the poets to angry frustration. Sassoon wrote of the cheap music-hall show:

I'd like to see a Tank come down the
stalls,
Lurching to rag-time tunes, or 'Home,
Sweet Home' –
And there'd be no more jokes in Music-
Halls
To mock the riddled corpses round
Bapaume.

Owen wrote from Scarborough in July 1918: 'I wish the Boche would have the pluck to come right in and make a clean sweep of the pleasure boats, and the promenaders on the Spa, and all the stinking Leeds and Bradford war-profiteers, now reading *John Bull* on Scarborough Sands.' England and the trenches were different worlds. The poets' hate was reserved not for the Germans but for the profiteers and the general staff. At home everyone was patriotic. 'Patriotism, in the trenches,' wrote Graves, 'was too remote a sentiment, and at once rejected as fit only for civilians. . . . Great Britain was a quiet, easy place for getting back to out of the present foreign misery; but as a nation it included not only the trench-soldiers themselves and those who had gone home wounded, but the staff, Army Service Corps, lines of communication troops, base units, home-service units, and all civilians down to the detested grades of journalists, profiteers, "starred" men exempted from enlistment, conscientious objectors, and members of the Government.' If the trench-soldiers were fighting for anyone, it was for each other. The trench poets were on their side.

After his protest, Sassoon was sent to Craiglockhart War Hospital to recover from neurasthenia. There Wilfred Owen, also convalescent, showed him his early war poems. Sassoon's encouragement and friendship gave Owen the self-confidence and inspiration he needed. With Sassoon's approval, Owen returned to the front in August 1918. He was killed on 4th November, a week before the armistice, while taking his company across the Sambre canal in the face of determined German machine-gun fire. In the few months before his death Owen produced most of those poems which mark him out as the greatest war poet of the First World War. He embraced the futility, the waste of life and spirit, the boredom, the blood, and the pity of the trenches in a vision which raised his verses high above the outraged satire of his master Sassoon. He saw his function as to warn his generation, by depicting the truth and the pity of war. From one side of the front, Owen pictured a 'sad land. . . . Gray, cratered like the moon with hollow woe,/ And pitted with great pocks and scabs of plagues'; from the other, the German poet Anton Schnack described the dead, 'heavy, fossilized, their hands full of spiders, their mouths red with scabs'. It was the same no man's land, the same corpses, for both. They felt the same horror, yet they fought. Political protest, like Sassoon's, had proved useless. In the end, all the poet could do was to describe.

Exercise

Vers un village de l'arrière
S'en allaient quatre bombardiers
Ils étaient couverts de poussière
Depuis la tête jusqu'aux pieds

Ils regardaient la vaste plaine
En parlant entre eux du passé
Et ne se retournaient qu'à peine
Quand un obus avait toussé

Tous quatre de la classe seize
Parlaient d'antan non d'avenir
Ainsi se prolongeait l'ascèse
Qui les exerçait à mourir

(Four gunners were going towards a village behind the front. They were covered with dust from head to foot. They looked at the vast plain, talking among themselves of the past, and when a shell coughed they hardly turned their heads. All four of the 1916 class talked of the past not the future – and so the ascetic discipline which trained them for death was carried on.)
From *Calligrammes* by Apollinaire

Preface
(found, unfinished, among Owen's papers)

This book is not about heroes. English
Poetry is not yet fit to speak of them.
Nor is it about deeds or lands, nor
anything about glory, honour, dominion
or power,
except War.
Above all, this book is not concerned
with Poetry.
The subject of it is War, and the pity
of War.
The Poetry is in the pity.
Yet these elegies are not to this
generation,
This is in no sense consolatory.
They may be to the next.
All the poet can do to-day is to warn.
That is why the true Poets must be
truthful.
If I thought the letter of this book would
last,
I might have used proper names; but if
the spirit of it survives Prussia, – my
ambition and those names will be content;
for they will have achieved themselves
fresher fields than Flanders.

From *Poems* by Wilfred Owen, published 1920
By permission, Harold Owen and Chatto & Windus, Ltd

Finished with the war
A Soldier's Declaration

(This statement was made to his commanding officer by Second-Lieutenant S.L. Sassoon, Military Cross, recommended for D.S.O., Third Battalion Royal Welch Fusiliers. . . .)

I am making this statement as an act of wilful defiance of military authority, because I believe that the war is being deliberately prolonged by those who have the power to end it.

I am a soldier, convinced that I am acting on behalf of soldiers. I believe that this war, upon which I entered as a war of defence and liberation, has now become a war of aggression and conquest. I believe that the purposes for which I and my fellow-soldiers entered upon this war should have been so clearly stated as to have made it impossible to change them, and that, had this been done, the objects which actuated us would now be attainable by negotiation.

I have seen and endured the sufferings of the troops, and I can no longer be a party to prolong these sufferings for ends which I believe to be evil and unjust.

I am not protesting against the conduct of the war, but against the political errors and insincerities for which the fighting men are being sacrificed.

On behalf of those who are suffering now I make this protest against the deception which is being practised on them: also I believe that I may help to destroy the callous complacency with which the majority of those at home regard the continuation of agonies which they do not share, and which they have not sufficient imagination to realize.
From the *Bradford Pioneer*, 27th July 1917

Chapter 24

Introduction by J.M.Roberts

Bismarck is supposed once to have said that the most important fact of world politics in the 19th century was that the Americans and the British spoke the same language. Important as this may have been and be, many people in both countries have always been too ready to take for granted a 'special relationship'. In the early years of the First World War, this made it hard for the British to understand United States' policy. This Chapter is about the changes which that policy underwent down to the climax of entry into the war, and about some of the consequences which flowed from that event.

Hugh Brogan's article on **The American People and the War** describes the context of American policy-making. Their attitudes were among the factors which the President, Woodrow Wilson, had to take into account. They go a long way towards explaining the complicated and confusing appearance which American policy often presented to Europeans in these years. The President, too, was a complex, curious man. The leading authority on his life, his biographer, Arthur S.Link, contributes to this Chapter a study of **Wilson and the Ordeal of Neutrality**.

In the end, the entry of the United States to the war was determined by the German general staff. Once again in 1916, as in 1914, German foreign policy was subordinated to technical and strategic considerations. The adoption of the Schlieffen plan had made Great Britain's entry to a Franco-German war almost inevitable, as German military planning had recognized. Now, the adoption of the strategy of unrestricted war by U-boat—described by Wolfgang Steglich in **The Fatal Decision**—equally made the entry of the United States to the war inevitable. **Declaration of War**, the subject of an article by Robert H.Ferrell, came almost at once.

Ludendorff and his advisers had calculated that the U-boats would bring Great Britain to heel before the enormous manpower of the Americans could make itself felt in France. This calculation was wrong: the U-boats did not prove able to do the job given to them. Yet the Germans were right in thinking that the American armies would take a long time to reach the battlefield. That is why **The New Military Balance** which followed the American declaration of war (analysed in this Chapter by Correlli Barnett) is a more complicated matter than appears at first sight.

Nevertheless, the American entry to the war was decisive. It was also symbolic of the ending of an age. Four centuries of European world domination were coming to a close. The New World had entered the European ring to decide quarrels the Old could no longer settle for itself.

Ullstein

Blockade by submarine. A U-boat stops an Italian ship in the Mediterranean

The sentence of defeat for Germany—Wilson asks Congress to declare war

Culver Pictures

American soldiers, setting out to fight on the Western Front, look back at New York

Germany

1915 4th February: Germans announce that they will use submarines against all merchant shipping in war zones.
1st May: first American ship, *Gulflight*, sunk without warning.
7th May: Walther Schwieger in German submarine U20 sinks the *Lusitania*. 128 Americans are drowned. Wilson sends notes of protest.
6th June: the Kaiser insists that all passenger lines must be spared.
19th August: Germans sink British liner *Arabic*.
18th September: the new chief of naval staff, Holtzendorff, orders that U-boat commerce war should be carried out on 'cruiser' system.

1916 29th February: Holtzendorff gives permission for armed merchantships to be sunk.
4th March: Falkenhayn says he must use unrestricted submarine warfare to finish war by the end of 1916.
13th March: orders are given that both armed and unarmed merchantships are to be sunk.
15th March: Tirpitz resigns.
24th March: U-boat torpedoes French packet steamer *Sussex* with heavy loss of life.
18th April: Wilson threatens to break off diplomatic relations with Germany in protest about the sinking of the *Sussex*.
4th May: German government agrees to demands of USA that submarines should adhere to 'cruiser' rules of warfare, on condition that Great Britain abandons illegal methods of blockade.
29th August: Hindenburg and Ludendorff replace Falkenhayn.
6th October: U-boats are told to act on 'cruiser' rules.
12th December: the Central powers make a peace offer to the Allies.
End of December: Hindenburg and Ludendorff demand unrestricted submarine warfare.

1917 9th January: at Pless Bethmann Hollweg agrees to unrestricted submarine warfare.

United States

1914 4th August: Wilson says USA will stay neutral.

1915 House visits London to work for Anglo-American peace drive.

1916 18th January: US asks Allies to disarm their merchantships if Germany agrees to warn such ships before sinking them. Wilson has to abandon this plan.
22nd February: Grey and House sign Memorandum on Wilson's plan of mediation.
5th March: House returns to Washington to say that British and French wish for peace.
27th May: Wilson declares that USA will join a post-war league of nations, as part of plan for settlement of war.
7th November: Wilson is re-elected on peace programme.
18th December: Wilson asks belligerents to state terms on which they would be prepared to cease fighting.

1917 Mid-January: Wilson tries to persuade British and German governments to accept his mediation.
26th January: Great Britain tells Wilson it is prepared to accept his mediation.
31st January: Bernstorff informs USA of German decision to renew unrestricted submarine warfare on 1st February.
3rd February: Wilson informs Congress that he is breaking off diplomatic relations with Germany.
25th February: three Americans lose their lives when the Germans sink *Laconia*.
1st March: Zimmermann telegram is published in the American press.
2nd April: Wilson asks Congress to declare war.
6th April: USA enters war.
June: 1st Division of the American Expeditionary Force lands in France.

Elsewhere

1916 At the battles of Verdun and the Somme, French, British, and Germans all sustain appalling losses.
June: Brusilov's Offensive gives Russia victory over Austria-Hungary.
27th August: Rumania declares war on Austria-Hungary.
6th December: Rumanian capital, Bucharest, occupied by Central powers.

1917 March: revolution starts in Russia. Tsar Nicholas II is forced to abdicate.
April and May: French army under Nivelle is repulsed by the Germans.

1918 21st March: Germans launch first of a series of offensives on Western Front. These last until July.
18th July: the French launch attack on Villers-Cotterêt. The tide starts to turn against the Germans.

Germany 1915-17 / Wolfgang Steglich

The Fatal Decision

For two-and-a-half years the Kaiser and his chancellor, Bethmann Hollweg, held out against the demand of the generals and admirals for unrestricted submarine warfare. Then at Pless, in January 1917, they succumbed, in a 'world-shattering decision', to the arguments of Hindenburg and Ludendorff

At long last, on 9th January 1917, Bethmann Hollweg, the German chancellor, at a conference at GHQ, Pless in Upper Silesia, signified his concurrence with the resolution in favour of unrestricted submarine warfare, that is he agreed to the torpedoing of enemy and neutral merchant and passenger ships without warning. His feelings were similar to those which had burdened him during the crisis of July 1914. For him the Pless decision was a leap in the dark, like the action of Austria-Hungary against Serbia in July 1914. On that occasion he realized that any attempt to overthrow Serbia might well lead to a European war. Now he was tormented by anxiety lest the reckless use of the U-boats result in war with the United States. And on both occasions his fears were justified.

In 1914 it was the growing consolidation of the Triple Entente, the increasing strength of Russia, and the critical situation in the Balkans which drove the German government to approve and guarantee the Austro-Hungarian attack on Serbia regardless of the risk of a European war. In 1917 the German government was impelled by the hopelessness of the land war to agree to unrestricted submarine warfare and thereby to run the risk of a conflict with the USA. In 1917, as in 1914, Bethmann Hollweg yielded to the military demands through a mixture of fatalism and a hope that the general situation might be changed by violent action. Bethmann Hollweg's two shattering decisions resembled each other in that each was based on a collapse of political leadership and an excessive regard for the military standpoint.

The arguments about U-boat warfare among the military and political leaders of the German empire had begun as far back as late 1914. The first impulse was given by the unsatisfactory progress of the naval war. At enormous cost a German battle fleet had been built up in sharp rivalry with Great Britain (p. 170). On the outbreak of war, however, any large-scale naval enterprise was discouraged by the government, which needed to maintain the German fleet intact as a political instrument. It was not until 1916 that the naval commanders ventured to engage the Royal Navy, and the battle of Jutland (p. 543) showed that Germany had not enough naval power to defeat the great

A U-boat puts out to sea, festooned with garlands, the tribute of the German people's faith in its destructive power. Almost all the press and the people believed, like the high command, that unrestricted submarine warfare could bring Great Britain to her knees

British fleet in a battle on the high seas. The pretensions of the German naval leaders were badly injured because of the limited effectiveness of the fleet since 1914, and Germany was driven more and more to rely on submarine warfare against British seaborne commerce. The aim was to destroy the economic life and supply lines of Great Britain and thus force it to sue for peace. But this strategical switch was by no means due solely to the German navy's ambition to play some part in the war. It was forced on the naval leaders by the grim fact that in a few months Great Britain had won complete command of the world's seas and was trying to cut off Germany's overseas imports by a distant blockade. It seemed essential not to accept this gigantic British success meekly but to find some counterstroke in reply. In the first months of the war German U-boats had destroyed several large British warships by underwater torpedo attacks, and these brilliant successes led to an over-estimation of the U-boat weapon, which in fact was still comparatively undeveloped. The chief of the naval staff, Admiral von Pohl, pressed for a blockade of the British coasts as early as the beginning of November 1914. And a little later Admiral von Tirpitz, state secretary of the imperial navy office, gave an interview to Karl von Wiegand, a representative of the American press, in which he drew the world's attention to the possibility of a German blockade of Great Britain by submarines. Among the German people an impression grew that the U-boats were an infallible weapon in the war with Great Britain. The result was a violent public agitation concerning U-boats.

Commercial warfare by U-boat actually began as far back as February 1915 and was consistently carried on in various forms for two years, until January 1917. During this period the German government had time and again to justify the employment of a novel method of warfare in face of the vehement complaints of the European neutrals and, especially, of the United States. Yielding to such opposition, it set its face, until 9th January 1917, against the unrestricted use of the U-boat weapon demanded by the naval authorities. But at the same time, in internal debates, it repeatedly asserted that its negative attitude was not due to consideration for international law but was purely for military and political reasons. When, in January 1917, the ruthless exploitation of U-boat warfare was finally decided upon, Bethmann Hollweg expressly declared that he had never opposed it on principle, but had always been governed by the general situation and the respective strengths of U-boat weapons. In the various deliberations it was the Kaiser Wilhelm II alone who expressed humanitarian scruples. For him the drowning of innocent passengers was 'a frightful thought'.

As the U-boat was a new weapon, there were in 1914 no international rules regarding its use in commercial warfare. The German government should have striven to obtain international recognition for the new weapon, for both the present and any future war. But instead, the Germans admitted the illegality of U-boat commerce war from the first by describing it as a reprisal measure against the illegal methods adopted by the British in their commercial blockade. For Great Britain, like Germany, had been forced by the advance of weapon technique to break the traditional international rules dealing with blockades. Because of the danger to its naval forces it could not carry on a close blockade of the German coasts—hitherto the only permissible method—but had to engage in a distant blockade directed at neutral as well as German ports. For this purpose the British declared the whole of the North Sea to be a war zone and prescribed for neutral shipping fixed navigational routes which could be supervised by British naval vessels. Moreover, Great Britain extended the regulations about war contraband and the confiscation of cargoes in neutral vessels. Liable to seizure were not only goods useful for the arming and supply of enemy forces, but all foodstuffs and raw materials intended for the Central powers. It was immaterial whether the cargoes were being carried direct to enemy ports or through neutral countries.

The new British contraband regulations initiated an economic and hunger blockade which was aimed at the enemy's civilian population. The German reprisal measure, commercial war by U-boat, was similarly directed against the civilian population. It might therefore be considered as merely a similar measure, by way of reprisal. But in fact there was one great difference. The British blockade was merely a confiscation of material goods, but the German submarine attacks endangered the lives of crews and passengers. When an underwater torpedo was fired without warning, it was impossible to take any steps to save the lives of those on board. And if the ship was attacked from the surface the crew and passengers taking to the lifeboats were exposed to the perils of wind and wave on the open seas, for the U-boat was in no position to pick them up and bring them to a place of safety.

The most difficult thing to justify was the effect of commercial war by U-boat on the neutrals, in whose case there was, of course, no question of reprisal. Instead, the German government demanded that the neutrals submit to submarine warfare as they had submitted to the British blockade of the North Sea. But there was only partial justification for this demand. True, neutral shipping used the prescribed routes through the English Channel and submitted to examination of cargoes in British ports. Nevertheless, the European neutrals, in spite of the British blockade, had delivered large food cargoes to Germany down to 1916. On the German side there was no desire to suppress neutral shipping by submarine warfare, but only to drive it out of certain sea areas. In the proclamation of 4th February 1915, which initiated submarine warfare, the waters around Great Britain and Ireland, including the whole of the English Channel, were declared a war zone. Every enemy merchant ship encountered in the war zone would be destroyed. Neutral ships were advised to avoid it, as attacks on enemy ships might, in the uncertainties of naval warfare, well affect neutral ships also. It was hoped that this warning might frighten neutral shipping off trade with Great Britain. Admiral von Pohl wanted to emphasize this warning by ordering all ships within the war zone to be sunk without distinction, a step which meant unrestricted submarine warfare. He actually wanted a few neutral ships to be sunk without warning at the outset of the U-boat operations so that there should be general uncertainty and neutral trade with Great Britain stopped as soon as possible. In subsequent deliberations the deterrent effect on neutral shipping was an important factor.

Bethmann Hollweg, who struggled in vain against the demands of the high command

At the beginning of 1915, and again at the beginning of 1916, such intimidation seemed especially necessary, for Germany at those times was far from possessing enough U-boats to carry on a successful economic war with Great Britain. In February 1915 there were only twenty-one U-boats available for watching the shipping lanes to Great Britain. As the voyage to the war zone, the return journey, and the overhaul afterwards, took a considerable time, there were never more than three or four boats operating at any one time on the coasts of Great Britain. Obviously there were not enough of them to inflict any considerable damage to Great Britain's trade by direct action. Thus it was very important to keep neutral ships, and as many enemy ships as possible out of the war zone. But the Germans had no success. Even before the announced U-boat commerce war started on 18th February, very firmly worded notes of protest reached Berlin from the neutral maritime powers affected. Most serious of all, the American government held the German government strictly accountable for all measures that might involve the destruction of any merchant vessel belonging to the United States or for the death of any American subject. The war situation of the Central powers in February 1915 was much too strained to risk complications with powerful neutral states. The chancellor therefore persuaded the Kaiser to order the U-boats to spare neutral ships, especially those belonging to the United States or Italy. The U-boat commerce war began four days late, on 22nd February 1915, in this modified form. In March 1915, out of 5,000 vessels entering and leaving British ports only twenty-one were sunk. Neutral shipping soon resumed trade with Great Britain.

Imperial War Museum

Arming at sea – a U-boat takes ammunition on board. From May 1915 U-boats were fitted with deck guns as well as with torpedoes, and surfaced before attacking an enemy ship

The Lusitania *incident*

In spite of precautions taken during the period of restricted submarine warfare, a grave incident occurred on 7th May 1915, when a German U-boat sank the British ocean liner *Lusitania* with an underwater torpedo (p. 521). Among the drowned were 128 American citizens. The sinking of the *Lusitania* aroused intense indignation in the United States, and a sharp exchange of notes between the American and German governments ensued. President Wilson had no desire to precipitate an armed conflict with Germany by his *Lusitania* notes, but he feared that a continuation of the U-boat war would one day leave him no other choice. He tried repeatedly to persuade Great Britain to allow food imports into Germany through neutral countries. At the same time he took a firm stand against the contempt for humane principles shown in the kind of warfare used by the U-boats. The first *Lusitania* note of the American government on 15th May 1915 denied the legality in international law of any form of U-boat commerce war, inasmuch as in neither an underwater nor a surface attack could the safety of passengers and crew be guaranteed. In the third *Lusitania* note of 23rd July 1915 Wilson conceded that submarines were a novelty in naval warfare and that no provision could have been made for them in the international regulations. At the same time it was admitted that the German submarine operations of the last two months had complied with the customs of war and had demonstrated the possibility of eliminating the chief causes of offence. This remarkable concession on the part of the Americans was based on the fact that since May 1915 the U-boats had been fitted with deck guns and, owing to the uncertainty of hitting the target with torpedoes, had carried on the commerce war in 'cruiser' style, according to the rules laid down for the taking of prizes. The U-boat came to the surface when attacking a ship and before sinking it allowed the persons on board to take to the boats. All enemy vessels were sunk without exception, but neutral ships were sunk only when they were carrying contraband.

Although this was the actual method of operation during the *Lusitania* crisis, the German naval authorities obstinately opposed any restriction being placed on submarine warfare and especially any attempt to confine U-boats to the rules of 'cruiser' warfare. They maintained that such methods were an intolerable danger to the submarine and its crew. They named as the chief dangers attempts of the merchant ships to ram the submarine, concealed guns on the ships, the use of a neutral flag by British ships, and attacks by enemy warships during the necessarily lengthy searches. The German government was not informed by the navy that in the period May-July 1915 eighty-six per cent of the merchant vessels that were sunk were dealt with according to the cruiser warfare rules, and that from February to July 1915 250 merchant ships carrying a neutral flag were examined and only on three occasions was any misuse of the flag discovered. By its policy of secrecy the navy apparently wanted to avoid being permanently restricted to 'cruiser' warfare and losing for ever the chance of unrestricted submarine warfare. On 6th June 1915 the Kaiser ordered that all large passenger liners, whether enemy or neutral, must be spared. Nevertheless, on 19th August, the British liner, *Arabic,* was sunk without warning, two more American citizens losing their lives. The Kaiser then ordered that no passenger liner was to be sunk until it had been warned and the passengers and crew given a chance to escape. During the arguments about U-boat methods in the summer of 1915 Tirpitz, in order to put pressure on the Kaiser, twice offered his resignation. His offers were abruptly refused. Yet the Kaiser changed his chief of naval staff at the beginning of September. Vice-Admiral Bachmann, a Tirpitz adherent who had held the office since February 1915, was replaced by Admiral von Holtzendorff, who was more amenable to the political views of the chancellor. On 18th September 1915 Holtzendorff gave orders that the U-boat commerce war on the west coast of Great Britain and in the Channel should be carried out on the 'cruiser' system. The naval commanders were not ready for this step and brought the U-boat war around Great Britain to a standstill. Thus ended the first phase of the U-boat war. The *Arabic* case was settled on 6th October by German compliance. The German government did not defend the action of the U-boat commander, which infringed the order of 6th June. The *Lusitania* case remained unsettled. The German government refused to admit that the U-boat attack on the *Lusitania* was contrary to international law, for if it did so future unrestricted submarine warfare would be impossible.

In 1915 several U-boats, large and small, were sent to the Austro-Hungarian naval base of Pola, and also to Constantinople. These carried on trade war in the Mediterranean and the Black Sea with great success, limiting their actions to the 'cruiser' rules. They restricted the flow of supplies to the Anglo-French forces in the Dardanelles and Salonika. But at the beginning of 1916 U-boat activities were severely handicapped by the progressive arming of the enemy's merchant vessels. The U-boat flotilla at Pola therefore asked the naval staff for permission to sink any armed merchant ship without warning. Holtzendorff granted the request, but with the proviso that passenger ships should continue to be exempt. At the same time he re-opened the trade war around Great Britain by issuing the same orders. A new phase in the submarine war was begun on 29th February 1916 and was termed 'intensified' U-boat war.

The high-ranking officers of the German navy looked on the new measures as a mere transitional phase. Since the beginning of the year the prospects for unrestricted submarine war had considerably improved, for General von Falkenhayn, chief of the army general staff, was now expressly demanding it. Since the autumn of 1914 the German armies, in co-operation with those of Austria-Hungary, Turkey, and Bulgaria, had created firm front lines on enemy territory; they had driven the Russians far back to the east, and by the occupation of Serbia had opened the way to Constantinople. Falkenhayn was at the peak of his military successes. In February 1916 he intended to deliver an all-out offensive on the Western Front, starting with a holding attack on Verdun. In the summer and autumn of 1915 he had firmly advised against the ruthless use of the U-boat weapon because he thought that a break with the United States might produce unfavourable reactions from the European neutrals and in particular might make Bulgarian assistance in the campaign against Serbia doubtful. In 1916, on the other hand, when the Balkan situation had been stabilized, such considerations were no longer valid. He believed that unrestricted submarine warfare directed against Great Britain would help his offensive on the Western Front. The U-boat action was timed to start in the middle of March. Almost the whole of the German press advocated ruthless use of the U-boats. The alliance between Falkenhayn and the navy on this point put Bethmann Hollweg in a very difficult position, and he spent the first weeks of the New Year in a very worried state. He feared that the adoption of unrestricted submarine warfare 'might result in condemnation by the whole civilized world and a sort of crusade against Germany'.

The Charleville conference

In the decisive conference with the Kaiser on 4th March 1916 at GHQ, Charleville, Falkenhayn declared that, in view of the dwindling resistance of the German allies and the German civil population, the war must be brought to an end before the year was out. The only means of achieving this was by unrestricted submarine warfare. On his part Bethmann Hollweg argued that Germany could stand another winter campaign. He would rather have a compromise peace than risk prolonging the war indefinitely by challenging America. In his opinion there were still insufficient U-boats. In the middle of March 1916 there were only fourteen large submarines capable of carrying on a commerce war in British waters.

On 4th March 1916 the Kaiser, unable to make up his mind, postponed his final decision until the beginning of April and then indefinitely. Nevertheless, with the agreement of the chancellor, a further tightening of the U-boat blockade was ordered on 13th March 1916. In the war zone both armed and unarmed merchant ships were to be destroyed without warning. Outside the war zone the previous orders remained in force. Tirpitz, who had not been called to the Charleville conference, reported sick to the Kaiser in protest and on 15th March he agreed to resign. One of Bethmann Hollweg's chief opponents had left the scene.

Whereas the instruction for the sinking of armed merchant ships was made public, the new order of 13th March was kept secret. Its effects, however, were viewed by the neutrals with growing alarm. Washington suspected that Germany had already started unrestricted submarine warfare. A new incident soon gave rise to another German-American crisis. On 24th March 1916 two Americans were injured when the cross-Channel passenger steamer, *Sussex,* was torpedoed without warning. In the erroneous belief that American citizens had lost their lives in the sinking President Wilson sent a note on 18th April threatening to break off diplomatic relations with Germany if it did not abandon its current methods of submarine warfare. Under pressure from this ultimatum the Kaiser gave orders, at Bethmann Hollweg's request, cancelling the tightened-up rules for submarine warfare in the combat zone around Great Britain. The rules of the 'cruiser' system were to be observed until further notice. The commanding officers on the naval front declared that such a procedure was unworkable, because of the danger to the U-boats, and they brought the submarine war in British waters to a complete standstill. In the Mediterranean the U-boats continued the campaign according to the new rules.

Cynical German cartoon protesting against the outcry over the drowning of passengers—a 'blind' American passenger on an 'unarmed' merchant ship

At the end of April 1916, when the reply to the American note had to be drafted, Falkenhayn again tried to persuade the Kaiser to agree to unrestricted submarine warfare. He asserted that he would have to forego action against Verdun if the U-boat war was suspended. Bethmann Hollweg indignantly rejected such an alternative and after a bitter dispute he once again convinced the Kaiser. In a note dated 4th May 1916 the German government agreed to the demands of the American government and informed it that the German naval forces had been instructed to observe the canons of international law with regard to the stopping, searching, and destruction of merchant vessels. At the same time it expressed its expectation that the United States would now induce the British government to abandon as soon as possible such of its methods of waging naval war as were contrary to international law. The German government reserved its complete freedom to alter its decision if this were not done. Wilson at once protested against the German claim to make respect for the rights of American citizens on the high seas dependent on the behaviour of the British government. Responsibility in such matters was individual not joint, absolute not relative. The two opposing standpoints were thus definitely laid down. If Germany again intensified the submarine war, it was to be expected that the

United States would promptly enter the war.

It was but a few months after the settlement of the *Sussex* case that the problem of unrestricted submarine warfare once again became acute. During the summer of 1916 the war situation was completely transformed. The Central powers, who had held the initiative for a whole year, were now forced into defensive battles lasting for months by the persistent offensive of the Russians in Volhynia and eastern Galicia and of the British and French on the Somme (p. 562), which could only be withstood by enormous efforts and casualties. Falkenhayn had to break off the battle for Verdun, which was bleeding not only France but also Germany to death. His prestige was shattered, and when Rumania entered the war against the Central powers on 27th August 1916 he was replaced by Hindenburg and Ludendorff. Hindenburg, who was the most popular of the German military leaders, became chief of the general staff. Bethmann Hollweg had worked for Hindenburg's appointment to this post during the critical summer months of 1916 because he thought that a moderate peace could be made acceptable to the German people, so misled by exaggerated hopes, only if it were covered by the name of Hindenburg. In other words, Bethmann Hollweg hoped to use the great authority of the field marshal in his efforts towards a peace of understanding. But Hindenburg's authority was fatal to Bethmann Hollweg's policy. Hindenburg and Ludendorff were advocates of unrestricted submarine warfare. After they had been summoned to take up the highest posts in the army they pleaded for a temporary postponement of this war measure only with respect to the difficult military situation. For at the moment great danger threatened from Rumania, and sufficient troops had to be made available as security against the European neutrals, who might regard unrestricted submarine warfare as a challenge. By the end of December 1916 the Rumanian army was defeated and in the following months military deployments against European neutrals could be initiated.

'This is how your money can fight—turn it into U-boats.' An appeal for war loans. In the background is a sinking enemy ship

Bibliothek für Zeitgeschichte, Stuttgart

Bethmann Hollweg had previously been able to stifle the arguments of Falkenhayn and the naval authorities in favour of unrestricted submarine warfare because the war situation in the spring of 1916 did not make such a risky measure absolutely essential. By the summer, however, the war was threatening to become one of attrition of man power and exhaustion of resources. Germany would not be strong enough in 1917 to undertake a large-scale offensive with the land forces available. A weapon that might well win the war was offered by the U-boats.

In these circumstances Bethmann Hollweg, in the latter part of 1916, tried to avoid the necessity of unrestricted submarine warfare by bringing about an early peace of compromise. President Wilson was working for the same end, because he wanted to keep America out of the war. On 12th December 1916 the Central powers made a peace offer to the Allies. On the 21st President Wilson invited the belligerents to state their war aims and announced his willingness to take part in the discussions. Hindenburg and Ludendorff had notified their concurrence with the peace offer of the Central powers, but as soon as the first negative reports began to arrive from the camp of the Allies they demanded, at the end of December 1916, speedy and energetic action at sea.

The prospects for unrestricted submarine warfare at the beginning of 1917 were much better than they had been a year before. Germany now had 105 U-boats, of which 46 large and 23 small vessels were available for the campaign in British waters. In view of the bad world harvests of 1916 unrestricted submarine warfare, if started before the chief overseas transport season began in early February, would foreseeably have a grave effect on Great Britain's grain supplies. Since 6th October 1916 the U-boats had carried on the commerce war in British waters on the 'cruiser' rules. Total sinkings were reckoned at 400,000 tons a month (in actual fact the figure was round about 325,000). By the removal of restrictions one expected an increase to 600,000 tons. The navy estimated that such a figure, enhanced by the consideration that neutral shipping would be frightened away, would in five months reduce the trade with Great Britain by thirty-nine per cent. This would force Great Britain to sue for peace. About the results of an American intervention in the war there was wide difference of opinion. The army thought that any great increase in the supply of American war material to the Allies was impossible, nor did it expect the arrival in Europe of large numbers of American troops. The politicians, however, thought that the American entry would encourage the Allied nations to hold out, would put large financial resources at their disposal, and would bring many American volunteers to join the Allies in Europe.

On the question of U-boat warfare Hindenburg and Ludendorff found their views supported by the vast majority of the German people. The largest party in the Reichstag, the Centre Party, passed a resolution on 7th October 1916 saying that the decision of the chancellor regarding submarine warfare must be based on the views of the supreme army command. As the Conservatives and National Liberals were in any case outright champions of unrestricted submarine warfare, Bethmann Hollweg knew that if he refused to make use of the U-boat weapon in opposition to Hindenburg and Ludendorff he could no longer count on a majority in the Reichstag. The feeling of the people was summed up by Bethmann Hollweg in his memoirs: 'No nation will stand for not winning a war when it is convinced that it can win.' He himself, in spite of his constant resistance to unrestricted submarine warfare, seems at times to have wondered whether, after all, the use of this extreme weapon might not achieve a turn for the better.

For the moment Bethmann Hollweg left the problem unsolved. When on 9th January 1917 he went to Pless to discuss the ever more pressing problem, he found the naval staff and the supreme army command united against him and they had already won over the Kaiser to their side. Hindenburg and Ludendorff saw no possibility of bringing the war to a victorious end unless the U-boats were used without restrictions. They declared themselves ready to shoulder all responsibility for any results caused by this war measure. The chief of the naval staff guaranteed that he could force Great Britain to its knees before the next harvest. Once again Bethmann Hollweg produced all his objections, but after the failure of the Central powers' peace move all hopes for a peace of understanding seemed to have vanished. Bethmann Hollweg could no longer maintain his opposition to the demands of the military and he told the Kaiser that he could not recommend him to oppose the vote of his military advisers. He felt he must refrain from offering his resignation, so as not to expose the inner dissensions in the German leadership to all the world. Until the last moment, however, he continued to doubt the wisdom of the decision of 9th January 1917. When towards the end of the month the prospects for a successful outcome of Wilson's peace efforts seemed more favourable, he tried to secure a postponement of unrestricted submarine warfare, but the naval staff assured him that most of the U-boats had already been despatched.

The beginning of unrestricted submarine warfare on 1st February 1917 was at first countered by Wilson with the rupture of diplomatic relations, whereby he hoped to bring Germany to its senses. The political tension between the two countries was increased at the beginning of March by the publication of a German offer of alliance to Mexico (intercepted by the British intelligence service) should the United States enter the war because of the submarine war. The sinking of seven American merchant ships by U-boats by 21st March finally obliged Wilson to summon Congress, which on 4th and 6th April approved a declaration of war.

At first the figures of sinkings by the U-boats surpassed the forecasts and expectations of the German naval authorities, reaching its maximum in April 1917. But when in the course of the summer merchant ships sailing for Great Britain were assembled in convoys and protected by destroyers the number of successes dwindled. Nevertheless, unrestricted submarine warfare brought Great Britain difficulties which led the British government to begin to take an interest in political solutions. But on the whole the strong urge towards peace that was expected from the U-boat menace failed to materialize. Looking back, it is clear that the German military leaders and politicians regarded the unrestricted submarine warfare as a failure. For from March 1917 onwards the Central powers were relieved of a great burden by the Russian Revolution. Russia dropped out of the war in the winter of 1917-18, and negotiations for a general peace of understanding might have been possible had not the Allies been encouraged to hold on by the prospect of American armed assistance. But the principal effect of unrestricted submarine warfare was on America itself, for it caused the abandonment of America's policy of isolation and its entry into world politics. *(Translation)*

'Shelling a merchantman' by H.R.Butler. This U-boat has warned the crew before firing, and they are escaping in lifeboats

Smithsonian Institute, Washington / Photo: Henry Beville

USA, 1914-17/Arthur S.Link

Wilson and the Ordeal of Neutrality

President Wilson had almost undisputed control of the foreign affairs of the greatest of the neutral powers, and America's actions would vitally affect the major powers of Europe and the outcome of the war. Could America stay neutral?

Opposite page: *President Wilson holding up a baseball at a World Series match, 1915. He 'played a part in the fate of nations incomparably more direct and personal than any other man'. Although he was an intellectual and an idealist, in this vital period Wilson understood and shared the attitudes of the majority of his fellow-countrymen*

Different views of Wilson's conduct. ***Below:*** *The British view, from a* Punch *cartoon. 'Hail Columba! President Wilson (to American Eagle): "Gee! What a dove I've made of you!"'* ***Bottom:*** *A German view. Big Chief Old Serpent letting out a war-cry. The Germans felt that Wilson was threatening Berlin*

Punch

Kladdereradatsch

The outbreak of war in Europe in August 1914 came, in its suddenness, to President Wilson like a bolt of lightning out of a clear sky. To be sure, Wilson had not been unaware of the possibility of a conflagration, for his confidential adviser and sometime agent, Colonel Edward M.House, writing from Berlin in May 1914, had warned that Europe was a powder keg about to explode. However, House's talks with German and British leaders had raised the tantalizing possibility of an Anglo-American-German entente under Wilson's auspices. No one in Washington (or in European capitals, for that matter) saw that the fuse was burning rapidly after the murder of the heir to the Austrian and Hungarian thrones and his young wife by a Serbian nationalist in Sarajevo on 28th June 1914. Moreover, when the great European powers went over the brink in late July and early August, Wilson was mired in controversy with Congress and in deep despair over the fatal illness of his wife. He could only wait in fascinated horror as Sir Edward Grey, the British foreign minister, wept as he told the American ambassador in London, Walter Page, about the British ultimatum to Germany, and King George exclaimed, 'My God, Mr Page, what else could we do?' One American well expressed what was surely Wilson's reaction when he wrote: 'The horror of it all kept me awake for weeks, nor has the awfulness of it all deserted me, but at first it seemed a horrid dream.'

But Armageddon *had* come. Wilson, as head of the greatest neutral power, whose interests would be vitally affected by belligerent measures, had perforce to work out his policies towards the warring powers.

Throughout the long months of American neutrality, from August 1914 to April 1917, Wilson, whatever his own predispositions, had to work within limits imposed by American public opinion. That opinion was so divided in its preferences for various belligerents during the first months of the war that any policy for the United States other than a strict neutrality would have been inconceivable. Wilson remarked to the German ambassador, Count Johann von Bernstorff, that 'we definitely have to be neutral, since otherwise our mixed populations would wage war on each other'. More important still, in spite of the attachments of various national and ethnic minorities, and of all the efforts of British, French, and German propagandists in the United States, the predominant American public opinion was consistently neutral before 1917. But Americans, even though they clung doggedly to their traditional isolationism and refused to believe that their vital interests were sufficiently involved in the outcome of the war to justify voluntary intervention, were none the less jealous of their sovereignty and international prestige. In other words, they would tolerate only a certain amount of provocation, and no more. To an extraordinary degree Wilson understood and shared the attitudes of the majority of his fellow-countrymen. Both expediency and conviction dictated policies that were agreeable to the great majority of Americans.

Although Wilson had strong emotional attachments to the Allies, particularly Great Britain, he profoundly admired German contributions to modern civilization. As a sophisticated student of modern history, he well understood that the causes of the war were complex and never imputed exclusive responsibility to either side. He was able to detach emotions from decisions and policies and, self-consciously, to make decisions on the basis of what he considered to be the best interests of America and Europe.

Wilson exercised greater personal control over foreign policy than any other chief of state among the great powers of the world. Constitutionally, as President he was sovereign in the conduct of foreign relations, subject only to the Senate's veto on treaties. Weak Presidents have abdicated their responsibilities to strong secretaries of state or congressional leaders. But Wilson was a 'strong' President. He believed that the people had invested their sovereignty in foreign affairs in him. He not only refused to delegate this responsibility, but insisted upon conducting foreign relations himself. Because he used his full constitutional powers to execute policies that the great majority desired, Wilson not only held the conduct of foreign affairs in his own hands, but was irresistible while doing so. 'It seems no exaggeration,' Churchill later wrote, 'to pronounce that the action of the United States with its repercussions on the history of the world depended, during the awful period of Armageddon, upon the workings of this man's mind and spirit to the exclusion of almost every other factor; and that he played a part in the fate of nations incomparably more direct and personal than any other man.'

Wilson's whole world came tumbling down in the first week of August 1914. Ellen Axson Wilson, his beloved wife since 1885, died on 6th August. Great Britain,

which he loved, and Germany, which he admired, were already beginning to tear at each other's throats. Near hysteria reigned in Wall Street as a consequence of the disruption of international trade and exchange.

With his customary iron self-control, the President moved confidently and serenely to meet emergencies and establish American neutrality. The formalities were observed easily enough. Wilson proclaimed official neutrality on 4th August and, two weeks later, admonished his fellow-countrymen to be 'impartial in thought as well as in action'.

However, being neutral in the midst of a great war was easier said than done. For example, should the American government permit its citizens to sell vital raw materials and munitions to the Allies when British cruisers prevented the Germans from having access to such supplies? More difficult still, should the government permit American bankers to lend money, which the secretary of state, William Jennings Bryan, called the 'worst of all contrabands', to the belligerents?

Having decided upon a policy of strict neutrality, Wilson, helped by Bryan and the counselor of the State Department, Robert Lansing, proceeded as systematically and as impartially as possible to be neutral in every circumstance. Hence he permitted the Allies to purchase as much contraband as they pleased, for to have denied them access to American markets and the benefits that flowed from dominant seapower would have been not only unneutral, but tantamount to undeclared war. For the same reason he permitted American bankers to lend money both to the Allied and German governments.

Wilson followed the rush of the German army through Belgium into northern France and was obviously relieved when the French and British were able to establish a secure defensive line by early autumn. At this point, at any rate, Germany seemed to threaten neither America's vital interests nor her neutral rights. Wilson's main problem in late 1914 was defending American trading rights against British seapower, or, to put the matter more realistically, coming to terms with the British maritime system.

Acting as neutrals always have during wartime, Wilson wanted to keep the channels of commerce to all of Europe open as widely as possible to American ships and goods. Acting as dominant seapowers always have, the British set about to cut off the flow of life-giving supplies from the United States to Germany and Austria-Hungary. Consequently, dispatches about these matters passed frequently between Washington and London, not only during the first months of the war, but as late as 1916. There was much talk of 'freedom of the seas' on the one side and of legitimate belligerent rights on the other. Actually, what sounded like the rhetoric of developing crisis masked the fact that there was substantial goodwill and accommodation on both sides. For their part, the British instituted maritime measures that were not only largely legitimate, but also were based upon precedents established by the United States government itself during the American Civil War of 1861-65. For his part, Wilson, understanding these facts, rejected demands of highly partisan German Americans and American economic interests with a large stake in free trade with Germany for measures to break the British blockade or prevent the Anglo-American trade in contraband.

Having passed through troubles that might have burgeoned into serious Anglo-American crisis, Wilson, at the end of 1914, could view the general state of American relations with the belligerents with some equanimity. There seemed to be no chance of serious conflict with Germany: there were simply no points of contact between the two nations. By Wilson's reckoning, the war would end either in stalemate or, more likely, in an Allied victory. He told a reporter for the *New York Times,* in an off-the-record interview on 14th December 1914, that he hoped ardently for a peace of reconciliation based upon negotiation. But, Wilson added, he did not think that it would 'greatly hurt' the interests of the United States if the Allies won a decisive victory and dictated the settlement.

Between the cruiser and the submarine

The German decision, announced on 4th February 1915, to use an untried weapon, the submarine, in a war against merchant shipping in the English Channel and a broad zone around the British Isles, created an entirely new situation, fraught with peril for the United States. Actually, at this time, the German navy did not possess enough submarines to prosecute an effective campaign, even against Allied merchant ships. But the Germans had compounded the blunder of acting prematurely, largely in bluff, by adding that *neutral* ships might be torpedoed because of the Allied use of neutral flags. It was only the first of a series of blunders by the German admiralty and the high command that would drive the United States into the war.

President Wilson replied to Berlin on 10th February with a stern warning that the United States would hold the German government to a 'strict accountability' and probably go to war if German submarines indiscriminately and illegally attacked American vessels on the high seas.

As it turned out, the gravest German blunder was to provide the British and French governments with a good excuse for doing what they had already planned to do—severely to tighten their blockade measures. Now they need fear no serious American reprisal. Invoking the ancient right of reprisal, the London and Paris authorities announced on 1st March that, in retaliation against the illegal and ruthless German submarine campaign, they would stop *all* commerce of whatever character to the Central powers, even commerce through neutral ports.

Wilson and Bryan worked hard to arrange an Anglo-American agreement that would provide some protection for American shipping against the cruisers and submarines. Their efforts foundered upon the shoals of the German refusal to give up the submarine campaign except at the price of virtual abandonment by the British of an effective blockade. Wilson was in fact now helpless; he could only acquiesce in the new Anglo-French blockade so long as the sword of the submarine hung over his head.

The President waited in uncertainty all through the early spring of 1915 to see what the Germans would do. There were several attacks against American ships that might have set off a crisis. However, the submarine issue was brought to a head suddenly and dramatically when *U20,* Kapitänleutnant Walther Schwieger, without warning torpedoed the pride of the Cunard Line, the unarmed *Lusitania,* in the Irish Sea on 7th May 1915, killing 128 American citizens among many others.

It was impossible for Wilson to temporize, so violent was the reaction in the United States. Yet what could he do? It was evident after the first shock that a majority of Americans wanted their President to be firm and yet avoid war if possible. This, actually, was Wilson's own intention. In three notes between May and early July, Wilson eloquently appealed to the imperial German government to abandon what was obviously a campaign of sheer terror against *unarmed Allied passenger ships.* In the last note he warned that he would probably break diplomatic relations if the Germans did not abandon that campaign. To each of Wilson's pleas, the German foreign office replied by truculently refusing to admit the illegality of the destruction of *Lusitania.* The impasse was broken by a second incident that came hard on the heels of the *Lusitania* affair—the torpedoing without warning of the White Star liner, *Arabic,* outward bound from Liverpool, on 19th August. Only when they saw that Wilson was on the brink did the Germans yield and promise not to sink unarmed Allied passenger liners without warning. Indeed, Wilson's firmness, and the lack of enough submarines to prosecute a decisive underseas campaign, paid even larger dividends in the form of guarantees that the German navy would sink American ships only after making full provision for the safety of human life, and that compensation would be made for all ships and cargoes captured or destroyed.

The subsequent German-American *détente* (encouraged by a temporary abandonment of the submarine campaign in general) set off demands in the United States, primarily by southern cotton producers in deep depression on account of the closing of their central European markets, for action against the total Allied blockade as firm as that taken against the German submarine campaign. Bryan had resigned in the middle of the *Lusitania* crisis, because he feared that Wilson's notes might lead the Germans to declare war against the United States. The new secretary of state, Robert Lansing, did prepare a formidable indictment of the British maritime measure, and Wilson permitted it to go to London on 5th November. But the President had no intention of enforcing the note's demands until German-American differences were clarified.

On the face of it, American relations with Great Britain and Germany had reached a state of tolerable equilibrium by the end of 1915. The Germans had quietly abandoned their submarine campaign in the North Atlantic, hence there were no incidents in that area to exacerbate German-American relations. For their part, the British had gone to extraordinary (and successful) lengths to support American cotton prices and to come to terms with other American producers who had been hard hit by the Allied blockade. But Wilson and his two principal diplomatic advisers, Colonel House and Lansing, were not reassured as they contemplated potential dangers in the months immediately ahead. The Allies were beginning to arm not only passenger liners but ordinary merchantmen as well, and, apparently, were ordering these ships to attack submarines upon sight. Second, reports from Berlin made it unmistakably clear that there had been only a respite in the submarine campaign, and that the Germans were preparing to use the arming of Allied ships as an excuse for an all-out campaign. So far *ad hoc* solutions had sufficed to preserve the peace, but it now seemed that events might develop which would remove all options. For example, a really ruthless submarine campaign might drive the United States, willy-nilly, into war, without any other purpose than sheer defence of national rights.

Wilson and House pondered long about the situation in the hope of gaining some initiative and of giving some purpose to American belligerency if it had to come. Sir Edward Grey had said only two months before that his government might be willing to consider a negotiated settlement if the United States would promise to join a post-war league of nations and guarantee to help maintain future peace. Seizing the seeming opportunity offered by Grey's suggestion, Wilson sent House to London in late December 1915 with instructions to work for Anglo-American agreement to co-operate in a drive for peace under Wilson's auspices. If that *démarche* should fail on account of German obduracy, Wilson said, the United States would probably enter the war on the Allied side.

While House was in London opening negotiations, Lansing and Wilson launched their own campaign to get the United States off the submarine hook. The secretary of state, on 18th January 1916, urged the Allies to disarm their merchantmen if the Germans would agree to warn such vessels and evacuate their crews before

***Bottom:** An election truck decorated with Wilson's claim for the trust of his country. In 1916 a wave of neutralist feeling swept the USA and persuaded Wilson to stand as a 'peace' candidate*

sinking them. Lansing added that his government was contemplating treating armed merchantmen as warships, which would mean that they could not engage in commerce at American ports. The Germans, gleefully agreeing with the secretary of state, announced that submarines would sink all armed merchantmen without warning after 28th February.

Reaction in London to what was called Lansing's *modus vivendi* was so violent that it threatened to wreck House's negotiations. Wilson thereupon hastily withdrew the *modus vivendi*. This action in turn set off a panic in Congress that the United States would go to war to protect the right of citizens to travel on armed ships. Wilson beat back a congressional resolution warning Americans against travelling on armed ships, but he made it clear that only lightly-armed merchantmen would be permitted to use American ports, and, more important, that he did not intend to make a great issue with the German government over armed ships in any event.

There was considerable relief both on Capitol Hill and in Whitehall. In London, Sir Edward Grey and House initialled, on 22nd February 1916, what is known as the House-Grey Memorandum embodying Wilson's plan of mediation.

Colonel House returned to Washington on 5th March in high excitement to tell the President that the British and French were eager to move as rapidly as possible for peace under Wilson's aegis. While Wilson and House were in the midst of planning for the great venture, a German submarine torpedoed a French packet steamer, *Sussex,* in the English Channel on 24th March with heavy loss of life. Reports of ruthless attacks against unarmed merchantmen followed in rapid succession.

After much backing and filling, and mainly in order to pave the way for his mediation, Wilson sent an ultimatum to Berlin on 18th April warning that he would break relations with Germany if she did not agree hereafter to require her submarine commanders to observe the rules of visit and search before sinking all unarmed ships, whether passenger liners or merchantmen. The German admiralty lacked enough U-boats to justify the risk of war with the United States and European neutrals like Holland and Denmark. Consequently, the imperial chancellor, Theobald von Bethmann Hollweg, won the Kaiser's support for submission to Wilson's demand. However, while yielding the Germans reserved the 'right' to resume freedom of decision on the use of submarines if the American government failed to compel the Allies to respect international law in the conduct of their blockade.

The happy settlement of the *Sussex* crisis, coupled with intimations that the Germans were eager for peace talks, spurred Wilson to action to put the House-Grey Memorandum into operation. His first public move was to announce, in an address in Washington on 27th May, that the United States was prepared to abandon its traditional isolationism and join a post-war league of nations. Privately, through Colonel House, he exerted heavy pressure on Grey to put the memorandum's machinery into motion by signalling his government's readiness for Wilson's mediation. Grey responded evasively at first; but Wilson would not be diverted, and then Grey had to tell him frankly that neither the British nor the French governments would consent to peace talks at this time or in the foreseeable future.

Grey's refusal to execute the House-Grey Memorandum, a crushing blow to the President's hopes for an early peace in itself, combined with other developments to cause Wilson to effect what would turn out to be an almost radical change in his policies towards the European belligerents.

First, the British government not only refused to relax its controls over American commerce, but, on the contrary, intensified its maritime and economic warfare in the spring and summer of 1916. In retrospect, the new British measures (including search and seizure of American mail on neutral ships and publication in the United States of a 'blacklist' of American firms still doing business with the Central powers) seem trivial when compared with policies in which the Washington administration had already acquiesced. However, Wilson and a majority of Americans resented the new measures as direct affronts to their national sovereignty. Second, the British army's severe repression of the Easter Rising in Dublin in April (p. 596) not only inflamed Irish Americans, but also caused a tremendous diminution in Great Britain's moral standing throughout the United States. Finally, the German-American *détente* following the *Sussex* crisis sent a wave of neutralism across the country, one so strong that it engulfed the Democratic national convention that re-nominated Wilson for the presidency.

These developments, of course, had their most important impact upon the man in the White House. They convinced him that the American people did not want to go to war over the alleged right of Americans to travel and work on belligerent ships. They forced Wilson to stand as the 'peace' candidate and to accuse his Republican opponent, Charles Evans Hughes, of wanting war. More important, they caused a very considerable hardening of Wilson's attitudes against the Allies, particularly the British. By the early autumn, Wilson believed that the Allies were fighting for victory and spoils, not for a just peace.

Wilson could do nothing, of course, while the presidential campaign was in progress. However, once the voters, on 7th November 1916, invested him with their sovereignty for another four years, Wilson was free to act. And action of some kind seemed to be imperative, for it was growing increasingly evident that both sides were preparing to use desperate measures to break the stalemate that was consuming human life and resources at a prodigious rate. For the British, this would mean further intensification of economic warfare; for the Germans, it would mean revoking the *Sussex* pledge and launching a wholesale campaign against maritime commerce. The only way to peace and safety, Wilson concluded, was to bring the war to an end through his independent mediation.

Diverted briefly by domestic developments and Germany's own offer to negotiate, Wilson launched his peace bolt on 18th December 1916 by asking the belligerents to state the terms upon which they would be willing to end the fighting. The British and French were stunned and furious. But they were helpless to resist, so dependent had they become upon American credit and supplies for continuation of their war efforts. Then Lansing intervened. Committed emotionally to the Allied cause, he set out to sabotage the President's peace move by encouraging the British and French governments to state such terms as could be won only by a decisive military victory. The Germans, who very much wanted Wilson to force the Allies to the peace table but did not want him meddling once the conference had begun, returned an evasive reply.

Wilson was undisturbed. In mid-January 1917 he launched the second and decisive move in his campaign for peace – high-level, direct, and secret negotiations with the British and German governments to obtain their consent to his mediation. While waiting for their replies, the President went before the Senate on 22nd January to tell the world what kind of settlement he had in mind and the American people would support by membership in a league of nations. The peace to be made, Wilson said, had to be a peace of reconciliation, a 'peace without victory', for a victor's peace would leave 'a sting, a resentment, a bitter memory upon which terms of peace would rest, not permanently, but only as upon quicksand'.

For reasons that are still obscure, the new British cabinet headed by David Lloyd George sent word on 26th January to Wilson that it was prepared to accept the President's mediation. The Austro-Hungarians were desperately eager for peace. But on 31st January Wilson was informed of the German decision to adopt unrestricted submarine warfare.

USA, 1914-17/Hugh Brogan

The American People and the War

In this great democracy the opinion of its people was of vital importance. How was it that a peace-loving, isolationist people of 1914 could in 1917 willingly embark on a crusade to keep the world 'free for democracy'

Few hours in history have been so full of real and self-conscious drama as that on 2nd April 1917 when President Woodrow Wilson came before the United States Congress, sitting in joint session, to recommend the declaration of war on Germany. The hall of the House of Representatives, where the scene took place, overflowed with listeners. Immediately below the rostrum sat the members of the cabinet, the justices of the supreme court, the senators, and the representatives. The galleries were packed with distinguished visitors, as well as with the diplomats, wives, and reporters who always throng to great official occasions in Washington. All present knew what was coming, knew that this was to be far and away the most momentous occasion of its kind since Wilson revived George Washington's practice of presenting his most important messages to Congress in person. 'As the President proceeded in his address,' reports an eyewitness, 'the tension of suppressed excitement grew until it burst all bounds . . . As the President recommended the declaration of war, applause, which seemed universal, rolled through the whole assembly from floor to gallery. The audience rose to cheer when Chief Justice White waved his hands in the air as he, in effect, led the expression of unanimous approval.' The central figure was almost alone in resisting the tide of enthusiasm. Later, in deep distress, he remarked to his secretary that 'my message today was a message of death for our young men. How strange it seems to applaud that'. Few others were capable of such Lincolnian melancholy at such a moment, or of counting the cost of the decision that Congress promptly took, by an overwhelming majority, ▷ 660

American delegation bound for the International Women's Peace Conference at The Hague, 1915. They were given a tumultuous send-off by their peace-loving countrymen. The flag was presented to them by New York's mayor

Previous page: *Months of strain, of self-congratulation, isolationism, and praise of peace led, somehow, to this – American soldiers embarking at Southampton to take an active part in the internecine struggles of the Old World. (Painting by Thomas Derrick, Imperial War Museum)*

to follow the President's recommendation.

The rest of the country, it is true, did not respond with all the fervour of the capital. It flooded Congress with messages of support (and some of dissent), but recruiting was slow. The political strength of pacifism, which had been widespread and highly vocal up to the last minute, was broken, but pacifist sentiment persisted. However, opinion in general accepted the idea that the United States, under attack from German intrigue and German submarines, had no choice but to fight; and welcomed the President's declaration that the war was to be one 'to make the world safe for democracy'. One of Wilson's two bitterest political opponents, former President Theodore Roosevelt, spoke for the American people when he hailed the war message as 'a great state paper'; and the other, Senator Henry Cabot Lodge, Sr, echoed that message when he declared, 'What we want most of all by this victory which we shall help to win is to secure the world's peace, broad-based on freedom and democracy'. In this fashion the American people made the cause of the embattled French and British their own.

Only America at peace!

Very different had been the national consensus three years earlier, when news of Europe's collapse into war crossed the Atlantic. A peace-loving, optimistic, passionately democratic but not very well-informed people had been horrified by the dreadful tidings. One intelligent and representative lady (a congressman's wife) wrote: 'I feel as if some black-winged monster had come between us and the sun, breathing poison over all the lovely green things upon the earth that should be praising God and magnifying him forever.' Newspapers were immediately filled with news of a war which the *New York Times* characterized as the bloodiest ever fought on earth, and 'the least justified of all wars since man emerged from barbarism'. But such reactions were not, of course, confined to the United States. The essentially American note was struck by the *Chicago Herald,* which said that 'Peace-loving citizens of this country will now rise up and tender a hearty vote of thanks to Columbus for having discovered America', by the *Wabash Plain Dealer,* which 'never appreciated so keenly as now the foresight exercised by our forefathers in emigrating from Europe', and, above all, by the President, in 1914 as in 1917 the most eloquent spokesman for his fellow-citizens: 'Look abroad upon the troubled world. Only America at peace! Among all the great powers of the world, only America saving her power for her own people. . . . Do you not think it likely that the world will some time turn to America and say: "You were right and we were wrong . . ."?' Neutrality instantly became the cherished wish and policy of the American government and people. Wilson, or so he said, 'looked upon the war as a distant event, terrible and tragic, but one which did not concern us closely in the political sense'. No European leader could say the same. America had reason to congratulate itself.

The horror mounted, so did the self-congratulation. A note of doubt, it is true, crept in early, as the struggle for mastery of the Atlantic raged, and it became clear that America could not automatically depend on safety from the European turmoil. But the election of 1916, which was won by Wilson and the Democrats with the slogan 'He kept us out of the war', was sufficient evidence of the nation's sentiments. Almost till the last minute, it thought it could stay out of the war; before and after that minute, it wanted to.

So clear is all this, and so solid were the reasons for continuing American neutrality; so immense were the obstacles between the United States and belligerent status, that it is still extremely difficult to understand how the plunge into war came about. American belligerency may have been right or wrong. It was certainly not inevitable. It was immensely important. Not only did it decide the outcome of the First World War; it clearly enounced, for the first time, what was to be the major theme of the 20th, the American, century – the coming of the United States into its heritage of power. Yet, given its true significance, the event seems more baffling than ever. The Americans of 1914 were isolationist as well as innocent. They did not want world power. The contrast with 1917 is so sharp, so enormous as to make all explanations seem inadequate.

The truth seems to be that the change was more apparent than real. As their rejection of the League of Nations was to show, the people of the United States remained isolationist at heart. In 1917 they simply failed to realize the full significance of what they were doing, for otherwise they would probably not have done it. Had they been told that American participation in the First World War was not inevitable, but that close and permanent American participation in the affairs of the modern world was, they would have been appalled. They wanted to believe the opposite. The nation had lived undisturbed by European conflicts for a century, and wanted to continue like that. Even most of those who whole-heartedly echoed the Wilsonian eloquence that spoke of a fight 'for a universal dominion of right by such a concert of free peoples as shall bring peace and safety to all nations and make the world itself at last free' would have denied that this involved a future commit-

Culver Pictures

Above: *British cartoon showing the two faces of Wilson's policy of neutrality*

Culver Pictures

American magazine illustrations. ***Above:*** *New Year 1917 promises showers of Allied gold to America.* ***Below:*** *America impotent*

Puck

ment of indefinite duration to meddle in the affairs of the Old World. By 'a world made safe for democracy' the American people on the whole understood a world in which they could safely be isolationist, one in which there would be no more alliances, no more wars or fears of wars, no more troubling intrusion of lesser breeds without the law on the peaceful preoccupations of the Land of the Free. This was to be a war to safeguard American interests and redeem American honour; a war to punish the aggressor; but, above all, a war to end wars.

To the end of his life Woodrow Wilson believed that American strength and American virtue could be successfully applied to make the dream come true. His countrymen soon abandoned this idea; but they did not substitute for it any perception that, as G.K.Chesterton remarked, 'the world cannot be made safe for democracy: it is a dangerous trade'. Instead, they fell back on the belief that the old principles were right, that the United States could and should keep itself to itself, shunning all overseas adventures. The great crusade had failed, like the turn-of-the-century imperialism which had preceded it. Now Americans would once more heed the solemn warnings of George Washington that 'Europe has a set of primary interests which to us have none or a very remote relation. Hence she must be engaged in frequent controversies, the causes of which are essentially foreign to our concerns. Hence, therefore, it must be unwise in us to implicate ourselves by artificial ties in the ordinary vicissitudes of her politics or the ordinary combinations and collisions of her friendships or enmities . . .' They would ponder the experience of their second President, John Adams, who, when minister at Paris, was told by a Swedish diplomat that 'I take it for granted, that you will have sense enough to see us in Europe cut each other's throats with a philosophical tranquillity'. They would follow the advice of their third President, Thomas Jefferson, who urged 'peace, commerce, and honest friendship with all nations, entangling alliances with none'.

The bubble of this pretty dream was to be pricked forever not long after the period with which this article is concerned. But it was intact, whatever the appearance to the contrary, throughout the war.

That war, in short, did not turn the Americans into proponents of *Realpolitik:* it launched them on one of the most high-minded enterprises in their history.

In 1914 the issues of the struggle had at first seemed, to the transatlantic onlookers, perfectly plain. The first weeks produced a storm of moral indignation, in which rational reflection was almost swamped. The storm did not, however, unite the nation. Not all Americans responded alike. The greater number, English-speaking when not of British descent, and sentimentally attached, thanks to French assistance during the War of Independence, to France, had no doubt that the blame all attached to Germany. The rape of Belgium was the chief justification for this feeling. Even today, when we cannot easily echo the virtuous protests at conduct (such as the bombing of Antwerp) which seemed unforgivable at the time, but which, we now recognize, was the logical result of modern war, it must be conceded that there was a wantonness about much of Germany's conduct which invited denunciation. It got it. On the other hand, the stories which inflamed American opinion to fever point, like that of mutilated Belgian children, some minus fingers, other minus hands, arriving as refugees in Wales, were simply false. It was no wonder that Americans of German descent or origin (6,400,000 of them) resented and vociferously repudiated the charges – without much effect. The fate of Belgium remained, throughout the war, one of the most potent stimulants of anti-German feeling.

Still, the German-Americans, vigorously assisted by the German embassy, did their best to throw the charge of sin on to the other side: and so the moralist attitude to the war was established.

Second thoughts, however, soon modified the indignation. For instance, a certain anxiety was felt in high places about the possible consequences of pro- and anti-German feeling for the domestic peace of the United States. The President issued an appeal for neutrality 'in thought as well as in act'; the Mayor of Cleveland, Ohio, a future secretary of war, was afraid that there might be war in the streets between the factions. He tells us: 'The Chief of Police smiled at my naïveté and said: "Mr Mayor, I will, of course, do what you suggest, but there will be no trouble here. Most of these people came from Europe to escape the very thing now going on there and their chief emotion will be thankfulness that they have escaped it and are not involved." ' The chief of police was right. All over the United States citizens gradually came to conclusions about the European powers like those expressed by the *Philadelphia Public Ledger* in September, 1914: 'All, in a mad stampede for armament, trade, and territory, have sown swords and guns, and nourished harvests of death-dealing crops.' Scepticism about the absolute righteousness of the Entente cause (especially as it was also that of Tsarist Russia from which many Americans, initially Poles, Jews, Ukrainians, had fled), though not faith in the cause of the Central powers, steadily strengthened as the months passed into years, and became one of the strongest props of Wilson's efforts to preserve neutrality and mediate a peace.

The ebbing of emotions solved few problems. The institution of a British blockade of Europe threatened to hamper American trade grievously, and immediately knocked the bottom out of the cotton market. Soon German submarines began to threaten neutral trade with Great Britain, and neutral lives embarked in British vessels. Most insidious of all, the Entente powers began to shop for armaments and munitions in America. Under the stimulus of their orders American trade revived: soon it was booming. And soon Great Britain and France, having exhausted their financial resources, sought to pay for American goods by raising loans in New York.

At first they had no success: the federal government discouraged such loans. William Jennings Bryan, the secretary of state, felt that they were unneutral. 'Money,' he said, 'is the worst of all contrabands because it commands everything else.' Unfortunately, if it was unneutral to supply Germany's enemies, it was unneutral not to. Perhaps, if America had refused to become the arsenal of the Entente, the chief result would have been a more rational strategy on the Western Front: Haig might not have been allowed to waste so much ammunition as he did in futile bombardment. At the time it was only clear that France and Great Britain, since their proposal was perfectly legal, would have a legitimate grievance if America refused to supply them. The prospective profits were tempting. America took the easy way. The ban was lifted, loans were negotiated, and trade with the Entente powers rose from $824,000,000 in 1914 to $3,214,000,000 in 1916. At the same time, because of the blockade, trade with the Central powers shrank from $169,000,000 in 1914 to $1,159,000 in 1916. In a Europe that was growing desperately short both of money and of materials, this amounted to an indispensable underwriting by the Americans of the Western cause. It is small wonder that the Germans grew increasingly indifferent to American feelings.

Yet, essentially, those feelings worked in the German interest. Any sort of peace concluded before April, 1917, would have been favourable to the Central powers, since the Entente had proved unable to dislodge them from their conquests. And Americans were overwhelmingly in favour of an early peace, especially as the price would have to be paid by others. Peace had been one of their pet causes for years before 1914. One industrialist-philanthropist, Andrew Carnegie, had set up a $10,000,000 Endowment for International Peace. In 1915 another, Henry Ford, sent a 'peace ship', filled with pacifists, to Europe, her mission being 'to get the boys out of the trenches by Christmas'. The German ambassador at Washington, Bernstorff, was so well aware of the usefulness of all this to his country that he worked unceasingly to preserve good relations between America and Germany, and encouraged Wilson's attempts to bring an early end to the conflict by mediation. His masters were not so wise. On 7th May 1915 one of their submarines sank the great English liner *Lusitania*: 128 Americans were among those drowned. Emphatic protests at this and similar sinkings eventually induced the Germans to hold their hand for a while,

Punch *cartoon – the ship of pacifists Ford sent to Europe. A U-boat shouts 'Welcome'*

but on 9th January 1917 they decided to resort to unrestricted submarine warfare. Wilson severed diplomatic relations. Then in March an intercepted cable, the famous Zimmermann Telegram, revealed that the Germans were embarking on an intrigue to draw Mexico into an attack on the United States in order to recover some of the vast areas lost during the 19th century. Roused to fury, America went to war in the following month.

There is nothing very remarkable about this list of challenges and responses; but it is worth pointing out that the reactions of the American people were, throughout, even more important than those of their government, which in fact they determined to a unique extent. In some respects the people were more extreme, going to the human heart of issues which the Administration tended to approach in legalities. After the sinking of the *Lusitania* some (Bryan among them) said that persons voluntarily sailing in British ships in submarine-infested waters had no one to blame but themselves if they were drowned. Wilson argued stiffly that the undoubted legal rights of the dead Americans had been wantonly infringed. Public opinion simply held that innocent women and children ought not to be drowned at sea merely because their ship had small-arms ammunition in her cargo. 'The torpedo which sunk the *Lusitania*,' said the *Nation*, 'also sank Germany in the opinion of mankind.' For the first time interventionist sentiment developed – not, admittedly, on any great scale.

The pattern was repeated in all the subsequent crises. In every case Wilson may be said to have kept himself one step behind the nation, never taking an irretrievable step until it was demanded of him by the majority of Americans – never, that is, until America had actually entered the war. Only then did his Messianic instincts begin to get the better of his judgement.

It is easy to see now that the war could not be waged without action by the United States, and that the United States, without really intending to do so, early involved itself and its interests on the Allied side. It follows from this that Wilson early lost his most important freedom, the freedom to stay out, even though for most of the period of neutrality America consciously decided to put up with the inconveniences of being a bystander in the immense struggle. By the winter of 1916-17, at the latest, the decision as to whether America would go to war or not rested with Berlin. Germany took the decision for unrestricted submarine warfare, and hence for war with America (no pre-nuclear great power would tamely submit to be bullied) on the calculation that it could beat the Entente before American strength became effective. The calculation proved mistaken. It all seems almost inevitable.

In 1916, however, it seemed that another possibility existed. The Germans, it is true, had made themselves hopelessly unpopular in the previous year by their brutality. They were therefore on their best behaviour. On the other hand, the British were, and had been from the beginning, flouting the rights of property that were only a little less sacred than the right to live. Resentment could never be so fierce over the impounding of ships and goods as it was over the loss of life, even when there was all too much reason to suspect the Entente governments of wishing to sabotage American efforts to mediate. But Great Britain made itself odious to the 3,400,000 Irish-Americans by its bloody repression of the Easter Rising in Dublin (p. 596). In view of the long and extravagant series of German blunders it is inconceivable that America would ever have fought on the side of the Central powers; but it might very well have deserted the cause of the Entente. After all, in November 1916, the President, while saying that relations with Great Britain 'were more strained than with Germany', prodded the Federal Reserve Board into issuing a statement that, in effect, put a stop – for the time being – to Entente efforts to borrow money in New York. The Western cause could not have endured many more such blows. Yet, so far as public opinion in America was concerned, the President would not have been much blamed for launching them. Scepticism about the Franco-British cause had reached such a pitch that when at length the United States did go to war, one editor explained that one side (the Entente) was a gang of thieves, the other a gang of murderers. 'On the whole, we prefer the thieves, but only as the lesser of two evils.' The Americans went to war convinced that what high purpose and idealism there was in it they brought with them.

The American crusade

Nothing, in fact, is more striking than the identity of outlook which united the moralizing President and the people. The historian may think that the United States was drawn into the war just because it existed. The laws of geography proved stronger than the will of man, and America was drawn into the First World War as it had been drawn into the Napoleonic Wars, reluctantly but inevitably (though it must yet again be emphasized that involvement did not necessarily mean fighting). However, once it had in fact become a belligerent, it was bound to change the nature of the struggle. Not only was the United States fresh, strong, and rich. It was, or thought itself to be, a uniquely successful political society. Its commitment to democracy was more than a century old, and was still fervent. In Wilson this commitment found its perfect spokesman, for he utterly shared it. It was an elemental belief which made it possible (indeed, psychologically necessary) for Wilson, in all good faith, to propose a crusade to America, and for the Americans to respond. It is true that not all of them responded with maximum eagerness, and that the temperature perceptibly cooled when it emerged that a conscript army was to be sent across the Atlantic; but the prevailing tendency was a belief that an American war *must* be for some loftier purpose than the mere defence of territorial integrity and national honour. There was quite enough enthusiasm to fill the sails of Wilsonian idealism, with incalculable results, not merely for the course of the war and the nature of the peace, but for the future of the world. In April 1917 the Americans decisively threw their wealth, power, and energy into a quest for a peaceful, free, and democratic world order. It is a quest that seems little nearer success today than it was fifty years ago; but its continuing popularity makes it still possible to hope that it will one day succeed, and still impossible to regret the crisis which led the people of the United States to make their great decision.

USA, April 1917/Robert H.Ferrell

Declaration of War

It was the German decision to begin unrestricted submarine warfare which lay at the basis of America's entry into the war. But a 'Bathing Beauty Scandal' and a strange telegram to the Mexican government also had their part to play. . . .

It was Lloyd George who once remarked that Europe slithered into war in 1914, and this description, graphically accurate, applies equally well to the entrance of the United States into the World War in 1917. Prior to these separate if similar *dénouements,* neither the Europeans nor the Americans quite knew what they were doing. As late as January 1917, within weeks of the fateful date of the declaration of war on 6th April, President Woodrow Wilson was asking the belligerents for a peace without victory and hoping to achieve it through his efforts at mediation, while the United States remained outside the war as a neutral power. But then came a series of unexpected military, diplomatic, and political changes, none of them American in origin. Before long, Wilson, to use the description of Senator Henry Cabot Lodge, was 'in the grip of events'. On 6th April 1917 some of the election posters of November 1916 were still up on the billboards, and Americans could ponder the Democratic Party slogans which had helped re-elect the President: 'He Kept Us Out of War'; and 'War in the East, Peace in the West, Thank God for Wilson'. They were not, however, angry with Wilson, for they too had reacted to unforeseen events.

What were these events of early 1917 which moved the President and people? It is easy now to see that, given what had gone before, in January 1917 it would take only a few more blows from the German government to make America abandon her neutrality. Given that government's almost complete lack of understanding of the sensitivities of the American government and people, the wonder is that neutrality lasted as long as it did, that German blunders did not come sooner. It is also curious to observe, in retrospect, that Wilson and the American people believed in January 1917 that they still possessed freedom of manoeuvre. The President early that month told his confidant Colonel House that 'There will be no war'.

On 19th January 1917 the German government thoughtfully told Ambassador Johann von Bernstorff about the decision to resume unrestricted submarine warfare on 1st February but Bernstorff was to inform the American government, and duly did so, only on 31st January, at 4 pm. It was a crude beginning, this eight hours' notice. Bernstorff had done his best to prevent this stupidity, this tactic of loosing the submarines, which he knew would drive the Americans into war. It was not only the trans-Atlantic munitions trade, or the export of American food (harvests had been poor in 1916), that the Germans were seeking to prevent; they wanted to strangle British economic life by cutting off all imports. They did not have to use so thorough a submarine blockade, which would inevitably affront the Americans, Bernstorff thought. He had cabled his views,

Wild enthusiasm and waving flags on Broadway—America has entered the war

but the German leaders paid no attention.

Bernstorff meanwhile had lowered his stock with the American government and public, and with his own government (he deeply offended the Kaiser), by allowing a peccadillo to get into public print. On a vacation in the Adirondacks with a lady who often entertained him, he posed in a bathing suit for a photograph, with his arms intimately encircling two ladies similarly attired. At the very time when he needed whatever personal influence and dignity he could muster, this photograph found its way into the hands of the Russian ambassador who passed it to the newspapers. Americans snickered at the Bathing Beauty Scandal. Bernstorff was a generally competent diplomat to whom both the American and German governments should have listened. Instead this 'good German' found himself ignored on public matters and laughed at over private ones. 'I am not surprised,' he said upon the break of diplomatic relations when he received his passports. 'My government will not be surprised either. The people in Berlin knew what was bound to happen if they took the action they have taken. There was nothing else left for the United States to do.' In despair he told a press conference afterwards that he was through with politics.

Below: *The text of Wilson's declaration of war.* ***Bottom:*** *Bernstorff, the ladies' man – a diplomat discomfited by scandal*

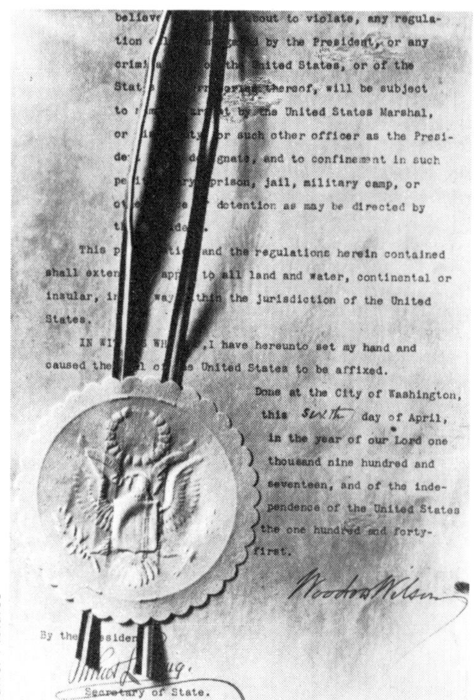
believe [illegible] about to violate, any regulation [illegible] by the President, or any crimi[illegible] the United States, or of the Stat[illegible] thereof, will be subject to [illegible] by the United States Marshal, or [illegible] or such other officer as the President [illegible] designate, and to confinement in such pe[illegible] prison, jail, military camp, or ot[illegible] detention as may be directed by t[illegible].

This p[illegible] and the regulations herein contained shall exten[illegible] to all land and water, continental or insular, in [illegible] the jurisdiction of the United States.

IN WI[illegible],I have hereunto set my hand and caused the [illegible] United States to be affixed.

Done at the City of Washington, this sixth day of April, in the year of our Lord one thousand nine hundred and seventeen, and of the independence of the United States the one hundred and forty-first.

Woodrow Wilson

By the [illegible]sident

[illegible]

Secretary of State.

Culver Pictures

Culver Pictures

After the formal break, two events followed which together pushed the country into war. The first was a clear-cut case of a German submarine sinking a passenger vessel with American citizens aboard. Wilson on 3rd February, when he informed Congress that he was breaking relations, had added that 'I refuse to believe that it is the intention of the German authorities to do in fact what they have warned us they will feel at liberty to do. . . . Only actual overt acts on their part can make me believe it even now'. For two weeks after resumption of unrestricted submarine warfare no incident occurred, no open violation of what Americans liked to believe was one of their principal neutral rights. There was no paralysis of shipping during the period, as American tonnage clearing United States ports dropped only from 1,019,396 in January to 847,786 in February. The day the fatal vessel, the 18,000-ton British liner *Laconia,* sailed from New York harbour, sixty-six ships of all nationalities were in the roadstead, loaded or loading for ports in the zone of war. Wilson spoke again to Congress on 26th February, reporting that 'The overt act which I have ventured to hope the German commanders would in fact avoid has not occurred'. That very moment, however, news of the sinking of the *Laconia* the day before was being flashed to Washington. It was whispered around the House chamber before the President finished his speech, and printed in the country's newspapers the next day. Three Americans, including two women, had lost their lives. The deaths of the women were not pretty to contemplate: a torpedoing at night, a lifeboat half stove-in as it swung down over the careening hull, this fragile craft itself slowly sinking while it wallowed off into the darkness, Mrs Albert H.Hoy and her daughter Elizabeth standing waist deep in icy water throughout the long night.

This was interpreted as an open challenge, by the German government which authorized it, and by the American government and people who had brought themselves into a frame of mind to oppose it.

The Zimmermann telegram

The second precipitating event came almost immediately when American newspapers on 1st March published the Zimmermann telegram. The *Laconia* disaster had proved that the Germans held no regard for international law and human rights. The Zimmermann telegram showed that they were guilty not merely of legal and moral turpitude but were enemies of the United States, willing to endanger the nation's very existence. In the annals of international stupidity during the 20th century, or any other century, this famous telegram hardly has an equal. It was a German proposal of an alliance to the government of Mexico (an alliance which was possibly to include the Japanese government as well). The Mexicans were to attack the United States during the hostilities now deemed imminent, in exchange for which the Germans promised a return of the 'lost territories' of the Mexican War of 1846-48: Texas, New Mexico, Arizona. The genesis of the proposal is now quite clear. The Americans had been giving Mexico much trouble in the past few years, even to the extent of sending in a punitive military expedition in 1916 under command of General Pershing. The Mexican regime of General Venustiano ('Don Venus') Carranza began to take interest in Mexican-German co-operation, and Don Venus in November made a suggestion, going so far as to offer submarine bases. An assistant in the German foreign office, one Kemnitz, turned the proposal into a project for an alliance. It was so preposterous a project that the German foreign secretary, Zimmermann, should have forgotten it. Instead he picked it up as a great idea.

Zimmermann sent his telegram to Mexico by several means, one of which was through the American embassy in Berlin and thence from Washington to Mexico City by Western Union. Ambassador Gerard transmitted this German message, in its original German code, as part of an arrangement which Colonel House had made, with Wilson's permission, for cable transmission of German messages pertaining to mediation. Ambassador Bernstorff had promised to use the arrangement only for peaceful purposes, but Zimmermann was not put off by that engagement.

The British government intercepted and decoded all three of Zimmermann's transmissions. Under the leadership of Admiral Sir William Reginald Hall, the Admiralty early in the war had set up a code and cipher-cracking operation, which triumphed with the deciphering of Zimmermann's idiotic telegram. Not wishing to show his knowledge of the German code, Hall at first was in a quandary about publishing, but ingenuity triumphed. One of his agents in Mexico City procured from the Mexican telegraph office a copy of the still-encoded telegram which Bernstorff had obtained from the American State Department and relayed from Washington. It contained certain small differences from the other intercepts, and upon publication the impression prevailed that someone had stolen or sold a decoded copy of the telegram, getting it from the German legation in Mexico City. The Germans reassured Hall that they were without suspicion by engaging in a lively inquiry with Eckhardt, the German minister in Mexico City, asking how many copies of the decode Eckhardt had made and who had handled them, using of course the same code which Hall had cracked. Hall found it amusing to read that Eckhardt tried to pass the blame off on to Bernstorff in Washington.

No denial

Even after the cat was out of the bag, the telegram published in every American newspaper, it was still possible for Zimmermann in Berlin to quiet the uproar, or at the very least to make the Americans disclose how they obtained the telegram, by baldly denying that he had sent it. President Wilson himself, the author in 1918 of 'open diplomacy', once in a confidential conversation with Colonel House said, admittedly for House's ears only (and, as it turned out, for House's diary), that a man was justified in lying for two purposes, to protect the honour of a lady and to preserve secrets of state. Had Zimmermann but known it, he could have cited the President in support of a diplomatic denial. Secretary Lansing in Washington was certain that Zimmermann would lie his way out, and was incredulous to learn that the German foreign secretary almost at once admitted authorship of the telegram in a burst of truthfulness as naïve as the composition which inspired it.

British postcard. For Great Britain, America's declaration promised men—and hope

What could the American government do after the publication of the telegram on 1st March? If Wilson does not go to war now, Theodore Roosevelt wrote to Lodge, 'I shall skin him alive'. The Prussian Invasion Plot, as the newspapers labelled the telegram, was transparently clear. Newspapers in the hitherto isolationist Middle West acknowledged the end of neutrality. The Chicago *Tribune* warned its readers to realize now, 'without delay, that Germany recognizes us an enemy', and that the country no longer could hope to keep out of 'active participation in the present conflict'. The Cleveland *Plain Dealer* said there was 'neither virtue nor dignity' in refusing to fight now. The Oshkosh (Wisconsin) *Northwestern,* an authentic voice from the Middle West, said that the telegram had turned pacifists, critics, and carpers into patriots overnight. Zimmermann, as Mrs Tuchman has written, 'shot an arrow in the air and brought down neutrality like a dead duck'.

The rest was anticlimax. The first Russian Revolution of March 1917 forced the abdication of the Tsar and the proclamation of a republic, and removed an embarrassing despotism from the ranks of the Allies, making it easier to say that the Allies were Democracy fighting the Central powers who represented Autocracy. About the same time, U-boats sank four American ships. The presidential decision to arm merchant ships, taken in mid-March, constituting a sort of armed neutrality, had no discernible effect on German policy. The President called a special session of Congress. On the evening of 2nd April 1917, Wilson went before both Houses, duly assembled in the Capitol building in Washington, and as the lights gleamed in the crowded chamber he asked his countrymen for what they were ready to give him. Many Senators had brought small American flags to the House chamber where the President spoke, and during the speech they clapped their hands and waved their flags.

JAMES MONTGOMERY FLAGG
I WANT YOU
FOR U.S. ARMY
NEAREST RECRUITING STATION

The Western Front, April 1917/Correlli Barnett

The New Military Balance

America's entry into the war was greeted by the Allies with almost hysterical relief. Russia was undergoing revolution, German submarines threatened Great Britain's power to stay in the war, and the French army had been demoralized. Yet the immediate military help which America could bring was much less than was generally realized. What she brought was hope

Imperial War Museum

***Left:** Recruiting poster. **Above:** On another poster a drowned mother and her child, the supposed victims of a U-boat, appeal for recruits to avenge her*

Lords Gallery

***Above:** Appeal for the war loan. **Below:** Tank Corps recruiting poster. At first the Americans tried to equip military units before sending them to France*

Huntingdon Hartford

On 6th April 1917 the United States entered the First World War. At the beginning of June General John J.Pershing, the commander-in-chief of the American Expeditionary Force arrived in England for a four-day visit, and then went on to France to began organizing his command. His reception by the British and French was warm to the point of hysteria: the King welcomed him, the crowds cheered and threw roses. The illustrated magazine *The London Graphic* caught the mood and the style of the time by surrounding a photograph of Pershing and his officers with a tabernacle in classical style, in which a luscious symbolic figure of a woman held a laurel wreath over Pershing's head; the caption read: 'Now is the winter of our discontent made glorious summer by this sun of (New) York.' (In fact, Pershing had been born in Missouri.)

The hopes, the great expectations, that were aroused in the British and French peoples by American entry into the war were understandable. The spring and early summer of 1917 saw Allied fortunes at their lowest ebb. The year 1916 had ended with apparently nothing to show for colossal losses but small territorial gains on the Somme and the preservation of Verdun. The expulsion of the Germans from French soil seemed as difficult and as far off as ever. The very real and heavy damage done to German power by the Allied offensives in the late summer and autumn of 1916 was hidden from view.

The third year of the war now unfolded for the Allies a prospect of catastrophe. On 1st February 1917 the Germans began unrestricted submarine warfare. The results of the first three months fully justified German calculations that before the end of the year Great Britain would be unable to prosecute the war because of lack of shipping to transport food, raw materials, and troops: the tonnage sunk rose from 470,000 in February to 837,000 in April. Admiral Jellicoe, the British first sea lord, believed that unless an answer to the submarine could be found—and in his estimation, none was in sight—the war was certainly lost. In March revolution exploded in Tsarist Russia and the Tsar Nicholas II abdicated. Although the Russian army had never fulfilled the hopes of 1914 that it would prove an irresistible steam-roller, it had nevertheless heavily engaged Germany's Austrian ally and brought her to the point of exhaustion, and had also drawn German resources away from the Western Front. In 1916 General Brusilov's Offensive (p. 577) had inflicted a smashing defeat in the east on the Central powers. Now that Russia was paralysed by revolution, no man could say what help, if any, she would bring.

Finally, at the end of April and the beginning of May 1917, the French army, under a new commander-in-chief, General Robert Nivelle, was crushingly, appallingly, repulsed in a general offensive on the Western Front which Nivelle had promised would lead to a swift breakthrough and a rapid, and victorious, end to the war. In the aftermath of this shattering disappointment, all the accumulated war-weariness and exhaustion of the French nation exploded in widespread army mutinies and civil disorders. It was no wonder that the Allied leaders and peoples alike greeted the belligerency of the richest, most industrially powerful nation in the world, with all its unblooded manpower, with somewhat hysterical relief. America brought on to the Allied side a population of 93,400,000 and a steel production of 45,060,607 tons. The human resources went far to make up for the 180 million Russians now perhaps lost to the Allied cause. The industrial power was overwhelming; American steel production alone was nearly three times as great as that of Germany and Austria together. However, all this was only *potential.* How long would it be before American resources, human and industrial, were translated into vast, superbly-equipped armies on the Western Front able to crush down the exhausted and outmatched Germans? In view of the German submarine successes and the manifest unsteadiness of the French army and nation, would there even *be* a Western Front by the time the Americans had deployed their power?

Whatever its enormous long-term importance in 20th-century history, the American entry into the First World War in April 1917 in fact was in itself of far smaller strategic significance at the time than the cheering British and French crowds supposed—or than American national myth claims. There was no progressive transformation of the war—no massive rescue operation. On the other hand, it is certain that without America, the Allies would have lost the war. The clue to this apparent paradox lies in that American help *before* her entry into the war was more vital than many recognize; and American help *after* her entry less vital, at least for some fifteen months.

The German and Austrian war effort was

1

2

Imperial War Museum

1 Medal awarded to American mothers whose sons were serving in the army. 2 Italian print—'Five million American citizens become soldiers to defend the world's freedom'. 3 American view of her fighting sons—crusaders keeping the world free for democracy. 4 'Our boys' in action: Doughboy Shooting in Street Combat, *painted by H.Dunn. It took a long while to mobilize the doughboys (infantry).* ***Opposite page:*** *A British tank, on Fifth Avenue, helping to campaign for funds for the American war effort—the 'Liberty loan'*

Crusading for democracy: with high hopes and a small army

entirely based on their own industries and technological skill. By the spring of 1915, after a temporary shortage of munitions, Germany had converted her vast chemical industry and her varied and highly modern engineering industries to the production of explosives, propellants, fuses, shells, ammunition, and weapons. Her machine-tool industry – the most modern and inventive in the world except for that of America – had no difficulty in equipping new munitions plants.

Great Britain and France, in sharp contrast, found when they tackled the problem of a massive expansion of war production that their industrial resources were largely out-of-date in equipment and techniques – and that they even lacked completely a whole range of the most modern kinds of industries. Thus, Great Britain and France before the war had been almost entirely dependent on Germany for chemical products, such as dyes, drugs, and photographic processing materials. It was plant that made dyes and drugs that could also easily make explosives. Great Britain had to create a chemical industry from scratch, based on seized German patents. While it was being built up, there was a bottleneck at the very base of shell manufacture – the propellant and the explosive.

British manufacturing industry was still largely mid-Victorian in its types of product, its methods of production, its skills and techniques. Mass-production plant, with lines of automatic or semi-automatic machines, producing all kinds of precision light-engineering work, was hardly known. Before 1914 Great Britain was dependent mostly on Germany, partly on America, for almost all the sophisticated products of the second phase of the industrial revolution – ball-bearings, magnetoes, sparking plugs, cameras, optical goods.

Great Britain therefore lacked both the general and the particular industries to sustain a modern war. Nor could her machine-tool industry equip the vast new factories that had to be created. Machine-tools were – and are – the basic industry of modern technological growth; they are the machines which make machines. The British machine-tool industry was also essentially mid-Victorian; it was small-scale, it made a limited range of tools to order by almost craft methods in small workshops. For the 'modern' kind of automatic or semi-automatic machine for a production-line, it contented itself in peacetime by acting as a distribution agent for American and German imports.

France was in no better case. Thus, American resources and know-how were, from the end of 1914, absolutely essential to the survival of the Allies. It was to America – and to a lesser extent to Sweden and Switzerland – that they looked to supply the specialized sophisticated products that they had imported from Germany. It was on American industry that Great Britain especially depended for shells and other munitions during 1915 and 1916, while Great Britain was still painfully creating her chemical and munitions industries. Even in 1915 a third of all shells issued to the British army were made in North America. In 1916 the debut of the mass British armies in battle was only made possible by shells from America and Canada. As the history of the ministry of munitions expressed it: 'During the early part of 1915, in fact, overseas contractors assumed a place of utmost importance, since upon them the War Office was forced to depend for the bulk of the shell supplies required for the 1916 campaign.'

The Allies were just as dependent on America for their longer-term needs in constructing their own munitions industries. The essential basis of the whole vast programme of national munitions factories, on which Lloyd George's fame as minister of munitions hangs, was the American machine-tool and the American methods and organization it made possible. In 1916, when Great Britain's new war industries were at last getting into full production, *The Times* wrote: 'One of the new factories has grown up on a spot which last November was green fields. Now there are 25 acres covered with buildings packed with machinery. Most of the machines are of American make, and some are marvels of ingenuity.'

The extent of Allied dependence on American technology, and also of their purchases (at the cost of their accumulated overseas investments) is illustrated by the increase in production of certain American industries *before* America began her own war-production programme. Between 1914 and 1917, American exports of iron, steel, and their products to Europe rose four-fold; American explosives production grew ten times between 1913 and 1917. Bernard Baruch, chairman of the US war industries board, wrote: 'Cincinnati is the greatest machine tool manufacturing center in the world. In 1913 the total value of the annual product of the United States was about $50,000,000. During the war period preceding our entrance, our productive capacity was more than doubled, but the expansion took place largely in the output of small and medium-sized machines—machines for the production of shells, rifles, fuses etc.'

It is therefore beyond question that without access to American resources, Great Britain and France would have lacked the material to sustain the war while their own industries were being created, and could not have created the industries at all. This indeed was acknowledged by the

Radio Times Hulton

Above left: *'This destroyer is needed to sink Hun submarines' reads the sign on the right. The destroyer was built in seventeen days.* ***Above right:*** *The American commanders of the army and the navy, General Pershing (on the left) and Admiral Sims (on the right)*

Ullstein

Above: *The first American prisoners to fall into German hands.* ***Below:*** *Loading a troopship for France. As the soldiers, fresh recruits for slaughter, tramp across the dock, girls in Red Cross uniform give each a last gift from the American people and wish them good luck*

Culver Pictures

British history of the ministry of munitions: 'Great Britain was practically dependent upon the United States of America for material for propellant manufacture, for a large proportion of her explosives material. She depended to a considerable extent upon the United States for shell steel and other steel . . . for machine tools.'

Thus America had proved a decisive influence on the course of the First World War long before her own entry into it.

However, by April 1917 the creation of the Allied – especially the British – war industries had been largely completed. Great Britain was now able to supply munitions freely to France and Italy. There was no longer so desperate or so large a need for American shells or machine-tools. The American declaration of war was therefore largely irrelevant and unimportant where Allied war production was concerned. Indeed, the flow of help was reversed once the American armies began to build up in France; it was France and Great Britain who largely equipped the American armies, as they were formed in France. The Americans made the capital mistake of deciding to produce their own designs of artillery pieces and aircraft, instead of adopting French or British designs for which many of their own factories were already producing ammunition or parts. The inevitable teething troubles of new designs were such that the American army received American guns just about in time to fire a salute in celebration of the armistice in November 1918. Not only this, but acute shortage of shipping space made it evidently more sensible to fill ships with men rather than guns, and then equip the men in Europe. So in the event the AEF was given French 75's for its field artillery, French 155-mm guns and howitzers for its medium artillery, and mostly British mortars. The British also supplied machine-guns, steel helmets, and even uniforms. The air component of the United States was equipped with French aircraft.

Obviously the prime fact about American *belligerency,* as opposed to mere industrial availability, was that United States armed forces would henceforth take part in the war. This indeed was the hope that inspired the civilian cheers, when the 1st Division, AEF, landed in France at the end of June 1917. These were the healthy men, from a nation twice as numerous as the British, or the French, who would take over the weight of the fighting from the tired, battle-shaken survivors of three terrible campaigns. Unfortunately, the American declaration of war was by no means followed by a breakneck expansion of the army and its swift deployment in France, such as the British had achieved in 1914-15. The 1st Division was not followed by the 2nd until September; by 31st October 1917 the AEF numbered only 6,064 officers and 80,969 men. Lloyd George has pointed out in his memoirs the poorness of the American performance compared with the British in creating an army: '. . . at the end of six months (after the outbreak of war) the British Expeditionary Force on the Western Front numbered 354,750. The First American Division was put into a quiet sector of the French front on 21st October 1917 – nearly seven months after the severance of diplomatic relations with Germany. The tide of American forces in France . . . mounted only in dribbling fashion during these early months. By the end of October it was 87,000; by the end of November, 126,000; and at the beginning of 1918, 175,000. That was nine months after the entry of America into the war. At that stage in our own war effort we had already thrown 659,104 into the various war theatres.'

Thus the United States exerted no military effect at all on the critical year of 1917, when Russia subsided more and more from the war, when Pétain strove to quell the mutinies in the French army and keep it together until such time as the Americans should arrive in force, when the Italians suffered a catastrophic defeat at Caporetto, when the *only* Allied army still capable of an offensive – the British – slogged doggedly forward towards Passchendaele. And, the Germans hoped and expected, 1917 was to be the decisive and final year of the war. For it was their calculation that the American army, as a great force, would never arrive because the U-boats would have destroyed the shipping that might have carried it across the Atlantic; if in fact the war itself had not been ended by the U-boat blockade before the Americans were ready to cross. In 1917 the Americans provided hope, little else to the Allies.

The Americans are not to be entirely blamed for the extreme slowness of their military mobilization. The peacetime American army had been even smaller than the British, and far less prepared for modern war. Whereas the British had at least trained and prepared an expeditionary force of six divisions for a European campaign, and completed all the staff studies about organization and methods necessary for subsequent expansion, the Americans started absolutely from scratch in every way. For example, the size, organization, and ancillary services of the basic infantry division had to be worked out and decided upon, as well as of corps and armies. In peacetime the United States army had numbered 190,000 officers and men spread in small detachments across the face of America and her own overseas dependencies. The very size of America posed its own problems, for before troops could go aboard the troopships, they had to be concentrated and accommodated near the eastern seaboard. This meant a vast programme of camp construction, on top of other programmes for training camps and training facilities. In France itself port facilities had to be enormously extended, and lines of communication built up from the ports allotted to the Americans to their designated sector in the right-centre of the Allied line, in the Argonne. This entailed major construction work to increase the carrying capacity of the rail links. Colossal supply depots had to be constructed and filled in France. The British had found that supporting an army in another country over twenty-two miles of sea involved enormous rearward services; America had to make war across 3,000 miles of sea. The major bottleneck however was shipping, both for troops and cargoes. The United States mercantile marine had nothing like enough ships available to move the American army across the Atlantic.

Culver Pictures

Industry steps up production for America's participation in the war – war workers making steel helmets for doughboys

Finally, there was a fundamental difference of views between Pershing on the one hand and Haig and Pétain on the other about the employment of American troops. Haig and Pétain at the beginning of 1918 were keenly aware that their armies were seriously under strength and without hope of adequate national reinforcements. They wanted American infantry to fill out their own divisions; they wanted help quickly. Pershing on the other hand (and his government) was resolved to build up a completely independent, self-contained American army in France, with its own divisions, corps, and armies. He was not prepared to see Americans swallowed up in Allied formations; he was prepared to wait, for months if need be, until all the artillery and supply services, the higher headquarters and staffs, necessary for an independent force were organized, trained, and equipped. Thus it was that when on 21st March 1918, the Germans launched the first and greatest of a series of titanic offensives on the Western Front, there was only one American division actually in the overstretched and outnumbered Allied line and three divisions in training areas.

The rate of the American build-up in France had been crucial to the calculations of the German high command in deciding on great offensives in the west in the spring of 1918. By November, 1917, when the German decision was taken, unrestricted U-boat warfare had failed in its object of knocking Great Britain out of the war; it had been beaten by the convoy system. Therefore, the Germans had to reckon on the entry into battle, sooner or later, of a mass and entirely fresh American army: certain defeat for Germany and her allies. Therefore, the war must be decided before that mass army arrived. Ludendorff told his colleagues: 'Our general situation requires that we should strike at the earliest moment, if possible at the end of February or beginning of March, before the Americans can throw strong forces into the scale.' In other words, since Russia had finally been knocked out of the war by the Treaty of Brest-Litovsk, the bulk of German strength could be concentrated on France and Great Britain before they could be rescued by their second great ally.

Culver Pictures

Big guns under construction. But the army only received the new American guns just before the armistice in November 1918

The crisis on the Western Front lasted from 21st March to 18th July, as the German onslaughts fell successively on different parts on the Allied front. Twice the British faced real danger of being driven into the Channel; once there was an acute risk of the French and British being separated; three times the French front was temporarily smashed and the French capital exposed again to possible occupation. In this largest, most violent, and most decisive campaign of the war, the American army played little part. Some units took part in the defence of the Amiens sector after 28th March; the 1st Division carried out a spirited counterattack at Cantigny, near Montdidier, on 28th May; in June the 2nd Division helped the French block the German drive across the Marne, and launched a successful counterattack which led to the recapture of Belleau Wood; units of the 3rd and 42nd Divisions fought defensively in the sector of Château-Thierry. These were very welcome, but hardly decisive contributions to a campaign against 192 German divisions.

What was far more important – indeed decisive – in terms of the issue of the war was the effect of the German offensive on the speed of the American build-up. A week after the Germans attacked on the Somme, on 28th March 1918, Pershing abandoned his somewhat deliberate and pedantic attempt to create an independent American army before entering the conflict, and offered Pétain as a temporary expedient all the troops he had, to use as Pétain wished. So the individual American units saw action under French or British corps and army command, not American. This immediate gesture was one sign of the American realization that the French and British might not last long enough to be rescued; that there was a need for desperate haste in getting American troops over to France and into battle. At the same time, Pershing still remained anxious that his Allies should not rob him of his own independent army by the feeding of Americans into their own divisions. It was only after long arguments between the Allied and American governments and commands, that it was finally agreed, at the beginning of June, that shipping space should be saved by bringing over men – infantry mostly – instead of complete divisions with all their space-occupying equipment. 170,000 combat troops were to come in June and 140,000 in July out of some 250,000 men ready to be transported in each of the two months. New divisions would be formed and equipped in France. These shipments of men were made possible by the British mercantile marine, made available as part of the bargain by the British government by cutting down British imports.

Whereas in March 84,000 Americans had crossed the Atlantic, 118,500 crossed in April, 246,000 in May, 278,800 in June, and 306,703 in July – nearly half of them in British ships. These figures, far higher than the German command had thought possible, spelt defeat for Germany.

On 15th-17th July the last phase of the great German 1918 offensive petered out in failure. On 18th July the French launched a surprise attack, led by massed tanks, from the Forest of Villers-Cotterêts. The attacking troops included two American divisions, each with a strength of 27,000 men, three times as large as a French or German division. The French attack marked the turn of the campaign; from then to the end of the war the Germans were to fight on the defensive.

It was now – and at very long last – that the American military presence in the war proved decisive. The great battles of March to July 1918, which the Allies had won virtually without American help, had left the British, French, and German armies all exhausted, with scant reserves and little hope of reinforcement from the homeland. For the original combatants of the war nothing remained but to break up divisions – to see their armies gradually decrease. A German battalion now numbered on average 660 men. The German gamble on victory had failed: neither the German army nor the German people (hungry, miserable, and despairing after years of blockade) had any further hopes to clutch at. In August, when the British offensive on the Somme (some American units took part), confirmed that the Allies now possessed the initiative, and confirmed also that the morale and discipline of the German army was beginning to disintegrate, there were nearly 1,500,000 Americans in France. The only German reservoir of fresh manpower lay in the 300,000 youths of the 1919 class called up in June. Whereas Allied leaders were planning for a campaign in 1919, whose principal weight was to be borne by a hundred American divisions, for Germany's leaders another year of battle was absolutely unthinkable.

Thus it was that even in the last months of the war, it was the American military *potential,* advertised by their limited offensives at St Mihiel and in the Argonne, rather than the actual fighting achievements of American troops, that affected the outcome of the Great War in 1918. In point of fact, the brunt of the fighting from July to November 1918 was borne by the tired but still dogged British, who took 188,700 prisoners as against 196,000 taken by the French, Belgians, and Americans together.

The American role in the First World War was therefore decisive: decisive industrially between 1914 and 1917, decisive in terms of military potential from midsummer 1918 onwards. It illustrated two facts of enormous importance to the future balance of power in Europe: that Germany was militarily the equal of the British and French empires together; and that Great Britain, the 19th-century 'work-shop of the world', was no longer a first-rank industrial and technological power, no longer able to defend herself and her empire out of her own resources.

Chapter 25

Introduction by J.M.Roberts

1917 brought two great changes: the United States entered the war and Russia began to leave it. Before Russia finally made peace in the following year she had suffered two changes of regime, a German invasion of remarkable depth and success, and the beginning of a civil war. Not surprisingly many observers thought her well on the way to national disintegration. The first step towards this had been the **Overthrow of the Tsar,** which David Floyd describes. Its preparation and its consequences are the subject of this chapter.

Of the three great European imperial dynasties, Russia's was the first to collapse because, whatever was said and believed about the corrupting effects of German sympathies and German gold, her government and people could no longer bear the harsh impact of two and a half years of fighting. On this topic we have asked for the collaboration of Soviet historians and one of them, Alexander Grunt, provides an article on **Russia at War** which describes the cumulative effect of defeat, privation, and suffering. They had imposed from the start enormous burdens on an overwhelmingly peasant society still only beginning to experience real industrial growth in 1914. After the last, glorious moment of success in the Brusilov Offensive, there came further defeats. As Geoffrey A.Hosking shows in **Rasputin and the 'Dark Forces'**, the regime could no longer escape responsibility in the eyes of the people for what was going wrong. The result was the revolution in March. It was much less a great offensive rising than the sudden collapse of a facade long since worm-eaten.

Russian politics in the summer which followed were essentially about the issue of peace or war. To Russia's allies, the moral and ideological advantage they won by the disappearance of a despot from their ranks was more than outweighed by the danger of Russia leaving the war altogether. She had saved her allies by making impossible the concentration of German effort on one front. Now this threat loomed up again. As a result, the precarious political health of the Provisional Government whose career is described in **Kerensky's Summer** by George Katkov was of great interest both to the Allies and the Central powers.

The ordinary Russian soldier saw things very differently. To him, only two things really mattered. The first was peace. The other was land. Those who fought in Petrograd for control of the crumbling state apparatus had to take this longing into account if they were to succeed. The Bolsheviks found it much easier to do so than most of their opponents. In large measure, this was because they were led by a political tactician of genius, Lenin.

Kladderadatsch

German cartoon: 'Russia'. Nicholas II with his enraged peasants at his heels

Radio Times

The Tsarina's 'holy man', whose amazing sexual excesses had political repercussions

Novosti

'Workers of all countries unite'. Workers demonstrate in Petrograd, May 1917

Russia

1914 1st August: Germany declares war on Russia.

1915 1st August: the Duma meets to consider the way the war is being conducted.
22nd August: six parties in the Duma form the Progressive Bloc, and demand a responsible ministry.
6th September: the Tsar assumes supreme command of the armed forces.
8th September: programme of moderate reform backed by Progressive Bloc is put before council of ministers.
15th September: Goremykin informs cabinet that Tsar has rejected proposal of ministers to resign so that ministry enjoying public confidence can be appointed.
16th September: the Tsar prorogues the Duma.

1916 15th February: the Duma meets. Goremykin is replaced by Stürmer.
September: new wave of strikes gathers momentum and continues throughout October.
30th December: Rasputin is murdered by Yusupov.

1917 19th February: Khabalov is appointed by Tsar to maintain order in Petrograd.
27th February: the Duma meets.
7th March: Tsar leaves Petrograd for army GHQ.
8th March: crowds start to demonstrate against the regime in Petrograd. Workers go on strike. Disorder spreads throughout 9th and 10th March.
11th March: soldiers sent against the crowds defect and join them. Tsar prorogues Duma.
12th March: Duma forms a committee to replace the Tsarist government. The Petrograd Soviet of Workers' and Soldiers' Deputies is formed.
13th March: Soviet news sheet *Izvestya* calls on people to take affairs into their own hands.
15th March: Milyukov explains to the crowds the formation of the Provisional Government. Tsar abdicates. 'Order No. 1' of the Soviet puts armed forces in Petrograd under its own command.
The Provisional Government forbids the use of force against rioting peasants.
May: units of Petrograd garrison demand the dismissal of Milyukov and Guchkov. Kornilov resigns his command of forces in Petrograd, and Milyukov and Guchkov resign from the government.
Kerensky initiates coalition government.
26th June: soldiers refuse to take offensive at their officers' commands and many of them desert.
Kornilov demands that the offensive be called off, and is appointed supreme commander-in-chief.
16th July: Bolsheviks organize armed demonstration of sailors and Red Guards. Troops are sent hastily from the front to suppress it.
20th July: Lvov and Kadet ministers resign.
3rd August: Kerensky resigns. Party leaders give him a free hand to form the government.
August: Kerensky holds Moscow State Conference to settle differences between Kornilov and the soviets. It fails.
8th September: Kerensky promises to put Kornilov's demands before the cabinet. Lvov misleads him about Kornilov's intentions, and he denounces Kornilov's 'plot' to overturn the government.
9th September: cavalry corps sent by Kornilov to Petrograd to maintain order is thrown into confusion by news of Kornilov's mutiny.
2nd November: pre-parliament refuses to give Kerensky powers to deal with the Bolsheviks.
7th November: Kerensky flees the Bolsheviks. The ministers of the provisional government are arrested by the Bolsheviks.

(All Russian dates are given in the new – western – style)

The Eastern Front

1914 26th August: battle of Tannenberg starts. Russia is resoundingly defeated by Germany.
5th September: Germans attack the Russians who suffer severe losses in the ensuing battle of the Masurian lakes.
3rd September: Russians take Lemberg. After the battle of Lemberg (8th-12th September) they force Austrians to leave Galicia.

1915 2nd May: Austro-German offensive in Galicia defeats and demoralizes the Russians.
1st July: Austro-German offensive against Russia starts. By the end of September Russia loses Poland, Lithuania, Courland, and a million men.

1916 Brusilov Offensive starts. The Russians fail to exploit their success and lose a million men.

1917 1st July: Brusilov starts offensive in Galicia.
18th July: battle of East Galicia opens. Germans and Austrians drive Russians back.
3rd September: the Germans attack and take Riga.

Russia 1914-16/Alexander Grunt

Russia at War

A Soviet historian shows how the Tsarist government failed to grapple with the immense problems posed by the war, and how the ground was being prepared for the revolution

For Russia 1st August 1914 was the last day of peace. At about seven o'clock in the evening of that day the car of the German ambassador, Count Pourtales, drew up outside the building of the Russian ministry of foreign affairs on Palace Square in St Petersburg. The ambassador entered the building, where he was received by S.D. Sazonov, the minister of foreign affairs, to whom he handed a statement to the effect that Germany considered herself in a state of war with Russia. A day later Germany declared war on France. At dawn on 5th August the British ambassador in St Petersburg, Sir George Buchanan, received a telegram from his government which read: 'War with Germany—take action.'

It had turned out to be impossible to resolve the tangle of conflicting interests, which had emerged at many different points of the globe, without resorting to war; and so began the most painful and bloody war of any that mankind had known. For the majority of people with little interest in politics the war came as a surprise. After all, what could the illiterate Russian peasant or factory worker know of the actual plans and aims of his own or of other governments? On the face of it one thing was clear: the German Kaiser had attacked Russia, and Russia must be defended. And it never occurred to those who were closer

Nicholas II, 'Autocrat of all the Russias', holds up an icon to be venerated by his troops. But under the strain of the war the traditional veneration for the Tsar was to melt away

to the centre of affairs and understood what was happening to try and explain the real significance of events to the ordinary people. At a ceremonial session of the State Duma everybody, from the monarchists to the representatives of the liberals and of the petit-bourgeois *Trudoviki* (who inclined towards the Socialist Revolutionaries and had until then been in opposition to the government, declared their full support for its actions, thus demonstrating the 'patriotic unity' of the Tsar with the people and of the people with the Tsar. The war suited them, because it promised the acquisition of new territories, markets for their goods, sources of raw materials, and huge profits. The sober voice of a Social Democratic deputy, who protested in the name of the working people against the fratricidal slaughter, was drowned in the general chorus of loyal speeches. The Social Democrats' refusal to vote for the military budget did not alter the situation. It was passed by an overwhelming majority. That is why in the first days of the war the country was swept by a wave of patriotic demonstrations in which the ordinary people also took part.

Only in time and after much suffering did the millions of ordinary people come to feel and understand how utterly unnecessary and senseless was the bloody slaughter into which they had been led by their rulers, that it was not for their native land but for the achievement of entirely selfish ends.

Meanwhile, the news from the front brought little consolation. An attempt by the Russian armies to drive deep into East Prussia ended in failure. They were forced to retreat, having lost 20,000 men dead and 60,000 prisoners. The situation was somewhat better on the south-western section of the front. The Russians had taken Galicia and thus threatened German Silesia, where a considerable part of German industry was concentrated. But they did not succeed in inflicting a final defeat on the Austro-Hungarian army. Towards the end of the year the exhausted troops on both sides went over to the defence. The front also became stabilized in the west, where the Germans had failed to inflict a decisive defeat on France. Hopes of a quick victory on one side or the other turned out to be illusory. All the warring countries found themselves faced with the necessity of waging a long and exhausting war which would require gigantic efforts of every kind.

Russia had entered the war without suffi-

cient preparation. Though a great power, with a population of over 150,000,000 and inexhaustible natural resources, she lagged considerably behind the foremost countries of western Europe in terms of economic and political development. The basic reason for this backwardness was the fact that the country's economic and political system had retained features handed down from the feudal past. The preservation of the inequitable form of land ownership was the principal economic survival of this nature. About 300,000 square miles of land belonged to 30,000 landowners. And a similar area of land was divided among 10,000,000 peasant holdings.

Survivals from the days of serfdom in the agrarian system acted as a brake on the development not only of agriculture but of industry as well. On the eve of the war, in 1913, Russia produced less than 4,000,000 tons of coal, and 9,000,000 tons of oil. Russia continued to be an agrarian country: eighty-six per cent of the total population of the empire was employed on the land, and agricultural output accounted for sixty per cent of the total national product.

The strain of war

Russia had remained an autocratic monarchy. The establishment of the State Duma, which the Tsar had been forced to accept during the first Russian revolution of 1905-07 (p. 78), had turned out to be no more than the semblance of a parliament. Even the bourgeoisie, let alone the working people in the population, were debarred from taking part in 'high politics'. The real power in the state was in the hands of the monarchy, which represented primarily the interests of the small and politically conservative class of courtiers and landowners. Civil rights were practically non-existent. All this naturally acted as a brake on the country's advancement and had a negative effect on all aspects of its life. The industrial bourgeoisie, though they disliked the situation in which they found themselves and could not come to terms with the 'extremes' of reactionary policy, still lacked the resolution to enter into open battle with the monarchy, fearing a violent upheaval by the masses, who had already demonstrated their strength in the first Russian revolution. The activity of the bourgeois parties did not go farther than modest parliamentary opposition in the Duma.

The first months of war had already shown that the Russian economy was not capable of satisfying the demands placed on it by the war. It was immediately affected by the call-up into the army which in the course of the war snatched 15,000,000 able-bodied men out of industry and agriculture. The stocks of arms and ammunition in the war department's stores were quickly used up, and industry could not make good the losses. Attempts on the part of the government to introduce controls over the economy and to mobilize industry for war production brought no substantial results and served in the end only to speed the collapse of the economic structure.

The exhaustion and gradual running down of the economy soon became apparent. Businesses were closed down one after the other. In 1915 alone 573 factories and mills stopped work. Only half the total number of plants were operating throughout the war. Production began to drop in the most important branches of the economy. By 1916 36 of the 151 blast-furnaces which the Russian iron and steel industry had at the beginning of the war had been shut down. The whole of the output of the iron and steel industry went to meet war needs, and this had a disastrous effect on those branches of industry which were not connected with the war. The country began to experience a fuel crisis, and a considerable proportion of the country's industrial plants came to a standstill through lack of fuel.

Transport, that most important element in the economy, was in a state of paralysis. At the beginning of 1916 there were 150,000 truck-loads of goods waiting to be moved on the railways. Five hundred and seventy-five railway stations were no longer capable of handling any goods at all. In the port at Archangel, through which communications were maintained with the Allies, the crates of goods literally sank into the ground under the weight of the fresh deliveries of various kinds of machinery and equipment piled on top of them. As a result of the disorganization of transport, there were food shortages in the towns of central Russia as early as 1915, while at the same time thousands of tons of grain, meat, and butter were rotting away at railway stations in Siberia. Following the February Revolution the former chairman of the council of ministers, B.V.Stürmer, said in his evidence before the special commission of investigation: 'There were so many trucks blocking the lines that we had to tip some of them down the embankments to move the ones that arrived later.'

The country's financial system was also disorganized. The conduct of the war involved enormous expenditure, which the normal pre-war budget was quite unable to cover. Increased taxes and the launching of domestic loans did not make up for the losses. The government had to resort to foreign loans and to increasing the circulation of paper money without adequate gold backing. This soon led to a fall in the value of the rouble, the disorganization of the whole financial system, and to an exceptional rise in the cost of living.

The war also had a very bad effect on agriculture. Large-scale mobilization left the countryside without man-power, while the requisitioning of horses deprived it of draught animals. Even before the war the manufacture of agricultural machinery had not been a very flourishing branch of industry. Now it came to a complete standstill, as did the production of chemical fertilizers. The result of all this was a sharp fall in the output of every kind of agricultural produce. The threat of famine hung over the country.

Rumblings of discontent

As is always the case, it was not the propertied classes but the labouring sections of the population who felt the burden and the deprivations of war soonest and most harshly.

As early as December 1914 prices of manufactured goods had risen by twenty-five per cent compared with 1913, while prices of consumer goods were up by eleven per cent. In 1915 prices of manufactured goods rose by 145 per cent and food prices rose by 122 per cent. Wage increases lagged far behind the catastrophic rise in the cost of living. Between 1914 and 1916 the working man's earnings rose on the average by 100 per cent, while prices of foodstuffs and consumer goods increased by from 300 per cent to 500 per cent.

Millions of ordinary people were bound sooner or later to ask themselves the purpose of all their suffering, the end to which they were sacrificing their lives and their health. They saw, and they knew from their own experience, that the war would bring them nothing but misfortune and privation. The first burst of patriotic excitement quickly passed, to be replaced among the masses of the people by a smouldering discontent with the war and the whole policy of Tsarism. This elemental discontent and ferment among the masses sought an outlet, and it could not fail ultimately to take the form of open revolt against the existing order. The police prepared alarming reports about the growth of the strike movement, which had practically ceased in the first months of the war. A particularly serious wave of strikes swept the country in June 1915, when 80,000 workers downed tools. A strike of textile workers in Kostroma in the same month ended in a bloody clash with the police. In August the blood of the working people was again flowing, when troops fired at a demonstration of textile workers in Ivanovo-Voznesensk. These repressive actions on the part of the authorities evoked indignation among the workers in many towns throughout the country. In September 200,000 working people were on strike.

The Russian revolutionary movement, which had gained great experience in the

Appeals for money to help the ramshackle Russian war effort. ***Below:*** *A Russian poster. 'Everything for the war. Subscribe to the 5½ per cent war loan.'* ***Bottom:*** *British propaganda poster appealing for help for her hard-pressed ally. But the Russian peasants wanted peace, not money for a longer war*

struggle against Tsarism during the years 1905-07, began once again, after a brief lull, to gather strength and to become a major factor in public life.

The growth of anti-war feeling was further encouraged by Russia's experiences in the war itself. Russian troops ended the campaign of 1914 in a state of extreme exhaustion. They had suffered great losses. The army had lost half a million men, and the situation with regard to the supply of arms and ammunition was bad. Reinforcements arriving at the fronts remained in their transports because there were no rifles to arm them with. The situation was just as bad when it came to providing the army with uniforms and food. 'We go about in ragged uniforms, and without boots. I have to go practically barefoot, just in my socks,' one soldier wrote home. 'Our infantry is so poor, they march in home-made boots', wrote another. This sort of thing could not fail to have its effect on the army's fighting qualities. Cases of desertion became more frequent; there was a sharp increase in the number of soldiers who deliberately inflicted wounds on themselves so as to avoid military service; and on every side could be heard comments on the futility of the war in which Russia's foolish rulers had involved the country.

Meanwhile, having failed to achieve a victory in the 1914 campaign, the German high command decided to concentrate its efforts on the Russian front, to inflict a defeat on Russia, put her out of the war, and then turn all its forces against Great Britain and France. In the first days of May 1915 German and Austrian troops succeeded in making a breach in the Russian front in Galicia, forced the Russians to withdraw from Galicia and Poland, and seized part of Russian territory. Altogether in the summer campaign of 1915 the Germans achieved several major successes, while the Russians suffered enormous losses, which now totalled, since the beginning of the war, no less than 3,400,000 men. Of these 300,000 were killed and 1,500,000 officers and men were taken prisoner.

Patriotic alarm

These defeats at the front brought about a sudden change in the relations between the bourgeois circles, for which the State Duma provided a platform, and the ruling group at the top. Hopes that the monarchy would be able to organize a victorious war, put an end to revolutionary ferment and, finally, involve the bourgeoisie in the business of governing the country were not borne out. 'Patriotic enthusiasm' gave way to 'patriotic alarm'.

The military machine turned out to be incapable of carrying out the tasks which faced it. Ominous signs of popular revolt became ever more evident. Efforts on the part of bourgeois circles to put their relations with the authorities on a proper business-like footing met with no success.

As they acquired a steadily increasing importance in the country's economy, the Russian bourgeoisie tried to find a place for themselves at the centre of the country's administration and to influence policy in the way they wanted it to go. In the first days of June 1915 a conference was held in Petrograd, as St Petersburg was now called in deference to anti-German feelings, of representatives of trade and industry to consider questions connected with the adaptation of industry to wartime needs. The conference decided to set up war industry committees which were to become one of the political centres of the bourgeoisie, in the same way as had the unions of the *zemstvos* and town councils which had been set up in the summer of 1914. From the very beginning these unions tried to interfere in the business of running the country's economy, but all their efforts were brought to nothing by the government, and were limited to rendering help to the sick and wounded. The leader of the central war industry committee was the energetic and determined A.I.Guchkov, the recognized leader of the upper bourgeoisie and one of the organizers of the Octobrist Party (the party of rich bourgeoisie and landowners formed in October 1905 which supported the Tsardom).

One of the principal demands put forward by the bourgeois community at the Petrograd conference was that the State Duma should be called into session. Since the beginning of the war the Duma had met on only two occasions—in August 1914, in connection with the outbreak of war, and in February 1915, for the formal approval of the budget. This did not suit the bourgeoisie in the least, because it regarded the Duma as the one institution able to exert pressure on the government.

'The State Duma,' said P.N.Milyukov, leader of the Kadet Party (Constitutional Democrats), at one of its meetings, 'is the only organizational centre of the national mind and will, the only institution which is capable of standing up to the bureaucracy.'

Insistent demands that the Duma should be summoned went along with a further demand that the government itself should be re-formed. The liberal bourgeoisie, in the form of the Kadet Party, was not prepared at that time to announce as part of its programme the demand for a 'responsible ministry', since it considered it possible to make do with changes in the membership of the council of ministers. After all, to enter into open battle with the authorities would have meant appealing to the masses and giving rein to the forces of revolution, which the bourgeoisie feared

no less than reaction. The frequent introduction of new people into the cabinet, 'to ensure the correct organization of the home front, the maintenance of internal peace in the country, and close collaboration between the government and the public', was put forward as a condition for summoning the Duma and one that would ensure that it worked effectively.

Defeats at the front and the growth of bourgeois opposition forced Nicholas II to make certain concessions. A group of people was formed within the council of ministers itself who considered it necessary to pay more attention to 'public opinion' and to adopt a more moderate policy towards the 'public'. It became ever more clear that the council of ministers could not, in its original composition, meet the Duma without coming into sharp conflict with it.

N.A.Maklakov, the minister for internal affairs, was the first to be dismissed. He was succeeded by Prince N.V.Shcherbatov, a member of the State Council, whom the liberal press described as 'a conservative in the European sense of the word', who respected the law and was opposed to any 'extremes'. However restrained were the opinions of the new minister, the departure of Maklakov gave great satisfaction to the middle classes who considered him, together with the war minister V.A.Sukhomlinov, one of the men principally responsible for all the troubles and misfortunes besetting Russia. Sukhomlinov, who had been in charge of the war department since 1909, was next to go after Maklakov. He was replaced by General A.A.Polivanov.

The campaign against Sukhomlinov had begun in the spring of 1915 when Russian troops were swept out of Galicia. His opponents dug up everything they could find against the minister: his compromising marriage with the wife of a Kiev landowner, Butovich, his close relations with a very doubtful character called Altschuller, and his connexion with the German spy Myasoyedov, who was hanged in the winter of 1915. The word 'treachery' was heard ever more frequently in connection with the war minister. One way or another Sukhomlinov had to be got rid of. As for Polivanov, it would have been difficult to think of a better sop to throw to the Duma. Even when he had been assistant to the war minister, from 1908 to 1912, Polivanov had won popularity for himself in the Duma through his ability to get along with the bourgeoisie, and had earned the reputation of being a 'leftist' in bureaucratic circles. The Tsar had no special liking for the man, but force of circumstances obliged him to agree to his appointment.

Two others to be dismissed were I.G. Shcheglovitov, the minister of justice, and V.K.Sabler, chief procurator of the Holy Synod (head of the church council). The former was replaced by A.A.Khvostov and the latter by A.D.Samarin, both completely conservative in their views but lacking the regard of the empress Alexandra Fedorovna and Rasputin, which was in itself an excellent recommendation in the eyes of the bourgeoisie. These appointments were the only changes which were made in the composition of the government on the eve of the new session of the Duma. The council of ministers was still headed by the very elderly I.L.Goremykin, who had long since earned himself the reputation of being an extreme reactionary and a persecutor of any kind of liberalism. The danger of a conflict between the 're-formed' government and the bourgeoisie had not been removed. This was fully confirmed by the events which followed.

The Duma meets again

It was on 1st August 1915, the first anniversary of the outbreak of war, that the State Duma met again. And, while the right-wing groups, representing the landowners, continued as before to give the government their unconditional support, the bourgeois section of the Duma made no attempt to conceal its dissatisfaction. The bourgeoisie was not interested in bringing about a radical change in the policy of the Tsarist regime. Their only concern was to introduce into the government people enjoying the unquestioned confidence of the middle classes, and able to represent their interests in it. A substantial majority of the factions in the Duma united around the slogan of 'a ministry of confidence'. The liberal Moscow newspaper *Morning Russia* even published a commentary under the heading 'A Cabinet of Defence' in which it gave the possible composition of a government which would suit the bourgeoisie. M.V. Rodzyanko, the Octobrist and chairman of the Duma, was named as premier, another Octobrist, A.I.Guchkov, was named as minister for internal affairs, and the Kadet P.N.Milyukov was named as minister for foreign affairs.

On 22nd August negotiations between the leaders of the factions in the Duma concluded, with the signature of a formal agreement among them. In this way a 'Progressive Bloc' came into being in the Duma – an organization which was fated to become the political centre of the whole bourgeois opposition. Many of the twenty-five members of its bureau – P.N.Milyukov, A.I.Shingarev, N.V.Nekrasov, V.N.Lvov, I.V.Godnev, and others later became members of the Provisional Government. Six of the factions in the Duma, from the Kadets to the 'progressive' nationalists – 236 of the 442 deputies – entered the Bloc. Those who remained outside it were, on the right, the extreme right wing and the nationalists, and, on the left, the Social Democrats and the Mensheviks, and the Socialist Revolutionaries. The Socialist Revolutionaries, though they did not formally enter the Bloc, always voted with it and supported its policies.

As for the Bloc's programme, its central point was the demand for the formation of a 'government of confidence'. The remaining points in it were very modest: changes in the personnel of local administration, a partial amnesty for religious and political offences, some initial steps towards removing the restrictions placed on Jews, the revival of trade-union activities, and so forth. There was nothing in it likely to undermine the power of the Tsar. The programme was not aimed at bringing about a breach with Tsarism, but at achieving agreement with it on the basis of liberal reforms and the organization of a victorious war with Germany. The central idea in the minds of the leaders of the Bloc was to bring about such a state of affairs in the country as would exclude the very possibility of a revolutionary outburst, which appeared to them as equivalent to utter chaos and anarchy. But even this

Victims of the war – Russian soldiers taken prisoner with their weapons near Lwów. 1,500,000 officers and men were taken prisoner during the terrible summer campaign of 1915. Heavy losses, added to hardships at home, increased the bitter resentment of the Russian people at the war and the foolish rulers who had involved them in it

extremely modest programme was too much for the monarchy. The formation in the Duma of a stable majority in opposition would put an end to any possibility of manoeuvring between the extreme flanks of the bourgeois landowning parties as the ruling group at the top had done since the first Russian revolution. Less than a month passed before the Tsar signed a decree dissolving the Duma. 'They brushed aside the hand that was offered them,' P.N.Milyukov recalled later. 'The conflict between the monarchy on the one hand and the representatives of the people and society on the other became an open breach.'

The leader of the opposition was obviously exaggerating when he said that what happened in September marked the end of efforts to find a compromise solution. Even before the final breach came about the bourgeoisie had more than once offered its hand to the government in the hope of arriving at a solution acceptable to both sides. But so far the monarchy had been quite unyielding. The sudden swing of policy away from partial concessions to reaction was not limited simply to the dissolution of the Duma. Before that Nicholas II had dismissed the Grand Duke Nikolay Nikolayevich from the post of supreme commander-in-chief and put himself in his place. It was quite clear that this change was in no way dictated by military considerations. Nicholas was not a military man and could be no more than a decorative figurehead. His assumption of the post of 'supremo' was unquestionably a political move, inspired by the Empress and Rasputin. Neither the objections of his ministers nor protests from members of the Tsar's family could make him alter his decision. The pro-German group led by the Empress Alexandra Fedorovna did its best to divert Nicholas's attention from domestic affairs, to put an end to the insignificant concessions being made to society, and to set course towards a separate peace with Germany.

This time it turned out to be not so difficult to deal with the bourgeois opposition. The concluding session of the Duma lasted just three minutes. The deputies listened in deathly silence to the words of the imperial decree pronouncing their dissolution, shouted a loyal 'hurrah', and dispersed without a single word of protest. They had too great a fear of the 'street', of any movement on the part of the masses, to embark on any open opposition to the whole system of government which had led the country to disaster.

Months passed. There were no signs of an end to the war, and the situation in the country became ever more tense. At the beginning of 1916 the strike movement flared up again on an even greater scale. Every year the working people of Russia went on strike in memory of those who died in the 'Bloody Sunday' of 22nd January 1905. On this occasion the traditional January strike assumed enormous proportions. In Petrograd alone at least 100,000 people went on strike. Neither police arrests nor the use of the army to guard the largest factories brought the movement to an end. The ferment of revolution spread even into the army. The people of the villages, crushed by the excessive requisitions, also began to raise their voice. An enormous quantity of inflammatory material was piling up, ready to burst into flame at any moment. The landowners and farmers began to be haunted by the memory of the things that had happened to them in 1905.

Government of tumblers

The Tsar and his government were helpless in the face of the approaching catastrophe. They were unable to avert either the economic crisis or the advance of the revolutionary movement. In their search for a solution the Tsar and those close to him had recourse to the dismissal of persons holding major posts in the government, and this only threw into relief the crisis among the men at the top, who had lost the capacity to assess the situation in a realistic and sober manner.

I.L.Goremykin, the prime minister, that faithful defender of the foundations of the monarchy, was the first to lose his seat in the government. It was the same story as in the summer of 1915. There was no question of any real change of policy in the direction of 'liberalization' but only of giving the Duma an opportunity to work off its anger on those who were dismissed. Goremykin's place was taken by the sixty-eight-year-old B.V.Stürmer, whose political reputation left no doubt that there was no reason to expect any changes for the better. Moreover, Stürmer's pro-German sentiments were widely known, which made it seem not unreasonable to regard his appointment as evidence of the Tsar's desire to start negotiations for a separate peace with Germany. The news was received with unconcealed alarm by the French and British ambassadors. Sir George Buchanan wrote: 'Possessed of only a second-class mind, having no experience of statesmanship, concerned exclusively with his own personal interests, and distinguished by his capacity to flatter and his extreme ambition, he owed his new appointment to the fact that he was a friend of Rasputin and enjoyed the support of the crowd of intriguers around the empress.'

There is a vast literature in existence about Rasputin. Innumerable legends have grown up around the name of that semi-literate peasant from Tobolsk who became the uncrowned ruler of Russia. Maybe not everything in them is true, but there can be no question about the tremendous influence which 'our friend', as the Tsarina called him, exerted on the country's policy. There can also be no doubt but that the emergence of Rasputin and all that Rasputin meant became possible only at a time when the whole system of autocracy was in decline and in a state of decomposition and decay.

Goremykin's replacement by Stürmer was not the end of the business. Sazonov, the minister for foreign affairs, and Polivanov, the war minister, were retired soon afterwards – both men with whom the bourgeoisie had had great hopes of collaborating. A real game of 'ministerial leap-frog' now began. Ministers were replaced one after the other. Two and a half years of war saw the removal of four prime ministers, six ministers of internal affairs, three war ministers, and three foreign ministers, among others. No wonder the council of ministers came to be known as the 'government of tumblers'.

The summer of 1916 appeared to bring some easing of the situation. There was some improvement in the way things were going at the front. Thanks to the energetic measures taken by General A.A.Brusilov, (p. 577), the talented commander of the south-western front, Russian troops had not only succeeded in breaching the Austro-German front in the Lutsk region, but also in turning the break-through into a strategic advance which led to the rout of the Austro-Hungarian army. The advance on the south-western front forced the Germans to transfer dozens of reserve divisions to the east and halt their attacks on Verdun. The Austrians were obliged, in their turn, to bring their advance in Italy to a halt. But, in the absence of support from the other fronts, the Russian advance did not affect the outcome of the war. Towards the end of the summer the armies had reverted again to trench warfare.

The tension within the country also appeared to have relaxed. There was some reduction in the wave of strikes by the proletariat, which raised hopes that the revolutionary movement would be suppressed. It is true that a spontaneous uprising broke out in the south-eastern regions of the country – in Kazakhstan and Central Asia – among the local population, which had been reduced to a state of desperation, but the government did not at first attach serious importance to it. The bourgeois opposition also appeared to have quietened down. In any case the so-called 'voluntary' organizations set up to manage wartime supplies and industry, who had formed the core of bourgeois opposition, now worked hard to establish contact with government circles.

▷682

Left: ***A homeless beggar.*** ***Above:*** *Barge-haulers on the banks of the Volga, unaffected by industrialization. The war increased the burden that fell on Russia's peasants, born to hard labour and deprivation*

The Subjects of the Tsar

In 1914 Russian society and institutions still bore the stamp of her feudal past. The Tsar, supported by a highly privileged nobility and church, ruled absolutely over a huge people who were mostly primitive peasants. But industrialization was shaking the traditional structure of 'Holy Mother Russia'. To factory workers socialism promised power as the reward for organization. Those who had made money through industry wanted power to correspond with their wealth. And Russia's long-suffering peasants had been driven to the point of rebellion by their misery.

Right: *Figure of 'Holy Mother Russia' on a Russian sticker protesting against German atrocities.* ***Below:*** *Workers and peasants – raw material of revolution. They are at a sale of boots in a provincial market*

Novosti

Left: *The world of toil: a quarryman breaking stones.* ***Above:*** *The world of privilege: ministers of the imperial court in a procession commemorating the 300th anniversary of the Romanov dynasty, 1913*

Above: *Leader of the Holy Synod, the high council of the Russian Orthodox Church. The Tsardom and the church were linked. The first Tsars saw themselves as heirs of Orthodox Byzantium.* ***Right:*** *Music at a peasant fair.* ***Below:*** *Beginnings of industry: a carrying ramp at a gold mine*

Disaster strikes

But all this was no more than a passing, and to a large extent illusory, period of calm. By the end of 1916 the catastrophic situation in which Russia found herself became fully apparent. Disaster struck every single branch of the economy. Industry, transport, finance, and agriculture were all in a state of complete collapse. One of the signs of the general economic disorganization was the severe food crisis which broke out in the autumn of 1916.

The grave economic situation, the severe shortage of foodstuffs, and the government's repressive measures led the workers to embark on a new wave of strikes on a larger scale than anything that had gone before.

In September 1916 the strike movement had not involved more than 50,000 working people. But in October 1916 nearly 200,000 people were on strike. No less than 1,542 strikes were recorded in the course of 1916, involving more than 1,000,000 workers—that is, roughly twice as many as in the previous year, 1915. The strikes assumed an ever larger scale and the strikers' demands became ever more insistent, with workers being drawn into the movement from the remoter districts as well as from the industrial centres. It was not, however, simply that the strike movement became a real mass movement, embracing the whole country; in the final months of 1916 it took on a clearly defined political colouring. What had been a struggle for the satisfaction of limited economic demands became a struggle against the existing system of monarchic rule, against the war and those who had brought it on the people.

The Bolshevik section of the Russian Social Democratic Party played a great part in giving this spontaneous movement an organized and purposeful character. The Bolshevik party had close links with the more advanced, most intelligent, and most active part of the working class, and it was in effect the only one of the socialist parties to have fought consistently and uncompromisingly against the war and against Tsarism. It regarded revolution and a complete break with the domestic and foreign policy of Tsarism as the only way to save the country from ruin.

But the party had to work in unbelievably difficult conditions. As far back as November 1914 the five Bolshevik deputies to the State Duma had been arrested and exiled to Siberia, and this meant the loss of a most important legal centre and platform from which the party could put forward its views. It therefore had to operate in conditions of complete secrecy. But despite all the difficulties and dangers besetting the Bolsheviks at every step, their revolutionary anti-war activity was not halted. It is sufficient to say that, from the beginning of the war and up to the February Revolution, local branches of the party put out more than 600 leaflets totalling around 2,000,000 copies. They were published in eighty towns and distributed throughout the country. In Petrograd, Moscow, Riga, Kharkov, and several other towns the Bolsheviks even succeeded in publishing illegal newspapers, and although these publications were usually soon shut down by the police, they did their job of educating the people and exposing the truth about the war. Bolshevik slogans became steadily more popular with the masses who were exhausted by the intolerable burden of war.

Imperial War Museum

General Sukhomlinov (left) a minister of war so corrupt that he was suspected of treason. He was tried and found guilty of having neglected the supply of munitions before the war

Despite the obstacles to communication put up by the censor, news of the tense situation at home, and of the growth of the revolutionary mood and revolutionary ferment got through to the front. Indignation grew in the army at the actions of the government and the Tsar in bringing the country to disaster. Instead of being an instrument for pacifying and suppressing the emancipation movement, the army became a part of the revolutionary people, ready for an assault on a regime which had outlived its day.

'We shall be crushed'

The ruling and owning classes found themselves faced with an inexorably approaching revolutionary explosion. Both the supporters of the Tsarist system and the opposition-minded bourgeoisie started feverishly to look for a way out of the crisis. The state in which the ruling group at the top found themselves towards the end of 1916 can be described in one word—isolation. They were isolated even from those classes and social groups whose interests they had represented and defended for many long years. Even the landowners, that most conservative of all the classes in Russian society, backed away from the group of intriguers around the throne who were all heavily under the baleful influence of Rasputin. Significantly, even V.M.Purishkevich, one of the most violent reactionaries and an opponent of any kind of freedom, who hated the liberals hardly less than he did the revolutionaries, appealed publicly for the Tsar's attention to be drawn to the 'terrible reality' and for Russia to be 'rid of Rasputin and supporters of Rasputin, both big and small'. The landowners wanted to preserve the monarchy, but not in the person of the indecisive and weak-willed Nicholas II, who was surrounded by rogues and careerists and who 'decided' on policies at the dictation of his wife and the black-bearded 'monk' Rasputin. In such circumstances there remained only one thing for the intriguers at the court to do: to carry the policy of repression to the very extreme and at the same time to conclude a separate peace with Germany as quickly as possible and, with the help of their old friend 'Willy', Wilhelm II of Germany, to put an end once and for all to both the 'revolutionary infection' and the liberals. This is the path on which the clique at the court decided. From autumn 1916 efforts to get talks going with the German government were transferred to the realm of practical politics.

The possibility of such a solution to the situation in no way suited the Russian bourgeoisie, for it would only prevent them from achieving the objectives at which they were aiming in the war, and they feared the political consequences of such a step for the country's internal order. The class which dominated the country economically could not, and certainly did not want to, find itself cut off from the centre of power. On this issue the bourgeoisie had a large and very important account to settle with the monarchy, and to achieve this long-cherished aim they were ready to resort to anything – anything, that is, except an appeal to the masses.

Fear of the masses, the fear of revolution, pushed the bourgeois opposition into making sharp attacks on a government which was incapable of dealing with revolution. But that same fear forced them at the same time to refuse to enter into conflict with the government. They feared that harsh words spoken in the State Duma might serve as a spark to start the conflagration which would destroy the throne, the government, and the bourgeoisie itself. It was V.V. Shulgin, one of the leaders of the Progressive Bloc, who put the situation remarkably neatly when he said: 'The crowd is pushing us in the back. . . . We are being pushed and we have to move, though we resist as far as the strength lies in us, but all the same we must move. . . . If we stop moving we shall be crushed, the crowd will break through and rush for that thing which we are trying to preserve – to preserve, despite all our protests, complaints, and reproaches – and that thing is power.'

The hopelessness of the situation became more apparent every day. Nicholas remained deaf to appeals by members of the Duma and the more reasonable of his officials. Neither he nor the clique of maniacs grouped so tightly around him would retreat a single step from the reactionary course they had set in domestic affairs and insisted on working for the conclusion of a separate peace with Germany. But outside the palace, in the working-class districts, the tide of popular discontent was rising and was ready at any moment to reach the flood. It was in these conditions that the bourgeoisie, having lost faith in the possibility of 'persuading' the monarchy to make concessions, embarked on the preparation of a palace revolution. The idea of such a step had been broached some time previously. One evening in the autumn of 1915 when one of the usual attempts to come to an agreement with the government had failed, a member of the Bloc said 'I am relying on 23rd March'. More than one hundred years before, on 23rd March 1801, conspirators had murdered Paul I and enthroned a new emperor. This was the recollection of men who could not and would not fight the Tsarist regime together with and at the head of the people. But at that time it was just talk.

In the autumn of 1916, however, such a solution turned out to be the only one possible. Leaders of the Progressive Bloc and of the bourgeois voluntary organizations joined the circle of conspirators. Generals Krymov, Denikin, Ruzsky, and others were also drawn into the affair. According to A.I.Guchkov, one of the active participants in the plot, it was proposed to seize the imperial train between GHQ and Tsarskoye Selo with the help of reliable guards' units, to force Nicholas to abdicate, then with the same forces to arrest the government in Petrograd, and then to announce what had taken place. If the Tsar refused to sign the abdication, his 'physical removal' would have to be carried out, as Denikin wrote later. Those were the plans and the immediate future would show how practicable they were.

The murder of Rasputin

On the frosty night of 30th December one more event occurred which was an interesting and not insignificant page in the historical drama which unfolded towards the end of 1916. On that night Grigory Rasputin was murdered in Prince Felix Yusupov's private residence in Petrograd by a small group of conspirators, Yusupov himself, Grand Duke Dmitry Pavlovich, and the deputy V.M.Purishkevich. Although the direct participants in the murder were few, behind them stood a wide circle of men interested in the elimination of the all-powerful favourite of the imperial couple. The idea of removing Rasputin and the Empress from affairs had been debated in aristocratic circles from the beginning of 1916, and towards the autumn of 1916 the idea began to assume its final form.

After Rasputin's murder the wife of the chairman of the Duma, Rodzyanko, wrote to Princess Yusupova: 'I am told that there are 106 persons under suspicion . . .' It was not, however, only the aristocracy, but members of the Duma too who were drawn into the conspiracy against the 'monk'. Quite apart from Purishkevich, a direct part was played in the preparations for the murder by V.A.Maklakov, a prominent member of the Kadet Party and brother of the former minister for internal affairs. It was he who gave the conspirators the potassium cynanide which they put in the food and into the madeira with which Rasputin was to be 'entertained'. It was he also who gave Felix Yusupov 'just in case' a rubber truncheon, which, incidentally, came in useful. A few days before the murder Purishkevich told his friend V.V.Shulgin about what was being planned. Other members of the Duma must also have known about it.

The drama which took place in the Yusupov mansion became public knowledge on the following day, when the body was hauled out of the Moyka into which it had been thrown. The Empress was beside herself and demanded severe punishment for the murderers. But Nicholas did not care to go very far, since it was found that members of the imperial household were involved in the affair. The Grand Duke Dmitry Pavlovich was exiled to Persia, Felix Yusupov was banished to his own estate in the Kursk *guberniya,* and Purishkevich, without any let or hindrance, got into his own hospital train and set off for the front. The Grand Duke Nikolay Mikhaylovich, who was also exiled as one of the people mixed up in the affair, wrote in his diary: 'Alexandra Fedorovna is triumphant, but I wonder if the wretched woman will remain in power very long.'

The murder of Rasputin, which was part of the general conspiracy against Nicholas II, was an attempt to save the monarchy in the 'old Russian way', and, as V.Shulgin very shrewdly pointed out, it was a 'profoundly monarchistic act'. But in itself it could change nothing and save nothing. The whole Rasputin affair had sunk roots deep into every part of the organism of the state. As though in reply to the murder, there followed a further series of reshuffles in the government. The position of chairman of the council of ministers was taken by the last premier of a Tsarist government, the weak-willed and decrepit Prince N.D.Golitsyn. The Romanov empire was rushing headlong downhill. It was the beginning of 1917, a year of revolution. *(Translation)*

Ullstein

Radio Times

Above: *Water-tower destroyed by Russians retreating through Lithuania, 1915.* ***Left:*** *Wounded Russian soldiers carted into Lwów. The Tsar's ministers failed to equip his army for modern war*

The Soldiers of the Tsar

Fifteen million peasants were summoned to fight for the glory of the Tsar and Holy Mother Russia. The army showed in microcosm the weaknesses of Nicholas II's regime. The high command, responsible only to an ineffectual monarch, were negligent in organizing equipment and supplies. A rigid caste system separated the officers from the masses they commanded. As this unwieldy army was pushed back from Galicia (Austrian Poland) through Russian Poland and Lithuania, the peasants went hungry, the soldiers died in their thousands and the Tsar lost his throne

Below: *Nicholas II with his staff. In 1915 Nicholas assumed supreme command of the forces – a symbolic assertion of autocracy irrelevant to the needs of his army.* ***Bottom:*** *German troops enter the blackened streets of a smoking Russian town.* ***Right:*** *After an attack – troops relax in a captured German trench*

Novosti

Novosti

▽ Novosti

Novosti

Above left: *Grim conditions for the wounded. Russian officers visit a field hospital.* **Above:** *German gas attack on Russian trenches. German equipment and weapons were incomparably more sophisticated than those of the Russians.* **Left:** *French poster: 'On enemy territory Russian prisoners are dying of hunger'*

Ullstein

Above: *Placard displayed by Germans to the Poles of Galicia: 'Przemysl is in our hands. We captured 1,000 Russian officers and 300,000 men in May.'* **Right:** *Bridge blown up by Russians in retreat.* **Below:** *Russian troops assembled to leave Czernowitz, the capital of Bukovina, which the Russians had to evacuate in July 1917*

Bibliothek für Zeitgeschichte, Stuttgart

Imperial War Museum

'The Last Naval Hope of Russia. The Baltic Fleet preparing for Sea', painted by J.M.Price. But, like the army, the navy was disaffected. Sailors were to take a leading part in the later stages of the revolution

Россійскій
царствовавшій
домъ....

Russia, 1914-16/Geoffrey A.Hosking

Rasputin and the 'Dark Forces'

While the foundations of the Russian state were being shaken by the war, a crisis was developing at the top—a crisis which was symbolized by and embodied in the career of one of the most extraordinary men ever to have swayed a nation's destinies

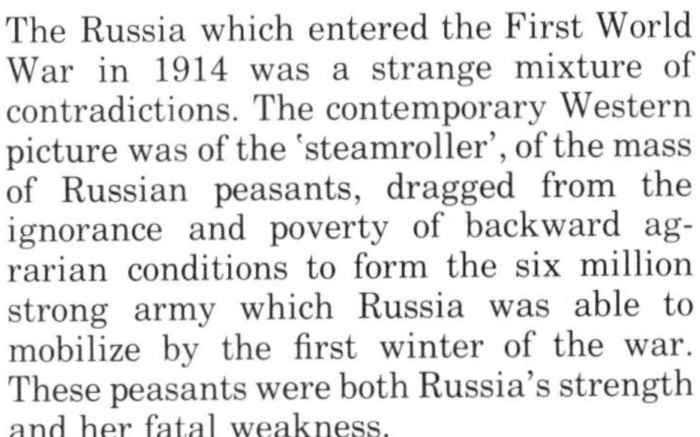

The Russia which entered the First World War in 1914 was a strange mixture of contradictions. The contemporary Western picture was of the 'steamroller', of the mass of Russian peasants, dragged from the ignorance and poverty of backward agrarian conditions to form the six million strong army which Russia was able to mobilize by the first winter of the war. These peasants were both Russia's strength and her fatal weakness.

Less known to the outside world was the new industrial and urban Russia which had grown fast in the last twenty or thirty years before the war, a Russia of coal, steel, and railways, of industrialists and financiers, of lawyers, doctors, and professors, and from 1905, of political parties, professional associations, and even trade unions. Tsarist Russia did not, as is often thought, 'decay' or 'decline': on the contrary, in its last years, it expanded and blossomed in a variety of conflicting forms which imposed an ultimately fatal strain on its structure.

The new Russia could find no place in traditional Tsarist society. Already in 1905 the peasants, urban workers, professional intelligentsia, and even part of the nobility, in uncertain alliance, had shaken the autocracy and compelled it to concede the establishment of a national parliament, the Duma (p. 78). This new body represented, however imperfectly, all classes of the nation, but gave the predominant voice to landowners and the wealthier urban elements. The aim of its establishment was to provide a forum in which the government could work with the more influential sections of Russian society to carry out the reforms which, during the 1905 revolution, were widely felt to be necessary. But as the revolution faded into the past the sense of urgency excited by this task weakened, and the old habits of autocracy reasserted themselves, strengthened by the fear of renewed social violence, by the memory of the Moscow barricades and of rural arson, lynchings, and murders. On the right wing of the Duma, and in the upper house, the State Council, strong groups emerged, on which the government came increasingly to rely for its majority, groups who were concerned to emasculate or indefinitely delay reforms which they feared might open the flood-gates of revolution. This process led among the intelligentsia and on the left wing of the Duma to growing disillusionment with political action and to a helpless and even irresponsible bitterness.

It is against this background of political stagnation and embitterment that we must view the emergence of the figure who for many historians has exemplified the ultimate decadence of Tsarism. Grigory Rasputin was a peasant from the village of Pokrovskoye in western Siberia. To describe him as a monk or a priest would be misleading, for he had no connexion with any organized church: yet he had gained from his early years of lonely wandering round Russia, the Balkans, and the Middle East a certain faith in himself as a spiritual healer, and had evolved for himself a doctrine of redemption through sin which has deep roots in Russian, and especially sectarian Russian, religious thought. When he first appeared in St Petersburg in 1903, his sturdy, unkempt peasant figure and his independent teaching and manner won him adherents at court (where traditionally mystical religions had been sought as a panacea for insoluble social ills).

A simple Russian peasant

There were special reasons why he should have attracted the attention of the imperial couple. Their long awaited male heir, the Tsarevich Alexey, had inherited haemophilia, and Rasputin's powerful, soothing personality proved able to staunch the painful and dangerous internal bleeding which characterizes this disease. In this way he won the devotion of the Empress, whose concern for her son had made her a lonely and hysterical woman. But there was more to the attachment than this. In the years of disillusionment, especially from 1911 onwards, which followed the failure of government and Duma to work constructively together, both Emperor and Empress came to see in Rasputin a representative of the simple Russian peasant folk, from whom, they felt aggrievedly, the Duma and the bureaucracy had separated them. To Dedyulin, palace commandant, who once expressed doubts about Rasputin's character, Nicholas replied: 'He is just a good, religious, simple-minded Russian. When in trouble or assailed by doubts I like to have a talk with him, and invariably feel at peace with myself afterwards.' Rasputin took care to cultivate his peasant image, going so far as to take part at court banquets unwashed

***Far left:** 'The Russian Royal Family'—the Tsar and Tsarina in the arms of their presiding evil genius—an irreverent Russian cartoon. **Above left:** Rasputin and his court followers—women found 'spiritual purification' through sexual intercourse with him. **Left:** 'The simple Russian peasant' with two other advisers of the Tsar*

The Tsarina and her son, Alexey. Rasputin owed his power over her—and in Russia—to his ability to soothe the pain haemophilia caused her beloved son

and plunging filthy hands into the soup tureen. Or he would talk to the imperial couple about the sufferings of the peasants and the measures which might be taken to alleviate them. In the uncertainty of the last years, the imperial couple liked to look on Rasputin as their link with the Russian people, and regarded the men of the Duma, the *zemstvos,* and the war-time voluntary organizations as selfish intriguers.

Rasputin was thus not only a symptom of the imperial couple's estrangement from the changing politics of contemporary Russia, he increased it. His arrogant behaviour in society, his religious unorthodoxy, and above all his overt sexual licence alienated many. Some of the national newspapers, in particular *Golos Moskvy (The Voice of Moscow),* mouthpiece of Guchkov, leader of the moderate liberal Octobrist Party in the Duma, began to publish regular reports of Rasputin's movements, written in an insinuating tone, as well as the 'confessions' of women who had sought spiritual purification through sexual intercourse with him. Early in 1912 a leading article appeared in *Golos Moskvy,* in which Novoselov, a specialist on religious sects, denounced Rasputin as a member of the *Khlysty* (a sect which practised flagellation as a means of erotic stimulation and of communion with God). This issue of the paper was confiscated, but Guchkov raised the question of Rasputin in the Duma, and circulated copies of letters from Rasputin to the Empress, containing expressions which might be interpreted to indicate sexual intimacy between them. *Golos Moskvy* even issued, in its illustrated supplement, a short biography of Rasputin, which ended: 'Representing himself as a saint, this blackguard and erotomaniac practises unbelievable debauchery in the village of Pokrovskoye, together with local girls, or with ladies who come to him for "instruction". Recently, Grigory Rasputin has settled in St Petersburg, where he has found himself powerful patrons and, more especially, patronesses. Here rumour has it that he has instituted the same "good works" as in his native village.'

This extract gives a good picture of the way in which liberal politicians vented their frustration through poisonous innuendo, extending even to the imperial family, and thus contributed to the atmosphere of suspicion and personal enmity in which politics were conducted in the last years of the empire.

Watchful unity

The outbreak of war restored temporary unity and a sense of common purpose. The Duma meekly accepted an indefinite prorogation, and the opposition parties declared their complete solidarity with the war effort. The *zemstvos* and town councils hastened to complement the government's war organization, first in the relief of the wounded and sick, and then increasingly in transport and supply. The government gave legal status to the body *(Zemgor)* which co-ordinated their work, and allocated treasury grants to it.

This unity and co-operation was, however, watchful and doubting. Russia's first major defeats, those of the spring and summer of 1915, when most of Poland and Galicia was lost, almost shattered it. Like all the combatant states, the Russian government had under-estimated the length and complexity of the war, with the result that, at an early stage, shortages of ammunition and supplies became apparent. *Zemgor* increasingly exceeded its functions in order to meet the most elementary needs of the army and the population. The civil and military branches of government were at loggerheads, and no supreme directing institution, except the Emperor, existed to co-ordinate their plans. The council of ministers, with its functions usurped on the one side by *Zemgor,* and on the other by the military command, felt powerless and isolated; at one of its meetings, Shcherbatov, minister of the interior, exclaimed with a sudden acute and anguished sense of reality: 'A government which has the confidence neither of the Emperor, nor of the army, nor of the towns, nor of the *zemstvos,* nor of the nobles, nor of the merchants, nor of the workers—not only cannot function, it cannot even exist! It's sheer absurdity. We're sitting here like a bunch of Don Quixotes!'

Some steps were taken to increase the effective co-operation of army, government, and society in the fields of industrial production and supplies. The unpopular war minister, Sukhomlinov, was replaced by Polivanov, who had worked with Guchkov and the Octobrists in the past over military questions. But the Duma parties wanted to go much farther and gain some ministerial posts for themselves at this time of national emergency. Milyukov, leader of the radical liberal Kadet (Constitutional Democratic) Party, and the most determined and subtle exponent of purely parliamentary forms of struggle, gathered a bloc of the moderate parties. In spite of the considerable political differences between them, they united, under the name of Progressive Bloc, on a programme of moderate reform and the demand for a ministry enjoying public confidence. On 8th September 1915 this programme came before the council of ministers, most of whom were agreed that the reform proposals were largely sensible. But the premier, Goremykin, aged and inert, though single-mindedly devoted to the autocratic ideal, was unwilling to meet members of the Bloc and insisted that the appointment of a future cabinet rested with the Emperor alone. Four ministers, led by Krivoshein, minister of agriculture, nevertheless consulted with leaders of the Bloc and as a result recommended the collective resignation of the cabinet to make way for a ministry enjoying public confidence. Goremykin reluctantly conveyed the proposal to the Emperor, who rejected it and ordered instead that the Duma be prorogued once more. Goremykin, relieved, reported the Emperor's decision to the cabinet on 15th September, remarking privately to the cabinet secretary: 'Let them abuse and slander me—I'm already old and have not long to live. But as long as I live, I shall fight for the inviolability of the Tsar's power. Russia's strength lies in autocracy alone. Without it there will be such chaos that everything will be lost.' The meeting was a stormy one: Polivanov and Krivoshein were embittered and little

Prince Yusupov. 'What remained, therefore, to save the Tsar and Russia from that evil genius? . . . There is only one way—to destroy that criminal "holy man" '

Imperial War Museum

The Tsar and his hated clique of advisers (Russian cartoon, 1916). Rasputin in particular made the Tsar the object of bitter personal enmities and contempt

short of offensive, while Sazonov, the temperamental foreign minister, refused to give Goremykin his hand at the end and staggered out shouting 'I refuse to shake hands with that senile idiot – *il est fou, ce vieillard!*'

The Emperor refused to receive petitions from the Duma or *Zemgor,* and with that any serious effort at conciliation between the monarchy and these social organizations came to an end. The Emperor had initiated plans of his own for meeting the crisis. Recognizing it correctly as a crisis of confidence between the monarchy and the various sections of his people, he attempted to solve it in the manner which background and upbringing suggested to him: by a re-affirmation of his autocratic power. On 6th September he announced that he was assuming personal supreme command of the armed forces. In this decision he was encouraged by his wife, who constantly urged him to be more authoritarian, and by Rasputin, whose views on government were identical with Goremykin's. But more than this, the traditions of autocratic imperial Russia, with which Nicholas was himself deeply imbued, had formed in his mind a paternalist vision of social cohesion, in which national unity was a matter of unquestioning obedience, of immaculate military reviews, of popular acclamations, and of religious ceremonies held in common (all of which he lovingly records in his diary and letters). Beside these things the demands of *zemstvo* organizations, political parties and recalcitrant ministers were no more than the tiresome intrigues of ambitious and petty troublemakers.

From August 1915, therefore, Nicholas asserted more consistently his personal rule. The situation, however, was much too complex for such a drastically simple solution, and the only result was that he became more and more isolated from men with a sense of responsibility and reality, and fell more exclusively under the influence of his beloved and unhappy wife, of her 'saviour', Rasputin, and of the sycophants who were prepared to minister to their common delusions.

The Duma parties and the social organizations were helpless. On the one hand, they felt the monarch's policy was leading to certain military defeat and probably revolution; and on the other, they were afraid to raise their hands against the monarch for fear of precipitating a mass revolution which they felt they had no means to control. They therefore vacillated between half-hearted co-operation and incipient conspiracy. Russian politics again became a murky world of suspicion and plotting, made the more sinister by the dual threat of national defeat and social revolution.

'Dark forces'

This was the world in which the legend of the 'dark forces' was born. As a succession of incompetent or even shady ministers was appointed on the strength of Rasputin's advice, the idea gradually took form, and became widely accepted, that he and 'the German woman' (the Empress, who was by origin a minor German princess) formed the centre of a court clique which was opposed to the war and was even passing secrets to the Germans. Some of the Emperor's closest advisers had indeed in 1914 advised against involvement on the side of Great Britain and France in a war which would 'undermine the monarchical principle'. But there was (and still is) no evidence to support the view that treasonable relations existed with Germany, or even that any serious attempt was being made to conclude a separate peace with her. Nevertheless, the members of the Progressive Bloc and the voluntary organizations co-ordinated by *Zemgor* had little else to unite them in their indecision except a virulent nationalist propaganda combined with insinuations about the patriotism of the monarchy. Liberal politicians, and even some of the Grand Dukes, began to discuss openly the possibility of a palace coup in which the Empress would be exiled or immured in a monastery and Nicholas forced to abdicate. Hints circulated on the possibility of regicide if all should fail.

The most convinced monarchists were not prepared to envisage such steps. But, determined to save the country from the evil which they felt was spreading over it, they settled on Rasputin as the single ulcer poisoning the whole body politic. Prince Yusupov, a wealthy young nobleman, who initiated the conspiracy which was to result in Rasputin's murder, described his feelings thus: 'From childhood I had been accustomed to regard the imperial family as special people, not like ourselves. I grew up to hold them in reverence, as higher beings, surrounded by some intangible halo. For that reason, everything that was said and passed around, all the rumours blackening their name, deeply offended me, and I did not want to believe what I heard.

Bowater Gallery

Bust by Naoum Aronson of Rasputin, spiritual healer and debauchee, unkempt peasant and political intriguer – the strange adviser of a doomed imperial court

'The war began . . . In spite of the general patriotic uplift inspired by the war, many were pessimistic. An atmosphere of gloom hovered around Tsarskoye Selo. The Emperor and Empress, cut off from the world, isolated from their subjects, and surrounded by Rasputin's clique, decided matters of world-shaking importance. One came to feel dread for Russia's fate.

'. . . There was no hope that the Emperor and Empress would understand the whole truth about Rasputin and dismiss him. What way remained, therefore, to save the Tsar and Russia from that evil genius? Inevitably the thought would run through one's mind: there is only one way – to destroy that criminal "holy man".'

Yusupov found two principal accomplices, Grand Duke Dmitry Pavlovich and Purishkevich, a flamboyant, erratic, and deeply patriotic member of the extreme right, monarchist wing of the Duma. With the help of these two men, Yusupov invited Rasputin to his home on the night of 29th-30th December 1916 and murdered him.

This murder was a futile and macabre melodrama. It solved none of the real problems facing Russia, and only increased the brooding bitterness which divided the imperial couple from almost all the nation. By so demonstratively removing a symptom in the guise of curing a disease, it left the Tsarist autocracy in all its nakedness, an idol no longer capable of attracting devotion, and ready to be deserted by all at the first breath of revolt in March 1917.

Russia, January to March 1917/David Floyd

Overthrow of the Tsar

After Rasputin's murder discontent with the monarchy gathered rapidly. Although he clung to his imagined authority Nicholas was powerless. Three months later, after a week of strikes and disturbances, and demands for bread, the end of autocracy and of the war, the Tsar was deposed

The murder of Rasputin did nothing to restore the fortunes of the monarchy or increase popular respect for the Tsar. If the removal of her 'friend' lessened the influence of the Tsarina on the nation's affairs, Nicholas showed no inclination to listen to the advice of the more liberal-minded of his ministers; on the contrary, he turned his back on both the government and the Duma and relied on his own imagined authority, exercised primarily through his minister of the interior, Protopopov, who dominated the administration.

Throughout January 1917 the storm of discontent gathered as the war continued to take its toll on the economy. Food shortages and a rapidly rising cost of living resulted in widespread unrest among the industrial workers, particularly in Petrograd and Moscow. There were as many strikes in the first six weeks of 1917 as in the whole of the previous year. But discontent with the monarchy and the conduct of affairs extended far beyond the working-class and the peasantry, into the ranks of the middle class, the progressive deputies to the Duma, the military leaders, and even the Grand Dukes themselves.

In January the Grand Duke Alexander wrote to Nicholas to persuade him to set up a government capable of inspiring confidence in the people. 'The Tsar alone cannot govern a country like Russia', he wrote. Rodzyanko, the chairman of the Duma, warned the Tsar on 20th January that 'very serious outbreaks' were to be expected. Russia wanted a change of government because, he said, 'there is not one honest man left in your entourage; all the decent people have either been dismissed or have left'. But such warnings had no effect on the obstinate and autocratic Tsar. His only reaction to the increasing threat of trouble in the capital was, on 19th February, to place the city under the command of General Khabalov, who was made directly responsible to the Tsar alone for

An enthusiastic welcome to the February Revolution. Soldiers at the front cheer at the news that the days of Tsardom are over. 'Nowhere in the country,' wrote Trotsky later, 'were there any popular groups, parties, institutions, or military units prepared to defend the old regime. Neither at the front nor in the rear was there to be found a brigade or a regiment ready to fight for Nicholas II'

Right: *March 1917. Revolutionary newspapers handed out.* ***Centre right:*** *Funeral procession for 'Victims of the Revolution'. But only two hundred people died in the revolution.* ***Bottom right:*** *German cartoon. Tolstoy's ghost asks: 'People of Russia, are you happy now that you are freed? You are not free as long as you are the soldiers of England'*

the maintenance of order. The Petrograd garrison was reinforced and equipped with artillery and machine guns. For the first fortnight of February an uneasy peace reigned in the capital; the police and the military appeared to have the situation in hand.

But Rodzyanko knew that the situation was deteriorating, and on 23rd February he told the Tsar he thought a revolution was possible. Nicholas brushed the warning aside and told Rodzyanko that, if the deputies did not watch their words, the Duma would be dissolved. It met, nevertheless, in the Tauride Palace on 27th February, and the government, expecting trouble during the session, stiffened the censorship, arrested all potential troublemakers and braced itself against the popular wrath. Tension in the capital rose. A week later, on 7th March, the Tsar decided to leave Petrograd for the army GHQ in Mogilev.

Next day disorders broke out in the capital which were to lead only a week later to the overthrow of the monarchy. Apparently without any central direction, and initially without any clear political aims, the workers of several large factories in Petrograd came out on strike. Their action was mainly a protest at the breakdown in food supplies, but the nervous reaction of the authorities soon turned industrial and economic unrest into political protest.

Troops were sent immediately to back up the police in the working-class districts of the city, with the result that next day, 9th March, the disturbances spread to the whole city, and protests against the continuation of the war were added to the demand for bread. The central Nevsky Prospect became a mass of marching people, some of whom were now shouting 'Down with the autocracy!'. By the third day, a Saturday, 10th March, a quarter of a million workers were on strike, the city's transport was at a standstill, and the authorities were desperate.

But for Nicholas the situation presented no problem. From the remoteness of Mogilev he cabled Khabalov: 'I order that the disorders in the capital shall be ended tomorrow; they are quite inadmissible at this grave moment of war with Germany and Austria'. But Khabalov, faced with the whole population in revolt, was no longer in a position to carry out his monarch's orders.

It was not that he had scruples about using force to suppress the revolt. The fact was that he could no longer be sure he had the necessary force at his disposal, and that what he had was rapidly slipping out of his control. The normally trustworthy and brutal Cossacks he had sent into action against the crowds had simply

Novosti

Novosti

Simplicissimus

L'Illustration

Novosti

Imperial War Museum

been lost among the demonstrators. The police had started to fire on the crowds, only to incense them still further and make them bolder in their resistance to brutality. The wave of arrests had continued, but the protest movement had no obvious outstanding leaders, and Khabalov could not arrest the whole population.

An affair of the capital

What ultimately decided the outcome of the revolt and the collapse of the regime, however, was the defection of the soldiery to the side of the revolution. It began with isolated cases of 'fraternization' between soldiers and demonstrators on the Sunday of 11th March and then spread like wildfire throughout the Petrograd garrison, so that by the Monday evening the whole force of 150,000 men had disintegrated. And when, in despair, Khabalov formed a special detachment of a thousand picked men and sent them into action, they too disappeared among the crowds. Whole regiments revolted, shot their officers, and threw in their lot with the working people, taking their weapons with them. On the Monday evening the workers seized the arsenal, where they found 40,000 rifles which were quickly distributed round the city.

The government was helpless. A decision to have Khabalov declare a state of siege was rendered ineffective by the fact that the authorities no longer controlled a printing press on which the declaration could be produced. The Duma was equally incapable of taking effective action. When Rodzyanko, its chairman, sent the Tsar a message saying that the fate of both the country and the monarchy was in the balance, and that urgent steps must be taken, Nicholas replied on 11th March with an order dissolving the Duma. Though it feared to defy the Tsar outright, the Duma remained in informal session and on 12th March elected a 'Provisional Committee' of twelve members, including representatives of the Progressive Bloc, with Alexander Kerensky, the Socialist Revolutionary, and Chkheidze, the Social Democrat. The Committee assumed the impossible task of 'restoring order'.

On the same day and in the same place—the Tauride Palace—another new body came into existence. It was the Petrograd Soviet (Council) of Workers' and Soldiers' Deputies, representing in a rough and ready way the interests of the rebelling factory workers, soldiers, and 'democratic and socialist parties and groups'. Such real power as could be said to exist in the capital—and in the country as a whole—was now vested in these two *ad hoc* bodies; the central government and the administration of the country had already collapsed. On the morning of Tuesday, 13th March, the Soviet issued a news sheet—*Izvestya* (News)—bearing a proclamation announcing its existence and calling on the people everywhere to take the conduct of affairs into their own hands. 'We shall fight to wipe out the old system completely and to summon a constituent assembly elected on the basis of universal, equal, secret, and direct suffrage.'

Rodzyanko kept the Tsar informed of the disastrous course events had taken, urging him first to institute reforms and then, when the situation worsened, to abdicate in the interests of the monarchy as an institution. Isolated and deprived of friends and supporters, Nicholas made his decision with surprising speed and lack of emotion. He left Mogilev to return to his capital on 13th March, but was diverted by the revolutionaries to Pskov. There, still in his royal train, on 15th March, he signed a document abdicating the throne in favour of his son Alexey and nominating his brother, the Grand Duke Michael, as regent. But before the two delegates from the Duma could reach Pskov Nicholas had changed his mind and finally handed them a document which said: 'We hereby transmit our succession to our brother, the Grand Duke Michael, and give him our blessing for his accession to the throne of the Russian empire'.

But, after some thought, Michael refused, and with that the Russian monarchy was at an end. It had been overthrown by the ordinary people of the capital with extraordinary little loss of life. Total casualties were estimated at less than 1,500, with less than 200 people killed. As Trotsky later pointed out, the revolution was almost exclusively an affair of the capital. 'The rest of the country simply followed its lead. Nowhere in the country were there any popular groups, parties, institutions, or military units prepared to defend the old regime. Neither at the front nor in the rear was there to be found a brigade or a regiment ready to fight for Nicholas II.'

The same day as Nicholas signed his act of abdication a Provisional Government was set up in Petrograd. But it had to share power with the Soviet, and the conflict between the two bodies was to occupy the next eight months of 1917.

Top left: *Sentries stand guard over the bodies of men killed during the revolution.* ***Centre left:*** *The burned shell of a police building. The police, instruments of Tsarist repression, represented everything the revolutionaries wanted to destroy.* ***Left:*** *A baker tramples on his old shop sign, 'By appointment to the Tsar'. (Russian postcard, 1917.) Even the* petit bourgeois *climbed on the band-wagon of revolution*

Russia, March to November 1917/George Katkov

Kerensky's Summer

The overthrow of the Tsar brought to power the ill-starred Provisional Government, and eventually Alexander Kerensky as its leader. Why did it fail? Did it deserve its failure?

On 15th March 1917 a large crowd of dishevelled soldiers, enthusiastic intellectuals and students, and glum-looking workers – a typical cross-section of the people who had been demonstrating in the streets of the capital since 8th March – milled around in the large Catherine Hall of the Tauride Palace in Petrograd. They knew that after the prorogation of the Duma by the Tsar on 11th March, a committee of its members had replaced the Tsarist government, which had ceased to exist after failing to control street rioting and the mutiny of a part of the Petrograd garrison.

The leader of the influential liberal Kadets (Constitutional Democrats), and of the parliamentary opposition to the autocratic regime, P.N.Milyukov, addressed the crowd, announcing that a Provisional Government had been set up and giving the names of its members. He was warmly applauded when he said that A.F.Kerensky (the head of the socialist, though non-Marxist, Labour faction of the Duma) had agreed to become minister of justice. Names of other ministers were greeted with surprise and disappointment in the crowd, and Milyukov was asked 'who appointed you?'. He answered that the Government had been appointed 'by the Revolution itself'. The crowd's suspicions were not allayed, and Milyukov was asked what was to become of the dynasty. When he disclosed the plan – which never materialized – to proclaim the infant Alexey Tsar under the regency of his uncle, indignant cries rose from the audience and Milyukov was at pains to point out the necessity of a gradual and orderly transition to a democratic regime. As soon as things were settled, he

Alexander Kerensky (left) takes a salute at a military parade. Kerensky, volatile and flexible, was for six months the dominant figure in Russian politics

said, the people would elect a Constituent Assembly by universal suffrage, and it would decide on the future of Russia. Democratic freedoms would be introduced immediately. This assurance restored the original delirious enthusiasm of the crowd and Milyukov was given an ovation and carried shoulder high from the hall.

Some eight months later, after a turbulent history in which the Provisional Government underwent at least four major reconstructions, only three of its original members remained in office. But the convocation of a Constituent Assembly, to secure a democratic regime for Russia, was still the aim of the government and the polling date was fixed for 28th November.

The footsteps of fate

Yet on 7th November 1917, on the eve of the elections to the Assembly, which could be expected to endorse its policy, the Provisional Government was reduced to a dozen distraught men, huddled in a room of the Winter Palace, with nothing but a group of cadet officers and a women's battalion to defend them from an assault of Red Guards and rebellious sailors led by Bolsheviks. As the approaching steps of the invaders rang through the endless corridors of the Winter Palace, the Provisional Government was asked whether the officer cadets should fight to prevent its falling into the hands of the rebels. The answer was that the Provisional Government would rather yield to force than have blood shed in its defence. And so the ministers were arrested and led off to prison in the Peter and Paul Fortress. The premier, Kerensky, was not among them; a few hours earlier he had left the capital to rally troops to fight the Bolshevik rebellion.

We may well ask what happened in these eight months to reduce the Provisional Government by the beginning of November to this sorry state of isolation and impotence. The Provisional Government was still vested with powers far exceeding those of the last Tsar; it still had under its orders a rudimentary administrative apparatus inherited from the old regime; Kerensky, the prime minister, was supreme commander of all Russian armed forces, at least in name. All political parties, except the monarchists and the Bolsheviks, were in some way represented in the government. And yet the people, whose will and aspirations the Provisional Government claimed to champion, made no move to support it in its hour of trial and Kerensky could not muster the few hundred soldiers needed to suppress the weak and poorly organized Bolshevik rising.

The government which was formed under the wavering and diffident leadership of Prince Lvov in March 1917, combined the highest executive power with full

Historical Research Unit

Above: The armband worn by the followers of Kornilov. ***Right:*** *German cartoon, July 1917. Nicholas from his prison listens as Lloyd George, President Wilson of the United States, and Ribot, prime minister of France, exclaim: 'We never deal with an autocratic government, never.' Nicholas muses: 'Once these rascals were like brothers to me.'* ***Below:*** *Dutch drawing of Nicholas on his way to Siberia, where the Provisional Government sent him and his family in August 1917*

legislative powers; and it soon arrogated to itself the right to interfere with the judiciary. Its claim that it was entitled to act as head of state, replacing the monarch and assuming all his prerogatives, soon brought it into conflict with Finland and other national minorities of the Russian empire.

This concentration of power, the government claimed, was necessary for introducing reforms – such as putting an end to national and religious discrimination – without which no democratic election to the Constituent Assembly was possible. In fact there was more to it than that: the collapse of the monarchy and the promise of every kind of democratic liberty brought about spontaneous changes and threatened a general landslide in the social and legal structures of the country. In order to stem and canalize this revolutionary flood the Provisional Government sought to give a legal form to what were then known as 'the conquests of the Revolution'. But the former revolutionary parties which surfaced from the underground after the Revolution now insisted on 'taking it farther' by destroying every vestige of the 'accursed past' in the shape of state and public institutions, all privileges and prerogatives, and social and army discipline. The popular appeal of these parties, known as the 'revolutionary democracy', was considerable; they dominated the soviets (councils) of workers', soldiers', and peasants' deputies, as well as the trade unions and other rapidly proliferating professional organizations; and they infiltrated the newly formed soldiers' and officers' committees of army units, both at the front and in the rear. Their demands went beyond what the Provisional Government could concede if it was to maintain the fighting capacity of the army and guarantee freedom of decision to the future Constituent Assembly.

It soon became obvious that a certain amount of coercion was necessary to prevent anarchy. For this, however, the Provisional Government lacked both the will and the means of enforcement. The Provisional Government admitted its reluctance to resort to force when, in mid-March, it received the first news of agrarian disorders in the countryside. The government instructed its commissars that force could not be used against looting and rioting peasants: agrarian anarchy was to be prevented by local land committees who were instructed to prepare for the nationalization of land and exhort the peasants to be patient and await the decision of the Constituent Assembly on land reform. Similarly, when told that a mob of soldiers, whose train had been delayed at a station for half an hour, had beaten the stationmaster to death, the Provisional Government ordered the railway authorities to explain to the soldiers that delays were sometimes necessary to prevent collisions and loss of life to passengers. At the same time, the Provisional Government, though it had forbidden them, acquiesced in the unauthorized arrests of former Tsarist officials and army officers; some of them were kept for months in inhuman conditions in the naval fortress of Kronstadt in defiance of government orders.

Disorder in the army

Even if the government had been willing to use force in order to prevent 'revolutionary democracy' from interfering with its administration, it would have found itself without the proper means of doing so. One of the first actions of the Provisional Government had been to disband the police and gendarmerie – bodies which had been guilty of persecuting revolutionaries in the past. Local authorities were told to organize a 'people's militia' for the maintenance of order; but, lacking experience and training, this militia proved to be unequal to the task. There remained the army, but the Provisional Government was unlucky in its relations with the armed forces right from the beginning. In Petrograd, which had a garrison of just under 200,000, the Provisional Government pledged itself in its first proclamation not to transfer any of the units stationed in the capital. This was done to reassure those soldiers who had rebelled against the Tsar and had even killed some of their officers, and who were, therefore, afraid of possible reprisals if they were sent to the front.

The Provisional Government's control over the army was further weakened by the publication on 15th March of the notorious Order No. I of the Petrograd Soviet. This introduced elected soldiers' committees in all units and boldly stated that orders of the Duma Committee were only to be obeyed when they conformed to the instructions of the Petrograd Soviet. Although addressed only to the troops in the capital, Order No. I soon set the pattern for 'revolutionizing' other garrisons and front-line units. It also put the armed forces in the capital virtually under the command of the Soviet, strengthening it against the Provisional Government.

Nor was the Provisional Government successful in its efforts to control the army in the field or in establishing good working relations with the successive supreme commanders whom it appointed. The 'revolutionary democracy' suspected the army, which had played no part in the February Revolution, of a lukewarm attitude to it, and was bent on 'revolutionizing' the rank and file. These efforts, made on the eve of a general offensive agreed upon with the Allies, met with resistance both from GHQ and from officers at the front. A horde of propagandists from Petrograd and other revolutionary centres in the rear descended on the troops at the front where they undermined discipline and relations between officers and men.

The first minister of war of the Provisional Government, Guchkov, did nothing to remedy this situation. He himself had fomented discontent and organized sedition against the Tsar before the Revolution, and now, on becoming minister of war, he started a purge of the officers' corps without consideration for the stability so necessary for an army in the field. Dismissed officers crowded GHQ, where they were joined by others who had lost their commands on the insistence of soldiers' committees infiltrated by Bolsheviks. They were resentful and bitter men looking for leadership in order to stop the process of 'deepening' the Revolution.

The Petrograd Soviet had issued at the end of March an appeal to all warring nations to conclude an early peace renouncing any aggressive war aims. The Provisional Government endorsed this in principle, at the same time assuring the Allies, through the minister of foreign affairs, Milyukov, that Russia would stand by its international obligations. Out of this hardly explicit discrepancy a conflict arose between Milyukov and Kerensky – who felt himself the representative of the Soviet attitude – and this led at the beginning of May to open demonstrations, some demanding and some opposing the resignation of the ministers of foreign affairs and war, Milyukov and Guchkov. Units of the Petrograd garrison took part in one of the demonstrations demanding their resignation. General Kornilov, whom the government had appointed commander-in-chief in Petrograd, had not authorized the demonstration and asked the government to support him and stop the Petrograd Soviet interfering with the troops under his command. Having failed to get satisfaction he resigned his post and returned to the army at the front. His departure coincided with the first ministerial crisis of the Provisional Government. Guchkov and Milyukov resigned, less as a concession to popular clamour than as a result of profound dissensions and divided loyalties inside the government itself. Party ties between Kadet and other liberal ministers proved less binding than the allegiance of some of them to the political masonic organization to which they belonged. Milyukov found himself 'betrayed' by his former deputy party chairman, Nekrasov, who like other Russian masons supported Kerensky in his conflict with Milyukov. His and Guchkov's departure opened the way to the entry of socialists into the cabinet and Kerensky emerged as the initiator of the first coalition government, in which he became minister of war.

▷ 698

An inglorious story of vacillation, betrayal, and misunderstanding

Novosti

Kerensky decided to instil into the army a new revolutionary spirit and a new faith in the justice of the cause for which it was fighting. The supreme commander, General Alexeyev, was dismissed without further ceremony and replaced by General Brusilov, known for his famous offensive in 1916 (p. 577). Kerensky instituted government commissars attached to various headquarters of the army, who would assist officers in all political matters, including contacts with soldiers' committees, and keep the government informed of the state of the army. The main weapon in Kerensky's arsenal was direct contact with the soldiers at army delegates' conferences and meetings of army units. Mesmerizing them by his eloquence, he impressed on his listeners that they had now become the army of a new-born world. With the proclamation of a 'just peace without annexations or indemnities' by the Revolutionary Democracy of Russia the war, he said, had changed its purpose and had obtained a new historical significance. The soldiers had always readily sacrificed their lives under the knout wielded by the tyrannical, autocratic regime. With how much more enthusiasm would they do so now, Kerensky claimed, as free citizens of a liberated Russia which would lead the world towards a new and happier era. Kerensky's exhortations flattered the other ranks who greeted him with ovations. The officers naturally resented being accused of having used cruel methods in the past to force their men to fight for the unworthy cause of the Rasputin clique: but they were willing to put up with anything which might raise the morale of the army.

When, however, the order for the offensive was given on 26th June, Bolshevik propaganda, supported by a fraternization campaign cleverly carried on by the German high command, proved stronger than Kerensky's oratory; soldiers' committees units at company, regiment, or even divisional level discussed battle orders and questioned their commanders' decisions to take the offensive in a war which supposedly had no aggressive aim. After an initial success, mainly due to patriotic volunteer detachments, the offensive collapsed ignominiously through the defection of whole units. The entire 11th Army deserted the front, lynching its officers, disrupting communications, looting, raping, and burning down whole villages. General Kornilov, who had been transferred from Petrograd to the south-western front, demanded that the government should call off the offensive and reintroduce the death penalty at the front as an emergency measure. In this he was supported by the government commissars attached to the units under his command, in particular by Savinkov, a Socialist Revolutionary (like Kerensky), and a former leading terrorist. In view of the desperate situation the Provisional Government not only met all Kornilov's demands but appointed him supreme commander-in-chief.

The need for a return to sanity in the army was forcefully impressed on the Provisional Government by the Bolshevik attempt to seize power on 16th July, which coincided with the German break-through in Galicia. The Bolsheviks organized a so-called 'spontaneous' peaceful, armed demonstration under the slogan 'All power to the soviets'. The Soviet and the Provisional Government, unable to rely on the capital's garrison, were faced with a rebellion of armed workers organized as Red Guards and Kronstadt sailors who had invaded the capital at the call of the Bolsheviks. The position of the Provisional Government, however, was quickly restored by the arrival of a few reliable troops from the front. But it had been a narrow escape, and the first coalition government never recovered from the shock.

The abortive Bolshevik coup sharpened the internal dissensions in the government between those who, like Prince Lvov and the Kadets, wanted to strengthen the authority of the government and those who, like Kerensky and the representatives of 'revolutionary democracy', sought to increase the government's popularity by initiating further revolutionary changes. On 20th July Prince Lvov and the Kadet ministers resigned, leaving Kerensky with the task of reconstructing the cabinet. After trying unsuccessfully for a whole fortnight to bridge the differences between the liberal and socialist camps, Kerensky himself resigned on 3rd August, leaving the country virtually without leadership. That same night his deputy, Nekrasov, summoned a memorable joint session of the cabinet and the party leaders in the Malachite Hall of the Winter Palace. After a torrent of speeches it was decided to accept and support a cabinet of Kerensky's choice. He was left free to define his programme, and the ministers were to be free of all control by their party committees and the Soviet.

Except for some changes of personnel, of which the departure of the 'defensist' Menshevik, Tsereteli, was the most important, the second coalition government differed little from the first. Premier Kerensky remained minister of war, but appointed Savinkov, the commissar at Kornilov's headquarters, to be his deputy in charge of the ministry. In practice, delicate political questions were dealt with by an unofficial 'inner cabinet', consisting of Kerensky, the minister of foreign affairs, Tereshchenko, and Nekrasov.

Kornilov himself, on accepting his appointment from a shaky and divided government, demanded that there should be no

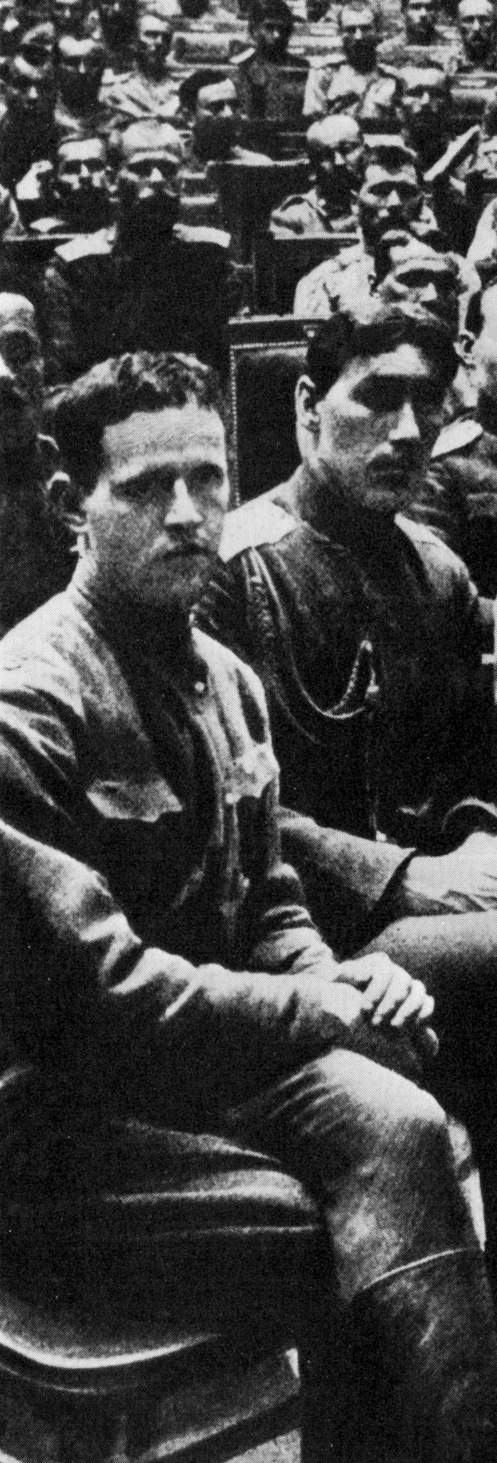
Ullstein

Mansell

Above left: ***June 1917: Demonstration of soldiers' wives demanding votes for women.*** ***Above right:*** *Kerensky (centre) at the funeral of cossacks killed in the Petrograd riots, July 1917. They had been recalled from the front to deal with Bolshevik-organized armed workers and sailors.* ***Below:*** *Kornilov—determined to restore the fighting capacity of the army*

Herman Axelbank

Below: *Kerensky. His hesitation won him the mistrust of both the officers' corps and the revolutionaries.* ***Left:*** *Delegates from the army in Petrograd. Some, the radicals, have torn the bands off their shoulders to show their scorn for authority.* ***Right:*** *July demonstration. The banner says: 'Down with the capitalist ministers. All power to the Soviets'*

Herman Axelbank

Novosti

L'Illustration

The Duma in session before (inset) and after the revolution. The trappings of Tsardom, the portrait and the imperial coat of arms had been removed by April

interference with his choice of commanding officers and claimed that as supreme commander he would be responsible only to his conscience and to the nation as a whole. He then urged the government to take the measures which he claimed were indispensable for restoring order in the country and the fighting capacity of the army. These measures, including the death penalty for sedition in the rear, spelled a curtailment of democratic freedoms – for instance freedom of propaganda, which was one of the 'conquests of the revolution' – which were deemed essential by the soviets for free elections. Kerensky hesitated, in spite of pressure from Savinkov who mediated between him and the supreme commander. Kerensky hoped to overcome the split in public opinion between supporters of Kornilov and those of the soviets at a monster debating rally, the Moscow State Conference, in late August. The conference only showed the chasm, presaging the possibility of civil war.

The Kornilov affair

After the failure of the conference, Kerensky decided, without consulting his cabinet, to approach Kornilov through Savinkov, asking for his loyal co-operation in fighting anarchy. He agreed to meet Kornilov's demands. If the publication of the new laws embodying them caused an outbreak of civil disobedience in Petrograd, it was to be suppressed by troops which Kornilov was to send to the capital and put at the disposal of the Provisional Government. A cavalry army corps was concentrated at the approaches to Petrograd on 9th September. Kerensky had not yet, however, put Kornilov's demands before the cabinet, despite Savinkov's urging. On 8th September he promised to do so that night, when the cabinet was to meet. Shortly before the meeting was due to start, Vladimir Lvov, a former member of the first two Provisional Government cabinets, an unbalanced, excitable, and totally irresponsible character, came to see Kerensky. Lvov had been acting as a self-appointed go-between posing both to Kerensky and Kornilov as a secret emissary of the other. From Lvov's confused and mendacious statement, Kerensky understood that Kornilov was now demanding the resignation of the government and the surrender of all power to him. The idea of a 'Kornilov ultimatum' henceforth dominated all Kerensky's actions at the helm of his foundering government, and was to be the major theme of everything he wrote during the next fifty years. When the cabinet met the same night, Kerensky denounced Kornilov's 'plot' and ultimatum and asked for a free hand to deal with the insubordination of the supreme commander. The ministers who had been given no information of the preceding developments, agreed, but, horrified by the new ordeal threatening Russia, handed in their resignations. Just before the meeting, Kerensky had been communicating with Kornilov by teleprinter, but failed to ascertain whether what he understood Lvov to have reported was correct: he feigned, however, to be in full agreement with Kornilov and promised to join him at GHQ the next day. Instead, after the cabinet meeting, he sent a curt informal telegram dismissing Kornilov from his post and summoning him to Petrograd. Indignantly Kornilov refused to submit and was backed by the overwhelming majority of his senior officers. The conflict had still not been made public and might have been settled, had not a proclamation of the Provisional Government denouncing Kornilov been released to the press prematurely. Kornilov appealed to the country, calling Kerensky's account a complete lie.

Neither Kornilov nor Kerensky disposed of sufficient forces to escalate their exchange of insults into a real trial of strength. The troops sent by Kornilov to Petrograd believed that they were going to support the Provisional Government and were shocked by the announcement of Kornilov's alleged mutiny: they refused to obey marching orders and broke up in confusion. Kerensky was not effectively in control of the capital's garrison; this and the Kronstadt sailors' detachments, ostensibly under the orders of the Soviet, were in fact controlled by the Bolsheviks.

The Kornilov affair petered out ingloriously. Kornilov called the whole thing off and allowed himself to be put under arrest. Kerensky appointed himself supreme commander. A committee of lawyers set up to investigate the alleged mutiny was appalled by the double-crossing and the lack of dignity on all sides, but was unable to complete its work before the collapse of the Provisional Government.

Kerensky is right in referring to the Kornilov affair as the 'prelude to Bolshevism'. But the return of the Bolsheviks to active politics and their final victory in November were made possible not by Kornilov's pressure on the Provisional Government to strengthen its authority, nor by his military measures to back up that pressure, nor even by his angry gesture of insubordination on being suddenly without warning denounced as a mutineer. These actions of Kornilov, who was widely supported by public opinion outside Soviet circles – even by socialists, such as Plekhanov and Argunov – were all brought about by the indecision and procrastination of Kerensky and his closest friends in the cabinet. While conceding in secret negotiations the urgency of the measures demanded by Kornilov, Kerensky seems never to have wanted to implement them and was relieved when he could interpret V.Lvov's incoherent innuendoes as an insolent and arrogant ultimatum by Kornilov, which released him from the promise he had just made to Savinkov to comply with the supreme commander's demands. Kerensky has only himself to blame that both his contemporaries and historians have shown so little sympathy with his behaviour at that critical moment. For after it he was considered by the officers' corps and the Kadets as one who had provoked Kornilov to rise in open rebellion and by the 'revolutionary democracy' as one who had had secret dealings with counter-revolutionary conspirators. Not even the ties binding Nekrasov, Kerensky, and Tereshchenko survived the Kornilov episode, and Nekrasov had to leave the government.

Kerensky's assumption of the highest functions of the state could not restore his popularity nor strengthen his authority. His attempt at establishing a kind of pre-parliament, from appointed representatives of various party and public organizations, led to a final humiliation: when Kerensky demanded full powers from the pre-parliament to deal with the incipient Bolshevik rising, he was rebuffed and told by the representatives of 'revolutionary democracy' that the Bolsheviks could best be fought by the acceptance of a government programme of immediate revolutionary reforms – reforms of a kind which were supposed to be decided by the future Constituent Assembly. Two days after his defeat in the pre-parliament, Kerensky was in flight from the Bolsheviks and the members of his government were incarcerated in the Peter and Paul Fortress.

Chapter 26

Introduction by J.M.Roberts

1916 had been a terrible year for Great Britain and France, yet 1917 was to be even blacker. It was some relief that fighting of quite the scale and intensity which had developed in the early days of the Somme offensive and at Verdun was not repeated. But the scars left by these great struggles had not healed before the Entente had fresh strains to bear while it was still enfeebled from the disasters of 1916.

France's most dangerous moment of the war came when, after the failure of the ill-judged Nivelle offensive, the French soldier suddenly turned on his leaders. In **The French Army Mutinies** John Williams describes this widespread movement which seemed to place the whole Allied front in jeopardy. It enhanced the prestige of Pétain who nursed his soldiers' morale back to health and promised no further vainglorious attacks. Much was later to be said about the part the mutinies played in influencing British strategy in 1917. During the summer and autumn this produced another great offensive, this time in Flanders, where for four months the British armies desperately struggled forward in a series of great battles (described by Brian Bond) and which are usually lumped together under one all-embracing name – **Passchendaele**. This was properly speaking the name of the last of the series, but its horror dominated the popular memory.

This struggle on the Western Front must be seen against a wide background of events almost all of which were deeply depressing for the Allied leaders. The moment of exaltation when the United States entered the war was soon forgotten in the weary wait for the American armies to arrive in France. In the east, Russia was more and more obviously a spent force. In November she was again to undergo a revolution which, this time, would take her out of the war altogether. In the Balkans, Rumania had been overrun and the Allied army at Salonika seemed incapable of taking decisive action. Finally, there came the last great military disaster of the year, **Caporetto**, the subject of an article by Ronald Seth. Italy, the once-courted ally, now became a liability requiring the diversion of men and material to keep her on her feet.

Yet, in spite of appearances, the Allies put something on the other side of the balance-sheet. The German home front was soon more pressed by blockade than the British. The war could only end in a German defeat unless the German army attacked and won in the west before the Americans could arrive. The great offensive could be expected in the spring of 1918; on which of the weary Allied armies it would fall no-one knew as 1917 came to its gloomy end.

Bibliothèque Nationale, Paris

In a German cartoon: poilus implore premier Ribot to lead them to Alsace-Lorraine

Imperial War Museum

After a bombardment a dead British soldier is searched for his papers of identification

Italian troops stop to talk with peasants during the headlong flight from Caporetto

France: Western Front

1916 12th December: Joffre is replaced by Nivelle, who plans offensive on Western Front towards Laon.

1917 23rd February: Germans start to withdraw to the Hindenburg Line.
March: Germans realize that the French are building up troops behind the Aisne for an offensive.
8th March: riots and strikes start the Russian Revolution. This helps demoralize French troops.
9th April: British start attack at Arras as prelude to French offensive.
16th April-21st May: French attack in the 2nd battle of the Aisne and the 3rd battle of Champagne.
They take the Chemin des Dames and lose 200,000 men.
29th April-10th June: wave of army mutinies breaks out, affecting sixteen corps. In May the unrest spreads to civilians; strikes become frequent.

1917 4th May: number of infantrymen in the Chemin des Dames desert and colonial troops circulate anti-war leaflets.
15th May: Pétain succeeds Nivelle as commander-in-chief and decides to keep French troops on the defensive until American reinforcements arrive.
September: unrest in army comes to an end.
16th November: Clemenceau becomes prime minister and rallies the country for victory.

Great Britain: Western Front

1917 4th May: at Paris meeting of French and British leaders Haig expounds plan for attack through Ypres salient.
7th June: Haig launches the first phase of an offensive and gains the Messines Ridge. This encourages him to press for the main offensive.
19th June: Jellicoe insists the army must clear Flanders coast to help the navy. The war cabinet decides to back Haig's offensive.
25th July: Haig's plan is finally approved.
31st July: 3rd Ypres campaign begins. On 10th August the British fight battle of Gheluvelt Plateau, and on 16th the battle of Langemarck. In these three battles they have limited success.
September: finding a breakthrough impossible, GHQ decide on battles of attrition.
1st September: Plumer starts to plan attack on Passchendaele-Staden Ridge.
20th September: British gain Menin Road Ridge.
26th September: they win battle at Polygon Wood.
4th October: in the battle of Broodseinde the British gain a bare foothold on the ridge.
Attempts to capture Passchendaele village start.
It rains unceasingly. On 6th November the village is captured by Canadian troops.
7th November: it becomes clear there is no question of continuing the campaign to the coast. Through the winter the Allies defend what they have won.

1918 April: the Germans recapture the ridge in a few hours' fighting.

Italian Front

1917 23rd January: General Arz von Straussenburg replaces General Conrad von Hötzendorff as chief of the Austrian general staff.
25th August: General Waldstatten is sent to German headquarters to obtain German support for Austrian attack on Italy.
20th September: Cadorna informs British and French military missions that he is going on to the defensive along the Isonzo.
24th October: Austro-German artillery opens fire with gas shells on the Italian batteries and forward trenches.
General Krauss pierces the front of the Italian 4th Corps.
Stein occupies the village of Caporetto.
25th October: Cadorna and Capello agree to a retreat to the Tagliamento.
The Italians refuse to go on fighting.
26th October: order to retreat is given.
Italians withdraw in confusion but Austrian and German forces taken by surprise and fail to exploit the advantage.
31st October: with the exception of a quarter of a million men lost as prisoners, all Italian forces have reached the Tagliamento.
9th November: Italians stand in good order behind the Piave after Germans breach Tagliamento line.
Cadorna succeeded by General Diaz.

1918 June: Germans re-open their offensive. It ends in complete victory for the Italians.
24th October: Diaz goes over to the offensive and inflicts crushing defeat on Austrians at the battle of Vittorio Veneto.

The French Army Mutinies

At Verdun and on the Somme the French soldier had shown unparalleled courage. Yet, a few months later, mutiny broke out in the French army and some of the most heroic units refused to go back to the front. After months of futile fighting on the Western Front, Nivelle, the new commander-in-chief, had promised quick and spectacular success in a fresh offensive. When he failed the army's spirit finally broke, bringing chaos to the front and crisis to the government

Below: *Nivelle offensive. The map shows what happened to Nivelle's attack. The broad white path shows the intended area of breakthrough.* ***Opposite:*** *'Poilus', painted by G.Pierre in 1917, captures the gloom and disillusion of the French soldier. The French army was in fact close to breaking point*

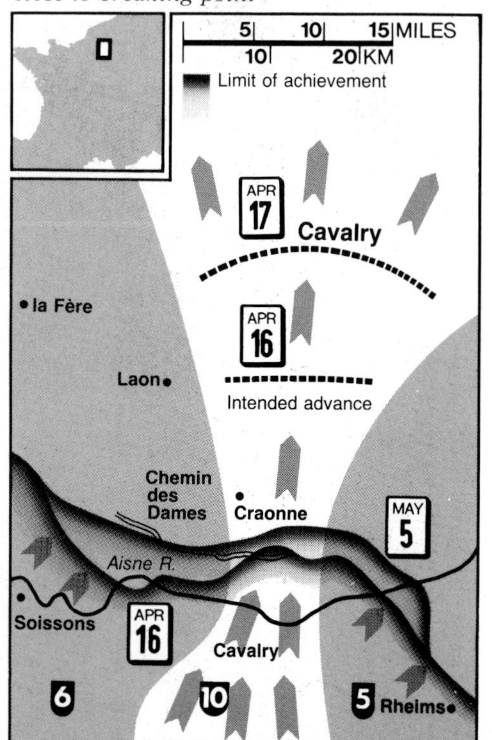

By the start of 1917 the war on the Western Front had settled into a state of apparently endless stalemate. For over two years the opposing sides had faced each other across the hardly shifting no man's land of northern France, wearing themselves down in a series of costly and ineffective offensives – Artois, Champagne, Verdun, the Somme. In this prolonged struggle of attrition no nation had suffered more than France. Not only was the war being fought on French soil, with all that this meant in devastation and loss of coal, iron ore, and other industrial resources, but her troops had suffered relatively the highest casualties of any belligerent power, amounting to some two and a quarter million men. As January 1917 dawned, with no promise of decisive action – let alone victory – in sight, the strain on the nation was beginning to tell. Soldiers and civilians alike were becoming weary and disillusioned. The current mood was expressed by a French officer from general headquarters, Colonel Emile Herbillon. 'The year is opening in a grim atmosphere,' he wrote on the 2nd January 1917. 'Promises and hopes have been followed by too many disappointments.'

Joffre dismissed

All that the Allied war leaders could plan for 1917 was another great Franco-British offensive just as they had ordained for 1915 and 1916. The stage seemed set for a repetition of the great attrition battles of those years. But one significant change had just occurred. Sixty-four-year-old General César Joffre, commander-in-chief of the French army and the main advocate of the attrition strategy, had been replaced. Bulky and imperturbable, 'Papa' Joffre had won enormous prestige as the victor of the Marne in 1914 and since then, at his Chantilly headquarters, had reigned supreme in Allied military affairs. But late in 1916 French deputies, resenting his autocratic powers, had attacked him – ostensibly for his mishandling of the recent Verdun and Somme campaigns (p. 562) – and had virtually forced Aristide Briand, the French prime minister, to dismiss him. With Joffre honorifically created a marshal of France and shunted into the post of the government's military adviser in Paris, General Robert Nivelle was appointed as his successor.

General Nivelle, a dapper, dynamic artilleryman aged sixty, had risen to rapid fame as an army commander at Verdun. 'We have the formula!' he had proclaimed on assuming command. His aggressive spirit and bounding self-confidence had so impressed Briand and his colleagues – now anxiously seeking a leader who would end the impasse on the Western Front – that he was promoted over the heads of France's most senior generals, Ferdinand Foch, Henri-Philippe Pétain, and Edouard de Curières de Castelnau. Nominated commander-in-chief of the armies of the north and north-east, Nivelle caused an immediate stir by brusquely re-shaping the Allied offensive plans for 1917. Now, as at Verdun, he was convinced he had the 'formula' for success, but on a much larger scale. Instead of Joffre's scheme for a combined Franco-British attack on a broad front to take place in February, he prescribed, as the principal operation, a massive French assault on the thirty-mile Soissons-Rheims sector, flanking the river Aisne, to be launched in April. This was to be supported by British and French attacks designed to contain the German reserves. By this plan, reversing Joffre's aim to let the British take some of the weight off the tired French troops, Nivelle envisaged a spectacular French break-through that might even lead quickly to victory in the west.

Nivelle's formula

Almost a million men were to take part in the main assault – a force commanded by General Micheler, consisting of three armies, the 5th (General Mazel), the 6th (General Mangin), and the 10th (General Duchêne). In support would be 5,000 guns. After a preliminary bombardment the 5th and 6th Armies were to attack and break the German line, and the 10th Army would then advance in the centre to exploit the rupture. The conception ran counter to all current military thinking. It relied on swift, sudden, surprise attack, delivered with overwhelming force and calculated to destroy the main enemy force – as Nivelle emphasized – within forty-eight hours. Considering the formidable power of the defensive as developed by 1917, it was a bold plan by any standards. But seen in relation to the enemy's Soissons-Rheims line it was foolhardy. The terrain was difficult, comprising a series of plateaux and ridges rising 200 feet above the Aisne; and the entire sector, held by the Germans for two years, was honeycombed with elaborate fortifications and bristled with guns and automatic weapons. Yet, dubious as the scheme was, Nivelle obtained approval

Musée de l'Armée, Paris

for it, in both Paris and London, through sheer persuasiveness and his personal conviction that it would succeed.

From the first, fate seemed to be against Nivelle. In January unprecedented cold descended on the Western Front, hindering offensive preparations, intensifying the troops' hardships as they huddled in their frozen trenches, and depressing still further their already low morale. Then Nivelle's whole plan was jeopardized by a major German withdrawal. In February the Germans began retiring from the ninety-mile Arras-Noyon-Soissons sector (west of the Soissons-Rheims line) to the heavily defended Hindenburg Line. They were thus eliminating a dangerous salient, shortening their front, and breaking contact with the French over a large part of Nivelle's projected field of operations (though a secondary one). Meanwhile they increased the number of their divisions in the Soissons-Rheims line from nine to forty. These moves radically changed the strategic picture; and doubts now arose about the wisdom of Nivelle's scheme. In Paris members of Alexandre Ribot's new government, especially the war minister, Paul Painlevé, received the plan with marked uneasiness. So did some of Nivelle's own generals and, on the British side, commander-in-chief Sir Douglas Haig and his colleagues. But Nivelle, fervently backed by his *chef de cabinet* (chief of staff), the fiery Colonel d'Alenson, refused to modify his main assault plan.

Building false hopes

But as the massive build-up proceeded behind the Aisne's left bank in the continuing wintry weather of March, one element essential to French success – surprise – had already been lost. It was impossible to hide the preparations from the enemy. And among the French troops, faced with yet another offensive that they had no reason to think would end any differently from previous ones, enthusiasm was at rock-bottom. But here Nivelle scored a psychological triumph. By a concentrated morale-boosting drive he wrought a spectacular change in the army's mood. In anticipation of his promised break-through, apathy disappeared and discipline and bearing noticeably improved. At last, the troops believed, there was a goal worth fighting for: this attack would achieve results. There was striking evidence of the new spirit in letters from the front, as examined by army postal control. In contrast to their earlier gloomy, bitter tone, these now expressed hope and confidence.

Security about the coming offensive was almost non-existent. In the Paris bars and bistros it was discussed openly – and with extravagant optimism. But no such optimism was felt by the French war cabinet, or by an increasing number of Nivelle's officers, senior and junior. Many of these wrote to Painlevé at the war ministry, reporting their misgivings. And so apprehensive were Ribot and his colleagues that, on the 6th April, an emergency top-level council was held at Compiègne (to whose historic Palace Nivelle had just transferred his headquarters) to decide whether the attack should go ahead as planned or not. President Poincaré, ministers, and army chiefs, including Nivelle, assembled in the President's special railway coach at Compiègne station. In a tense discussion almost all present voiced doubts about the operation. Nivelle forcibly argued that it would succeed: he even promised that if his armies had not broken through within forty-eight hours he would call off the assault. Finally, realizing he had no support, he angrily offered his resignation. Amid the general dismay, Poincaré hastened to reassure Nivelle that he had the government's confidence, and full responsibility for proceeding with the offensive.

Craonne, April 1917. A painting by François Flameng. It was here in atrocious weather conditions that Nivelle's ill-starred offensive predictably foundered

The bubble bursts

Nivelle had got his way; and in the sleet-filled dawn of Monday 16th April – a week after a preliminary British attack at Arras – the assault was launched. It turned out to be a disaster. Within a fortnight it had ground to a halt (though local operations continued), broken on the deadly Craonne plateau, the slopes of the Chemin des Dames and the heavily defended heights all along the front. Its failure was evident in the first hours: there were ghastly scenes as French troops struggled against uncut barbed wire and were mown down by withering automatic fire from undestroyed strong-points, and misdirected fire from the French 75s fell among panicking French Senegalese. Poor security, ineffective artillery preparation, and atrocious weather had – quite apart from the basic weakness of the whole conception – all combined to doom the operation from the start. Instead of the promised break-through, Nivelle's troops gained a few miles of ground at the price of almost 200,000 casualties. Their new-found euphoria collapsed like a pricked bubble. The reaction was catastrophic but in the circumstances predictable. In bitter frustration and resentment at their 'betrayal', the men of Nivelle's armies rebelled.

For some six weeks in the spring of 1917 much of the French army was in a state of mutiny. Elements of fifty-four divisions refused to obey orders, demonstrated, deserted, called for peace, brandished red flags, threatened or attempted to march on

Musée de la Guerre, Paris

French line-drawing 1917: 'The Grumble'. When Nivelle's offensive yielded only a few miles of ground at a cost of 200,000 casualties the grumble became a mutiny

Paris and overthrow the government. At the gravest moment, in early June, only two entirely dependable divisions stood between Soissons and the capital sixty-five miles away. The wonder is that the Germans did not take advantage of the situation to launch a counter-attack on the Soissons-Rheims front. Had they done so the course of the war must have been incalculably altered. But equally remarkable is the factor that prevented them from doing this – the maintenance of almost total secrecy which concealed news of the mutinies from the enemy and the French home front, to say nothing of the British high command and government. Such scant information as the Germans received through agents or escaped German prisoners they demonstrably discounted.

Dark episode

The official secrecy over the mutinies has never been relaxed. French military archives are virtually inaccessible and the official French war history *(Les Armées Françaises dans la Grande Guerre)* reveals little detail. Something of the story can be gleaned from contemporary diaries and memoirs; but the fullest and most reliable account comes from Marshal (then General) Philippe Pétain who, as commander-in-chief in succession to Nivelle, was called on to restore order in the demoralized armies. Pétain's record (which he entrusted to Major-General Sir Edward Spears, and which Spears published in his book, *Two Men Who Saved France,* Eyre and Spottiswoode, 1966) throws much light on this dark episode, even to the naming of individual units involved.

The main wave of mutinies lasted from 29th April to 10th June. They reached their height on 2nd June, with seventeen separate outbreaks. Of the 151 incidents recorded (some occurred after the 10th June) 110 were listed as 'grave', and altogether 110 units were affected, mostly in the camps and barracks of the Aisne region behind the Chemin des Dames sector. There were also disorders on over 100 troop trains and at 130 railway stations. The first outbreak took place east of Rheims, where an infantry regiment refused to parade on being ordered back to the line after only five days' rest. On the 4th May a number of infantrymen in the Chemin des Dames area suddenly deserted, and men of a colonial regiment circulated anti-war leaflets and noisily refused to fight. The tempo of revolt now quickened. On the 16th and 17th a Chasseur battalion and an infantry regiment rebelled. On the 19th another Chasseur unit demonstrated, and next day two entire infantry regiments refused to march. Violence had so far been absent; but on the 22nd and 27th, near Tardenois (in the Aisne region), there were two cases of officers being assaulted. On the 28th seven regiments and a Chasseur battalion from five different divisions mutinied. And as the month ended, disorder swept through eight divisions which had fought at Chemin des Dames or were about to move there.

Mutiny spreads

One mutiny was, in Pétain's words, 'conceived in cold blood'. This involved a crack infantry regiment which had fought gallantly at Verdun and since then been in almost constant action until February 1917. Told to stand by for the front, on 27th May it moved from rest quarters to billets near Soissons. On the 29th over 800 men paraded – in excellent order – to protest against making further useless and costly attacks. Rejecting the pleas and threats of their divisional and corps commanders, they recruited more followers with the aim of seizing trains, travelling to Paris and putting their demands before the Chamber of Deputies. The officers, who had stood by helplessly, now managed to control the situation. At dawn next day the mutineers were ordered into lorries and driven, still demonstrating, to a quiet area and finally to Verdun. The sequel: courts-martial in which four men were sentenced to death, and the ceremonial stripping of the regiment's colours.

Early June brought more and worse outbreaks. On the 1st one regiment near Tardenois – again with a fine fighting record – was ordered to the front after a brief rest period. Chanting the *Internationale,* the men marched in angry protest to the local town hall. The brigade commander, who tried to stop them, was attacked and his insignia ripped off. The divisional commander intervened but was shouted down. Then the ringleaders freed prisoners from a detention camp and the troops ran wild, overturning lorries and smashing windows. By next evening a 2,000-strong mob was on the march, waving red flags and calling for peace and revolution. On the 3rd the regiment was moved to another camp and the agitation quickly subsided.

Their brief duration was often a feature of these outbursts – even the violent ones. On the 2nd a Chasseur battalion rioted in the same area, opened fire on the commanding officer's quarters and burned the huts of a unit that tried to restrain them. But by nightfall the mutiny had fizzled out and there was no repetition. Meanwhile trouble was rife on leave trains and at railway stations in the rear. Pétain cites two typical cases. At Château-Thierry, on 7th June, police battled with rebellious leave-men from Paris who finally had to be controlled by armed troops. Next day, in a clash at Esternay station, soldiers mobbed and assaulted railway officials who tried to shepherd them back to their trains.

Russian influence

The disorder had now passed its peak, subsiding almost suddenly, like a worked-out fever. From the 10th to the 30th June incidents averaged one a day; and by September had ceased altogether. The whole uprising was essentially a spontaneous protest by desperate and overtried troops rather than a concerted rebellion. Many men saw themselves as strikers, not mutineers. Heinous though this collective indiscipline of an army was in military terms, it should be remembered in mitigation that some mutinying units – among the French army's best – had fought with heroism in previous battles. And the mutinies had their moments of pathos, as when captured rebel formations marched back to face court-martial and the direst penalties with their uniform spruce and their boots shined. French troops already had a list of long-standing grievances over vast and seemingly needless losses, derisory pay, exiguous leave, harsh discipline, wretched welfare conditions. Coming on top of these, the Aisne *débâcle* was the crowning blow. 'The fighting troops were at the end of their tether,' wrote Pétain. A GHQ officer, Lieutenant Henry Bordeaux, reporting on the state of one rear division, observed 'a sort of moral nihilism'. 'It is an army without faith,' he added.

Below: *French soldier with wooden crosses sets out to mark graves during the offensive.* ***Bottom:*** *General Nivelle. It was hoped that his aggressive spirit would end the impasse on the Western Front*

London Express

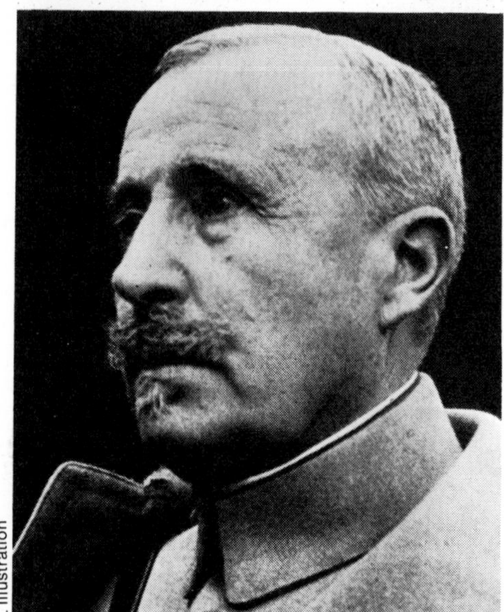

L'Illustration

Yet the mutinies were at least encouraged by two external factors. One was the Russian Revolution, which shook the world in mid-March (p. 692). In France it inspired a wild revolutionary spirit among the two Russian brigades – Russia's small expeditionary force – serving alongside the French. This mood infected many less steadfast *poilus* (French 'Tommies') in the nearby camps – the more so when the Russians, suffering crippling losses in the Aisne offensive, staged their own mutiny. Moved first to bases in the rear, they were then isolated in central France, where they were finally shelled into submission by other Russian troops. The frequent waving of red flags, chanting of the *Internationale,* and calls for revolution by the French mutineers testified to the influence the Russians had on them.

Defeatist campaign

The other factor was more sinister: subversive propaganda spread by civilian agitators in the rear. Active since the previous November (and even earlier) in conjunction with labour troubles in the war plants, it had intensified in the New Year. Military security produced strong evidence of a defeatist campaign being directed at the troops through anti-war tracts and newspaper articles, and illicit meetings and inflammatory speeches in the leave centres. Late in February Nivelle unavailingly requested the minister of the interior, Louis-Jean Malvy, to suppress the traffic and its chief instigators, whom he named. It was only Nivelle's forceful boosting of the troops' morale before the Aisne offensive that damped down the defeatist threat at this crucial moment. But when disorder swept the armies in May, the agitators renewed their assault. They haunted the Paris termini distributing anti-war leaflets to troops in transit; incited them to desert (there were desertion agencies near the stations, where men could obtain civilian clothes); used every means to push the disaffected *poilus* into revolt, including the clandestine dispatch to the army zone of extremist, left-wing news-sheets – like *Le Bonnet Rouge* and *La Tranchée Républicaine* – that defied the censor's ban.

But the anti-war campaign was also being waged against the home front. Playing on the war-weariness of French civilians – and these were almost as spiritless and disillusioned as the soldiers, especially after the hope-shattering fiasco of the Aisne offensive – the saboteurs were provoking labour unrest and infiltrating the war factories with their defeatist-pacifist propaganda. From mid-May – when militant *midinettes* (Parisian working-girls) paraded the Paris boulevards – onwards, demonstrations and strikes became frequent, until by the end of June there were over 170 stoppages in war plants in Paris and the provinces. Sympathizing troops joined in some marches. Occasionally violence erupted, incited by agitators. Beneath the capital's workaday surface there was unwonted tension. Never in the war had national morale been so uneasy. Through the June weeks Ribot's war cabinet met in an atmosphere of constant crisis. The corridors of the Chamber of Deputies buzzed with alarm and pessimism. And in two stormy secret sessions of the Chamber, left-wing members bitterly attacked the government and high command, questioned France's ability to continue fighting and canvassed the possibility of peace. 'The fever is spreading,' wrote President Poincaré. 'Must we await a new victory of the Marne to be healed?'

France's whole war-making capacity was undermined by a grave *malaise.* The superficial unity she had achieved in August 1914 – burying her acute political, social, and labour differences in face of the national emergency – was breaking down under the exhausting strain of nearly three years of war. But the particular defeatist-pacifist menace that now threatened her might have been minimized if, at the outset, the government had taken a different decision about national security.

Lukewarm reprisals

Instead of arresting, as intended, some 2,500 potential troublemakers – listed in the police dossier, *Carnet B,* which had been compiled for just this eventuality – the authorities had detained only the known spies, largely on the ground that action against left-wing labour leaders and other suspects might antagonize the workers and impede the call-up. This policy had paid ill. A mixed assortment of pacifists, internationalists, left-wing extremists, Marxists, and anarchists – each with their own pretexts for sabotaging France's war-effort—were left free to disseminate their propaganda. They ranged from Merrheim, the trade union chief, to sponsors of illicit newssheets like Faure, Duval, and Almereyda, and a host of other undesirables, many of them aliens. And behind them were traitors such as the notorious Bolo Pasha, Lenoir and the police chief Leymarie, working directly for Germany. Under the complacent tolerance of Louis-Jean Malvy, minister of the interior, these men operated with almost total immunity. Their task was made easier by continued government reluctance to suppress them for fear of provoking labour disturbances. The treason trials of 1918, bringing Malvy and many lesser fry to justice, were to expose the full extent of the internal danger assailing France.

Pétain to the rescue

How far was the defeatist propaganda responsible for the mutinies? The answer seems to be that while it was not the root cause, it was a strong contributory element. This at least was the verdict of General Pétain, who succeeded Nivelle as commander-in-chief as the troubles were boiling up in mid-May. Nivelle had been dismissed amid a resounding command crisis. Sixty-one-year-old General Philippe Pétain, famous as the saviour of Verdun, was undoubtedly the right man to replace him. Aloof and reserved, he hid beneath his cold exterior an unsuspected warmth: he understood the troops and they trusted him. His method of handling the mutinies was a mixture of sternness and humanity. First he moved ruthlessly to stamp out disorder and punish the ringleaders. He stiffened the faltering authority of his officers. He took vigorous steps to curb the prevalent drunkenness—a potent factor in inflaming the revolts. And he vehemently attacked the 'contamination' from the rear. Furious at the government's failure to suppress the defeatist groups, he bombarded ministers with demands for action, warning them that if the agitation continued he could not answer for the army's recovery. But Pétain knew that much was wrong within the army itself. Thus he set about a whole range of welfare reforms.

Perhaps most effective of all were Pétain's contacts with the troops themselves. Almost daily in these weeks his white-pennanted car left GHQ, Compiègne, on a comprehensive tour of formations. In about a month he covered over ninety divisions. A tall, magisterial figure with his flowing moustache and frosty blue eyes, he addressed officers and men, exhorting, encouraging, explaining his plans for limited operations designed to avoid heavy losses. He talked with individual soldiers, listening sympathetically to complaints and suggestions. The visits were of inestimable value. At last the men felt that someone was caring for their interests, that they counted as human beings. By late summer the French army was well on the way to restoration. The price it had paid for mutiny was not, in the circumstances, high. While many convicted mutineers were sentenced to long terms, of the 412 men condemned to death between May and October, only 55 were executed.

Now the home front remained to be purged. As with Pétain and her army, France providentially possessed the right man for the task. Late in 1917 the elderly Georges Clemenceau emerged from the political wilderness to become prime minister. None of France's previous wartime premiers—René Viviani, Aristide Briand, Alexandre Ribot, and latterly Paul Painlevé—had been able to command a sustained, united war-effort. But Clemenceau was a leader of different calibre. A merciless enemy of all anti-patriotic elements, he feared no party or faction. Having denounced Malvy in the Senate in July, as prime minister he proceeded to liquidate the defeatist cliques, silence the pessimists and doubters, and renew France's bruised and battered fighting spirit. His one aim was victory. 'Home policy? I wage war! Foreign policy? I wage war!' he bluntly stated. 'All the time I wage war!' As 1917 ended, France seemed to have narrowly surmounted her gravest crisis.

Below: *The commander-in-chief sympathizes with a soldier's complaint. Pétain handled the mutinies with sternness and humanity, but he knew much was wrong with the army.* ***Bottom:*** *Militant* midinettes *on the march. Even Parisian working girls were restive*

Bibliothèque Nationale, Paris

Western Front, June-November 1917/Brian Bond

Passchendaele

One of the hell-holes of the First World War, Passchendaele was to be known for all time as 'the battle of the mud'. Planned by Haig as part of a clean break-through to clear the Flanders coast, it turned into a battle of attrition of the worse kind, where men drowned in shell-holes filled with rain and mules and horses literally disappeared into craters of Flemish ooze

The name 'Passchendaele' applies, strictly speaking, to the last phase of the 3rd Ypres campaign of July-November 1917. But it is far more usual to find it used as a damning synonym for prolonged battles of attrition in the Flanders mud during the First World War. Half a century later, people are still arguing passionately about whether the offensive should ever have been undertaken in the first place, why it was allowed to go on for so long, and what effect it had on the course of the war as a whole.

On 15th November 1916 General Joseph Joffre, the French commander-in-chief, assembled a conference of the Entente military representatives at Chantilly to determine Anglo-French strategy for the coming year. He and Sir Douglas Haig, the British commander-in-chief, agreed that the attrition battles of the Somme and Verdun in 1916 had left the German army on the Western Front near to breaking point. Joffre feared that the French army could undertake only one more major offensive, but he hoped this would be decisive. He proposed a concerted offensive on all fronts in the spring of 1917 with the British cast for the leading role in the west. In December, however, General Joffre was replaced by the most junior of the French army commanders, General Robert Nivelle, who had persuaded both the French prime minister Aristide Briand and the British prime minister David Lloyd George that he could achieve a complete break-through in under forty-eight hours – a feat which had eluded both sides since September 1914. In Nivelle's plan the French were to strike the major blow on the Aisne sector, while Haig launched diversionary attacks near Arras and took over part of the French line south of the Somme.

Opposite page: 'Canadian gunners in Mud', a painting of Passchendaele by Bastier. 'Passchendaele' assumed the importance of historical myth – a myth of men smothered and helpless in mud, sacrificed for nothing. ***Below left:*** *Gough, the young 'thruster' put in charge of the opening offensive.* ***Below right:*** *Robertson, chief of the imperial general staff. 'It is now a question of wearing down and exhausting the enemy's resistance.'* ***Bottom:*** *Haig, Joffre, and Lloyd George. Haig and Joffre agreed in 1916 that the Germans on the Western Front were near breaking point. To this misjudgement Haig owed his confidence, and his disastrous persistence in Flanders*

Imperial War Museum

Nivelle fails

In February and March 1917 the effective German director of strategy, General Erich Ludendorff, forestalled Nivelle's planned offensive for the spring by withdrawing between fifteen and twenty-two miles on a front of about seventy miles to a strong defensive position known – after the nominal commander – as the Hindenburg Line. Nivelle was reluctant to adjust his aims and – oblivious of the need for surprise – made no secret of his highly ambitious plan. The French offensive began on April 16th in an atmosphere of political and military mistrust between the Allies and lasted until May 7th. It penetrated up to four miles on a sixteen mile front, but this limited success contrasted too sharply with Nivelle's personal promises. Frustrated by failure, the French armies began to disintegrate. Long-festering grievances came to a head in mutinies that broke out in May and June in nearly half the units in the French army. General Henri-Philippe Pétain, the hero of Verdun, who replaced Nivelle on 15th May, quickly restored order, but also dropped strong hints that the French would have to remain largely on the defensive for the rest of the year until they could be backed up by American divisions and more tanks and heavy artillery. Meanwhile, after prolonging the gruelling battle at Arras to shield the French during their offensive on the Aisne, the British had to take a fresh look at the projected Flanders offensive in the light of conditions very different from those that had applied when the Allies had planned their strategy earlier in the year.

On May 4th, the French and British civilian war leaders and their military advisers met at Paris to revise their strategy after Nivelle's failure and the Russian February Revolution. The military chiefs agreed unanimously that offensive operations must be continued on the Western Front. Allied attacks, they believed, had already exhausted a large proportion of Germany's reserves and she must be prevented from throwing her full weight against either Russia or Italy. But, in the words of the chief of the imperial general staff, Sir William Robertson: 'It is no longer a question of aiming at breaking through the enemy's front and aiming at distant objectives. It is now a question of wearing down and exhausting the enemy's resistance. . . . We are all of the opinion that our object can be obtained by relentlessly attacking with limited objectives, while making the fullest use of our artillery. By this means we hope to gain our ends and with the minimum loss possible.' Both the British and French governments gave their approval to these recommendations. Before the seriousness of the French army mutinies began to be revealed to him early in June, the British commander-in-chief, Sir Douglas Haig, was already contemplating a bold stroke in Flanders very different in spirit from the cautious policy outlined above. The British government had laid down in November 1916 that the clearing of German submarine bases from the Flanders coast was a strategic objective of the first importance.

Haig believed that such a break-through could be achieved from the Ypres salient, assisted by a supporting advance along the coast and an amphibious landing near Ostend. This aim rested on a very optimistic view of weakening German morale and reserves. It also assumed full French co-operation in supporting offensives, and this Pétain – who had just replaced Nivelle – promised on May 18th.

French support crumbles

But on 1st June the picture changed. General Debeney brought Haig a message from Pétain which mentioned euphemistically that 'the French army was in a bad state of discipline' and would not be able to fulfil the promise to attack in support of the opening of the British offensive at Ypres. A week later Pétain himself revealed in more detail the gravity of the situation but added that things were improving – as indeed they were. Thereafter, though hopes of really active French participation faded, Haig remained confident that the British army (assisted by six French divisions) could gain a major victory in Flanders. Lloyd George who, incidentally, knew even less about the breakdown of French discipline than Haig, grew increasingly sceptical about French co-operation. By 13th June he was harrying Robertson with a plan to remove twelve divisions from Haig's command 'to settle the war in Italy'. Robertson, a firm 'Westerner' who usually saw eye to eye with Haig, nevertheless cautioned him against 'large and costly attacks without full co-operation by the French'; and on 13th June he wrote: 'Don't argue that you can finish the war this year, or that the German is already beaten. Argue that your plan [the concentration of all available troops and material on the Western Front] is the best plan – as it is – that no other would be *safe* let alone decisive, and then leave them to reject your advice and mine. They dare not do that'.

Why in these unpropitious circumstances, with even the loyal Robertson urging caution, did Haig decide to launch the Ypres offensive? It had long been apparent to the British commander-in-chief that the French war effort was flagging, so that the collapse of morale after Nivelle's abortive offensive came as no surprise to him. Judging from his diary entries Haig's motives were mixed: he wished to shield and encourage the French, but was also eager to gain a great victory for the British army which had now, at last, become the predominant partner. What needs to be stressed, however, is that the senior French commanders had no enthusiasm for a major offensive in Flanders designed to clear the Channel coast. Pétain, in fact, was opposed to any major

National Gallery of Canada

'The whole surface of the ground consisted of nothing but a series of overlapping shell-craters, half full of yellow, slimy water. . . . The original roads had almost ceased to exist and it was necessary to lay down corduroy tracks . . . These and the "duck board" walks were daily machine-gunned by low-flying aeroplanes. Every yard of ground had been carefully "registered" by the enemy's guns, and a peculiarly effective form of gas shell, containing "mustard gas", had been evolved . . .' (Brigadier General Baker Carr.) ***Above:*** *'Void', painted by Wellard.* ***Below:*** *'Gassed. "In Arduis Fidelis"' by Gilbert Rogers*

Imperial War Museum

offensive on the Western Front in 1917, and on 19th May he told Sir Henry Wilson – who had been attached to Nivelle's headquarters – that Haig's projected advance towards Ostend was certain to fail. General Ferdinand Foch, chief of the French general staff, was, if possible, even less encouraging and sarcastically referred to the campaign as 'a duck's march'.

Jellicoe's bombshell

The crucial incident, as far as the indecisive British war cabinet committee was concerned, occurred at a meeting on 19th June; namely 'Jellicoe's bombshell'. Not a single member of the committee, consisting of David Lloyd George, Andrew Bonar Law, Sir Alfred Milner, Lord Curzon, and General J.C.Smuts, favoured a major offensive on the Western Front in 1917, but the first sea lord shattered their assumption that time was on their side by declaring that German submarines were taking such a toll of merchant shipping that it would be impossible for Great Britain to continue the war into 1918. The Royal Navy would be in grave difficulty unless the Belgian coast could be cleared by the Army. Although this alarmist prediction suited Haig's own military views, it is very doubtful if he took Jellicoe's warning as seriously as is often supposed. As recently as 7th May Haig had described Jellicoe in a letter to his wife as 'an old woman', and after the meeting on 19th June he noted: 'No one present shared Jellicoe's view, and all seemed satisfied that the food reserves in Great Britain are adequate'. Even more revealingly General Charteris, Haig's chief of intelligence, recorded in his diary on 28th June: 'No one believed this [Jellicoe's] rather amazing view, but it had sufficient weight to make the Cabinet agree to our attack going on.'

The fundamental reason for Haig's determination to launch the Flanders offensive was, it seems clear, neither the necessity to shield the French nor to clear the Channel coast of enemy submarine bases. It was rather his conviction that the Germans were so near to collapse that six months of fighting at the present intensity on the Western Front could end the war that year. His confidence was increased by the auspicious beginning of operations on 7th June, when General Sir Herbert Plumer's 2nd Army – assisted by the explosion of nineteen enormous mines under the German front line – was brilliantly successful in carrying out a limited advance to seize the Messines Ridge and so straighten out the salient south of Ypres.

The interval of fifty-three days which then occurred between this successful preliminary advance and the opening of the main offensive on 31st July was to prove fatal. Haig's plans were not finally approved until 25th July and then only after the desirability of reinforcing the Italian Front in preference to Flanders had been endlessly debated by the war cabinet. Haig certainly had grounds for the bitter remark that he would have liked such confidence and support as the prime minister had recently given to Nivelle. More important however, as Haig's most recent biographer, John Terraine, has pointed out, Haig had intended even in the preliminary planning stage that there would be a delay of some six weeks between Messines and the main attack. Moreover, as the same author has written, Haig made his 'gravest and most fatal error' in 1917 of entrusting the main role in the Flanders battle to the 5th Army commanded by General Sir Hubert Gough. It could be argued that Gough was the obvious choice for the bold strategy envisaged. He was, at forty-seven, the youngest army commander (whereas Plumer at sixty was by far the eldest); he was a cavalryman and a 'thruster' whereas Plumer – rather like Pétain – was noted for his cautious approach to planning and tactics, and his great concern to minimize casualties. Yet, quite apart from criticisms levelled at Gough and his staff for revising and mishandling Haig's plans, the transfer of command at such a time was bound to cause administrative complications and delays, particularly as the French contingent (General Anthoine's 1st Army) had to be fitted in on Gough's left between the 5th Army and Rawlinson's 4th Army on the coast.

Third Ypres opens

Like so many campaigns of the First World War, the actual operations of Third Ypres – which at last began on 31st July after a fortnight's preparatory bombardment and several postponements at the request of the army and corps commanders – soon ceased to bear much resemblance to the original plan. Essentially Haig had assumed that after eight days the 5th Army would have advanced fifteen miles and would have got control of the Ypres-Roulers-Thourout railway. Only when this was done would the 4th Army begin to attack along the coast, assisted by amphibious landings and, with Gough's support, would turn the German defences. Meanwhile the 2nd Army, after playing only a minor supporting role in the opening days, would advance to the north-east to secure the whole Passchendaele ridge.

This schedule proved to be far too optimistic. The campaign degenerated into a struggle for control of a plateau some sixty metres high. The operation fell into three distinct phases each containing three major actions. In the first phase Gough's 5th Army played the major role, and fought the battles of Pilckem Ridge (31st July), Gheluvelt Plateau (10th August) and Langemarck (16th August). The British had deliberately thrown away the chance of a surprise attack and they were hampered by driving rain. But despite this the first day, unlike the opening of the Somme battle on 1st July 1916, was far from being a disaster. The main assault was made by fourteen British and two French divisions supported by over 2,000 guns and howitzers on a very wide front of nearly twenty miles. The troops in the centre and to the left managed to reach the third and farthest target lines, and the only real check was suffered on the right of 5th Army's frontage. Here, from the Gheluvelt Plateau, specially trained German divisions made a fierce counter-attack, while the strength of the enemy's counter-bombardment during the battle as a whole showed how little real damage the British army's 'softening-up process' had done. Yet even if GHQ's initial assessment of British casualties at 15,000 was too low, it still compared very favourably with nearly 60,000 on the first day of the Somme.

Unfortunately atrocious weather had already begun to hamper further advance. On the first day the weather had completely prevented the British from using their superior air force for artillery reconnaissance. Far worse, as Colonel Fuller noted at Tank Corps headquarters: 'By July 31st from the Polygone de Zonnebeke through St Julien and northwards past Langemarck the Steenbeck had become a wide moat of liquid mud.' The British were unlucky in that the weather broke on the very first day. But meteorological reports for the previous eighty years could have showed GHQ that Flanders was notoriously wet in August. Rapidly, the swamp expanded, greatly assisted by the bombardment which had effectively destroyed the already precarious drainage system. Tank Corps headquarters daily sent a 'swamp map' to GHQ until instructed not to send any more. It seems unlikely that Haig ever saw these maps, and neither he nor Gough at this stage grasped the full significance of the appalling ground conditions. As early as 4th August General Charteris noted: 'All my fears about the weather have been realised. It has killed this attack. Every day's delay tells against us. We lose, hour by hour, the advantage of attack. . . . Even if the weather were to clear now, it will take days for the ground to harden, if indeed it ever can before the winter frost. . . . I went up to the front line this morning. Every brook is swollen and the ground is a quagmire. . . .'

Although there were some fine days in August, the weather and the terrain dictated the course of operations: Gough's second and third attempts to press forward

Pages 714-715: 'The Harvest of Battle' by C.R.W.Nevinson. Normally it took two men to carry a stretcher: by October it took sixteen. Mules and horses sank beneath the mud with their loads. A survivor wrote: '. . . we had often to drink shell-hole water, not knowing what would be at the bottom. Many a lot I helped to pull out of shell holes, where fellows were sinking and could not move'

(on 10th and 16th August) were thrown back by fierce counter-attacks. In his book *The Fifth Army,* Gough wrote that after 16th August he 'informed the Commander-in-Chief that tactical success was not possible, or would be too costly under such conditions, and advised that the attack should now be abandoned'. This advice was consistent with Lloyd George's prior condition that the attack should be discontinued if casualties were incommensurate with the amount of ground gained. In ignoring this condition and advice, Haig may still have been concerned to assist the French, but another explanation seems more likely. To call off the offensive at this

Imperial War Museum

German prisoner captured in the successful battle of the Messines Ridge, an auspicious opening for Haig's campaign

stage would have entailed surrender to Lloyd George's nagging pressure to divert large forces to Italy. Haig and Robertson were fully agreed that such a move might result in losing the war on the Western Front.

Plumer plans carefully

At the end of August Haig transferred the main role in further operations from Gough to Plumer. This signified a return to a more cautious approach based on concentrating overwhelming artillery cover for each short infantry advance. Contrary to the caricature presented by his extreme critics, Haig did not favour remorseless tactical attrition once the initial attempt at a breakthrough had lost its impetus. Indeed he criticized Gough for ordering too many small attacks on isolated farmhouses and strong points since they were seldom effective and were too costly in lives and ammunition. It was ironic that although September was to be generally dry, in sharp contrast to August, Plumer spent the first three weeks of it meticulously preparing the next short step forward. The main sector of the offensive was limited to 4,000 yards with four divisions packed into the front line. The depth of the advance was restricted to 1,500 yards when a halt would be made to hold off counter-attacks and to await the ponderous advance of the huge mass of artillery. Plumer, and his chief of staff General Sir Charles Harington, calculated that the Passchendaele-Staden ridge could be cleared by four such limited attacks.

Anzac advance

The first of the three battles of the second phase – that of the Menin Road Ridge on 20th September – resulted in a clear victory. This was essentially an artillery triumph. General Birdwood, who commanded the 1st Anzac Corps in the battle, recalled that it was quite the best artillery barrage the Australians had ever seen. 'Creeping forward exactly according to plan, the barrage won the ground, while the infantry followed behind and occupied all the important points with a minimum of resistance.' The attack began at 5.40 am, and by mid-day the final objectives had been reached. The Germans were unable to counter-attack before 3.15 pm and were successfully beaten off. In bright sunshine British aircraft were able to report nearly four hundred objectives to the artillery. Ludendorff recorded: 'Another terrible assault was made on our lines on September 20th. . . . The enemy's onslaught was successful, which proved the superiority of the attack over the defence. . . .'

Plumer's second offensive – at Polygon Wood on 26th September – closely resembled the Menin Road battle both in its careful preparation and encouraging results. It too was fought in good weather. Prince Rupprecht of Bavaria, commanding the German forces in Flanders, now began to worry about his defensive tactics and the scarcity of reserves. General Charteris, whose optimistic reports fed and fortified the convictions of his chief, noted that the situation at the end of September closely resembled that on the Somme the previous year. 'Now, as then, we had worn down the German resistance to very near breaking point; then as now the weather went against us. It is a race with time and a fight with the weather. One thing is certain, no other army but ours could fight on as we are fighting. D.H. is asking for the last ounce from it and getting a wonderful response.' Encouraged by Plumer's gains and Charteris's assessment of German exhaustion, Haig on 28th September revived the idea that the next advance should be immediately exploited. 'I am of the opinion that the enemy is tottering, and that a good vigorous blow might lead to decisive results. If we could destroy, or interrupt for 48 hours, the railway at Roulers there would probably be a débâcle, because the enemy would then have to rely on only one railway line for the supply of his troops between Ghent and the sea. . . .'

Plumer's third attack, the battle of Broodseinde on 4th October, followed the same pattern as the previous two: it was a heartening tactical victory but showed no signs of yielding those 'decisive results' which Haig had mentioned to his army commanders. It also marked the zenith of the artillery's contribution to the Third Ypres campaign before casualties, loss of guns, and the sheer impossibility of movement reduced its effectiveness. The Germans suffered particularly heavy casualties in this battle because the British barrage fell on five divisions just as they themselves were forming up to attack. This battle at last afforded the 2nd Army a foothold on the Passchendaele ridge. But a decision now had to be quickly made as to whether to halt the advance, particularly as the amphibious operations against Ostend had by now been abandoned and with them any real hope of reaching the Channel coast that year.

The day after Broodseinde Haig conferred with his army commanders. Charteris noted: 'We are far enough on now to stop for the winter, and there is much to be said for that. Unless we get fine weather for all this month, there is now no chance of clearing the coast. If we could be sure that the Germans would attack us here, it would be far better to stand fast. But they would probably be now only too glad to remain quiet here and try elsewhere. . . . Most of those at the conference, though willing to go on, would welcome a stop.'

Passchendaele – a 'porridge of mud'

The final phase of the campaign from 4th October to 6th November was fought for the almost obliterated village of Passchendaele, and as John Terraine rightly stresses, it 'bore throughout the characteristics which have generally been associated with the whole of it'. After the respite in September rain fell almost unceasingly through October and, with the continuing barrage, destroyed the few remaining signs of roads and tracks. By this time the whole area had reverted to a 'porridge of mud': mules and horses were known to have sunk beneath it with their loads; guns could find no solid ground to fire from; and it took sixteen bearers instead of two to carry each stretcher case the 4,000 yards to the field dressing stations. These conditions characterized the battle of Poelcapelle (9th October), the two battles ▷ **717**

'It was no longer life at all. It was mere unspeakable suffering'—Ludendorff

Above: *Desolation after a battle—a strafed wood.* ***Left:*** *The dying huddled with the dead, after the battle of the Messines Ridge.* ***Below left:*** *A soldier struggles forward. 'Even if the rainfall had been below instead of above the average, the destruction of the drains would have sufficed. . . . The drenching rains simply helped the broken drains to convert a reclaimed marsh into an impassable quagmire' (Lloyd George). By September, Gough wrote, 'Men of the strongest physique could hardly move forward at all and became easy victims to the enemy's snipers. Stumbling forward as best they could, their rifles also soon became so caked and clogged with mud as to be useless.'* ***Below right:*** *Reserves waiting in the trenches to advance on the village of Veldhoek*

Bibliothek für Zeitgeschichte, Stuttgart

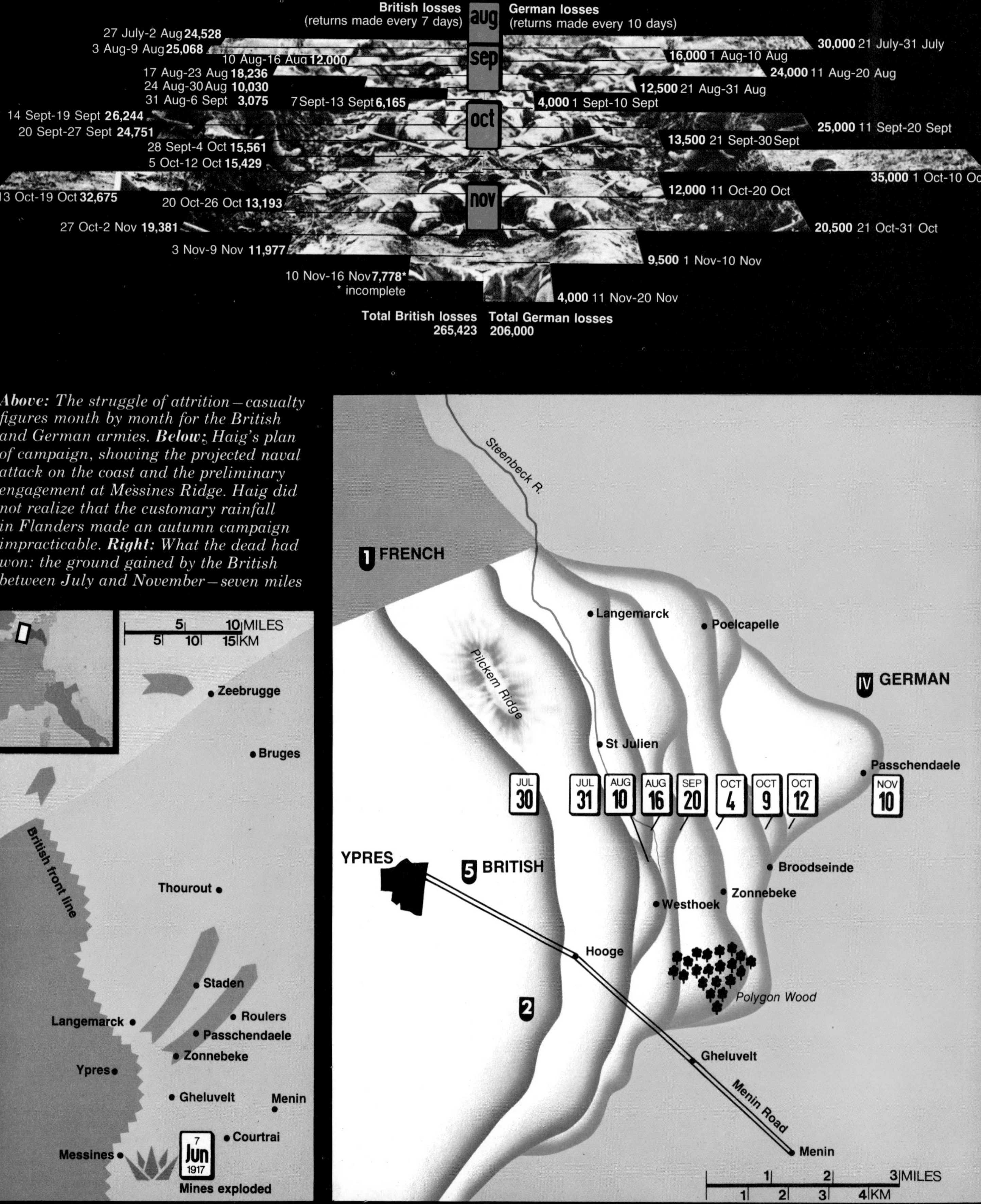

Above: The struggle of attrition – casualty figures month by month for the British and German armies. *Below:* Haig's plan of campaign, showing the projected naval attack on the coast and the preliminary engagement at Messines Ridge. Haig did not realize that the customary rainfall in Flanders made an autumn campaign impracticable. *Right:* What the dead had won: the ground gained by the British between July and November – seven miles for Passchendaele (12th and 26th October) and the eventual capture of the village by the Canadians on 6th November. For the troops it was, in Terraine's succinct phrase 'a month of dire misery and absolute frustration'. The Germans, as the defenders, at least had less problems of movement, but conditions were not much better for them. Ludendorff did not exaggerate when he wrote: 'It was no longer life at all. It was mere unspeakable suffering.'

Had Haig decided to halt after Broodseinde it is unlikely that even the abominable conditions which characterized much of the fighting in August would have given the campaign its terrible reputation. Even Haig's warmest defenders have been obliged to look beyond the borders of Flanders in order to justify the Passchendaele battles. Thus Charteris wrote on 7th November: 'We have now got to where, with good weather, we should have been in early September, and with two months in front of us to carry on the operation and clear the coast. Now, from the purely local point of view, it is rather a barren victory, and if the home people decide on a defensive next year, it will be almost lives and labour thrown away.' The campaign had pushed out the Ypres salient to a maximum depth of seven miles and ended without capturing the whole Passchendaele-Staden ridge—which had been the first objective. Had Jellicoe's prediction—that Great Britain's ability to continue the war depended on the army clearing the Belgian coast—been well-founded the war would have been lost. Nor did the German IV Army voluntarily retire, as after the Somme campaign, to give the attackers the illusion of victory. Instead the Allies were obliged to defend the Ypres salient through yet another winter while the Germans were reinforced from the Eastern Front. The campaign had failed to realize Haig's hope of inflicting a decisive defeat on the German army.

Defending the disaster

There is a deep-rooted belief that Haig continued to fight at Passchendaele 'to save the French'. Haig's diaries contain several references in the summer to the need to 'encourage the French to keep fighting', and to give the Germans no opportunity to exploit their weakness. That the Germans were not actually planning to attack the French is no reflection on Haig's sincerity, though it was a surprising misjudgement by so experienced a staff officer. For the later phases however, Haig's own diaries reveal that his assessment of French capabilities changed. Thus on 1st September he noted: 'The result of our pressure at Ypres is shown by the slackening of German efforts on the Chemin des Dames, and the comparatively weak resistance which they have made to the French attack at Verdun. The French army has consequently had the quiet time desired by General Pétain in which to recover from the Nivelle offensive.' Moreover after Pétain had proved reluctant to attack in support of the British in September, Haig wrote to Robertson (on 8th October): 'Though the French cannot be expected to admit it officially, we know that the state of their armies and of the reserve manpower behind the armies is such that neither the French government nor the military authorities will venture to call on their troops for any further great and sustained offensive effort, at any rate before it becomes evident that the enemy's strength has been definitely and finally broken. Though they are staunch in defence and will carry out useful local offensives against limited objectives, the French armies would not respond to a call for more than that, and the authorities are well aware of it.'

Ten years after the campaign Haig asserted that Pétain had repeatedly urged him to attack 'on account of the awful state of the French troops'. But Haig meticulously recorded meetings with all important soldiers and statesmen and there is no suggestion that in his four meetings with Pétain *during the campaign* such a request was even hinted at. Pétain denied the postwar rumour, while Haig never mentioned this crucial piece of intelligence to the British government. Possibly Haig was confusing French requests during the Arras operations in April and May with later events in Flanders.

Counting the cost

It does not seem likely that by prolonging the Flanders offensive Haig gave indirect help to the Allies on other fronts. The Passchendaele phase prevented neither the final collapse of the Russian armies during the autumn of 1917 nor the rout of the Italians at Caporetto towards the end of October. Indeed Ludendorff was actually able to detach several divisions from the Western Front during the British offensive. There is plentiful evidence, including the war memoirs of Prince Rupprecht and Ludendorff, to support Haig's conviction that the Flanders attrition was having a serious effect on the IV Army's morale. But the Allies also suffered severely. Indeed, since the Germans were for the most part defending, and for much of the campaign adopted economical tactics of defence in depth from dispersed strong points, it would not be surprising if the attackers' morale was the more severely strained of the two. Moreover, Haig and his staff (though not Robertson) seem to have underrated the tonic effect on morale of Germany's tremendous victory over Russia

Imperial War Museum

The wounded in a bleak and sodden world. ***Above:*** *Stretcher-bearers carry a wounded man through mud which reaches their knees.* ***Below:*** *Wounded German carried on a stretcher by South African Scots*

Imperial War Museum

Below: *Canadian and German 'walking wounded' on their way to a dressing station. They are resting on the devastated ground just outside Passchendaele*

Imperial War Museum

'Never again should British troops be subjected to such a battle of attrition for anything short of national survival'

Imperial War Museum

The town of Ypres, its houses ruined and deserted, pitted by huge water-filled shell craters

which became ever more certain as the Flanders fighting dragged on inconclusively. Victory in the east gave the Germans vastly increased numbers – forty divisions were transferred to the Western Front from Russia and Rumania between 1st November and the middle of March and more followed later. And it gave them renewed hope – for a decisive blow in the spring of 1918.

Confusion and controversy over casualty statistics spring not only from gaps in the reliable first-hand sources against which differing estimates can be checked, but also from the different methods used by the belligerents in reckoning their losses. The British total of 245,000 killed and wounded given by the *British Official History* has been widely accepted as approximately correct, though in August 1918 the general staff gave the war cabinet an estimated total of just over 265,000, and Sir Basil Liddell Hart puts it as high as 300,000. The higher of the two German estimates (in their *Official History*) for their IV Army between 1st July and mid-November – covering a much wider front than the Ypres sector – is 202,000 including missing. The *German Medical History,* however, puts the total as low as 175,000. Even if the *British Official History* is accurate for British losses, and the higher German total is on the low side, it would still be impossible to argue that in the gruesome computation of casualties the third battle of Ypres had resulted in a clear gain for the British and French.

Haig misjudges Germany

Although at the time the gradual effects of attrition on enemy numbers and morale was regarded by GHQ as a valid reason for prolonging the battle, Haig himself appears to have been motivated chiefly by his persistent belief that Germany was near to total collapse. The baneful influence of General Charteris in sustaining this illusion has been widely recognized. 'In retrospect,' as one careful historian has written, 'we can say with certainty that General Charteris's estimates of enemy strength and morale were almost criminally optimistic, and that Haig was badly misled in basing his plans upon them.' Well-founded though this criticism is, it would be unjust to make the chief of intelligence a scapegoat for the commander-in-chief. Haig's extremely powerful and self-confident personality could be a source of a weakness as well as of strength: once his mind was made up on a subject he was not easily swayed. In his book *At G.H.Q.,* Charteris, without seeking to denigrate his former commander, cites more than one instance of Haig going well beyond his (already over-optimistic) intelligence reports and predictions. Haig's published papers, while they show clearly the size of the problems he faced also show that he just did not have the critical intelligence needed to judge objectively the enemy's capacity to go on fighting.

Civil-military relations, and Allied co-operation were strikingly defective during the campaign. Lloyd George and the war cabinet committee had little faith in Haig or his plan yet they neither felt able to replace him nor gave him their full support. In turn the commander-in-chief had no confidence in the prime minister and consequently appears to have withheld information about the French mutinies lest it should provide justification for weakening the Western Front. The French war minister and later prime minister, Paul Painlevé, gave Lloyd George stronger assurance than was proper that the French armies could and would give full support to Haig's offensive, and the commander-in-chief Pétain, similarly made promises which he was reluctant to fulfil. Robertson was perhaps in the least enviable position, for in trying to restrain Lloyd George in his obsession with the Italian front and at the same time caution Haig against attempting too much in Flanders, he earned the former's hostility and the latter's suspicion. Haig did nothing to prevent his removal from office early in 1918.

Tragic waste

In legend, the battles of the Third Ypres campaign appear as nothing but ill-prepared bloodbaths. But they were more than this. Where conditions permitted they were carefully planned and skilfully executed. In particular Plumer's set-piece advances in June and September, and Pétain's operations on the Verdun sector, showed what could be achieved if objectives were strictly limited and superior artillery cover could be concentrated. Yet the Ypres salient was particularly unsuitable for an attempted break-through because of the precarious drainage system, the climate, and the terrain. Indeed, the faint possibility of a break-through to the Channel coast probably depended not only on the complete success of Gough's opening offensive, but also on the simultaneous launching of amphibious operations. Although the latter were carefully planned, the obstacles remained so formidable that it was probably a wise decision to cancel the operation when the land advance failed to make good progress.

The 1914-18 War still retains much of its terrible reputation because, on reflection, so much waste and suffering seem to have been exacted for no sufficient cause. Three years of indecisive slaughter, and the frailty of human judgements combined to produce the tragedy of the Third Ypres campaign in which the heroic endeavour of the troops appeared to yield only negligible results. No one, however, can be certain that the lives lost in Flanders were sacrificed in vain. Also, in changed circumstances – and because he had grown wiser from experience – Haig showed in 1918 that he could fight a more mobile and less costly campaign, culminating in the final victory which he had falsely anticipated in 1916 and 1917. 'Passchendaele', however, transcended the historical reality of an inconclusive campaign and became a potent historical myth. As such its influence reached far beyond 1918. Statesmen and soldiers are activated by such historical myths as well as by present realities. In 1939-45 Churchill and many of his generals had the memory of Passchendaele vividly before them: never again, they were resolved, should British troops be subjected to such a battle of attrition for anything short of national survival.

Above: *German prisoners and wounded Tommies – sculpture by F. Derwent-Wood.*
Left: *German bunker taken by the Welsh during the battle of Pilckem Ridge. The blast wall was added to the original bunker by the British in preparation for the long winter during which they had to defend their hard-won gains.*
Below: *Post-war photograph of the rows of gravestones in the cemetery of Polygon Wood, Zonnebeke*

Photo: Chris Barker

Italian Front, May 1915-October 1918/Ronald Seth

Caporetto

On 26th October 400,000 Italian soldiers decided to go home, 'with the determination that for them at least the war was ended'. For three years they had fought bravely but in the eleven battles of the Isonzo they had won a bare seven miles. And now a reinvigorated enemy was upon them

Women leaving their homes in Caporetto. The Austrians had broken through the Italian lines, and soldiers and civilians were crowding down the valleys in headlong flight from the front

General Conrad von Hötzendorff, while chief of the Austrian general staff, had an obsession. He was firmly convinced that an all-out offensive against Italy, if properly equipped and timed, would be so effective that she would have to withdraw from the war. He had held this view long before Italy had joined the Allies, and time and again he had urged the old Emperor Franz Josef to let him launch such an attack on Italy. He argued that if she were reduced to military impotence she would more easily resist the temptation to jettison her neutrality in favour of the Allies. Franz Josef, who still believed that the rules governing the conduct of nations must be observed, and that a nation's neutrality must be respected unless she wantonly provoked retaliation, had refused to pander to his chief of staff's whim.

After Italy's entry into the war, Conrad had become more convinced than ever that his plan for a really massive attack on Italy was the only way in which the Italian Front could be eliminated. There is little doubt that if he had had sufficient forces to mount such an offensive without withdrawing the Austro-Hungarian troops on the Eastern Front opposite the Russians, and if he had not had to bow always to the will of the German high command, he would have acted as he proposed. But he had not enough forces; the Germans would not agree to his withdrawing his units

on the Eastern Front; and every time he brought the matter up, they persistently maintained that they had no divisions to spare to give him the numbers which he needed.

But the longer the war went on, the more obsessed Conrad became. He flatly refused to believe that the unrestricted U-boat campaign which the Germans were planning, would end the war, as they were insisting it would; and he became such an embarrassment to his colleagues that a month after he last broached the subject—on 23rd January 1917—the new young Emperor Karl, who had succeeded when Franz Josef died in November 1916, replaced him with General Arz von Straussenburg, a much younger man.

Karl did not, however, retire Conrad; he sent him to command the western (Trentino) sector of the Austro-Italian Front.

The Italian Front

The Italian Front stretched from the Swiss-Italian borders in the west to the eastern frontier between Italy and Austria, via the line of the Alps. The eastern frontier more or less followed the course of the River Isonzo. The Isonzo enters the Adriatic Sea west of Trieste, and to get there from its source in the Julian Alps, winds along the eastern edge of the Friulian plain.

Except for about fifteen miles at its southern end, the Isonzo front was guarded by a spur of the main Alpine chain the Julian Alps, which, as it sweeps southwards, broadens out into plateaux and limestone hills. Running more or less parallel with this spur for half its length, the Isonzo cuts its way through a deep and rocky valley, which is separated from the Julian Alps by limestone uplands. Though the slope of these uplands is a fairly gentle gradient, they are deeply incised by a network of valleys and ridges.

South of the town of Tolmino, and rising out of the spur, is what the Italians call the Bainsizza plateau. The word plateau usually describes a flat mountain-top; but the Bainsizza is not flat; it is crossed and recrossed by ridges which rise steeply above the average level.

To the south of the Bainsizza is the Carso plateau, which has been described as 'a howling wilderness of stones, sharp as knives'. Between these two plateaux, but lying to the east, is the Selva di Ternova plateau, which is not so high as the other two, but is densely wooded.

Along the whole length of the front, the Austrians held the high ground and looked down on to the Friulian plain. This meant that unless the Italians attacked only on the fifteen mile coastal strip in the direction of Trieste, everywhere else they would be attacking uphill.

Eleven battles for seven miles

When the Italians came into the war in May 1915, General Cadorna had thirty-five divisions. This was a respectable force, as far as man-power went, but it was sadly short of artillery. In contrast, the Austro-Hungarians had ten divisions fewer; but were vastly superior in artillery.

Between the two sectors of the front where fighting was possible—at the western end north of Verona, and at the eastern end on the Isonzo—Cadorna deployed his forces. While the 1st and 4th Armies guarded the Venetian plain in the west, the 2nd and 3rd Armies took up positions on the Isonzo, together with the Carnia Group, comprising nineteen battalions of Alpine troops, at the very northern end of the front.

Cadorna decided to make his main effort on the Isonzo front. There were historical as well as military reasons for this. The Austrian provinces east of the Isonzo had once belonged to Italy, and since Italy had been transformed into a united kingdom in 1870, she had been asking for them to be restored to her; while on the military side, Italian pressure here would relieve Austrian pressure on Serbia.

Cadorna's general strategy on the Isonzo was to go forward in a series of what he called offensive bounds. He would attack the Austrians with limited objectives, pause to consolidate and re-form, and then leap forward again.

The plan, however, did not succeed. Between 23rd June 1915, when he launched his first offensive bound, and 29th August 1917, the Italian armies attacked the Austrians eleven times—the first to eleventh battles of the Isonzo—and by the end of the eleventh battle had gained a maximum of seven miles.

The reasons for so small a return for so great an effort were many and various. Discipline among the higher echelons of officers was faulty, chiefly because Cadorna ruthlessly eliminated any commander who failed to obtain the objectives set him. In the nineteen months before Caporetto he dismissed 217 generals, 255 colonels and 335 battalion commanders. The effect of this was to engender in his senior officers such a sense of insecurity that they became over-cautious, and in their caution failed their commander-in-chief. At the same time it created a lack of contact between the supreme command and the field commanders which had the result of imprisoning Cadorna in an ivory tower by which he was denied all knowledge of the reactions of both officers and men to the war in general and their own problems in particular.

Equally serious, however, was the lack of equipment, and especially of artillery and heavy ammunition. At the vital moment there were not enough guns to press home the advantage, or ammunition supplies would fail.

This situation was partly due to the fact that the switch-over of Italian industry from peace-time to war-time production was difficult and slow; and partly due, particularly as the war developed, to sabotage of the military war-effort by extreme socialists, who were opposed to the war.

In addition, in the pauses between battles, the morale of the soldiers deteriorated. Until after Caporetto, absolutely nothing was done for the leisure entertainment of the troops. The men passed all their time in their dug-outs or tents, with nothing to divert them, and this situation was a breeding-ground for the wildest rumours purporting to describe what was going on behind the fronts. The Italian, with his tremendous attachment to family, grew fearful about his family's welfare, now that he was not there to protect it. ▷722

Visitors to the Italian Front, 1917.
Below: *Cadorna (centre). His intolerance prevented him understanding his army.*
Bottom: *Emperors Karl (far left) and Wilhelm II, hoping to knock Italy out of the war*

Ullstein

On the other hand, things were not much better on the Austrian side. The lack of a decisive victory and the extremely hard conditions imposed by the terrain and the weather conditions, particularly in the winter campaigns, had their effect on the morale of the Austrian soldier.

This was especially true after the Italian success, limited though it was, on the Bainsizza sector in the eleventh Isonzo battle of August 1917. After the conclusion of that battle, the Austrian military commanders seriously doubted whether their armies would be able to withstand a twelfth Isonzo battle, should Cadorna decide that the Italian army should launch one.

It was at this point that they recalled the old military adage that the best form of defence is attack. It also came back to them that Conrad had had a plan; and someone remembered that when he had last outlined his plan in detail he had suggested that the Caporetto sector of the Isonzo front should receive the main weight of the Austrian attack, since the Italian line was weakest there. A little elementary intelligence showed that this sector was still the weak link in the Italian Isonzo chain.

However, German help would still be needed, so on 25th August General Waldstatten was despatched to German general headquarters with instructions to use all his efforts to obtain German approval of and the required assistance for an offensive on the Isonzo.

The German Kaiser informed the Austrian Emperor that he could count on the whole of Germany to crush Italy. His high command had other ideas, but after some argument it was agreed that if Lieutenant-General Krafft von Dellmensingen, an expert in mountain warfare, having inspected the Isonzo at Caporetto, thought such a plan could succeed, then serious German consideration would be given to the proposals.

Dellmensingen went to the Isonzo, looked

Troops and wagons move down a military road in Venezia towards the River Tagliamento. The order for retreat has been given and the Italian army is retiring to lick its wounds after Caporetto

and reported. 'In view of the prevailing difficulties,' he wrote, 'success lies only just on the border of possibility.' This was sufficient for the Germans and practical plans were put in hand.

As it happened, Cadorna had no plans for launching a twelfth battle on the Isonzo. On 20th September he surprised the British and French military missions by telling them that he had abandoned his plans to renew his offensive and was going on to the defensive on the Isonzo – at least for the time being. He gave as his reason the necessity to conserve his supplies of ammunition.

In response to Cadorna's earlier pleas for artillery, the British and French had just sent a few heavy batteries to Italy 'on loan for the sole purpose of offensive operations'. When they heard that Cadorna intended to abandon the offensive, Lloyd George and his French opposite number Painlevé, in a fit of pique, accused Cadorna of getting the guns under false pretences and ordered them to be withdrawn. All the French batteries were recalled and two out of the three British batteries.

In his memoirs Cadorna explains what caused his decision. The intelligence he had received showed that the Austrians were going to make a tremendous effort to put Italy out of the war, and that they were going to make this effort soon, and not in the spring of 1918, as German agents in Switzerland were putting it about.

By 6th October forty-three enemy divisions had been identified on the Isonzo front. After this date the intelligence gradually became more precise. There were many troops on the Bainsizza sector and German troops were assembling in the Sava valley, sixty miles east of Caporetto.

On 9th October, the intelligence bulletin said that 'the last week of October might be accepted as the most probable date for the beginning of the enemy offensive'.

On 14th October General Capello, commander-in-chief of the Italian 2nd

Ullstein

Army, on whose sector Caporetto was situated, was ordered to Padua by his doctors for a change of air and rest. This was a blow of the first order, for Capello had the total confidence of his troops, and his absence at a time when they were receiving the full force of the enemy attack could easily place the whole Isonzo front in jeopardy.

A week later Cadorna informed the British director of military operations: 'The attack is coming, but I am confident of being able to meet it. Owing to the very difficult country on the Tolmino sector, I am of opinion that an attack there can be checked without difficulty and I am consequently holding that sector lightly.' (Caporetto is north of Tolmino.)

In making this fatal decision, Cadorna had made serious errors of appreciation. He had accepted at face value the information given by a Czech deserter that the main attack would be made at Tolmino, and allowed this to colour his appreciation of more detailed information given by Austrian deserters. He had also allowed his knowledge of the Tolmino terrain to underestimate the probable weight of the enemy attack. Most serious of all, because of his confidence, he had failed to send out scouts to the area north of Tolmino – that is, in the neighbourhood of Caporetto – and so did not know that four Austro-German divisions were assembled, one behind the other, in the valley running northward of Plezzo.

The Austrians break through

Cadorna and Capello were two very different characters, and had had several differences of opinion throughout the war. Now they differed again about the plans for countering the enemy attack. Cadorna issued instructions for a defensive attitude with local counter-attacks; Capello favoured an offensive-defensive action, with a large-scale counter-attack, northwest from the Bainsizza.

Disregarding his supreme commander's instructions, Capello deployed his troops in readiness to carry out his own plan, with his three second-line corps *south* of Caporetto.

Though still in a high fever, Capello insisted on returning to his headquarters on the evening of 23rd October, but he grew worse. After dictating orders, he had to retire again. He had been gone only an hour or two, when, at 2 am on 24th October, the artillery of the Austro-German XIV Army on the Tolmino-Plezzo sector, opened fire with gas-shells on the Italian batteries and forward trenches. After two hours there was a two-hour pause. The Italian artillery replied, but after an initial fierceness it weakened and did little harm to the opposing infantry.

A member of the Bersaglieri, crack troops of the Italian army, with his portable bicycle folded on his shoulder. The Italian soldiers had fought with staunch courage, but Cadorna did not believe in pandering to the comfort of his troops, and, since no information was given them about the course or purpose of the war, the wildest rumours flourished. Morale had already begun to crack before Caporetto

Below: Carving made by an Italian prisoner-of-war depicting the punishments inflicted by the Austrians on Italian-speaking subjects who had deserted to fight against them. The most famous of these was Cesare Battisti (p. 499)

Soon after the bombardment began, light rain started to fall. Within a short time it changed to a heavy downpour, while on the heights there were snow-storms, and in the bottoms of the valleys thick mist. By dawn visibility everywhere was low.

At 6.30 am the bombardment was resumed with high explosive. From Plezzo down the whole length of the front to the sea, guns of every calibre opened up. Never before on the Isonzo had there been such an intense bombardment, and in a very short time the Italian defences had been reduced to rubble, while men's lungs were seized with a cruel agony which paralyzed their thoughts and actions as their gas-masks let through copious draughts of German poison gas.

And—calamity of calamities at such a time—all communications between commands and advance lines were destroyed.

At 8 am the firing of two giant mines gave the German XIV Army the signal to advance from Plezzo and Tolmino. To his surprise, General Krauss, at Plezzo, met no resistance from the Italians. By 9.30 am the front of the Italian 4th Corps had been pierced.

Meantime, General Stein, just north of Tolmino, had advanced with his divisions. He had been opposite the weakest spot in the Italian front.

In his pre-battle orders, Cadorna had instructed General Badoglio, who was to become famous in the Second World War as Marshal Badoglio, and who was commander of the 18th Corps covering the line from Plezzo to Tolmino, to withdraw his troops to the west bank of the Isonzo. For some reason never subsequently clarified, Badoglio deferred carrying out this order until shortly before the battle began, with the result that only a small force met Stein, and the remainder of the corps was cut off on the east bank.

Stein obliterated this small Italian force, and by doing so opened up a way across the river. By 4 pm he had occupied the village of Caporetto.

Thus, by mid-afternoon a fifteen-mile gap had been punched in the Italian line; and now, on the very first day, in the very sector where Cadorna had not expected an attack, the rot began.

The bogeyman comes

Up to this time the Italians had encountered only Austrians of whom they had no great opinion. In contrast, the reputation of the Germans as fighters was immense. Italian commanders had been wont to use it as a bogeyman to frighten recalcitrant troops into obedience.

Now the Germans were actually here!

When the truth dawned on the Italian troops, their morale, such as it was, snapped completely. In this they were matched by their junior commanders who did not know how to deal with tactics they had not been taught to counter.

The four divisions of General Cavaciocchi's 4th Corps melted away in flight, carrying with them Badoglio's 19th Division. Most of these troops fell prisoner in the next few days.

By nightfall, Krauss was making for Monte Stol, northwest of Caporetto and Stein had the greater part of his divisions on the west bank of the Isonzo. Only south of Tolmino had the Italian forces under General Caviglia held; and as soon as Cadorna heard of the disaster in the north, he ordered them to fall back, too. At the same time he ordered the Duke of Aosta, commanding the 3rd Army, and General Capello to put the defences of the line of the Tagliamento river into a state of readiness with civilian labour, and 'with the utmost speed and maximum secrecy'. He explained that in order to save the 3rd Army and the remainder of the 2nd Army that had held firm, they might have to fall back on that line.

The next morning broke bright and clear, and the sun came out. The situation could be seen a little more clearly now, and Capello, who had returned to take command when the battle began, was forced to inform Cadorna that all positions on 2nd Army's front east of the Isonzo had been lost.

Cadorna ordered the Duke of Aosta to send back the less mobile of the 3rd Army's heavy and medium artillery to the River Piave, in the rear of the Tagliamento line. With the remainder he was to withdraw west of the Carso valley and prepare a line there to cover a general retreat.

At noon, Capello arrived at Cadorna's headquarters at Udine to discuss the situation. He was desperately ill and on the point of collapse. He told Cadorna that in his opinion all contact with the enemy should be broken off and a withdrawal made to the Tagliamento without delay. For once the two men agreed. But Cadorna did not issue the orders for the retreat for another twenty-four hours.

There have been many descriptions given of the flight of the Italian 6th and 27th Corps from Caporetto. Even put baldly and briefly it presents an almost unbelievable situation.

In his *History of the Great War*, C.R.M.F. Cruttwell has written: '400,000 soldiers were going home, with the determination that for them at least the war was ended. The reports of their behaviour are most curious. Having broken contact with the enemy, they were in no hurry; they stopped to eat and drink and pillage. One observer notes their air of "tranquil indifference", another that while they had all thrown away their arms, they kept their ▷ **728**

Museo Storico dei Granatieri, Rome

Chaotic retreat – amazing revival

Commando 1ª Divisione Carabinieri Pastrengo, Milan

Left: *A trench on the Carso, painted by G.A.Sartorio. The Carso plateau, 'a howling wilderness of stones, sharp as knives', had eventually been taken by the Italians for a terrifying loss of lives and of morale.* ***Above:*** *Two flags of Italian commando troops.* ***Below:*** *King Victor Emmanuel III meets the Allies at Peschiera in November 1917. It was agreed that the Italian army should stay behind the River Piave to build up its organization and morale. It did so, and a year later the Italians took their revenge for the defeat of Caporetto*

Radio Times Hulton

Illustrazione Italiana

Above: **Flotsam from an army**—the dead bodies of horses washed up in the river bed of the Tagliamento after the collapse of the Italian army and its hasty retreat to the bank of the river

Above: *Exhausted soldiers rest after their hasty week-long march to the Tagliamento. Fortunately the Austro-German army was confused and did not fully exploit the chaotic Italian retreat*

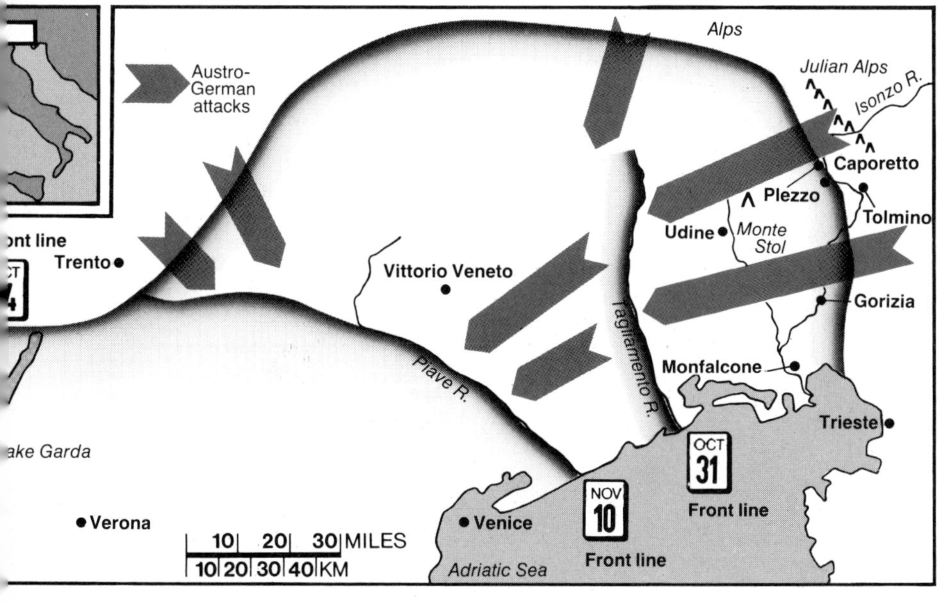

Nationalbibliothek, Vienna

Above: *The Austro-German attack. The forces which routed the Italians at Caporetto pursued them to the Tagliamento and then to the Piave. By 3rd November forces had come south from the Alps, and on 9th November Conrad ordered forces to attack from Trento.* ***Below:*** *Italian corpse on the bank of the Piave*

Above: *Germans and Austrians tending their wounded.* ***Below:*** *The skeleton of an Italian sniper still at his post, with his helmet, his rifle, and unused cartridges. But the courage of the Italians had been sorely tried before Caporetto, and many surrendered their arms after making only a feeble resistance to the enemy*

Museo Storico Italiano della Guerra, Rovereto

Museo Bersagliere, Rome

gas-masks; nearly as many civilians were fleeing, more wildly, from the face of the enemy, blocking what remained of the road space with their carts and household goods.'

Soldiers and civilians crowded down the valleys, using the only roads by which supplies and reinforcements could have reached them. They held up troops moving over to new lines. They had no thought for honour or country, they who had fought with amazing courage in the eleven battles of the Isonzo.

Yet there was something peculiarly Italian in this mass defection. General Raffaele Cadorna has told the author that his father related that there was no attempt to threaten officers, only a refusal to obey; and that when he himself rode among them, no one lifted a finger against him; on the contrary, as soon as they recognized him they stiffened and saluted.

Vengeance

The retreat, when ordered, took the 3rd Army commanders by surprise. It took the Austrian commander opposite equally by surprise, and he made no attempt to pursue. This was just as well, for there was a certain amount of initial disorder which could have been made worse had the rearguard had to fight.

The retreat of the 2nd Army, however, was extremely chaotic. This was scarcely to be wondered at, in view of the previous headlong flight of half that Army, and the fact that the German commander Berrer did pursue. He succeeded in splitting the 2nd Army irreparably in two.

On the other hand, all was not well with the Austro-Germans. The speed of their advance took them unprepared, and there were no orders which allowed for the full exploitation of the situation. As a result, orders were issued, then changed, and this gave rise to friction which bad staff work did not help to eradicate. In addition, army commanders and divisional commanders began to issue their own orders, and soon, they, too, were in a hopeless confusion.

This helped Cadorna considerably, and by 31st October, he had all his forces, except for the quarter million lost as prisoners, across the Tagliamento, and the Germans were still so mixed up that he was able to pause and take breath.

With the broad torrent of the river between them and the enemy, the Italian soldiers also took breath – for the first time for a week – and looked about them. What they saw seems to have brought them up short, and soon it was apparent to all observers that a new spirit was beginning to move them. Within a few days an amazing transformation was visible; military order and discipline were being quickly restored.

But the Germans also recovered, and when they made a large hole in the Tagliamento line, Cadorna decided to withdraw to the line of the River Piave. This further retreat was not without difficulties, but on 9th November all Italian armies stood in good order behind the Piave.

On that same day Cadorna was dismissed and was succeeded by General Diaz.

Throughout the remainder of the winter and the spring of the next year, Diaz regrouped, reinforced, resupplied, and retrained his armies. The lessons of Caporetto were studied and heeded. New tactics were devised, designed to remove the weaknesses of the old which had been responsible for the heavy losses of men and had made Caporetto inevitable.

In June the Germans reopened their offensive. Eight days later it ended in complete victory for the Italians.

In October, Diaz went over to the offensive, and exactly a year to the day from Caporetto, he launched the battle of Vittorio Veneto and inflicted on the Austrians a far worse disgrace than they had inflicted on the Italians on the Isonzo.

Caporetto had been avenged.

Retreat from Caporetto – the weary march of humiliated men. Drawing by Max Gualo

Chapter 27

Introduction by J.M.Roberts

Everyone knows that the effects of the Great War were revolutionary. We have been living ever since in the new world of politics and economics which it left behind or made possible. In coming Chapters many of the transformations it detonated will be discussed. Usually, the crumbling of the old empires or the discrediting of old principles are the changes that come most easily to our minds in such a connexion. This Chapter, on the other hand, will deal with other senses in which the war was revolutionary.

In the first place come transformations in the nature of warfare itself. Even after the outbreak it was becoming clear that the war might bring sweeping changes in military and naval technique. We have asked our adviser on military history, Captain Sir Basil Liddell Hart, teacher of a whole generation of military writers, to discuss this crucial topic. **The New Warfare** is an important study in this History; it sums up the content of many of our accounts of individual campaigns. It explains the appearance of a mode of warfare whose outlines can be traced back to the American Civil War, but for which most Europeans were still utterly unprepared in 1914. We sometimes forget that for more than forty years the British and French armies had only fought colonial wars and only a tiny contingent of the German army had ever fired a shot in anger – and that was in China.

One characteristic of the new warfare was its unprecedented mobilization of scientific and technical skills. The repercussions of this were to go on long after 1918: technical and scientific progress were enormously accelerated by the war. In **The Way War Altered Peace**, Ronald W.Clark describes the far-reaching scope of many innovations whose significance was at first purely military or naval. Ironically, science benefited from the conduct of a war whose conduct was often the negation of anything that could be called scientific.

It was one of the few unqualified benefits of the war that medical services, too, improved out of recognition. In most earlier wars, the chance of a soldier dying from disease was far greater than his chance of being killed by his enemy. If he were wounded, the odds against his recovery were heavy. Armies carried disease about with them like extra baggage and spread it wherever they marched. Yet the filth, lice, mud, and damp of the Western Front did nothing like the execution wrought by far milder conditions in earlier wars. Christopher Spry surveys the role of **Medicine at War** and explains some of the ways in which this beneficial change came about. Here, too, necessity forced the rate of progress.

Staatsbibliothek, Berlin

French workers assemble bomb casings, 1916. Aircraft added a new aspect to war

Imperial War Museum

A dazed and wounded German is guided to a stretcher by a comrade, Amiens 1918

Bibliothek für Zeitgeschichte, Stuttgart

German pioneer ascertaining the height of enemy aircraft for anti-aircraft battery

War seen from hospital

'When one shoots at a wooden figure, it makes a hole,' reflected one of the women who had volunteered for medical service with the Voluntary Aid Detachments (VADs). 'When one shoots at a man it makes a hole, and the doctor must make seven others.' As fast as scientists laboured in the laboratories to produce more effective ways of killing men, the doctors and nurses worked to repair the damage. Some of them left records of war seen from the hospitals.

'In Braila there were 11,000 wounded and 7 doctors. . . The people here had been working 36 hours without stopping. . . Of the seven doctors – only one was a surgeon. . . It was just a case of going on dressing blindly and the wounded coming in and in and in. . .

'They have twenty hospitals in running order – and there were still men lying about in empty houses with their uniforms on – and the horrible smell of sepsis from their wounds. We opened a temporary dressing station that afternoon. No more doctors have arrived but they have given me an operating theatre'

Report of Dr Elsie Inglis, leader of a Scottish Woman's Hospital Unit in Rumania, by permission of the Fawcett Library. Copied from MS.

'The leg I was holding came off with a jerk and I sat down still clasping the foot. I stuffed the leg into the dressing pail beside the other arms and legs. The marquee grew hotter and hotter and the sweat ran off the surgeons' faces'

VAD Lesley Smith, helping in the operating theatre of a field hospital in France

'The hospital is very heavy now – as heavy as when I came; the fighting is continuing very long this year, and the convoys keep coming down, two or three a night. . . . Sometimes in the middle of the night we have to turn people out of bed and make them sleep on the floor to make room for more seriously ill ones that have come down from the line. We have heaps of gassed cases present who came in a day or two ago; there are 10 in this ward alone . . . the poor things burnt and blistered all over with great mustard-coloured suppurating blisters, with blind eyes – sometimes temporally (sic), sometimes permanently – all sticky and stuck together, and always fighting for breath, with voices a mere whisper, saying that their throats are closing and they know they will choke. The only thing one can say is that such severe cases don't last long; either they die soon or else improve – usually the former; they certainly never reach England in the state we have them here. . .'

VAD Vera Brittain, working in a hospital in France, after the battle of Cambrai

Warfare, 1914-18/Captain Sir Basil Liddell Hart

The New Warfare

'The military mind always imagines that the next war will be on the same lines as the last. That has never been the case and never will be,' wrote Foch in 1926. He was speaking from his own experience of shock during the First World War. Almost every theory that the military leaders had held at the outbreak of war of how it would be fought and could be won were disproved

The Western Front, 1917. A British soldier contemplates a German artillery bombardment of the British reserve trenches. This was the grim aspect of the new warfare: a shattered landscape, battered trenches—the graveyard, in fact, of the war of movement

In 1914 the armies marched to the battlefield on foot as they had done for centuries. The only difference was that they were taken part of the way by rail, and that their reserves could be switched from one flank to another by that same mechanical means. The main effect of this change was that such large numbers were poured on to the roads beyond railheads as to impede their own manoeuvre, while a supplementary effect, due to more rapid switching, was that an enemy's manoeuvre could be more easily blocked.

The war gave a tremendous impetus to the growth of mechanical transport, both road and roadless. Motor vehicles multiplied by scores of thousands, but this acceleration of movement only improved the capacity of supply; it did not markedly affect strategy since it could not alter the immobility of fighting troops who had already been driven, by the machine-gun, to

bury themselves in trenches. The possibility of moving at 30 mph was of little avail to soldiers who had been reduced by a tactical obstacle to 0 mph.

To resurrect movement in face of fire, the fire-support of the attackers was developed by multiplication – of guns – and by addition – of new weapons, the light machine-gun, the mortar, the grenade, together with gas, smoke, and flame-projectors. Some of them contributed to defence as much as to the attack, and none of them succeeded so far as to revive a war of movement.

Eventually the tracked and armour-clad vehicle, known as the tank, was introduced; this went farther than any other means to overcome the machine-gun obstacle, and by German admission proved the most important military factor in the final phase of the war. But the end came, after a gradual withdrawal, before the tank had been developed far enough to produce more than a local acceleration of movement. In the army that retired, and in the armies that followed it up, a mass of motor vehicles were mingled with a greater mass of horse vehicles.

It is a question whether movement as a whole could have been much quicker even if the machine-gun brake had been lifted. Retardation may have averted confusion. On the other fronts – Bulgarian, Turkish, and Austrian – the brake was less effective, with the consequence that the new air weapon found dense targets. And under its blows the retreating armies dissolved in chaos.

The navies of 1914 showed a greater advance on the past than the armies. They were also less tested. Battleships and cruisers were the natural heirs of the old wooden ships of the line and frigates, but through steam and armour they had been so transformed that their properties were difficult to gauge owing to the paucity of naval actions since the mechanized age of naval warfare had dawned. With the invention of the torpedo they had been confronted with a new menace, at first projected by the torpedo-boat, to which the

Imperial War Museum

destroyer, developed as a counter, became a successor.

If the new weapon had a certain likeness to the old fireship, it had much wider possibilities. These were increased by the advent of the submarine, while the movement of fleets suffered a fresh restriction by the development of mines. It was more difficult to estimate the change of conditions because of the controversy that raged round the torpedo. The conflict of enthusiasm and prejudice produced an atmosphere in which scientific study was suffocated – if it was ever possible among a class who were men of action and had never been educated in a scientific way of thought. The natural result was a compromise by which the maintenance of the existing order was mixed with concessions to the new idea. Destroyers were added to the battlefleet, but were tied to its protection rather than applied to an offensive role.

As for submarines, at the outbreak of war in 1914 Germany had only twenty-eight, and by 1917 little more than a hundred, out of which only about a third were operating at any particular time. Yet, even apart from their deadly action against commerce, the effect of their latent menace to battleships was such that by the summer of 1916 the British naval authorities were agreed that the Grand Fleet must be kept out of their reach. To quote the British Official Naval History they had 'so restricted the movements of a fleet of super-Dreadnoughts – each one of which could steam several thousands of miles without refuelling – that the waters opposite one-third of the eastern coastline of Great Britain, and about half of the North Sea, were outside its zone of effective action'.

Farce on horseback

The course of land warfare proved so different from the expectation of the military leaders that a fuller discussion of their pre-war views is necessary.

If there was one feature of the half-century preceding 1914 that would seem impossible to misjudge, it was the increasing advantage of the defensive, due to the growing power of infantry firearms – first the magazine rifle and then the machine-gun. An obvious corollary was the limitation placed on cavalry action. The American Civil War, as it advanced, made these new factors plain. It was not to be expected that European generals would profit by this second-hand experience, since the great Field-Marshal von Moltke dismissed it as no more than 'two armed mobs chasing each other round the country, from which nothing could be learned'. But the Franco-German War, despite its brevity, demonstrated at Gravelotte and elsewhere the same change of conditions. Nevertheless in 1883 we find the German protagonist of the 'Nation in Arms', the future Field-Marshal von der Goltz, declaring that 'the idea of the greater strength of the defensive is a mere delusion'. The Boer War might surely have suggested a doubt of this dictum, yet in 1903 the future Marshal Foch, already acting as the official mould of French military ideas, committed himself to the confident prediction that 'any improvement in firearms is bound to strengthen the offensive'.

He at least had not been a participant in any real test, but the future Field-Marshal Haig, called upon by the royal commission, when fresh from the South African battlefields, to give account of the light that he had gained, was confident that 'cavalry will have a larger sphere of action in future wars'. His forecast might have been more intelligible if he had been thinking merely of mounted troops, which had been necessary to cope with Boer mobility. But he showed that his mind was fixed on the cavalry charge by the stress he laid on mounted *action,* and he confirmed this subsequently by the severe measures he took to curb the tendency to turn cavalry into mounted riflemen.

His view was shared by the military authorities of all the Continental powers, with the result that in 1914 Germany, France, Russia, and Austria-Hungary each deployed over a hundred thousand cavalry. With what result? The French relied for their information mainly on their cavalry, but, as has been officially related: 'This immense mass of cavalry discovered nothing of the enemy's advance . . . and the French Armies were everywhere surprised.' The most important effect that the German cavalry achieved was that, by their reckless destruction of telegraph lines everywhere, they did much to paralyse their own command during the advance into France. The Austrians' advance was 'preceded by a great mass of cavalry'; their official history records that most of them never came within sight of the enemy, owing to their horses being disabled through sore backs. They at least were luckier than those who did make contact. For since the Russian cavalry stayed behind, the remaining Austrian cavalry bumped into the Russian infantry; poor shots as these were they did not fail to hit such a target, and the Austrian cavalry came back with nothing to compensate their heavy casualties.

This cavalry prelude was overshadowed by the drama that followed, when the main armies clashed, but it was perhaps the hugest farce that has ever been enacted in a theatre of war.

The generals were no more fortunate in gauging the possibilities of newer instruments. Not many years before 1914, when the attention of a member of the British Army Council was drawn to a note on the development of aircraft, he endorsed it thus: 'We are no nearer the solution of the conquest of the air than we were in the days of Montgolfier's Fire Balloon.' A more comprehensive disbelief in change was expressed by General Sukhomlinov, the Russian war minister who warned the instructors at the staff college that he could 'not hear the words "modern war" without a feeling of annoyance. As war was, so it remains; all these things are vicious innovations'. Sukhomlinov was disappointed in his ambition to command the Russian armies in the war, but he could at least content himself with having helped to ensure that they marched blind and little better than armless to the slaughter.

Military myopia

Different in form, but fundamentally similar in nature, was the assurance of the French commander-in-chief, Joffre, when on 6th August, 1914, he serenely declared: 'It may be concluded that the Germans are executing a plan of which we have knowledge.' Hence it was with ample confidence that he launched his forces eastward into Lorraine, and into a trap, while the Germans swept through Belgium.

The German command thus scored an initial surprise, but they threw away the advantage through an over-confidence that verged on intoxication. They told the Austrians that if the French army took the offensive they counted on attaining a decision 'on the 21st day of mobilization', i.e. 23rd August. If the French army stayed on the defensive behind its frontier defence, they might take a week longer to achieve a decisive victory. They would then transfer their forces to the Russian front where they 'should arrive on the 41st day of mobilization'. The decision had not come when 22nd August came, although that day the French, advancing blindly, ran into the advancing Germans in the Ardennes, and were thrown back. Although mauled, they slipped away. Yet the German command was sufficiently persuaded that the decisive victory had already been won that, on the 25th, it began transferring forces to Russia from the right wing. By the time this reached the Marne, it was much weaker than the forces opposing it. And on the 41st day of mobilization, 11th September, it was in full retreat!

The decisive turn had come with the penetration of the British Expeditionary Force into a thirty-mile gap between the two German armies of the right wing. This gives an ironical turn to the fact that the German command had rebuffed the offer of their navy to interfere with the shipment of the BEF, saying that 'it would be of advantage to settle with the 160,000 British at the same time as the French and Belgians'.

Below: *Painting of U-53 on Atlantic patrol by Claus Bergen. The Germans were not slow to appreciate the revolutionary addition of submarines to their naval armoury*

The blindness of generalship, especially towards new developments, was not cured by sharp contact with reality—partly, perhaps, because that contact was at second-hand. The German machine-guns had paralysed movement on the battlefield for months when Haig (now commander of the British First Army), resisting a proposal for increasing the British strength in these weapons, remarked that: 'The machine-gun was a much overrated weapon and two per battalion were more than sufficient.' Called upon for his judgment, Field-Marshal Lord Kitchener, now made war minister, conceded that four per battalion might be useful, but anything 'above four may be counted a luxury'. Long before the war ended, there would be a scale of more than forty heavy and light machine-guns per battalion—but that was due to the foresight and forceful pressure of a civilian minister, Lloyd George.

Military myopia likewise prevailed when means were mooted to overcome the defensive barrier formed by the hostile machine-guns. When the project of building tanks was submitted to the British engineer-in-chief in June 1915, he icily remarked: 'Before considering this proposal we should descend from the realms of imagination to solid facts.' Eight months later, when the first tank performed in front of Lord Kitchener, his comment was: 'A pretty mechanical toy.' 'The war,' he added, 'would never be won by such machines.'

Most of the generals were confident that it would be won long before such unnecessary aids could be produced. They had been confident from the earliest months, and they remained so despite constant disproof.

On 13th September, 1914, General Henry Wilson, the right hand of the British commander-in-chief, Sir John French, unwisely noted in his diary a conversation he had had with the guiding brain of the French commander-in-chief: 'Berthelot asked me when I thought we should cross into Germany, and I replied . . . in four weeks. He thought three weeks.' That very day the Allied armies were held up on the line of the Aisne, where they remained for the next four years.

The following June, Poincaré, the French President, pathetically complained to Kitchener: 'Joffre and Sir John told me in November they were going to push the Germans back over the frontier; they gave me the same assurance in December, March, and May. What have they done? The attacks are very costly and end in nothing.'

Lest it might be imagined that these optimistic forecasts were merely, if rashly, uttered to encourage ministerial morale, one must record a few more prophecies in which the generals indulged in their own circle. Thus, in November 1914, Sir John

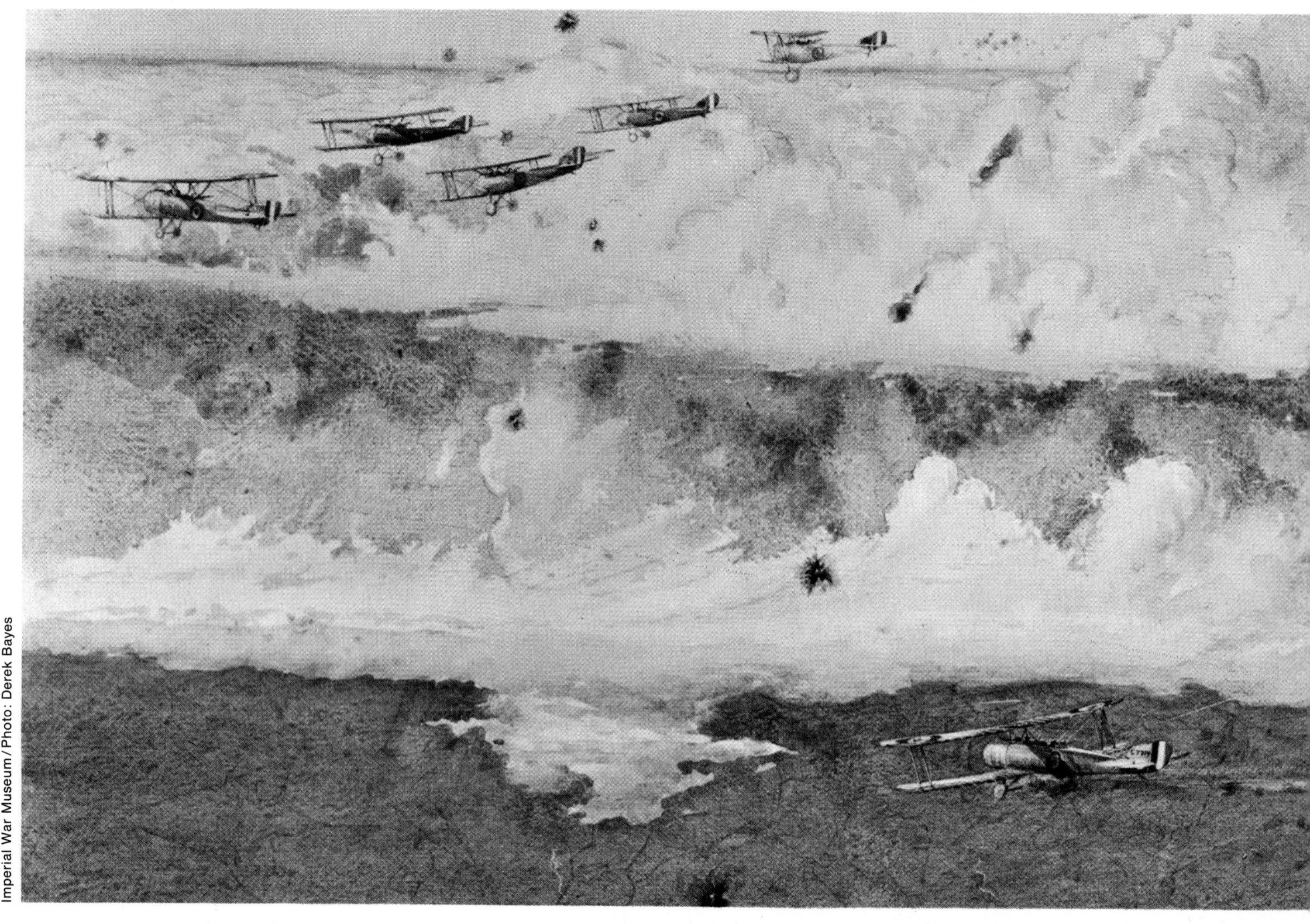

Imperial War Museum/Photo: Derek Bayes

French asserted that all the hard fighting of the war was over; in January 1915, he expressed the opinion that the war would be over by July; in March, Haig felt sure that the Germans would be wanting peace before the end of July; in August, he declared that he would not be surprised to see the enemy give in by November, and that in any case they could not go on after January 1916.

But in September 1915 the great Allied offensive proved a failure, and at the end of a dismal year French was replaced by Haig as British commander-in-chief.

The Allied commanders had by now come to the conclusion that the solution of the entrenched deadlock lay in multiplying artillery, and the weight of the preparatory bombardment – overestimating its potentialities while disregarding the fact that the heavier it became the worse it would tear up the ground over which they were planning to advance.

The main role in the British summer offensive of 1916 was entrusted to the Fourth Army under Rawlinson. Haig and he, as the British Official History records, 'impressed on all, at conferences and other times, that the infantry would only have to walk over and take possession of the enemy trenches'. The opening assault on 1st July was a complete failure on the greater part of the front, with a loss of 60,000 men in a single day. But the offensive was continued, and by November, when it was at last suspended, the British loss had risen to over 400,000 men, while the French had lost 200,000 – the German loss being about four hundred thousand.

At the end of 1916, continued disappointment led to the replacement of Joffre by Nivelle, who planned a great offensive for 1917, declaring: 'We shall break the German front when we wish.' When his executive subordinate, General Micheler, reported that the enemy were building a new third line of defence out of reach of his artillery, Nivelle lightheartedly retorted: 'Don't be anxious, you won't find a German in those trenches; they only want to be off!' He confidently asserted that he would break through the Germans' first two positions 'with insignificant loss', that in three days at most his armies would be in open country, beginning the great pursuit to the Rhine. The offensive was duly launched and at nightfall had progressed about 600 yards instead of the six miles anticipated in Nivelle's programme; its continuation on subsequent days did little more than increase the loss to a total of 120,000. The chief effect was to strain the morale of the French troops to breaking-point, producing a dangerous series of mutinies in the attack-sickened army. It was crippled for the rest of the summer and had to be nursed for the rest of the war.

Notwithstanding the paralysis of his allies, Haig told the British cabinet in June 1917, that 'if the fighting were kept up at its present intensity for six months Germany would be at the end of her available man-power'. By such assurances he gained a dubious sanction for his own continued offensive at Ypres. On 21st August he reported to the government that 'the time is fast approaching when Germany will be unable to maintain her armies'. On 8th October, arguing for permission to push deeper into the shell-torn morass there, he declared that the enemy might collapse 'at any moment'. With obvious doubt, as if making a concession to pessimistic politicians, he prefaced his view of 1918 prospects with the remark: 'Even if they hold out until next year.' But even if they did, and were able to transfer troops from the Russian front, he did not contemplate any serious check to his offensive. Not by a single word did he suggest the possibility that the Germans might take the offensive. As late as 7th January, 1918, when he came home to see the cabinet, he expressed the opinion that the Germans would not attack. But on 21st March, they refuted his forecast, by breaking through his overstrained troops and penetrating his front to a depth of nearly forty miles.

While the series of crises that followed were retrieved, and the scales of the war turned, by the arrival of American reinforcements, it was basically the pressure of seapower that undermined Germany's resistance and ensured her collapse. This fact lends significance to the French command's pre-war estimate of the help that the British navy would afford. Colonel Repington, the military critic, had written in *The Times* that it was 'worth 500,000 bayonets to the French'. But Henry Wilson, then the strategic brain of the British War Office, retorted that 'our Navy was not worth 500 bayonets'. After consulting the three leading French soldiers, he wrote:

'Castelnau and Joffre did not value it at one bayonet . . . Foch is of exactly the same opinion.'

Prophets unheard

It is not true to stay that the trend of warfare is impossible to gauge – at least of warfare hitherto. Marshal Foch was making an appropriate confession rather than a scientific statement when he declared in 1926: 'The military mind always imagines that the next war will be on the same lines as the last. That has never been the case and never will be.' One can well understand that in retrospect the war looked different to him from anything he had ever conceived, or prophesied of it, beforehand. But the conditions that dumbfounded him and his fellows were only the climax of an evolutionary process which they could have detected, but did not. Every war for half a century, since 1861, had made it plainer. Others did perceive them.

M. Bloch, a civilian banker of Warsaw, gave a remarkably accurate diagnosis of their essential elements in his *War of the Future,* published on the eve of the 20th century, before he had even the data of South Africa and the Russo-Japanese war in Manchuria to confirm his deductions. There were also military minds, even if these belonged to men not in the seats of authority, that foresaw the coming stalemate and pointed out its chain of causation. Captain Mayer, the French military critic, was provoked by Foch's fiery advocacy of the offensive to predict, only too well, the siege war that would engulf generals who were dreaming of mobile war without the means of mobility. He was boycotted for his audacity. So was the eminent military historian, Lieutenant-Colonel Grouard, when he turned from the past to the future, and forecast in 1911 exactly what would happen if the French command adopted such a plan as they did, in 1914. And, as we have seen, the British military critic, Colonel Repington, had a far wider grasp than either the French or British general staffs of the factors that would influence the issue of the war.

The war was filled with battles, yet the most that the historian can fairly say is that they were a contributory factor – one of many – the main factor in the collapse of Germany being economic pressure. On this point there is Haig's own admission, at the end of October 1918: 'Germany is not broken in a military sense. During the last weeks her armies have withdrawn . . . in excellent order.' The Allied armies were exhausted and needed to be reorganized before they could follow up. But Germany was broken internally by hunger, sickness, and despair. Her breakdown developed directly from military disappointment, from the depression which spread when her own offensive in the spring failed to bring the victory that Ludendorff had promised. But the foundations of her resistance had been undermined by the Allied blockade.

The abortiveness of battle as a means of winning wars can be traced to the declining power of the attack to overcome defence. This condition was due to the growing power of modern firearms, and had been long in evolution. It was first manifest in the American Civil War, where it came to be a standard calculation that one man in a trench was equal to three or four in an assault. In Europe the wars of 1866 and 1870 brought fresh evidence of the paralysing influence of fire, although the brevity of both wars tended to obscure it. Nevertheless, after the second, the winning strategist of those two wars, Moltke, drew the conclusion that his victory could not be repeated, and enunciated the lesson that: 'As a result of the improvement of firearms, the tactical defensive has acquired a great advantage over the offensive. . . . It seems to be more advantageous to proceed to an attack only after having repelled several attacks by the enemy.'

Then came the Russo-Japanese War (p. 68) which foreshadowed nearly all the factors which upset military calculations in 1914 – the paralysing power of machine-guns, the hopelessness of frontal attacks, and the consequent relapse of the armies into trenches. But military optimism was even more impregnable – to the assault of facts. To ardent soldiers war was unthinkable without successful attack, so that they were able to persuade themselves that attacks could succeed. The delusive basis of that faith was quickly exposed when the First World War began, and was made clearer still when the trench deadlock set in – for four years. And it is significant that

Air warfare, 1917. The aeroplane, used mostly as an army auxiliary, formed part of the revolutionary growth in mobility

Relics of the trenches

Millions experienced the new warfare—from the trenches, into which soldiers were driven by the tactical stalemate and the supremacy of the defensive. The weapons and equipment they were given to fight with varied: from near medieval maces and mail to gas masks designed to combat one of the most sinister of the new weapons

__1__ German helmet, wire cutters, and spiked club. __2__ A fearsome collection of Italian maces. Trench raiding parties armed themselves with clubs and maces for night forays when the ability to deal a swift and silent death was essential. __3__ Typical British equipment: steel helmet, gas mask, Mills grenade, ·455 Webley, and trench mirror

1

Imperial War Museum/Photo: Chris Barker

3

Imperial War Museum/Photo: Alan Spain

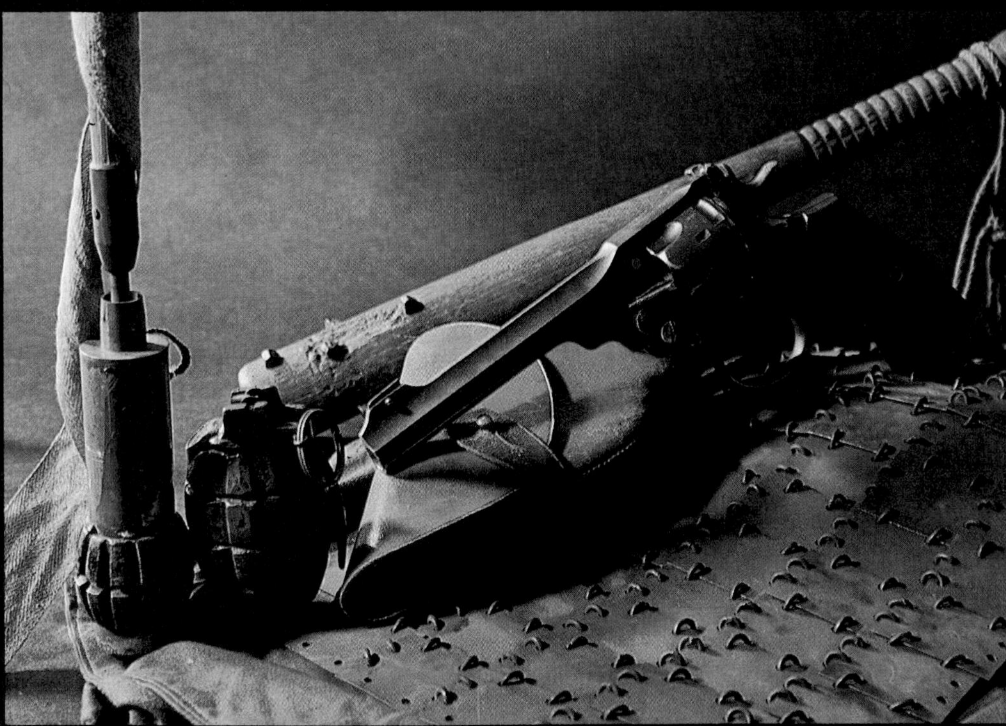

__4__ Other British trench weaponry: a hobnailed cudgel and No. 2 Mk. 1 grenade, together with bullet-proof vest, Mills grenade, ·455 Webley and holster. The Mills grenade or Mills bomb was developed for hand and rifle launching. __5__ Austrian bugle, German Navy Luger, and German gas mask. __6__ Corroding artifacts of war. An Italian lamp, meal-box, revolver, and mail vest

5

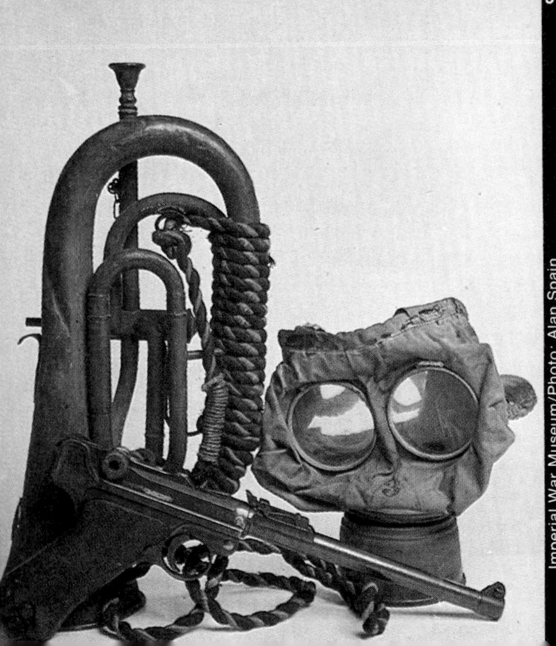

Imperial War Museum/Photo: Alan Spain

the only great battles which had far-reaching results before morale had broken down were those which took the form of a counter-stroke after the enemy had spent himself in vain attacks – the Allied victories in the first and second battles of the Marne, the German victories at Tannenberg, Gorlice, and Caporetto. Yet none of the commanders at the outset, and hardly any later, showed remembrance of Moltke's advice, or were willing to delay their own offensive dreams until they had dispelled the enemy's.

The historical basis of the belief in the hand-to-hand fight was equally false, and it reacted on the belief in numbers. For a century the military manuals of Europe had continued to emphasize the decisive importance of physical shock, echoing Clausewitz's dictum: 'The close combat, man to man, is plainly to be regarded as the real basis of combat.' The French doctrine of 1914 fervently declared that the object of all attacks was 'to charge the enemy with the bayonet in order to destroy him'. Something might be claimed for it if the emphasis had been on the psychological effect of a close-quarter threat, but the time and attention devoted to bayonet-training showed that the bayonet-fight was regarded as a reality. Yet even in the 18th century a practical soldier like Guibert had remarked its rarity, while Jomini was but one of a number of witnesses of the Napoleonic battles who said that, except in villages and defiles, he had 'never seen two forces cross bayonets'. Half a century later Moltke would point out the fallacy of the French assertion that their victory at Solferino had been won by the bayonet. In 1870 their troops were to pay heavily against Prussian fire for this delusion among their leaders, yet Boguslawski records that in actual fact 'bayonets were never crossed in open fight'.

Only in conditions where shock was a practical possibility could the theory of massing superior numbers be effective. It was difficult to adjust it to conditions where one man with a machine-gun might count for more than a much larger number who were advancing upon him with the bayonet. The fallacy was proved most emphatically of all by the Germans against the Russians; by their superior weapons and technique the Germans discounted the vastly superior numbers of their Eastern Front opponent.

The gradualness of evolution owed much to the stout resistance which the military profession has always offered to novelty. The impetus of science in the 19th century did not suffice to storm these ramparts. The obstruction that the tank had to overcome on paper before it took the field in 1916 is well known; less familiar is the fact that it might have been available before the war began. There was Mr de Mole's tank, superior in design to the one that was actually produced. But the design had been submitted to the War Office and was there pigeon-holed – until the war was over. There was also the promising idea contained in drawings submitted by a plumber of Nottingham. It also was unearthed after the war; the file bore the brief but decisive verdict: 'The man's mad.' Similar blindness marked the attitude of even the more thoughtful among leading soldiers to the possibilities of the air. When Foch watched the 1910 *Circuit de l'Est,* which proved the reliability of the new invention, he exclaimed: 'That is good sport, but for the Army the aeroplane is no use.'

The lessons of the war

In sum, there were four main features of the 'new warfare' that, developing in the 19th century, came to dominate the course of the First World War from 1914 onwards.

First, was the growth of size. From France under the Revolution and Napoleon, through America in the Civil War and Prussia under Moltke, the armies swelled to the millions of 1914. Yet back in the 18th century Marshal Saxe had foreseen the hindrances of size: 'Multitudes serve only to perplex and embarrass.'

Second, came the growth of fire-power, beginning with the adoption of rifles and breech-loading weapons. This, imposed on size, conduced to a growing paralysis of warfare on land and sea.

Third, was the growth of industrialization. The change from well-distributed agricultural communities to a concentration of population and an interdependence of areas, together with the more complex needs of such a civilization, gave more influence in war to economic objectives. By acting against those, even in the comparatively primitive South, Sherman decided the issue of the American Civil War. Soldiers in Europe, however, remained unable to see much beyond the opposing army. Their eyes were bloodshot. Yet in the end it was the economic pressure, mainly applied by the navy, which decided the issue of the World War.

A fourth was the revolutionary growth of mobility, due in turn to the steam engine and the motor. Paradoxically, its chief effect when added to the other tendencies was to reduce the effective mobility of armies. The railway – which had speed but not flexibility, the other constituent of mobility – fostered the accumulation of masses, and these were hampered not only by their own bulk but by the growth of fire. The road-motor, a much later development, was neglected until the war came and was then at first applied merely to the service of mass. Not until it was embodied in the tank did it begin to assist the recovery of mobility – by making it possible for men to advance in face of bullets.

The aeroplane likewise began as a mere auxiliary, and to this minor role it was still mainly confined as its numbers grew. Even in the greatest bombing raid on London only thirty-three machines were employed, although four thousand were in use for the narrower duties of army co-operation. But in the last phase of the war, aircraft showed their powers at the expense of armies by frustrating the escape of the defeated Bulgarian, Turkish, and Austrian armies; they turned the ebbing tide into a stagnant shambles.

What were the outstanding lessons of the war along these lines of evolution? The first, certainly, was that the huge conscript armies tended to make war inevitable, just as, when war was engaged, they tended to make it immobile. 'Mobilization means war,' the German ambassador threateningly said to the Russian foreign minister with more profound truth than he intended. For, once the mass of the people were summoned to arms from their normal occupation, an atmosphere was created in which peace-feelers were stifled.

Moreover, these armies were so cumbrous, their movement so complex, that even direction could not be modified. Thus, when the Kaiser, clutching at a report that France might forsake Russia's side and remain neutral, said to Moltke the younger, who had now been appointed to his famous uncle's place as chief of the German general staff: 'We march, then, only towards the East?' Moltke replied that this was 'impossible. The advance of armies formed of millions of men was the result of years of intricate work. Once planned it could not possibly be changed'. So the millions went forward.

But when they reached the battlefield, they were stopped by the machine-guns, few as these were. Back in 1884, a military prophet had acclaimed the machine-gun as 'concentrated essence of infantry'. Military authorities had paid little attention to such prophecies – until the war came in 1914. Then it was shown that one man sitting behind a machine-gun was equal to ten, a hundred, even a thousand, who were rushing on him with the bayonet. The generals were puzzled. They had always counted strength by count of heads.

It was the machine-gun that made infantry advance hopeless and cavalry futile. The next four years were spent in trying to overcome this obstacle.

First, the generals, true to their theory of mass, tried masses of artillery. This method achieved poor results in proportion to the effort. It made a short advance possible but forbade a long one – by ploughing up the ground over which the advance had to be made.

A new method dawned in 1915 – the use

Imperial War Museum

Left: Protected against gas attack, a German machine-gun crew stand by to open fire. German machine-guns paralysed movement on the Western Front and exploded conventional theories of warfare. ***Below:*** *Loading British gas projectors. The efficacy of the new weapon depended on which way the wind blew.* ***Opposite:*** *German flame-throwers going into action*

Imperial War Museum

of tanks. Reluctantly accepted by authority, it did not receive a real opportunity in the field until the last year of the war. Then it produced longer and quicker advances than had hitherto been made, and proved, by German admission, the most effective land weapon yet employed.

The Germans had also tried, in 1915, a new means to overcome the barrier. This was gas. Luckily for the Allies, the German soldiers thwarted the German chemists, and the best chance of a decisive result was forfeited. Still, by ringing the changes on various types, gas continued to play an important part. The most effective, by far, was mustard gas, which disabled by blistering the skin and took effect even after a long interval. The strategic effect, however, was more in hampering an enemy's attack than in assisting one's own. Thus it tended to increase the paralysis in which the war was already gripped.

One possibility of overcoming machine-guns was largely neglected – the advance in obscurity. Night attacks were rare, for fear of confusion – although this was a lesser risk than a daylight advance in face of defending machine-guns. Smoke screens were never fully developed. When first suggested in 1914, Kitchener had emphatically declared that they 'would be of no use for land operations'! Yet in 1918, it was under cover of fog – nature's smoke – that the Germans repeatedly broke through the Allied front. When fog was lacking, they failed. It is strange that neither side sought to produce artificial fog on a great scale.

At sea likewise the same lines of evolution led to the same conclusion – a state of general paralysis. The traditional purpose of destroying the enemy's main forces in battle was never fulfilled, and although the fleets were once within range of each other, at Jutland, analysis of that tactically ineffective encounter tends to emphasize the factors that made for paralysis.

Naval development had been marked by swelling as on land, although this elephantiasis at sea affected the size of individual ships rather than the numbers of a fleet. Battleships became so large, and hence so few compared with Nelson's day, that admirals became more reluctant to risk them. And the growth of fire-power tended to keep the fleets apart; fighting at long ranges made a decision more difficult. To this check was added that of a new weapon, the torpedo; if it did not attain the results in sea fighting that had been anticipated by the prophets, this was largely because the fear of it made the admirals shy of pursuing an offensive movement – and thereby exposed the ineffectiveness of a battle-fleet. The lighter craft, too, were in consequence diverted to the unprofitable duty of chaperoning their big sisters. The British official history candidly confesses: 'The Grand Fleet could only put to sea with an escort of nearly one hundred destroyers . . . the German U-boats had hampered our squadrons to an extent which the most expert and far-sighted naval officer had never foreseen.' A few months after the 'victory' of Jutland, the danger of a German invasion of Denmark loomed on the horizon of the British government; after examination by the Admiralty, the conclusion was reached that 'for naval reasons it would be almost impossible to support the Danes at all'. What a humiliating confession of impotence: The shadow of the German submarine was longer than the shadow of Nelson's column.

Nor was that all. The growth of industrialization had made nations, Great Britain above all, more dependent on overseas supply. By multiplying commerce it had multiplied the targets for indirect attack. While British destroyers were chaperoning battleships, the German submarines were sinking British mercantile shipping – until Great Britain herself was in sight of collapse. When part of the destroyers were diverted to protect commerce, the Grand Fleet had to be practically locked up for its own safety! It was history's most ironical case of 'protective arrest'.

The Germans' paucity of submarines led in turn to the self-imprisonment of their fleet when the available submarines were wanted for the new unrestricted campaign against merchant shipping. The farcical result was thus reached that 'for the future the two great battle-fleets could but lie inactive, watching one another across a kind of "No Man's Sea", where attack and defence were concerned only with transport and commerce'.

This direct action against the supplies upon which Great Britain depended for her existence, was carried so far that by the following spring, of 1917, she was in sight of collapse before the danger was brought under control – through the introduction of the convoy system, which in turn depended on the additional destroyers provided by America.

This near-fatal menace was created by a comparative handful of submarines, operating under most disadvantageous geographical conditions, and in waters guarded by 3,000 destroyers and light craft – odds of 30 to 1 against the submarines.

As for the growth of mobility, through the supersession of sails by steam, its influence is to be traced throughout the stalemate that prevailed. Its effect was to engender a fundamental immobility. In the case of the outer and greater naval power this prevented it destroying the enemy's fleet; in the case of the inner and weaker, Germany, it ensured her ultimate collapse from pernicious anaemia.

The man in the trenches—raw material of the new warfare

'Same old trenches, same old view,
Same old rats as blooming tame,
Same old dugouts, nothing new,
Same old smells, the very same,
Same old bodies out in front,
Same old strafe from two till four,
Same old scratching, same old 'unt,
Same old bloody war.'
A.A.Milne. Fought in the Somme

'Up there, in uncompleted lines the boys stand in mud and water through the night—there had been much snow and the rain completes its evaporation into water . . . A peg of wood will help suspend a ground sheet against the dripping clay wall and a man may flatten himself under this looking like part of the trench. Rain, pitiless rain, soaking and numbing—and so to wear the night away. . . . I've just come from where fifty thousand bodies lie, bones and barbed wire everywhere, skeletons bleached if one takes a walk over the frightfully contested and blown up hill. Boots and bones protruding from one's dug-out walls, and yet—one is merry there.'
Sergeant Ernest Broughton

'I am still stuck in this trench. . . . I haven't washed or had my clothes off at all, and my average of sleep has been 2½ hours in the twenty-four. I don't think I've started to crawl yet, but I don't suppose I should notice it if I had; it is a matter of such small importance.'
Captain Edwin Gerard Venning, France

'I have been talking to one of my stretcher bearers. He has a foot swollen to three times its normal size: a great helpless bright pink lump. He has been stretcher-bearing over that awful ground almost the whole of four days. Changing his socks did no good. . . . Poor beggar! I shall be surprised if he doesn't lose that foot.'

'Our rations came to Bull's Trench in bags of ten, per mules, and were carried thence by human mules. No water was brought, but the ice in the shell-holes was melted to obtain water. . . . An axe would soon be the means of filling the dixies with lumps of ice. We used it for tea several days until one chap noticed a pair of boots sticking out . . . and discovered they were attached to a body. . . . We generally managed to sleep warm by sleeping close together and sharing blankets—each man carried two. The cold, however, was far preferable to the mud. . . . We could move about.'
Sergeant E.W.Simon, from the Somme

'The rats interrupted me. They are fat and grey and bold. One came and looked at me and squealed at about 3 o'clock in the morning when I could see no prospect of going to bed ever, and so infuriated me that I slashed at him with my stick and splashed my whole face so with mud that I had to spend the next hour or so trying to get a lump of it out of my eye. I missed the rat, and imagined him with a paw to his horrible nose—laughing at me.'
Captain T P C Wilson, France, 1st March 1916

1

2

Imperial War Museum

1 *Bearded German soldiers swathed in greatcoats huddle in a damp trench for a hurried meal.* **2** *A British officer inspects stew for the trenches.* **3** *Kindly gesture amid unspeakable horror. A German soldier lights his prisoner's cigarette.* **4** *The stew must get through. Not even a gas attack can prevent this German soldier carrying long-awaited hot food into his dugout*

3

Südd-Verlag, Munich

5

Museo di Storia, Milan

6

Press Association

7

Bibliothek für Zeitgeschichte, Stuttgart

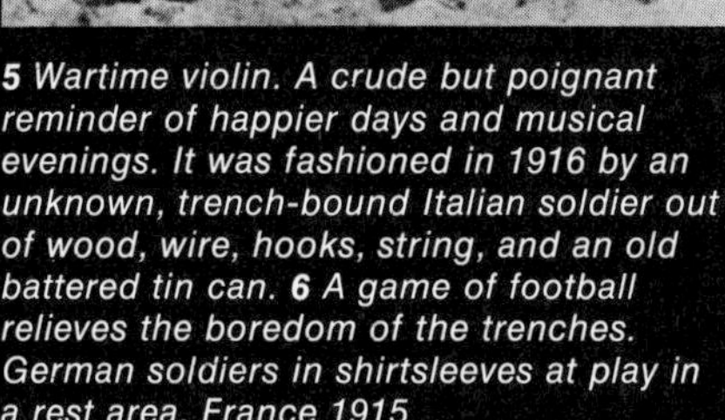

__5__ Wartime violin. A crude but poignant reminder of happier days and musical evenings. It was fashioned in 1916 by an unknown, trench-bound Italian soldier out of wood, wire, hooks, string, and an old battered tin can. __6__ A game of football relieves the boredom of the trenches. German soldiers in shirtsleeves at play in a rest area, France 1915

__7__ German soldiers breakfasting on bread and tinned meat in a characteristically comfortable dugout. __8__ Officers' quarters —not luxurious, but better than a trench. The British staff officer and French colonel in Sir William Orpen's painting have not had to share the frequently nightmarish life of their men. Senior officers' lives were too precious

Imperial War Museum

8

In a painting by Gilbert Rogers, Royal Army Medical Corps personnel move among captured trenches comforting the dying and removing the wounded during the battle of Messines Ridge, June 1917. Trenches were often morasses of reeking mud, but some of the dugouts were remarkably snug

Imperial War Museum

Science, 1914-18/Ronald W.Clark

The Way War Altered Peace

The conscription of science and technology took on a new impetus during the First World War. The results were to affect the way men lived when peace came even more radically than the way they died while war lasted

It is significant that the link between science and technology and the First World War should be worthy of comment at all. Early Bronze Age men discovered that metal weapons were more useful than stone and flint. The Greeks used flame, smoke, and Greek fire, a mixture of sulphur, pitch, nitre, petrol, and quicklime which was the ancient equivalent of napalm. The Chinese employed gunpowder for their 13th-century rockets. Both the Romans and Leonardo can claim ancestry for the tank and

The most advanced bomber produced before the armistice—the Handley Page V/1500. *It was to have been used for bombing Berlin, but instead it was redesigned for use in the early post-war civilian air services. Advances in the design of aircraft which might not have been made in twenty years of peace-time were made in four under the pressure of war. Flying became a science*

Imperial War Museum

the panzer division. Sir Frederick Abel was chemist to the Royal Military College, Woolwich, more than a century ago, and the links between science and the Admiralty go back to the days of Pepys.

But the impact of science and technology on the struggle between the Allies and the Central powers in the First World War was of a totally different order. It did really alter the way in which men fought and died, as surely as the long bow brought down the feudal system. More importantly, it helped shape the two decades that followed the peace, the decades of the day before yesterday. Most significantly of all, science and technology made the equipping and provisioning of armies an industrial enterprise involving whole nations. Thus they helped, between 1914 and 1918, to abolish the clear line between combatant and non-combatant; they made total war inevitable in the future and total destruction more likely. Between them, they succeeded in putting back the clock so that war implicated entire populations in a way which had been unknown since the religious wars of previous centuries.

In the First World War neither side exploited the new possibilities very well, very quickly, or without the constant prodding of disaster. Neither the politicians nor the service chiefs had the ability to see that the industrial and scientific revolutions of the 19th century had made their ideas out-of-date. Thus the German high command bungled the use of gas and the British high command bungled the use of the tank. Both sides awoke too late to the fact that when the Wright brothers became airborne at Kittyhawk they added a third dimension to warfare.

Despite this reluctance of governments and high commands to alter their accepted methods, the direct impact of science and technology on the fighting man was in the long run pervasive and spectacular, if less important than its long-term effect on industry and post-war civilian life. It began early in the operations, as the traditional war of movement ended. One result of this transformation into static warfare was to encourage the development of sound-ranging. With the formation of trench systems it became more important to pin-point enemy artillery, and it was found that this could be done by using microphones in which a tiny platinum wire was heated by an electrical current. Arrival of a sound wave cooled the wire and altered the electrical resistance. This change could be timed to within a hundredth of a second and, since the speed of sound was known, records from a number of such microphones could accurately locate a gun-battery by a simple process of triangulation.

Development of heavier artillery – and of the techniques and steels required for it – was but one other result of the stalemate which by the autumn of 1914 had bogged down both armies in deep defensive positions which ran 500 miles from the Channel coast to the Swiss frontier. During the next four years each side turned to its scientists and technologists to produce new ways of breaking the stalemate. But the German high command was unprepared for the success of its first gas attack, and had failed to learn the lesson when its chemists provided a second chance by the use of the radically different mustard gas two years later. The Allied high command never understood the tank or believed that it would displace the cavalry as queen of the battlefield.

Poison gas

The Germans struck first. Fritz Haber, who had already solved Germany's nitrate shortage, had by the spring of 1915 prepared with Walther Nernst, professor of chemistry at the University of Berlin, enough chlorine for a gas attack. Although the Allies had ample warning – details from a prisoner who carried a gas-mask; messages from Martha McKenna, the Belgian spy, who was told to stick to troop movements – no precautions were taken. When the gas was first used north of Ypres on 22nd April, the Allies were so surprised by the attack that two divisions broke; the Germans were so surprised by success that they failed to follow-up. Five months later the British, who had protested against the illegality and inhumanity of gas, used it themselves at Loos – this time adding to its effect by mixing smoke with it. Three months later the Germans replied with phosgene, an easily made by-product of their huge dyeing industry. Diphosgene, chloropicrin, and hydrocyanic acid which attacked the central nervous system, all followed. The Germans scored a second surprise when in 1917 they first used mustard gas, which injured by contact as well as ingestion. Invented by a British chemist half a century earlier but thought to be useless, its employment was half-hearted and its exploitation amateur.

In the short run the Germans might have utilized gas to make a decisive breakthrough on the Western Front. In the long run two things went against them; one was the prevailing wind, which favoured the Allies in the westernmost of the two defensive systems; the other was the blockade and the size of the Allied world's chemical industry.

The British were quite as hidebound in their exploitation of the tank. A development of Leonardo's 'covered chariots which are invulnerable', it was only made practicable by the internal combustion engine. Colonel Swinton, who first conceived the idea of marrying the virtues of the farm tractor and the armoured car; Churchill, who from the Admiralty irregularly diverted £75,000 to the director of naval construction to experiment with the vehicles after the War Office had shelved the idea; and Foster's, the engineering firm of Lincoln who made the new vehicles, all share the credit for pushing the tank in the face of opposition. Developing it demanded technological rather than scientific flair. Using it demanded something more – an act of the imagination. Lack of this, combined with a desire to see what happened, caused eleven of the new machines, still beset with teething troubles, to be used prematurely in September 1916. The secret was out. Just as Cherwell, thirty years later, was to bring about the loss of the H_2S bombing device with dire results for bomber command, so the high command had now let the tanks out of the bag. Even so, when nearly 400 of them were used a year later at Cambrai, they broke through three lines of defence and penetrated four miles, leaving only a thin half-finished trench line before them. But nearly half the tanks were by that time out of action. Only the cavalry was available to follow up. Another year was to pass before the tank played its vital part in the eventual breakthrough.

At sea, the impact of both technological and scientific change was varied and lasting. Judged by any yardstick, the development of wireless was among the most important results and in this, as in other improvements of communications, all three services shared. In the army's newly-created Signal Corps, where the young Edward Appleton was first turned towards the problems which ended in his discovery of the ionosphere, Colonel Fuller devised his ingenious 'fullerphone'. In this early form of scrambler device, the alternating current in a telephone circuit was converted to direct current by a 'chopper' arrangement before being sent to the line and then re-established at the receiving end. In the Royal Flying Corps the need for lightness helped to revolutionize radio communications. And in the Royal Navy itself the war witnessed both the fundamental change from the spark system to the continuous wave system, and the evolution of directional wireless equipment which was to revolutionize post-war maritime navigation. A navigational footnote is provided by the Leader Gear developed by the navy. This consisted of a cable fed with alternating current and laid on the sea-floor, plus receiving gear on the ship with which the captain could tell whether he strayed from a course above the cable. Forty miles of it, laid mainly at difficult harbour entrances, was in use when the war ended. ▷ 750

Cambrai, 1917: the coming of the tank

On 20th November 1917 a British tank armada lumbered out of the morning mist opposite Cambrai and scythed through the massive fortifications of the Hindenburg Line. The traditional preliminary bombardment had been dispensed with and the Germans further misled by a series of diversionary raids and feints.

Seven months earlier a handful of tanks had been cautiously deployed on the Somme. At Cambrai they proved disconcertingly successful. Supported by six divisions and the creeping barrage of 1,000 guns the unwieldy machines flailed aside the wire entanglements and vaulted the broad trenches with the aid of brushwood fascines. By nightfall the British attack had yielded 10,000 German prisoners and 200 guns. It was a rare success, and in London, for the first and only time during the war, bells were rung to acclaim victory.

'The immediate onset of the tanks inevitably was overwhelming,' wrote D.G.Brown of the Tank Corps. 'The German outposts, dazed or annihilated by the sudden deluge of shells, were overrun in an instant. The triple belts of wire were crossed as if they had been beds of nettles, and 350 pathways were sheared through them for the infantry. The defenders of the front trench, scrambling out of dug-outs and shelters to meet the crash and flame of the barrage, saw the leading tanks almost upon them, their appearance made the more grotesque and terrifying by the huge black bundles they carried on their cabs. As these tanks swung left-handed and fired down into the trench, others, also surmounted by these appalling objects, appeared in multitudes behind them out of the mist. It is small wonder that the front Hindenburg Line, that fabulous excavation which was to be the bulwark of Germany, gave little trouble. The great fascines were loosed and rolled over the parapets to the trench floor; and down the whole line tanks were dipping and rearing up and clawing their way across into the almost unravaged country beyond. The defenders of the line were running panic-stricken, casting away arms and equipment.'

The attack, conceived as a lightning raid, had assumed the proportions of a full-scale offensive for which the 3rd Army was materially unprepared (there were no infantry reserves or machines to exploit the offensive). The entire tank force had been deployed along the length of the salient rather than against selected priority objectives. And as German divisions raced to the threatened sector the British offensive began to falter.

'But where were the Cavalry?' demanded Stephen Foot of the Tank Corps. 'It was nearly eleven o'clock. All the tanks and infantry had reached their objective in our part of the line. Marcoing had been captured. The Germans were in flight. When would the Cavalry arrive to exploit the success? . . . And what was the Cavalry doing? Why, carrying out regular tactics for advancing by stages into an enemy's country! . . . It was really too absurd. Ribecourt had been captured at 7 a.m., the R.E. were loading up material from a German dump just outside the village at 9 a.m., and now, four hours later, the Cavalry were advancing as cautiously as if Germans might be expected round the corner. . . . The Cavalry squadrons were only just crossing No Man's Land and it was nearly 2 p.m., just six hours after the barbed-wire entanglements had been cleared for them by special tanks detailed for that purpose. We heard afterwards that the head of the Cavalry column did not start until noon from Fins, which was four miles behind our original front line!'

Bottom: *Wounded war-horse of a new age of warfare: a broken-down British tank photographed by the Germans after its participation in the battle of Cambrai*

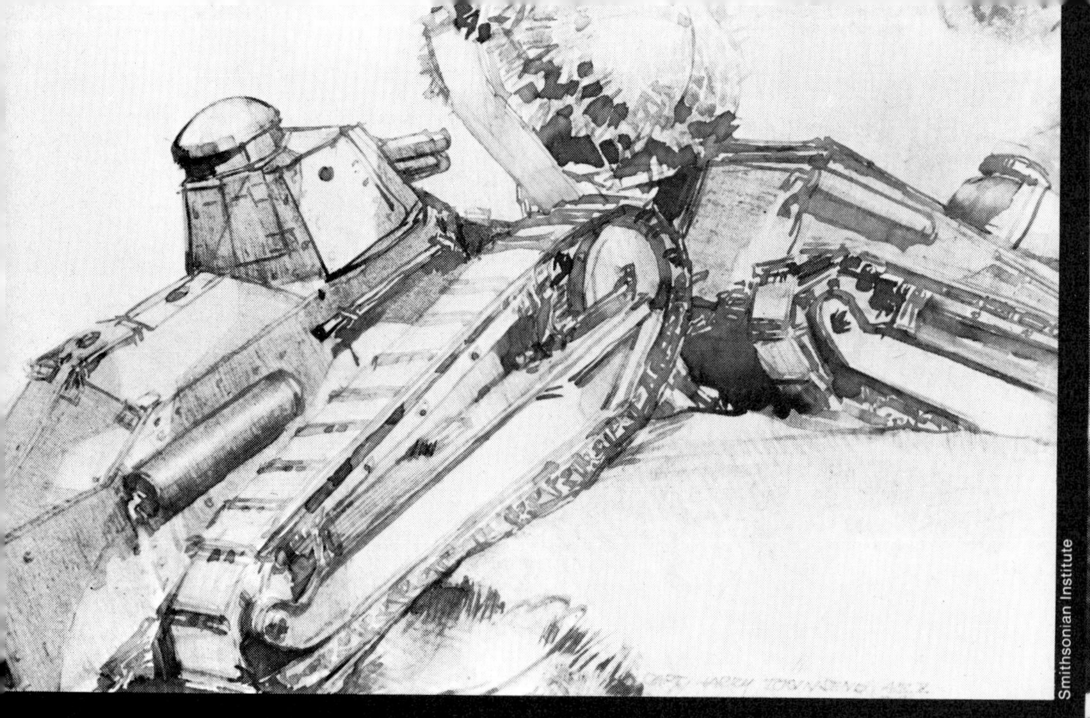

Smithsonian Institute

Musée Royal de l'Armée, Brussels

The tank in action

At Cambrai the tank proved itself. Previously British military experts had been sceptical – Kitchener called it 'a pretty mechanical toy'. Yet in 1918 Ludendorff was to call tanks 'our most dangerous enemies'. They had broken the stalemate of the trenches. ***Above:*** French Renault *light tanks climb a hill.* ***Left:*** *Captured British* Mark IV *tank, used by the Germans, overturned by a shell. Germany did not use her own tanks until 1918.* ***Below:*** Renault *light tanks, 1918. The French developed tanks independently, later than the British.*

Südd-Verlag, Munich

Ullstein

THE TANK
is a travelling fortress that clears the way for our soldiers.

It cuts through the wire - under fir
It saves lives
It is *our* War discovery
It is a matter of pride to help to build Tanks.

Imperial War Museum

Far left: *German tank soldier in uniform. His mask, made of steel mesh, is for protection against shrapnel. A German tank of the kind behind him held eighteen men.* ***Left:*** *Queen Mary, visiting a tankdrome at the front, stops beside a* Mark VII *male tank. 'Male' tanks carried heavy guns, 'female' tanks only machine-guns.* ***Above:*** *British poster appealing for money to build tanks. The basic idea of developing a machine like a Holt tractor into an 'armoured moving fortress' was suggested to the British military authorities in October 1914.* ***Below:*** *French* St Chamond *tanks, painted by François Fl: meng, 1918*

Imperial War Museum

Imperial War Museum/Photo: Alan Spain

Left: ***French Morane.*** *The metal plates on the propeller were to deflect the bullets the pilot shot from the aircraft. Not until Fokker invented his synchronizing gear could pilots shoot accurately.* ***Above:*** *Optical science applied to war – British trench periscope, German range charts, compass, and range-finder.* ***Below:*** *British Royal Flying Corps examine aerial photographs taken over enemy territory.* ***Opposite page:*** *A new dimension to war – German Hannoveranas fight British Martinsydes*

Imperial War Museum

The change to oil-firing from the less efficient coal-firing, adopted progressively in the Royal Navy between 1914 and 1918, was a process in which the Germans, due to their comparative shortage of good steam coal, already had a head start; and the first problem tackled by the Admiralty Engineering Laboratory, set up in 1917, was that of obtaining higher power per cylinder from fast-running diesel engines. Here, as in a score of similar fields, the technological advances of the Admiralty were to be utilized by the post-war merchant navy. Improved boilers, the application of the impulse design of turbine for marine work, automatic feed regulators and valves were but some of the items developed for war and utilized afterwards.

The ripples from such work went farther. Gear-cutting practice and the manufacture of gear-cutting machines were both stimulated by naval demands. Comparably, it can be argued that one of the most significant technological results of the war was the revolution in the accuracy of screw gauges, brought about when the National Physical Laboratory at Teddington had to set radically new standards to meet the demands of the munitions industry.

In the early months of the war the Admiralty concerned itself mainly with the German High Seas Fleet, but the submarine threat soon became apparent and it was here that the opportunities for 'pure' science seemed greatest. By the end of 1916 Admiral Sir Percy Scott, already important for his gunnery inventions, had suggested construction of an electro-magnet that would be a combination of magnetic mine and submarine detector. There had been suggestions for a 'walking mine' which would carry itself across the floor of the North Sea to the German coast. Trawls and magnetic detectors had been proposed, while on 31st July 1916 officers soberly gathered at Horsea Island to watch a Mr Ashmore unsuccessfully try to detect submerged oil with a divining rod.

Hydrophones which could detect a submarine's engines, depth charges, and a special type of shell which finally ended attack by a surfaced submarine, only reduced the danger. The submarine menace was eventually beaten by the increased use of small attacking craft and by the convoy system – introduced after a hit-and-miss attempt at what would now be called operational research.

Only towards the end of the war came two anti-submarine devices that were to go into cold storage for twenty years. One was the magnetic mine, samples of which were laid in the North Sea. The other was Asdic, named after the Anti-Submarine Detection Investigation Committee.

When the *Titanic* had been sunk in 1912 after collision with an iceberg, it had ▷ **752**

Domenica del Corriere

been suggested that sound-waves emitted by a ship might be reflected by such floating masses and thereby give warning of danger. Soon after the outbreak of war, the Asdic Committee, which included Professor (later Sir William) Bragg, the French Professor Langevin, and Professor (later Lord) Rutherford, was set up to discover whether some such principle might be applied to submarine detection. By 1915 Langevin had found that the piezo-electric effect—the vibration of certain crystals when they are subjected to an electric field—could be utilized to make a quartz crystal emit sound waves. If this were done under water, and in the right way, the sound waves would be reflected by an underwater obstacle and their echoes detected with the help of the same crystal. The method was developed throughout the war years and was becoming operational in 1918.

War takes flight

But it was in the air that the results of science and technology were most spectacular. This was largely due to the timing of history. It was as recently as 1903 that the Wrights had made their first flight; and just as Otto Hahn's discovery of nuclear fission in 1938 stood ready for exploitation from 1939 onwards, so did flight hold out opportunities for the services from the outbreak of the First World War.

Five years earlier Lord Haldane, then secretary of state for war, had set up a special scientific committee at the National Physical Laboratory to deal with aeronautics since, as he wrote, 'we were at a profound disadvantage with the Germans, who were building up the structure of the Air Service on a foundation of science'. The NPL had by 1913 enabled E.T.Busk to build the first really stable aeroplane, the RE1 which was developed into the BE2c, the standard two-seat biplane of the Royal Flying Corps at the outbreak of war. This, like many other types, was built at the Royal Aircraft Establishment, Farnborough, a brain-box for the aeronautical advance, in whose mess there was concentrated at one time F.A.Lindemann (later Lord Cherwell), G.P. (later Sir George) Thomson, E.D. (later Lord) Adrian, William (later Sir William) Farren, and G.I. (later Sir Geoffrey) Taylor.

Despite Great Britain's interest in aeronautics, her application of the new science to war was tardy. Even Colonel Seely, Haldane's own parliamentary private secretary dismissed aircraft manufacturers in 1908 with the statement that 'we do not consider that aeroplanes will be of any possible use for war purposes'. When war came, Great Britain could apparently muster only some sixty-three machines compared with the 156 of France and the 260 of Germany. The army had about eleven pilots, the Royal Navy even fewer. 'France has about 263', said Seely, 'so we are what you might call behind.' This disadvantage was compounded by the first-rate German equipment—hand-operated magnetic engine-starters, accurate compasses, pressure petrol gauges, speed and altitude recorders, and a small independent screw mounted on one of the main planes which drove the dynamo. The British had more primitive equipment—and also supply difficulties; the ever-popular Bosch magneto was made by the Germans.

As the war went on, a series of improvements in design, engine-power, and materials, each comparatively small in itself, combined to bring first the British ahead, then the Germans, then the British again. This leap-frogging in the technological race thus gave each side temporary command of the air for short periods. But it was a close thing, and the tide was finally turned not by science but by the overwhelming resources of the Americans, the British, and the French, and the shortage of materials imposed on the Germans by the Allied blockade.

The Germans, however, introduced two of the more important developments of the war in the air. The first was the synchronizing gear designed by the Dutchman Anthony Fokker, which allowed a pilot to fire forward between the revolving blades of his propeller. 'The obvious thing to do was to make the propeller shoot the gun, instead of trying to shoot the bullets through the propeller,' as he put it. The device gave the Germans an unparalleled advantage, only lost when one of their planes was captured and the synchronizing gear copied by the British.

Of greater long-term importance was the

Horses and men masked against the new horror scientists had given soldiers – gas. Though this picture looks fanciful, horses were in fact given gas masks. It was for the discovery of gas that the war effort of German scientists was remembered in the post-war years.

idea of the cantilever-sectioned strutless wing, incorporated in the Junkers J1 in 1915, and the low-wing monoplane made entirely from metal – at first iron and steel but later duralumin – which evolved from it. The Zeppelin, which without the development of the aeroplane might have had a significant impact on the war, ceased to be alarming once the British realized that its hydrogen-filled gasbags were spectacularly vulnerable to explosive bullets.

The need to gain mastery of the air spurred on the combatants to make advances in four years which they might not otherwise have made in twenty. Air photography was developed. Wind tunnels were built. While a 100 hp engine would weigh about 400 lb at the beginning of the war, an engine developing three times the horsepower at the end of the war would weigh less than twice as much. Weight for weight, speed and rate of climb were increased. And while the heaviest all-up weight of a plane in 1914 was about two tons it had risen to about ten tons by 1918. In many essential ways the war had transformed flying from an art into a science.

This new power to strike at the enemy was only sparingly used. In the autumn of 1914 the British had destroyed the airship sheds at Friedrichschafen. In the summer of 1916 the Germans carried out a highly damaging raid which destroyed 8,000 tons of British ammunition at Audruicq. But because they had little faith in strategic bombing it was not until the last months of the war that Great Britain mounted a major attack on German targets. And the German air assault on London was not pressed home – first because of limitations imposed by the Kaiser; later, when the improved 'Elektron' bomb became available in quantity, because of political reasons invoked by the German high command. Both sides were less wise twenty-five years later.

Between 1914 and 1918 science and technology thus began to alter the shape of war on land, at sea, and in the air. The eternal infantryman remained, jokily resigned to the new methods being used to kill him. But now he had to think as well as to obey. The British still shipped more fodder than ammunition to the Western Front; but this was to be the last time. The mechanic from the factory was beginning to take over from the yeomanry; it was no longer 'bugles calling for them from sad shires' but a ghostly clatter from the production line. The chemists and the metallurgists, the aerodynamicists and the electricians were, for better or for worse, becoming more useful to a nation than field commanders.

Yet this transformation of the battle was less important than the transformation on the home front. At the start of the war Great Britain had found herself almost totally unequipped to fight it industrially. She imported from Germany the 30,000 tons of potash she needed annually, and was dependent on the same enemy for the tungsten needed by steel-makers, and even for zinc smelted from ore produced in the empire. She made barely a tenth of the dye-stuffs she needed. She was producing only 1,140 magnetos a year; the rest came from Germany. 'This country,' said F.G. Kellaway, parliamentary secretary to the ministry of munitions, speaking in 1919, 'very nearly lost the war owing to the fact that it was almost entirely dependent on Germany and Austria for scientific and optical glass.' In 1914 a considerable part of British army artillery used gun-sights exclusively made by Goerz of Berlin.

Industrial ground regained

To remove what had been a humiliating dependence on the enemy, a committee was set up in London in September 1914 'to consider and advise as to the best means of obtaining for the use of British industries sufficient supplies of chemical products, colours, and dye-stuffs of kinds hitherto largely imported from countries with which we are at present at war'. Less than a year later the government rushed through a 'scheme for the organization and development of Scientific and Industrial Research'; at the last moment of the eleventh hour, industry was kicked into the 20th century. The result was that by 1919 Great Britain had regained much of the industrial ground lost during the previous three decades. She faced the peace more able to compete with the rest of the world, less willing, at last, to live off her Victorian fat.

There were also the specific peace-time results of a war which, in the words of the president of the Royal Society of Canada, Dr A.S.Mackenzie, had 'accomplished for science what thirty years of peace might not have done'. Alcock and Brown made their historic transatlantic flight in a converted bomber. The first regular civilian flights between London and Paris were organized to carry passengers and mail to and from the Peace Conference. The giant Handley Page bombers which were to have blasted Berlin if the war had continued were redesigned to provide the backbone of the early post-war civilian services. The development of vehicles to help supply the armies locked together between the Channel ports and the Swiss frontier led to the 'motoring age' of the 1920's; and the improvement of the petrol engine, together with the work on tracked vehicles, established the farm tractor in post-war Great Britain. War-time food rationing pushed scientists into a study of nutritional problems and the value of vitamins, while the transformation of the primitive wireless transmitters of 1914 made post-war commercial broadcasting possible.

In Germany the impact of science and technology had different, though equally drastic, peace-time results. The ground work for the revolutionary German synthetics industry had been laid before the war when, by a single stroke of genius, Fritz Haber had solved the country's nitrate problem. Huge quantities were being imported from South America and used for the production of ammonia which was essential to both the fertilizer and the explosive industries. Haber discovered that ammonia could be made by combining hydrogen with nitrogen if the two gases were circulated under great pressure in the presence of a catalyst – the process for which he was later awarded the Nobel Prize. An additional bonus for Germany came from the new steels needed for the high-pressure chambers required.

Development of oil-from-coal processes, the synthesizing of artificial rubber, and the utilization of ingenious synthetic materials devised by the German chemical industry to replace those cut off by the blockade, all followed. As late as 26th September 1918 *Nature* reported an expert French industrial summary from which it was concluded that 'The new industries which have been created, and the great development of those already in existence, would, apparently, enable Germany to prosecute the war almost indefinitely'. Germany, as well as Great Britain, had been forced to take a great industrial leap forward.

So far as the scientists themselves were concerned they had taken the first steps outside the ivory enclosure formed by the Royal Society and the learned institutions. They still kept their eyes primarily fixed on what they regarded as pure science, a point well illustrated by Rutherford who in 1919 apologized for being late at a meeting of the successor to the Asdic Committee. He explained in a letter to Karl Compton, the US physicist then in charge, that he had been delayed by an item of pure research. He appeared to have done something important. 'If this is true,' he wrote, 'it is a fact of far greater importance than the war.' It seemed that he had disintegrated the nucleus of the atom.

Yet it was not by such apparently pure and unapplicable work that the scientists were to be remembered during the years that followed the war. Just as they were to be thought of, after the Second World War, as the men who made the bomb, so did the words 'poison gas' stick to the scientists after the First. All the rest, which helped to make the 1920's and the 1930's, was, for the most part, forgotten.

Imperial War Museum

Medicine, 1914-18 / Christopher Spry

Medicine at War

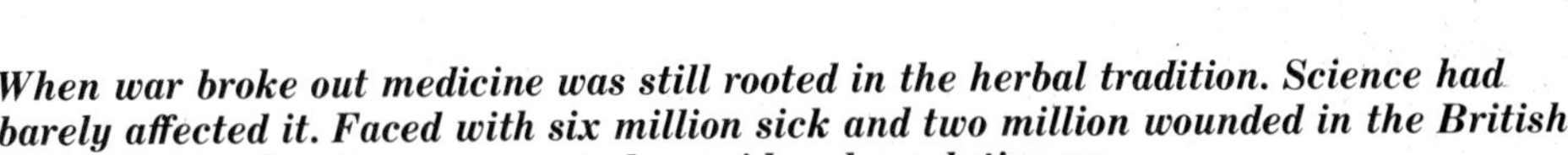

When war broke out medicine was still rooted in the herbal tradition. Science had barely affected it. Faced with six million sick and two million wounded in the British empire alone the changes were to be rapid and revolutionary

Medicine had changed little between 1900 and 1914. In Great Britain state control of medicine had just begun with the introduction of compulsory National Health Insurance for men earning less than £2 a week. By contrast there had been a compulsory medical insurance scheme in Germany since the previous century. Those in the upper income groups were well looked after in private practices or in private nursing homes. Many poorer patients could afford only occasional visits to doctors, and their in-patient treatment was in local hospitals, many of which still retained the traditions of charity institutions. Science had hardly touched medicine. For example, X-rays were only used occasionally, there were no antibiotics, and treatment was still in the herbal tradition. Blood transfusions were a novelty. There were no 'specialists' but well-known doctors were called in as 'consultants' and were expected to cover the whole spectrum of disease. When the war broke out provision for the wounded was very inadequate. There were only 18,000 hospital beds in the whole of the British empire for a war which left six million sick, and two million wounded in the British empire. Problems occurred frequently, and mistakes, such as the failure to send any dentists with the British Expeditionary Force to France in 1914, were numerous. In Great Britain the response from the medical profession was such that no compulsory enlistment of doctors was needed until 1916, and women provided remarkably effective voluntary medical assistance. At the end of the war there were over 144,000 British Medical Service personnel with 637,000 hospital beds.

High velocity bullets and shrapnel produced severe wounds. While the soldiers lay in French fields, their wounds often became infected with gas-gangrene and tetanus. Only after two years did it become apparent that the best treatment was to remove casualties rapidly to hospital, and to cut out all the dead tissue. X-rays of bones became commonplace. Bone surgery developed as a highly skilled branch of surgery, and this led to the foundation of the British Orthopaedic Society in 1918. Despite steel helmets, ten per cent of all injuries were to the head. Surgery of the eye, face, ear, nose, and throat, and brain and plastic surgery developed rapidly under war stimulus and many surgeons who gained the necessary knowledge and experience of this surgery later set up as 'specialists'. Abdominal surgery advanced little. Infections killed over half those who had been shot in the stomach. Many lives might have been saved if a blood transfusion service had been provided, but, surprisingly, none appeared.

As in previous wars, diseases produced more casualties than the enemy. In the South African war there were fifteen non-battle casualties per wounded man. In the First World War the number of non-battle casualties was reduced to two sick for each wounded man mainly as the result of control of the water-borne diseases, cholera, typhoid, and dysentery, which were prevented by chlorination of drinking water. Typhoid immunization was also begun at the same time. Insect-borne diseases remained important on fronts in the Mediterranean and tropics. There were a million deaths in the Balkans from typhus which is spread by the louse, and in German East Africa over half the forces were constantly prostrate with malaria. This contrasts markedly with conditions in the Second World War following the discovery of DDT.

The public in Great Britain was shocked to discover that one soldier in twenty had to be admitted to hospital for treatment of venereal diseases. However, this rate was no greater than the incidence in the general population before the war, and half of the cases were infected before they went abroad. Lord Kitchener had written a leaflet which was given to all British troops going abroad advocating continence, but once in France the armies frequented 'maisons de tolérance' (officially recognized brothels), and in Le Havre 171,000 men are known to have visited the houses in one street in a year. By 1918 strong public feeling in Great Britain led to their closure. The treatment of venereal diseases was primitive, and hepatitis was often transmitted when unsterile needles were used. A later consequence was the introduction of venereal disease eradication programmes in the USA.

The war presented many new medical problems. Among the most distressing were psychiatric disorders. Strain, stress, and exhaustion at the front produced 'shell shock'. Soldiers suffering from this had often been under heavy bombardment in

Over twenty-one million men were wounded during the First World War. Doctors needed not only their old skills but turned to science to provide new ones to aid a mutilated generation. ***Far left:*** *A captured German doctor dresses the wound of a British Tommy.* ***Left:*** *Equipped to live in a post-war world – a mutilated Austrian fitted out with artificial lower legs, and forearms*

Will Dyson/Odhams Press Ltd.

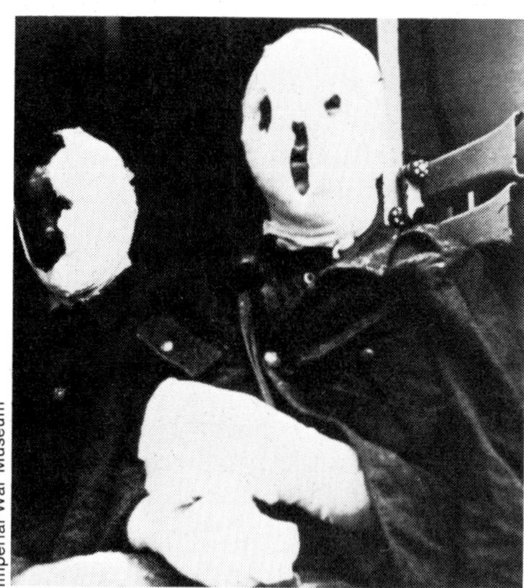

Imperial War Museum

Above left: *British cartoon: 'The Secret Invader'–disease, which in war-time killed more men than died in battle. In the First World War cholera and water-borne diseases were partly controlled.* ***Above right:*** *Wounded being taken to hospital by motor ambulance*

Ullstein

Above: *German victims of the war at a castle, turned into a hospital, doing physical exercises designed to teach them how to walk again.* ***Below:*** *Wounded from a special hospital for French colonial soldiers being decorated for their 'conspicuous gallantry' under fire*

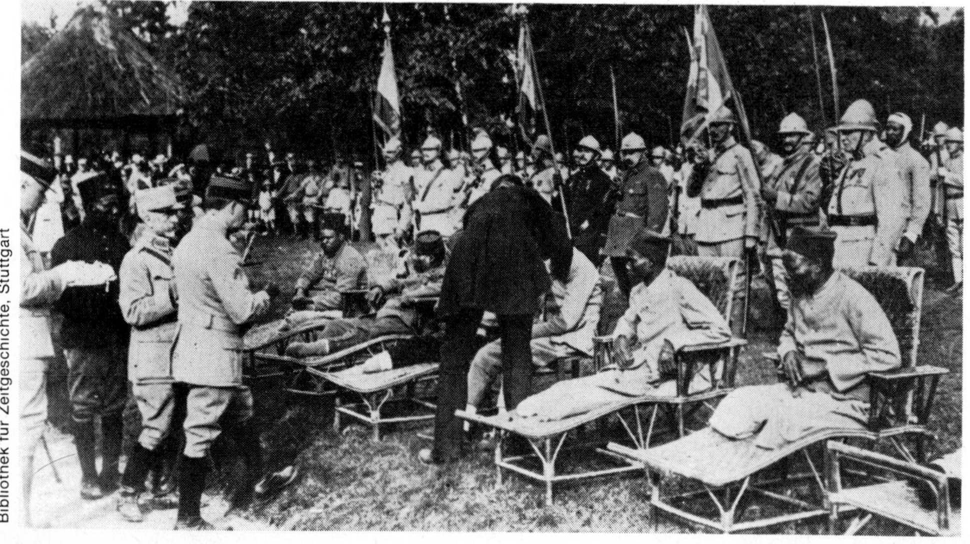

Bibliothek für Zeitgeschichte, Stuttgart

the trenches, but only a fifth had actually been involved in explosions. At the end of the first year of the war, ten per cent of the officers and five per cent of the soldiers admitted to a hospital in Boulogne were sent back to Great Britain suffering from 'shell shock'. Psychiatrists were called in to help the French and British armies who had the most cases and by 1917 ninety-one per cent of these patients returned to duty. The success of their treatment resulted not only in the gradual disappearance of 'shell shock' as an important cause of invalidism, but also achieved general recognition for psychiatry. The relationship between desertion at the front and the effects of 'shell shock' caused difficulties. Desertion was punished by shooting, but in fact eighty-nine per cent of those who were sentenced to death were diagnosed as suffering from 'shell shock', and joined others in special hospitals. In 1921 there were 65,000 men still receiving pensions for the effects of 'shell shock'. Another new disease, 'trench fever', occurred. It had many features in common with severe influenza. Sir David Bruce carried out experiments on volunteers in a hospital in Hampstead, London and found there was a factor in louse excreta which caused the disease.

Gas warfare suddenly added a total of 185,000 casualties to the heavy load in the hospitals. Nine thousand died from the effects of gas. The gases either burned the skin, or affected the lungs and air passages about an hour after they had been inhaled. Pneumonia and fluid in the lungs produced death or permanent destruction of lung tissue. Chemical warfare stimulated an enormous amount of research which added to knowledge in biochemistry and pharmacology. Several new drugs were discovered including emetine bismuth iodide which is one of the most powerful forms of treatment for amoebic dysentery. The introduction of flying stimulated studies into the functions of the heart and lungs. Liquid oxygen was produced and became available for use in anaesthetics.

In the previous century Germany had been the major contributor to medicine and surgery, but this was destroyed by the war. The disillusion of defeat coupled with the financial attraction of private practice distracted doctors and prevented the recovery of German medicine, and many scientists emigrated. In Great Britain 'specialists' gave a new impetus to medicine while in the USA group medical practices were set up because of the success of units of this kind in the war. Above all, the war forced new problems on medicine which could only be solved by scientific methods, and this produced the fusion of science and medicine which transformed life in the next fifty years.

Chapter 28

Introduction by J.M.Roberts

It is still very hard to arrive at a satisfying judgement about the historical importance of the Bolshevik revolution. But of its immense symbolic and mythical importance there can be no doubt. In many countries other than the USSR it is an inspiration to millions and is seen as an example. To the Russians themselves, most of whom have been born since 1917, it is the fountainhead from which have flowed the benefits of Soviet society. An entire chapter is devoted to this major theme.

Soviet historians have given much time to the revolution. We have welcomed the opportunity of making their views available in Y.N.Gorodetsky's article on **The Bolshevik Revolution**. This article, like others by Soviet historians in subsequent chapters, is written from the standpoint of a tradition of historiography unfamiliar to many of our readers. It is both Russian and Marxist. Many of the assumptions taken for granted by Soviet historians will also be unfamiliar and it is worthwhile to draw attention here to some of these.

First of all, there is the basic Marxist assumption that the decisive factors at work in any historical situation are the material conditions in which men have to act. These conditions shape the class conflict which is the essential dynamo of historic change. Those who choose the 'right' side in this conflict – that is, the side whose eventual victory is predetermined by the material evolution of society – are progressive and may be praised; those who choose the other side are bound to lose and must be condemned. This framework gives a very clear and simple outline to many historical episodes in Soviet eyes. Western historians are usually more reluctant to come down decisively and unambiguously in favour of one 'true' explanation of what happened than are their Soviet colleagues.

Russian assumptions are also often rooted in what is believed to be experience – for instance, the distrust of the outside world which goes back to the period of intervention in Soviet affairs by outside powers after the revolution – as well as in Marxist theory. This does not always fit very logically into Marxist categories: if, after all, capitalist countries are bound to strive to overthrow a socialist state, there is not much point in condemning them morally for doing so. Nevertheless, past antagonisms do much to condition Soviet thinking today. We have two articles which illustrate this. William V.Wallace tells the extraordinary story of **The Czechoslovak Legion** and the complications it provoked. Finally, in **The Treaty of Brest Litovsk** Jaroslav Valenta explains the full rigour of the peace imposed on Russia by the victorious Germans, an example, to some Russian eyes, of the treatment they might expect from the countries of the West.

Ullstein

Bolshevik banner, 'Workers of the World Unite', carried by Russian demonstrators

Imperial War Museum

Skoropadsky, Hetman of the Ukraine, with Hindenburg (left) and Ludendorff (right)

VHU, Praha

Czech Legion, promised safe passage to Vladivostok, hands over arms to Red Army

Russia: internal affairs

1917 September: Bolsheviks prevent a *putsch* by Kornilov. They gain power in Moscow and Petrograd Soviets. The peasants start to rise against the landlords.
October: discontent spreads among soldiers, soviets, and peasant organizations. The government's attempt to take military action fails.
23rd October: Bolshevik Central Committee passes a resolution saying the time is ripe for an armed uprising.
29th October: the Bolshevik Party appoints a Military-Revolutionary Centre to supervise the Soviet's Military-Revolutionary Committee.
1st November: the Provisional Government tries to remove units from the Petrograd garrison. The Military-Revolutionary Committee appoints commissars to units of Petrograd garrison.
6th November: Central Committee of Bolsheviks organizes headquarters in Peter and Paul Fortress, Petrograd. Garrison and Red Guards seize strategic points. Lenin takes command.
7th November: Lenin announces the transfer of power to the Military-Revolutionary Committee and the victory of the socialist revolution.
The second All-Russian Congress of Soviets meets in the Smolny Institute. The *Aurora* fires a shot, the signal for the seizure of the Provisional Government in the Winter Palace.
8th November: Lenin makes the Decree on Peace – an appeal for a just peace without annexations and indemnities – and the Decree on Land (saying that all land is the property of the whole people).
A Bolshevik government is formed.

Russia: external affairs

1917 17th December: Russia and Germany agree to a ceasefire and start negotiations for a peace treaty in Brest Litovsk.
1918 7th January: Trotsky goes to Brest Litovsk.
10th February: the Germans deliver an ultimatum: peace or war. Trotsky answers, neither peace nor war. He leaves Brest Litovsk.
9th February: Germans sign separate peace with the Central Council of the Ukraine in exchange for promises of grain.
18th February: the Germans reopen hostilities.
24th February: the Soviet government decides to accept German peace ultimatum.
25th February: Germans take Pskov, and on 4th March they take Narva.
3rd March: the Russians sign the Treaty of Brest Litovsk, giving up Poland, Lithuania, Courland, Riga, part of Belorussia, and parts of Transcaucasia.
March: German troops invade the central Russian districts of Voronezh and Kursk, and in May the Crimea.
27th August: Soviet Russia signs a protocol surrendering part of her gold reserve.
November: Soviet government denounces the Treaty of Brest Litovsk.

The Czechoslovak Legion

1917 July: permission is given to establish the Czechoslovak Legion on Russian territory.
1918 February: Masaryk gains Bolshevik permission for the Legion to travel east to Vladivostok, to be brought to France, on condition that it gives up its Russian arms.
March: the Legion agrees to move east from Penza with only a very few arms.
April: the first contingent reaches Vladivostok.
14th May: Czechoslovaks quarrel with local soviet and take over Chelyabinsk. Trotsky orders all soviets to disarm the Legion and arrests two members of the Czechoslovak National Council in Moscow.
20th May: the Czechoslovaks summon National Congress to Chelyabinsk and refuse to disarm without a guarantee of unimpeded departure.
25th May: Trotsky orders that every armed Czechoslovak be shot on sight.
By end of June the Legion seizes the Trans-Siberian Railway from Penza to Vladivostok.
In the summer some join in an anti-Bolshevik state set up in the Samara region.
August: British, Japanese, and American forces land at Vladivostok to secure the Legion's exit.
November: the war ends. The Legion stays in Russia because there is no Allied shipping to evacuate it.
1920 January: the Czechoslovaks supporting the reactionary Kolchak hand him to the Communist government.
February: the Legion is allowed to return home.
(All Russian dates are given in the new-western-style. According to this calendar the revolutions popularly referred to as the February and October Revolutions took place respectively in March and November.)

'Ten days that shook the world'

The repercussions of the events in Petrograd in October and November 1917 are still with us today. These are eyewitness accounts of men and women who lived through those momentous days

The Provisional Government which had ruled Russia since the revolution of March 1917 was proving no more capable of controlling the economy nor of improving the military situation than the Tsarist government had been (p. 674). Hampered by the Petrograd Soviet for all the eight months of its existence the Provisional Government was weakened further by the revolt of General Kornilov in September. A socialist coalition under Kerensky did not give a war-weary people the peace it craved nor the economic and agricultural reforms which the Bolsheviks offered.

In May Lenin had won acceptance at the party conference for his 'April Theses' calling for non-co-operation with the Provisional Government, for peace, and for the transference of power from the bourgeois Provisional Government to the soviets once they were dominated by the proletarian Bolsheviks. These soviets (councils) of workers' and soldiers' deputies had sprung up all over the country after the February Revolution (a few had existed for a short time in 1905). Their members were elected on the factory-floor and in the barracks, and a few were formed in the countryside. They enjoyed more popular support than the Provisional Government.

By September the Bolsheviks had secured majorities on the Petrograd and Moscow Soviets, although Mensheviks and Socialist Revolutionaries still dominated the Central Executive Committee of the All-Russian Congress of Soviets which had first met and elected its governing body in June. Lenin now considered that conditions were ripe for the socialist revolution. 'All power to the soviets' became the slogan of the day.

On 23rd October at a meeting of the Central Committee of the Bolshevik Party a decision was taken to prepare for an armed insurrection. A political bureau (Politburo) was formed to carry out the decision. Two days later the Petrograd Soviet created a Military-Revolutionary Committee under the chairmanship of Trotsky, and it was this body rather than the party Politburo which prepared for and executed the subsequent coup. On 3rd November the troops of the Petrograd garrison acknowledged the Petrograd Soviet as sole power, and on 5th the Peter and Paul Fortress, containing an arsenal of 100,000 rifles, went over to the soviet. On the night of 6th-7th November the Military-Revolutionary Committee at the Smolny Institute gave the go-ahead.

'The main operation began at two o'clock in the morning. Small military parties, usually with a nucleus of armed workers or sailors under the leadership of commissars, occupied simultaneously, or in regular order, the railroad stations, the lighting plant, the munition and food stores, the waterworks, Dvortsovy Bridge, the Telephone Exchange, the State Bank, the big printing plants. The Telegraph Station and the Post Office were completely taken over. Reliable guards were placed everywhere.'
Trotsky, 'History of the Russian Revolution'.

'Towards four in the morning I met Zorin in the outer hall, a rifle slung from his shoulder.

'"We're moving!" said he calmly, but with satisfaction. "We pinched the Assistant Minister of Justice and the Minister of Religions. They're down cellar now. One regiment is on the march to capture the Telephone Exchange, another the Telegraph Agency, another the State Bank. The Red Guard is out. . . ."

'On the steps of Smolny, in the chill dark, we first saw the Red Guards – a huddled group of boys in workmen's clothes, carrying guns with bayonets, talking nervously together.

'Far over the still roofs westward came the sound of scattered rifle fire, where the yunkers [*officer cadets*] were trying to open the bridges over the Neva, to prevent the factory workers and soldiers of the Viborg quarter from joining the Soviet forces in the centre of the city; and the Kronstadt sailors were closing them.

'Behind us great Smolny, bright with lights, hummed like a gigantic hive. . . .'
John Reed, 'Ten Days That Shook the World'.

'Wednesday, 7 November, I rose very late. The noon cannon boomed from Peter-Paul as I went down the Nevsky. It was a raw, chill day. In front of the State Bank some soldiers with fixed bayonets were standing at the closed gates.

'"What side do you belong to?" I asked. "The Government?"

'"No more government," one answered with a grin. "*Slava Bogu!* Glory to God!"

'The street cars were running on the Nevsky, men, women, and small boys hanging on every projection. Shops were open, and there seemed even less uneasiness among the street crowds than there had been the day before. A whole crop of new appeals against insurrection had blossomed out on the walls during the night – to the peasants, to the soldiers at the front, to the workmen of Petrograd.'
John Reed

Although the revolution was carried out in the name of the soviets, Lenin viewed the victory as

Below: *Delegates to the Congress of Soviets examine documents outside the Smolny Institute*
Bottom: *Heroes-to-be of the new Russia – Red Guards warm themselves at a street corner*

S.C.R. Photo Library

S.C.R. Photo Library

one of his party and its militant arm, the Red Guard. Trotsky, however, had insisted that the seizure of power should coincide with the forthcoming Congress of Soviets, and when, in the late evening of 7th November, the Second All-Russian Congress of Soviets went into session it set the seal of legality on the Bolshevik revolution.

'First comes the election of the governing body of the congress (the presidium). The Bolsheviks get 14 members. All other parties get 11. The old governing body steps down and the Bolshevik leaders, recently the outcasts and outlaws of Russia, take their places. . . .

'Then suddenly out of the night, a rumbling shock brings the delegates to their feet, wondering. It is the boom of cannon, the cruiser *Aurora* firing over the Winter Palace.'

Albert Rhys Williams, 'Through the Russian Revolution'.

The attack on the Winter Palace had begun. Defended by a handful of cadets and by a women's battalion, the ministers of the Provisional Government huddled in a back-room hoping that their prime minister, Kerensky, would return with loyal troops to crush the rebellion before the palace fell to the insurrectionary mob. The Winter Palace fell to the Bolsheviks during the night.

'At the Red Arch soldiers informed us that the Winter Palace had just surrendered. We ran across the Square after the Bolshevik troops. . . . Only a small entrance was open and we poured through the narrow door.

'Inside the Junkers were being given their liberty. . . . The Ministers of the Provisional Government . . . were sent to Peter and Paul Fortress. We sat on a long bench by the door and watched them going out.

'Tereschenko impressed me more than the others. He looked so ridiculous and out of place; he was so well groomed and so outraged. . . .

'Everyone leaving the palace was searched, no matter on what side he was. There were priceless treasures all about and it was a great temptation to pick up souvenirs. . . .

'A young Bolshevik lieutenant stood by the only unlocked door, and in front of him was a great table. Two soldiers did the searching. The lieutenant delivered a sort of sermon while this was going on. I wrote down part of his speech:

'"Comrades, this is the people's palace. This is our palace. Do not steal from the people. . . . Do not disgrace the people. . . ."'

Louise Bryant, 'Six Red Months in Russia'.

'Thursday, 8th November. Day broke on a city in the wildest excitement and confusion, a whole nation heaving up in long hissing swells of storm. Superficially all was quiet; hundreds of thousands of people retired at a prudent hour, got up early and went to work. In Petrograd the street-cars were running, the stores and restaurants open, theatres going, an exhibition of paintings advertised. . . . All the complex routine of common life – humdrum even in war-time – proceeded as usual. . . .

'The air was full of rumours about Kerensky, who was said to have raised the front, and to be leading a great army against the capital.'

John Reed

The British ambassador wrote in his diary:

'I walked out this afternoon to see the damage that had been done to the Winter Palace by the prolonged bombardment of the previous evening.

'In the evening two officer instructors of the women's battalion came to my wife and beseeched her to try and save the women-defenders of the Winter Palace, who, after they had surrendered, had been sent to one of the barracks, where they were being most brutally treated by the soldiers. General Knox at once drove to the Bolshevik headquarters at the Smolny Institute. His demands for their immediate release were at first refused on the ground that they had resisted desperately, fighting to the last with bombs and revolvers. Thanks, however, to his firmness and persistency, the order for their release was eventually signed, and the women were saved from the fate that would have inevitably befallen them had they spent the night at the barracks.'

Sir George Buchanan, 'My Mission to Russia'.

In the evening the second session of the Congress of Soviets met. Bolsheviks moved forward to fulfil their promises.

'It was just 8.40 when a thundering wave of cheers announced the entrance of the presidium, with Lenin – great Lenin – among them. A short, stocky figure, with a big head set down on his shoulders, bald and bulging. Little eyes, a snubbish nose, wide generous mouth, and heavy chin; clean-shaven now but already beginning to bristle with the well-known beard of his past and future. Dressed in shabby clothes, his trousers much too long for him. Unimpressive, to be the idol of a mob, loved and revered as perhaps few leaders in history have been. A strange popular leader – a leader purely by virtue of intellect; colourless, humourless, uncompromising and detached, without picturesque idiosyncrasies – but with the power of explaining profound ideas in simple terms, of analysing a concrete situation. And combined with shrewdness, the greatest intellectual audacity.'

John Reed

Below: *In the streets of Petrograd soldiers discuss the latest rumours. In the early days of November 1917, days of troubled uncertainty, Russia's capital hummed with conflicting revolutionary theories*

S.C.R. Photo Library

Lenin read the draft of an appeal by the Soviet government to all the nations at war, calling for immediate negotiations for a just and democratic peace.

'It was exactly 10.35 when Kameniev asked all in favour of the proclamation to hold up their cards. One delegate dared to raise his hand against, but the sudden outburst around him brought it swiftly down. . . . Unanimous.

'Suddenly, by common impulse, we found ourselves on our feet, mumbling together into the smooth lifting unison of the *Internationale*. A grizzled old soldier was sobbing like a child. . . . "The war is ended! The war is ended!" said a young workman near me, his face shining. And when it was over, as we stood there in a kind of awkward hush, someone in the back of the room shouted, "Comrades, let us remember those who have died for liberty!" So we began to sing the Funeral March, that slow, melancholy, and yet triumphant chant, so Russian and so moving.'

John Reed

Lenin then read his Decree on Land, abolishing all property in land and forbidding hired labour. Without discussion or amendment the decree was passed. The congress then approved the constitution of a provisional workers' and peasants' government, the Council of People's Commissars.

The Bolsheviks controlled Petrograd but the city was rife with rumours about Kerensky—indeed the middle class was eagerly awaiting the counter-revolution.

'During the whole of the 28th [*10th November*] very disquieting news of Kerensky's offensive continued to be received. . . .

'Smolny took feverish action. From morning till night troops, mostly Red Army men, were being moved to the front. . . . Masses of workers were sent outside the town to dig trenches. Petersburg was festooned with barbed-wire entanglements. . . .

'On the 30th [*12th*] it was decided to finish with Kerensky at one blow. The Kronstadt and Helsingfors sailors' detachments were moved *en bloc* to the front. Trotsky himself went too; from now on he was invariably to be present at the most critical points all over the country. . . . And by the end of that night Trotsky was already reporting to Petersburg from Pulkov: "KERENSKY IS IN RETREAT—we are advancing." . . .

'The liquidation of Kerensky consummated the October Revolution. Moscow was still an arena of bitter struggle, and the enemies of the Bolsheviks were still far from laying down their arms. Now, however, there was in Smolny a unified and indivisible Government of the Republic, and its armed enemies had become rebels and nothing more.

'The revolution that had placed a proletarian party at the head of a first-class world Power was accomplished. A new chapter had opened in the working-class movement of the world and in the history of the Russian State.'

N.N.Sukhanov 'The Russian Revolution, 1917'.

Extracts reprinted by kind permission of: Margaret Bonnet; Lawrence & Wishart and the Communist Party of Great Britain; International Publishers, New York; Liveright Publishing Corporation; Doubleday & Co. Inc.; Cassell; and Oxford University Press.

The New Rulers of Russia
—profiles of ten of Lenin's followers

BUKHARIN—
executed, 1938
Bukharin, born in 1888, was the youngest of the leaders of the revolution. He joined the Bolshevik wing of the Russian Social Democratic Workers' Party in 1906. He was a member of the party's Central Committee from 1917. He was a leading theoretician in the party and openly opposed any policy he considered a deviation from Marxism. Thus as leader of the 'Left Communists' in 1918 he led the opposition to the Treaty of Brest Litovsk, and advocated the immediate control by the workers of industry. However, after the Civil War he swung to the right of the party and ardently supported Lenin's New Economic Policy (NEP), which gave the peasants freedom in cultivating the land and in marketing their crops. From 1919 to 1929 he was a member of the Politburo and editor of *Pravda*, the party organ. Bukharin supported Stalin in the latter's struggle for power with Trotsky, Zinovyev, and Kamenev, and succeeded Zinovyev as president of the Communist International in 1926. When Stalin rejected NEP, Bukharin joined Rykov and Tomsky in the Right Opposition to the collectivization of the peasantry. He was dismissed from his party and government posts in 1929. He was partially rehabilitated in 1932 but was arrested in 1937. At his trial in 1938 he 'admitted' to counter-revolutionary activities and was executed.

DZERZHINSKY—
death from natural causes, 1926
Dzerzhinsky, born in 1877, was of aristocratic Polish descent. He joined the Lithuanian Social Democratic Party in 1895. He spent fifteen of the next twenty-two years in Siberia. Freed by the February Revolution, he became a member of the Central Committee of the Bolshevik Party and of the Military Revolutionary Committee of the Petrograd Soviet. In December 1917 he was called on by Lenin to organize the Cheka, the political police of the new regime, and, as commissar for internal affairs in 1922, became head of the Cheka's successor, the GPU. His fanaticism in the cause of communism was reflected in the brutality of his methods. He became chairman of the Council of National Economy in 1924. He died of a heart attack in 1926 after a violent speech against Zinovyev at a meeting of the Central Committee.

KAMENEV—
executed, 1936
Kamenev was born in 1883, the son of a Jewish railway engineer. He joined the Russian Social Democratic Workers' Party in 1901. He returned from Siberia to Petrograd with Stalin after the February Revolution and led the opposition within the party to Lenin's call to revolution. In spite of this he was appointed to the seven-man Politburo, formed by the party to carry out the *coup*. Opposing Lenin's refusal to form a socialist coalition, Kamenev resigned from the Central Committee of the party and from the presidency of the Central Executive Committee of the Soviets in November 1917.

He was re-elected to the Central Committee and to the Politburo in 1919. He was party boss in Moscow and chairman of the Moscow Soviet, and became a member of the *troika* which took over during Lenin's last illness. Kamenev was a man of sincere convictions untainted by personal ambition, but his moderation and doubt of his own judgement caused him to seek a leader. Thus he followed the less intelligent but more unscrupulous Zinovyev to their mutual destruction. He was expelled from the party in 1927, and in 1936 was tried for plotting acts of terrorism against the party leadership and was shot.

RADEK—
disappeared after 1937
Radek was born in Galicia in 1885. From 1906 to 1913 he wrote for the social democratic press in Poland and Germany. He met Lenin in Switzerland during the First World War. In 1917 he went to Stockholm and became the Bolsheviks' link with the outside world. In 1918 he travelled secretly to Germany to organize the German Communist

Party. He returned to Russia in 1920 and became the foremost Soviet journalist. He was a leading member of the Comintern, chiefly responsible for central Europe, and was blamed for the failure of the communist revolution in Germany in 1923. He was relieved of his posts and expelled from the party in 1927. Re-admitted to the party in 1930 he became foreign editor of *Pravda*. In 1937 he was tried for 'Trotskyist' activities and was sentenced to ten years' imprisonment. It is not known for certain how he died.

RYKOV–
executed, 1938
Rykov, the son of a peasant, was first arrested in 1900 for organizing a 1st May demonstration. He visited Lenin in Geneva in 1902 and became a Bolshevik the next year. After the revolution in February 1917 he returned from exile

in Siberia and became a member of the Central Committee of the Bolshevik Party. He was commissar for internal affairs in 1917, chairman of the Council of National Economy *(Sovnarkhoz)* in 1918, member of the Politburo from 1923 to 1929, and chairman of the Council of People's Commissars *(Sovnarkom)*–prime minister–after the death of Lenin in 1924.

Opposing collectivization he joined Bukharin and Tomsky in the Right Opposition to Stalin in 1928. He was replaced as chairman of *Sovnarkom* by Molotov in 1930. In 1937 he was expelled from the party and arrested. In 1938 he was tried and executed with Bukharin.

STALIN–
death from natural causes, 1953
Stalin was born in 1879 in Georgia, the son of a cobbler. Editor of *Pravda* in 1913, he was arrested and sent to Siberia. Returning from exile after the February Revolution, he supported Lenin's call for a proletarian revolution and was admitted to the party's Central Committee and Politburo. In 1922 Stalin was appointed general secretary of the party and he built the secretariat into a powerful servant to his ambitions, as yet unnoticed. He first destroyed the left-wing leaders of the party and then turned on the leaders of the right.

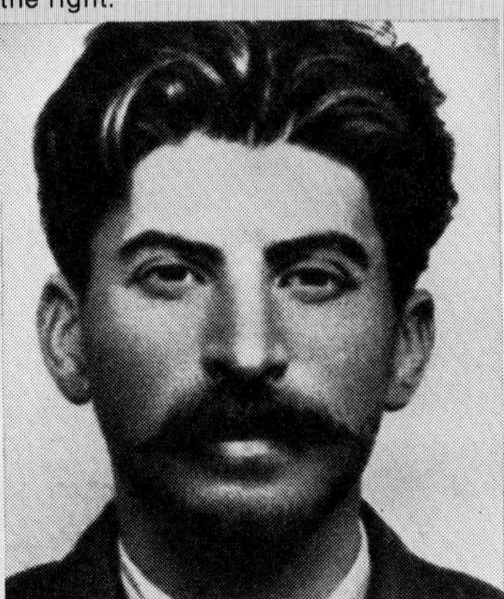

Stalin was the least Europeanized of the leaders of the revolution and the most nationalist in outlook. He was a practical politician rather than a theorist, unlike his rivals, and the party in the 1920's was beginning to reject the traditional internationalism and intellectualism of the revolution. He introduced the first of his five-year plans in 1929 and set about the rapid industrialization of Russia and the collectivization of the peasantry. Stalin's dictatorship utterly transformed the Soviet economy, but at the cost of millions of lives. It was necessarily accompanied by a reign of terror which eliminated all possible opposition to him. However, it was the basic strength of Soviet industry which saved the USSR in 1941. After the purges of the 'thirties he was unchallenged within the party and absolute ruler of the USSR.

SVERDLOV–
death from natural causes, 1919
Sverdlov was born in 1885, the son of a Jewish artisan. He joined the Russian Social Democratic Workers' Party in 1900, and the Bolshevik wing of that party in 1903. He was arrested five

times. Freed by the February Revolution from exile in Siberia, he became a member of the Central Committee in August 1917, and was a constant supporter of Lenin's policies. As secretary of the Central Committee of the Bolshevik Party and president of the Central Executive Committee of the Soviets he ensured party control over the state apparatus. But after his death in 1919 it was decided to separate the two organs of power and to build up official party control over the state administration.

TOMSKY–
suicide, 1936
Tomsky was born in 1880 and began working in a factory at the age of twelve. In 1905 he was the Bolshevik chairman of the Reval (Tallinn) Soviet. He escaped from arrest in 1906 and attended party congresses abroad. He took part in the July demonstrations in Petrograd in 1917 and in the October Revolution in Moscow. He became a member of the Central Committee in 1919 and of the Politburo in 1922. From 1917 to 1929 he was chairman of the Central Trade-Union Council. Allied with Bukharin and Rykov in the Right Opposition to Stalin, he was dismissed from his posts in 1929. He shot himself following accusations of complicity in the treason of Zinovyev and Kamenev.

TROTSKY–
assassinated, 1940
Trotsky was born in 1879, the son of a Jewish farmer. He became a Marxist in 1897. In 1902 he escaped from Siberia and went abroad. He took part in the 1905 Revolution and was vice-chairman of the short-lived St Petersburg Soviet. After another escape from imprisonment he again left Russia. When he

returned to Russia in 1917 he joined the Bolshevik Party. As chairman of the Petrograd Soviet and the Military Revolutionary Committee, he organized and directed the successful seizure of power by the Bolsheviks in November 1917. He was commissar for foreign affairs in the new Soviet government and headed the Russian delegation to Brest Litovsk. As commissar for war from 1918 to 1925 he crushed the Kronstadt Rising with his customary severity, and led the Red Army through the Civil War. The struggle for power with Stalin, foreseen by Lenin, began during the leader's last illness in 1923. Trotsky was more intelligent than Stalin, was a brilliant revolutionary theoretician, had been favoured by Lenin as his successor, and had played an outstanding role in the revolution and in the Civil War. Stalin used every means to discredit Trotsky and destroy him politically. The power that Stalin had built up within the party prevailed and Trotsky was expelled from the party in 1927. He was exiled from the Soviet Union in 1929. A thorn in the side of Stalin's dictatorship, he was assassinated by an agent of Stalin in Mexico in 1940.

ZINOVYEV–
executed, 1936
Zinovyev was born in 1883 of a Jewish *petit-bourgeois* family. He became Lenin's closest associate in exile. He was a member of the Politburo in October 1917, despite his opposition to the armed insurrection planned by the Bolsheviks. In 1919 he was appointed president of the Communist International, which was founded to promote

worldwide communist revolution. He was party boss in Petrograd and chairman of the Petrograd Soviet.

With Kamenev and Stalin he was a member of the *troika* (triumvirate) which came into being following Lenin's illness. Making no secret of his ambition to succeed Lenin, Zinovyev emerged as its leading member. Although he was a powerful orator and a hard worker, he incurred the hostility of the party by his vanity and his intellectual shallowness and lack of conviction. He led the Left Opposition to Stalin at the Fourteenth Party Conference in April 1925, and joined Trotsky a year later in a last bid for political survival. He was removed from his posts in the government and was expelled from the party in November 1927. In 1936 he was accused of conspiracy at the first of the Moscow trials and was executed.

Russia, October-December 1917 / Y.N.Gorodetsky

The Bolshevik Revolution

Revolutionary ideas had broken the structure of Russian society. In the country land-hungry peasants were attacking their landlords. The soldiers at the front refused to fight. The workers went on strike. But their first revolution had not given Russia's people what they wanted – land and peace. And this Lenin's Bolsheviks promised them

'October' – sculpture by P.A.Balandin, of Lenin, the hero of the Bolshevik ('October') Revolution, with the workers turned soldiers who helped him into power in Russia

The overthrow of the autocratic Tsarist regime in March (February by the Julian Calender) 1917 was a great victory for the peoples of Russia. In alliance with the army, the working class of Russia fought for and won political freedom. The whole country was covered by a network of 'soviets' (councils) and of committees of soldiers and peasants. Power in the country was divided, but as early as June the Provisional Government had established a dictatorship with the help of the Mensheviks and Socialist Revolutionaries (SRs). Not a single one of the social aims of the revolution had been met. Neither the government of Prince Lvov nor Kerensky's government which followed it gave land to the peasants or rid them of their servitude to the landowners. Workers in the mills and factories continued to be cruelly exploited, their standard of living declined sharply, their wages were cut, and there was hunger in the towns. A country which had been exhausted by the First World War was now thirsting for peace, yet the Provisional Government's policy was to continue the war.

Russia was torn by violent contradictions. The progress of agriculture was held back by the fact that enormous areas remained in the hands of the landowners. At the same time modern industry was developing in the country, with a high level of concentration of production and manpower. The urban working class which amounted to about 20,000,000 of the country's population of over 150,000,000, was organized into trade unions and had learned a great deal about political struggle in the first Russian revolution of 1905 (p. 78).

The Bolshevik Party

The Bolshevik Party, led by Vladimir Ilyich Lenin, directed the struggle of the working class towards the acquisition of power, the solution of the land question, bringing the war to an end, establishing workers' control over production, and nationalizing banks and the more important branches of industry. But this struggle on the part of the workers and peasants came up against bitter resistance from representatives of the ruling classes.

In September 1917 the party of the Russian bourgeoisie, the Constitutional Democrats (Kadets), and the reactionary military circles led by General Kornilov tried to carry out a counter-revolutionary *putsch* and to set up a military dictatorship (p. 698). This plot evoked general opposition among the people and rallied the revolutionary forces to the Bolshevik Party. At the beginning of September the Petrograd and Moscow soviets of workers' and peasants' deputies passed resolutions proposed by the Bolsheviks. The Moscow Soviet was led by one of the oldest members of the Bolshevik Party, V.P.Nogin, while L.D.Trotsky, who had only recently joined the Party, was elected chairman of the Petrograd Soviet.

The influence of the Bolsheviks in the soviets throughout the country spread rapidly in September and October. The Bolsheviks became the leading element in the soviets almost everywhere.

In the autumn of 1917 the revolution in Russia entered on its decisive stage.

All classes and all social groups in Russian society were drawn into the most far-reaching revolutionary crisis. It was a crisis affecting the whole nation, because it became apparent in all spheres of the nation's life, involving the working people, the ruling classes, and the political parties. With merciless precision Lenin revealed the inevitability of the collapse of a Russian economy dominated by the bourgeoisie and landowners and of the economic policy of the Provisional Government. It was not individual mistakes that brought the government to the brink of disaster. At a time when there was a tremendous growth in the revolutionary activity of the masses all efforts on the part of the Provisional Government to regulate economic life by reactionary bureaucratic means were doomed to failure. The government's whole policy was leading to famine and the disorganization of production, the destruction of economic contacts, and the creation of a state of chaos in the country. To carry out genuinely democratic measures for regulating the economy, to nationalize the banks and syndicates, and control production and demand would have meant taking a step forward – to socialism.

The collapse of the Provisional Government's food policy had an especially serious effect on the condition of the mass of ordinary people. Memories of the March days of 1917, which had started with food riots, were still very fresh in the people's minds. On the eve of the October Revolution the country's food situation worsened considerably as a result of the policy of the Kerensky government which paid no attention to the needs of the people.

The collapse of the Provisional Government's economic policy was seen in its most concentrated form in the breakdown of transport. This was the bloodstream sustaining the country's whole economic life and binding it together into a single organism, and it collapsed with tremendous speed. Towards the end of October 1917 the minister of transport, A.V.Liverovsky, admitted that the transport situation 'threatened to bring to a halt the major railroads which supplied the country with essential services'.

One very clear sign of the nationwide crisis was the break-up of the ruling parties of Socialist Revolutionaries (SRs) and the Social Democrats (Mensheviks). The formation of left-wing groups among the SRs and Mensheviks, the sharp intensification of conflicts between the leadership of these parties and the rank and file of their members and between the party headquarters and their local organizations, and the enforced rejection by the local committees of SRs and Mensheviks of the slogan of coalition with the bourgeoisie was the direct result of the collapse of those parties' reformist policy. On 4th November the soldiers' section of the All-Russian Central Executive Committee, led by SRs and Mensheviks, demanded peace and the transfer of land to the peasants, but proposed that power should be handed over to 'the democratic majority in the pre-parliament' – that spurious, representative body set up by the Provisional Goverment.

S.C.R. Photo Library

Lenin, on his way to Petrograd to direct the revolution. On 28th October he and the Bolshevik Central Committee finally announced: 'The time is fully ripe'

Traitors to the revolution

From the middle of October 1917 open warfare on the part of all the working people against the Provisional Government became a daily occurrence in the nation's life. The workers everywhere were arming themselves, the number of workers' armed detachments – the Red Guards – increased rapidly, and they developed their contacts and their plans for common action with the garrisons in the major towns. The workers had a tremendously revolutionizing effect on the troops at the fronts, especially on the Western and Northern Fronts. Sailors of the Baltic Fleet declared the Kerensky government to be a government of betrayal of the revolution. Councils of

Left: *'The Word of Lenin' by V.Liminov, Soviet painter. Soldiers read a news-sheet. Bolshevik propaganda fanned their discontent with the war. Lenin's programme of peace and land, rather than his politics, expressed the longings of the people of Russia.* ***Bottom left:*** *'Working people arise!' by Soviet painter V.Serov. The Bolsheviks exploited working-class discontent*

workers' and soldiers' deputies, regimental and divisional committees, and peasants' organizations proclaimed at the numerous conferences they held that none of the tasks of the revolution could be solved without the overthrow of the Provisional Government and the transfer of power to the soviets. A resolution passed at a congress of soviets of the Vladimir province on 29th October declared the Provisional Government and all the parties which supported it to be traitors to the cause of revolution and all the soviets in the province to be in a state of open and determined warfare with the Provisional Government. This was only one of the moves in this general process of decisive and ruthless warfare between the people and the government. The same resolution was supported by the soviets in Moscow, Ivanovo-Voznesensk, Aleksandrov, Kovrov, Ryazan, and other towns. When a congress of soviets in the Ryazan province decided to hand power over to the soviets immediately, Nikitin, the minister of the interior, demanded that armed force should be used against the people of Ryazan. On 31st October the minister cabled the commander of the Moscow military region: 'Impossible to take counteraction with resources of the civil authority.' But the military commander was also unable to render any assistance, because he had no dependable troops at his disposal. The soviet of the Moscow province proposed that all the soviets in the province should ignore the orders issued by the Provisional Government. The Vladivostok Soviet, some 6,000 miles from Moscow, issued instructions to the effect that failure to obey the soviet's orders would be regarded as a counter-revolutionary act. Soviets in the Urals declared that the main task was to overthrow the Provisional Government.

It was the industrial working class and its party which took the lead in this popular movement. Factory committees sprang up everywhere and quickly gathered strength, and they were everywhere dominated by the Bolsheviks. In Petrograd on 30th October-4th November there took place the first All-Russian Conference of Factory Committees. Ninety-six of the 167 delegates belonged to the Bolsheviks.

Strikes and peasant revolt

The strike movement in the autumn of 1917 was closely connected with the soviets' struggle for power. There were strikes of metal-workers and woodworkers, of chemist-shop assistants and railway workers, of textile workers and miners. A general strike of 300,000 textile workers in the central industrial region (Moscow), which began on 3rd November, affected every branch of life in the region. The workers took control of the plants, occupied the telephone exchange, mounted guard over the warehouses and offices. It was more than a strike: the workers not only faced up directly to the problem of assuming power, they began to solve it. But in 1917 the strike was only one of many weapons used by the proletariat in its struggle. The Red Guards and the workers' militia, the establishment of factory guards and workers' control, the factory committees and the bold acts of intervention in the management of industrial plants – all these forms of organization and means of struggle gave the working class tremendous possibilities for influencing the course of events and leading them on a nationwide scale.

The strength of the working-class movement was multiplied by virtue of the fact that the industrial workers exercised a tremendous influence over the peasantry and themselves received in return support in the form of a spreading peasant war against the landowners. In September and October 1917 there were something like 2,000 cases in which the peasants took political action, killing the landlords and seizing the land.

'If, in a country of peasants, after seven months of a democratic republic, things could come to the point of a peasant revolt, this demonstrates unquestionably the nationwide collapse of the revolution, the crisis it is in, which has reached unprecedented proportions, and the fact that the counter-revolutionary forces are reaching the limit of their resources,' Lenin wrote in mid-October 1917.

But the peasantry's official representative at the time was the All-Russian Council of Peasants' Deputies, which had been elected at the peasants' congress back in May and had long since lost any right to represent anybody. The executive committee of the All-Russian Council of Peasants' Deputies sanctioned punitive expeditions against the peasants, and supported the policy of hostility to the peasantry pursued by the government (in which the prime minister was the SR Kerensky and the minister of agriculture the SR Maslov). The peasant masses who had risen in revolt against the landowners took decisive action. In the main centres of peasant uprisings the struggle against the landowners acquired, under the influence of the industrial workers, both organization and a clear purpose. The 332 delegates to a peasant congress in the Tver province took a unanimous decision to hand over the land immediately to the management of land committees. The local land committees in the Tambov province seized land belonging to the Church and the landowners and rented it out to peasants who had very little or no land. Similar acts were repeated throughout the country.

S.C.R. Photo Library

Women queuing outside a food-store in Moscow. The bread ration, a pound a day in the spring, was cut to half a pound just before the October Revolution

Government force

How did the Provisional Government reply to these demands by the peasants? It organized punitive expeditions and drew up various legislative proposals providing for eventual reforms, the aim of which was to 'pacify' the peasants and certainly not to satisfy their demand that the land should be handed over to them.

The forces at the disposal of the Provisional Government for undertaking such punitive expeditions were limited, consisting mainly of Cossack and cavalry units. The actions undertaken by the peasants forced the Provisional Government to split up its troops between numerous areas in which there had been uprisings: in the Ryazan, Kursk, Tambov, Kiev, Tula, Saratov, Samara, Minsk, Kazan, Podolsk, Volhynia, and other provinces. Squadrons of Cossacks and cavalry detachments which were dispatched to particular districts became submerged in the vast sea of peasant revolt. Meanwhile, the provincial commissars of the Provisional Government demanded that soldiers be sent to *all* districts to suppress peasant disorders.

But even the local authorities soon realized the futility of using force against the peasantry. In the course of the peasant uprising even those land committees which supported the government's policy were forced to take over the property of the landowners and distribute it among the poorer peasants. The Kadets, the SRs, and the Mensheviks tried in every way to minimize the importance of the peasants' struggle, making out that it was just 'wild anarchy' and talking about 'pogroms' and 'disorders'. This falsification of the truth is disproved by the facts: in the main centres of the uprising the peasants transferred the land to the poor peasants in an organized manner. In those places where the SR party obstructed the work of the peasant committees the movement did indeed assume anarchistic forms. But the peasants had thoroughly learned the lessons of the first Russian revolution of 1905. The more advanced forms of peasant protest and revolt (the seizure of arable land and landowners' property) were three or four times as widespread in 1917 as they had been in 1905-07. In the autumn of 1917 between sixty and ninety per cent of all peasant actions included the seizure of land.

As for the proposed reforms, their essence is apparent from the final bill put forward by S.L.Maslov, the minister of agriculture. According to this bill, which was the most 'left-wing' for the Provisional Government, the landowners were to retain the right to own the land. The 'land-lease fund' to be set up under this bill was to take over only 'land not being cultivated by the resources of the owners'. The rent to be paid by the peasants was to go to the landowner.

The whole experience of the eight months during which the Provisional Government was in power demonstrated that without a further revolution the peasantry would not receive any land or rid itself of oppression by the landowners. It was this experience which pushed the peasantry to carry out an uprising which, when linked with the struggle of the industrial workers, created the most favourable conditions for the victory of the socialist revolution.

Petrograd workers with an armoured car captured from Kerensky's troops. On the fatal night of 7th November Kerensky was searching for loyal troops to support his government

Novosti

The revolutionary structure

By November 1917 the Bolshevik Party had about 350,000 members. But its strength was to be measured rather by its influence over the many millions of people embraced by the soviets, the trade unions, the factory committees, and the soldiers' and peasants' committees. At a time when an armed revolt was developing on a nationwide scale the task of Lenin's revolutionary party was to take care of the political and military organization of the forces of revolt. At the centre of this preparatory work stood the working class. The Red Guards were acquiring fighting experience, were learning the tactics of street fighting, and were establishing and strengthening their contacts with the revolutionary units in the army. In the districts inhabited by other nationalities the Bolsheviks gained the support of the oppressed peoples, who saw in the victory of a socialist revolution a guarantee of national and social emancipation. Major centres of revolutionary struggle were set up in all these districts and they linked the national liberation movement with the workers' and peasants' movement, bringing Petrograd and Moscow together with the outlying regions in a single revolutionary front. One such centre in central Asia was Tashkent, which as early as September 1917 raised the banner of struggle against the Kerensky government. In the Trans-Caucasus the centre was the industrial city of Baku; in the Ukraine Kharkov and the Donbass; in the Western territories of the country it was Minsk. The Bolsheviks were clearly the dominant force in the decisive places in the country: in the capital, in the industrial centres, on the Western and Northern Fronts, and in the major garrison towns in the interior. The seventy-five Bolshevik newspapers and periodicals which were published in all these regions were a very important organizing force.

The decision to work for an uprising, which was taken at the Sixth Congress of the Bolshevik Party in August 1917, was put consistently into practice. At a meeting on 23rd October, in which Lenin took part, the Central Committee of the Bolsheviks passed a resolution concerning the uprising. This decision did not set a date for the uprising, but it did stress that 'an armed uprising is inevitable and the time for it is fully ripe'. The Central Committee advised all the branches of the party to be guided by this fact and to consider and decide all practical issues with this in mind. The resolution was passed with Zinovyev and Kamenev voting against it. A week later Kamenev wrote an article opposing the decision in the Menshevik paper *Novaya Zhizn* (New Life). L.D. Trotsky voted in favour of the resolution on the uprising, but his later position amounted to delaying the beginning of the revolt until the All-Russian Congress of Soviets, which was to deal with the question of power. This attitude of Trotsky's was subjected to severe criticism by Lenin, who emphasized that to postpone the uprising until the Congress of Soviets would be to give the counter-revolutionary forces an opportunity of organizing themselves and dispersing the soviets.

On 29th October an enlarged session of the Central Committee of the Bolsheviks, attended by representatives of the Petrograd committee, the Bolsheviks' military organization, factory committees, and trade unions, approved the decision to organize an armed uprising and appointed from its number a Military-Revolutionary Centre composed of A.S.Bubnov, F.E. Dzerzhinsky, Y.M.Sverdlov, I.V.Stalin, and S.M.Uritsky. The leading spirit and organizer of the work of the Military-Revolutionary Committee was Yakov Sverdlov, a thirty-two-year-old Bolshevik who already had behind him seventeen years of revolutionary activity, prison, penal servitude, and seven escapes from deportation. This centre consisting of five men formed part of the Soviet's legal headquarters for the armed uprising – the Military-Revolutionary Committee of the Petrograd Soviet. A major part in the Committee was played by Bolsheviks N.I. Podvoysky and V.A.Antonov-Ovseyenko, and by the left-wing SR, P.E.Lazimir.

In late October provincial and district conferences and congresses of soviets, factory committees, and army and frontline committees took place throughout the country. History had never before seen such a mass mobilization of popular forces around the working class for a decisive attack on the capitalist system.

Meanwhile, the Provisional Government was trying to regain the initiative. On 1st November it dispersed the soviet in Kaluga, encircled Moscow and Minsk with Cossack troops, and tried to remove the revolutionary units of the capital's garrison from Petrograd. The only effect of these actions was that the revolutionary forces became even more active.

The Military-Revolutionary Committee appointed its own commissars to all units of the Petrograd garrison and to all the more important offices. The revolutionary troops and the Red Guards were brought to a state of readiness for battle. On 6th November the avalanche of popular wrath descended on the government which had betrayed the revolution. On that day the Central Committee of the Bolsheviks organized an alternative headquarters in the Peter and Paul Fortress and took decisions concerning the control of the postal and telegraph services, of the rail junction, and of the food supplies to the capital. The Petrograd garrison and the Red Guards went over to direct military action to bring about the immediate overthrow of the Provisional Government.

Red Guards outside the Smolny Institute. Inside on 7th November the hall was seething with people. The Congress of Soviets was deciding the future course of the revolution

Gérard Oriol

The Bolsheviks seize power

The city of Petrograd is situated on a number of islands, joined together by bridges. Hence the great strategic importance of the bridges. During the day of 6th November units of the Red Guards seized practically all the bridges and defeated efforts on the part of the officer cadets to cut the working-class districts off from the centre. Revolutionary troops occupied the central telegraph office, the central news agency, and the Baltic (Finland) station. Ships of the Baltic Fleet put out from Helsingfors and Kronstadt to come to the help of revolutionary Petrograd.

On the evening of 6th November Lenin left his secret hiding place and arrived at the headquarters of the armed uprising, and under his leadership the uprising developed at much greater speed. Troops of the Military-Revolutionary Committee occupied, on the night of 6th-7th November and the following morning, the telephone exchange, a number of railway stations, and the State Bank. The capital of Russia was in the hands of a people in revolt. ▷**768**

On the morning of 7th November Lenin wrote his appeal *To the Citizens of Russia,* which announced the transfer of power in the state into the hands of the Military-Revolutionary Committee. This, the first document to emerge from the victorious revolution, was immediately printed and posted up in the streets of Petrograd.

At two thirty-five on the afternoon of the same day the Petrograd Soviet went into session. There Lenin proclaimed the victory of the socialist revolution. In a short, moving speech he defined the main tasks of the revolution: the setting up of a Soviet government, the dismantling of the old state administration and the organization of new, Soviet administration, the ending of the war, a just and immediate peace, the confiscation of the property of the landowners, and genuine workers' control over industrial production.

Throughout the day of 7th November meetings of the party factions from the Congress of Soviets were taking place in the Smolny Institute. Details of the party composition of the second All-Russian Congress of Soviets bear witness to the depth and the extent of the process of Bolshevization among the ordinary people. At the first Congress the Bolsheviks had accounted for only ten per cent of the delegates, but at the second Congress they embraced fifty-two per cent of the delegates. The Bolsheviks carried with them a large group of left-wing SRs – more than fifteen per cent of the delegates, whereas there had been no left-wing SRs at all at the first All-Russian Congress of Soviets. Mensheviks and right-wing SRs of all shades of opinion, who had unquestionably dominated the first Congress of Soviets (eighty-four per cent of the delegates), accounted for only twenty-six per cent of the delegates at the second Congress.

There is no need to produce any more precise evidence to demonstrate the extent to which the *petit-bourgeois* parties had disintegrated; the decline from eighty-four per cent in June 1917 to twenty-six per cent in October is sufficiently clear. All the same, the Bolsheviks did not try to antagonize or isolate the other parties which formed part of the soviets.

The first session of the second All-Russian Congress of Soviets began at 10.40 pm on 7th November and came to an end just after five next morning.

The white-pillared hall of the Smolny Institute was seething with people. Within its walls were to be found representatives of the whole of Russia, of her industrial centres and farming regions, national territories, Cossack regions, and of all the war fronts and garrisons in the interior. It was a representative assembly from the whole of Russia, which had to decide the future course of the revolution.

Sitting on the platform were the downcast leaders of the old Central Executive Committee – Bogdanov, Gots, Dan, Filippovsky – but this was their last appearance as leaders of the supreme organ of the soviets. It was, at the same time, an admission of defeat for their policy of resistance to the popular will and an admission of the legitimacy of the Congress, to which, by the very fact of the official opening, the old Executive Committee was handing over its very reduced authority.

The Congress elected a presidium from among the Bolsheviks and the left-wing SRs, and Dan and his friends departed. Then the work of the Congress began.

There was, in the long stream of speeches, in the heated dispute about the revolution which had taken place, and in the sharp conflict between the political parties, a certain strict logic and system which reflected the relationship of social forces in the vast country stretching out beyond the confines of the Smolny Institute.

The Provisional Government, meeting in the Winter Palace in the centre of Petrograd, was utterly isolated from the country. The palace was defended by detachments of officer cadets, Cossacks, and women's battalions. As the ring of rebel forces drew closer round the Winter Palace, and as the reports from the war fronts grew ever more hopeless, so the speeches of the more conciliatory statesmen became more nervous and their actions became more devoid of logic. By continually walking out of the congress and then coming back to it the Mensheviks and the right-wing SRs tried to disorganize its work. The result of their efforts was very painful for them.

After some noisy demonstrations and much hysterical shouting and appeals the right-wing SRs and Mensheviks succeeded in taking with them out of the congress an insignificant group of people – about fifty of the delegates. At the same time there took place a significant regrouping of forces at the congress. The number of SRs was reduced by seven, but the group of left-wing SRs increased to eighty-one. The Mensheviks disappeared altogether, but the group of Menshevik-internationalists rose to twenty-one. This means that many members of the faction of Mensheviks and SRs did not obey the decision of their leaders to leave the congress, but preferred to switch over to the left-wing groups.

At about ten in the evening of 7th November the revolutionary troops surrounding the Winter Palace went over to the attack for which the signal was a shot fired by the cruiser *Aurora.* The Winter Palace was taken. Antonov-Ovseyenko arrested the members of the Provisional Government and put them in charge of the Red Guards to be taken to the Peter and Paul Fortress.

Pleading

Meanwhile, the forces of the counter-revolution – the Mensheviks, and right-wing SRs, pinned their hopes on the units at the front. During 6th and 7th November General Dukhonin from the General HQ and a representative of the war ministry, Tolstoy, sent messages from Petrograd demanding, begging, and pleading with the commanders of the fronts to send troops as quickly as possible to Petrograd to put down the uprising. The commanders of the South-Western and Rumanian Fronts, where the influence of the conciliators and nationalists seemed to be especially strong, declared that there were no units to be found which were suitable for the job of 'pacifying' Petrograd. And those regiments which they had succeeded by a trick in moving towards Petrograd were held up on the way by the railwaymen, the workers, and revolutionary soldiers. A strict revolutionary control was set up in Orsha, so that no trains were allowed through to Petrograd. The armoured trains which were sent off for Moscow were held up in Minsk. Vyazma and Gomel not only refused to let troops through but even held up telegrams from the staff of the Western Front.

Contrary to the hopes of the forces of counter-revolution, the soldiers on all fronts came out in defence of the soviets.

At 5.17 am N.V.Krylenko, an officer and a Bolshevik, representing the revolutionary forces of the Northern Front, went up on to the platform of the congress to speak; he was staggering from fatigue. He was soon to be made supreme commander-in-chief of the Russian army. The congress listened with enthusiasm to his statement that a Military-Revolutionary Committee had been set up on the Northern Front, which had taken over the command and intended to prevent the movement of trainloads of counter-revolutionary troops in the direction of Petrograd. Delegations were continually arriving from the trains sent to Petrograd and declaring their support for the Petrograd garrison.

The first official state document of the socialist revolution – the *Appeal to the Workers, Soldiers, and Peasants* – was drawn up by Lenin. It proclaimed that the Congress of Soviets was taking power into its own hands and that all power throughout the country was passing into the hands of the soviets of workers', soldiers', and peasants' deputies. This was how the main question of the revolution was resolved in legislative terms – the power of the soviets was established.

The most difficult problems, around which a bitter struggle had been fought throughout the eight months of the revolution – the questions of peace, land, workers' control, the self-determination of

Two Soviet paintings of the revolution. ***Below:*** *The signal for revolution – a shot is fired from the cruiser* Aurora. *The attack on the Winter Palace is to begin.* ***Bottom:*** *'The Inevitable' (by S.Lukin). The Winter Palace has been stormed. The members of the Provisional Government are under arrest. A Red Guard, one of the victors, stands in the throne-room of the Tsars*

Overleaf: *Soviet painting of the storming of the Winter Palace. The Bolshevik Revolution was almost bloodless. There were scuffles in the corridors between the invading Red Guards and the defending women's battalion and officer cadets. But when the ministers surrendered, only five soldiers, one sailor, and none of the defenders had been killed*

S.C.R. Photo Library

S.C.R. Photo Library

nations, the democratization of the army – were posed and decided openly and straightforwardly in that document.

The *Appeal to the Workers, Soldiers, and Peasants* was approved with only two opposing votes and twelve abstentions. This represented a complete victory for Lenin's idea of transferring all power to the soviets.

The first decree approved by the second All-Russian Congress of Soviets was the decree concerning the peace.

Peace

Certain critics were later to assert, quite unfairly, that Russia could have had peace even without the Bolshevik Revolution, and that if it did not come about it was only because of mistakes committed by the governments of the Entente powers and the Provisional Government who did not succeed in seizing the initiative in deciding the question of war or peace.

There can be no question but that the Provisional Government committed plenty of 'mistakes' of every kind. But it was by no means a matter of the weakness of certain individuals or of their personal mistakes. Those mistakes were dictated by the class nature of the policy of the Provisional Government, its loathing of the revolutionary movement and its fear in the face of that movement, and its dependence on the governments of the Entente powers. The growth of this dependence led even to the expulsion from the government of the war minister, A.I.Verkhovsky, who suggested a negotiated peace with the German bloc so as to concentrate forces against the revolution.

At 9 pm on 8th November the second session of the Congress of Soviets opened. Lenin went up on to the platform. 'Next Lenin, gripping the edge of the reading stand, letting his little winking eyes travel over the crowd as he stood there waiting, apparently oblivious to the long-rolling ovation, which lasted several minutes' – recalls the American journalist John Reed, who was an eye-witness of the events and a participant in them.

'The question of peace is the burning question, the most pressing question of the present time,' Lenin began. The proletarian revolution was not decked out in the flamboyant clothes of beautiful words, nor was it concealed behind noisy manifestoes and impossible promises. It got down in a businesslike way to the great and difficult job of liberating the peoples of Russia and of the whole world from bloody slaughter. There was a note of confidence and firmness in the words of Lenin's decree, which proposed that all the warring peoples and their governments should enter immediately into talks concerning a just peace, without annexations or indemnities. ▷**773**

ИНТЕРНАЦIОНАЛ
30
РАКОВСКIЙ
ВЪ ЖЕРТВУ

***Left:** 'Burial of victims of the Russian revolution' by B.E.Lintoff. There were, in fact, very few Bolshevik martyrs in November 1918. **Bottom left:** Russia sacrificed on the altar of the International – anti-Bolshevik poster. Lenin directs the sacrifice: Trotsky brandishes a knife. Other Bolsheviks, a Jew (with thirty pieces of silver), and Kerensky (far left) look on*

The Decree on Peace gave legislative form to new principles of foreign policy – the principles of equality and respect for the sovereignty of all peoples, the abandonment of secret diplomacy, and the coexistence of different social systems. The decree was addressed not only to the governments but also to the peoples of the warring nations.

The diplomatic representatives of the Entente powers tried to ignore the Decree on Peace and pretend that the document 'did not exist'. But the decree became the property of hundreds of millions of working people. Evidence of this is to be found in the strikes and demonstrations which swept through many countries of the world at the end of 1917 and in 1918.

The Decree on Peace was approved unanimously by the congress.

The congress turned immediately to the second question: the immediate abolition of landlord property rights. The yearnings of the people, their century-long dreams of being free from the oppression of the landlords were expressed in the Decree on Land.

'Landlord property rights are abolished, immediately and without any compensation,' the decree said. All land was declared to be the property of the whole people. It was made the duty of the local soviets to draw up an accurate account of all property and to organize the strictest revolutionary protection for everything that was handed over to the national economy. There was a special point which proclaimed that the land of the ordinary peasants and Cossacks would not be confiscated. Part of the decree consisted of the peasants' demands, drawn up on the basis of 242 local peasant demands.

The Decree on Land was approved by a general vote of the delegates, with only one delegate voting against and eight abstaining. Thus the Bolsheviks won a complete victory on this cardinal question of the revolution as well. The peasantry received land from the hands of the victorious urban working class. This turned the alliance between the proletariat and the peasantry into a tremendous force promoting the further progress of the revolution. What the proletariat had failed to achieve in 1905 – to unite its struggle for socialism with the democratic movement of the peasantry for land – was achieved triumphantly in November 1917.

Since it was by its nature an expression of revolutionary democracy, the Decree on Land was put into practice by methods which were both revolutionary and socialist. This is to say, it rid the land of the survivals of serfdom more resolutely and thoroughly than any bourgeois revolution had yet done. By abolishing the private ownership of land the Decree on Land took the first step towards the liquidation of capitalist ownership of banks, industrial undertakings, transport, and so on.

As a result of the agrarian reforms carried out on the basis of the Decree on Land and the subsequent legislation the poor and middle peasants received 540,000,000 acres of land. The big landowners, the royal family and the Church lost all their land – 400,000,000 acres – and the rich peasants (kulaks) lost 135,000,000 of the 216,000,000 they had owned in 1914.

This revolutionary redistribution of land served as the basis for further reforms in agriculture and for the development of a socialist farming system.

Bolshevik government

Since it enjoyed an overwhelming majority, it was natural that Lenin's party should form the new government. During the Congress the Central Committee of the Bolshevik Party had carried on intensive negotiations with the left-wing SRs about their participation in the government. The left-wing SRs had been members of the Military-Revolutionary Committee and they had – though, it is true, not without some hesitation – taken part in the armed uprising and supported the principal decisions taken by the Congress. But the left-wing SRs were too closely connected with their right-wing colleagues in the party and were too dependent on them in an ideological and organizational sense to be able to make up their minds immediately to join the Soviet government. It was a month later that they took this step.

At this point the Bolsheviks assumed the responsibility for forming a new government. 'We wanted a Soviet coalition government,' Lenin said. 'We did not exclude anyone from the Soviet. If they (the SRs and Mensheviks) did not wish to work together with us, so much the worse for them. The masses of the soldiers and peasants will not follow the Mensheviks and SRs.'

The decree which the Congress passed concerning the formation of a workers' and peasants' government headed by V.I.Lenin became in effect a constitutional document. It determined the name of the new government: the Soviet (Council) of People's Commissars, a name which reflected the fact that the new government was closely linked with the people and had developed out of the soviets. The decree laid down in general terms that the new government was subject to the control of the All-Russian Congress of Soviets and its Central Executive Committee. Thus the decree set out the constitutional principle regarding the responsibility of the workers' and peasants' government to the supreme bodies of the Soviet regime: the Congress of Soviets and the All-Russian Central Executive Committee, which had the right to remove people's commissars.

Once it had proved victorious in Petrograd the revolution spread quickly throughout the country. Immediately after Petrograd, the soviets were victorious in Moscow, where the battles for power were very violent and lasted for five days, ending on 16th November 1917 with the complete victory of the soviets.

In the course of three months the socialist revolution was victorious throughout the vast country. From the line of the Western Front to the shores of the Pacific Ocean and from the White Sea to the Black Sea. The ways in which the revolutionary power of the soviets was established varied greatly from place to place. In Smolensk, Voronezh, Kazan, Chernigov, Zhitomir, and Kiev the workers and peasants took power only after armed struggle with the counter-revolutionaries. In Minsk, Yaroslavl, Nizhny Novgorod, Samara, Kursk, and Perm the soviets came to power by peaceful means.

Imperial War Museum

Soldiers of the revolution, the ragged bootless men who enabled a party of 350,000 to gain control over a country of a hundred and fifty million people

At the very beginning of its course the socialist revolution in Russia succeeded in doing what the Paris Commune tried but failed to do. The workers, peasants, and soldiers of Russia set up a new administration, formed their own government at the All-Russian Congress of Soviets, uniting millions of working people, resolved the questions of peace and land, and offered all the peoples of Russia the possibility of national independence.

Such was the victory of the Bolshevik Revolution, which changed the face of the world and had a decisive influence on the fate of mankind. *(Translation)*

Russia, December 1917-November 1918/Jaroslav Valenta

The Treaty of Brest Litovsk

Russia needed peace. Her army had disintegrated, her western subject peoples – Finland, Estonia, Bessarabia, and the Ukraine – had declared their independence. Lenin had called for a general armistice, but only the Germans responded. On 17th December an armistice with Germany came into effect, and the two sides met in Brest Litovsk to discuss peace terms

__Bottom:__ A professional revolutionary on his way to talk peace with a Prussian general – Trotsky sets off for Brest Litovsk. The Germans knew that Russia could not stop their armies; but Trotsky looked for a revolution in Germany that would cripple her military might

No more than eight months separated the victorious peace settlement imposed on Russia by Kaiser Wilhelm's Germany at Brest Litovsk from Germany's capitulation at Compiègne. For eight months her rulers could dream that at last a decisive turning point had been reached in the war and that the most far-ranging aspirations would now be fulfilled – plans for establishing a ruling position for Germany throughout the world. The great power on Germany's eastern border, Russia, had been abased and compelled to sign a separate peace and her vast territory, seized by revolution and debilitated by civil war, appeared to be an easy prey.

The Peace of Brest Litovsk had wider implications than its effect on German-Russian relations. On 3rd March when Sokolnikov signed the treaty as Soviet representative it seemed that more had happened than the mere winning of the first round in the war; most contemporaries thought the balance had definitely shifted in favour of Germany and the Central powers. It looked as if willingness to risk a fight on two fronts had paid off. It seemed to have justified those military circles that favoured expansion and adventure.

The fanfares of triumph in Berlin and Vienna inevitably caused serious alarm among the Allies. Wheat from the Ukraine would make the sea blockade of the Central powers impotent, and there was reason to fear the transfer of huge contingents from the German and Austro-Hungarian armies to the French and Italian theatres before the American Expeditionary Force could arrive. In some Allied countries voices were again raised, suggesting that it would be better to reach a compromise than face a long drawn out war. The spokesmen for the national liberation movements among the suppressed peoples of Austria-Hungary were worried, and with reason.

The road from the ceasefire signed in December 1917 to the Treaty of Brest Litovsk was neither short nor easy. Each

side needed time to analyse the actions of the other in order to clarify its expectations of what peace might bring. The Central powers, and in particular their economies, were on the verge of complete exhaustion. Ludendorff admits in his memoirs that he was waiting for a 'miracle', for a revolution in Russia to eliminate from the war an enemy whose endless territory had been swallowing up division after division. The problem of making peace on the Eastern Front was a double-edged one. As good a balance as possible had to be struck between the expansionist ambitions of some circles, particularly military ones, and more realistic intentions to bite off only as much as the Central powers could chew. Russia's withdrawal from the war had helped to spark off a highly unwelcome surge of discontent and revolutionary unrest in Austria-Hungary and Germany, which would be fanned by the conclusion of a palpably annexationist treaty.

Among the foremost exponents of a relatively realistic line were Richard von Kühlmann, first secretary in the German foreign office, and the Austrian foreign minister, Count Czernin. It would be wrong of course to imagine that there was any idyllic measure of agreement between Berlin and Vienna about the approach to peace with Russia. Early in December Czernin threatened to sign a separate treaty if necessary, regardless of Berlin's policy. This he hoped would eliminate the influence of extremist circles in Germany whose exaggerated demands were likely to prevent any peace settlement with Russia – a settlement which the Danubian monarchy needed even more urgently than its ally. Czernin seems to have realized that the insatiability of the German imperialists outran their real capabilities. This does not mean, however, that he was prepared to abandon all plans of annexation; he agreed with Kühlmann that Poland, Lithuania, Courland, and the greater part of Livonia should stay in the hands of the Central powers.

In Petrograd, similarly, the views of the Soviet government about the peace problem were slowly changing. The Bolsheviks had gone into the revolution with the slogan of 'peace without annexations or indemnities', a policy of dissociation from both sides in the war and rejection of the aims of both great power alliances. Refusing to fight on, the Soviet government 'declared war on war'. It nevertheless made intensive efforts to avoid being identified in its peace offers with either side in the battle and proposed terms to all the contestants. Even after signing a ceasefire with the Central powers – who in view of their military, economic, and domestic political plight were in no position to reject any proposals out of hand – the revolutionary government in Petrograd continued to urge the Allies to join in the negotiations. It was reluctant to embark on a separate peace and its spokesmen went so far as to get the German negotiators to undertake that there would be no transfers of troops from the Russian to the Western Front. Indeed, even after the Brest negotiations had been broken off in February 1918 and the German offensive had started, the Bolsheviks appealed for help to the Allied missions in Russia.

Revolutionary hopes

Not even the Bolshevik Party was untouched by disagreements about the whole complex of issues involved in making peace with the Central powers. One wing of the party, and similarly one wing of the coalition partners in the government and in the Central Executive Committee of Soviets, was sharply opposed to the conclusion of the Brest Litovsk Treaty. Bukharin, as leader of the Left Communists, declared that the first proletarian state in the world must not sign an agreement which would betray the revolutionary movement in the other countries and repress the rising wave of revolutionary action. Similar arguments were used by the Left Socialist Revolutionaries, who were anti-German and pro-Allied in their sympathies. Without a close familiarity with the political theories then prevailing in Soviet Russia it is hard to understand how these ideas of a 'revolutionary war' could have been used in protest against the Brest negotiations – especially since the Russian army had virtually disintegrated.

It must be admitted that there were many illusions and unrealistic, though revolutionarily optimistic, assessments of the situation on the Soviet side. One illusion was that the curtain was about to go up on a pan-European, if not worldwide, revolution arising from the extraordinary intensification of political, class, and social antagonisms and conflicts brought about by the war. Even before the victorious October Revolution in Russia, Lenin had formulated his theory of the 'prologue', the theory that the Russian events would be a spark setting fire to a revolutionary conflagration throughout the main industrial countries of Europe – all of which were involved in the war – and above all in Germany. The spate of demonstrations and manifestations that followed the opening of negotiations in Brest Litovsk, both in Germany and still more in Austria-Hungary, seemed to bear out this expectation, and this was bound to influence decision-making quarters in Soviet Russia.

The first few weeks of negotiation, in December 1917 and January 1918, gave no indication of the slightest approximation of views between the two sides. On the contrary it became ever more clear that the real dictator at the conference was not Kühlmann, the titular head of the German delegation, but the brutal Prussian general Max Hoffmann, a spokesman of the most extreme imperialist and militarist circles in Germany. His *extempore* outbursts, culminating in the famous moment when he banged the table with his fist and demanded that the remaining Baltic territories should be evacuated by the Russians and taken under German 'protection', caused a crisis in the negotiations.

From January 1918 the Soviet peace delegation was headed by Trotsky, who shared Lenin's view that from a purely military standpoint Soviet Russia had no chance at all in a conflict with the Central powers. He agreed that a treaty must be signed as soon as Germany presented an ultimatum, and before leaving for Brest he assured Lenin that he had no intention of putting over a doctrine of 'revolutionary war'. But at the same time Trotsky considered that the radical mood of the population had made the home front of the Central powers so unstable that their armies would be incapable of launching an effective anti-Soviet offensive. It was therefore his policy to postpone the conclusion of an agreement until it might appear plain that the Central powers were not only determined, but actually able, to start large-scale military operations against Russia. When the German ultimatum was delivered, then, he declared the standpoint of the Soviet government to be 'neither peace nor war'; with that, the Soviet delegation went back to Petrograd.

The subsequent course of events fully bore out Lenin's attitude, which had previously failed to win majority support. The German and Austrian armies of intervention advanced without meeting serious obstacles, and the assumption that there would be a revolutionary upheaval inside Germany proved false. Soviet historians have recently considered the question of the magnitude of the opposition put up by improvised Red Army units and some at least now take the view that the much-vaunted victories of Narva and Pskov were isolated phenomena compared with the general abandonment of positions by the army. At the Seventh Congress of the Bolshevik Party Lenin ruefully described the capture by the enemy of railway stations which no one attempted to defend. 'Yes, we shall live to see worldwide revolution,' he remarked. 'But so far it is only a pretty fairy-tale, a most attractive fairy-tale.' Not that Lenin had ceased to believe in the forthcoming world revolution, but he recognized that revolution in Europe was not probable at that moment.

During the night of 23rd-24th February 1918 the Central Executive Committee of

'Limitless and overweening rapacity, together with the crudest contempt for the rules of international life'

the Congress of Soviets ended a lively debate by voting 116 to 84 in approval of the earlier decision of the Bolshevik Party's Central Committee to accept the German peace ultimatum. A telegram in these terms was immediately despatched to the German headquarters, where meanwhile fresh and still stiffer conditions had been drafted. For Trotsky's previous reply had caused consternation among the German politicians. At the meeting of the Imperial Council called to seek a way out of the unexpected situation ('Are we to go running after the Russians, pen in hand?' Kühlmann had exclaimed) the state secretary had proposed taking note of Trotsky's declaration and awaiting further developments. Kühlmann felt obliged to take account of domestic reaction and to avoid needless exacerbation of the anti-war mood of the masses by any aggressive prolongation of the war. But as usual in such moments of decision, it was the intransigent, expansionist, and annexationist views of the general staff that won the day, demanding the formal signature of a treaty incorporating further annexations. The same quarters were even playing with the idea of continuing the war, overthrowing the Bolsheviks, and setting up a new 'national' government of supporters of the monarchy to guarantee pro-German policies for the future—for the whole German offensive had virtually become a technical problem of organization rather than one of military strategy. German military circles were well aware that the Soviet government was 'inwardly hostile' to them.

After making a declaration that he was signing the document not as a negotiated peace treaty but as a *Diktat* under the pressure of *force majeure,* the Soviet representative put his name to the list of demands presented by the Central powers and by Germany in particular. The hostilities between the Central powers and Soviet Russia were formally at an end. For the temporary victors, the booty was enormous. Russia gave up so-called Congress Poland, Lithuania, Courland, Riga, and part of Belorussia pending a decision by the Central powers about the fate of these lands; in the Caucasus Kars, Ardahan, and Batum fell to Turkey; some million square kilometres with a pre-war population of forty-six million was ceded. Reparations totalling three thousand million roubles in gold were imposed on Russia.

The Treaty of Brest Litovsk had an immediate effect, of course, on the course of the war elsewhere. So far events had not been dominated by revolution, but by the war itself, whose general course determined the pattern and outcome of happenings that seemed to be only marginally connected with it. It is not surprising, then, that so many voices were raised immediately after the signing of the treaty, especially in the Allied countries, accusing the Soviet government of being a lackey to Germany. The dictated settlement was quoted as evidence that Lenin and his Bolsheviks, far from being a defeated party obliged by circumstances to swallow humiliating peace terms, were in fact the instrument and partner of Germany and of its general staff in their fight for world domination. Even in Soviet Russia itself, indeed, not everyone saw the force of Lenin's argument that Russia had to sign the Treaty of Brest Litovsk because she had at this point to give way before superior force since she lacked the military strength to defend herself.

Bread at bayonet point

It soon became apparent, however, that the Brest Litovsk Treaty involved deep and insuperable contradictions which made cooperation between the parties impossible. The contrast in attitudes toward the peace, toward its short-term and long-term aims alike, condemned the agreement to failure before the signatures were even dry. Representatives of two social systems, one imperial and nationalist, the other proletarian and internationalist, based their attitudes on doctrines which promised ultimate results on an international scale. Germany, the undoubted leader of the Central powers, had a rapacious and undisguised desire to become the leader of Europe and so lay the foundations of world domination. The Soviet government, on the other hand, sought to be a beacon for pan-European, if not worldwide, revolutionary upheavals. Both aims were at the time unrealistic. Germany failed to foresee all kinds of developments latent in the situation of the moment, Russia paid no attention to anything except that its partner in the newly signed peace treaty would not be its partner for long. A relationship founded on such a basis was practically doomed to be short-lived and could not even furnish a practicable *modus vivendi* for forces which, however antagonistic to each other, continued to recognize to some extent a certain appreciation of the realities of power and the basic purposes of the other side. So the Treaty of Brest Litovsk could not outlast the First World War.

It was the Central powers, and especially Germany, who were the first to realize (and that very speedily) that the optimism they had invested in the treaty, loudly proclaimed on the home front as the *Brotfrieden* or Bread Peace, was built upon sand. The only hopes that were fulfilled were those associated with the freeing of part of their troops. By June 1918 there were over 200 divisions on the Western Front and only 40 on the Eastern. This transfer made possible the Germans' spring offensive, which the Allies required the utmost effort to withstand; for the Allies victory and peace now seemed distant indeed, a prospect for 1919 at the earliest.

The German hope that failed most completely was that of turning Russia, particularly the Ukraine, into an economic hinterland for the supply of food and raw materials to the Central powers, so that the catastrophic effects of the Allied blockade would be removed. Germany made a secret agreement with the Viennese government about economic policy in the eastern areas previously belonging to Russia. Since December a special office had also been set up under the former state secretary Helfferich not only to do the preparatory work, particularly on the economic and financial side, for the impending peace treaty, but in the long run to lay the ground for the complete domination of Russia's food and raw material supplies, by German industry. The meeting of 16th May 1918 held between leaders of German economic and industrial life, showed that the permanent influence of Germany in Russia was to rest, above all, on the bayonets of the German army and the assistance of the entire military machine. But Germany's ruling circles had overestimated her strength and they mistook a temporary pattern of power for a valid foundation of long-term policy. The idea of basing economic exploitation on a military apparatus proved quite ineffective even during the course of 1918; the classic instance of this was the experience that befell the Austro-Hungarian occupying forces in the Ukraine.

The Ukrainian Central Council led by Hetman Skoropadsky had induced the Central powers without any difficulty to sign a separate peace recognizing its independent status, and the Brest Litovsk Treaty incorporated a commitment on the part of the Soviet government to come to terms with the Central Council too. But who was there to make peace with? The German politicians were well aware that they were treating with a fictitious government fully justifying Trotsky's sarcastic remark that the only territory the Central Council ruled over was the suite its delegates occupied in the Brest Litovsk hotel. In fact on the day before the signature of the separate peace with the Ukraine the entire Central Council had to flee from Kiev. The treaty was nevertheless signed, such was the beguiling effect of the delegates' 'personal guarantee' to deliver 'at least one million bushels of grain' to the Central powers.

Military requisitioning of grain in the countryside took too many soldiers and was ineffective anyway, while for normal trade relations there were not the most elemen-

Far left: *The humiliation of Russia by the Central powers. By the terms of a 'dictated' peace Russia lost Poland, Courland, Riga, and parts of Lithuania and Bessarabia. Then the Germans and Austrians moved in to occupy the Ukraine.* ***Above:*** *Germans and Russians sign the ceasefire in December 1917.* ***Left:*** *Skoropadsky, Hetman of the Ukraine, talks to the Kaiser. Germany signed a separate peace treaty with the Ukraine—but Skoropadsky had not the power to fulfil his promises to supply Germany with badly needed food.* ***Below:*** *Captured Cossack guerrilla leaders being interrogated by German officers in Tiflis*

tary economic conditions. The occupying power was unable to carry out any commercial acquisition of grain because its own militarized industry was incapable of furnishing capital or consumer goods in exchange, and had too few roubles for ordinary purchases in the villages.

Between the German and Austrian purchasing organizations there arose with increasing frequency not merely rivalry but mutual deception and fraud. In Kiev the German representatives were forever complaining that their Austrian colleagues were unfairly outbidding them, in violation of their agreement. The Austrians, moreover, exploited the more favourable communications between their own country and the Ukraine in order to seize the lion's share of the grain purchases, such as they were. In mid-May 1918 the German military inspectors reported that a mere 4,000 tons of grain had been exported to Germany to date, whereas Austria had procured 25,000 tons from the Ukraine. In all, the German and Austro-Hungarian conquerors were only able to squeeze out of the Ukraine about a fifth of the expected quantities of foodstuffs and agricultural products. In absolute terms the procurements were pretty sizeable, but they looked small in comparison with the conquerors' requirements and, indeed, with the hopes invested in the conquest of the Ukraine's 'black earth' belt. German officers and diplomats based on Kiev came gradually to the conclusion that the Central Council's authority was 'not to be taken seriously', for it showed itself incapable of organizing even the foundations of a viable economy. Ironically enough, one of the major problems of implementing the *Brotfrieden* in the Ukraine was rail transport. Although the Central powers had acquired among other things the whole hard-coal minefield of the Donets, they had to import 80,000 tons of coal month by month from Germany to keep transport going.

Hopes of economic profit from Soviet Russian deliveries likewise fell far short of expectations. The commercial attaché in Moscow, Lista, found that the Soviet government was putting a number of obstacles in the way of trade with Germany. In the summer of 1918 a practical barter operation was started up, but it remained small in scope and had no serious effect on Germany's food and raw material shortages. Nor did the forced surrender of part of Russia's gold reserve demanded by the Protocol of 27th August 1918, which supplemented the Brest Litovsk Treaty with provisions concerning reparation for German property nationalized or confiscated in Soviet Russia.

German political plans for Russia's future also underwent an interesting development after the Brest Litovsk Treaty, under the influence of extreme annexationist views, especially those represented by the military clique around General Ludendorff. To be fair, these views were not shared by some of the more sober civilian politicians like Kühlmann who (it has been said), when it came to argument over eastern policy, 'must always have felt doomed to defeat in any dispute with Ludendorff'.

Foretaste of Nazism

In recent years the attention of historians has been drawn not only to the nature of German aims at the beginning of the First World War, but also to a detailed examination of German objectives in the east after the signing of the Brest Litovsk Treaty. The subject is all the more important because of the number of similarities, in scope and strategy, between the annexationist aims of that period and those of Nazi Germany formulated a quarter of a century later at the zenith of the *Wehrmacht*'s successes. In both periods we find the same limitless and overweening rapacity, together with the crudest contempt for the basic rules of international life: the respect for treaties and for the rights of other countries. The appetite of the German high command ranged from Finland and the Baltic to Murmansk, from the Ukraine and the Crimea to the Caucasus, Georgia, and Baku. These ideas were fully supported by the still decisive influence of the court in the First World War; Wilhelm II was delighted by the *élan* of his generals. Objections raised against such flagrant violation of the recently concluded peace settlement were imperiously dismissed as 'fear politics', on the grounds that 'peace with Russia can only last as long as they are afraid of us'. In the spring of 1918, pursuing this strategy of fear, German troops crossed the arbitrarily fixed frontiers and entered the central Russian districts of Voronezh and Kursk, lending aid in money and arms to the Cossack leader Krasnov on the Don. Ludendorff even toyed with the idea of setting up a 'South-Eastern League', covering the whole area between the Don and the Caucasus, under German surveillance.

The policies of Ludendorff and the high command in the Crimea, after the peninsula had been occupied in the summer of 1918 by German troops from the Ukraine, were the very prototype of Nazi ambitions to establish a German enclave there. The original plan was to assign a certain influence on the Crimea to Germany's ally Turkey, as her Pan-Ottoman enthusiasts, remembering the former glories of the Ottoman empire, wished; but this plan soon collapsed. Instead, the Kaiser's headquarters started to think about a 'State of Crimea and Tauris', perhaps in federation with the Ukraine; under this plan the Crimea, of course, was to be settled mainly by German colonists from the Caucasus, the Volga basin, Bessarabia, and so on. Germany would be given sole use of the port of Simferopol and exercise a dominating economic influence over this whole artificial entity. The purpose of this fantastic plan was evidently to guard the Ukraine from the rear and ensure its obedience to German orders. This is clear, for example, from Ludendorff's argument that it was in the interests of the *Reich* 'that there should exist on the Black Sea a state under chiefly German influence to serve as a buttress to our significant economic interests in the East'.

These wide-ranging militarist plans for the east were of course quite out of proportion to Germany's military means at the time and merely put further strains upon them as the situation developed. They were in the strictest sense 'boundless', as leading officials of the *Wilhelmstrasse* described them. In order to 'secure' existing territorial gains and hopes of further spheres of influence, these plans always required involvement in more and more distant regions. In the case of the Caucasus they even led to a conflict of interests within the camp, between Germany and Turkey. For in addition to her immediate territorial gains under the Brest Litovsk settlement Turkey was already trying, exactly in German style, to enlarge her own sphere of influence at Russian expense to the north of the Caucasus, where she proposed to set up a chain of vassal buffer-states. Berlin, however, did not intend to make way for these ambitions. For Germany regarded Transcaucasia as a bridge for further penetration into Central Asia; she wanted to 'use an opportunity which occurs perhaps once in many centuries'. Ludendorff was personally disposed at the beginning to leave the Turks a free hand in the Caucasus. But he soon swung round to the opposite policy, in its extreme form as usual, and proposed sending 'small forces' into Transcaucasia. These he described as mere 'training units' for a future Georgian army, yet in the same breath he defined their role as similar to that of the German expeditionary force in Finland – a force which took on a decisive role in the civil war there.

In June 1918 Ludendorff explained Germany's expansionist aims in the Caucasus quite pragmatically. He stressed the importance of securing rich mineral deposits and supplies for Germany's war economy. He hoped it would be possible to form a native army to fight side by side with Germany against Russia and to create another 'Caucasian Bloc', possibly in alliance with the above-mentioned 'South-Eastern League' and with various Cossack

Below: *The arrival of the first delivery of Russian gold to Berlin. Reparations totalling three thousand million roubles in gold were imposed on Russia, but neither this nor the requisition of wheat from the rich lands of the Ukraine made any real difference to the war economies of Austria-Hungary and Germany*

and other states to the south-east of Russia. The German militarists gave willing support, especially in arms, to the most dubious local and tribal leaders who now converged on Berlin with offers of collaboration (a 'Kalmuk Prince' amongst them); they were to accept German protection after their artificial states had been set up with the help of German bayonets. This fully accorded with Wilhelm's idea of breaking up the Russian state into four tsardoms—the Ukraine, Transcaucasia and the whole South-East, Great Russia (Muscovy), and Siberia. Such a programme of course, if ever attempted, would mean further protracted warfare with Russia.

The real loser—Germany

The real victor to emerge from the Peace of Brest Litovsk was not Germany, who had dictated its brutal conditions, but Soviet Russia, who had accepted them with all the humiliation they involved. Lenin's tactics of prevarication and temporary retreat brought their expected reward. They gave Soviet Russia the necessary time for consolidation at a critical stage. The economic gain the Central powers had anticipated from a separate peace remained, despite the best efforts of the occupying powers to purchase or requisition goods, far below the expected levels. The 35,000 waggons of corn and other foodstuffs and raw materials sent out of the occupied area, mainly the Ukraine, in the course of six months' exploitation were not enough to make any appreciable difference to the war economies of Germany and Austria-Hungary.

The treaty also spelt defeat for the Central powers in another and equally sensitive field. Multitudes of prisoners returned to Germany and Austria-Hungary after experiencing the revolution in Russia; they returned with very different scales of values and concepts than those they had had when they put on uniform in 1914. They were glad to be back home, of course—but not to get back into uniform and resume fighting. They became a source of infection in the army and doubtless accelerated its collapse as the Russian revolution itself and the dissemination of the politics and ideology, especially peace propaganda, that went with it undoubtedly did. The Austro-Hungarian army, like the state it served, broke up into its national components. In November 1918 German regiments started to set up military councils which took part in the revolutionary movements on German soil.

In November, too, the Soviet government denounced the Treaty of Brest Litovsk and Germany undertook to cancel it by signing peace terms at Compiègne. The time when she could enforce the conditions of a dictated peace had passed. The Soviet government no longer had to fear the possibility of German intervention. And official Berlin could no longer hope to maintain its hold in Russia with bayonets; it could not even maintain relations with the Soviet government when, under the impact of revolution at home, the very German soil was shaking under its feet.

The surprise and anxiety caused in the Allied countries by the signature of a separate peace in 1918 had a kind of epilogue in the fears aroused among some of the new post-war states of central Europe at the thought of a possible German-Soviet *rapprochement*. But these fears were groundless at the time when they occurred. The Brest Litovsk Treaty had left too sour a taste behind it to serve as a suitable psychological model for future policy. Besides, external circumstances had changed too much. When the November revolution broke out in Germany it seemed as if the moment which the Bolsheviks had prophesied, the moment of pan-European revolution, was finally approaching. Only gradually was it seen with sufficient clarity that none of the revolutionary outbursts in the rest of Europe had been powerful enough to overturn the existing structure of society. No link in Europe's social chain had been as weak as Tsarist Russia. The German-Soviet treaty later signed at Rapallo, some aspects of which were anticipated as early as 1920, was in no way a continuation of the Brest Litovsk pattern; it was not a *Diktat* but a treaty between equal partners. It implied a new approach to international problems and it signalled the creation of a new and more permanent constellation of forces. *(Translation)*

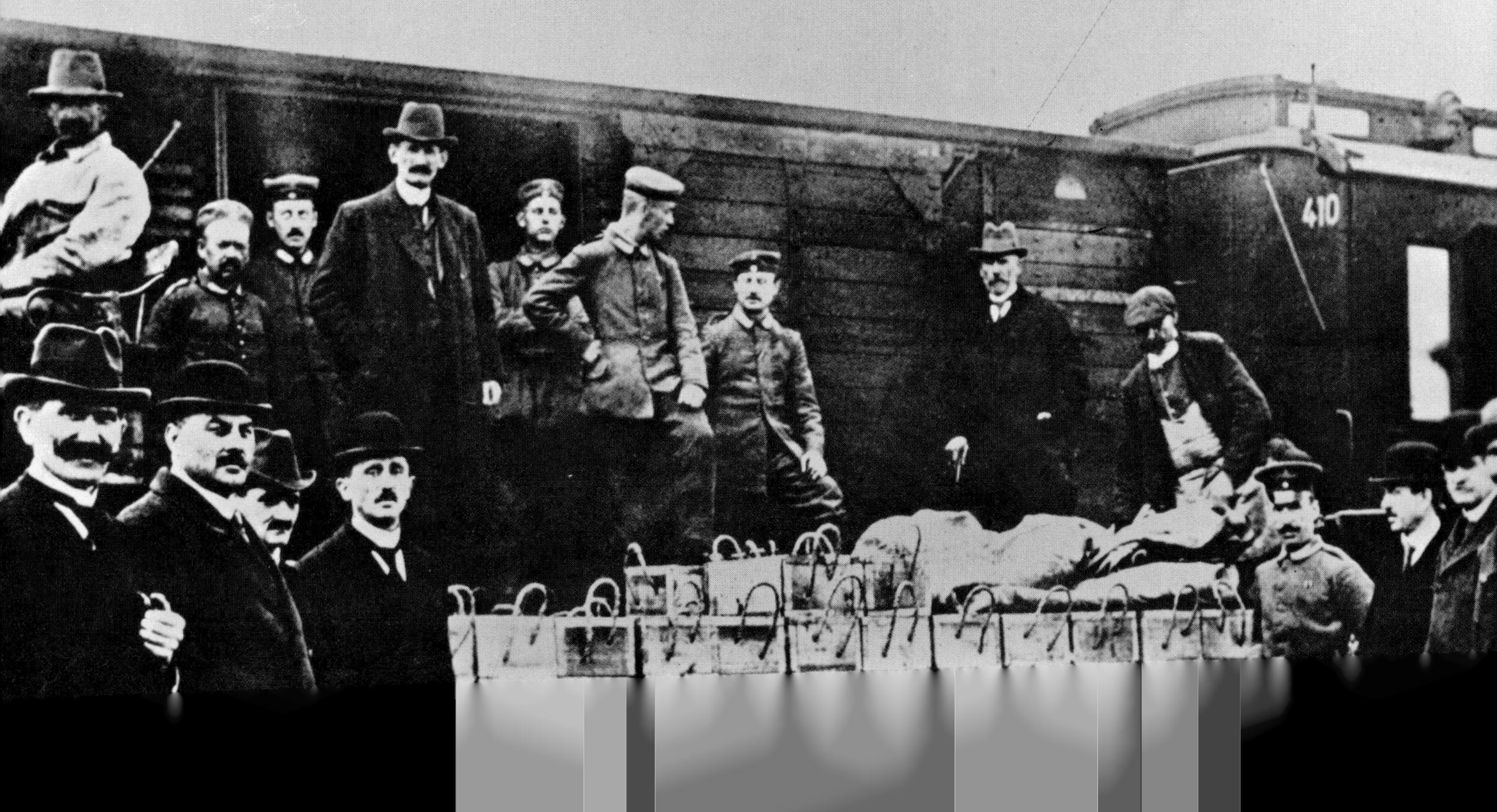

VHÚ, Praha

Above: *Presenting the colours to the first Czech unit in the Russian army. It won a victory in 1917, but trouble started when the Bolsheviks seized power*

Below: *'In a Ukrainian Cottage' painted by Czech legionary Štěpán Váca in 1919 in Siberia. It shows Czechoslovak volunteers visiting Ukrainian peasants*

Above: *Czechoslovak recruiting poster from the United States. Masaryk built up the legion in France in order to win Allied recognition for the Czechoslovak nation*

Russia, 1917-18 / William V.Wallace

The Czechoslovak Legion

The rumble of the Soviet tanks in Prague in August 1968 was an echo of the conflict between the Czechoslovaks and the Soviets fifty years previously. For the epic of the Czechoslovak Legion was an uncanny presage of the history of Czechoslovakia itself

Below: Czechoslovak volunteers in the trenches near Zborov before the battle they fought and won as part of the Russian army in July 1917. *Bottom:* Thorns in the side of Russia's new masters, the Bolsheviks – Czechoslovak Legionaries, wrapped well against a temperature of −40°C, guard a train in Siberia. By June 1918 they controlled most of the Trans-Siberian Railway and had set up a state within a state

VHÚ, Praha

VHÚ, Praha

At the beginning of the First World War Czechoslovakia was not even a name. There were people in the west who had heard of Bohemia, some indeed who were acquainted with its glorious past. But there were none at first who sensed its future; and at home in Bohemia and Slovakia there were few in 1914 who realized that the moment for complete and united independence had arrived. Yet, by the end of the war, Czechoslovakia was not only a feature of the political map of the new Europe, the Czechoslovaks were almost a household word in the political conversation of the west. Much of this was due to the action and the legend of the Czechoslovak Legion. 'The story of the adventures and triumphs of this small army,' wrote Lloyd George to Thomas Masaryk, the first President of Czechoslovakia, 'is one of the greatest epics of history . . . Your nation has rendered inestimable service to Russia and to the Allies in their struggle to free the world from despotism; we shall never forget it.'

The Legion in Russia was only one section of a bigger Czechoslovak military force. Units were also formed in France and Italy. All told, there were finally about 180,000 Legionaries. The inspiration was mainly that of Thomas Masaryk (p. 611). A professor of philosophy and for some years before the war a member of the smallest Bohemian political party in the Austrian Reichsrat, he was nonetheless the most hard-headed and influential leader of the Czech national movement. He was the first to go abroad in 1914 to work for the final destruction of Austria-Hungary and he ultimately built around himself a sufficiently representative group of Czechs and Slovaks to win for them the title of the Czechoslovak National Council in the summer of 1918. He realized that the key to political success lay in the possession of military power, and he built up the Legion as a means of winning recognition for the Czechoslovak nation from the Allied governments.

The Legions were recruited from three main sources. Some Czechs and Slovaks had been living abroad, often for more than a generation, as fugitives from the political oppression or economic backwardness of Austria-Hungary; others slipped abroad in the course of the war; and many more deserted on the Italian and Russian fronts rather than fight for a Germanic victory. Although there were considerable initial difficulties in cutting through diplomatic and military niceties, Masaryk was eventually able to utilize the mounting Allied need for manpower to secure recognition for the Czechoslovak Legion both as a fighting unit under Allied command and as a political unit under the control of the Czechoslovak National Council.

In this manner the Legion was a means to the end of Czechoslovak nationhood. The majority of those who volunteered did so for patriotic reasons and the Legion became the symbol of a nation fighting for its existence. After the war the Legionaries were to act as guardians of a hard-won independence. Under the distinguished editorship of Dr Lev Sychrava, a lawyer by training and one of Masaryk's original team, they ran their own newspaper, *Národní Osvobození* (National Liberaton), which had a standing much like the old *Manchester Guardian* in Great Britain, and they generally influenced national politics in the direction of sensible moderation. But in its heyday it was the Czechoslovak Legion in Russia that attracted most attention. It numbered over 90,000 men, it won worldwide fame and made a marked contribution to history.

Despite the Slav racial affinities of the Czechoslovaks and the Russians it was harder for Masaryk to shape the Czechoslovak Legion in Russia than in the west. Masaryk's own sympathies were liberal and republican – he was an avid reader in French and he had an American wife. He found it difficult to negotiate with the Tsarist government which was not anxious to co-operate anyway. The legendary Slovak leader abroad, Milan Štefánik, achieved little success by a mission to Russia in 1916. After the February Revolution (p. 692) negotiations became easier. The Provisional Government was at least nominally democratic and Milyukov was a friend, although Kerensky was none too helpful. Masaryk visited Russia and a Czech brigade, formed in the Russian army, showed its paces in the little victory at Zborov in Galicia in July 1917. Permission was obtained to establish the Czechoslovak Legion in Russia. But the real complication set in with the Bolshevik Revolution in October.

Masaryk could be critical of social democracy. Ultimately, he was sharply critical of communism. But as the leader of a people fighting for its own independent nationhood, Masaryk was the last person to want to dictate the political beliefs of another people. He had absolutely no wish to get the Legion involved in the internal struggles of Russia. In any case his real concern in 1917 was to help to defeat Germany and Austria-Hungary. To this end he wanted to see the fast-growing Legion in Russia in action against the national enemy, preferably in the west. After the Bolshevik Revolution it was immediately apparent that the Legion could not fight on the Eastern Front because it was the primary aim of Lenin to secure peace with Germany. The Bolshevik Colonel (later General) Muraviev tried to use the Legion against the dissident Ukraine. So in February 1918 Masaryk negotiated Bolshevik permission for the Legion to travel east along the Trans-Siberian Railway to Vladivostok where Anglo-American shipping could transport it to the Western Front in France. The great Czechoslovak 'Anabasis', as it was later to be called, was to be nothing more than a train journey east, albeit one of 6,000 miles.

Victim of international politics

From Masaryk's point of view, of course, it also made political sense to bring the Legion to France. For the moment at any rate, the centre of international power lay in the west. But from this point onwards the Legion became as much the victim of international politics as an influence upon them. It took the heroic but unfortunate Czechoslovaks two whole years to complete those 6,000 miles.

The French were as anxious as Masaryk to see all the Czechoslovak Legionaries in the west. They regarded the whole of the Czechoslovak Legion, including the Russian section, as part of their own army. Early in 1918 the German threat was still very much on their doorstep and they were desperately short of reinforcements; it would be some time before the Americans could arrive in force. But the British attitude was more complicated. Although it was France that had pioneered the alliance with Russia, there was much more interest in Great Britain in diversionary attacks on Germany from the east. Even after the Bolshevik Revolution the British government was anxious to keep Russia locked in war with Germany. Again, with its blockade mentality, the British government was most concerned to keep Russian food and oil supplies out of German hands, and this could best be done by stiffening the Russian will to fight. Since the peace terms which the Germans offered the Bolsheviks in December 1917 were uncomfortably severe, there seemed for a month or two to be a chance that Russia would continue the war. The idea quite naturally occurred to the British government to suggest to the French that the Czechoslovak Legion should be retained in Russia as a bolster against Germany. Even when Lenin forced his colleagues to accept the humiliating terms of the Treaty of Brest Litovsk, signed on 3rd March, the British government still clung to its original notion. It was buoyed up by reports from Bruce Lockhart, the British agent in Moscow, that Trotsky in particular was still interested in winning help from the west to turn the tables on the Germans. A first British force landed in Murmansk in April after the conclusion of Brest Litovsk, and a second force followed in June, specifically to make contact with the Legion. A new role was being engineered for the Czechoslovaks, to rouse an unwilling Russian people to take up arms again against Germany.

Before Brest Litovsk the new Russian government was quite willing to let the Legion make its way east. It was not only powerless to do anything else, it was also anxious to have foreign troops off its soil (particularly when some of their leaders were former Tsarist officers) and equally anxious not to complicate the Brest Litovsk negotiations. The only condition laid down was the surrender of most of the Legion's Russian-supplied arms. Of course, the Bolsheviks would not have been true to their ideology if they had not tried to subvert some of the Czech and Slovak soldiers. Since most of the Czechoslovaks wanted to defeat Germany and go home, Bolshevik revolutionary propaganda had little immediate success. However, there were enough political defectors to form the first small Czechoslovak Communist Party in Moscow in May under a former tailor by the name of Alois Muna. There was a sudden epidemic of committees among the

Below: *Czechoslovak Legionaries in the Ukraine caught and executed as traitors by the invading Austrian military. Incidents like this strengthened the determination of the Czechoslovaks to go east fast and to 'shoot our way to Vladivostok if we have to'.*
Bottom: *Digging trenches for cannons for defence in the Urals in the winter of 1918*

VHÚ, Praha

VHÚ, Praha

rank and file of the Legion. But all the troops continued to sport the names and symbols of the Hussite Wars of the 15th century as an indication of their nationalistic if also democratic outlook and pressed on eastwards. The first contingent reached Vladivostok in April 1918 although many were still not across the Urals. The failure of their propaganda made the Bolsheviks a little irritable. Their irritation increased after Brest Litovsk as it became clear that the western Allies were not willing to accept Russia's withdrawal from the war. The Communist government gradually decided that the presence on its soil of foreign troops, including the Legionaries, amounted to intervention in its internal revolution. The Czechoslovak Legion was being cast in a role it never in fact played.

In the spring of 1918 the British concept of the Legion's possible role was put to the French in different ways. There was the need to harass the Germans in the rear; there was no shipping available in the Far East; the Legion could be evacuated westwards. The French were in part confused; they also had second thoughts. They began to feel that the Legion's presence in Russia might encourage Japanese intervention to deal with Germany. The result was an ambiguous agreement in May to divert part of the Legion north-west to Archangel where the British expected them to stay, whereas the French expected them to be evacuated. Coupled with this, at least on the British side, went a loose and in no way officially admitted feeling that intervention by the Legion to deal with Germany was in fact intervention to deal with the Bolshevik government itself.

Of all this the Czechoslovak National Council was not made aware. Edward Beneš, later Czechoslovakia's first foreign minister, did indeed agree to the re-routing of part of the Legion through Archangel; but he did so to avoid giving the impression that he was unco-operative and to hasten the passage of the Legion to the west. The Legionaries themselves were not apprised of what was being done.

The Legionaries had tasted military success in 1917. As they left the Ukraine in the wake of Brest Litovsk they had a further successful brush with the occupying German troops. Their numbers were growing daily as was their confidence and organization. War produces its heroes and *entrepreneurs*; the Czechoslovaks have never been short of either, even in peacetime. Before the February and October Revolutions of 1917 they had already felt themselves to be socially and economically superior to the Russians; the disintegration that the Legionaries now saw around them merely increased their pride in themselves and their self-sufficient organization. They threw up their own military leaders, men like Jan Syrovy, one-time bank clerk in Russian Warsaw and later commander-in-chief of the Czechoslovak army. They set up their own governing body. And they produced their own revolution.

The Legion in revolt

Initially they were quite prepared to keep to their agreement to hand over most of their arms and leave Russia. They accepted a new agreement in March; they would move east in trainloads from Penza, a mere 168 rifles and a single machine-gun per trainload. For funds they had some grants that miraculously reached them from France and they had the assistance of local soviets along the way. But the state of the railway was really so bad that they could not travel fast enough; they became annoyed with Bolshevik propaganda and began to suspect Bolshevik good faith—at this time Stalin was pressing for their total disarmament. Some became openly hostile to the Bolsheviks; most found their sympathies fading. The more they straggled out along the line, the more they wanted to get to France and finish their war.

A minor incident provoked the revolution. On 14th May 1918 two trains drew up at Chelyabinsk in the middle of Siberia, one carrying a unit of Czechoslovak Legionaries eastwards, the other carrying Hungarian prisoners-of-war westwards to join the Red Army. The Czechoslovaks had

Below: *The Trans-Siberian Railway. By June 1918 the Czechoslovak Legion was in control of the Trans-Siberian Railway from Penza to Vladivostok except for Irkutsk. At Samara they found the Tsar's gold reserves—a magnetic attraction for anti-Bolshevik leaders.* **Bottom:** *Czechoslovak machine-gunners on an armoured train at Ufa, near Chelyabinsk*

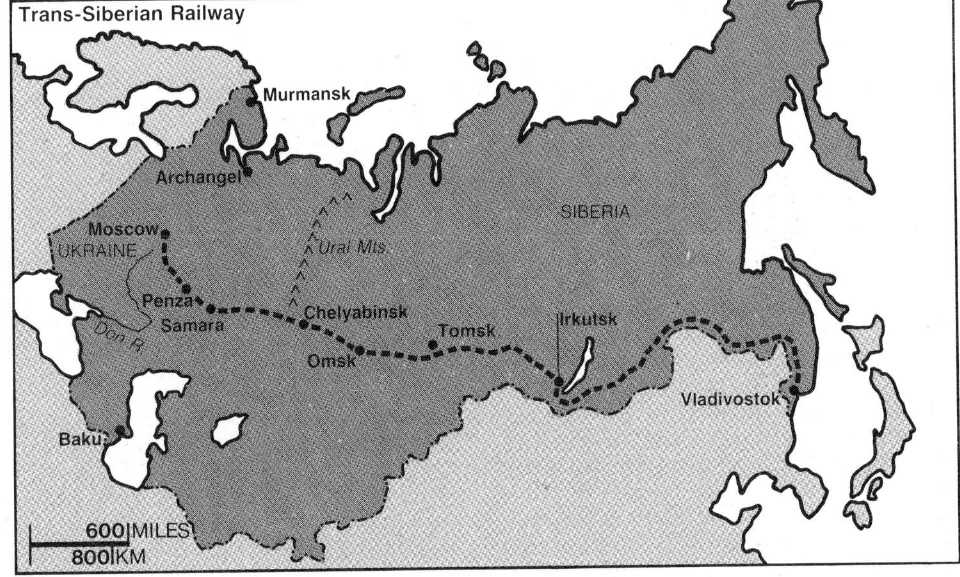

VHÚ, Praha

no particular love for the Hungarians who were not Slavs but who were one of the hated ruling peoples of Austria-Hungary. A Hungarian threw a crowbar which killed a Czechoslovak; the dead man's companions turned and murdered the Hungarian. The local soviet arrested the Czechoslovaks responsible and then arrested a delegation sent to seek their release. In retaliation the Czechoslovak unit arrested the soviet and took over the town. They were Czechoslovaks on their way to fight for their nation in Europe; they were not going to be pushed around.

Shoot on sight

The delicate relationship between the Czechoslovak Legion and the Communist government immediately collapsed. Within a few days Trotsky sent out orders to all soviets to disarm completely the Czechoslovak Legion; at the same time he arrested two leading members of the National Council in Moscow. The Czechoslovaks summoned their National Congress to Chelyabinsk on 20th May, elected a provisional executive committee, and, while expressing their sympathy with the Russians in their revolution, made it quite clear that they would not disarm until they had a satisfactory guarantee of unimpeded departure. Trotsky retaliated on 25th May by ordering every armed Czechoslovak to be shot on sight. Undeterred, the Czechoslovak Legion had by the end of June seized the Trans-Siberian Railway all the way from Penza through Chelyabinsk, Omsk, and Tomsk to Vladivostok with the one exception of Irkutsk. In effect the Legion had taken the law into its own hands and set up a temporary state within a state to ensure its escape.

To this end the Legionaries fought a number of battles with the Bolsheviks. In the summer of 1918 some of them in the extreme west joined with local Mensheviks and Socialist Revolutionaries in an anti-Bolshevik state set up in the Samara region; a Czechoslovak soldier, General Stanislav Čeček, actually took command of a combined Czechoslovak-Russian army. This was dangerously close to the kind of intervention that the Western powers had sought and the Legion had eschewed. The Legion also refused to divide and allow its westernmost units to go to France via Archangel. This seemed to be a denial of its declared purpose. But the truth was otherwise; the Legion was unwilling to expose itself to intervening directly in European Russia. Its action round Samara was also consistent with its major objective. Allied consular and military agents on the spot led it to believe that a large Allied force would soon land in Siberia to invade Germany from the east. The Legion waited.

The Legion went on waiting. But as the Allies did not come, it moved eastwards. The railway being what it was, the Legion could not move fast. There were still no Allied ships at the other end. But by contrast, British, Japanese, and American military forces had all landed at Vladivostok in August 1918; perhaps there might still be an Allied operation against Germany. Moreover, one of the things the Legion had come upon in the Samara region was the Tsarist government's gold reserve. This now became the point of power round which revolved a number of anti-Bolshevik governments, including that of the increasingly right-wing Admiral Kolchak in Omsk. Once the war was over in November 1918 the Legionaries had no purpose in remaining in Russia. They simply wanted to go home to the new nation, for the creation of which they had joined the Legion in the first place. But so long as there was an anti-Bolshevik government in Siberia the Western powers would not supply shipping to evacuate them. The Legion was still technically under French command; accordingly it stayed on until early in 1920. It still had no liking for the Bolsheviks but it soon became completely disillusioned with Kolchak because of his dictatorial abuses and military shortcomings. It remained aloof and ran its own little state along the railway, with its own enterprises, its own bank, and its own newspaper. Finally, in disgust, the Legionaries surrendered Kolchak to the Communist government in the moment of his defeat in January 1920. The intervention was over; a month later the Legionaries could go home.

They were never intentionally interventionists themselves. Undoubtedly they served their own nation well. The Czechoslovak diplomats at Versailles had an army in Russia and therefore had negotiating strength. But essentially the Legion became an international pawn. Most subtly of all, perhaps, its plight in the early summer of 1918, when it was still split into two straggling halves one on either side of Irkutsk, was used by the British and French governments to persuade the United States to intervene.

President Wilson liked creating other nations in the American image. But in 1917-18 he drew the line at Russia; it was enough that Tsarist autocracy had been overthrown. He was anxious not to get involved in the Bolshevik Revolution. But the British, and to some extent the French, were determined to make America's weight felt in every theatre of war and therefore tried to get America engaged in a revived Eastern Front. And what moved him in the end was not an array of anti-German or anti-Bolshevik arguments and pressure-groups but simply the need, as he was made to see it, of rescuing the Czechoslovak Legion from disaster. While the Legion was still cut in two at Irkutsk, it was put to him by the British and French—and also by some of his own advisers—that American troops were essential to help the Czechoslovak Legion to reunite and escape from Russia. Wilson had already set himself up as the terrestrial patron saint of the emerging nations. He had a particular fondness for the Czechoslovaks and for Masaryk himself, whom he saw as a kindred intellectual and political spirit. And he was under great pressure from East European immigrant groups whose entry into the war against Germany and Austria-Hungary had at last made them politically influential. In August 1918 Wilson authorized the dispatch of 7,000 soldiers to Vladivostok to hold the Legion's port of exit. It was part of the irony of the situation that the Americans landed almost exactly at the same time as the Czechoslovak Legion closed the gap in its lines. But America was now involved in intervention.

The legacy of intervention

The Czechoslovak Legion proved its own qualities in the fighting in Siberia and it tested the mettle of the new Red Army. If it brought near-disaster to the Russian Revolution, it also helped to strengthen it. Unaccountably, one of its units failed at one stage to open fire on Trotsky! More important, it never really turned on the Bolsheviks though it was the one force that could have caused them serious damage. When it finally sailed from Russia, it left behind a legacy of hatred, not so much for the Czechoslovaks themselves as for the idea of foreign intervention. This had not been forgotten by the time of Munich, nor of Vietnam. The Czechoslovak Legion was an object lesson in the dangers of idealism exploited for wrongful ends.

There was a legacy for Czechoslovakia, too. The majority of the Legionaries returning from Russia were convinced of the folly of getting caught up in east-west battles. They were the ones who shaped Czechoslovakia's policy of depending on east and west together or not at all. Yet this was a policy that failed in 1938 at Munich and again in 1948 when the Communists came to power. It was not given to the Czechoslovak state any more than it had been given to the Czechoslovak Legion to pursue a course of its own. In any case, among the Legionaries who returned were both anti-Bolsheviks who refused to fight on the side of the Soviet Union in 1938 and pro-Bolsheviks who helped to found the Communist Party of Czechoslovakia which eventually came to power in 1948.

The story of the Czechoslovak Legion was a microcosm of world history in the years 1917 to 1920 and an uncanny presage of the subsequent history of Czechoslovakia.

The Home Fronts

Chapter 29

Introduction by J.M.Roberts

Because of its scale and nature the war broke directly into many more people's lives than any earlier struggle and it continued to bend them and interfere with them, year after year. As states threw more and more burdens on their subjects, and undertook more and more direction of their lives, the struggle seemed more and more to resemble a combat between great economic systems and whole societies. It far transcended the clash of armies and navies.

It was such a view of the struggle that underlay and justified the attacks on the economy and the civilian population launched through the rival blockades. In an earlier chapter we explained the intensification of submarine warfare by the Germans and in his article, **Blockade Bites Deep**, Arthur Marwick describes the damage being done by this weapon and its effects on the outlook for 1918. Indisputably, the Germans were coming off worst. They had depended less on imported food than the British before 1914, but their mortality rates now showed them to be nearer starvation, in spite of the heavy losses they had inflicted on Allied shipping in 1917. As the shortages of food, fuel and clothes pinched more and more, so did the national unity with which Germany entered the war show signs of cracking. In these circumstances it was likely, if not certain, that the SPD, the old 'enemies of the Reich' in the eyes of Prussian conservatives, would again begin to think about opposition. They would have to, if they were not to lose their members to other leaders. What happened and the troubles which the war had already brought to the party, are described in J.R.C.Wright's article, **Socialism and Unrest**.

Partly because of the strains imposed by war on this scale and partly because of the nature of mass societies, great efforts were made to use public opinion as a weapon. This had begun early in the war. Even then neutrals had to be won over and placated, the morale of the home population kept up, and that of the enemy's civilians attacked. On the whole the battle of propaganda was won hands down by the Allies. Lord Francis-Williams describes for us the general nature of propaganda warfare early in the war, in his article **Propaganda 1914-15**, which analyses mass war in an age of mass literacy. Z.A.B.Zeman then describes other ways in which this weapon was used against the Central powers in **Propaganda and Subversion**. Such propaganda epitomized the war's total demands on society—even on its mental life—in a democratic age. It also presaged further and even more startling advances in techniques which would be increasingly used in both cold and hot wars in the next fifty years.

Radio Times

Pulling sugar-beets in Britain, 1916. They had once come from Germany and Austria

Herman Axelbank

Anti-war rally in Germany. The resentful, deprived mass of the populace wanted peace

Martyred Nurse Cavell, by Louis Raemaekers. Public opinion was now a weapon of war

Blockade

1915 42,000 working days lost in Germany through strikes.

1916 Quarter of a million working days lost in Germany through strikes.
98 strikes involving 9,344 strikers in France.
29th August: Hindenburg succeeds Falkenhayn as German chief-of-staff with Ludendorff as quartermaster general.
December: 'Hindenburg Programme' instituted to surmount manpower problem.
4th December: Lloyd George becomes British prime minister.
5th December: all German males between seventeen and sixty not on active service to be drafted into 'Patriotic Auxiliary Service'.

1917 689 strikes involving 293,810 strikers in France.
1st February: Germany launches unrestricted submarine warfare.
3rd February: voluntary rationing scheme announced in Great Britain.
16th April: German government proposal for a reduction in bread ration is met with first of a waves of strikes.
10th May: 'May Strikes' last a fortnight in Great Britain.
13th June: British government appoints commission of enquiry into industrial unrest.
15th November: Clemenceau becomes French prime minister.

1918 January: Germany hit by third and largest wave of strikes.

Propaganda and Subversion

1914 4th August: HMS *Telconia* cuts cables between Hamburg and New York.
7th August: Churchill announces that a press bureau is being set up in Great Britain to censor press reports and issue information to the press.
September: Charles Masterman sets up propaganda office in Wellington House, London.
16th September: *Dumfries Standard* prints story of atrocious treatment of Nurse Hume which many other newspapers pick up.
16th September: Grand Duke Nikolay Nikolayevich publishes declaration saying Russia had entered war to fulfil national desires of Slav peoples of Austria-Hungary.
30th September: Sir Stanley Buckmaster takes over directorship of press bureau from F.E.Smith.
December: 170,000 copies of Grand Duke Nikolay Nikolayevich's manifesto are distributed in Prague.

1915 March: Helphand writes memorandum on Russian revolutionary movement for Germans.
May: Colonel Repington, military correspondent of *The Times* writes article criticizing supply of munitions to British forces.
14th May: Masterman publishes the Bryce report in thirty languages on the conduct of the Germans in Belgium.
6th November-20th November: *The Globe* forced to suspend publication until it issues an apology for publishing a false report that Kitchener had resigned.
20th November: Lord Northcliffe writes leader critical of Kitchener in the *Daily Mail*.

1917 April: Germans provide a sealed train to take Lenin back to Russia.

1918 Lord Beaverbrook is put in charge of the new ministry of information.
April: an Allied commission is set up at Italian headquarters including representatives of South Slav, Czechoslovak, and Polish exiles committees.

Germany

1914 3rd August: SPD parliamentary party decides to vote for government bill designed to raise money for war.
4th August: SPD unites behind government.
December: Liebknecht votes against war finances.

1915 December: group of SPD deputies go into open opposition to the war and the SPD leadership.

1916 September: conference of the whole SPD fails to restore unity.

1917 January: those opposed to official SPD policy hold their own conference and eventually form their own party—the Independent Social Democratic Party (USPD).
19th July: SPD, Catholic Centre, and Progressive parties pass a resolution for peace in the Reichstag.

1918 March: SPD does not vote against the Treaty of Brest Litovsk, which proposes sweeping annexations of Russian territory, contrary to its principles.

Imperial War Museum

Home Fronts, 1917/Arthur Marwick

Blockade Bites Deep

What was it like for the civilian populations of Great Britain, France, and Germany during 1917, the year of shortages? The most dramatic result of the German submarine campaign was that it brought the USA into the war. But perhaps the most interesting effect was what it revealed about the economy and morale of the three countries involved

Ullstein

Left: Ratings load a torpedo tube aboard a German U-boat. Unrestricted submarine warfare threw the Allied war effort into dire jeopardy, bringing high prices, scarcity, and profiteering in its wake. ***Far left:*** *British soldier examines French candlesticks once meant for Germany. Metal shortages hampered the German war effort*

None of the great powers was really prepared or equipped to wage a protracted war in which the rival blockades would increasingly impose siege conditions on the domestic populations. France, though industrially under-developed, came nearest in 1914 to self-sufficiency, with forty-two per cent of her active population still employed in agriculture; but the balance was totally distorted by the German invasion which involved a loss to France of almost ten per cent of her territory and fourteen per cent of her industrial potential. What France thus lost had to be supplied from outside. As the war dragged on into 1917 the situation became more and more critical. There was little scope for bringing more land under cultivation, and agricultural productivity steadily declined as the soil grew tired and the men who once had worked it were slaughtered on the field of battle.

Great Britain had been prodigal in her neglect of agriculture in the pre-war years, so that she had to depend on imports for four-fifths of her wheat and forty per cent of her meat, and relied on Austria and Germany for almost all of her beet sugar. For the island nation more than any other, trade was life: the unrestricted submarine campaign launched by Germany on 1st February 1917 threw the whole Allied war effort into dire jeopardy.

Submarine warfare

Before the war Germany had efficiently developed her agricultural and industrial resources and in 1914 was producing two-thirds of her own food and fodder requirements. Through scientific inventiveness and the use of *Ersatz* ('substitute') materials she was able to overcome many immediate shortages. The initial advantage was Germany's, but as the war continued that advantage slowly, implacably, wasted away. It was as vital to Germany that her submarine campaign should achieve a quick kill as it was to the Allies to ward off that fate.

By Easter 1917 German submarines were doing such deadly business that one out of every four ships sailing out of British ports was doomed to destruction. Disruption in basic imports meant scarcity, high prices, profiteering, and austerity. Life in Great Britain and France took on the hue of battleship grey: 'Paris is no longer Paris,' a contemporary lamented; *l'année des privations* ('the year of privations'), was how another described 1917. Day and night were reversed. Once the streets had been filled, during the day, with breathless bustle; now they were deserted – for everyone had work to do, whether in a munitions factory or the local forces canteen. At night there was now complete darkness where once there had been a constellation of lights, and the sounds of steam-hammers and factory machinery where once there had been total silence. And the night was full of the noise of rumbling convoys and the long, ominous-looking trains that carried munitions or delivered the shattered bodies of soldiers straight to the sidings at the military hospitals.

Although the strain on civilian morale was severe, the crisis point in Great Britain was limited to a few anxious weeks in the summer of 1917 when it seemed likely that the entire war effort might founder. Then the last-minute adoption of the convoy system eased the situation. But in France hardship and social strains were more intense, and these, added to the terrible slaughter at the battle of Verdun, the previous year, created a condition in which a complete collapse of morale was always a possibility – a collapse which would have struck the foundations of the whole Allied effort.

Shortages everywhere

The first real shortages, and first queues appeared in Great Britain in the early months of 1917. The press described the kind of scene which became common everywhere: at Wrexham a farm-wagon laden with potatoes 'was surrounded by hundreds of clamouring people, chiefly women, who scrambled on to the vehicle in the eagerness to buy. Several women fainted in the struggle and the police were sent for to restore order'.

In December 1916 David Lloyd George took over the government. He appointed a food controller who established himself amid the splendour of Grosvenor House where the suggestive flesh of the famous Rubens paintings was covered up to protect the morals of the girls recruited as typists for the new ministry. A scheme of voluntary rationing, whereby each citizen was to restrict himself to four pounds of

DON'T WASTE BREAD!

SAVE TWO THICK SLICES EVERY DAY, and Defeat the 'U' Boat

Bibliothek für Zeitgeschichte, Stuttgart

Musée Royal de l'Armée, Brussels

'Life . . . took on the hue of battleship grey'

***Above:** French peasant women harvesting the potato crop in place of their menfolk who had gone to the front. The real brunt of the war was borne by the peasantry and their bitterness against their urban compatriots introduced a new and dangerous tension into France in 1917.* ***Above right:** British appeal for economy in face of the U-boat menace. By Easter 1917 German submarines were doing such deadly business that one out of every four ships sailing out of British ports was doomed to destruction.* ***Below:** Pineapples with everything? They were cheaper than potatoes in Great Britain in February 1917*

Radio Times

bread, two-and-a-half pounds of meat, and three-quarters of a pound of sugar a week was announced on 3rd February – two days, it may be noted, after the start of unrestricted submarine warfare. At the beginning of May a Royal Proclamation on the saving of grain was read on successive Sundays in churches and chapels throughout the land, and a special food economy campaign was mounted. Some shops and local authorities established their own rationing schemes and these were reinforced by statutory food control committees formed throughout the country. Margarine, fats, milk, and bacon became very scarce. Sugar and butter were practically unobtainable. Even 'Government Control Tea' – often likened to sweepings off the floor – was very hard to get. Towards the end of the year there was a 'meat famine', followed by meat rationing early in the new year. Upper and middle-class families turned to substitute dishes. To them shepherd's pie still seemed something of an outrage: 'but mummy, it's a particularly nasty piece of shepherd', lamented a little boy in one of the many cartoons which concentrated on the food situation. For working-class families the biggest hardship was the steep rise in the price of bread: to make matters worse bread was 'Government Bread' whose various strange ingredients tended to go bad in warm weather.

Bombs, strikes and scandals

To ram home the consequence of their submarine blockade the Germans unleashed the heaviest civilian bombing raids of the entire war: the underfed, war-weary citizens of London took to the tubes for shelter. Across the Channel there was little bombing in 1917 but in other respects France did not fare so well. During the harsh winter of 1916-17 coal supplies gave out. This was the topic upon which French cartoons concentrated: in one a lackey is depicted bowing obsequiously before the coalman – 'Coal,' he says, indicating a richly carpeted stairway, 'take it up by the main staircase.' In various parts of the country coal wagons were forcibly commandeered by members of the public. *Pâtisseries* were closed, and restaurant menus subject to severe restriction. Because of flagrant profiteering, the government encouraged the founding of co-operative and civic restaurants and industrial canteens with *prix fixe* ('fixed price') menus. The cost of living had gone up by at least eighty per cent since 1914, causing special hardship to the million or so refugees from the German-occupied areas scattered throughout the main centres of population.

Farmers and many small tradesmen were able to do well for themselves (American troops became a particularly good

Collection René Dazy

Bibliothek für Zeitgeschichte, Stuttgart

***Above:** British poster stigmatizes indolent luxury. But upper and middle-class families did turn to substitute foods. Even so, shepherd's pie still seemed something of an outrage. 'But mummy, it's a particularly nasty piece of shepherd,' lamented a little boy in one of the many cartoons. **Above centre:** Poster devised and drawn by a French schoolgirl appealing for economy in the use of gas lighting. Gas supplies relied on coal and during the harsh winter of 1916-17 coal reserves gave out. **Above right:** Gunners and heavy artillery piece silhouetted against the unearthly glare of war on an Austrian poster offering to buy nickel, copper, and brass. These metals, it stated, were desperately needed for munitions. **Bottom left:** Etonians fighting the U-boats, not on the playing fields, but on nearby potato patches. **Below right:** A sugar registration card. A scheme of voluntary rationing was begun in February 1917*

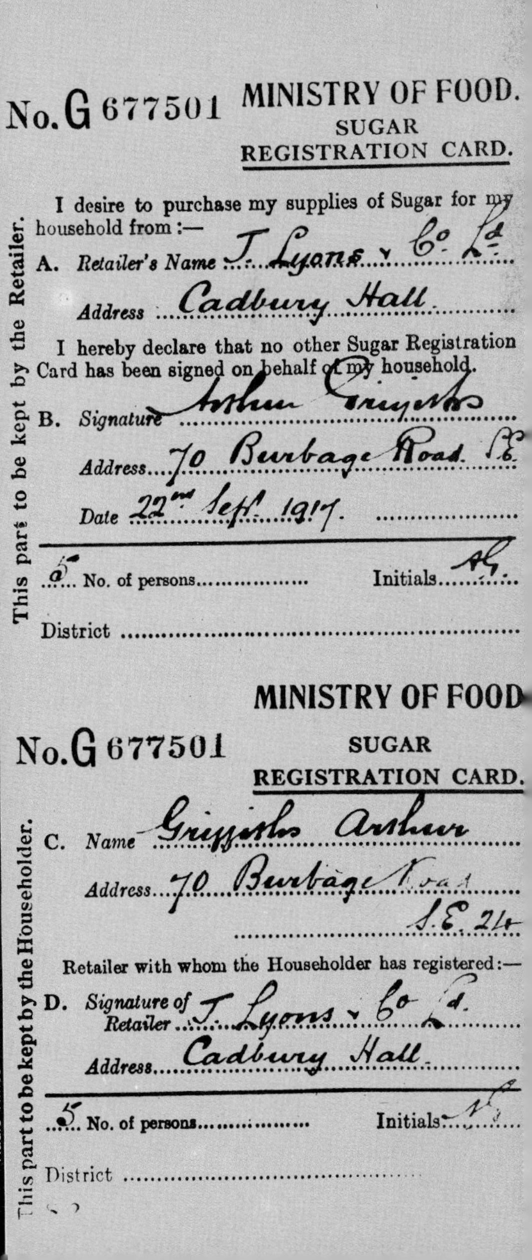

No. G 677501 MINISTRY OF FOOD.
SUGAR
REGISTRATION CARD.

This part to be kept by the Retailer.

I desire to purchase my supplies of Sugar for my household from :—

A. Retailer's Name J. Lyons & Co Ld
Address Cadbury Hall

I hereby declare that no other Sugar Registration Card has been signed on behalf of my household.

B. Signature Arthur Griffiths
Address 70 Burbage Road SE
Date 22nd Sept 1917.

5 No. of persons .... Initials AG

District ....

MINISTRY OF FOOD
No. G 677501 SUGAR
REGISTRATION CARD.

This part to be kept by the Householder.

C. Name Griffiths Arthur
Address 70 Burbage Road
S.E. 24

Retailer with whom the Householder has registered:—

D. Signature of Retailer J. Lyons & Co Ld
Address Cadbury Hall

5 No. of persons .... Initials

District ....

Radio Times

source of quick profit) but many bakers, adversely affected by government price control, went bankrupt. The salaried middle class suffered severely from the rising cost of living. While sections of the working classes, protected by government minimum wage laws, did not do too badly, the real brunt of the war was borne by the peasantry, and their bitterness against their urban compatriots introduced a new and dangerous social tension.

The February and October revolutions in Russia, by which eventually a major country was lost to the Allied cause, spread a tremor of excitement throughout the

Ullstein

Berlin in 1917. The public parks lose their flowerbeds and take on the appearance of allotments. All food was desperately scarce

working-class movement in Great Britain and France, though war weariness and the high cost of living were probably sufficient to account for the great outbreak of industrial unrest which characterized 1917. In France there were 689 strikes involving 293,810 strikers (compared with only 98 strikes and 9,344 strikers in 1916). In Great Britain the 'May strikes', breaking out on the 10th of the month and lasting for a fortnight, caused such dislocation of war production that on 13th June the government appointed commissions of enquiry into industrial unrest. The commissioners for the north-east declared that 'the high price of staple commodities have undoubtedly laid a severe strain upon the majority of the working classes, and in some instances have resulted in hardship and actual privation'.

Other commissions noted food prices and profiteering as the main grievances. In Great Britain the political structure, reactivated by Lloyd George, just managed to survive the test, though there were bitter struggles between politicians and military leaders. In France there was a succession of political scandals, some dangerously tainted with defeatism. By the end of the year three prime ministers had resigned: Aristide Briand in March, Alexandre Ribot in September, and Paul Painlevé in November. Only the accession on 15th November of the seventy-six-year-old Clemenceau gave promise of any restoration of leadership and stability.

The razor and the noose

In her use of submarine warfare Germany just failed to slash open the jugular vein of the Allied powers. But if the German weapon against the Allies was the razor, the Allies weapon against the Germans was the noose – and it was already applying slow strangulation. There were no bloodstains but the life was being squeezed from the German nation. As the war continued, so Germany's initial advantage disappeared: food imports from neutral countries came to a halt, and whatever requisitions Germany might make from conquered territories these fell far short of redressing the balance. By the winter of 1916-17 the German people were already suffering hardships beyond anything endured in Great Britain or France. Yet, while the Allied press did occasionally carry stories of shortages and hunger in Berlin, they more usually concentrated on praising the thoroughness of Teutonic organization, setting it up as an example for the Allies to follow. In fact, even since August 1916 when the dominion of General Erich Ludendorff (the new quartermaster general) and General Paul von Hindenburg (the new chief-of-staff) had been established, Teutonic organization was not doing too well against the vested interests which were stronger in the loose confederation known as the German empire than in more homogeneous countries like Great Britain and France. Part cause, more symptom, of Germany's troubles was the bad harvest of 1916: for all the pre-war advances farming was now in decay because of a shortage of farm workers and, thanks to the blockade, of a shortage of fertilizers and farm implements.

No men, no trains

The problem upon which the new military rulers concentrated was that of Germany's manpower shortage, staggeringly revealed in a census of 1916 which showed that although there were a million more women and thousands more children in employment, total numbers in productive employment were three-and-a-half million less than before the war. The 'Hindenburg Programme' of December 1916 was basically intended to surmount the manpower problem. Under the terms of a law of 5th December every male German citizen aged between seventeen and sixty not on active service, was to be drafted into 'Patriotic Auxiliary Service'. Because of the resistance of employers, who were as reluctant to employ women as they were to release their skilled men, and because there were many routes through which wealthier citizens could escape their obligations (by, for instance, joining some voluntary wartime committee), the law was not very successful. The early months of 1917 revealed the 'Hindenburg Programme' to be falling far short of its targets. Manpower was the topic of the

Bread ration book for itinerant German. A bad harvest in 1916 further added to decay in German agriculture induced by war

moment, rather as coal was in France and austerity food in Great Britain: one German cartoon pictured two ageing spinsters lamenting, 'If only compulsory female service would come – then perhaps the marriageable age would also be extended to fifty years.'

Undue attention to manpower concealed the chaos which was developing in German transport. Before the war German imports had come inland from the North Sea ports by river and canal: now, with these ports blockaded, the main transport burden lay on the rail connections to the Ruhr and Silesian coalfields, to the iron deposits of occupied France, and to the food-stores of the east. Trains simply began to go missing as the various state and local authorities raided them for the provisions they needed. Close on the heels of the transport crisis there followed a widespread coal deficiency.

Poor German production figures – thirty to forty per cent less than before the war by 1917 – revealed not so much inefficient leadership as the weariness of an underfed people. Etched deep into the German consciousness was the bitter 'Turnip Winter' of 1916-17 when in place of potatoes the people ate fodder beets – and there was not always a lot else to eat. For Germans it was not a question of the imposition of rationing – for two years they had had cards for bread, fats, milk, meat, and butter – but a question of whether the ration to which they were officially entitled would in fact be obtainable. At the beginning of 1917 men were subsisting on a basic ration of a quarter of a loaf of bread (200 grams) per day, and less than a quarter of a pound of fats per week; the procurement of other

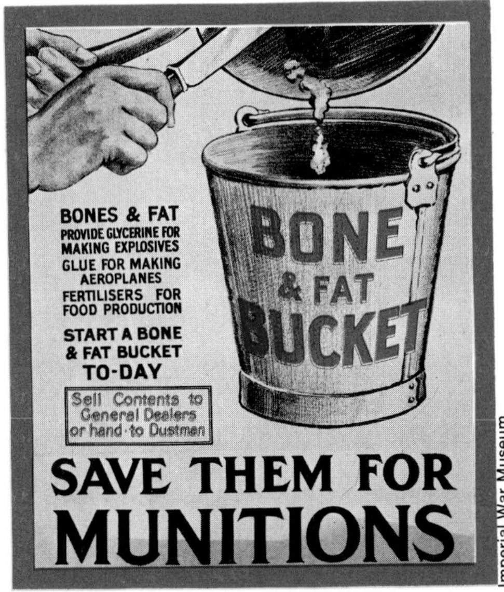

Imperial War Museum

British poster appealing for what was once considered refuse. Only in wartime was the value of such commodities fully appreciated

commodities was difficult and sporadic. Total German consumption of meat in 1917 was one quarter of what it had been in pre-war years, and what was available was most inequitably distributed.

Throughout the year schoolchildren and women's organizations collected kitchen waste, coffee-grounds, hawthorn fruits, kernels of fruit, acorns and chestnuts, stinging nettles, pine cones, green leaves (as fodder), paper waste, rubber waste, cork and cork waste, tin waste, metals, parts of bulbs, bones, bottles, celluloid, rags and tatters, photographic silver residues, platinum (from discarded sets of teeth, or from jewellery), gramophone records, women's hair. Most notorious example of all of German thoroughness was the conversion of dead horses into soap. This prompted the Allied atrocity story that Germany was building 'corpse-conversion factories' to make soap from dead soldiers.

To the pains of hunger and squalor was added anger over profiteering and black marketeering. Price control, in the hands of over a thousand separate agencies, was totally inadequate. 'The black market,' said a speaker in the Reichstag, 'has become the one really successful organization in our food supply system'. The famous memorandum from the Neukölln municipal council to the war food department, pirated in the left-wing press, revealed clearly what was happening. Big firms, using their economic power, or access to desirable commodities, were directly cornering food for their own employees; occasionally municipalities were able to do likewise, creating conditions of bitter local rivalry, and a complete breakdown of any pretence at food distribution. The memorandum predicted that from 'shortage and famine' the country would go to 'catastrophe'.

Even those allowed extra rations by virtue of their heavy manual work were getting less than half the necessary intake of calories. By late 1917 milk was practically unobtainable. Scarcity of soap brought a new menace: lice. The toll in disease and premature death was heavy. Death among those under five increased by fifty per cent in 1917; deaths from tuberculosis doubled. On 16th April the government had planned a reduction in the meagre bread ration. Working-class opinion was not mollified by announcements in various localities that such extras as sauerkraut, barley groats or smoked herring (one quarter of a herring per week) would be made available, and the proposed cut was met by the first wave in what, as in France and Great Britain, was to prove a year of strikes. Altogether nearly two million working days were lost, compared with less than a quarter of a million in 1916 and 42,000 in 1915. In the German navy, bottled up in its own ports, frustration, privation, and bitterness were at boiling point. Sailors, as well as workmen and food rioters, participated in the second wave of strikes which broke out in June.

German morale crumbles

Social and industrial troubles, naturally, bubbled over into politics. The political crisis of July began with various vague promises of reform: if the workers had no bread, then they must have political rights – that was the argument of politicians. It ended with the resignation of the chancellor, Theobald von Bethmann Hollweg. But conditions got worse, especially for the farmers – who had earlier done reasonably well, but who were now subject to food searches, regulations, and enforced slaughter of their stock – officials, who in some cases were, literally, worked to death, and the salaried middle class. Relatively speaking the upper strata of the industrial working class did better, because in official circles the industrial worker was valued more highly than any other class in the community, except the military. One bitter middle-class comment was typical: 'A family with two munitions workers normally enjoyed not only extra rations but a higher purchasing power than the family of a professor (whose war value, if he was a physiologist, was limited to the writing of articles proving the scientific adequacy of wartime standards of nutrition).'

The blockade, on both sides, brought home to the civilian populations some of the grim truths of war. From governments it brought, in a curious way, certain positive responses. Minimum wage laws and

Bibliothek für Zeitgeschichte, Stuttgart

Poster glibly assuring Germans that their army would win the freedom of the seas. Yet the Allied blockade strangled the country

social welfare, designed to meet some of the grievances of the industrial worker were now seen to be as vital to the nation's survival as the man in the trenches. France was sorely tried. One more bloody reverse on the field of battle might well have been sufficient to let loose civil disorder. But on the whole civic loyalty in Great Britain and in France withstood the test. It was in Germany, apparently the efficient, disciplined nation, that the pressures of economic warfare exposed the selfishness of the employers, the jealousies of the different localities, the class antagonisms, and the hollow facade of the parliamentary structure.

In January 1918 Germany was hit by the third and mightiest wave of strikes. Subsiding before the priority needs of the last great German offensive, it was, nonetheless, a clear sign that while Britain and France had, by a hair's breadth, managed to survive their worst year, 1917, the existing German system was approaching collapse and revolution.

THE DAILY
MIRROR

"THREE CHEERS

FOR BELGIUM!"

Propaganda 1914-15

The press had been powerful in peacetime. But in a time of great events and high emotions it acquired a new significance

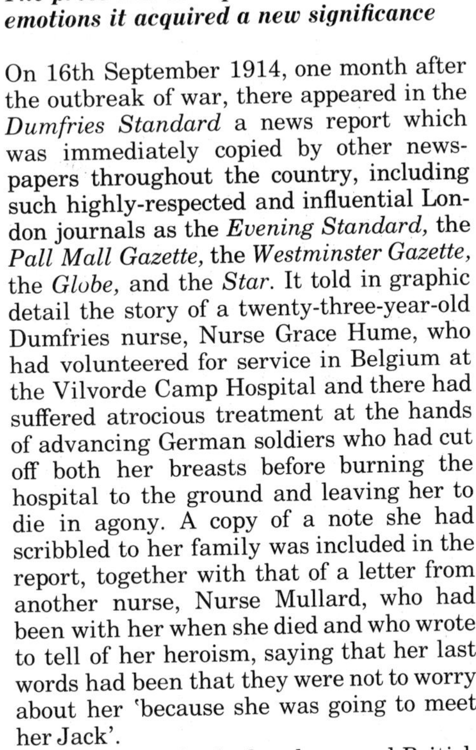

On 16th September 1914, one month after the outbreak of war, there appeared in the *Dumfries Standard* a news report which was immediately copied by other newspapers throughout the country, including such highly-respected and influential London journals as the *Evening Standard,* the *Pall Mall Gazette,* the *Westminster Gazette,* the *Globe,* and the *Star*. It told in graphic detail the story of a twenty-three-year-old Dumfries nurse, Nurse Grace Hume, who had volunteered for service in Belgium at the Vilvorde Camp Hospital and there had suffered atrocious treatment at the hands of advancing German soldiers who had cut off both her breasts before burning the hospital to the ground and leaving her to die in agony. A copy of a note she had scribbled to her family was included in the report, together with that of a letter from another nurse, Nurse Mullard, who had been with her when she died and who wrote to tell of her heroism, saying that her last words had been that they were not to worry about her 'because she was going to meet her Jack'.

This report shocked and enraged British opinion, confirming the popular belief that Great Britain was engaged in a war for civilization against a savage and brutal enemy possessed of neither pity nor humanity.

There was not one word of truth in it. Subsequent inquiries showed that so far from being tortured and murdered by German soldiers in Belgium, Nurse Hume, although she had volunteered for service at the front, was still in England on the staff of the Huddersfield Hospital. No such person as Nurse Mullard existed. The whole story was the fabrication of an hysterical seventeen-year-old girl, Nurse Hume's younger sister Kate, and had been swallowed whole by the press. But even after its perpetrator had been brought to court and charged, the story continued to circulate. It reappeared, intermittently, in one form or another throughout most of the war.

It was one of the first of the great atrocity stories. It was by no means the last. Even before the story of the Dumfries nurse, *The Times* had published a dispatch from its Paris correspondent reporting that 'an official of the Catholic Society' had recently interviewed a man who 'had seen with his own eyes German soldiery chop off the arms of a baby which clung to its mother's skirts'. This was soon amplified. A clergyman on 7th October 1914 told the Manchester Geographical Society (an odd audience): 'You will hear only one hundredth part of the actual atrocities this war has produced. . . . There are up and down England today, scores – I am understating the number – of Belgian girls who have had their hands cut off.' And a report published by the *Sunday Chronicle* on 2nd May 1915 described how 'a charitable great lady' was visiting a home for Belgian refugees in Paris when she noticed a little girl of ten who, although the room was hot, kept her hands hidden 'in a pitiful little worn muff'. 'Suddenly,' the report continued, 'the child said to her mother "Mamma, please blow my nose for me".' At this the great lady protested that surely such a big girl could use her own handkerchief, to be told by the mother in a dull, matter-of-fact tone, 'She has not any hands now, ma'am'.

Rape and mutilation

Other stories told of the raping and mutilation of nuns, and of a peasant in Sempst who had been compelled by five German soldiers to watch while they assaulted and ravished his thirteen-year-old daughter before bayoneting her and shooting his wife and small son. Wounded Canadian soldiers had been forced to watch one of their officers being crucified: 'He was pinned to a wall with bayonets through his hands and feet and then another bayonet was driven through his throat.' This appeared in *The Times* of 10th May 1915.

Germany had her own crop of atrocity stories. One of the most successful was issued by the Wolff Bureau, the German news agency, a few months after the war began. It reported that a French doctor, assisted by two French officers in disguise, had been arrested attempting to infect a well at Metz with plague and cholera bacilli. Many versions of this subsequently appeared.

In Great Britain and France particular attention was given to the propaganda value of reports of the cutting off of children's arms and the raping and mutilation of nurses and nuns; in Germany one of the most popular told of the gouging out of the eyes of captured German soldiers. A hospital in Aix-la-Chapelle was stated to contain a ward entirely devoted to such cases, and the *Weser Zeitung* of Bremen

Opposite page: *Great Britain's* Daily Mirror *helped rally opinion at the outbreak of war with 'Three Cheers for Belgium'. But the British press was indiscriminate and often irresponsible.* **Above left:** *Lord Northcliffe: 'Napoleon of the Press.' His searing attack on Kitchener outraged the country.* **Left:** *French troops catch up on the war news. British reports were heavily relied on*

reported similar instances in a Berlin hospital of soldiers mutilated on the battlefield. Later investigation proved all these stories to be untrue.

Atrocity stories have existed in every war. What gave them their particular significance in this war was the existence of large-circulation newspapers. For the most part these stories were born in the popular imagination, the products of unconscious anxieties and passions given new force by war hysteria. They were picked up by the newspapers and given wide publicity because the newspapers knew that this was what their readers wanted to hear—and, under the powerful influence of the emotions of war, were themselves persuaded, in every country, that these were the sort of acts of which the hated enemy was capable, and that anything that furthered resistance was justified.

Although atrocity stories played a significant part in forming popular attitudes in all countries, particularly at the beginning of the war, they represented only a comparatively small part of the uses to which mass media was put for propaganda purposes by all the warring nations. For the first time mass warfare and mass literacy coincided. As a result, the influencing of popular opinion both at home and abroad took on a new significance.

'The Siege of Portsmouth'

Such influencing had begun well before the start of war. More than nine years previously, for example, readers of the *Portsmouth Evening Mail* had found themselves invited to think of their fate, if a German invasion came, through the medium of a sensational serial, 'The Siege of Portsmouth', which used the actual names of prominent citizens of the town in order to give the story verisimilitude. The paper had been bought by Alfred Harmsworth, later Lord Northcliffe (p. 143), to help him in a parliamentary election in which he was standing as a Conservative candidate. Despite lurid posters showing the Portsmouth Town Hall being shelled, the serial was not very successful, nor did Harmsworth win the seat. But the theme of Great Britain's danger from German ambitions was continued on a much greater scale when Northcliffe launched his halfpenny national daily, the *Daily Mail*, a year later, and was supported there by a series of scarifying articles by the popular socialist writer, Robert Blatchford, founder of the *Clarion*, whom Northcliffe commissioned.

Even before Northcliffe bought control of *The Times* in 1908 that paper had been prominent in seeking to rouse public opinion to the dangers of German military and naval ambitions, and its Berlin correspondent, George Saunders, had been denounced by the Kaiser as a 'first-class

swine' (*'Erzschweinehund erster Klasse'*) for doing so. J.L.Garvin in the *Observer* was equally insistent in his warnings. With the aid of confidential material secretly fed to him by Admiral Sir John Fisher, the first sea lord, he led a campaign for more British dreadnoughts, which received powerful reinforcement in the popular music-hall song, 'We want eight and we won't wait'.

However, at this stage the press was divided. Against the voices of the *Daily Mail, The Times,* and the *Observer* were set those of almost the entire Liberal press, headed by the *Daily News,* the *Daily Chronicle,* and the *Westminster Gazette,* who trusted Germany's pacific intentions and believed that the other three were deliberately trying to foment war hysteria. There were similar, although smaller, divisions in the French press. In Germany the major newspapers took their line from the official German press bureau, which, while denying thoughts of war, constantly preached the need for German expansion. But the strong German Social Democratic movement and its newspapers were very pacifist and suspicious of the intentions of the German military command.

Censorship

With the outbreak of war all such divisions of press opinion on both sides vanished. But the relationship between press and authority—particularly in the more democratic nations—could not but be ambivalent. The whole inclination of the professional military—and naval—mind was to keep the press in ignorance and to publish only what seemed good to authority. In Great Britain even the newspapers' requests for accredited war correspondents with the troops were at first refused, although later the value of the dispatches of such men as Philip Gibbs was fully recognized. Even when newspaper correspondents were allowed, they were at first kept at base, well behind the lines and treated, in Northcliffe's angry phrase, as despised camp followers.

The need for censorship of material which might give information to the enemy was from the start recognized by government and newspapers alike. On 7th August 1914, Winston Churchill, the first lord of the Admiralty, announced in the House of Commons the setting up of a press bureau with the dual task of censoring press re-

La Baïonnette

Left: *'Homage to the Mother of the Crucified Canadian Soldier' by D.G.Widhopff. The artist was probably inspired by a tendentious report that some Canadian troops had been forced to watch one of their officers being crucified.*
Right: *A French depiction of mythical German atrocity*

Above: Northcliffe's Daily Mail *aided military charities. Before the war the newspaper had attempted to draw public attention to the threat of German militarism. In war it demonstrated the power and responsibility the new mass press could wield.* ***Below:*** *Although raids by Zeppelins and Gotha bombers were rare the* Daily Chronicle *knew what its readers wanted to see.*
Opposite page: *Heart-rending appeal became a compelling recruiting poster*

ports and of issuing to the press 'all information relating to the war which any of the Departments of State think it right to issue'.

The first head of the press bureau was Mr F.E.Smith (later Lord Birkenhead), a leading Conservative MP and one of the most brilliant lawyers of his time. However, he soon proved singularly unsuited to the task – and this for an unforeseen reason. Although often unnecessarily strict with routine material submitted to it, the press bureau under him turned out to be far too liberal for the comfort of the military mind where larger matters which roused F.E.Smith's own personal and political interest were concerned.

Things came to a climax at the end of August when a dispatch was submitted by *The Times* from its correspondent in France, Arthur Moore, describing the extent and consequences of the Allied retreat at the battle of Mons. The dispatch was so damning in its disclosures and judgements that *The Times* assumed that the censorship would automatically cut out most of it. Instead, to its amazement, it came back not only approved practically in its entirety but with additions written in by F.E.Smith himself which made the total impact even more disturbing. It was accompanied by a note from 'F.E.' to the editor of *The Times*. This apologized for the 'clumsy journalistic suggestions' made, but urged that they should be used 'to enforce the lesson – reinforcements and reinforcements at once'.

The dispatch was the first revelation of the extent of the blow inflicted by the Germans on the Allies in one of the first major battles of the war and it created a public sensation. Much to the anger of *The Times,* it was described as grossly exaggerated by Asquith, the prime minister, in the House of Commons and denounced by him as likely to spread alarm and confusion. It was clear that a new head of the press bureau must be found.

This proved to be another political lawyer, but a less contentious one, the solicitor general, Sir Stanley Buckmaster. He took over as director on 30th September 1914 and at once appointed to help him as assistant director an eminent journalist, Sir Edward Cook, formerly editor of the *Westminster Gazette* and later of the *Daily News,* who became joint director when Buckmaster moved to higher things as lord chancellor in May 1915. Thereafter although press censorship was sometimes criticized for delay in issuing news or for passing an item of information for one paper and stopping it for another, this was due far more to the difficulty of finding competent staff than to any original sin and it gradually became an efficient organization working on principles which proved so acceptable that they were adopted almost in their entirety for press censorship in the Second World War.

Censorship of cables and foreign letters, both in-coming and out-going, was compulsory. All other press censorship was voluntary. No censors were posted in the offices of the newspapers themselves and they made their own decisions as to what should be submitted to the press bureau. However, although news censorship was voluntary this was more a matter of principle than of practice. The Defence of the Realm Act (DORA) specified the matters on which publication was an offence, such as the disposition, and number of troops, movements of ships, details of munitions and war material, plans of future operations and – the most difficult part of censorship to operate – the publication of false statements about the war. The press bureau itself contributed notices amplifying or particularizing areas of information to which DORA applied.

There were, therefore, substantial legal sanctions behind the censorship. Moreover, since it was a complete defence against a charge under DORA if a newspaper could show that what it had published had been submitted to, and passed by, censorship, newspapers had a strong incentive to submit all war news to the press bureau and abide by its decisions. There were few prosecutions.

One of the few was in November 1915 when *The Globe* published a statement that Lord Kitchener had resigned as secretary of state for war and repeated it two days later after an official denial had been issued by the press bureau. Thereupon the police raided the newspaper and, acting under section 51 of the Act, seized its printing machinery. The newspaper was forced to suspend publication until it agreed to issue a retraction and apology.

At no time did press censorship extend to opinion. Newspapers were allowed freedom to say what they liked in leading articles or expert commentaries – and often did so, with considerable courage in the face of strong public opinion to the contrary.

The most famous instance of this came in May 1915. It arose from an article by Colonel Repington, the authoritative military correspondent of *The Times,* who was in close touch with Sir John French, the commander-in-chief of the British army, strongly criticizing the supply of munitions to the British forces.

What Repington had to say confirmed what was being hinted at in many heavily censored letters home from soldiers at the front. It confirmed also what Northcliffe, owner of the *Daily Mail, The Times,* the *Daily Mirror,* and many publications, and the biggest press power in the country, had learned from officers in the ▷800

Will they never come?

REPRINTED FROM

"THE WEEKLY DISPATCH"

(November 22nd, 1914)

Zeichnet die Sechste Kriegsanleihe

BRITAIN · NEEDS

YOU · AT · ONCE

Previous pages: *Age of chivalry recalled for propaganda purposes. Gallant Christian knights battle to suppress enemy heresy and wickedness.*
Left: *Austrian poster appealing for war-loan subscriptions.* ***Right:*** *British recruiting poster*

hospital run by Lady Northcliffe in their house, Sutton Place, near Guildford.

Northcliffe decided to act. He had originally campaigned excitedly for Kitchener to be minister of war and had helped to make him a popular idol: the strong silent soldier whose picture with pointing finger and the caption 'Your King and Country Need You' glowered down from every hoarding.

But Northcliffe was by now disenchanted with his hero. In office he had proved inefficient, pig-headed and narrow-minded. He sat like a stubborn toad on war news, refusing to allow any truthful account of reverses to be issued, in the mistaken belief that ordinary men and women, of whom he had little understanding, could not be trusted with bad news. Most of the worst censorship restrictions in the early days of the war could be traced to him. This was bad enough; but Northcliffe was now convinced that the failure to provide the fighting soldiers with the shells they needed was directly due to Kitchener's inability to adapt himself to modern war.

David Drummond

The British press stigmatized Germany as a treaty breaker with the slogan 'A Scrap of Paper'. A postcard echoes the disgust felt for German violation of Belgian neutrality

Late in the afternoon of 20th May Northcliffe closeted himself in his room at the *Daily Mail* offices and there wrote by hand a leading article, a column and a half in length, headed, 'The Tragedy of the Shells: Lord Kitchener's Grave Error'. 'The admitted fact,' it declared, 'is that Lord Kitchener *ordered the wrong kind of shell*– the same kind of shell which he used against the Boers in 1900. He persisted in sending shrapnel–a useless weapon in trench warfare. . . .' When the leader was finished and sent to the printers, Northcliffe gave orders that the only placard issued by the *Mail* that day should be 'Kitchener's Tragic Blunder'.

This attack on a public idol shocked the country. The *Daily Mail* was burnt on the London Stock Exchange and banned in leading London clubs and public libraries. Thousands of readers cancelled their subscriptions. 'If this country were Russia, Germany, or Austria,' said the *Daily Chronicle,* 'Lord Northcliffe would have been taken out into a courtyard and shot within 48 hours. . . . If it were France or Italy he would probably have been lynched within a shorter interval.' 'Either that frenzied office boy must be suppressed or no government can live,' declared the *Daily News,* 'we have to choose between responsible government and a press dictatorship.'

Yet in the end the truth of Northcliffe's criticism was accepted. It contributed to the fall of the Liberal government and the formation of a coalition–although still at this stage under Asquith–and the creation of a ministry of munitions under Lloyd George. It was a classic example of the influence the mass press could exercise.

This influence was, however, indiscriminate and often irresponsibly employed. It helped to rally opinion at the outbreak of war with the cry of 'Brave Little Belgium', stigmatized Germany as a treaty-breaker with the slogan, 'A Scrap of Paper', nicknamed the Kaiser 'The Mad Dog of Europe' and stirred British patriotism by the widely publicized, but, as far as could subsequently be discovered, untrue, allegation that he had referred to the British Expeditionary Force as this 'contemptible little army'–a phrase transformed into a kind of battle honour by the press as 'The Old Contemptibles'.

But press power was also used to drive Lord Haldane, one of the most efficient war ministers in modern history, out of public life because he had once expressed admiration for Hegel and other German philosophers, to force Churchill from office after the failure of the Dardanelles campaign, to ruin many innocent peoples' lives by promoting indiscriminate spy hysteria, and to conduct a vicious campaign against even the most genuine conscientious objectors.

News from the German front

The British press had a bigger impact than either the French or German in the first two years of the war. It was freer and it had a larger circulation. The French press was from the first subjected to a much tighter censorship–it was, indeed, because the French insisted that the same regulations should apply to British correspondents as to their own that all correspondents were at first excluded from the lines of the Allied armies. French newspapers were smaller than British and lacked the same opportunities for display and throughout the war the flow of official news to them was small. Many of them found themselves forced to depend on British reports.

The German press was kept under even tighter control by the military command. The official press bureau *(Pressekonferenz)* was headed by a military officer and no news that suggested inefficiency or lack of military success was permitted. The number of casualties was deliberately minimized. Thus on 15th November, 1914, when the official list of casualties already totalled some 55,000, all that the *Pressekonferenz* permitted the newspapers to publish was the story that killed and wounded might number a few hundred. Successes were consistently exaggerated and reverses minimized with the result that when the truth came out the effect on civilian morale was much greater than it would otherwise have been.

There was, however, one area of press publicity in which the German authorities were, rather surprisingly, much more wide-awake than either the British or the French. They were quick to recognize the advantage of giving facilities to neutral war correspondents, particularly American ones, at a time when the Allied command would have nothing to do with them.

The contrast was so striking that in January 1915 Theodore Roosevelt, the former American President, who was strongly pro-British, wrote to Sir Edward Grey, the British foreign secretary, reporting 'a distinct lessening of the feeling for the Allies and a growth of pro-German feeling'. This, he said, was due in large

Staatsbibliothek, Berlin

A lavishly equipped American pressman meeting German soldiers. The Germans saw the advantages of giving facilities to neutral journalists when the Allies totally ignored them

part to the 'very striking contrast between the lavish attentions showered on American war correspondents by the German military authorities and the blank refusal to have anything whatever to do with them by the British and French Governments. . . . The only real war news written by Americans who are known to and trusted by the American public comes from the German side; as a result of this the sympathizers with the cause of the Allies can hear nothing whatever about the trials and achievements of the British and French armies. . . .'

This protest and that of the British newspapers helped to bring some reform. As initial military resistance to war correspondents was broken down American journalists were given facilities alongside the newly accredited British correspondents. They were soon joined by photographers. Pictorial journalism, brilliantly exploited by Northcliffe's *Daily Mirror* among others, became an increasing feature of war reporting – and war propaganda.

Bidding for American support

By 1915 the need to gain American support was fully recognized by both sides and the fact, also, that to gain it the maximum possible use must be made of every available system of mass communication – of the press above all.

The Germans had certain initial advantages. There were tightly knit groups of German immigrants, particularly in the middle west, anxious to help the Fatherland. Many of the American-Irish active in politics in Boston, New York, and elsewhere were also strongly anti-British, so was the biggest newspaper chain in the country, the Hearst press, and the even more Anglo-phobe *Chicago Tribune*, controlled by Colonel Robert McCormick. To make additionally sure of favourable press coverage German sympathizers were secretly provided with official German funds to buy the *New York Mail* and provide a newspaper in which German propaganda stories could be published and then quoted as from an American source.

The French, also, could draw on a good deal of traditional American sympathy, going back to Lafayette and the War of Independence and nurtured by university and other groups which made much of France's contribution to civilization. This was well utilized.

The British, on the other hand, had certain initial disadvantages springing from American popular suspicion of British colonialism and from the fear that Great Britain was trying to embroil America in a war that was none of her concern. Most informed official and financial opinion was pro-British. But it was popular opinion that had to be won over.

Great Britain had one big advantage. London was the junction for the trans-Atlantic cable service. German news cables were thus cut off and, since there was a compulsory cable censorship, the transmission of any anti-British news could be prevented. To counter this, the Germans started a wireless press service to send news to America. But although it was used by a number of American newspapers, wireless was still at too early a stage to compete seriously with the trans-Atlantic cable service.

British propaganda proved in the end much the most successful, partly because it was skilfully directed to getting over a number of simple themes likely to appeal to American idealism, such as that this was a war to protect the rights of small nations and to make the world safe for democracy, but also because it was much more flexible than the German in exploiting news and events as they came along. Moreover, whereas the head of German propaganda in America, Dr Dernburg, a former minister for the colonies who set up a press bureau in New York, operated in a blaze of crude publicity, the British made use of friendly Americans to do their propaganda and themselves remained in the background.

Not only were they always at the service of the big metropolitan newspapers but they sent a weekly news report to some 360 newspapers in the smaller towns across America. Interviews with prominent Americans and with British personalities known to the American public, including well-known novelists, were circulated.

American sympathizers were mobilized and provided with facts for letters to their local papers, particularly in answer to criticisms. American lecturers were briefed with British material. Free war photographs were distributed widely to local American newspapers which might not otherwise have been able to afford them.

Also the British were much quicker than the Germans in appreciating the opportunities of the cinema. Films on 'Britain Prepared', on scenes from the front, on life in Great Britain in war-time, were made and sent over for American distribution. Later leading Hollywood producers, including the famous D.W.Griffith, were persuaded to make pro-Allied feature films.

But above all, events, and Germany's own actions, favoured the British propaganda effort. When the *Lusitania* was torpedoed by a German submarine on 7th May 1915 (p. 521), Great Britain needed to do little to fan American shock and anger beyond helping the American press to secure as many human stories from survivors as possible. The news itself was sufficient.

Propaganda was to be intensified as the war proceeded. But by the end of 1915 the pattern of mass warfare in conditions of mass literacy, and the powerful means that could be used to shape public opinion both in the warring nations and in the rest of the world had been well established.

War could no longer be kept as the private possession of professional soldiers provided with civilian armies to use as they wished. The mass media had moved in. Public opinion had taken its place among the chief munitions of war.

Mass Communications, 1914-18/Z.A.B.Zeman

Propaganda and Subversion

When the military failed to win the war for either side, the diplomats and the newspaper men were called in to help. Stories of atrocities were told to Americans and the alien subjects of the Romanovs and Habsburgs were encouraged to demand their independence. The war of slogans, subversion, and ideas was to have a profound affect. It helped Lenin into Russia, and perhaps into power, it helped America into the war, and ultimately it gave new boundaries to Europe

Had the war run according to the plans of the military, it would have ended in a few weeks or, at worst, months. There would have been no need for either propaganda or subversion. Instead, the war went on for more than four years, and the belligerents had to keep up their own morale and destroy the enemy's. So propaganda and subversion came into their own.

Initially, war-time propaganda was developed during the attempts to influence opinion in the neutral states. The United States became the principal target and here the Germans were at a disadvantage from the very beginning of the war. The first British naval action took place a few hours after midnight on 4th August 1914. Off the North Sea coast where the Dutch and German frontiers met, HMS *Telconia* ripped up the cables between Hamburg and New York. After that the Germans had to use either a clumsy, round-about cable route, or wireless messages anyone could pick up. As far as communications were concerned, the British held America in the palm of their hand.

In London an office specializing in propaganda was organized in September 1914. Asquith, the prime minister, invited a member of his cabinet, Charles Masterman, Chancellor of the Duchy of Lancaster, to take charge of propaganda. The chairman of the national insurance commission at Wellington House, Masterman set up his inconspicuous propaganda headquarters at the same address.

Barrage of persuasion. A Louis Raemaekers cartoon on the propaganda reaching German soldiers in the trenches

A former Cambridge don whose best-known book was *The Condition of England* published in 1909, Masterman was a high-minded, high churchman who lacked the common touch in politics. He was, however, a first-rate publicist. The production of pamphlets and books constituted a large part of the Wellington House activities, and most of them were aimed at the American public. The Bryce report on the conduct of the Germans in Belgium was the best-known of Masterman's publications. It was printed in some thirty languages, appearing on 14th May 1915, a week after the sinking of the *Lusitania* (p. 521).

As long as Asquith was in power and the politicians were either disinterested or suspicious of the value of propaganda, Masterman remained undisturbed. By autumn 1916 a number of government departments had, however, acquired their own information services and then, in November, Asquith, Masterman's friend and protector, left office. The situation remained unsettled until early in 1918, when Lord Beaverbrook was put in charge of the new ministry of information. By that time Masterman's originally modest enterprise had developed into a big government industry. Lloyd George talked about 'our propaganda, costing I dare not tell the government how much . . .' In fact, Lord Beaverbrook, by getting rid of the Wellington House office, was able to cut the proposed budget of his ministry from £1,800,000 to £1,200,000.

'Hands across the sea'

Though it made a later start than German publicity, British propaganda in America was more effective. Its touch was uncertain on one occasion only. After the Easter Rising in Dublin in 1916 (p. 596), the sudden, stark announcement of the executions of the revolutionaries outraged Irish America. The Germans, however, kept on making blunders all this time. The British had on their side the common language and, often, similar attitudes and ideals. More Americans knew their Shakespeare than their Goethe, and believed that the Duke of Wellington rather than Blücher won the battle of Waterloo. Masterman made the most of such lucky coincidences; he coined the inspired slogan 'Hands Across the Sea', and pioneered the technique of creation, by propaganda, of popular, simple images. The bestiality of the enemy was packaged and sold under the labels *'Lusitania'*, or 'Belgium', or 'Edith Cavell' (the nurse executed by the Germans for helping Allied soldiers escape). The Germans had a lot to learn from the simple, crisp appeal of Masterman's propaganda, which made an important contribution to preparing the Americans for their entry in the war.

Masterman's work was later carried on by the press lords, Beaverbrook, Rothermere, and Northcliffe. Among them, they commanded a formidable pool of talent. In Great Britain, their knowledge of the audience they had courted for many years before the war undoubtedly helped to create the kind of publicity that eased the soldiers and civilians alike over the last, difficult months of the war. The functions of the newspaper owners in the ministry of information were, however, specialized. While Beaverbrook looked after the overall running of his ministry, Rothermere specialized in propaganda to neutral countries, and Northcliffe looked after enemy territories.

Propaganda to the enemy, if it also aimed at undermining and then overthrowing the government, crossed the borderline and became subversion. In that regard, too, the Great War produced some remarkable and lasting results.

The Tsarist authorities were the first to experiment with subversion. As far as the Ukrainians in Austria-Hungary were concerned, the Russians simply continued their pre-war policy of trying to convert them to the Orthodox religion and disloyalty to the Habsburg state. The curious blend of religious and nationalist propaganda went on being turned out by the monasteries on the Russian side of the border after the outbreak of the war. Then, on 16th September 1914, the supreme commander, Grand Duke Nikolay Nikolayevich, published a declaration addressed to the Slav peoples of Austria-Hungary. It was printed as a leaflet in all their various languages, and it announced that Russia, 'who has sacrificed on several occasions the blood of her sons for the liberation of nations' had entered the war so as to bring freedom as well as 'fulfilment of national desires' to the peoples of Austria-Hungary.

From the end of September 1914 various Russian leaflets were in circulation in Bohemia, Moravia, and in the parts of Bukovina and Galicia the Russians hadn't already occupied. In December some 170,000 copies of the Grand Duke's manifesto were distributed in Prague. It raised hopes among the pro-Russian Czechs and gave the Austrian military authorities another excuse for taking punitive measures against the Slav peoples of Austria-Hungary. Apart from costing the lives of several hundred people, the Grand Duke's declaration and other Russian propaganda activities early in the war made no lasting impact. The spring and summer of 1915 saw the first series of Russian defeats and, as the front was pushed farther and farther east, the popularity of Tsarist Russia among the Slavs in Austria-Hungary declined.

Grand Duke Nikolay Nikolayevich probably did not appreciate the double-edged nature of the weapon he was using. Like Austria-Hungary, the Russian empire consisted of many nations; it had suffered a revolution less than ten years before the outbreak of the war. The Germans made full use of their opportunity: at several points, subversion, resulting in a revolution, was their one hope of winning the war.

German help for Lenin

Towards the end of November 1914 the Germans realized that the army and the Schlieffen plan had failed to win the war for them. The plan for an early knock-out blow against France and a swift subsequent reckoning with Russia did not materialize. Where the army had failed, the diplomats were called in to help. The chain of enemy alliances, the Germans now argued, had to be broken, by knocking out its weakest link. There were some differences about this among Germany's rulers, but the consensus of opinion pointed in the end to Russia as the weakest link.

The Germans could either try to conclude a separate peace with Tsarist Russia or try to weaken and overthrow it by subversion and then conclude peace with its successor. The war lords never took a clear-cut choice between the two courses open to them in regard to Russia. They favoured one or the other at different times, but they never completely dropped either. They did not set up a special office to deal with subversion and propaganda. Subversion in Russia was supervised by the foreign ministry, with a special section of the general staff in Berlin sometimes assisting the diplomats, but more often acting independently. There was at first no one at the Wilhelmstrasse – the foreign ministry – even remotely acquainted with the Russian revolutionary movement. It was not usual for the diplomats to move in such circles. They had to rely on outside advice.

They could have done worse than getting it from Alexander Helphand, better known to European socialists under his pen-name, Parvus. A Russian Jew, Helphand had studied in Switzerland, arriving in Germany in 1891. He joined the socialist movement and all its stormy controversies of that decade. He became young Léon Trotsky's friend and teacher and ran with him the first soviet in St Petersburg in 1905, becoming its last chairman. A difficult man to please, Parvus was satisfied with neither the advance nor the rewards of socialism. In 1910 he went to Constantinople where he made a fortune as a merchant. In 1915 he reappeared in Berlin and early in March wrote a memorandum on the Russian revolutionary movenent, now a classic in the literature of subversion. He recommended the Germans o encourage national movements on the ringes of the Tsarist empire, chiefly in the Jkraine and the Caucasus. The Germans nad been doing that for some time, and Helphand was able only to fill in a few letails in that regard. But the essential service he did for the Germans was that he lrew to their attention the disruptive force of Russian Social Democracy, and especially of its Bolshevik faction.

In this way Parvus brought together the nost incongruous allies in the Great War. Lenin wanted defeat and revolution in Russia that would remove the Tsarist egime he hated; the Germans pursued the same aim in order to break the British-French-Russian alliance and reduce the war to a one-front engagement. With Helphand's encouragement, the Germans were prepared to do a lot for Lenin and his party. Some Bolshevik journalism and propaganda was printed, probably without Lenin's knowledge, by official printing presses in Berlin. In April 1917, after the revolution, Lenin was desperately trying o find a way of getting back to Russia. He elt, according to his wife, 'as if corked up n a bottle' in Switzerland. The Germans provided the 'sealed train' to take Lenin and some of his comrades across the Reich o Sweden and back home. Without that service, Trotsky wrote later, there probably would have been no Bolshevik revolution. n addition, the government in Berlin was ever ready to spend millions of marks on he Bolsheviks and their subversive activities in Russia.

The question of the extent to which the Germans helped Lenin and the Bolsheviks on their way to power will probably remain a matter of controversy. Be it as it may. he three years' effort on the part of the Germans was rewarded by a late but spectacular success. In December 1917 hey concluded an armistice, and in March 918 peace, with the new Bolshevik government. They transferred some forty divisions from the east to the Western Front, and on 21st March 1918 launched their great offensive in France, their last bid for victory.

Dismembering the Habsburg empire

n the winter 1917-18, their fortunes at the owest ebb, the Allies were impressed by Germany's success in Russia. At a conference of propagandists in London in February 1918, a French expert on central European affairs thought it essential that he Allies launch a 'war of ideas' on Germany. He then complimented the Germans on their effort in regard to Russia. He hought German propaganda had a powerful impact, that it 'had been conceived and carried out by a metaphysician ▷808

Tasiemka

Above: *The clipped perforation on this Austrian stamp was no accident. It conveyed a message to Italian intelligence officers who received it from an agent spying for Italy in Austria*

Above: *The German way with spies: an unceremonious lynching.* **Below:** *A German cartoon ridicules British interrogation. 'For the last time have you got a Zeppelin on you?' the tearful German spy is asked*

APOLLO THEATRE
THE GREAT SPY PLAY
THE FLEET IN PERIL
INSIDE THE LINES

Imperial War Museum

Propaganda and spy-hysteria

Spies, it was imagined, lurked everywhere – in marshalling yards, recording the movement of troop trains and *matériel*; in naval bases observing fleet departures; and in industrial centres assessing war production. If a few did, the rest existed exclusively in the popular imagination. And notably in Great Britain. The violent spasm of spy-scares and alien-hunting which marked the opening months of the war never entirely subsided as these illustrations testify. Disaster abroad and mismanagement at home could so easily be blamed on the insidious activities of agents in the employ of enemy powers. But the lives of many innocent people were ruined by the promotion of this indiscriminate spy-hysteria which had virtually no basis in reality

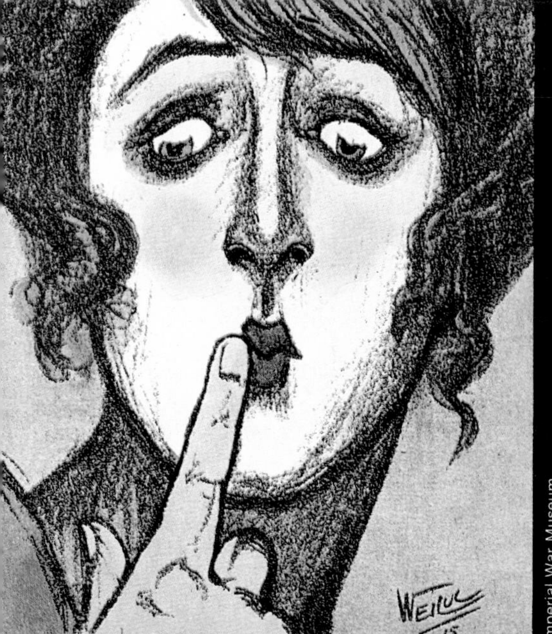

Above: *French magazine cover warns that careless talk costs lives. The aims of the Nivelle offensive had been openly discussed in Parisian cafés with little thought for security*

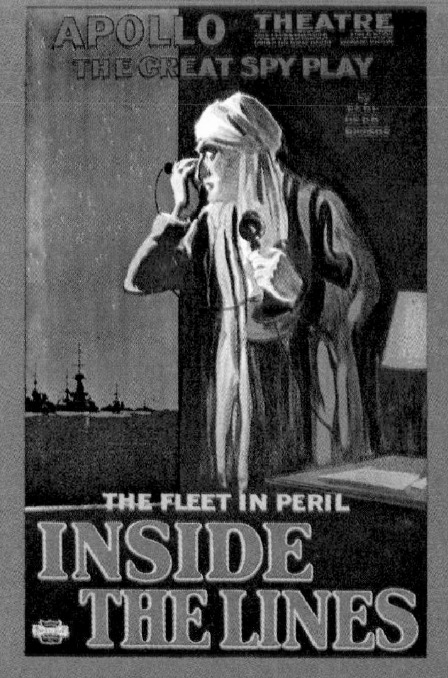

Above: *British playbill. The theatre fed spy-hysteria in Great Britain by presenting sinister enemy agents in fanciful situations.* ***Below:*** *Counter-intelligence. 'Interrogation' by Francis Dodd*

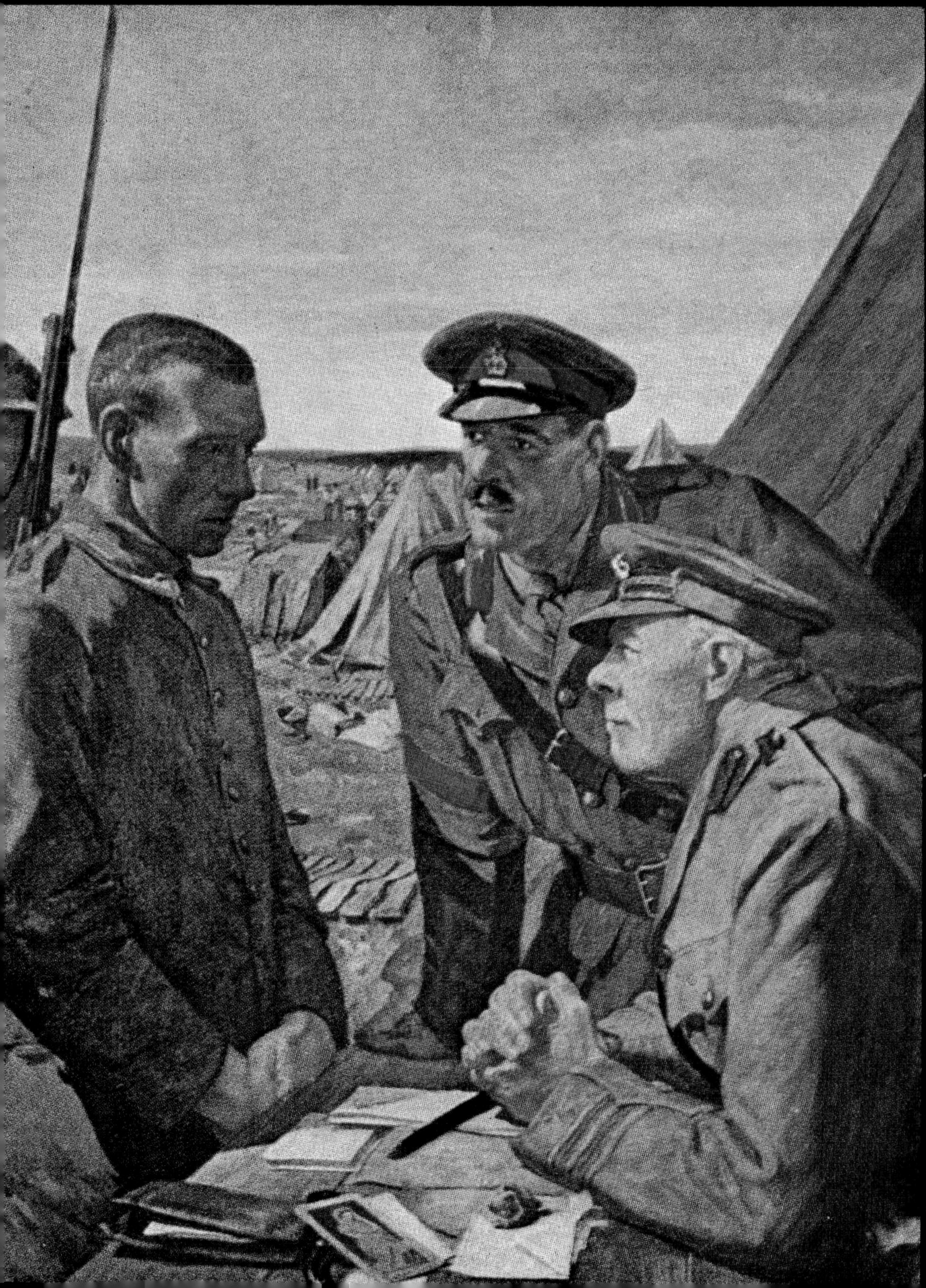

Imperial War Museum

Achtung!
Feind hört mit!
Decknamen verwenden!

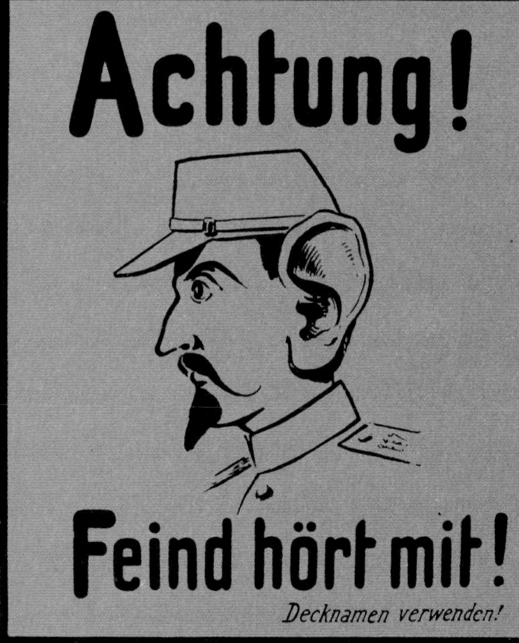

Tasiemka

Great stress was laid on the overriding need for secrecy. ***Above:*** *A German poster warns against conversation within French earshot.* ***Below:*** *British reminder. A lot could be learned from lonely soldiers*

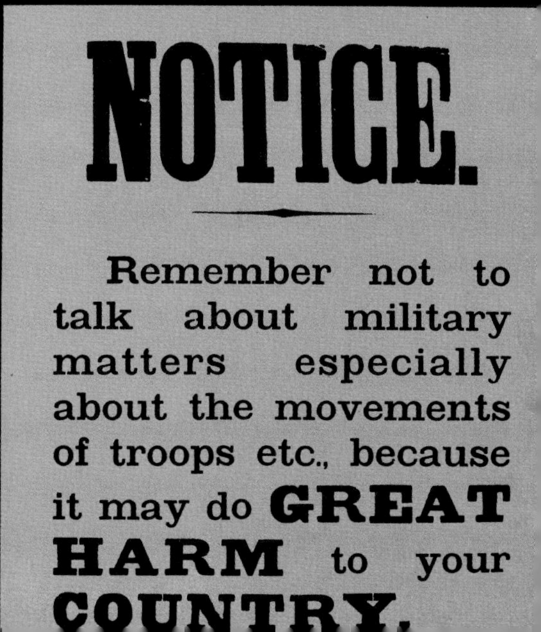
NOTICE.
Remember not to talk about military matters especially about the movements of troops etc., because it may do GREAT HARM to your COUNTRY.

ILLUSTRIRTE·ZEITUNG

Kriegs Anleihe
Helft den Hütern Eures Glückes
Georgi 1918.

Musée Royal de l'Armée, Brussels

'The beastly Hun'

Public opinion had taken its place alongside the guns as a potent war weapon and it became the aim of Allied propaganda to convince the world, and particularly the neutral world of Germany's bestiality. If her soldiers behaved no better and no worse than their Allied counterparts, they were portrayed as pitiless butchers who took a peculiar delight in blood-letting. Public opinion had become a significant weapon of war and with skilful use it might be used to recruit American power and prestige to the Allied cause. Understandably, the Germans did not see themselves as the ogres of Allied propaganda. Their war was just, their soldiers noble

Above: *Archetypal German soldier. A confident, muscular engineer adorns a German magazine cover. The wholesomeness of their soldiers was a theme popular among Germans*

Above: *'Help the Protector of Your Joy' urges a German war-loan poster. A blond, blue-eyed Nordic warrior shields racially-pure German motherhood*

Below: *How the public saw their army. Photograph of laughing German soldiers with Frenchwomen and baby from the pages of a popular German magazine*

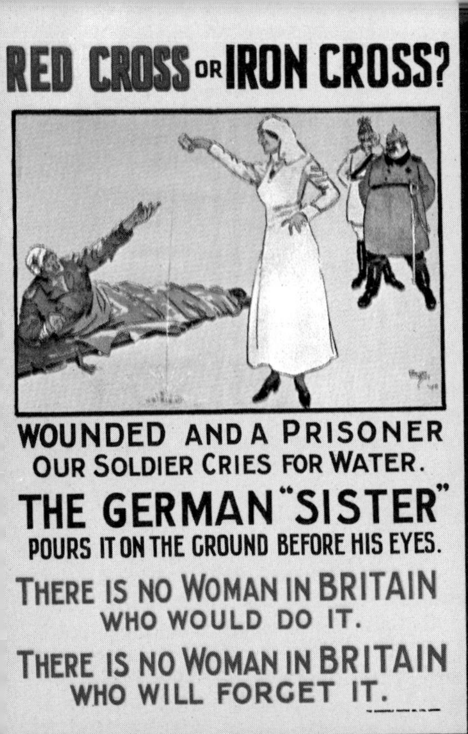
RED CROSS OR IRON CROSS?
WOUNDED AND A PRISONER
OUR SOLDIER CRIES FOR WATER.
THE GERMAN "SISTER"
POURS IT ON THE GROUND BEFORE HIS EYES.
THERE IS NO WOMAN IN BRITAIN
WHO WOULD DO IT.
THERE IS NO WOMAN IN BRITAIN
WHO WILL FORGET IT.

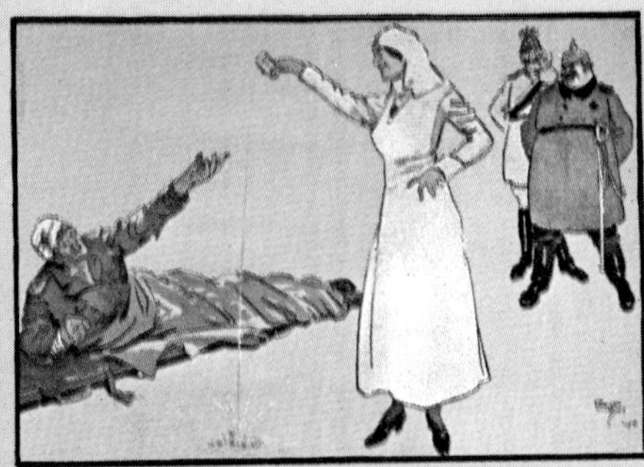

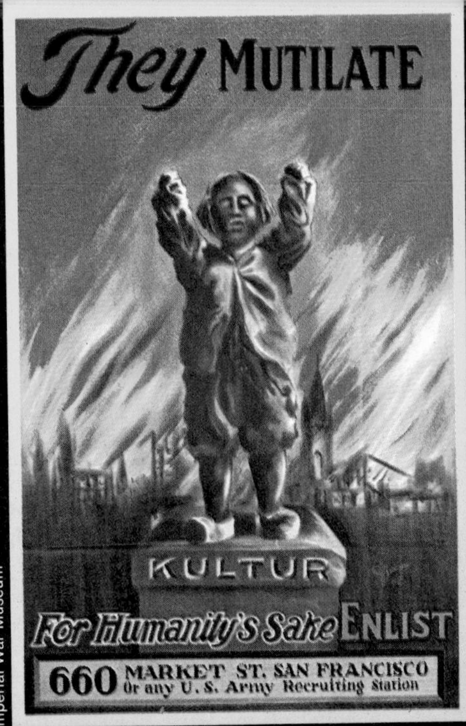

Imperial War Museum

They MUTILATE
KULTUR
For Humanity's Sake ENLIST
660 MARKET ST. SAN FRANCISCO
Or any U. S. Army Recruiting Station

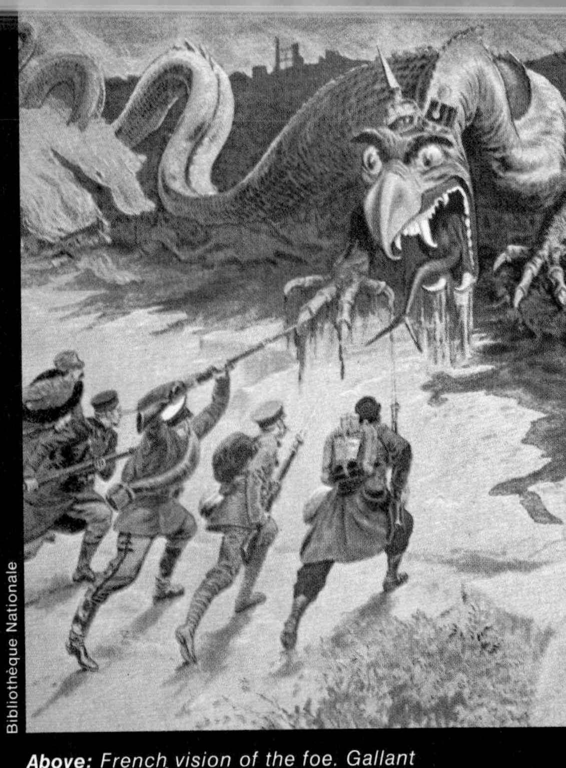

Bibliothèque Nationale

Above: British poster illustrates alleged Teutonic callousness towards a prisoner. People believed that this was the sort of act of which the hated enemy was capable

Above: Monument to culture. A blind, mutilated Belgian child on an American recruiting poster. Allied propaganda convinced America of German inhumanity

Above: French vision of the foe. Gallant Allies confront the Austro-German beast. **Below:** German contempt for Christianity suggested in British war bond campaign

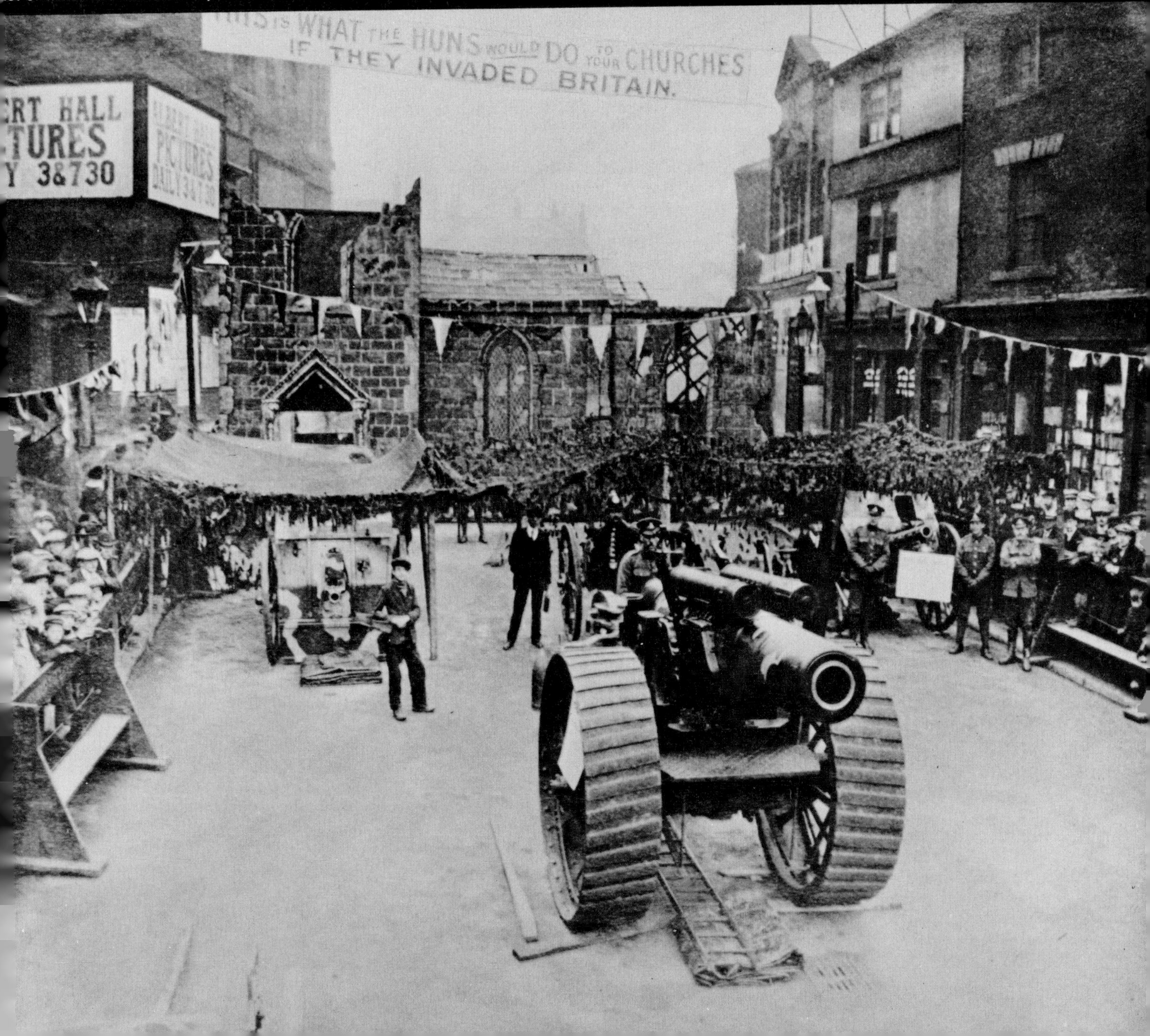
WHAT THE HUNS WOULD DO TO YOUR CHURCHES
IF THEY INVADED BRITAIN.
ERT HALL
TURES
Y 3&730

Musée Royal de l'Armée, Brussels

Illustration from British propaganda leaflet dropped over the German lines: a jovial German prisoner savouring one of the delights of captivity

who had clearly foreseen the shattering effect of Bolshevik doctrine on Russian minds'. He went on to say that 'in view of the military position, Allied propaganda must aim on the one hand at quick results, and, on the other, at the transformation of the state of mind prevailing in enemy countries. Therefore it should be directed in the first place against Austria-Hungary and be based upon the aspirations of the subject Habsburg races without forgetting that even among the Magyars there were potentially anti-Habsburg elements'.

In the winter of 1917-18, with the possibility of military disaster never absent from their minds, the Allied governments had begun to use the exiles from the Habsburg empire and the forces they represented in order to embarass the Central empires. Wickham Steed, the foreign editor of *The Times* and the key figure in Northcliffe's department in the ministry of information, had maintained that Austria-Hungary was the pivot in the struggle against the enemy alliance, and that unless she were 'discomfited and transformed, if not dismembered' Germany could not be defeated. The Italian front became the main theatre for Allied propaganda against Austria-Hungary. Early in April 1918 an Allied commission was set up at the Italian headquarters, which included representatives of the South Slav, Czechoslovak, and Polish exiles' committees; they were consulted on questions concerning propaganda, which took mainly the form of leaflets encouraging refractory national movements.

It was the second onslaught on the morale of the Austro-Hungarian troops within a few months. The first had come from Russia, when Trotsky started using the peace negotiations with the Germans for spreading subversive Bolshevik ideas to western Europe. Both Lenin and Trotsky were convinced that revolutions abroad would follow their own, and from the first day in power they put themselves out to promote them. The commissariat of foreign affairs set up a department for foreign propaganda, and two million roubles were allocated for the promotion of revolutions abroad. In order to undermine foreign governments by showing the wickedness of old diplomacy, the Soviets began publishing the secret treaties of the Tsarist government. Again and again, in his speeches and proclamations, Trotsky tried to create or broaden the antagonism between the rulers and the ruled. Though not revolutionary in intention, the effect of President Wilson's simultaneous appeals to the 'silent masses' of Europe occasionally reinforced the Bolshevik agitation. In the important question of self-determination of peoples, Bolshevik and American publicity in the winter of 1917-18 coincided and made a powerful impact, especially in Austria-Hungary.

Ironically, the collapse of the Russian army and the armistice had released enough Austro-Hungarian forces to deal with internal unrest. Contrary to Lenin's views and despite Trotsky's intensive agitation, no revolutions took place to the west of Russia before the end of the war. A wave of strikes swept Europe, but that was all. Though the Bolshevik leaders were right in assuming that the revolution could not remain confined to one country, they overestimated its potential impact.

From books to banners

The 1914-18 war was the first total war in the history of the world. For the first time, both soldiers and civilians took part and were directly affected. The armies were however organized for war and protected against some of its most degrading features. The Allied blockade, for instance, hit the civilians in Germany and Austria-Hungary a long time before their armies. The civilians were also affected by subversive propaganda much more than the troops. The situation in Russia in 1917 had shown that the armies nearest the revolutionary centres—Petrograd and Moscow—were the least reliable while the most remote military units and especially those stationed on foreign soil, in Rumania, were almost unaffected by revolutionary agitation. It was the assault of peace propaganda, from the hinterland and from the German lines, on the Russian troops culminating late in the summer of 1917, that made the Russian army melt away.

In the spring of 1918 the Allies started using the exiles from the Habsburg empire, Masaryk and Beneš, Trumbić and Paderewski, as the Germans had used the Bolsheviks and the national movements in the Tsarist empire. There existed political sympathies between the Allies and the exiles, where there were none in the case of Lenin and the German government. But in both cases the support given to the exiles was developed under the fire of military necessity. The exiles from the Habsburg monarchy had spent the war fighting for the recognition of the right of their peoples to independence without much success. Now, in the spring and summer of 1918 they could hardly believe their good fortune. Recognition of their aims, even recognition of their committees as the future governments of their independent countries—not yet in existence—by one Allied state was followed by another. The exiles let their peoples in the Habsburg empire know of their successes. Soon, the Habsburg empire disappeared under the tide of popular enthusiasm for national independence.

The impression on the Europeans of wartime propaganda was deep and lasting. Many of its slogans can now be recognized as the seeds of future political developments. What the propagandists sowed during the war the politicians reaped after its end. They all had to come to terms with the slogans of national self-determination, of national unity obliterating party divisions, of land and social reforms. They, of course, had all been there before the war. Propaganda, especially in 1917 and 1918, forced their growth. It took them out of books and party programmes, and put them on to banners and took them out into the streets, so that nobody could ever forget them.

Like many other weapons used in the First World War subversion was still passing through its experimental stages. Few people knew how to use it and many overestimated its effectiveness. Its employment had been greatly stimulated by the pressures of the war and especially of military emergency. But it proved most effective at times of military triumph. It deepened the panic of a hard-pressed enemy, perhaps speeding up the course of events leading to total victory. But it never turned the tide of defeat.

Germany, 1914-18/J.R.C.Wright

Socialism and Unrest

In 1914 the German socialist party rallied to the defence of the fatherland, and voted funds to the government for war. Never, it seemed, had Germany been so united. But the socialists themselves were bitterly divided. Some wanted national security, some peace, some revolution

At the outbreak of war in 1914 the German trade union leadership and the German Social Democratic Party (SPD) in the Reichstag decided to support the German government and not to oppose the war. They abandoned the class struggle and joined the middle class and conservative parties to defend the German fatherland. This action marked a break with many of the principles proclaimed by the German labour movement in the past and it led to a split in its ranks which was never closed. From 1914 until 1918 the German labour movement was not only at war for Germany against foreign enemies; it was also at war with itself. The national war was lost in 1918; the civil war between the two parties which emerged within the labour movement is still being fought. How did the division within the party come about?

The origins of this division may be traced before 1914 to the foundation of the German working-class movement in the 1860's and 1870's. The most famous German socialist, Karl Marx, had only a limited influence on the movement. His theory of the inevitable collapse of the capitalist order and the duty of the proletariat to prepare for revolution commanded great reverence in Germany, but it did not stimulate much action. Marx himself did not specify the type of revolution to be aimed at: he did not advocate a foolhardy recourse to the barricades which was certain to end in disaster, and he had no time for the isolated acts of violence practised by the anarchists, but equally he rejected the idea that the working class should be content to acquire rights within the existing system. This last policy was recommended by another famous personality in the early history of the German labour movement, Ferdinand Lassalle. His colourful career ended in a duel fought for love. Unlike Marx he believed that social revolution could be won within the Prussian state and even with its help: he was ready to co-operate with Bismarck

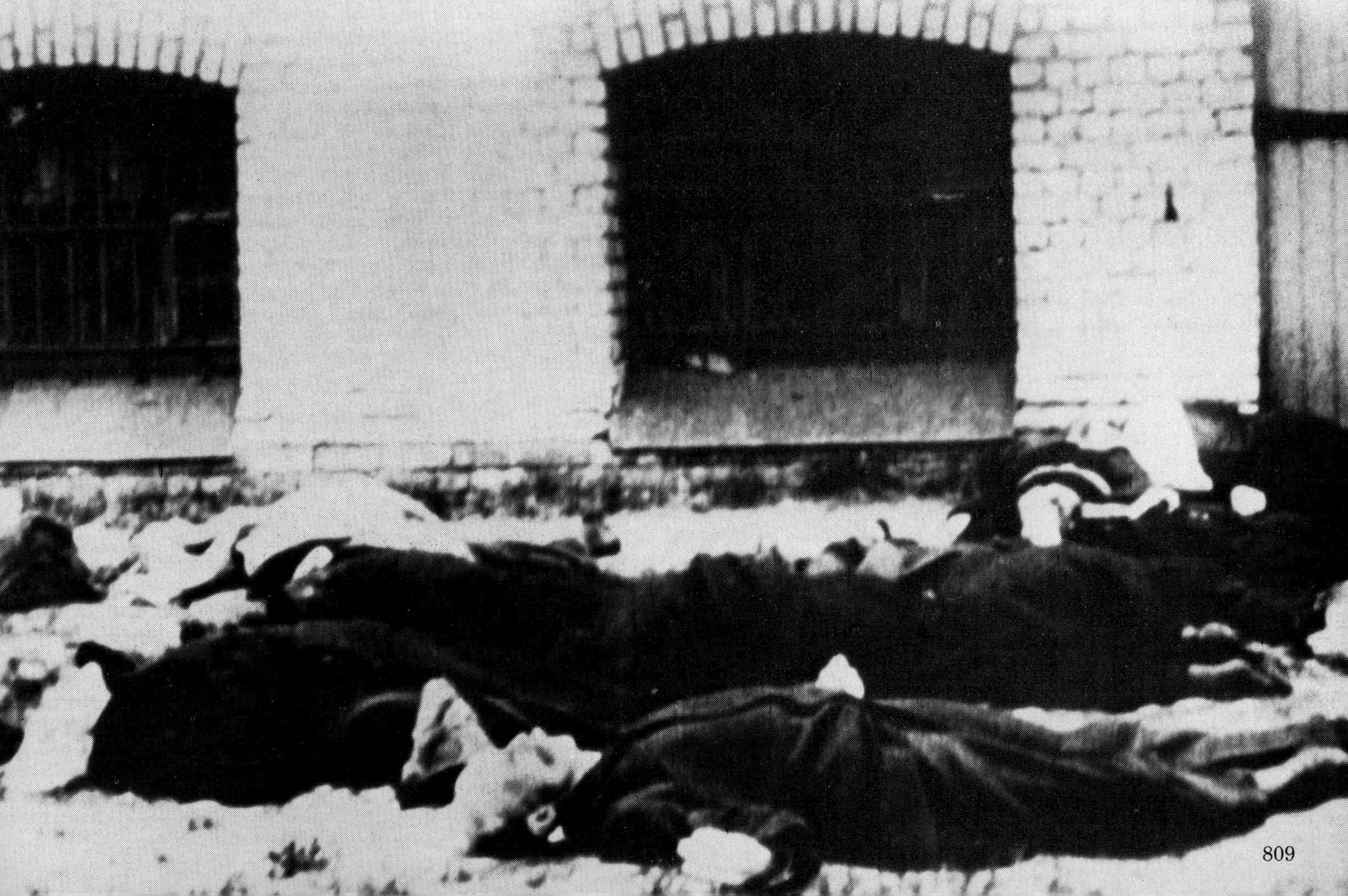

Dead German strikers, 1918. They demanded better food and conditions, peace without annexations, the release of political prisoners, and democratic reforms. They were met with violence

Bibliothek für Zeitgeschichte, Stuttgart

Imperial War Museum

Ullstein

1 A swaggering caricature of a British officer on a German poster which asserted 'He is Guilty'. Great Britain, it claimed, was the principal enemy and appealed for unity to defeat her. 2 An attempt to avert revolution: German poster appealing for peace and order

to gain political rights for the working man.

The question of whether to prepare to overthrow the existing state or to work for reform within it remained at the centre of disputes within the German labour movement. No agreement was reached either before the war or after it. Nevertheless, the labour movement did not divide into two separate parties before the war: unity was maintained by compromise and evasion. The war led the movement to commit itself more definitely and this broke it. After the war the division became formalized in two separate parties, the old SPD and the German Communist Party (KPD).

The world of make-believe

There were good reasons why the SPD did not choose between peaceful or aggressive methods of changing society before the war. There were arguments in favour of each method and objections to each of them. Bismarck's anti-socialist legislation, enforced between 1878 and 1890, showed both the need for revolution and the danger of attempting it. At the same time his social insurance measures gave Germany a system of social welfare twenty years in advance of Great Britain. In the 1890's it did not look as though the capitalist world would collapse. Germany was experiencing a period of great industrial expansion – by 1900 Germany produced more steel than Great Britain – and the German working class benefited from the increase in national wealth brought by economic growth. Friedrich Engels, a close friend of Marx, tried to interpret Marx's theories to suit a situation in which revolution seemed a distant prospect. He believed that the development of large working class political parties like the SPD was the correct policy. Eduard Bernstein, a member of the SPD, challenged Marx's theories directly – for instance he said that the standard of living of the working class was rising not falling.

Between 1900 and 1913 there was a spectacular rise in trade union membership (p. 121). This gave the trade unions great influence within the working-class movement as a whole: in 1914 about a third of the SPD parliamentary party consisted of trade union officials. Under the leadership of Carl Legien they were a conservative body favouring moderate and not revolutionary policies. They were suspicious of party 'intellectuals' like Karl Liebknecht or Rosa Luxemburg (p. 262) who advocated mass strikes. The trade union leaders believed that such strikes would fail and that union organization would be ruined in the process. Some of the right-wing leaders thought that the interests of the working man would be better served by the expansion of German industry and the extension of German power to other parts of the world.

The SPD, like the trade unions, grew fast. In the 1912 elections it won a great victory, receiving over four million votes (a third of the total number cast) and 110 seats in the Reichstag. Like the trade unions, the more the party grew, the more conservative its officials became. Friedrich Ebert, a man of working-class origin, later to be the first President of the German Republic established in 1918, typified this outlook. He is reported to have said that he hated social revolution like sin.

Those who favoured peaceful reform were probably right in thinking that more aggressive policies would not be successful: the power of the German state was too great. There was also much to be said for sharing in the benefits of the existing society. The weakness of this argument was that the benefits were not shared equally. Although Germany had a parliamentary system, its parliament did not have the same power as in France or Great Britain: it was not able to appoint ministers. In the greatest of the German states, Prussia, the state parliament was not elected on a democratic basis: the franchise was weighted in favour of landowners and industrialists. In this situation the SPD did not have the influence on public policy which its strength merited; in addition its members were discriminated against, for instance in appointments to the higher civil service. There were also restrictions on trade union activity: unions were not allowed in the agricultural and railway industries. Despite its parliamentary strength the SPD was unable to effect reform. This gave force to the argument that the exercise of parliamentary rights was not enough.

It is not surprising, given the difficulties facing the party, that the SPD leadership did not commit itself to either of the policies open to it. In theory it remained true to the goal of revolution; in practice it pursued policies of moderation. The party programme of 1891 allowed for both. Karl Kautsky, who undertook the unenviable task of reconciling theory and practice in a new theory, summarized the position by saying that the SPD was a revolutionary but not a revolution-making party. Although this was a natural position to take, it was also a false one. The party had failed to win power but it could not admit defeat. It lived in a world of make-believe, standing apart from the state which it had failed to conquer but which it was unwilling to join.

The impact of war

The war forced the German labour movement to choose between Germany and the international socialist movement. It could no longer simply stand aside, and its decision exposed the contradictions in its pre-war attitude. The war also made the support of the German working class much more important to the government than it had been before. Once the chance of a quick victory had faded, the continuation of the war required the mobilization of the whole

4

Staatsbibliothek, Berlin

3 Colossus in the Tiergarten. Berliners, like Lilliputians, gaze in awe at an iron effigy of Hindenburg. Germany's brave exterior concealed disease, starvation and disillusion. 4 Karl Liebknecht (with wheelbarrow). He was sentenced to hard labour for agitation in 1916

of the nation's resources. This meant that the bargaining power of German labour was greatly increased. The SPD leaders could hope to win the concessions which had been denied them in peace in return for their support of the war. At last there seemed a real prospect of achieving reform through co-operation with the existing state. Yet, at the same time, the war offered new hope and opportunity to those who believed that the grievances of the German working class could be put right only by revolution. For the war put a strain on the German state and the German people which weakened the government and increased the revolutionary temper of the working class. Before the war neither the supporters of moderate policies nor those who advocated revolution had looked like succeeding; now both thought their hour had come. This made each side more determined to go its own way and increased the hostility between them.

On 3rd August 1914 the SPD parliamentary party decided at a private meeting to vote in favour of the government bill to raise money for the war. The voting was seventy-eight in favour, fourteen against. On the following day, accepting the decision of the majority of its members as binding on them all, the SPD gave its united support to the government in the Reichstag. The majority saw the war as a war of national defence against Russian Tsarism, the traditional enemy of the European Left. The decision of the party to support the war was a great relief to many of its members: Eduard David, a member of the right wing of the party, wrote in his diary on 4th August: 'After this storm I had the feeling that the world war was over, that peace had again returned'. If the party had opposed the war, David continued, its resistance would have been speedily overcome by military force but wide sections of the army and population would have been discouraged and embittered in the process. 'Now,' he concluded, 'we have won a common basis for influential activity during and after the war and we must not let ourselves be excluded again.'

The split in the Party

The victory of the SPD majority did not long go unchallenged. In December 1914 the most extreme opponent of the war policy within the parliamentary party, Karl Liebknecht, ignored the rules of party discipline and voted against war finance in the Reichstag. In 1915 he defended his action by saying that it was his loyalty to socialist principles which had led him to disobey the party line. At a meeting of the international socialist movement in Stuttgart in 1907 the SPD had agreed that if war broke out it would be their duty 'to intercede for its speedy end, and to strive with all their power to make use of the violent economic and political crisis brought about by the war to rouse the people, and thereby to hasten the abolition of capitalist rule'. This now became the programme of a small group of radicals, including Liebknecht, who were known as Spartacists (after the leader of a revolt of gladiators and slaves during the Roman Empire) and who later formed the nucleus of the KPD. Their source of inspiration was Rosa Luxemburg, a Jewess from Russian Poland, a woman of great humanity and determination. She applied to herself words attributed to Martin Luther when he was asked to retract his heretical teaching at the Diet of Worms in 1521, 'Here I stand, I can do no other, God help me'. She was a devastating critic, feared by the SPD leaders and the government alike. She spent three of the war years in prison and was murdered together with Liebknecht by a group of soldiers in January 1919.

During 1915 more members of the SPD began to have doubts about the wisdom of supporting the government. Their opposition became focused on the question of whether the war was a war of defence. Those who believed that Germany had been encircled by hostile powers before the war thought that they must gain more by the peace settlement than a return to the pre-war frontiers: otherwise, they argued, Germany would be just as insecure in the future. This led to the demand for annexation of new territory to make Germany the dominant power in Europe. The SPD leaders were confused on this issue: they accepted the aim of national security but they could not endorse a war of conquest. There was a growing feeling within the party from 1915 that the war had become an imperialist venture and that the party should withdraw its support and press for peace without annexations. The chancellor of the Reich, Bethmann Hollweg, refused to give a clear assurance that the German government did not intend to annex new territory, and in December 1915 twenty SPD deputies went into open opposition against both the war and the Social Democratic leadership.

The action of this opposition minority led to bitter debates within the parliamentary party. Haase, a lawyer and one of the leaders of the opposition, explaining why the minority intended to challenge the party line, said that it would be different if the party were fighting the enemy but that it was not. By the 'enemy' he meant the class enemy; he was echoing a slogan of Liebknecht's, 'The chief enemy is at home'. One of the party 'intellectuals' accused the majority of hypocrisy on the issue of annexations and another member of the minority described the war finance bills as 'blood bills' and 'murder credits'; '700,000 men have already been killed in Germany', he said. 'I will not take responsibility for this any longer.' On the other hand, another lawyer argued that the majority must be allowed to decide whether it was a war of defence or not. Noske, a man of working-class background who was to earn notoriety within the socialist world by using right-wing volunteer troops against the Spartacists in 1919, said that a class war was absurd in the present situation and that the front was against the country's enemies. Legien, the trade union leader, demanded that in the interests of party unity the minority should be separated from the parliamentary party. Otherwise, he said, there would be chaos. He likened the minority to strike-breakers, adding, 'When someone has spat in my face once, I do not turn my face towards him again'.

Between 1915 and 1917 members of the SPD opposition to the war attended meetings in neutral Switzerland with other anti-war socialists including Lenin. In September 1916 a conference of the whole SPD failed to restore unity. In January 1917 the minority called a conference of their own. The SPD leadership ruled that by doing this the opposition had separated itself from the main party. This forced the minority to found a new party, which was called the Independent Social Democratic Party (USPD). This new party contained people with different aims although they all opposed the policy of co-operation with the government. The main division within the USPD was between those whose first interest was peace and the Spartacist minority who eagerly expected revolution. Rosa Luxemburg in a letter to the wife of one of the more moderate leaders dismissed them as a 'company of singing toads'.

The fruits of co-operation

The SPD leaders had little influence on the course of the war. They were unable to prevent the policy of unrestricted submarine warfare being adopted although they disagreed with it. After the American declaration of war in April 1917 and the failure of the German government to make peace with the new regime in Russia established by the February Revolution of March 1917, the SPD became critical and pessimistic. At a private meeting of the parliamentary party on 5th July 1917 one member said that no one believed that Germany could win the war; it was only a question of how long she could hold out. Another member condemned government policy as 'insane and criminal'.

The SPD tried to put pressure on the government by acting in concert with the Catholic Centre and liberal Progressive parties; together they had a majority in the Reichstag. In July 1917 these three parties succeeded in getting a peace resolution passed by the Reichstag, but the resolution did not commit the government to anything definite. In March 1918 the weakness of the SPD was revealed when it decided merely to abstain from voting on the Treaty of Brest Litovsk which proposed sweeping annexation of Russian territory. The reason for the SPD's abstention was its fear of alienating the Centre and Progressive parties which voted for the Treaty. The same fear led the SPD to continue to vote for the war finance bills.

The efforts of the SPD to force democratic reform on Prussia were also unsuccessful. Despite the support of the Centre and Progressive parties and a promise of reform from the Kaiser, the SPD was thwarted by Prussian conservatives with the backing of General Ludendorff. However, the three parties of reform (SPD, Centre, and Progressive) were successful in the last year of the war in increasing the power of the Reichstag over the chancellor.

The SPD was also able to defend the interests of the trade unions during the war. In this the party was helped by the military authorities on the home front who appreciated the importance of union co-operation. The Auxiliary Service Law of December 1916 applied the principle of conscription to labour, but it did not control wages and it allowed workers' committees in the war industries and arbitration committees on which workers and employers were equally represented.

To an increasing number of SPD voters during 1917 and 1918 the failures of the party seemed to outweigh its successes. Large sections of the German working class turned against the SPD and rejected its appeals to them to 'stick it out' in the national interest. This working-class opposition to the war was influenced by the USPD and the Spartacists but it also had its own leaders, a group of radical shop-stewards under Richard Müller, centred on the Berlin metal industry.

The workers' strikes

The main causes of unrest were economic. Germany imported a third of her food supply before the war; the war, the Allied blockade (p. 557), and the failures of organization soon resulted in serious shortages. The severe 'turnip winter' of 1916-17 (so-called because during it the population had to eat turnips instead of potatoes) led to strikes for more food and higher wages (with which to buy food on the black market). As the war progressed the strain of working long hours with inadequate nutrition began to tell. To the casualties of battle were added the casualties of disease and starvation. To food shortages were added shortages of housing, clothing, and soap. The resentment of the deprived mass of the population was intensified by the scandal of war profiteers. As the conviction grew that opportunities of peace had been missed to satisfy the ambitions of those who wished to annex new territory and as it became plain that promises of democratic reform would not be fulfilled, so the sacrifices imposed by the war seemed hollow and feeling against the government hardened. The example of Liebknecht was honoured; in 1916 when he was sentenced to two and a half years hard labour for agitation against the war and the government, the radical shop-stewards organized a demonstration strike which was supported by 55,000 Berlin workers.

The groups within the German labour movement which opposed the war were no more successful than the SPD in influencing its course. The opposition was not powerful enough to threaten the government or to make it modify its war aims. The most serious strike waves (which were later to form the basis of the right-wing myth that the German army had been defeated by a 'stab in the back') occurred in April 1917 and January 1918. The strikers demanded better food and conditions, peace without annexations, the release of political prisoners, and democratic reform. In 1917 the strikers appealed to the working class throughout Germany to set up workers' councils, on the model of the Russian soviets, to protect their interests. The most important centres in 1917 were Berlin and Leipzig, and in 1918 some 400,000 Berlin workers were involved. In 1917 the government promised economic improvement but did not meet the political demands. In Berlin, where the strike continued, it was suppressed by force: some of the munitions factories were taken over by the army and strike leaders were drafted to serve at the front. In 1918 the government refused to negotiate with the workers' council in Berlin although the Social Democrats as well as the USPD was represented on it. Again force was used and the strike collapsed.

During the great German offensive of the spring and early summer of 1918 the home front was quiet although conditions were no less severe than in the previous year: so long as there was a prospect of victory the German government was able to contain the forces of opposition. In the autumn of 1918, however, when it became clear that the war had been lost, the old regime was critically weakened. By November, in the words of Richard Müller (the leader of the radical shop-stewards), 'Germany was like a powder-barrel – a spark was enough and the explosion was there'.

The defeat of Germany gave the German labour movement the opportunity of power which had eluded it so long. This did not restore its unity. The divisions which had grown up in the search for power and which had been brought into the open by the pressure of war were perpetuated by differences which now arose over how power was to be used.